Physical Education Activities for Women

Even if the day ever dawns in which muscular vigor will not be needed for fighting the old heavy battles against nature, it will still always be needed to furnish the background of sanity, serenity, and cheerfulness of life, [and] give moral elasticity to our disposition . . .

William James

Physical Education Activities for Women

Betty Foster McCue

PROFESSOR OF PHYSICAL EDUCATION, UNIVERSITY OF OREGON

The Macmillan Company
Collier-Macmillan Limited, London

First Printing

Library of Congress catalog card number: 69-10022

THE MACMILLAN COMPANY
COLLIER-MACMILLAN CANADA, LTD., TORONTO,
ONTARIO

Printed in the United States of America

Preface

Can one profit by reading a book about physical education activities? Some persons say that in the performance of motor skills we learn only by doing; yet in today's world few individuals are self-taught in relation to anything. A teacher's instruction, the encouragement and assistance of one's companions, and participation and practice are essentials for good performance of physical education activities. But comprehension and readiness for participation can be enhanced by preparation through reading. May your reading lead to understanding and prepare you for *doing*.

With a few exceptions where appropriate, chapters in this book use the following pattern: general description and brief history of the activity; a listing of goals or what one can hope to accomplish in learning the activity; equipment needed; etiquette, good sportsmanship, and safety; description and illustration of skills; a résumé of rules or citing of sources where they can be found; mechanics of movement when analysis is helpful; self-evaluation processes for the participant; terminology; and a selected list of references for those who desire further study of the activity. Unless otherwise specified, directions are given for the right-handed participant.

No presentation of a physical education activity can wholly and exhaustively cover the activity presented. Each contributor to this book, a teacher of the activity of which she writes, has been diligent in making every effort to comply with editorial suggestions. With goals in mind, however, the editor still shares the dilemma of Arthur Guiterman, who, when he wrote *Gaily the Troubadour*, used the following epigram:

> Go, little book, and leave me still in doubt
>   Which afterthought implies the greater sin:
> "I wonder if I should have left that out?"
>   Or, "Was it well to put that poem in?"

Today we have increasing help from sophisticated audiovisual equipment and improved analysis and understanding of the scientific principles of human movement; and world performance records in sports are regularly broken. But how can the beginner and novice best be helped? This book aims to give one general concepts, an understanding of possible goals, and background information to both arouse and, at least in part, satisfy the reader's curiosity.

We appreciate the advice and help given by friends; we are especially grateful to Ellen Griffin, Tankie Holton, Sara Houston, Dorene Leonard, Ruth Mixon, Claire Noyes, Dot Spangler, Nancy Williamson, and Julia Wray. Mrs. Jill Macduff and Mrs. Betty Hilliard gave yeoman service in preparing the manuscript, and without the assistance of Helen Domonkos this book would not have been completed.

It was a pleasure to work with friends and colleagues on this project. May we help you to help yourself, and may you enjoy a lifetime of activity.

B. F. M.

Acknowledgments

Grateful acknowledgment is made to the following schools and individuals for their assistance and/or permission in securing photographs. Numbers following names refer to chapters or figures in which the pictures are reproduced.

Berea College, Berea, Ky., Chap. 20, Figs. 29, 30, 31

Kathleen Black, Edmond, Okla., Chap. 5, pictures of Mrs. Grant

Carroll Dick, Durham, N.C., Chap. 6

Neil Doherty, Holyoke, Mass., Chap. 13

Duke University, Durham, N.C., Thad Sparks, photographer, Chaps. 5, 21

Ruth Eddy, Durham, N.C., Chaps. 2, 4, 8, 10, 19

Fairleigh Dickinson University, Rutherford, N.J., Evelyn F. Terhune, Chap. 7

Folk Dance House, New York, Mary Ann Herman, Chap. 20

J. Ray George, Arvada, Colo., Chap. 9

Kent State University, Kent, Ohio, Photographic Department, Chaps. 15, 18

Verna Klye, Melbourne, Australia, Chap. 16, "Field Hockey"

Mt. Tom Ski Area, Holyoke, Mass., Chap. 13

Oberlin College, Oberlin, Ohio, Department of Physical Education for Women, and A. E. Princehorn, photographer, Chaps. 3, 20

Southern Illinois University, Carbondale, Ill., Photographic Service, Chap. 17.

Andrew Stofan, Oberlin, Ohio, Chap. 12

University of Connecticut, Storrs, Conn., Women's Physical Education Association, Chap. 21, Fig. 3

University of Illinois, Urbana, Ill., Photographic Department, Chap. 11

University of North Carolina, Greensboro, N.C., Photography Department, Chap. 16, "Lacrosse"

Contents

PART ONE

What Do You Need?

Chapter **1**

Why Exercise?

You Need Exercise—Why Not Enjoy It?

Do you enjoy sports? Are you a tennis player who revels in serving an ace that your opponent fails to return, a swimmer who swims a half mile because it feels good, or an ardent golfer who goes back for more even after a four-putt? Do you enjoy walking in the out of doors, or climbing steps two at a time even if you aren't in a hurry?

If you haven't found *some* sport or physical activity you can do well and enjoy, it's because you haven't had the opportunity or just haven't found the right activity for you. Individual preferences for sport activities vary greatly. We all enjoy doing that which we do well, and we want to do what our friends are doing. But don't let these factors predetermine and limit your activity experiences. Try a variety of activities. Enjoyment comes with the acquisition of a performance level acceptable to you; and this you can acquire. Whatever your choice, start now.

You need a variety of physical action for your own well-being. Physical exertion is no longer required to accomplish the tasks of our daily living, but vigorous muscular activity remains a requirement of our physical bodies. Physiologists, psychologists, and sociologists attest to this basic need for exercise.

How does one meet the need for exercise? This is a decision that each individual makes for oneself. Whether you choose tennis, golf, swimming, horseback riding, walking, some other means of exercise, or no activity at all

(worst possible decision!) is up to you. If you have had some instruction and experience in a sport, you are more likely to enjoy it and seek further participation. For the student in school, this is a last opportunity to receive instruction in physical education activities without a special effort on her own to seek it out later on.

Activity Demands Function of All Vital Organs—Benefits of Exercise

Physical activity involving the large muscle masses of the body places demands on all the vital organs (Fig. 1). The trained body, free from disease and accustomed to regular amounts of vigorous activity, is the healthy body. Exercise can improve circulation, and the circulatory system in turn provides nourishment for all body parts; but vigorous activity also stimulates each vital organ to function at its optimum. Exercise, in stimulating circulation for example, brings about good bone nutrition; but bone growth is also affected by exercise in another way. The stress and strain placed on the bones by contracting muscles cause a strengthening of the bones along their lines of stress. The physically active person, then, can achieve optimal functioning of all body parts in response to the demands placed upon the body.

EXERCISE AND YOUR HEART

Your heart is a muscle. It differs in structure and function from skeletal muscle, but like skeletal muscle, it improves with exercise.

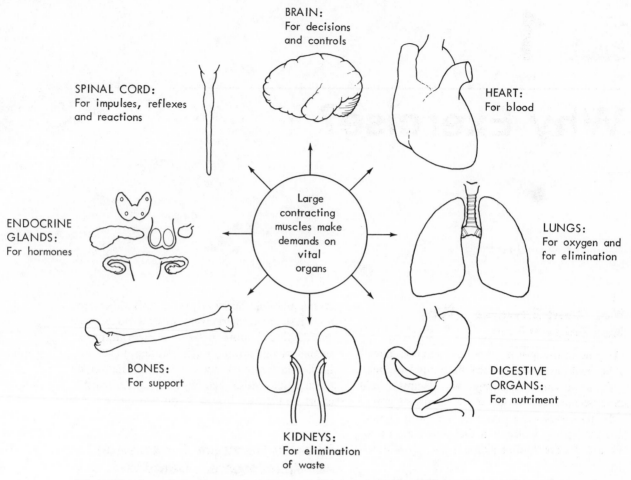

BRAIN:
For decisions
and controls

SPINAL CORD:
For impulses, reflexes
and reactions

HEART:
For blood

ENDOCRINE
GLANDS:
For hormones

Large
contracting
muscles make
demands on
vital
organs

LUNGS:
For oxygen and
for elimination

BONES:
For support

DIGESTIVE
ORGANS:
For nutriment

KIDNEYS:
For elimination
of waste

(1) Activity demands function of all vital organs. (From Jesse Feiring Williams, *The Principles of Physical Education*, 8th ed. Philadelphia: W. B. Saunders, 1964.)

Proper physical activity results in a trained heart that functions more effectively in several ways. With training in regular and vigorous activity, the heart, even during strenuous exercise, will perform at more efficient levels. Improvement includes a slower heart beat, thereby delaying the onset of fatigue, the pumping of more blood per beat, and return to a normal pace more quickly after hard work. Thus a person who exercises regularly is a person who can work longer with less expenditure of effort.

A myth, perpetuated even by the dictionary definition, holds that athlete's heart is a heart condition in which there is some enlargement caused by continued physical exertion and strain. The heart is a muscle, and it is true that it may increase somewhat in size with regular and strenuous exercise, but this hypertrophy or enlargement of the heart is an indication of its healthful development. A sound heart is not injured by exercise or physical conditioning.

A heart weakened by some earlier disease could be strained with excessive exercise, but in many cases even this pathologically weakened heart can be strengthened if the patient follows his doctor's recommendation for a gradual build up of exercise.

MUSCLE ACTION BENEFITS CIRCULATION

Any kind of activity or physical movement that is self-initiated is caused by the contraction of some skeletal muscles and the relaxation or stretching of the opposing muscles. Our muscles work in pairs. While one muscle is contracting to cause a movement, the muscle that would bring about the opposite action is relaxing. For example, if you bend your elbow as you lift this book, muscle fibers in your biceps on the front part of your upper arm contract, while the triceps on the other side of the same arm relax, or stretch slightly if you bend your arm to more than 90 degrees. This muscle action produces a massaging effect on surrounding body tissue in general and on the small blood vessels in particular. The massaging effect of muscle action aids the circulation of the blood in the extremities of the body. Studies have shown that frequent physical exercise also causes an increase in the number of capillaries or small blood vessels, so in this manner, too, the circulatory system is improved with exercise.

BLOOD CHOLESTEROL LEVEL

Atherosclerosis, a narrowing of blood vessels caused by fatty deposits on their walls, is more apt to occur in individuals who have a high blood cholesterol level. Emotional strain and a diet high in animal fats are two factors known to raise cholesterol levels in some persons. Both exercise and proper diet are aids in controlling the cholesterol level; and exercise, by keeping the blood flow strong in the circulatory system, breaks down the fatty deposits. Thus exercise assists in maintaining blood cholesterol level within the normal range. Individuals with atherosclerosis or other types of cardiac disease should of course follow their physician's recommendation in regard to the desirable amount of exercise.

EFFICIENCY IN BREATHING

Exercising regularly can effect changes in the respiratory system. With practice, scuba divers can markedly increase their endurance for the amount of time spent under water. Not only breath holding, but over-all breathing efficiency improves with strenuous exercise that is continued over a period of weeks. There will be a slower rate of breathing; and the trained or regularly exercising person may take as little as six to eight breaths a minute, whereas the untrained person may be taking as many as eighteen to twenty breaths per minute. With exercise that is strenuous enough to make one breathless or panting, the depth of the chest is increased, the diaphragm is more fully used, and the blood is exposed to oxygen over a greater area. Smaller amounts of air are needed by the trained individual because a larger proportion of the oxygen from the air can be absorbed by the lungs. These physiological changes create a greater efficiency in breathing, but the benefits accrue only with regularity of participation in moderate to strenuous exercise. Deep breathing unaccompanied by exercise will not effect the change.

EXERCISE AND MUSCLE CONTOUR

Why do we need exercise? The human body, unlike a machine, wears out with *lack* of use. Skeletal muscles, the muscles that help you to move, atrophy and lose strength when they are not used; they lose normal contour and become flabby. If you have ever had an arm or leg in a cast, you realized when the cast was removed that after only a few weeks of immobilization you had less strength in that part than you formerly had. Fortunately, this loss of strength can be overcome by starting with mild daily exercise and gradually, over a period of several weeks, increasing the effort involved. Less dramatic but similar circumstances occur when an individual leads a sedentary life. When a person moves her body only enough to walk a few feet from home or dormitory to automobile, to elevator, and to classroom or office desk, her skeletal muscles are used very little. Loss in strength and muscle tone (firmness) can come to even a young person who fails to be physically active. Weakness and flabbiness can come in the abdominal and back muscles as well as in the arms and legs.

Why is lack of activity and a resultant loss of muscular strength undesirable? Muscle strain and imbalance or lopsidedness in posture are apt to occur with weak muscles. Muscle flaccidity, or an appearance of flabbiness, may be apparent even in a slim person. Normal muscle contour, and the muscle strength required for balanced posture and avoidance of muscle strain, necessitates the regular use of all of the skeletal muscles of one's body. The body will wear out from lack of activity. You need exercise for your appearance. (See Chapter 2 for details on muscle strength and avoidance of strain.)

EXERCISE AND ENERGY

Physical activity develops the stamina necessary to carry on daily work without undue strain and fatigue. It has been demonstrated that individuals who lead sedentary lives experience less feeling of fatigue and develop a greater tolerance for their work when they add regular daily physical activity to their pattern of living. Surely this is increasingly important as more and more young women of today combine a career with the complexities of housekeeping and taking care of their families.

The inactive person may be tired simply because she is inactive. This type of fatigue is not counteracted by rest, but rather by activity. The sedentary person who rests more and more because of fatigue can reach a point of very low tolerance for any activity at all. With the slightest exertion she is weary. On the other hand, the person who is active in a sport or some type of regular vigorous physical activity can meet the demands of her daily life with greater ease.

TOLERANCE OF STRESS

What kind of situations cause stress, worry, and tension in an individual? Is it tomorrow's exam, unattained social goals, or poor organization of one's daily schedule? This depends on the person; but all individuals have limits to the number and type of stressful situations which they can stand.

Our bodies react to stress with changes in circulation, respiration, metabolism, temperature, and body chemistry. Some individuals have much more violent and wearing reactions to stressful situations than others. Inability of the organism to adjust to stress results in exhaustion, and continued lack of physiological adjustment to stress can even be the cause of death.

Exercise and sports are beneficial in relation to stress in two ways. Hans Selye, Canadian physiologist, has shown that exercise serves as an aid in counteracting or working off the physiological effects of stress. Emotional stress can frequently be relieved by activity. It can be relaxing to the physiological systems of the body to go for a walk or to play in a volleyball tournament. On the other hand, if that volleyball tournament is highly competitive with much emphasis on winning, instead of releasing tension, it may be a cause of tension. Stressful situations in sports can serve as a small sample of life and act as the proving ground on which the body learns to adapt itself to stress. Today we recognize the interrelatedness of mind and body. Inherent in physical activity is the potential for the release of mental and physiological stress. The House of Delegates of the American Medical Association states that "in an age of mounting tensions, enjoyable physical activity can be helpful in the relief of stress and strain, and consequently in preserving mental health."

WEIGHT CONTROL THROUGH EXERCISE

Exercise, or physical activity, can contribute to weight control. Two fallacies exist in relation to exercise and weight control. Many individuals believe that exercise requires so few calories that it has little effect on maintaining desirable weight and that, as soon as one is physically active, appetite increases so that the increased amount of food consumed offsets any weight loss that might have occurred with the exercise. When we realize that men engaged in hard labor may eat as much as 6,000 calories of food per day without gaining weight, we know that activity makes a difference. The energy cost of physical activity varies with the strenuousness of the activity, and there is also variation according to the individual's size, age, skill level in performance of activity, nutritional condition, and environmental conditions. Nevertheless, for the sake of comparison, here are some average energy costs: walking two miles in half an hour uses about 100 calories; bicycle riding for the same amount of time, 150 calories; fencing, 300; swimming the crawl, 400; and over 1,000 calories are used in running at the rate of seven miles per half hour. Exercise does use calories; the more strenuous the exercise, the more calories used. A person who wishes to lose weight should eat less, but using more calories through activity can also be of significant help.

We need to put appetite into proper perspective in relation to exercise. Obesity is most likely to start when physical activity is decreased. In other words, appetite fails to drop off when a person becomes less active. Jean Mayer, nutritionist at the Harvard School of Public Health, says that "adaptation to today's mechanized living, without development of obesity, means that the individual will either have to step up his activity or be mildly or actually hungry all his life."

One must continue with accustomed amounts of activity in order to maintain a constant weight. The person who suddenly or gradually becomes less active uses less energy and will gain weight unless caloric intake is decreased. However, the underweight individual also needs exercise because a moderate amount of daily activity can stimulate his appetite and of course also provide the other physiological benefits regularly gained from exercise.

EXERCISE DURING MENSTRUATION

In the past, conflicting opinions have been expressed in relation to the wisdom of activity during the menstrual period. We now know that, unless pathological or structural defects are present, the female benefits from mild to moderate exercise during menstruation. Mild physical activity is beneficial even in cases of dysmenorrhea (painful menstruation), because the activity will aid in offsetting psychic factors and relieve congestion, which is often the cause of the discomfort. If the dysmenorrhea is caused by inadequate abdominal strength, this can of course be corrected by strengthening exercises. Only jumping, which results in hard vertical landings, and heavy lifting are to be avoided during the menstrual period, for these activities can place increased pressure on the pelvic floor of the abdominal area. The female may continue with her accustomed amount of activity during menstruation even if this activity is highly competitive. Research has shown that the female who is used to strenuous sport participation need not modify her schedule during her menstrual cycle providing: "her menstrual cycle does not show unfavorable change, and her sports performance during the period is not worse than her usual average."[1]

Specific exercises often prove helpful for dysmenorrhea. However, if pain is persistent or severe, a physician should be consulted. The following exercises can be used regularly throughout the month:

1. Back lying with knees bent and feet on the mat. Contract the abdominal muscles slowly and forcefully, hold for three counts, then relax for three counts. Repeat ten times.
2. From a kneeling position, keep the hips directly above the knees while bending forward so that the hands, side of face, and chest touch the mat. Stretch one leg backward until the knee is straight and the foot is above the mat, then bend that leg and extend the other leg. Bend and extend alternate legs ten times.
3. The Billig Exercise. Stand sideways to the wall, feet together. Place the near arm against the wall at shoulder level with elbow bent and fingers pointing forward. Push the hips toward the wall until they touch it; stretch in the middle, do not twist the hips. Repeat on the other side. Perform several times daily.

POISE AND BALANCE

Time, space, and force are all factors that determine the quality of movement. Some people have an innate capacity for moving beautifully, but all can acquire the capacity through knowledge of the principles of good body mechanics, analysis of one's own habit patterns of movement, and practice for the correction of faults. Once acquired, effective patterns for movement must be used in order to be maintained. Thus another benefit that develops from participation in sports is the maintenance and/or improvement of balance and agility. The small child loves to experiment and explore, and he accomplishes feats of balance and movement that amaze and sometimes frighten observing parents. Most children discover their own abilities through exploration and practice. If, as adults, we cease being active and no longer use our bodies in a variety of movements, we gradually lose our ability to move efficiently and effectively. The old saying goes that "once you have learned to swim, you will always know how." This is comforting, but at least mildly misleading. If you have not used roller skates or a bicycle for five years, how well can you now perform on them?

YOUR PERSONALITY

The development of personality can be a wholesome outcome of participation in sports. Robert J. Havinghurst, Professor of Education at the University of Chicago, says that "personality is the valuing aspect of human behavior, while intellect is the knowing aspect." Your personality is you, particularly *you* in the actions that bring about the reactions of others. Either by design, or just in response to contact with people, you mold and make changes in your personality. What can be gained through participation in sports? This question was answered by some students: Jean said that dancing with strangers in her folk dance class gave her courage to become acquainted with people in other situations as well. Carol lost the golf match but found that she had gained self-control even under pressure. Dede won the tennis match and found that her competitors appreciated her thoughtfulness and modesty.

Play can bring emotional stability to the adult as well as the child. For children play offers an outlet for aggressions and hostilities. This can also be true for the adult. Striking, batting, kicking, and throwing in game situations all permit socially acceptable ways to release hostile emotions.

In physical education activities the dignity

[1] Dr. James C. H. Russell, *Sports for Girls*, Wisconsin DGWS, October, 1964, p. 11.

and worth of the individual are recognized. Group relations can be improved through physical education activities as participants learn cooperation, courtesy, fair play, good sportsmanship, initiative, perseverance, courage, and self-control. Physical education activities can also foster alertness, the ability to interpret human actions and to gain insight and understanding of the behavior of others. Surely the game of life can be enhanced if these attributes are practiced and learned in physical education activities.

SENSORY PERCEPTION

We perform movements and motor skills with our bodies in order to explore and understand our environment. Understandings of relationships in space are important for the child in the acquisition of reading skills. A child first feels, and then understands, the spatial relationships of up and down, front and back, and right and left. These concepts must come in terms of self, and then are transferred to reading and writing.

Our motor movements orient us to our world, but we also gain fun and satisfaction from the movement itself. The values of physical activity are considered by Eleanor Metheny of the University of Southern California in terms of sensory perception when she says,

Why do intelligent people like us spend many hours in the hot sun batting a tennis ball back and forth across a net? Why do we walk miles on tired feet in pursuit of a golf ball? . . . Why do we bounce on trampolines, circle high bars, dive from diving boards into cold water, and stretch our ligaments on the practice bar in a dance studio? . . .

Why do we do these things? To become physically fit? To develop our ability to learn by doing? To improve our human relationships? Certainly all of these things can and do result from these movement experiences—but even more certainly, these are not our basic motivations in seeking those experiences. We do them because we find these movement experiences meaningful in their own right.

We play tennis for the same reason that men paint pictures, sing, play musical instruments, devise and solve algebraic equations, and fly airplanes. We play tennis because it satisfies our human need to use our human abilities, to experience ourselves as significant, creative, and, therefore, personalized beings in an impersonal world. We do these things to intensify, structure, and enhance the sensory perceptions that are our only direct source of information about ourselves and the world we live in; and these sensory perceptions are the source of the human meanings we find in our human lives.[2]

Summary

Why do we need exercise? We need it to maintain or increase muscular strength and to maintain or improve heart and lung efficiency. Exercise can contribute to the maintenance of a desirable blood cholesterol level, can aid in weight control, can be a factor in relieving dysmenorrhea, and contribute to the maintenance of agility and sense of balance in motor movement. The physically active person not only enjoys increased stamina, but also has greater endurance for the demands of her day-by-day living. Dr. Fred V. Hein of the American Medical Association says, "What has always been suspected is beginning to be scientifically demonstrated. Exercise may still be considered good 'medicine'."

We recognize the totality of the individual, the wholeness of man. We take our bodies to the classroom along with our minds. We know that we are more than a summing up of parts. The physical and mental together make up a total being; and our physical activity experiences affect all the aspects of our lives.

The physiological benefits of exercise are significant, and the contributions of physical activity to the psychological and sociological aspects of the individual's life are also important. The developing of personality through the give and take of game situations enables one to know oneself. Playing with a partner, on a team or against an opponent provides insight for working with others. One's personality is always showing; one always works on some kind of a team!

What do you need? You need daily participation in physical activity that is strenuous enough to keep you at the level of physiological efficiency that you desire for your daily living. You should sample various sports and activities until you find some that are enjoyable and satisfying to you so that you will continue to be an active participant for the rest of your life. You do need frequent and invigorating exercise.

[2] Eleanor Metheny, *Connotations of Movement in Sport and Dance* (Dubuque, Iowa: William C. Brown, 1965), pp. 103–104. Copyright © 1965 by William C. Brown Company, Publishers.

What Is Physical Education?[3]

The experience of physical education is—or may be—

The joy of action;

The aesthetic delight in the ease and harmony and beauty of movement of one's own body or that of others;

The pride and self-confidence in the skillful and expressive use of one's own body;

The poise of the body, the spring of the step, the sparkle in the eye.

It is—or may be—

The sun and the wind; it is water and snow and ice; it is the cinder track, the grassy field, the rippling stream, the wooded hill, the rocky slope, the other side of the mountain.

It is—or may be—

The thrill of achievement;

The ability to keep going when all seems lost;

The ability to start over when all is lost;

Picking one's self up with a laugh after a tumble;

The knowing one can be counted on.

It is—or may be—

The deep satisfaction of cooperative work and play, of concerted action and camaraderie;

The ability to say a hearty "well-played" to one's opponents, to one's teammates and to one's self;

The ability to say, with a smile, "Let me help you," "Let's do it together," "Won't you join us?";

With apologies and a thank-you to E. B. White, it is the "don't in don't shove, the line that forms to the right, the seventh inning stretch, the score at the beginning of the ninth."

It is—or may be—

Fun;

A strong, skillful, sensitive body;

A courageous and generous spirit.

Test Yourself

Following are three simple ways to assess yourself in relation to physical activity. Physiological functioning is variable within the individual; the following procedures provide estimates of present status. Other suggestions for testing yourself are included in Chapter 2.

[3] Written by and permission for publication granted by Pauline Hodgson.

CARDIOVASCULAR EFFICIENCY

Taking your pulse rate after exercise is a means of assessing cardiovascular adjustment to activity. Hodgkins and Skubic have standardized a step test for women and have presented norms for performance. The exercise to be performed is stepping up and down on an 18-inch bench at the rate of twenty-four steps per minute for a period of three minutes. After one minute of rest following the exercise, the performer's pulse rate is taken for thirty seconds.

The following table by Hodgkins and Skubic enables you to convert your thirty-second pulse rate to a scale based on 100 points, and to a ranking based on standards of performance.

Table for Conversion of Pulse Rates to Cardiovascular Efficiency Scores for those Completing the Three-Minute Step Test*

Standard	Score	30-sec. Pulse
Excellent	96 and above	32 and below
	91–95	34–35
	86–90	36–37
	81–85	38–39
	76–80	40–42
	71–75	43–45
Very good	66–70	46–49
	60–65	50–54
Good	55–59	55–58
	49–54	59–66
Fair	44–48	67–73
	39–43	74–83
Poor	33–38	84–98
	28–32	99–116
Very poor	0–27	117–120

*Reprinted from Jean Hodgkins and Vera Skubic, "Cardiovascular Efficiency Test Scores for College Women in the United States," *Research Quarterly*, December 1963, p. 461. Copyright, 1963, by the American Association for Health, Physical Education and Recreation, National Education Association. By permission of *Research Quarterly* and AAHPER.

The table represents standardized scores for college women. Slight differences were observed for high school girls at the lower end of the scale. A formula was established to convert pulse rates of those unable to complete three minutes of stepping.

ENERGY REQUIREMENTS

You can readily determine the comparative strenuousness of the activities in which you participate. Take your pulse rate just prior to activity. It should be close to your normal resting pulse rate in order to have a reliable comparison. Your pulse rate should then be taken immediately following the most strenuous part of an activity. Comparing this rate with your pulse rate for other activities will indicate the relative strenuousness of your participation.

WEIGHT LOSS WITH EXERCISE

Weigh yourself before and after exercise; then again in two hours. Comparison of the first two weighings will show loss of weight due to exercise and loss of weight accompanying the loss of body fluids if there has been sweating. The third weight figure, taken two hours after exercise, will be an indication of loss due to the exercise alone, provided weight has not been altered through eating and a fluid intake greater than the fluid loss of the exercise.

Selected References

Davis, Elwood Craig, Gene A. Logan, and Wayne C. McKinney. *Biosphysical Values of Muscular Activity*. Dubuque, Iowa: William C. Brown, 1965.

Johnson, Perry B., *et al. Physical Education—A Problem-Solving Approach to Health and Fitness*. New York: Holt, Rinehart and Winston, 1966.

Karpovich, Peter. *Physiology of Muscular Activity*. Philadelphia: W. B. Saunders, 1965.

Morehouse, Laurence E., and Augustus T. Miller. *Physiology of Exercise*. St. Louis, Mo.: C. V. Mosby, 1963.

Paterson, Ann, and Edmond C. Hallberg. *Background Readings for Physical Education*. New York: Holt, Rinehart and Winston, 1965.

Selye, Hans. *The Stress of Life*. New York: McGraw-Hill, 1956.

Chapter 2

Your Figure
and How You Move

Posture—What Is It?

Your posture and how you appear to others is determined by the alignment of the segments of your body and the action of your muscles. Your posture is the "you" that people recognize— all the characteristic positions and movements that you assume as you walk, run, sit, or move in any way are part of your posture.

Suppose you were caught by a candid camera. Would you look pretty good? Remember— your posture goes with you all the time (Fig. 1): as you make your bed (Fig. 2), wash your hair (Fig. 3), or talk on the phone (Fig. 4). Figure 5 shows *her* favorite position for theme writing. Consider the many postures you get into to study. Your posture is not just the position that you hold for ten seconds for a posture picture; it is the many poses you assume all day, every day. These habitual postures are what really matter.

(1) Your posture is with you all the time.

(2) As you make your bed.

(3) As you wash your hair.

(4) As you talk on the phone.

(5) For theme writing?

WHAT IS CORRECT

The feet

Starting with the feet, let's consider what good posture means. Figure 6 shows the bony structure of the foot. The inner border of the foot is arched so that it can absorb shock; the outer border is flat for weight bearing. Figure 7 shows the foot in a normal position with the weight slightly to the outside. Good use of the feet implies toeing straight ahead, receiving the weight of the body on the heels, and allowing the weight to flow forward along the outside to the ball of the foot. The heel cord should be straight at the back of the ankle (Fig. 8).

Many people roll on the inside borders of their feet. If the weight falls on the inside, the normal function of the arch is lost as the arch is flattened and weakened; the heel cords curve in rather than remain straight (Fig. 9). There is strain on the ankle as it rolls in, a condition called pronation of the foot. In severe cases there can also be strain on the inside of the knee.

Check yourself. How do your empty shoes look? The owner of the pair pictured in Figure 10 obviously has pronation. The way the heel is worn down does not always indicate pronation, but if the inner border of the shoe is worn, and if the shoes tilt inward, pronation certainly exists. If the heel is worn on the outside, this means only that the outside of the heel strikes the ground first, but pronation *may* occur after impact by rolling the weight to the inside.

Toeing out increases the probability of pronation because placing the foot in this position causes the weight to fall to the inside of the foot (Fig. 11). Also, it is difficult for the person who toes out to move well in going straight ahead because the foot thrust is to the side rather than backward against the ground.

Walking

In walking, the toes should point almost straight ahead (Fig. 12). The feet follow two parallel lines. One should not attempt to walk on a single line with one foot taking up a position directly ahead of the other.

The heel strikes the floor first. The whole leg is swung forward freely from the hip with the upper leg leading, knee relaxed (Fig. 13). The weight is transferred smoothly along the outer border to the ball of the foot. Then the toes are used as the weight is transferred (Fig. 14).

Knees

Another shock absorber is in the knee, that is, if the knee is used correctly rather than being thrust back as far as it will go. A margin of safety is maintained if the knee is very slightly bent (Fig. 15). When the knee is hyperextended, it has reached the danger point. There is no give (Fig. 16). This position also causes an increased pelvic tilt or tipping of the hips down and forward with a hollowing of the lower back and relaxed abdominals. From the front, the knees should face in the same direction as the toes (Fig. 17).

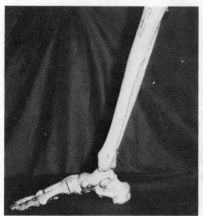

(6) Bone structure of the foot.

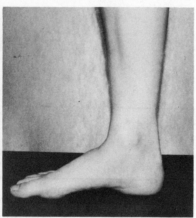

(7) Foot in normal position.

(8) Good alignment.

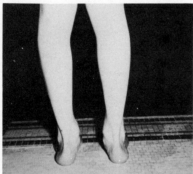

(9) Pronation.

(10) Shoe wear caused by pronation.

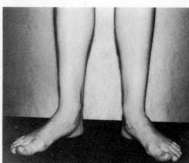

(11) Poor position.

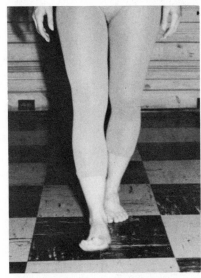

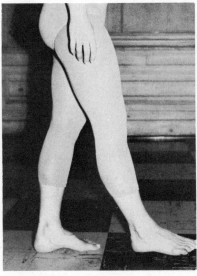

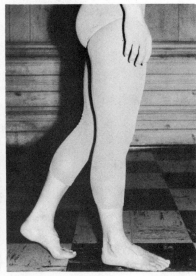

(12) Placement of the feet in walking.

(13) Heel first.

(14) Push-off from toes.

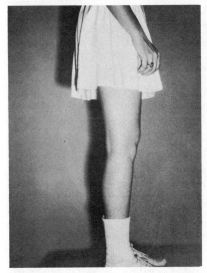

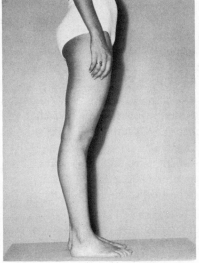

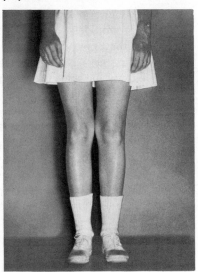

(15) Good position—knees slightly bent.

(16) Poor position—knees hyperextended.

(17) Good alignment.

Pelvis and spine

A side view of the skeleton shows the structure of the pelvis (Fig. 18). Feel the large bones in the front of your hips. When these are allowed to go down in front and abdominal muscles are relaxed, the angulation of the pelvis is increased and the curve in the lower back, called the lumbar curve, is increased.

In the infant who is just beginning to walk, the increased pelvic tilt is pronounced and the abdomen is prominent. Even the seven- or eight-year old normally has an increased pelvic tilt (Fig. 19). Some increase in pelvic tilt is to be expected at an early age, but it is a postural error at college age and older (Fig. 20). Unfortunately it's easy to assume an increased pelvic tilt—just lock your knees. But as in most postural errors, there can also be an overcorrection—a decreased pelvic tilt or tipping of the hips down and back. Some young women have a decreased pelvic tilt and flattened lower back (Fig. 21). Either of these errors can cause back trouble and loss of the shock absorbing potential of the spine. A third error is that of throwing the hips forward with a resultant leaning back from the waist up. Usually a forward head accompanies this condition (Fig. 22).

In the correct standing position a vertical line should pass just in front of the ankle joint,

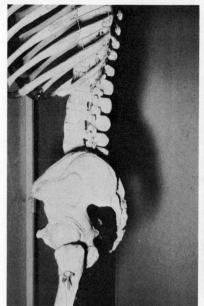

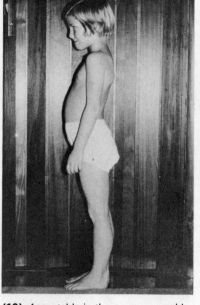

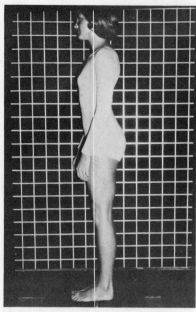

(18) Pelvis and spine.

(19) Acceptable in the seven-year-old.

(20) Increased pelvic tilt—Not acceptable at college age.

through the knee joint, and the center of the hip, shoulder, and ear (Fig. 23). The four curves of the spine should be moderate. From the back, the skeleton (Fig. 24) shows that at the base of the spine the sacrum is convex; then the lumbar curve of the lower back is slightly concave; the dorsal spine, the upper back, curves out slightly; and the fourth curve, the cervical curve or back of the neck, goes in. When one or more of these curves is too great or is flat, the back is weakened and abnormal; a change in one curve will cause compensatory changes in the other curves. If one stands in a well-balanced

position with the four natural curves, the head can also be easily centered over the shoulders, and the shoulders relaxed.

Lateral balance

When viewed from the back, the body should be in balance. As one stands with the weight evenly balanced on both feet, the spine should be straight as in the back view of the skeleton (Fig. 25). Some lateral deviations are structural, but habitually standing with most of the weight on one foot may cause one hip to be higher than the other (Fig. 26). The spine,

(21) Decreased pelvic tilt—too far the other way.

(22) Poor position—Leaning backward from the waist.

(23) Good alignment.

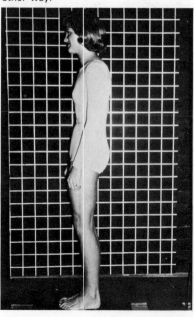

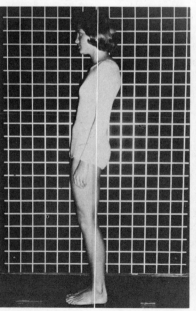

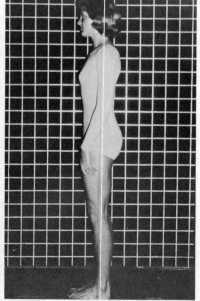

What Do You Need?

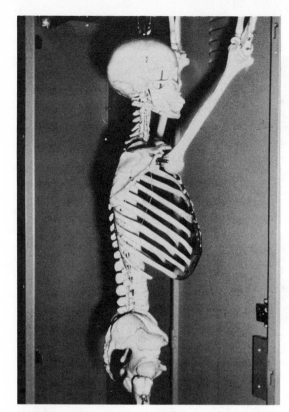

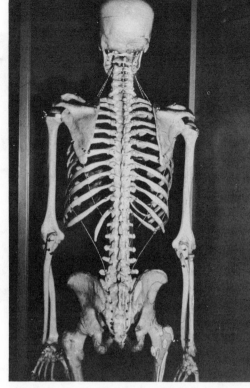

(24) Four curves in spinal column.

(25) Rear view—spinal column should be straight.

adjusting to this inequality of weight distribution, compensates by curving to the side. This condition is called *scoliosis*, or lateral deviation of the spine. Figure 27 shows a slight scoliosis. The right shoulder is lower than the left, and consequently the right hand is lower than the left. Some inequality in hip level can be spotted by noting the differences in the spaces between

hips and arms. This particular scoliosis was a result of slight difference in the length of the two legs. In well-balanced standing, the weight is equal on both feet, the hips are level, the spine is straight, shoulders are the same height, and the head is centered. Notice how the plumb line falls right through the center in this balanced posture (Fig. 28).

(26) One hip higher than other.   **(27)** Scoliosis.   **(28)** Good alignment.

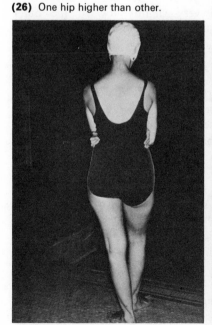
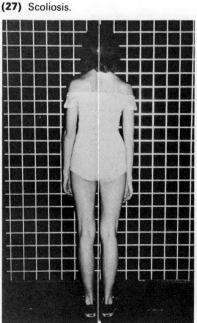
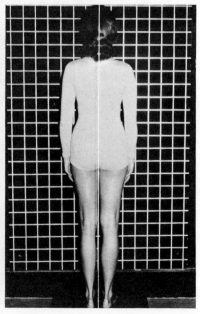

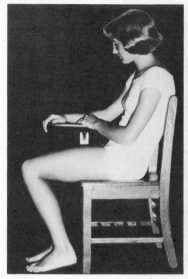  

(29) Poor posture. **(30)** Poor posture. **(31)** Poor posture.

Sitting Posture

In most of our everyday living, one does more sitting than standing. Long hours of studying sometimes produce the postures shown in Figures 29 and 30. Notice how the weight is incorrectly borne on the spine rather than on the seat. Then sometimes one sits on the floor and makes a *C* of the spine instead of maintaining good alignment (Fig. 31). Prolonged sitting in an asymmetrical position strains joints and ligaments. Whether sitting on the floor or in a chair, attention should be given to equal distri-

(32) Good alignment.

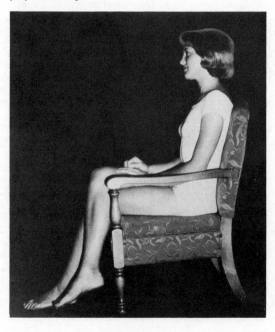

bution of weight. Both hips should be level. Correct sitting means that the seat is well back in the chair and the upper body is aligned over the hips (Fig. 32).

POSTURE IN ACTION

Most of us can assume a correct posture at a given moment, but what is more important is the way we move and how we do things day in and day out. How good is your posture when you move?

Feet

How well do your feet move? The weight should fall very slightly toward the outer borders of the feet and the feet should point straight ahead; this footwork is essential in bowling. If your left foot turns out when you bowl, the ball will probably go to the left. But, more important, there is also a strain on the foot and leg (Fig. 33). One should slide as the ball is released. To slide straight is essential for a controlled ball and good foot action (Fig. 34).

Knees

The knee should point in the same direction as the foot. A tennis player can put terrific strain on her feet, ankles, and knees. Figure 35 is a posed position to illustrate a point. This movement is painful to watch and painful to do. Compare it with action in which the foot and knee go in the same direction (Fig. 36). The technical demands for aesthetic quality in dance often require turning the toes out. If this is done

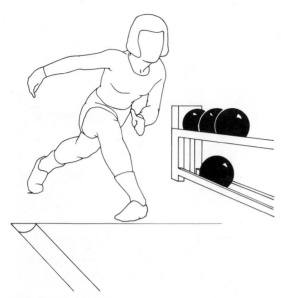

(33) Poor foot position.

(34) A straight slide.

(35) Straining feet, ankles, and knees.

(37) Good alignment of hip, knee, and foot.

(36) Good position—foot and knee go in same direction.

correctly, the whole leg is rotated outward at the hip joint; so, of course, the knee and foot are aligned (Fig. 37).

Let us look at knee posture from the side. The archer who locks her knees throws her alignment off (Fig. 38). A good archer has her knees straight, but easy. Only in this way can she have good alignment (Fig. 39). Locked knees not only cause poor posture and look bad, but they decrease efficiency of movement and may even subject the player to injury (Fig. 40). When the knees are flexed, the back is not in a strained

(38) Poor alignment—knees hyperextended.

(39) Good alignment.

(43) Knees and lower back strained.

(40) Knees and lower back strained.

(41) Good position—ready to move.

(44) Decreased pelvic tilt and round upper back.

(42) Easy knee action.

(45) Good alignment.

(46) Placing strain on lower back.   **(47)** Leg muscles used to avoid strain.   **(48)** Good alignment.

position; and in softball the take-off for first base can be started more quickly (Fig. 41). Easy knee action is essential in all sports (Fig. 42).

Pelvis

Golf is a difficult skill to master and is made more difficult by standing incorrectly. Figure 43 shows an increased pelvic tilt. The opposite, a decreased pelvic tilt with resultant round upper back, makes it impossible to swing freely (Fig. 44). With good alignment, one is in position for a good swing (Fig. 45).

Lifting

Avoid lifting a heavy suitcase the wrong way (Fig. 46). Lifting is done the correct way when leg muscles are used instead of back muscles; the legs are bent, and the upper body keeps its alignment. Many a strained back muscle could be avoided if lifting were done by legs instead of backs (Figs. 47 and 48).

Alignment for standing posture

After seeing various postures, do you prefer to have good alignment with: toes straight, knees easy, hips level, abdomen flat, four natural spinal curves, shoulders relaxed, and head centered (Fig. 49)? It certainly looks better. It's up to you.

Body Mechanics—How Should One Move?

PRINCIPLES OF BODY MECHANICS

The way one moves about in daily living not only gives others an impression of gracefulness

or awkwardness, but also can provide ease of movement in the use of one's muscles and joints or can cause continual mild strain. The following mechanical principles relate to the use of one's body in movement.

Maintenance of balance. In movements of all kinds, one continually makes adjustments in order to maintain balance.

Opposition. As one part of the body moves beyond the edge of the supporting base, the

(49) Good alignment.

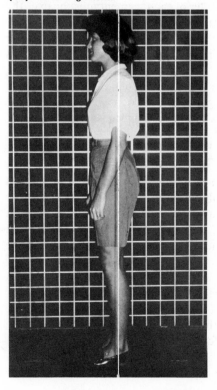

balance in the entire body will be lost unless some other part is moved out of line in the opposite direction, or unless an opposing force is applied to maintain the body in the unbalanced position. For every movement of a part of the body forward, backward, or sideways, there should be a counteraction of an equal amount with another part in the same rhythm but in the opposite direction. Opposition aids in balancing movement. In walking, for example, the swinging of an arm with the opposing leg reduces excessive trunk rotation; whereas in the broad jump, both arms oppose both legs to give added force to the foot push-off.

Additional weight. When lifting, supporting, or carrying an object, that object becomes a part of the body weight insofar as the maintaining of balance is concerned. Therefore the object should be as nearly in line with the center of the body as possible.

Base of support. If balance is threatened by some external force, it can be more easily maintained when the base is large. The base, when standing, should be increased by placing the feet farther apart forward-backward or sideways, depending on the direction of the outside force.

Gravity. Gravity is constantly acting on the body as a whole and through the individual parts. The head, neck, shoulders, trunk, hips, and legs each have their own center of gravity and the center of each segment must be over the center of the segment just below it. The center of gravity for the total body-mass is just above the hip joint in the middle of the body. When this center is lowered, as in bending the knees, balance is more easily maintained; when the center of gravity is raised, as in rising on tiptoe with arms overhead, balance is more difficult.

Economic use of force

Inertia and momentum. When starting to move, the body must overcome inertia. Once a movement is started, it takes less effort, because of momentum, to maintain a given speed than to change the speed. The more momentum can be used advantageously, the less effort will be required.

Muscle strength. Strong muscles will perform a movement more efficiently than weaker muscles. The muscles of the legs and thighs have greater strength than the muscles of the back, thus the former should be used in stooping and lifting.

Energy required. When lifting, supporting, or carrying an object, the closer the load is kept to the center of gravity of the body and the more directly over the base of support, the less the expenditure of energy.

Application of force. In moving a load, less energy is expended if the force is applied through the center of gravity of the load.

Vertical lift. The greater the vertical distance required to lift one's body, an object, or both, the greater the amount of work and the more energy required. When stooping to a load, one's body should be lowered only so far as is necessary to reach the desired object.

Muscle action. If first placed on a slight stretch, a muscle will contract with greater force. Therefore one bends the knees and ankles to stretch the working (extensor) muscles before using them in jumping or lifting.

Transfer of weight. When using any part of the body, force can be added from the entire body by shifting the body weight from one foot to the other. Power is gained in throwing, softball batting, and golf and tennis swings by the transfer of weight from one foot forward to the other foot.

Sequential action. Greater force results when the muscular contraction for a movement is initiated in the trunk muscles and flows in sequence to the periphery. For maximum force, each more *peripheral* segment should be activated at the peak of the more central one and should move at a faster rate than the preceding one. In throwing, the contraction progresses from the muscles of the back, to the shoulder, to the elbow, to the wrist, and finally to the fingers, each segment moving with greater force and speed than the previous one.

Absorption of force. To avoid jarring one's body and to dissipate force gradually in landing from a jump or in falling, the movement should be spread over as great a distance as possible. When falling, one should curl and roll. Upon landing from a jump, one should "give" with the ankles, knees, and hips.

Differential relaxation. Only those muscles necessary to an action should be contracted; other parts of the body should be relaxed.

Control of direction of movement

Force, applied in line with an object's center of gravity, will move it in a straight line. If force is applied "off-center" to an object, it causes the object to turn. To minimize the effect of friction on an object that is being pushed, the force should be applied slightly below the center of gravity of the object and in line with the desired direction.

APPLICATION OF PRINCIPLES OF MOVEMENT TO SELECTED MOVEMENTS

If one applies the principles pertaining to balance, force, and direction, correct body mechanics will result.

Sitting in a straight chair

1. The pelvis is well back in the chair.
2. The trunk is balanced over the pelvis.
3. The back of the chair is used for support.
4. The feet are close to the chair.
5. The knees and ankles are close together.

Sitting down in a chair

1. The feet are apart in a forward-backward stride position.
2. One leg touches the chair.
3. No more than 90-degree flexion at the hip joints—avoid reaching back with the hips.
4. Use the arms only for balance.
5. Control the bending of the knees.

Rising from a chair

1. Separate the feet into a forward-backward position before rising.
2. Use the arms only for balance.
3. Maintain balance and good alignment.

Sitting at a desk

1. The body is inclined forward from the hips.
2. The feet are close to the chair and on the floor.
3. The arms rest lightly on the desk for balance.
4. Reading material should be tilted to almost 45-degrees to prevent a forward head position.

Climbing stairs

1. The body is inclined forward from the ankles.
2. If the hands are used on the rail, they should be used lightly for balance only.
3. Both knee and hip joints become straightened as one pushes upward.
4. The feet are placed in the center of the tread.

Descending stairs

1. The movement is smooth.
2. The body is in good alignment.
3. The feet are placed in the center of the tread.
4. The hands are used lightly on the rail.

Jumping

1. The trunk is inclined forward.

2. The arms swing to assist in moving the body in the desired direction.
3. With the push-off there is a straightening of hip, knee, and ankle joints and the toes point straight ahead.
4. The knees and feet are slightly apart on landing.
5. Ankles, knees, and hips bend at landing to absorb the force.

Stooping and lifting

1. Hips, knees, and ankles bend in stooping.
2. The trunk is inclined slightly forward.
3. The load is centered before lifting.
4. The leg muscles are used in lifting.

Carrying

1. The load is carried close to the body.
2. When carrying with one arm, the free arm is used for balance.
3. Adjustment in balance is made at the ankles.

Reaching overhead

1. The body is close to the object with the feet in a forward-backward stride.
2. The adjustment in alignment is made at the ankles.
3. The object is grasped near its center of gravity.

Pushing and pulling

1. The feet are in a forward-backward stride.
2. The trunk is inclined forward with the back straight.
3. Force is applied through the center of gravity of the object.
4. The body weight is used to advantage.

For What Purposes Should One Exercise?

Everyone should participate in daily, vigorous physical activity. The benefits of exercise were presented in Chapter 1. But what are your personal needs? How do you measure up in flexibility, endurance, strength, balance, weight, posture and body line, and ability to relax? The simple tests on page 22 will give you some indication of your present status.

EXERCISES FOR SELF-IMPROVEMENT

The right exercises, correctly performed, can bring about self-improvement. By increasing muscle tonus and permitting better alignment, exercise can aid in correcting poor body position

Can you—	If you cannot, you need to—
1. Close your eyes, cross arms on chest, and stand on one foot for ten seconds while sole of the free foot rests against the inside of the opposite knee? Perform on both right and left foot.	Participate in activities to improve balance.
2. Do fifteen sit-ups from a back-lying position with the knees bent?	Perform exercises to strengthen abdominal muscles.
3. Sit erect on the floor with legs outstretched and forming a right angle to the body.	Perform exercises for leg, hip, and lower back flexibility.
4. Lie on back and stretch arms overhead to touch elbows on the floor?	Perform exercises to increase shoulder flexibility and upper back strength.
5. Lie on face with knees bent at right angles and push up to hands and knees ten times?	Perform exercises to increase arm strength.
6. Assume and be able to maintain a squat position with knees together and heels on floor?	Perform exercises for leg flexibility and balance. Achilles tendon at back of ankle is tight.
7. Assume a squat position with hands on ankles and elbows straight; while keeping the elbows straight, bounce with the feet—seventy-five times—high enough so that both feet leave the floor?	Strengthen the feet and legs.
8. Stand against the wall with the lower back just one hand's thickness away from the wall?	Stretch lower back muscles and correct pelvic tilt. Lower back is too curved.
9. From standing position, bend forward to a squat and place hands on floor, then spring the feet into a backward thrust position with legs straight; return to squat, then stand with knees straight? Repeat 12 times in 30 seconds.	Improve endurance.
10. Check standing posture for alignment of segments?	Be aware of posture improvements needed.
11. Lie still and relaxed on a mat, feeling comfortable, for one minute?	Learn to release muscle tension.
12. Show correct weight for age, height, and body build?	Gain or lose weight through planned diet and regular exercise.

and contour. For improved body form and performance one may also need greater endurance and, in specific body areas, an increase of flexibility or strength. What may be vigorous exercise for one individual may be moderate exercise for another. Capacities vary enormously. This is one reason why no one series or system of exercise and activity meets the needs of all individuals. Variation in individuals and their needs requires, for effective performance, a knowledge of principles:

1. Muscle tonus relates to the length of muscle fiber in its resting state. Good muscle tonus requires the regular use of all body parts. Disuse results in poor muscle tonus and flabbiness of contour.
2. To increase flexibility, a gradual attempt must be made to increase range of movement through its full range of joint motion in a continuous, easy manner. Forceful, jerky movements can cause muscles to contract and shorten, rather than to lengthen. Poor habitual posture can be the reason for the shortness of some muscles; this in turn causes lack of flexibility.
3. Muscle strength is increased by 1) increasing the resistance or weight against which the muscle group is performing, 2) increasing the number of times an exercise is performed, and 3) increasing the speed of performance. Mere repetition of an exercise does not increase muscular strength.
4. Building endurance benefits the functioning of the internal systems of the body. Unless participation in activity is strenuous enough to make one breathless, no circulatory or respiratory extension occurs and hence endurance is not improved.
5. General suggestions for exercising—
   a. Exercise a little each day.
   b. Push yourself a little more three times a week by repeating each exercise until you begin to tire.
   c. Each week increase the number of repetitions beyond the number done the previous week; this should not necessarily increase the length of time needed to do the exercises.
   d. It takes less time and energy to keep fit than to develop or redevelop physical fitness.

(50) Correcting a slump.

(51) Correcting a slump: giant lift.

(52) Correcting a slump.

(53) Correcting hips forward.

(54) Correcting head forward.

EXERCISES FOR SPECIFIC CONDITIONS

For improvement of alignment

When the *fault* is a *slump*,

1. With heels 6 inches from wall, bend forward from hips; slowly extend spine up against wall. Gradually bring feet back up to wall and then stand away from wall. Get the feeling of pushing head up against imaginary resistance. Lift the rib cage, but keep arms and shoulders relaxed (Fig. 50).
2. Giant lift (an isometric exercise[1]). Put rope under feet and, with the body in well-aligned position, pull up strongly. Hold six seconds (Fig. 51).
3. Cross leg sitting, body relaxed forward over legs. Starting at base of spine, extend

[1] An isometric exercise—a contraction of muscles in which there is an increase in tension without shortening of the muscle. It is done with maximal tightening of the muscle without moving, usually by pushing or pulling against an immovable resistance.

vertebrae one by one to an upright position, lifting arms and expanding rib cage. Return to starting position and repeat (Fig. 52).

When the *fault* is *hips forward*,

1. Stand facing wall with toes, chest and nose touching. Retract abdominals, pull head *straight* back—leaving only toes and chest touching wall (Fig. 53).

When the *fault* is *head forward* (with increased cervical curve),

1. Stand or sit with back to wall, towel held against wall behind head. Try to *flatten back* of neck to wall as strongly as possible. Use maximum effort and hold six to nine seconds.
2. Hold towel behind neck. Slowly retract back of neck against resistance of towel. Keep head level. Do not raise chin (Fig. 54).

(55) Correcting forward shoulders.

(56) Correcting forward shoulders: arm circling.

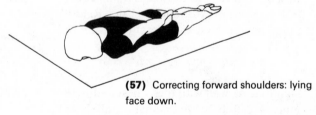

(57) Correcting forward shoulders: lying face down.

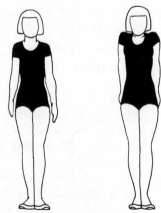

(58) Correcting shoulders high.

When the *fault* is *forward shoulders* and/or *protruding shoulder blades,*

1. Sit with upper back flattened against wall, arms extended overhead. Keeping arms against wall, slowly pull elbows down (Fig. 55).
2. Arm circling. Sitting or standing with arms stretched sideward, circle arms up and backward. Be sure to keep head erect and still (Fig. 56).
3. Sitting with wand, towel, or rope held behind head, lower the object behind shoulders. Keep head erect.
4. Lying face down. Clasp hands behind hips and pull shoulders down and shoulder blades together (Fig. 57).

When the *fault* is *shoulders high,*

1. Gradually hunch shoulders up as high as possible, feeling muscular tension which is created. Then allow them to drop and completely relax (Fig. 58).

When the *fault* is *increased curve of dorsal spine,*

1. Back lying, knees bent, with arms extended sideward, palms up, small pillow under dorsal spine. Take this position on the floor for two ten-minute periods a day. Make an effort to relax completely and allow muscles across chest to stretch.
2. Uncurling. Kneeling with hips resting on heels, insteps flat on floor, trunk resting on knees, arms at side. Starting with the lower back, gradually straighten to an upright position by uncurling spine. Then bend forward from the hips with back extended and chest leading until trunk is parallel with floor. Round body, drop head and repeat (Fig. 59).

To strengthen abdominal muscles

1. a. Back lying with knees bent, ½ sit-up with arms extended forward; if this is impossible, tuck the toes under a piece of heavy furniture and perform the exercise. In this exercise and in the sit-ups that follow, the head is lifted first and you *curl* up to a half-sitting position. The movement is smooth and controlled. You return by slowly uncurling. There is no benefit from jerking up with a straight or arched back.

b. Back lying with knees bent, ½ sit-up with arms behind neck (Fig. 60).

c. Same as 1(a) or 1(b) except done with a twist: first to right, then to left.

2. An isometric exercise for abdominal strengthening: Sit erect in a straight-backed chair. Clasp arms around the back of the chair. Tuck the chin down and try to pull the head forward and downward toward your thighs. Hold a *maximal* pull for six seconds. Relax. Repeat maximally. (You should feel that you are shortening the distance between your rib cage and your pelvis.)

Pelvic tilt and lumbar spine

When the *fault* is *increased curve*,

1. a. Lie on back with knees bent. Press lower back toward the floor by contracting the abdominal muscles. Get the feeling of pulling up in front with abdominals and down in the lower back.

   b. Lie on back with legs straight. The pelvic tilt is always increased in this position. Decrease the tilt by the same two pulls used in 1(a) (Fig. 61).

2. a. Lie on back with knees bent. Reduce pelvic tilt and keep it reduced. Lift one knee to chest. Straighten that leg and lower it slowly. Be sure the lower back remains near the floor.

   b. Same as 2(a), except move both legs. Bend knees up; straighten legs. Lower them *only* as far as you can go without losing pelvic control. If the lower back starts to arch, bend the knees up and start over. Repeat, attempting further maintenance of pelvic control (Fig. 62). (Note: It is unwise to do this exercise in reverse, i.e., to lift straight legs from the floor.)

3. Stand side to mirror. Place one hand on abdomen, the other on back of hips. Increase and decrease pelvic tilt. Do not hold the breath. Try to feel the correct mid-position between increased and decreased tilt. If you have increased tilt, you should practice exercises 1(a)(b) and 2(a)(b), and also those exercises for improving abdominal strength.

When the *fault* is *decreased curve*,

1. Lying face down, arms extended overhead. Raise straight arms and legs ten times.

(59) Correcting increased curve of dorsal spine: uncurling.

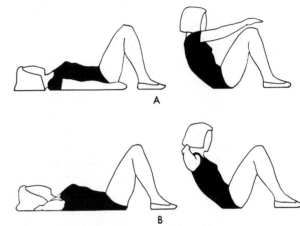

(60) Strengthening abdominal muscles.

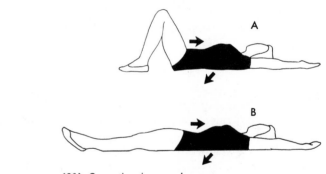

(61) Correcting increased curve.

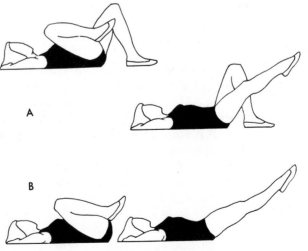

(62) Correcting increased curve.

Your Figure and How You Move   **25**

Knees hyperextended or flexed

The best and only exercise for correcting hyperextended or flexed knee positions is maintenance of the correct position. This will probably take constant reminding and correction by checking in a mirror.

To correct inward rotation of legs

1. Stand, toes straight ahead. Tighten gluteals (muscles of the seat), rotating legs so that kneecaps face straight ahead, without moving feet.

To correct foot pronation

1. Stand with feet straight ahead 3 to 4 inches apart. Keep big toe and heel on floor. Strongly pull the inner borders of the feet up, at the same time pinching gluteal muscles together and rotating the knees outward.
2. Writing with toes, holding pencil under toes with point out beyond the *little* toe.
3. Footcircling. Sit with one leg crossed over the other. Point the toes down; circle the foot in the direction of the large toe, i.e., clockwise with the right foot, counterclockwise with left foot. Contract muscles under arches strongly during the inner part of the circling motion.

MOVING POSTURE—WALKING

Occasionally, standing posture is good, but when one starts to move, postural faults occur. If this is true with you, start the correction in the static position. Some of these faults are probably slump, hips forward, head forward, shoulders forward or high, increased or decreased pelvic tilt, knees hyperextended, pronation, and asymmetries.

If your moving posture reveals new errors, here are some hints for improvement:

1. Arm swing. When the arms are relaxed, it is normal for them to swing in opposition to the legs. The amount of arm swing is proportional to the speed of the gait. If *excessive*, it is accompanied by excessive sway of the whole shoulder girdle. Both arms should swing through the same range of motion, but an unequal swing is commonly seen. It may come from always carrying books or packages in the same arm. If either of these errors is habitual with you, becoming aware of them is the first step. Practice in front of a mirror and also have a friend check you.

2. Pelvic movements. (a) If your pelvic tilt changes from increased to decreased with your gait, you may have too long a stride or weak abdominal muscles. Shorten your stride and use exercises indicated to strengthen your abdominal muscles. (b) Excessive movement in the frontal plane is to be avoided because it creates a seesaw motion of the hips. This occurs when the pelvis is allowed to sag over the side of the swinging or non-support leg. Excessive movement in the horizontal plane occurs when the hip is allowed to move forward too much with the moving leg.

You may check for both of these by taping a yardstick across your hip bones (horizontal to the floor). Walk toward a mirror and note whether the ends of the yardstick move up and down or backward and forward as you proceed.

3. Stride. The stride or distance between toe of back foot and heel of forward foot should be about the length of the foot; this will also depend on the length of your leg. Check your wet footprints. If needed, make a conscious effort to either shorten or lengthen your stride. The lateral distance between the feet should be from 1 to 2 inches.

4. Rhythm. Beauty of the body in walking depends to a large extent on smooth flowing rhythm and the absence of unnecessary movements. Speed, flow of energy, and evenness are elements of rhythm:
   a. Speed. Although individuals vary their walking speed according to the immediate purpose of walking, the speed of footwork in relation to total progress is worthy of examination. Short, therefore fast, steps tend to give a choppy effect to the gait and to induce excessive swing of the shoulders and hips because more momentum is created than can be used in total forward propulsion. Unusually long steps give a sauntering, loping effect in which the body rises and falls excessively.
   b. Flow of energy and evenness. By listening to the sound of your own walking on a hard surface you can detect whether the feet have a smooth flow of energy or whether one foot hits more forcefully and thus accents its beat; and also whether there is evenness in the timing or if the left-right sequence is longer than the right-left, or vice-versa.

5. Feet and legs. From the moment of the push-off until the heel is placed on the ground, the leg should swing in a straight line. This movement can easily be checked by walking towards a mirror, observing one foot at a time. If the foot is thrown around, lift the leg a little more.

EXERCISES FOR GENERAL CONDITIONING

The body needs daily vigorous activity. It can be gained by brief periods of swimming, tennis, or any active sport; it can also be gained, with self-discipline, through calisthenics. In the latter case one should select a group of exercises that use practically all the skeletal muscles. It is especially important, for the sake of good posture, to include exercises to keep strong those muscles which must work constantly against gravity, i.e., the muscles that keep the spine and head erect, the abdomen firm, and the feet in a normally arched position. For women, exercise of the arms and shoulders are usually needed because these muscles get very little strengthening in everyday activity.

Sample of a daily exercise program:

1. Standing erect with feet slightly apart, slowly rise on toes and stretch the arms as high overhead as possible for two or three seconds. Then collapse into this position (Fig. 63).

(63) Position for collapse.

Shake the head, shoulders, and arms loosely. Repeat the stretch and relaxation several times.
2. Run in place for two or three minutes. Lift the knees high and land lightly on the floor. Breathe easily and regularly. Keep the arms and trunk easily relaxed.
3. Select one of the exercises listed previously under "Shoulders" or "Dorsal spine."
4. Select one of the abdominal exercises, preferably the strongest one you can do well.
5. Check your posture, side and front view, at your mirror and stretch tall as you check, but be sure to keep arms and shoulders relaxed, pelvic tilt normal.
6. Grasp the top of the door frame or a substantial shower curtain bar and swing vigorously back and forth for a minute or two. Lift the knees on the forward swing. Do not do this exercise until you are proficient with push-ups and have enough hand and arm strength to maintain the grasp and swing.

RELAXATION

The ability to relax at will is becoming increasingly important to well-being, especially in view of the fact that neuromuscular hypertension is a common malady of the times. Knowing how to relax can help one to reduce fatigue, to fall asleep faster and to sleep more soundly, to perform tasks with the minimum of energy, and to meet critical situations with ease and poise. The word *relaxation* has three interpretations: diversion, exercise to relieve tension, and complete inactivity.

Diversion, a change from one activity to another is the most common form of relaxation. It may mean different things to different people, but it is most beneficial if it implies a change of pace and scene. For a very active person it may mean a game of bridge. For the office worker or student it may be a sport. The result is most beneficial when the diversion is a complete contrast to the usual routine.

Activity to release muscular tension is, perhaps, a less known kind of relaxation. The particular movements are usually for flexibility and are of a rhythmic nature. One of the most simple of this type of activity is the stretching of the muscles of the back of the neck and circling the head to release the strain of maintaining a sitting position for a long time.

The following exercises are suggested for learning to release muscular tension:

1. Back lying, vigorous shaking of hand, and release. Repeat using arm, shoulder, foot, and leg.
2. Back lying, stretch whole body, hold, then release.
3. Sitting, chest expansion with inhalation, then release.
4. Same as No. 3 except add lifting of upper arm, then whole arm.
5. Sports examples of partial relaxation:
   a. bowling
   b. recovery of arms in crawl stroke

c. release of tension before any carefully coordinated action.

The third type of relaxation is the ability to let go completely and to prevent muscular activity not only in the large muscle groups but also in the eye and the speech muscles. Acquiring this ability may take a great deal of practice.

1. Lie on the back. Tense all the muscles in the body (clench fist, grit teeth, hunch shoulders, frown, stiffen legs, and so on). Suddenly let go and feel the difference as the tension leaves (fingers uncurl, jaw drops, shoulders lower, eyelids are barely closed).
2. Progressive relaxation. Starting position: Lie on back (all muscular effort against gravity is eliminated) with the head very slightly tilted to the side, arms at the sides with the palms down, fingers touching the floor, wrists high, and elbows slightly bent. The legs are rotated outward slightly and the knees slightly bent to relieve strain on lower back.
   a. Observe the breathing without changing the depth or the rhythm and concentrate on letting it come and go naturally. Make the chest feel heavy during exhalation.
   b. Shift the concentration to one arm, and with exhalation, let the muscles of the arm become heavy and inactive.
   c. Increase the area of relaxation to both arms, shoulders, hips, and so on, until able to relax the whole body. Individuals vary in the time it takes to achieve com-

plete relaxation in one part of the body. Progress to complete relaxation will depend on the individual.

Selected References

BOOKS

Barney, Vermon S., Cyntha C. Hirst, and Clayne R. Jensen. *Conditioning Exercises.* St. Louis: C. V. Mosby, 1965.

Barratt, Marcia, *et al. Foundations for Movement.* Dubuque, Iowa: William C. Brown, 1964.

Broer, Marion. *Efficiency of Human Movement.* Philadelphia: W. B. Saunders, 1966.

Drury, Blanche J. *Posture and Figure Control Through Physical Education.* Palo Alto, Calif.: National Press, 1961.

Rodahl, Kaare. *Be Fit for Life.* New York: Harper & Row, 1966.

Wallis, Earl L. and Gene A. Logan. *Figure Improvement and Body Conditioning Through Exercise.* Englewood Cliffs, N.J.: Prentice-Hall, 1964.

Wessel, Janet A. *Movement Fundamentals, Figure, Form, Fun.* Englewood Cliffs, N.J.: Prentice-Hall, 1961.

White, Patricia. *Body Contouring, Fitness, and Poise.* Palo Alto, Calif.: Peek Publications, 1966.

PAMPHLETS

Frost, Loraine. *Posture and Body Mechanics.* Extension Bulletin Number 792. Iowa City, Iowa: University of Iowa Press, 1962.

Leverton, Ruth M. *A Girl and Her Figure.* Chicago: National Dairy Council, 1955.

President's Council on Physical Fitness. *Adult Physical Fitness.* Washington, D.C.: United States Government Printing Office, 1965.

Royal Canadian Air Force. *Exercise Plans for Physical Fitness.* New York: Pocket Books Publishers, 1962.

PART TWO

Individual Sports

Chapter 3

Archery *Helen E. Domonkos*

History. Goals. Equipment. Bracing the Bow. Shooting. Safety. Rules. Correction of Errors. Archery Activities. Terminology. Archery Organizations.

The objective in archery is to hit the target by shooting arrows with a bow. It is a fascinating test of skill that can be practiced alone, in informal groups, or in organized competition. The sport requires discipline of one's mind and muscles in order to hit the mark and gives great satisfaction as one achieves his goal. Because the strength involved can be adapted to one's capabilities, even individuals with physical limitations can participate with great enjoyment.

History

Archery has a colorful background, beginning as a means of survival before recorded history and changing to an ultramodern sport of the present century. No one knows who used the first crude bow and arrow, but it was probably made at least one hundred thousand years ago. The *Encyclopedia Britannica* ranks the bow and arrow along with the discovery of fire and the development of speech as the three most important cultural advances in the history of mankind. Other authorities have ranked the importance of archery with fire and the wheel.

Mrs. Domonkos has her B.A. from Ohio Wesleyan University, and her M.S. and Teacher's Certificate from Wellesley College. She has just retired from Oberlin College where she taught archery for thirty years. Mrs. Domonkos has attended Teela-Wooket Archery Camp many times and is a Teela-Wooket Certified Instructor.

All agree that the discovery of the bow and arrow made a significant contribution to the cultural advance of the human race, for it lifted man above the level of beasts.

Archaeological studies show that man through the ages has devised and used some form of a bow and arrow on every continent with the possible exception of Australia. The use of the bow has changed to fit man's needs: from a means of procuring food and clothing, to warfare of organized archery battalions, to a modern recreational activity. Archery is a part of our heritage and is vicariously enjoyed by all, as shown by the popularity of stories of Robin Hood, William Tell, and Hiawatha.

Although archery was practiced in some form in almost every country, it flourished to the greatest extent in England. The earliest record of the founding of an archery club is the Royal Edinburgh Archery in 1600. The Scorton Archers, founded in 1673, are particularly famous because that club has held the oldest continual archery tournaments in existence. The Royal Toxophilite Society of Archers, founded in 1781, made a great impact on English archery, but this later waned, probably because of the Napoleonic wars and the war with the American colonies. In 1844 the Grand National Archery Society was organized and became the governing body of archery in the United Kingdom. Annual tournaments have been held since 1844 with the exception of the First World War years.

In the United States, the oldest club for which records have been kept, the United Bowmen of Philadelphia, was organized in 1828. After sixty years of colorful activity, they disbanded and their treasured trophy was deposited with the Historical Society of Pennsylvania. This club has again become active under the leadership of Dr. Howard Baier.

In 1877 and 1878 a series of articles entitled "The Witchery of Archery" by Maurice Thompson appeared in *Harper's Magazine*. These articles fascinated many readers interested in a game more active than croquet, and resulted in a lively correspondence with the author. Maurice and his lawyer brother, Will, invited these "mail archers" to come to Crawfordsville, Indiana, to talk and shoot. Out of this informal gathering the decision was made to call a meeting in Crawfordsville on January 23, 1879, for the express purpose of drafting a national archery constitution. The new organization, the National Archery Association, held its first tournament the following August in Chicago.[1] Annual tournaments have continued every year, although during some war years instead of meeting, the tournaments were held as postal matches with scores mailed in to the association headquarters.

The National Field Archery Association, founded in 1939, is entirely separate from the NAA. The NFAA fosters sportsmanship in hunting, issues current information regarding state game laws as they apply to bowhunting, and annually conducts tournaments to determine the national field archery championships.

ARCHERY ACTIVITIES

The many ways that bows and arrows can be used appeal to a wide range of interests. For those who like to walk through woodland and shoot at targets at different distances and elevations, where one must estimate through light and shadow the distance to the target, where the terrain is rugged with trees and rocks, field archery is the answer.

Each year the hunting of game attracts an increasing number of archers. Game laws in practically every state permit bowhunting before the regular season is open. Such a sportsman must know wood and animal lore intimately in

[1] It is interesting to note that the NAA predates the United States Lawn Tennis Association by two years, and the United States Golf Association by fifteen years.

addition to being able to shoot instantaneously at unknown distances at a target that is often moving. All bowhunters assiduously practice field archery.

Bowfishing is another form of hunting that appeals to many. A reel on the bow with a line attached to the barbed arrow makes the arrow and fish retrievable. Shooting through water, which changes the line of vision, is intriguing.

The Pope-Young Round is an advanced round which hunters, field, and target archers enjoy because of the fascinating combination of speed and accuracy involved. Six arrows are shot within forty-five seconds at six different targets, which range from 20 to 80 yards. After each set of six arrows is shot, all contestants rotate to a different starting station, making a different range for each of the thirty-six arrows shot.

For those who like to try their skill and strength in shooting arrows for distance (in a field laid out for such activity), there is flight shooting. This is done in either the standard form of shooting or free style (holding the bow with the feet and the string with both hands).

Clout shooting is a form of archery where thirty-six arrows are shot in a trajectory through the air toward a target 120 or 140 yards away (men's range is 180 yards). Beginning players can shoot a modified clout of 80 to 100 yards. The target is a 48-foot diameter circle on the ground with a white flag to mark its center.

Novelty meets are very popular; they can be as varied as the imagination desires, with safety factors and physical facilities being the only limitations.

With such a large variety of ways to use the bow and arrow, it is important to realize that attaining good form in standard target shooting is the best possible foundation on which to achieve success in all the other phases.

Goals

BEGINNING ARCHERY

1. Learn how to brace a bow.
2. Learn selection and care of equipment.
3. Learn safety rules.
4. Learn the seven steps of shooting and have fair form.
5. Learn the principles of using a point of aim and bowsight.
6. Be an intelligent spectator at archery events.

7. Be able to shoot a Junior Columbia Round, using either a point of aim or bowsight, with a score of 200 or over.
8. Learn the basic tournament rules.
9. Participate in a tournament and act as one of the target officials.

INTERMEDIATE ARCHERY

1. Have improved form in shooting.
2. Know the principles of using point of aim, bowsight, and instinctive sighting.
3. Shoot a Columbia Round in a tournament, using bowsight, with score of 200 or over and act as one of the target officials.
4. Participate in a novelty meet using instinctive sighting.
5. Participate in a modified clout tournament using a bowsight.

Equipment

BOWS

The weight of the bow is the single most important factor. Choose a bow that is light (eighteen to twenty pounds), and gradually increase the weight as shooting technique improves (twenty to twenty-five pounds). The weight is determined by the number of pounds of force required to pull the bow a specific distance. Inasmuch as most bows are weighted for a 28-inch draw, the actual weight is approximately one to two pounds less per inch for arrows shorter than 28 inches.

There are many different materials and designs of bows. Straight bows of lemonwood have a tendency to dry out and are being replaced by fiberglass bows, which may be straight (Fig. 1) or recurved (Fig. 2). For those who wish to buy their own bow, the laminated recurved center shot fiberglass bow with hardwood core is recommended.

Bowstrings may be single looped as in Figure 1, or double looped as in Figure 2. The timber hitch knot is used to tie the lower end of a single looped string (Fig. 3).

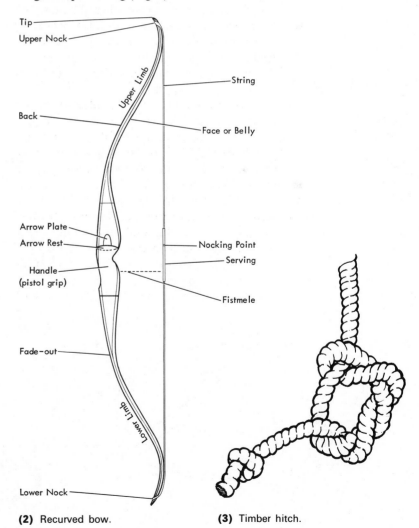

Upper Nock

Upper Limb

Back

Face or Belly

Arrow Plate
Arrow Rest
Handle

Fistmele 6"

Serving

Lower Limb

Lower Nock

Tie End of String

Timber Hitch

(1) Straight bow.

Tip
Upper Nock

Upper Limb

Back

String

Face or Belly

Arrow Plate
Arrow Rest

Handle
(pistol grip)

Nocking Point
Serving

Fistmele

Fade-out

Lower Limb

Lower Nock

(2) Recurved bow.

(3) Timber hitch.

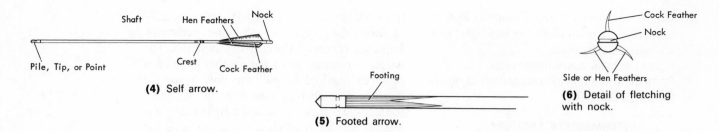

Shaft — Hen Feathers — Nock

Pile, Tip, or Point — Crest — Cock Feather

(4) Self arrow.

Footing

(5) Footed arrow.

Cock Feather — Nock

Side or Hen Feathers

(6) Detail of fletching with nock.

ARROWS

The correct length of arrows is most important. Too short an arrow is not safe, and too long an arrow is not accurate. The desired length of an arrow can be determined by holding the bow arm in the correct shooting position and measuring from tip of chin to base of the index finger. Another means of measuring is the breastbone method. Place the nock end of an arrow against the breastbone and extend both arms forward on each side of the arrow. The arrow is the correct length when the fingertips touch the metal point. If undecided between a longer or shorter length, start with the longer length. Arrow lengths for women vary between 23 and 27 inches, with an occasional need for 22- and 28-inch lengths.

Wood arrows, usually made of Port Orford cedar, are either self (one piece of wood) (Fig. 4) or footed (a fine grain hardwood spliced into the foreshaft) (Fig. 5). Footed wood arrows have greater durability and balance than self wood arrows but their cost is almost as great as fiberglass. Fiberglass, tubular glass, or aluminum arrows are the choice of skilled archers, because they are more durable and can be more closely matched in spine and weight.

Arrows are fletched so the slight spiral of the feathers is always in the same direction (Fig. 6). The "cock" feather is at right angles to the nock and is more easily distinguished if it is a different color from the "hen" or side feathers.

Archers beyond the very beginning level should use matched arrows. Such arrows have very slight deviation in spine (degree of stiffness), and are the same length, weight, and shaft diameter, with feathers of identical size and shape, thus giving greater accuracy in shooting. The spine of the arrows to be used should be determined by the weight of the bow, the heavier bows requiring arrows with a stiffer spine.

FINGER TABS OR SHOOTING GLOVES

Finger protection is an absolute necessity in order to avoid blisters as well as to permit the smoothest possible release. Best tabs are made of cordovan leather, which is firm yet pliable. Good protection is secured with double tabs (Fig. 7), which may be cordovan with the same or felt backing, or hair-calf facing with cordovan backing. Finger gloves (Fig. 8) give more protection to the sides of the fingers, but each

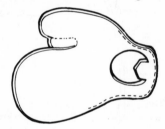

(7) Finger tab.

(8) Shooting glove.

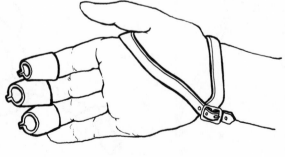

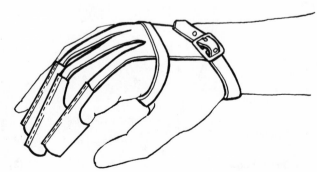

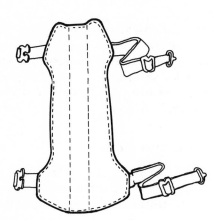

(9) Arm guard.

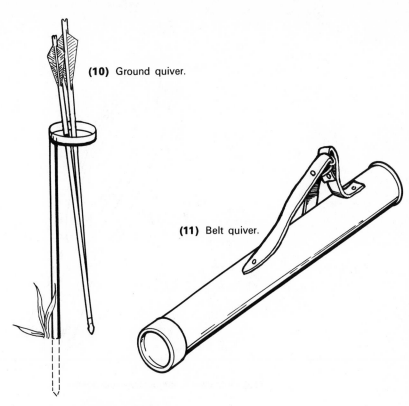

(10) Ground quiver.

(11) Belt quiver.

individual should have her glove molded to her particular finger shape, whereas tabs are interchangeable. *There must be absolutely no shooting without finger protection.*

ARM GUARDS

A guard (Fig. 9) is worn to protect the inner forearm of the bow arm against the recoil of the string and to hold the sleeve close to the wrist. Guards are made of leather or plastic reinforced with steel ribs. *It is imperative to wear an arm guard at all times.*

QUIVERS

Metal ground quivers with a pointed tip at the bottom, and circle-shaped at the top (Fig. 10), may be used to hold arrows for target shooting and can support the bow as well. However, bows are out of the way when a bow rack, stationed back of the shooting line, is used. Belt or shoulder quivers (Fig. 11) are standard equipment for field shooting and may also be used for target shooting. For indoor ranges, tennis cans may be used as quivers with sand for weighting, or a square block of wood may be nailed to the bottom of the can for support.

TARGETS

Indian grass or rye straw wound tightly in a coil and held together by tarred twine makes the best target. The standard size is 48 inches in diameter. The target face (Fig. 12) is painted in nonglaring colors with a gold center 9.6 inches wide, and each successive ring (red, light blue, black, and white) 4.8 inches wide. On official NAA faces, each colored ring is divided at center with a black line.

(12) Target with scoring values.

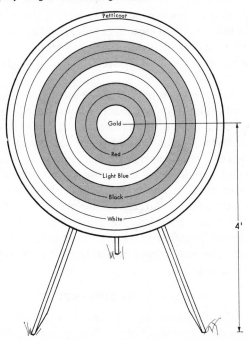

Target Value for Five Ring Scoring		Target Values for Ten Ring Scoring	
Gold	9	Gold	10 / 9
Red	7	Red	8 / 7
Blue	5	Blue	6 / 5
Black	3	Black	4 / 3
White	1	White	2 / 1

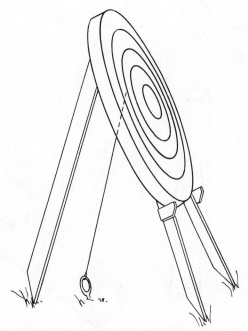

(13) Side view of target stand and anchor.

The target stand should be made of soft white pine. It is always necessary to anchor the target so that it will not blow over (Fig. 13). The center of the gold area of the target is 4 feet from the ground, and the target itself should tip slightly backward.

The range should be in an area away from traffic with 20 to 30 yards of unobstructed open space in back of the target line. A hill in back of the targets is an additional safeguard and makes retrieving arrows easier. Between targets there should be a minimum of 10 feet and preferably 15. The range should run north and south with the targets at the north end. The target line and shooting lines 10 yards apart should be clearly marked and the grass closely cut. The area should be marked off with ropes for safety.

ACCESSORY EQUIPMENT

The following sundry equipment should be available: toe markers, points of aim, tongue depressors (for range finders), small black-headed pins (for bowsights), adhesive tape, spring scales (for weighing bows), extra bow-strings of varying lengths, pencils and score-sheets, bowyer's wax, individual tassels or towels back of each target (for wiping off arrows), wide elastic bands (for slipping over bulky sleeves at the elbow), band-aids, tincture of benzoin (for toughening fingers), pliers (for removing arrows from target stand), file (for

sharpening dulled arrow points), paint, feathers (for fletching), Duco cement, fletching jig, button and carpet thread (for serving strings) or special nylon serving thread, paraffin (to rub on serving), rope (for tying up stray dogs that can be a hazard to safety).

Bracing the Bow

Bracing the bow, also called bending or stringing the bow, requires slipping the upper loop of the string into the upper nock of the bow in preparation for shooting. Two methods of bracing the bow are the push-pull (Fig. 14) and the step-in.

(14) Push-pull method of bracing bow. (Courtesy of the Department of Physical Education for Women, Oberlin College.)

PUSH-PULL METHOD

1. Hold bow at handle with left hand while back of bow is toward body. Elbow rests on hip bone.
2. Place lower limb against left instep with contact just above the nock and toward self with left hand on handle. Do not let the bow touch the ground. Check to be sure that the loop of the string is in the lower nock.
3. Place heel of right hand on upper limb and press downward (Fig. 15) while pulling toward self with the left hand on the handle, twisting body to the left to help bend the bow.
4. While maintaining this push-pull pressure, the forefinger and thumb of the right hand slip the loop into the nock (Fig. 16).
5. Check the bow nock of the upper limb to be sure that the loop is completely seated in the upper nock before removing pressure of the right hand.

To unbrace the bow, use the same body position. The string is lifted from the nock by the index finger and slipped down (not off) the upper limb as push-pull leverage is applied.

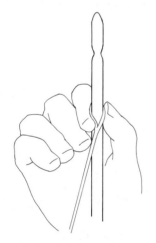

(15) Right hand pressing against upper nock.

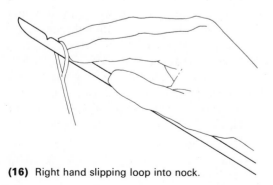

(16) Right hand slipping loop into nock.

(17) Step-in method of bracing recurved bow. (Courtesy of the Department of Physical Education for Women, Oberlin College.)

STEP-IN METHOD

The step-in method is used on recurved bows and then only with caution (Fig. 17).

1. With the bowstring uppermost and lower nock of bow to the left, step in with right leg.
2. Carefully place lower end of bow across the top of left instep so that limb is *flat*.
3. Pressure against belly side of bow handle is given by the back of the right thigh.
4. Right hand pushes upper end of bow forward while the left hand slips the string into the nock. *Avoid twisting the lower limb*.
5. Check bow nock of each limb to be sure that loop is completely seated before releasing pressure.

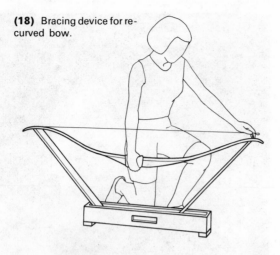

(18) Bracing device for re-curved bow.

Unbracing the Bow

To unbrace the bow, the push-pull method is recommended. This method is safe for use on all bows. Although the step-in method may be used successfully by some people, it is not without danger of damage to the bow, because there is apt to be twisting of the lower tip out of alignment. (Dealers will not replace a twisted bow if this method of bracing has been used.) Glass recurved bows are not as susceptible to twisting as the laminated glass-and-wood recurved bows.

If the recurved bow is too heavy to use the push-pull method for unbracing, there are commercial bracing devices (Fig. 18) on the market. If the school has many recurved bows, such a device is recommended.

Should You Be a Right- or Left-Handed Shooter?

Because both hands are active in archery, your dominant eye should determine which way you shoot. Try this test: raise your left hand with index finger pointed at a small object. Close your left eye. Does the finger remain on the object? If so, you have a dominant right eye and should shoot right-handed (holding the bow in your left hand). If you find that you have a dominant left eye, you should shoot left-handed. If your left eye is dominant but you prefer to shoot right-handed, it is absolutely imperative that you close your left eye while aiming and shooting.

Because right- and left-handed shooters have reverse hand positions, the terms *bow hand* and *string hand* will be used instead of left and right hands whenever possible.

The Seven Steps of Shooting[2]

Stance. Stand astride the line with feet no more than shoulder width apart (8 to 16 inches), toes pointing straight ahead, bow shoulder (left for right-handed) pointing toward target. Weight is evenly divided, body balanced and erect, but not tense. Face is turned toward target.

Nocking arrow (Fig. 19). Hold the bow horizontally with back of hand up. With the other hand take an arrow with thumb and fore-finger at the nock (avoid touching feathers), place arrow on top of bow at arrow plate above hand on handle, turn arrow so cock feather is up, then slip arrow nock onto the string at right angles. Index finger of bow hand helps to steady arrow until bowstring is partially drawn.

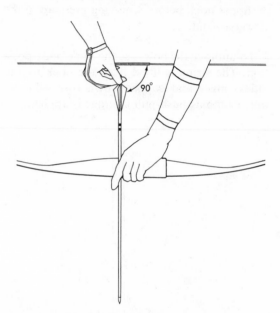

(19) Nocking arrow at right angle to string.

Drawing the bow. Bow hand is placed so that bow rests in heel of hand with the *V* formed by the index finger and thumb in the center of the bow; top of hand is even with top of handle (Fig. 20). Index finger and thumb (thumb on top) encircle bow loosely with lower fingers scarcely touching the bow. The wrist is straight, with fingers dropped slightly lower than wrist. Raise bow toward target with elbow of bow arm *almost* straight, elbow rotated down and out, in such a position that if the bend were continued

[2] Adaptation of material taught by Myrtle K. Miller, Teela-Wooket Archery Camp.

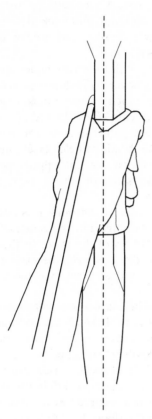

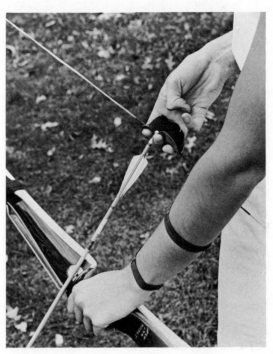

(21) Placement of shooting fingers on string.

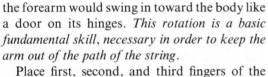

(20) Position of hand on bow handle as seen by archer.

the forearm would swing in toward the body like a door on its hinges. *This rotation is a basic fundamental skill, necessary in order to keep the arm out of the path of the string.*

Place first, second, and third fingers of the string hand on the string in the first joint or slightly in front of the joint. All three fingers must be at right angles to the string, with the same amount of each finger on the string. The arrow rests between first and second fingers with *very slight* contact. Bend fingers only at the first joint, keeping back of hand straight and in line with forearm. Relax thumb in palm of hand (Fig. 21).

Drawing the bow is done by use of the arm, shoulder, and upper back muscles increasing the spread between the arms. Think of pulling back from the tip of the string elbow in order to bring shoulder blades together. String elbow is back at full draw, with the arm parallel to the ground, making a continuation of the line of the arrow (Fig. 22). The fingers do not pull, they merely act as hooks on the bowstring. String fingers, hand, and forearm must not be tensed,

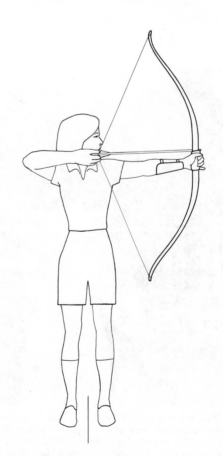

(22) Position at full draw.

(23) Draw and anchor (front view). Notice relaxed position of bow hand. (Courtesy of the Department of Physical Education for Women, Oberlin College.)

(24) Draw and anchor (back view). Notice tip of arrow in relation to back of bow; also notice firm anchor with string contacting center of chin and nose. (Courtesy of the Department of Physical Education for Women, Oberlin College.)

because the draw is accomplished by use of the upper arm, shoulder, and back muscles. Take a breath during drawing and hold it until after the arrow is released.

Anchoring. Pull the string under jaw bone so side of index finger is touching the under side of jaw bone at center. String touches tip of nose and center of chin (Figs. 23 and 24). Thumb is relaxed in the palm; it does not assist in the anchor. The head is held erect and turned toward the target but not tipped. The anchor must be the same on every shot, firm and comfortable.

With some facial contours, it is not possible to align the bowstring at the center of the chin and touch the tip of the nose. In this case the center of the chin becomes the anchor with the bowstring coming as close as possible to the tip of the nose.

Aiming. There are three different methods: (1) Point of Aim (POA) is the best method for beginners in order to avoid overdrawing the arrow. This will be explained first. (2) Bowsight is the method generally used after one has acquired a fair degree of skill in the draw. With the modern fast recurved bows, this method is more accurate than the POA (see following section, "Use of Bowsights"). (3) The so-called instinctive method is the most difficult, as it involves developing a fine kinesthetic feeling in the aiming process (see later section, "Field Archery").

Point of Aim (POA) Method involves using a spot on the ground, target, or background at which you point the arrow and sight in order to hit the target. Using the bowstring as a straight edge, line up POA with the center of the gold (Fig. 25). Place POA approximately two-thirds distance from shooter to target in line with the gold for close ranges. Refinement of exact spot comes only through trial and error.

For right-handed shooters, the right eye is the aiming eye (reverse for left-handed). Close the left eye. Sight with right eye to right of string, left of bow, to tip of arrow so you see the POA resting on top of the arrow point. Both eyes may remain open if your right eye is dominant (right-handed shooter) and you can focus clearly. If you have a dominant left eye, you must either shoot left-handed or close the left eye. After a little experience, one should, while sighting, be able to see the string lying close to the left side of the bow.

Hold the shooting position for two, three, or

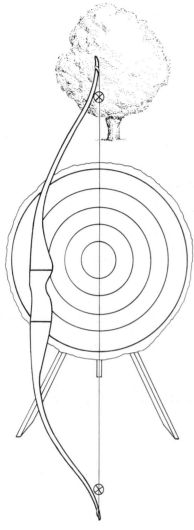

(25) Use of bowstring for alignment of POA with gold.

(26) Relase and follow-through. The lower limb of the bow swings forward if bow hand is relaxed. Notice string hand is still at neck. (Courtesy of the Department of Physical Education for Women, Oberlin College.)

more seconds to be sure muscles are steady. Maintain a steady push of the bow arm and pull of the string arm so that the arrow will not creep forward even slightly while you are concentrating on aiming.

Release. Relax fingers of string hand, allowing string to slide smoothly off the fingers. After tension of string is released, the back muscles will cause the right elbow to continue to move in the same direction, so the string hand will glide along the neck about 4 inches. The inside of the forearm and upper arm must remain close together and move backward as one segment.

The bow arm remains in the same careful alignment throughout. As soon as arrow is released, relax bow wrist and fingers, and let bow act naturally (Fig. 26). Avoid gripping bow, dropping arm, or throwing arm sideways. Keep the bow arm pointed toward the gold.

Follow-through or after-hold. Hold your position until after the arrow lands. Keep your eye on your POA. Analyze and check position of string hand and elbow, as well as position of bow hand, elbow, and shoulder.

EXPLANATION OF POA PRINCIPLE

There are two reasons why it is necessary to aim below the target at close range: (1) Because the nock end of the arrow is not at the eye but under it, the arrow is actually tipped upward. (2) A projectile flies in a trajectory or arc that first rises and then falls. At close range the arrow is still rising so the arrow must be aimed below the target; at long range the arrow is falling, so it must be aimed above the target. The sight line and the flight line always intersect at the tip of the arrow (Fig. 27).

A record of one's POA can be made by using a tongue depressor as a range finder. With the range finder in the bow hand, the bow arm is held in precise shooting position, with the top of the range finder at center of gold, and the edge bisecting the target (Fig. 28). Mark with thumb nail where the POA is in relation to the gold. The closer one is to the target the lower the POA.

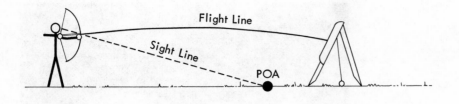

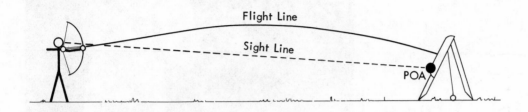

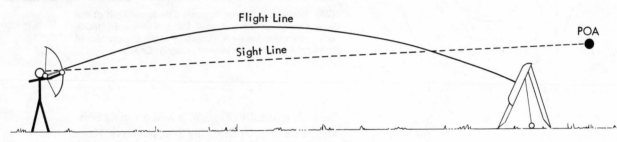

(27) POA principle for close range, point blank, and long range.

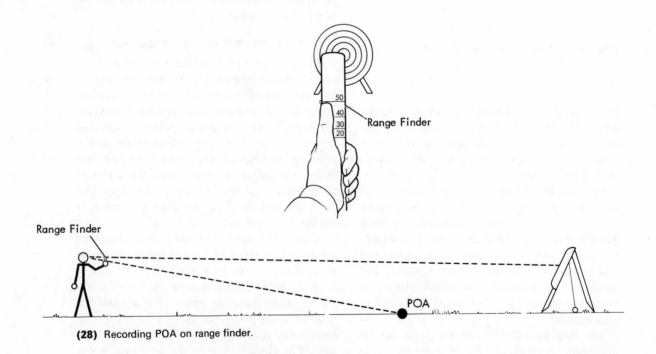

(28) Recording POA on range finder.

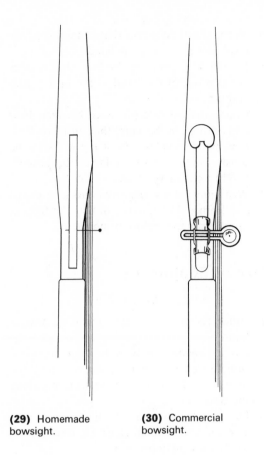

(29) Homemade bowsight.

(30) Commercial bowsight.

THE USE OF BOWSIGHTS

Bowsights may be used in the United States in "Free Style" tournaments, but not in tournaments designated as "Bare Bow." Sights may be simple home-made devices, such as an 8-inch strip of adhesive and a small black-headed straight pin (Fig. 29) or a commercial sight (Fig. 30). The sight is put above the handle on the back of the bow (or belly if it is smoother). If using a pin, it is inserted between the adhesive and the bow so the head is above the arrow. With a bowsight the sight line of the right eye (reverse for left-handed) is to the right of the string, through the head, to a definite small spot in the center of the gold. The aiming eye must see the string aligned along the left side of the bow.

The bead is adjusted for each range, being high on the upper limb for close ranges, and low for long ranges. Correction laterally may be made by pushing or pulling the bead in or out. Correction is always made in the direction of the error: for instance, if the group is high, the bead is raised; if it is low, bead is lowered. If the group is right, push the pin in; if left, pull the pin out (reverse for left-handed).

In the POA method, at full draw the tip of the arrow is brought into line just below the POA. One concentrates on the tip of the arrow at the base of the POA and sees the target in peripheral vision. In the bowsight method one looks at a definite small spot in the center of the gold with the tip of the arrow in peripheral vision. Holding steady is absolutely essential for accuracy in aiming. Throughout the release and after-hold, one must focus on a definite small spot in the center of the gold.

After one has recorded her POA on a range finder, it is an easy step to transfer the recorded perspective to the bowsight. In the POA method it is the distance between the center of the gold and the POA; in the bowsight method it is the distance between the center of the gold and the tip of the arrow when the bow is at full draw.

Safety Practices and Archery Etiquette

Inasmuch as bows and arrows are weapons, safety rules must be established at the start. Everyone must realize that the penetrating power of an arrow is greater than a bullet, as shown by tests of shooting at sand bags. *The importance of safety procedures cannot be over-emphasized.*

1. Everyone, when shooting, stands astride the shooting line.
2. No one nocks her arrow until the signal is given to begin shooting. A nocked arrow is like a cocked gun.
3. One blast of the whistle signifies the beginning of shooting, one blast for stopping, and two blasts for an emergency.
4. After the starting whistle, the archer shoots her six arrows, then steps three paces back of the shooting line.
5. No one crosses the line in front to retrieve an arrow that has fallen from a bow. If it can be reached by use of the bow without changing one's position, it may be retrieved and shot.
6. No tackle is taken back of the shooting line when people are shooting.
7. No one points an arrow at anybody, even in fun.
8. No one shoots for distance except on a specially marked field.
9. No one shoots straight up in the air.

10. When scoring and retrieving arrows, always stand to the side of the target rather than in front, unless you are the target captain, who withdraws all arrows.

11. In drawing arrows from the target, be sure no one is back of you, where she may be injured by a sudden removal of the arrow.

12. When retrieving arrows, target mates help look for lost arrows and all return together. Never return while target mates are still at or behind the targets.

13. When different ranges are desired for a group that is shooting at the same time on the same field, always use one shooting line and place the targets at the desired ranges (Fig. 31).

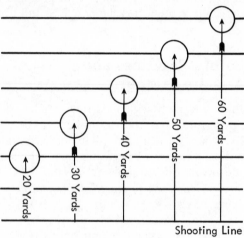

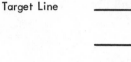

(31) Target arrangement when shooting at different ranges.

14. No one ever stands either to the right or left in front of the shooting line.

15. Wear clothing with no pins, buttons, pockets, or ruffles on the left (on the right for left-handed shooters), to interfere with the bowstring on release.

16. Wear clothing that fits the bow arm snugly (without being tight) so the string will not be deflected from its path.

17. Nock arrow so that cock feather is pointing away from the bow, not toward it.

18. Inspect arrows for glue deposit especially on the feather below the cock feather. This feather passes over the top of the bow hand and roughness at its base may scratch the hand. A band-aid should be placed over any scratch before continuing shooting.

19. Be sure that arrows are long enough to avoid pulling the arrow within the bow.

20. Never shoot an arrow that is splintered, as a splinter may enter the hand.

21. Be careful in bracing the bow that it does not slip out of the hand at the upper limb and hit one in the face.

22. Check the fistmele (distance between bow and string) to be sure that it is at least 6 inches. If it is less, the string will slap the wrist. Manufacturers indicate the bracing height on recurved bows.

23. Wear finger tabs or gloves and arm guard at all times. Use tincture of benzoin to help toughen fingers before blisters form.

Care of Equipment

BOWS

1. Brace the bow correctly, gripping bow at handle.

2. Do not bend the bow in the opposite direction to its curve. Attempting to straighten or reverse the curve may result in breaking the bow.

3. Do not release string without an arrow. The arrow absorbs the shock which, if submitted to the bow, may break it.

4. Do not overdraw bow. Only short people should use short bows (less than 58 inches). Bows ranging from 58 to 66 inches long are less apt to break, and will pinch the fingers less as the string is drawn.

5. Never shoot a bow upside down as it changes the stress on the bow. Paint an arrow pointing upward on upper limb of the bow to remind the shooter to avoid this error.

6. At the beginning of the season and in cold weather "work up" a bow by gradually increasing the bend several times before shooting.

7. Never let any part of the bow touch the ground, as dampness affects its cast and the bow may be stepped on. Place it on bow rack or ground quiver.

8. Always unbrace the bow after shooting.

9. Hang the bow vertically by bowstring near upper nock, or have it lie flat. Never let a bow stand, because it bends the lower limb.

10. Wipe off wooden bow with dry cloth if it gets wet in order to prevent splinters.

11. Keep in a cool, well-ventilated and not too dry place during the off-season (not near radiator or in a hot room).

ARROWS

Retrieve arrows from target correctly (Fig. 32). One hand with thumb and forefinger around arrow, palm forward, presses against target with back of hand. With other hand grasp arrow as close to target as possible and pull straight out. The drawn arrow is then placed in hand against target, between thumb and forefinger, with crest hanging down. Carry arrows fanned out so that feathers do not touch. Thumb pivots down the shafts with points in palm (Fig. 33). It is not necessary to place a finger between each arrow.

Retrieve arrows from the ground without bending arrow or touching feathers. Stoop, grasping arrow as near the ground as possible, and pull straight back. If the feathers are embedded in grass, pull the arrow on through. When retrieving arrows, pick up any arrow (not just your own) on the ground in front of the target as soon as discovered. Otherwise, someone may step on the arrow and crack it. Place arrow behind target under tripod for archer to claim. Never shoot at a target which has a "hanging" arrow.

In shooting, be sure that arrows are long enough so that they will not be drawn within the bow, as that can cause serious injury. Wipe off any mud and moisture with tassel or dry cloth. Mud spoils the arrow's balance and finish. Always keep arrows in a rack in such a way that feathers do not touch each other. Between seasons arrows need to be sprayed with moth repellent.

STRINGS

Keep strings well waxed, using bowyer's wax. If string is frayed, discard it, for in breaking it may also break the bow. Keep extra strings coiled rather than folded with a sharp bend. Replace serving if it is frayed or loose (Fig. 34).

TARGETS

Avoid rolling targets. Rolling is harder on targets than is shooting. Targets should be dampened with a spray mist of water in dry weather, because straw and grass break when dry. If target becomes loose and soft, it can be tightened by following string with which it is wound, pulling cord with a hook, working from the center out. Targets should be stored flat, face downward in a humid, cool place. Rye straw targets should be sprayed with rodent repellent and stored so that rats cannot get into them.

(32) Retrieving arrows from target. (Courtesy of the Department of Physical Education for Women, Oberlin College.)

(33) Carrying arrows fanned out. (Courtesy of the Department of Physical Education for Women, Oberlin College.)

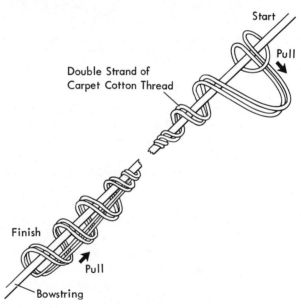

(34) How to start and finish serving bowstring.

Target Archery Rules and Tournament Procedures

1. Values of rings in five-ring scoring are gold, 9; red, 7; blue, 5; black, 3; white, 1. Values in ten-ring scoring are: gold, 10, 9; red, 8, 7; blue, 6, 5; black, 4, 3; white, 2, 1. An arrow that cuts through the black line between rings and *cuts into* the next ring is given the higher value except when the target face or arrow has been touched before the decision has been made.

Archery   **45**

(35) Four shooters at target scoring in tournament. (Courtesy of the Department of Physical Education for Women, Oberlin College.)

2. Arrow rebounding from scoring face, if witnessed, is 7 when shot from 60 yards or less, 5 when shot from a distance over 60 yards. On the score card, a circle is drawn around such a score to distinguish it from the usual 7 or 5.

3. Arrow that has passed through so that it is not visible from the front is 7 at 60 yards or less, 5 when shot from a distance of over 60 yards. Arrow passing completely through target, if witnessed, is scored the same. For either of these, a circle is drawn around such a score on the score card.

4. Arrow in petticoat has no value and is not considered a hit.

5. Tie scores are resolved in favor of the archer shooting the highest score at the longest distance, then the next longest distance, in descending order. If still tied, ties shall be resolved by the greatest number of golds, then reds, then blues, then blacks. If still tied, the tie shall be resolved by the greatest number of perfect ends. If still tied, it shall be so recorded.

6. An arrow leaving the bow shall be deemed shot if the archer, while standing where she has been shooting, cannot reach it with her bow.

7. When equipment breaks, an archer is not entitled to repeat a shot unless the misshot arrow can be reached from the archer's position on the shooting line by use of her bow.

8. If an archer shoots more than six arrows on an end, she shall forfeit as many of the highest scoring arrows as the number of extra arrows shot.

9. A hit on a target not assigned to the archer shall not be counted.

10. It is recommended that no more than four people shoot at the same target.

11. In official tournaments, two archers will shoot three arrows at the same time, then yield their positions to the other two. Then the first two shoot their remaining three arrows, followed by the second two. Thus witnessing is facilitated.

12. When four people are shooting at a target, one is captain, two are scorers, and the fourth is assistant captain (Fig. 35). The captain calls and draws each of her own arrows first, starting with the highest, then in score card sequence she does the same for each shooter. It is customary for the captain to give the number of hits for each archer as a summary before proceeding to pull the

Susan Smith — Round: Columbia — Date: Apr. 19, 1968	Hits	Score
At 50 yds.		
7 7 5 1	4	20
9 7 7 5 5 3	6	36
9 7 3 1 1	5	21
7 7 7 5 5	5	31
	20	108
At 40 yds.		
9 7 7 7 5	5	35
9 7 7 5 5 5	6	38
9 7 5 5 3 1	6	30
9 9 7 7 7 5	6	44
	23	147
At 30 yds.		
9 9 9 7 7 5	6	46
9 7 7 5 5 5	6	38
9 9 9 9 9 9	(6 L.M. 54)	
9 9 9 9 7 7	6	50
	24	188
Total Score	67	443

Jean Lowry — Round: Columbia — Date: Apr. 19, 1968	Hits	Score
At 50 yds.		
7 7 5 3	4	22
7 5 5 3 1	5	21
9 5 5 3 1 1	6	24
9 (7) 5 3 1	5	25
	20	92
At 40 yds.		
9 5 5 3 3	5	25
9 5 3 1	4	18
5 5 5 1 1	5	17
9 7 5 1	4	22
	18	82
At 30 yds.		
9 9 7 5 5 3	6	38
7 7 7 3 3	5	27
9 9 7 5 3 3	6	36
9 7 5 5 5	5	31
	22	132
Total Score	60	306

Stella Brennen — Round: Columbia — Date: Apr. 19, 1968	Hits	Score
At 50 yds.		
9 7 7 3 1	5	27
9 9 7 7 1 1	6	34
7 7 5 5 5 3	6	32
9 9 7 5 3	5	33
	22	126
At 40 yds.		
9 9 7 5 1	5	31
9 7 7 5 5 5	6	38
7 7 7 5 1 1	6	28
9 9 7 5 5 3	6	38
	23	135
At 30 yds.		
9 9 9 7 7 5	6	46
9 9 7 (7) 5 5	6	42
9 9 5 5 5 5	6	38
9 9 9 9 7 5	6	48
	24	174
Total Score	69	435

Mary Bliss — Round: Columbia — Date: Apr. 19, 1968	Hits	Score
At 50 yds.		
7 7 5 5	4	24
9 7 7 5 3	5	31
9 9 7 7 5 5	6	42
9 7 5 5 5	5	31
	20	128
At 40 yds.		
7 7 7 5 3	5	29
7 7 5 3 1 1	6	22
9 7 7 5 5 3	6	36
9 7 7 7 5 5	6	40
	23	127
At 30 yds.		
7 7 7 7 5 3	6	36
9 9 7 7 7 5	6	44
9 7 7 7 7 7	6	44
9 9 7 (7) 5 5	6	42
	24	166
Total Score	67	421
Team Score	263 – 1605	

(36) Sample scoresheet for five-ring scoring.

next person's arrows. The captain is in general charge of the target, also.

Two scorers score independently. One scorer repeats the value of each arrow and the total number of hits as the captain calls same. Assistant captain checks and assists the captain; she is also responsible for errors.

13. Double scoring shall be used. The two scorers shall check their records with each other after each end, range, and round. See sample scoresheet (Fig. 36) for five-ring scoring. (A quick check for mistakes in five-ring scoring: if hits are even, score must be even; if hits are odd, score must be odd.) For ten-ring scoring, see Figure 37.

14. Lady Paramount (the woman official in charge of a tournament) witnesses and signs the score card for perfect ends.

15. A round that requires shooting from more than one distance is started from the greatest distance, after which archers move forward to the next distance. No practice arrows may be taken between ranges.

16. When there is a "hanging arrow," Lady Paramount blows her whistle twice (emergency signal). All persons on the shooting line unnock their arrows. Then the person who shot the arrow goes to the target and places it firmly in the hole.

17. Any type of sighting device attached to the bow or any type of point of aim that does

Name *Janice Rudd*			Name				
Round *900 American*			Round				
Date *Oct. 24, 1968*			Date				
At *60* yds.		Hits	Score	At yds.		Hits	Score
7 5 4 4 2		5	22				
8 7 7 5 3 1		6	31				
9 5 5 4 1		5	24				
7 5 4 4 4 4		6	28				
9 8 7 5 2 2		6	31				
	28–142						
At *50* yds.				At yds.			
8 7 7 5 2 1		6	30				
9 7 ⑦ 5 2 1		6	31				
8 7 7 5 3 3		6	33				
9 6 6 4 4 1		6	30				
8 8 7 5 4 2		6	34				
	30–158						
At *40* yds.				At yds.			
8 8 7 4 2		5	29				
7 6 6 3 2 1		6	25				
9 7 7 4 3 2		6	32				
10 8 7 7 4 1		6	37				
8 7 5 4 4		6	32				
		29	155				
Total Score		87	455	Total Score			

(37) Sample scoresheet for ten-ring scoring.

not protrude more than 6 inches above the ground level may be used in a tournament, unless it is a "bare-bow" tournament.

18. Any type of bow except a crossbow may be used.

Popular Target Archery Rounds for Women

ROUNDS DESIGNED FOR SCHOOL USE

Scholastic Round: 24 arrows from 40 yards, 24 arrows from 30 yards, respectively.

Jr. Scholastic Round: 24 arrows from 30 yards, 24 arrows from 20 yards, respectively.

Range Round: 60 arrows from a single distance, which may be either 50 yards or 40 yards. If indoors, the distance is either 30 yards or 20 yards.

Miniature Round: 60 arrows from 15 yards on a 24-inch target, scaled to the same proportions as the regulation target. This type of round is designed for indoor shooting.

OFFICIAL ROUNDS OF THE NATIONAL ARCHERY ASSOCIATION

American Round: 30 arrows from 60 yards, 50 yards, and 40 yards, respectively. (5-ring scoring)

900 American Round: same as foregoing in every respect except 10-ring method is used for scoring.

Jr. American Round: 30 arrows from 50 yards, 40 yards, and 30 yards, respectively. (5-ring scoring)

Columbia Round: 24 arrows from 50 yards, 40 yards, and 30 yards, respectively. (5-ring scoring)

Jr. Columbia Round: 24 arrows from 40 yards, 30 yards, and 20 yards, respectively. (5-ring scoring)

INTERNATIONAL ROUND (Fédération Internationale de Tir à l'Arc)

The International Round is commonly called the FITA. Scoring is based on the following:

36 arrows from 70 meters on a 48-inch target;
36 arrows from 60 meters on a 48-inch target;
36 arrows from 50 meters on a $31\frac{1}{2}$-inch target;
36 arrows from 30 meters on a $31\frac{1}{2}$-inch target.

Ten-ring scoring is always used for the FITA Round. The quick check for mistakes in five-ring scoring does not apply to ten-ring scoring, however.

Some Common Beginning Errors with Suggested Corrections

The following are stated for right-handed shooters. It is essential to learn the correct coordinations at the start, as errors repeated become habits that lead only to discouragement. Each individual can check her form under the following seven steps.

Errors	Correction	Errors	Correction
I. Stance Twisting toward target at hips or shoulders.	Stand tall, turn only at neck. Do exercise of turning at neck to limber up neck muscles.	**IV. Anchor** 1. To right of center of chin. 2. Too high on face.	Practice draw and anchor in mirror to see if string is in center and under chin, and if possible, touching nose at tip without moving head.
II. Nock 1. Cock feather toward bow.	Check ridge on arrow nock in addition to finding feather that is at right angles to nock. (See Fig. 6.)	3. Thumb touching chin or jaw bone.	Relax thumb in palm of hand. It has no function in the anchor.
2. Arrow starts at right angles but string hand pushes nock up or down.	Mark nocking point on string above arrow with Scotch tape or thread. Avoid pressure on arrow nock.	4. Moving head toward string. 5. Mouth open or chewing gum.	Stand tall, contract back and abdominal muscles for a steady trunk position. Pull right elbow back, bringing shoulder blades together. Set teeth to get uniform anchor position.
III. Draw 1. Gripping bow tightly.	Place forefinger and thumb on handle with other fingers extended forward (not out at left side). Have bow rest in hand with pressure on belly of bow, not on back or sides.	**V. Aim** 1. Using wrong eye. 2. Not holding long enough to get steady aim.	Practice closing non-sighting eye in front of mirror. Practice draw, anchor, aim, and hold without release. Contract abdominal and back muscles to assist upper back and shoulder muscles.
2. Pinching arrow nock so arrow falls away from bow.	Think of pulling string, not arrow. Have *very light* contact on arrow. Practice drawing elbow back at beginning of draw. Relax fingers; they are only "dead hooks" on string.	3. Tipping head to look along arrow.	While looking straight ahead, pull bowstring back with hand under chin. Then turn head toward target and keep head in same position. Look only at tip of arrow.
3. Hunching left shoulder.	Hunch shoulder and drop it to sense correct and incorrect position. Practice mimetics of drawing with conscious use of abdominal muscles along with upper back and shoulder muscles, while keeping bow shoulder low. If fault persists, a lighter bow must be used.	**VI. Release** 1. String hand flies out dropping elbow. 2. String hand jerks out to right.	Without any tackle in your hands, practice release by pulling against other hand. Place bow hand at anchor point, palm forward, then with string hand pull against other hand as in shooting, releasing in a straight line and checking afterhold position.
4. Straightening left elbow with string slapping elbow or forearm.	Rotate elbow outward before draw and maintain this position during entire process. Emphasize pull of string arm more than push of bow arm.	3. Creeping forward.	Check on bow arm so that it continues to push, and keep string elbow *back*. Squeeze shoulder blades together until moment of release. If fault persists, change to a lighter bow.
5. Rolling bow wrist in or out.	Practice drawing string back only a few inches while concentrating on keeping bow wrist and forearm straight with *V* of thumb and forefinger in center of bow. (See Fig. 21.) Gradually increase length of draw.	4. Tossing action of bow arm.	Have POA or bowsight set so arrows will go far enough. Keep bow arm pointing toward gold.
6. Drawing string too far to right.	Draw string close to arm-pit.	5. Throwing bow arm to right or left.	Relax bow hand as soon as string is released, keeping arm pointing toward gold. Do not let bow shoulder go up or forward. Contract back and abdominal muscles to keep trunk steady while relaxing bow hand.
7. Tipping head and bow to right.	Keep head and bow in same plane as rest of body. Look at tip of arrow, not along arrow.		

Errors	Correction
6. Hitting shoulder, sleeve, pocket, or wrist with string.	Remove jewelry and objects in pocket on left. Tie cloth or use elastic band around elbow if sleeve is bulky. Have fistmele at least 6 inches to avoid wrist slap.
VII. *Follow-through*	
1. Shooting too fast.	Hold position longer than necessary and check on position of both arms.
2. Dropping bow arm.	
3. String hand moving out from neck.	Feel neck cord with index finger to be sure hand is touching neck.
4. Moving to see flight of arrow.	Hold steady until you hear sound of arrow hitting.

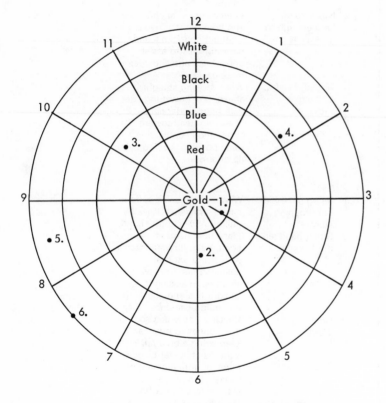

1. Gold at 4 o'clock
2. Red at 6 o'clock
3. Blue at 10 o'clock
4. Black at 2 o'clock
5. White at 8:30 o'clock
6. Petticoat at 7:30 o'clock

(38) How to describe location of shots.

Analysis of where your arrows are on the target will help you to improve. Description of exact spot can be made by naming color and designating place as though the target were the face of a clock (Fig. 38).

If arrows are widely dispersed, uniformity in shooting is lacking or muscles have not steadied down in aiming. If the arrows are in a "group," but off center, some one or more errors are the cause.

It is always necessary to check on one's position, because an error causing the arrow to go left may be offset by another error causing the arrow to go right. This may result temporarily in fair scores, but eventually causes lack of improvement and discouragement.

A diagrammatic listing of some common errors that cause arrows to go left, right, high, and low is given in Figure 39. By combining the faults listed, one can discover reasons for arrows going left and low, right and high, and so on.

Clout Shooting

Clout shooting is a fascinating variation of archery after one has developed sufficient strength and control to shoot the medium weight bows (approximately 22 pounds or heavier), and has learned to use a bowsight. One needs a heavier bow in order to shoot the greater distance. The arrow is sent in a high trajectory toward the white flag which marks the center of a 48-foot target on the ground.

The round consists of shooting thirty-six arrows (six ends). The standard distances are 120 and/or 140 yards for women, and 180 yards for men. Because it is recommended that beginners start with a light bow, many school bows may not be heavy enough to shoot that far; therefore, an unofficial modified range of 80 to 100 yards is often used.

An easy way to make the clout target is to use a rope the length of the radius of the target (24 feet) plus a couple of feet so that the rope can be carried low and taut in a circle around the flagpole. Regular target colors are painted on the rope, each color being 4.8 feet wide (same as the standard target in feet instead of inches).

Five people are appointed to be pullers of arrows, one for each color, and one person carries the rope in the circle. Two scorers record

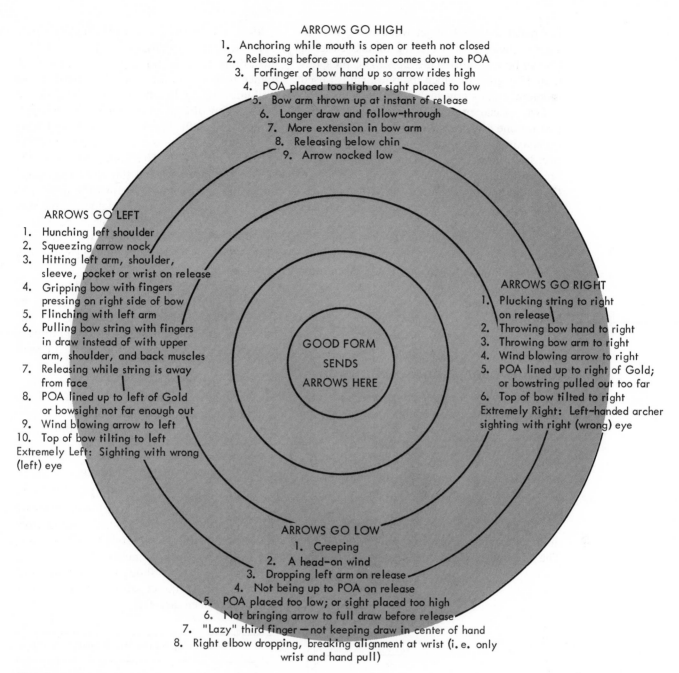

ARROWS GO HIGH
1. Anchoring while mouth is open or teeth not closed
2. Releasing before arrow point comes down to POA
3. Forfinger of bow hand up so arrow rides high
4. POA placed too high or sight placed to low
5. Bow arm thrown up at instant of release
6. Longer draw and follow-through
7. More extension in bow arm
8. Releasing below chin
9. Arrow nocked low

ARROWS GO LEFT
1. Hunching left shoulder
2. Squeezing arrow nock
3. Hitting left arm, shoulder, sleeve, pocket or wrist on release
4. Gripping bow with fingers pressing on right side of bow
5. Flinching with left arm
6. Pulling bow string with fingers in draw instead of with upper arm, shoulder, and back muscles
7. Releasing while string is away from face
8. POA lined up to left of Gold or bowsight not far enough out
9. Wind blowing arrow to left
10. Top of bow tilting to left
Extremely Left: Sighting with wrong (left) eye

GOOD FORM
SENDS
ARROWS HERE

ARROWS GO RIGHT
1. Plucking string to right on release
2. Throwing bow hand to right
3. Throwing bow arm to right
4. Wind blowing arrow to right
5. POA lined up to right of Gold; or bowstring pulled out too far
6. Top of bow tilted to right
Extremely Right: Left-handed archer sighting with right (wrong) eye

ARROWS GO LOW
1. Creeping
2. A head-on wind
3. Dropping left arm on release
4. Not being up to POA on release
5. POA placed too low; or sight placed too high
6. Not bringing arrow to full draw before release
7. "Lazy" third finger — not keeping draw in center of hand
8. Right elbow dropping, breaking alignment at wrist (i. e. only wrist and hand pull)

(39) Common causes of arrows going right, left, high, and low.

all scores. The five pullers walk behind the rope, each one pulling all arrows from her band. After completion, all arrows are laid on the rope side by side in their respective color with similar crests together. Scoring values are the same as in 5-ring target shooting. As the scorers call the name of the archers, each one claims her arrows and calls out the value received for each arrow, finishing with the total number of hits.

HOW TO SHOOT CLOUT

The form of shooting clout is the same as in target archery with the anchor under the chin, at the center and touching the chin. Aiming is usually done by putting a sight on the lower limb. If maximum distance is desired, the bow arm should be held at a 45-degree angle, in relation to the horizontal, with the bowsight placed so that it is on the flag. If one's arrows do not reach the clout target when using the 45-degree angle, it is necessary to use either a heavier bow or shorten the range. The angle less than 45 degrees to which the bow arm is raised is determined by how high one must aim.

Two special precautions are necessary: (1) that no one overdraws her arrow. Eagerness to get maximum distance often causes archers to overdraw the arrow within the bow. This breaks the arrow, may cause serious damage if the splintered pieces pierce the skin, and may break the bow. (2) Because the arrows are scattered over a wide area, there is danger that arrows may be stepped on in carelessness or haste.

Interest is added if recognition is given after each end (1) to the person with the highest score, (2) to those who had golds, and (3) to those who had all six arrows on the clout target.

Field Archery and Bowhunting

Field archery is an interesting variation from target archery. Besides being enjoyable simply for its own sake, it is basic training for bowhunting. In field archery one walks to various shooting stations placed at varying distances with different size targets (usually small targets for short ranges, and larger targets for longer ranges), often in a woodland setting. The shooting technique is fundamentally the same as in target archery except for the anchor and aim. The stance may vary depending on the terrain.

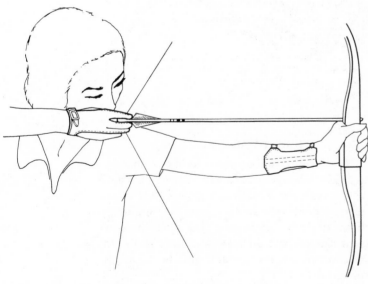

(40) Field archery anchor.

Most field archers use instinctive or "bare bow" method of sighting, which is by far the most difficult of the three sighting methods. A higher anchor than that used in target shooting facilitates aiming, because it brings the nock end of the arrow directly under the right eye (right-handed) (Fig. 40). The index finger is under the cheek bone with the other two fingers near the corner of the mouth. The hand rests against the side of the face with the thumb fitting snugly under the jaw bone and against the neck. The head is tipped slightly to the right, and the bow is canted (tipped) the same degree to the right so that the archer can see the target with both eyes open. (Distance is better estimated with both eyes focusing.)

This position literally fits the hand to the face and permits a snug unified anchor. Look at the smallest discernible spot in the center of the bull's eye and concentrate on it. A full draw is always taken. Aiming at objects at different distances requires a kinesthetic feeling in the bow arm for the correct degree of elevation. This feeling is developed only by great concentration. Much practice is necessary, too, because hunting bows are heavier and more difficult to control.

FIELD ARCHERY ROUNDS

Advanced archers shoot the Field Round,[3] which is a twenty-eight-target course (twice around fourteen targets). Distances range from 20 feet to 80 yards, with target faces varying in size from 6 inches to 24 inches.

Beginning archers shoot the Flint Round,[4] which is a seven-target setup or twice around, making fourteen targets.

Course Setup for the Flint Round		
Target 1	25 yards	12-inch face
Target 2	20 feet	6-inch face
Target 3	30 yards	12-inch face
Target 4	15 yards	6-inch face
Target 5	20 yards	12-inch face
Target 6	10 yards	6-inch face
Target 7	30, 25, 20, 15 yards (walk-up, one shot from each post)	12-inch face

[3] Specifications and rules may be secured from the National Field Archery Association, Box 514, Redlands, California.
[4] Ibid.

1. Archers shoot in groups of four people.
2. Archers shoot four arrows at each target.
3. Target faces are black and white with outer ring having a value of 3, inner ring 5, and the center spot 5X. Recording of 5X is of help in breaking ties, but does not add to total score.
4. Arrows that bisect a line count the higher value.
5. Arrows that penetrate through target face and are not visible from the front score 3.

Scholastic Field Archers' Round[5] is recommended for use where outdoor facilities are too limited for an official field course. A 30-yard archery range is all the space that is needed, with enough targets to accommodate the group with four at a target and range width suitable for class size. All archers shoot four arrows from the same distance at the same time. All are field targets; size can be adapted to the experience of the group. Suggested distances for this seven-target unit are

1. 25 yards
2. 10 yards
3. 30 yards
4. 20 yards
5. 25 yards
6. 10 yards
7. "Walk-up" 30, 25, 20, 10 yards, one arrow at each distance.

SAFETY

Field archery

Never shoot a strange field course without a "buddy," and never release an arrow unless you can see clearly your target and the area beyond. Call "timber" *before* drawing the bow, to make sure the complete area is clear.

When retrieving arrows, always leave bows in front of target face, or have one of the group remain in front of the target to be sure other archers hold their shooting. If shooting alone, tie a flag to your bow and stand it in front of target. Stay on the paths of the course and walk only in the designated direction of the course.

Bowhunting

Check hunting laws locally or through the NFAA. Wear safe clothing; do not wear white in deer hunting season. Never hunt with more

than one other companion. Be aware of location and destination of other hunting parties near you. Take a map, compass, and first-aid kit with you. A sportsman always assumes responsibility of finding wounded game, no matter how arduous the task.

Novelty Meets

Novelty meets are great fun when the group has attained a fair degree of skill. Instinctive or "bare bow" shooting is often used in novelty meets. Events can be scheduled with team or individual competition. A creative project can be assigned to groups of three or four students to plan, present, and officiate an original event for the rest of the class. Planning a novelty meet is also an excellent rainy day project. It is important to stress safety rules, because carelessness is apt to result from the excitement of the competition.

In the team events, prizes can be awarded to the winner of each event, or an accumulative score may be kept with five points for first place, three for second, and one for third.

SOME POPULAR NOVELTY EVENTS

In the *Halloween shoot*, cut-outs of witches, goblins, pumpkins, and cornstalks are fastened to each target. Four members on each team are lined up on the 30-yard line in front of a target. Each member has her six arrows and bow on the 20-yard line. First shooter runs to 20-yard line, shoots three arrows and returns to touch off next person, then goes to end of line. This is continued until all have shot their arrows. For scoring, hitting witches or goblins is minus ten points each; hitting pumpkins and cornstalks is plus ten points. Team finishing first gets ten additional points.

In the *song contest*,[6] the object is to collect a complete song and be the first team to sing it. Paper plates, with parts of several familiar songs written hodgepodge on them in short phrases or lines, are fastened face down to targets. After each end archers remove from target those plates which they hit. Shooting continues until they have collected an entire song. Teams may exchange plates, but must not know what words they are receiving. The winner is that team which first sings its completed song.

---

[5] Nellie S. Martin, "Schoolyard Field Archery," *DGWS Archery-Riding Guide* 1966–68.

[6] Myrtle K. Miller, *Archery Training Guide*, Teela-Wooket Archery Camp.

In the *balloon shoot*, balloons with strings tied to them, allowing free play, are fastened to each target off-center. Small prizes, such as apples or lollipops, are tied to the other end of the string and dropped back of the target. When a balloon is punctured, Lady Paramount blows her whistle to stop shooting and archer goes to target to collect her prize. When all balloons on a target have been punctured, archers may shoot at other targets which still have balloons.

The object in the *string event* is to have the team get the smallest group around their captain's arrow. Four team members line up with a target; the range can be according to the skill of the group.

The captain of each team shoots an arrow into her target. (If a captain misses the target, all captains are given the opportunity of shooting a second arrow and choosing which arrow they wish to use.) All members of teams then shoot their arrows as close as possible to captain's arrow.

Each team is given a length of string, which is placed close to target face encircling a specified number of arrows that are grouped around the captain's arrow. The team with the shortest string wins the event.

In the *20-yard target shoot* (*three targets*),[7] four team members line up with a target. Two members of the team shoot arrows at their own target and two at each of the other targets, followed by two members shooting their six arrows in the same way. Scores are the same as in regulation target archery.

For the next end teams rotate to next target, repeating the foregoing pattern. This is repeated until all teams have shot from all positions. Team with highest score wins.

The Robin Hood round is a standard team round. Each team shoots at its own target with only golds (or golds and reds) counting as hits. After each end the team with the lowest number of hits is eliminated and heckles the remaining teams. Shooting continues until the winning team is determined.

Terminology

Addressing the target: Standing with body turned at right angles to target.

American round: Shooting thirty arrows at each of three ranges, 60, 50, and 40 yards.

[7] *Ibid.*

Anchor: The position at which the string hand is fixed during the act of aiming to determine placement of nock of arrow.

Archery-golf: An adaptation of the game of golf to archery. Archers shoot for holes and score according to the number of shots required to hit the target (usually a 4-inch ball elevated 18 inches).

Arm guard: A piece of leather or other material worn on the forearm of bow arm to protect it from bowstring.

Arrowplate: A device used to mark the place where the arrow crosses the bow.

Arrow rest: A projection on the side of the bow, at the upper edge of the handle, used to keep the arrow steady on the arrowplate.

Back (of bow): The side of the bow away from the string.

Backed bow: A bow that has a thin strip of different material glued on the back throughout its length, designed to add strength.

Bare bow: No mark or sighting device on the bow for aid in aiming.

Belly: The side of the bow nearest the string, sometimes called front of bow.

Bending the bow: Process of slipping the bowstring into the bow nock in preparation for shooting. Synonymous with bracing or stringing the bow.

Bow arm: The arm that holds the bow while shooting.

Bowman: An archer.

Bowsight: A device on the bow designed for sighting.

Bowyer: One who makes bows.

Bracing the bow: *See* bending the bow.

Cast: The energy or power within a bow, determining distance arrows may be shot.

Clout target: A target 48 feet in diameter, laid out on the ground, the center of which is marked with a white flag.

Cock feather: The feather at right angles to the nock.

Columbia round: Twenty-four arrows at each of three ranges 50, 40, and 30 yards.

Composite bow: A bow made of layers of more than one kind of material.

Creep: To allow the string hand to move forward or bow arm to bend before or during release.

Crest: The color scheme applied to the feathered end of the arrow to distinguish sets of arrows.

Crossbow: A bow so arranged that it is shot similarly to a gun with a groove or barrel, which directs the arrow, and a trigger, which releases the string.

Double round: Any round shot twice in succession and scores added.

Draw: The act of pulling back the bowstring, as in shooting.

End: Six arrows, shot consecutively or in groups of three.

Eye: The loop that is woven into the string.

Field captain: Man in charge of a tournament.

Finger tab, stall, or **tip:** A leather protection used on the string fingers.

Fistmele: Width of hand with thumb raised, used for measuring the desirable distance of the string from the bow, approximately 6 inches or more for recurved bow. (Follow bow manufacturer's specifications when given.)

Fletch: To feather an arrow.

Fletching: The feathers on an arrow, usually three or four.

Flight arrow: A light arrow used for flight shooting.

Flight shot: A shot for greatest possible distance.

Follow the string: An expression to describe the curve taken by a bow if it does not return to a straight line when unstrung.

Follow-through: The act of maintaining the shooting position until arrow strikes the mark. Also called the *after-hold*.

Footed arrow: An arrow that has a piece of hardwood spliced on the point end, designed to give it additional weight and strength.

Grip: The handle of bow.

Group: A number of arrows placed in close proximity on the target.

Hen feathers: The two feathers that are not at right angles to the nock. Also called *side feathers*.

Hit: A shot within the scoring face of target.

Holding: Keeping an arrow at full draw while aiming.

Instinctive shooting: Aiming and shooting a bow without the aid of a point of aim, bowsight, or other mechanical means.

Lady Paramount: Woman on the range in charge of a tournament.

Limbs: The two arms of a bow, one above and one below the grip or handle.

Loose: To release the drawn string.

National round: Forty-eight arrows at 60 yards and twenty-four at 50 yards. Ladies' round.

Nock: The groove at the end of an arrow into which the string fits. Also the notches on either end of a bow that hold the string. To place an arrow on the string is "nocking the arrow."

Nocking point: The point on the string at which the arrow is nocked, often marked with a knot, thread, ink, or tape.

Overbowed: Using too strong a bow.

Overdraw: Drawing the bow so that the pile of the arrow is inside the bow; drawing the bow beyond its proper arrow length.

Petticoat: The black rim and the part of the face outside of the white ring; an arrow in the petticoat counts as a miss.

Pile: The head, tip, or point of an arrow.

Point-blank range: Distance at which the point of aim is the center of the gold.

Point of aim: An auxiliary mark used in indirect aiming at a target.

Quiver: A receptacle for arrows.

Range: Distance to be shot; a shooting ground, indoors or out.

Range finder: A marked device for resetting the point of aim after it has been established.

Recurved bow: A bow with tips that curve back in a graceful arc.

Reflexed bow: A bow that bends backward in its entirety when unstrung.

Round: General name applied to shooting a prescribed number of arrows at prescribed distances.

Self arrow: An arrow made from a single piece of wood.

Serving: The winding of thread around the center of a bowstring and its loops to protect it from wear by the fingers, arrow nock, and bow nocks.

Shaft: Main body of an arrow.

Shaftment: The part of the shaft occupied by the crest and feathers.

Shooting line: Line astride which the archer stands.

Sight: A device on the bow enabling the archer to aim directly at the gold.

Spine: The stiffness-flexibility combination of an arrow.

Stringing: *See* bending the bow.

Tab: A flat piece of leather used on the hand to protect the archer's fingers.

Tackle: General term referring to archery equipment.

Target face: The painted front of a target.

Tassel: A yarn tassel worn on the archer's belt, used to wipe arrows.

Timber: Term used in field archery to warn others that an arrow is about to be shot.

Timber hitch: The knot used to tie the lower end of a single looped string to bow.

Toxophilite: One who loves, studies, and practices archery.

Trajectory: The arched path of an arrow in flight.

Understrung: A bow not braced high enough.

Weight (of bow): The number of pounds required to draw the bowstring the length of its arrow. (The actual weight of an arrow is in grains.)

Windage: The influence of the wind on an arrow in flight.

Selected References

BOOKS

Burke, Edmund H. *Archery Handbook*. Book #316. Greenwich, Conn.: Fawcett Publications, 1956.

DGWS Archery-Riding Guide, current edition. Washington, D.C.: American Assoc. for Health, Physical Education, and Recreation.

Haugen, Arnold O., and Harlan G. Metcalf. *Field Archery and Bowhunting*. New York: Ronald Press, 1963.

Miller, Myrtle K. *Archery Training Guide*. Mimeographed, 1966. 67 Old Stone Church Road, Upper Saddle River, N.J. Used as textbook for Instructors' Course at Teela Wooket Archery Camp, Roxbury, Vt.

National Archery Association. *The Archer's Handbook* (published every four years). Ronks, Pa.: N.A.A.

Niemeyer, Roy K. *Beginning Archery*. Belmont, Calif.: Wadsworth Publishing Co., 1962.

PERIODICALS

The Archer's Magazine and *Archery World*, Donald Webb and Sherwood Shock, eds., 24 S. Reading Avenue, Boyertown, Pa. (official publication of National Archery Association; issued monthly).

Archery, Roy Hoff, ed., Box H, Palm Springs, Calif. (official publication of National Field Archery Association; issued monthly).

ARCHERY ORGANIZATIONS

National Archery Association, Exec. Secy Clayton Shenk, Ronks, Pa. Governing body of all target archery in the U.S. Individual membership $5.00 per year. Includes subscription to *Archery World* magazine.

National Field Archery Association, Box 514, Redlands, Calif. Governing body for field archery in the U.S. Individual membership $5.00 per year. Includes subscription to *Archery Magazine*.

Chapter 4

Badminton *Ruth B. Eddy*

History. Goals. Equipment. Etiquette. SKILLS: *Grip, Serves, Overhead Clear, Drop, Smash, Drive, Around the Head. Strategy. Mechanics of Movement. Evaluation. Terminology.*

Badminton is a fast racket sport played indoors or outdoors by two players (singles) or four players (doubles). Informal, outdoor badminton has become very popular because of the relatively small area needed for a court, the inexpensive equipment, and the rapidity with which beginners can learn to play. The feathered shuttle, which can be hit either very slowly or very fast, provides a game with extreme change of pace. Badminton allows beginners to enjoy hitting the shuttle back and forth at a slow tempo, and also provides a challenge to the expert who can make the shuttle travel with great speed.

History

A form of badminton was played in India by British military officers in the 1879's, but the game was not called badminton until it was played in 1873 at Badminton, the English country estate of the Duke of Beaufort, by army officers returning home from India. It was played under the rules that governed it in India until 1887, when the Bath Badminton Club was formed. The rules standardized by this group were further revised to approximately their present form about 1895 by the Badminton Association of England. Although there were All-England championships for men as early as 1899, the first official all-England matches were played in 1904. In the 1890's badminton was introduced to Canada and a few years later to the United States, although interest in this country was not widespread until 1930. In the meantime, badminton spread through Europe, Australia, and New Zealand.

The International Badminton Federation, formed in 1934, manages the Thomas Cup men's international competition, which is similar to the Davis Cup in tennis. The cup, presented by Sir George Thomas in 1940, is challenged once every three years by teams of four to six amateur players. There are five singles matches and four doubles matches.

In 1957, Mrs. H. S. Uber of England presented the Uber cup for international matches for women, which the United States won the first year. The Uber Cup, like the Thomas Cup, is contested once every three years.

Miss Eddy majored in English at Pembroke College, Brown University, and earned her M.S. in physical education at Smith College. For two years, as a member of the United States Naval Reserve, she was a Link Instrument Trainer Instructor. An associate professor at Duke University, Miss Eddy is an ardent badminton participant and teacher.

Goals

Because the equipment is so light, strength is not a prerequisite for learning badminton. The girl who moves well and knows how to throw can learn to play a fairly good game of singles and doubles in a beginning course. She should master the following skills:

1. Serve a long service. It should be high enough to clear a racket held as high as the opponent can reach when standing in the center of the receiving court and long enough so that it falls within 2 feet of the back line.
2. Serve a short low service that is low enough to clear the net by no more than 1 foot, descends as it clears the net, and is short enough to land within 1 foot of the short service line.
3. Hit the overhead clear on the forehand so that it will go over the opponent's reach and land within 2 feet of the back line.
4. Smash with speed to any part of the court from one's own midcourt.
5. Hit the overhead and underhand drop shots on both forehand and backhand sides so that they have a descending trajectory as soon as they pass over the net.

Facilities and Equipment

COURT

The badminton court is 44 feet long and 17 feet wide for singles (Fig. 1). It is divided by a firmly stretched mesh net 5 feet high at the center and 5 feet, 1 inch at the posts, which are placed at the side boundaries of the court. For doubles, the width of the court is increased by $1\frac{1}{2}$ feet at either side, making the court 44 by 20 feet. The service court is wider and shorter for doubles than for singles, but the total service area to be covered by one player is almost the same.

Because most of the footwork is within the court, the clearance space outside the court need be only about 6 feet. The total space required for one court is 56 by 32 feet. An overhead clearance of 25 feet is necessary; 30 feet or more is recommended.

RACKET

Although there are no specifications for badminton rackets, the usual weight is 5 ounces and the length 26 inches (compare with the tennis racket of 13 ounces and 27 inches). It is oval headed and strung with gut or nylon; gut stringing is most desirable because of its resiliency, but nylon strings are more durable and less expensive than gut. Metal rackets with synthetic strings are especially durable. Steel shafts are commonly used to reinforce wooden racket frames. The average grip size is $3\frac{3}{4}$ inches (compare with the average tennis grip of $4\frac{1}{2}$ inches).

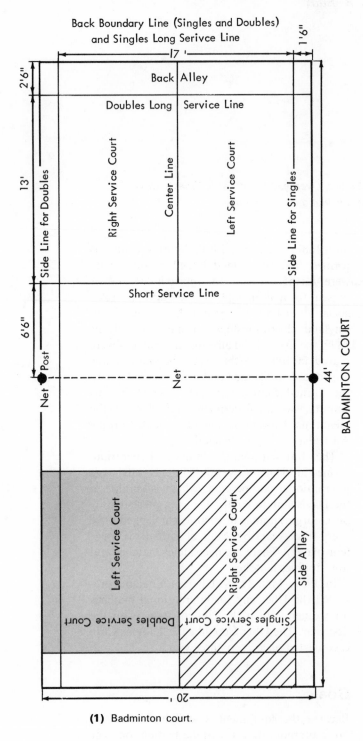

(1) Badminton court.

Feathered Shuttle   Plastic Shuttle

(2) Shuttle.

SHUTTLE

The shuttle (also called shuttlecock or bird) consists of a tiny cork ball, 1 inch to $1\frac{1}{8}$ inches in diameter with fourteen to sixteen goose feathers fixed in a circle on one half of its surface (Fig. 2). Only one badminton shuttle can be made from the feathers of one goose, because the feathers used must be a uniform $2\frac{1}{2}$ to $2\frac{3}{4}$ inches long. The feathered shuttles are therefore costly. Plastic ones are made which nearly duplicate the flight of the feathered shuttle and greatly increase durability. The official shuttle weighs 73 to 85 grains, or about $\frac{1}{6}$ of an ounce (compare with the tennis ball, which weighs about 2 ounces).

COSTUME

As in other court or racket sports, custom dictates white costumes for badminton. The costume for women is a white tennis dress, white shorts or short skirt and blouse, and flat-soled tennis shoes with heavy socks. The heavy socks are needed to protect the feet from blisters. Tennis shoes must fit well and have soles designed for gripping. Boating shoes have become popular because of their good support and nonskid soles.

Etiquette

Like all racket sports, badminton has some unwritten laws of etiquette. As in most individual sports, nothing is ever done that might distract the player's attention; for example, one never walks behind a court during play. Shuttles from adjoining courts are sent back as soon as possible. One doesn't retrieve one's own shuttle but waits until the neighboring player can return it. Applauding oneself or making excuses for one's play are marked lapses of etiquette. Rules of etiquette require handing or sending the shuttle directly to one's opponent when it is her turn to serve, and, as loser of a match, shaking hands with the winner.

To avoid strained muscles, a warm-up period should precede matches. During the preliminary warm-up period it is customary to rally with the opponent. If she asks for particular shots, they should be set up for her. However, no practice shots for service or any other strokes are to be taken after the warm-up period is terminated.

If there are no officials, the player should call any illegal hits on herself, that is, slings, carries, or catches on the racket. If a player is in doubt as to whether the shot landing on her side of the court is "out of court" (landing clear of and outside the boundary line), she should say so and have the point replayed. Without officials, the server should call the score before each serve. In doubles, "first service" and "second service" should also be called.

Spectators should remain unobtrusive during play. They should not evidence strong partiality. It is appropriate to applaud good play by either team, but one should not applaud when points are awarded because of poor play or obvious errors.

Skills

GRIP

The grip (Fig. 3) is assumed by holding the racket at the very end of the handle with its face perpendicular to the floor so that the *V* formed by the thumb and first finger is on the top and slightly to the left of the handle. As seen from the player's left side, the thumb is angled diagonally up along the handle (Fig. 4). The same grip is used for forehand and backhand.

Some players, however, prefer to use two different grips for the forehand and backhand. For the forehand the *V* is in the center of the top of the racket handle, rather than to the left as in the all-stroke grip. For the backhand, the hand shifts slightly farther to the left than in the all-stroke grip. The important factor in these slightly varying grips is that the player must have free use of the wrist joint. The fingers, spread and angled up toward the head of the racket, control the swing of the racket and keep the

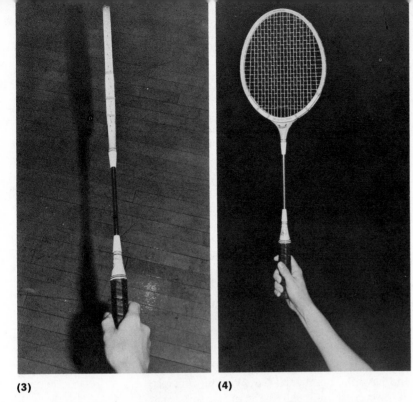

(3)   **(4)**

(3–4) Grip viewed from two different angles.

(5) Backswing.   **(6)** Forward swing.

(7) Contact.   **(8)** Follow-through.

(9) Completion of follow-through.

(5–9) The long serve.

racket from settling into the palm. The grip must be gentle but firm to control the racket but maintain freedom of wrist action.

THE LONG SERVE

Learning the long serve as one's first stroke gives the beginner a correct way to put the shuttle into play and provides an offensive skill (Figs. 5, 6, 7, 8, and 9). The rules require an underhand swing; the shuttle must be no higher than the server's waist with no part of the racket higher than the server's hand at the moment of impact. There is no limit on the height of the backswing or the follow-through. The swing should be a nearly vertical, up-back, down, and up-forward action (very much like the path of the golf swing) in order to be sure that it is legal.

The long serve should be hit high enough to clear the maximum reach of the opponent when she is midcourt, deep enough so that she must go to the very back of her court to retrieve it, and high and deep enough so that it descends almost straight down just inside the backline. Although it is not considered an outright winning shot, it should have this trajectory to force the defender to move to back court. The shuttle that is dropping straight down is harder to hit than one falling at a slant.

Position

For the singles game the server positions herself close to the center line and about a yard in back of the front service line. In case her service is returned, she is near the center of her own area ready to defend or attack. Her service must be directed to the court diagonally opposite her; that is, from her right court to her opponent's right court when her own score is zero or even, and from her left court to her opponent's left court when her score is odd. Therefore, she lines herself up on a diagonal. To simplify lining up, she imagines a line drawn from herself to the center of the opponent's service court, assumes a stride stance with the left foot nearer the net than the right, and puts her toes on this line (Fig. 5).

A correct stance and a preparatory position are essential to any good swing. To learn to hit the serve in the desired direction, the server assumes the follow-through position, as in Figure 8, then, without changing the position of the feet, goes into the backswing. (The rules do not allow a step to be taken when serving.)

Contact point

It is important to know the contact point or point in space at which the racket is to strike the shuttle. The contact is well ahead of the body, slightly to the hitting side, and near the floor to accommodate the reach of the hitting arm plus the length of the racket. Figure 10 illustrates a way of becoming familiar with the contact point by holding the shuttle on a string and adjusting its height to the path of the racket. Once the student is aware of the contact point, she is ready to toss or drop the shuttle to this point at the right moment. Most beginners have no difficulty with the serve, but some need a little practice in order to contact the shuttle in the right place at the right moment.

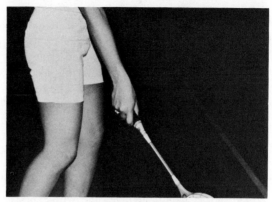

(11) Forearm supinated, wrist bent.

(12) Forearm pronated, wrist straightened.

(10) Position of shuttle for contact on long serve.

(13) Forearm pronated, wrist bent.

(11–13) Wrist action on forehand.

Wrist action

The backswing must be large enough to generate maximum forward speed in the racket at impact. Speed is built up not only by a shoulder turn and full armswing, but also by wrist action, sometimes regarded as a swing within a swing. Wrist action is essential for imparting distance and speed to the shuttle. It is similar to the lash of a whip, the flick of a fly rod, or the whip of a towel. It happens so fast that it is difficult to see or to analyze. The secret of wrist action is to rotate the forearm, quickly turning it in on the forehand and turning it out on the backhand as the hit is made. Figures 11, 12, and 13 show the wrist action of the forehand in sequence. Figure 11 shows the backswing with the forearm rolled back or supinated, i.e., inside of the arm and palm away from the body. The thumb points away from the net and the wrist is bent. Figure 12 shows the moment of impact. The arm has rolled halfway over and the wrist has straightened. In Figure 13 the arm has continued to turn over so that the hand has turned a full 180 degrees (from palm away from the body to palm toward the body), and the wrist bends up. The racket has moved through a half circle during the arm swing. By adding wrist action to the arm swing, a larger swing and greater speed are gained. The rolling-over action with the forearm is reversed for the backhand.

Swing

In the *backswing* (Fig. 5, page 60), the wrist action just described should be put into the larger swing, which involves the whole body. The body is first turned back to the right away from the target and the racket is taken back until the racket head points directly away from the target. The shuttle is held diagonally forward ready to be dropped. The weight shifts to the back foot.

The *forward swing* is initiated by the rotation of the body counterclockwise in order to face the target. The weight is well over the forward foot. The arm is pulled down near the hitting area but the wrist action is delayed. The right shoulder moves down and forward (Fig. 6, page 60). In Figure 7 (page 60) the forearm has rolled in, allowing the wrist to straighten at contact. In Figure 8 (page 60) the forearm finishes turning and the wrist bends again.

Figure 9 (page 60) shows a complete *follow-through* or continuation of the swing until it loses

its momentum naturally. The follow-through usually does not stop until the hand reaches a position above and near the left ear. Completed rotation of the forearm puts the back of the racket hand toward the server's head, palm facing out, and the racket head pointing back over the left shoulder away from the target.

The beginner must work toward increasing the speed of the racket on the long serve; wrist action, or the wrist flick, is essential for speed. Some students find it aids wrist action to make a *backward loop* with the racket before starting the forward swing. In this case the swing starts with the racket head pointing forward and the arm pronated (Fig. 14). The racket is started backward and swings in a loop before the forward movement for the serve occurs (Fig. 15). For some players this preparatory action loosens up the swing and aids in timing. Notice that the hand moves back first and the racket head lags behind; then the hand makes a circular move and is ahead of the racket on the forward swing. The beginner should add this loop only if it makes her swing feel more relaxed and if it aids her timing and racket acceleration.

SHORT SERVE

The short serve can be thought of as a slowed-down abbreviation of the long serve but with little wrist action. In order not to inform the opponent of the serve to be delivered, the back-swing for the short serve must look like that of a long serve; only on the forward swing does it differ. Instead of whipping the racket through fast on the forward motion, the arm swings slowly. The wrist straightens on the forward swing and remains straight as the racket continues on through until the tip points at the target with the face of the racket nearly perpendicular to the floor (Fig. 16). This is accomplished by a slow, deliberate turn of the body.

There are other ways to accomplish the short serve effectively. One is to flick the wrist and eliminate much of the body and arm action. Regardless of how the stroke is executed, the flight of the shuttle must be low and must force the opponent to return *up*, for if the flight of the serve is high enough to hit down, the receiver immediately has the advantage and is almost certain to win the rally. To guard against hitting this serve too high, the racket face must not be slanted up too much. The angle of the face of the racket determines the trajectory and an open racket face (turned upward) results in a high

(14–15) Backward loop for long serve.

(14) Starting position.

(15) Continuation of loop.

(16) Follow-through on short serve.

flight. Focusing on the net tape helps one to visualize the desired trajectory; the face of the racket must be square to that trajectory at the moment of impact.

OVERHEAD CLEAR

The flight of the overhead clear is like that of the long serve. The shuttle is hit up and deep so that it reaches its highest point above the back territory of the opposite court. The overhead clear is accomplished by the same swing pattern as the overhand throw.

The target for the clear is a point in space directly above the very back of the court and

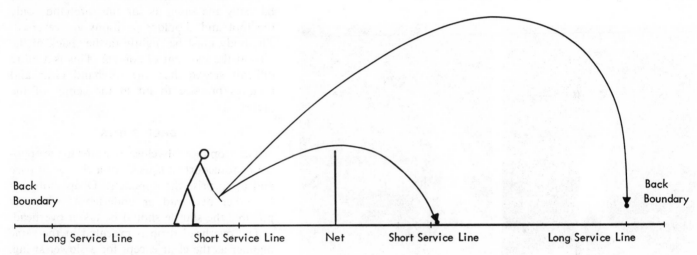

(17) Shuttle flight on long and short serves.

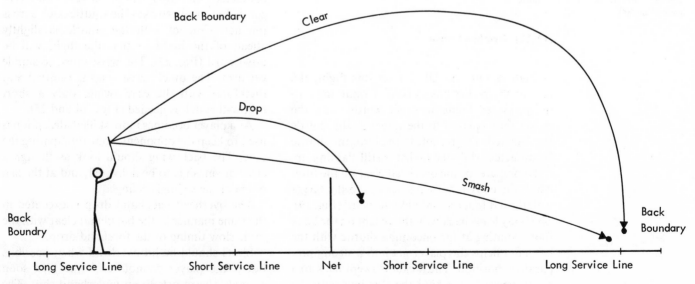

(18) Shuttle flight on overhead strokes.

(19) Backswing.

(20) Forward turn.

(21) Contact. (This swing is a little late. Contact should be made slightly in front of body.)

(22) Follow-through.

(19–22) Overhead clear.

as high as one can hit. To get this flight, the face of the racket has to be at a right angle to the proposed flight, in other words, with the racket face squared to the target as the shuttle is contacted. To give loft to the bird, the shuttle is contacted while the racket is still slanting up.

To prepare for the overhead clear on the forehand, the body is turned sideways to the target with the left foot and shoulder forward (Fig. 19). The body leans back with the weight on the back foot. Pointing at the oncoming shuttle with the left hand helps the player get into a strong preparatory position. The racket is swept back to a point where it is behind the shoulder with the racket head pointing down toward the floor. The elbow is bent and the forearm rolled outward so that the wrist can be bent back.

The forward swing is initiated by a strong rotation of the body counterclockwise, and the weight is transferred from the back (right) to the forward foot (Fig. 20). The arm and wrist actions are delayed until the last moment before contact, then both extend strongly and the forearm rolls over to impart speed and power. The racket is whipped forward to contact the shuttle when it is overhead and slightly to the right side of the body (Fig. 21). The racket continues out toward the target as far as possible in this shot, then with the completion of the wrist snap the racket comes down (Fig. 22).

For the backhand clear the execution is basically the same as for the forehand; only the foot and shoulder positions are reversed. The body must be slightly farther back of the bird at the moment of contact. This is a more difficult stroke than the forehand clear and requires practice to hit in the center of the racket.

DROP SHOTS

The drop shot falls close to the net in the opponent's forecourt; it is used for a change of pace and to surprise the opponent. Drop shots can be either overhead or underhand; whenever possible the shuttle should be taken overhead.

The overhead drop is executed in the same manner as the clear except for a slower swing, shorter follow-through of the racket, and a definite downward aiming. As the shuttle is contacted, the hitter lets up in force and very gently but firmly strokes the shuttle back across the net. Contact with the shuttle is slightly ahead of the body so that the flight will be downward (Fig. 23). The wrist must be supple yet firm. The quick wrist snap is omitted and therefore, with the easy swing, only a short follow-through is needed (Figs. 24 and 25).

As a player becomes more skilled, deception is used to keep the opponent from anticipating the play. The backswing should look as though a clear or smash is to be delivered, and at the last moment the swing is changed.

The overhead backhand drop is executed in the same manner as the backhand clear with the same slow timing of the forehand drop.

Shots should be hit overhead when possible, but if the player cannot reach the bird soon enough, she resorts to an underhand shot. The

(23) Contact.

(24–25) Follow-through.

(23–25) Overhead drop shot.

underhand drop shot is a defensive shot. If the player had been in position in time, she would have used the overhead. Usually the underhand drop requires great stretch to reach it in time. It can be converted into a winning shot by strategically angling it or by giving the shuttle a flight so close to the net that it is difficult to return without hitting the net or scooping up.

Inasmuch as power is not needed in this stroke, it is not necessary to turn the body sideways to the net unless one wishes to use deception. At the last possible moment, the speed of the swing is reduced and the shuttle is gently lifted up. The follow-through is short. A good net player is able to use the underhand drop on both the forehand and backhand.

THE SMASH

The smash is a powerful winning stroke in badminton. It begins in the same manner as the overhead swing of the clear, but the difference in point of contact imparts a swift downward flight to the shuttle. The backswing is similar to the backswing for the clear but with a little less lean back. The player is behind the approaching shuttle and the contact is high and slightly forward of the right shoulder so that the shuttle can be directed sharply downward (Fig. 26). The follow-through is continued until the racket passes the left side of the left knee. The finish is forward and down, with the racket arm pronated so that the racket face and palm of the

(26) Contact with shuttle.

(27) Follow-through.

(26–27) Smash.

hand turn in toward the left side of the body (Fig. 27).

Extending the arm and body for the clear and the smash can be practiced by hitting a shuttle suspended by a string high overhead. The shuttle can be adjusted to the appropriate level for the stroke. This practice promotes a feeling for the height and distance forward necessary for the body and racket to meet the shuttle (Fig. 28).

(28) Practice in reaching for shuttle.

(29) Contact.

(30) Follow-through.

(29–30) Drive.

(33) Follow-through.

(32) Contact.

(31) Backswing.

(31–33) Underhand clear on backhand.

←

(36) Forearm supinated, wrist bent.

(35) Forearm supinated, wrist straight.

(34) Pronation, wrist bent.

(34–36) Wrist action on backhand.

←

THE DRIVE

If the shuttle is too low to smash, a drive with a horizontal swing may be used. One can adjust to the height of the shuttle with the knees and the arm swing. Figure 29 illustrates a forehand drive hit at medium height. Figure 30 shows the follow-through of the drive.

To prepare to hit a shot on the backhand side, the body is rotated counterclockwise away from the target; the right shoulder is forward and the right foot is nearer the net. The weight goes to the back (left) foot as the racket is taken back (Fig. 31). Opposite faces of the racket contact the shuttle on the forehand and backhand. As with the forehand, the forward swing is initiated by a strong body turn toward the target and a step onto the forward foot. The shuttle is contacted ahead of the forward foot with a strong arm extension and forward swing and a wrist snap at the last moment (Fig. 32). The follow-through is in the direction of the desired flight (Fig. 33).

On the backswing the arm is pronated or turned in so that the palm of the hand is down (Fig. 34). On the forward swing the forearm begins to roll or supinate; just before impact, at the last moment, the wrist straightens (Fig. 35). After impact the arm continues to roll into supination and the wrist bends (Fig. 36). Supination is a strong movement that gives speed and depth to the flight of the shuttle. Whether the backhand is an underhand, drive, or overhead shot, the forearm and wrist actions are essentially the same.

ROUND-THE-HEAD

Because it is very difficult to smash on the backhand side of the body, a stroke called round-the-head has been devised so that the forehand swing can be used on the backhand side. It is possible only because of the light weight of the racket.

The body is rotated back clockwise for the backswing and the stance is similar to that of the smash (Fig. 37). With a little practice one finds that contact can be made with the shuttle above the head rather than sideways to the right, and gradually one is able to make contact when it is to the left of the head (Fig. 38). The follow-through is forward and somewhat to the right (Fig. 39). If the shuttle is not too far to the backhand side, the round-the-head shot can be very effective.

FOOTWORK

Badminton can be a game of great speed because of the velocity that is imparted to the shuttle by skilled racket work, the short distance the shuttle has to travel, and the fact that it may not contact the floor. This means that fast footwork is essential.

In the position in which one is ready to receive the service (called *ready position*), the player stands with the feet comfortably apart, one foot slightly ahead, weight forward on the balls of the feet, heels off the floor, both arms raised forward, and the racket head about head high. The player is on the verge of being off-balance so that she can lose her balance instantly and start

(37) Backswing.   **(38)** Contact.   **(39)** Follow-through.

(37–39) Round-the-head.

(40) Footwork for underhand drop shot—right forecourt.

(41) Footwork for underhand drop shot—left forecourt.

moving. After the service is delivered and the point is being played, the feet keep moving and the body must be balanced at all times. The player hops, skips, slides, and runs, with the feet close to the floor and taking short quick steps at the end of the approach in order to have perfect positioning.

It is of paramount importance to move quickly in order to take the shuttle as soon as possible at the highest point. The higher the shuttle is taken, the greater will be the area of the opponent's court for placement. If a player can gain the advantage by hitting down, the opponent is put on the defensive and must hit up. In addition, the earlier one can return a shot, the less time the opponent has to get into position.

To cover the entire court it is necessary to return to a position in center court after each

shot. One should be so aware of her position in relation to this center base that on the follow-through of a stroke the player moves directly to this base. Court coverage is much easier if the player watches the opponent's swing and racket to see the stroke in the making. The kind of shot, as well as its placement, will be more easily anticipated. The objective is to intercept shots rather than run after them.

When the shuttle falls toward the right forecourt, in order to return the shot, the player runs and reaches forward with her racket. By stepping on the right foot one can reach farther both to the right forecourt (Fig. 40) and to the left forecourt (Fig. 41). Moving forward or sideways is easier than moving backward. For strokes other than the short underhands near the net and the round-the-head shot, the

(44) Back with right foot.

(43) Feet together.

(42) Back with right foot.

(42–44) Footwork for sliding to back of court.

body should be sideways to the net when maneuvering to position so that the body weight can be used to give added power. To return a deep forehand, the player should pivot to turn the body sideways; then she takes a series of quick slides or runs, at the same time swinging the racket back to be ready for the stroke. Figures 42, 43, and 44 illustrate sliding to back court to return a deep forehand. Upon reaching the desired position, the player, already in a side-to-net position, strokes the shuttle as she shifts her weight forward.

To return a deep backhand the same general principles hold except that one has to go farther to get in position for the backhand. The pivot is reversed with the right shoulder toward the net and the left foot leading on the slides or runs. As a general rule, the foot in the direction of travel is the leading foot.

Rules Summary

The official laws of badminton, published in the DGWS Tennis-Badminton Guides, are determined by the International Badminton Association and copyrighted by The American Badminton Association.

Games consist of eleven points for women's singles and fifteen to twenty-one points, as arranged for men's singles and for doubles. A match is two out of three games. Before starting to play, opponents toss; the side winning the toss has the option of a) serving first, b) not serving first, or c) choosing the side of the court. Points are scored only by the side that is serving. If the serving side loses the rally, the other side gets the serve.

To start the game, the server in her own right court serves diagonally to her opponent's right court. She continues to serve, alternating courts after each point she wins, until she commits an error. Then the opponent serves, starting in her right court. Service is in the right court when the server's score is zero or an even number of points (left court for odd number of points).

On service, the shuttle at the moment of being struck must be no higher than the server's waist and no part of the racket higher than the server's hand. The feet of the server and receiver must be stationary within their respective courts until the service is delivered. The feet must not be touching any court line. If the shuttle hits the top of the net on the service, it is in play, providing it meets the other requirements of a legal serve.

In doubles, only one player of the side beginning the game is entitled to serve in the first term of service. Thereafter, both players have a chance to serve before the right to serve is lost. After one side has lost its right to serve, the service goes to the opponent who is in the right-hand court. After service is completed and received, either of the partners may hit the shuttle.

When the score becomes tied near the end of a game so that one or two points are needed to win, the side which reached the score first may set the game. In an eleven-point game the score may be set to three points at nine-all and two points at ten-all; in a fifteen point game, to five points at thirteen-all, and to three points at fourteen-all.

Strategy

THE SERVE

The long service is the basic serve in singles. The short serve is used occasionally, especially if the opponent stands back in anticipation of a long serve. In doubles the reverse is true: the short serve is the basic serve and the long serve is used occasionally.

Because the service court for singles is long and narrow, and for doubles wide and shallow, the strategy varies for the singles and doubles game and for the left and right service courts. In service the corners are the specific targets and their relative strategic value must be assessed in terms of the strengths and weaknesses of the opponent.

In a singles game a serve to corner A in Figure 45 would be to the opponent's backhand, but she would not have far to go to return to her center position; a serve to B would be to her forehand, but she is out of position for the next shot. Both of these corners, however, would keep the opponent away from an attacking position near the net. Serving to C would draw the opponent out of position, but from this side angle she has a wide range for return. Serving to D would be to the opponent's backhand but she could angle the shot to either side for her return; she is therefore in a most threatening position.

In doubles the serve is even more important than in singles; the receivers can gain a strong advantage on the first return which the servers may never be able to overcome. The basic low short service of doubles should not rise after passing the net, for the receiver can easily rush the net and gain a marked advantage. Deception in the serve is important, coupled with enough well-placed deep shots to forestall any inclination of the opponent to rush the net. The same careful analysis of the tactical value of each corner, as already suggested for singles, should be made for doubles play. Much depends on the type of team formation that has been decided upon.

CLASSIFICATION OF STROKES AND THEIR STRATEGIC USE

Strokes classified according to the flight are clear, drop, smash, drive, and round-the-head. With the exception of the last stroke, these are further divided into forehand and backhand. Strokes may be classified according to the relationship to the body: overhead and underhand with the sidearm action of the drive coming in between. Because the clear and drop can be either an overhead or underhand, the classification according to shuttle flight is more functional.

The *clear* is a basic stroke used to force the opponent to the back court and may be helpful to give one time to recover position. Its trajectory and distance must be accurately executed, for it must be high enough not to be intercepted and deep enough so that it will go near the back boundary line. If it is too low, it will go out; if it is too high, it will be an opening for a smash. One should learn to hit the clear with considerable power on both the forehand and backhand. It is better to take this stroke overhead and at the earliest possible moment. If the shuttle has to be taken underhand, this stroke is not effective from deeper than midcourt, because it travels too slowly.

Drop shots are combined with clear shots to keep the opponent on the run forward and backward and on the diagonal. If this shot is played close to the net and sent almost parallel to the net, it is called a *net* shot; if it is sent in a loop over the net, it is called a *hairpin*. The net shots can be accomplished by wrist action, which disguises their intended direction, and they are executed on both the forehand and backhand.

The *smash*, a powerful overhead shot used after an opening has developed, can finish the point. To be sent with power, it must have body

rotation and body weight back of it as the arm throws the racket head with maximum speed at the shuttle. The contact point should be at the height of one's reach. The smash should not be used unless one has time to get into the correct position. Its possibility of success diminishes in the back one-fourth of the court. It is likely to be netted because of its sharp downward angle. The speed of the racket should be developed gradually as one gains control. The term *half-smash* is used to describe a shot sent with less power but with great accuracy. Its downward angle makes it hard to intercept. Experts can execute a backhand smash but it is extremely difficult. The average player can, with practice, achieve a backhand half-smash in forecourt.

Drives are most effective when taken about shoulder level so that the shuttle can travel in a flat trajectory. The speed of the drive, which is second to the smash, makes it a strong attacking stroke. It is very effective when used to force a singles player to run from side to side. It should not be used if there is a possibility of interception, for its return would be too quick for recovery; for this reason its use in doubles is limited.

GENERAL STRATEGY

1. A dependable service weakens the opponent's morale and builds confidence in the server.
2. Serve to a specific corner and use that placement to advantage for strokes that follow; this should be in the plan of attack.
3. Clears to an opponent's backhand are especially effective, for if the shot is intercepted the return cannot be aggressive.
4. Analysis of the opponent's game enables one to give her the kind of shots she does not handle well. The same analysis on one's own game leads to practice of the shots that are weak.

SINGLES

The singles game is strenuous when played with a skilled opponent. The position of the server is near the center line approximately 3 feet from the short service line for serving in either court (Fig. 45). The receiver stands slightly to the left of the middle of her court, because she must move farther back on the deep backhand than for the deep forehand. She is in the ready position with racket up, weight forward, ready to move in any direction. Her center base (marked *X* in Figure 45) is a little left of center and varies according to the position from which she has come, i.e., if she has returned a shot near the net, she would go to a position more forward than if she has returned a deep shot. One's ability to anticipate and intercept shots determines whether one's base is an attacking or defensive one. Much depends on the opponent's skill and type of play.

The basic long high serve is usually returned by a clear to force the server back; if the return is not very deep, this may be followed by a drop shot to the near net corner. After the opponent has been maneuvered out of position or makes a weak return by hitting up in midcourt, the point may be finished by a smash.

DOUBLES

There are a number of different formations for partner play in doubles. All of the various systems have advantages and disadvantages, which depend on the players' abilities, their preference, and the opponents' weaknesses. Three of the basic doubles systems of play are side-by-side, up-and-back, and a combination system.

The *side-by-side* formation (Fig. 46) divides the court in half lengthwise with each player responsible for her half of the court. This is the easiest system for beginners to learn. If both players are right-handed, the player in the left court takes the shots hit down the center line because they are on her forehand. Players using this system should be proficient in all strokes; the difficult shots to cover are the net shots and clears from the back court. When serving, the player does not stand up as far as the short service line, for immediately after serving she must go to a position at the mid-point of her half of the court. The receiver, on the other hand, stands well forward in this system and is prepared to rush the net, while her partner stands somewhat deeper and near the center line ready to cover the back court in case the receiver is drawn forward on a short serve. After the first play the partners go to the side-by-side position. Disadvantages of this system include confusion as to who takes center shots and the difficulty of covering the full length of the half court forward and backward. The system provides a strong defensive formation, but lacks opportunities for offense.

The *up-and-back* formation (Fig. 47) is a strong offense system. It is customarily used in

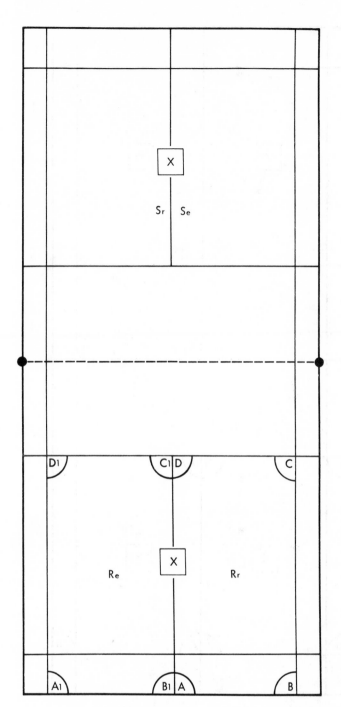

Sr—Server in rt. service ct.
Se—Server in lt. service ct.
Rr—Receiver in rt. service ct.
Re—Receiver in lt. service ct.
X —Center Base
A,B,C,D—Target corner for rt. service ct.
A1,B1,C1,D1—Target corner for lt. service ct.

(45) Court positions for singles.

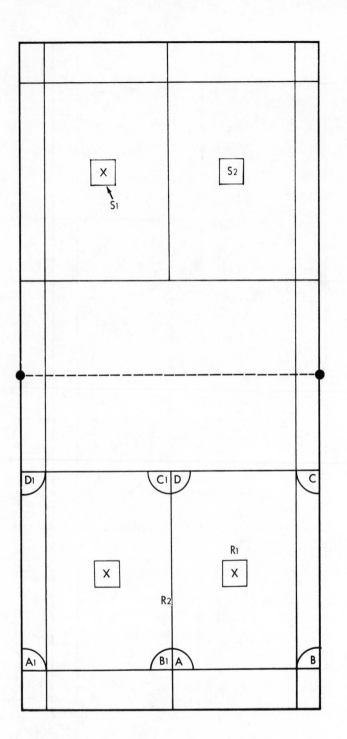

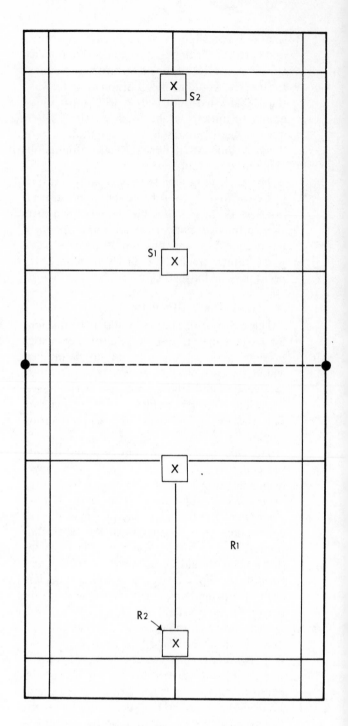

S1–Server
S2–Server's partner
R1–Receiver
R2–Receiver's partner
X –Center Base
A,B,C,D–Target corners for rt. service ct.
A1,B1,C1,D1–Target corners for lt. service ct.

S1–Server
S2–Server's partner
R1–Receiver
R2–Receiver's partner
X –Center Base

(46) Side-by-side system.

(47) Up-and-back system.

mixed doubles with the women playing the forward positions. The player who is "up" near the short service line is in a position to cut off any weak returns; the "back" player covers the entire back court. The vulnerable areas in this formation are the sidelines and the center court area just over the head of the net player and in front of the back player. The net player must have good racket work for net shots and be quick in her reaction, and the back player needs especially to be able to return sideline drives and to smash with accuracy. The server follows up a low serve and guards the net. The partner may take the position at back court across the center line while the serve is being delivered. After the opening play they each assume their prearranged up-and-back positions.

The *combination* system uses the side-by-side formation for defense, and the up-and-back for offense. The players may start with the side-by-side formation, and as soon as the opponents hit up or show signs of weakness, they change to the up-and-back system to press the attack. If a player is drawn to the net, the partner takes the back court; to return to the side-by-side position, the front person moves into the side position of the nearest court and the other player moves to the other side. Some players may prefer to start with the up-and-back position, using it for their basic formation until it is necessary to take a stronger defending position, at which time each takes the nearest court. This system is an advanced form of team play and requires practice with one's partner to avoid confusion when shifting. Also, each player must be skilled in all positions—whether intercepting at the net or smashing from back court.

Mechanics of Movement

The construction of the badminton shuttle does not make drawing the racket across the shuttle effective for a cut shot. There are no spins, slices, or chops, at least not for the beginner. Hits should be made with the racket at a right angle to the line of the swing at the moment of impact. This is done with the grip described earlier (similar to the Eastern forehand grip in tennis) and a side to the net position when taking the backswing. Mediocre results come from facing the net and making flat hits. The "backyard badminton" player who uses this latter technique also grips the racket with the hand rotated

too far to the right. A beginner may have initial success with this grip and stance but soon reaches a plateau of learning from which it is difficult to advance. The mechanical drawbacks are 1) swinging while facing the net precludes the possibility of a long backswing and thus limits build-up of racket speed, 2) hip and shoulder rotation are restricted so power cannot be gained in this manner, 3) the faulty grip prevents strong wrist action, and 4) there is little room for a follow-through.

The following principles of movement apply to badminton:

1. For every action there is an equal and opposite reaction. This principle affects all movement on the court. For example, as the weight goes forward to the left foot for a smash, the right foot pushes back against the floor. In serving, even though the feet must remain stationary, the principle also applies, for the weight shifts to the forward foot as the back foot pushes down and back.
2. The center of gravity must fall within the base of support for balance, but is advanced near the edge of the base for easy movement and quick changes of direction. This is apparent in the "ready" position where the weight is forward and the heels are raised.
3. The flatter the arc of a swing, the greater the possibility for accuracy in directing a hit. The arc of the swing is flattened by turning sideways to the net, transferring the weight from the back to the forward foot, and taking a long backswing and follow-through toward the target.
4. The longer the radius of the swing, the greater the speed and force that can be applied. In any badminton hit where speed and power are desired, the swing should start with body rotation and move out from the shoulder, elbow, and wrist. When the shuttle is contacted with only a bent elbow and swing of the lower arm there will be less power in the hit.
5. Sequential action, starting at the center of the body and radiating out through the arm with a last-moment snap of the wrist, gives smooth coordination to the swing.

Evaluation

Badminton skill tests can be used for practice and to evaluate performance. Details on scoring and scale scores are available for the short and long serve, clear, and volley.[1]

SHORT SERVE

The short serve can be practiced to the near corners of the service court by serving over the net and beneath a rope stretched 20 inches above the net.

LONG SERVE

A rope 8 feet high is extended across the court 14 feet back from the net. The player stands in the serving position and attempts to serve the shuttle so that it clears the rope and lands near the back of the court. The back alley can be used as the target, or the scoring system presented by Scott and French can be used.

CLEAR

The rope used in the long serve is also appropriate for clear practice. A player who stands under the rope can set-up to the person who attempts to clear from her midcourt. The shot must be above the rope and should land near the back court. The back alley can be used as the target, or the scoring system by Scott and French will give finer discrimination of ability.

WALL VOLLEY

Volleying the shuttle can be practiced against a wall. The shuttle is volleyed against the wall from a distance of 6 feet and consecutive hits are counted.

KEEP AWAY

A game of "keep away" provides clearing practice for four players who stand in the back courts and try to clear out of reach of two or four others who stand near the service lines.

Terminology

Alley: The narrow lengthwise area added to the singles court to form the doubles boundary.

Back alley: The area between the two back boundary lines.

Back boundary lines: Two lines 2½ feet apart. The outer line is the back boundary for the playing court in

---

[1] M. Gladys Scott and Esther French, *Measurement and Evaluation in Physical Education* (Dubuque, Iowa: William C. Brown Co., 1959).

singles and doubles. The inner line is the back boundary line for the doubles service court.

Balk: Any deceptive movement or "feint" made to disconcert an opponent before or during the serve. This is a fault.

Carry: Momentary holding of the shuttle on the racket during a stroke; also called a *sling* or *throw*. This is a fault.

Clear: A stroke that sends the shuttle high and deep to the back of the court.

Cross-court: A stroke that sends the shuttle over the net to the diagonally opposite court.

Double hit: Shuttle hit twice in succession by player or player and partner. This is a fault.

Down: The loss of serve by failure to score. In doubles each side has two downs before losing the serve to the opponents (except in the first inning when the serving side has one down).

Drive: A stroke that sends the shuttle in a fast nearly horizontal flight.

Drop shot: An overhead or underhand stroke that imparts little speed to the shuttle and causes it to fall close to the net on the opponent's side.

Fault: A violation of the rules. A fault made by the "in" side puts the server out; a fault made by the "out" side gives a point to the "in" side.

Hand-in: Term used to indicate that the player serving still retains the service.

Hand-out: Term used in doubles to indicate that one partner has had her turn at serving.

Inning: Term of service or time during which a player or side has the service.

In side: The side that is serving.

Let: The legal replay of a point.

Love-all: Score zero—zero.

Match: Best two out of three games.

Mixed doubles: A game in which a man and a woman play as partners on each side.

Net shot: Shot hit from the forecourt and just clearing the net.

Out side: The side that is receiving.

Round-the-head shot: A shot made with the forehand face of the racket but hit on the backhand side of the body.

Second service: Term used in doubles to indicate that one partner is "down" or has already had her turn at serving.

Setting: The playing of additional points when the score is tied at specified scores in a game.

Shuttlecock: The official name; more commonly referred to as *shuttle* or *bird*.

Smash: A hard hit overhead stroke that sends the shuttle down with great speed. The game's chief offensive stroke.

Wood shot: A legal shot in which the frame of the racket hits the base of the shuttle.

Selected References

Davidson, Kenneth R., and Leland R. Gustavson. *Winning Badminton*. New York: Ronald Press, 1964.

Davis, Dorothy, ed. *Selected Tennis-Badminton Articles*. Washington, D.C.: American Assoc. for Health, Physical Education and Recreation, 1963.

Devlin, Grace, ed. *Bird Chatter*. 2 Dolfield Rd. Owings Mills, Md. (periodical of the American Badminton Association).

DGWS Tennis-Badminton Guide, current Edition. Washington, D.C.: American Assoc. for Health, Physical Education, and Recreation.

Friedrich, John, and Abbie Rutledge. *Beginning Badminton*. Belmont, Calif.: Wadsworth Publishing Co., 1962.

Varner, Margaret. *Badminton*. Dubuque, Iowa: William C. Brown, 1966.

Chapter **5**

Bowling *Kathleen Black*

History. Goals. Equipment. Etiquette. SKILLS: *Grip, Stance, Aiming, Approach, Arm Swing, Release, Follow-through. Scoring. Fouls. Pin Fall. Organizations. Evaluation. Terminology. DUCKPINS.*

Bowling, a popular game of the day, is one sport in which participation is seldom limited; it is played by men, women, boys, girls, and even by the handicapped. Interestingly, bowling is one of the few sports in which all can be participating in the game together at the same time. It is truly a family sport. An indoor recreational activity, bowling knows no season but enjoys year-round participation.

The game of bowling combines the skill techniques necessary for participation with the restriction of rules to regulate play. Primary skills that are basic for success are control, rhythm, timing, and coordination. Because strength and endurance are only secondary, bowling is an ideal recreational activity for all.

Bowling is fun and the basics are easy to learn. With concentration and practice, you too can be a good bowler.

History

Bowling, as so many of our present-day sports and activities, had its beginning many centuries ago. Although it was not played with today's

precise rules or equipment, the basic objective of the game was the same—to knock down a pin or pins with a ball. The earliest records of bowling indicate that fourth-century Germans carried with them a small wooden club called a

(1) A good start.

Miss Black, an instructor of health and physical education at Central State College, Oklahoma, has also taught at El Reno High School and the University of Oklahoma. She has served as president of her local bowling league for five years and was a member of the league champion team for two years. In 1965 Miss Black was Oklahoma City Women's Class B Doubles Champion.

---

kegal which they used for recreation and, when the need arose, for self-defense. The kegal also played a part in the religious life of the day. If a man could knock over his kegal with a round stone, he proved to his priest that he had been living an honorable life. In the years that followed, the clergy adopted the kegal activity as a means of recreation. Martin Luther is credited with being an enthusiastic bowler.

In America, bowling was first mentioned in Washington Irving's "Rip Van Winkle." The early days of our country, however, found the sport in danger of being outlawed because of the unhealthy atmosphere created by professional gamblers. Participation in the game of ninepins, as bowling was then called, was in fact prohibited by the Connecticut legislature because of the gambling and rowdiness associated with the game. The modern-day version of bowling, with the triangle formation of ten pins, was created in order to legalize the game.

Goals

Through participation in bowling, it is hoped that you will develop the motor skills that will aid in the improved efficient use of your physical abilities. Bowling can assist in improvement of body balance, hand-eye coordination, and the timing of coordinated movements. Your growth will also include the abilities that are necessary in understanding pin and ball deflection, in calculating spares and splits, and in developing increased concentration on the techniques of skill movements and the strategy of the game.

Bowling will provide a recreational pursuit in which you can participate for the remainder of your life. Joining one of the many forms of organized bowling leagues will enhance your interest in this enjoyable leisure-time activity.

Clothing and Equipment

Only a minimum amount of equipment is required to enjoy participation in bowling. All equipment necessary (bowling ball and shoes) can be furnished by the bowling lane. Bowling has no required clothing in color or design; participation, however, will be more enjoyable if the bowler's blouse is loose in the shoulders and sleeves to allow free arm swing. The skirt should be somewhat full at the hem in order to

permit the proper striding distance in the approach.

A bowler's enjoyment of the sport will increase when she acquires her own personally fitted equipment. Regulation bowling balls may not exceed 27 inches in circumference or 16 pounds in weight. The weight of the ball should be matched to the bowler, because a ball that is too heavy will throw the bowler off balance. However, a ball that is too light for the bowler is also difficult to control.

A second factor in fitting the ball is the span —the distance from the thumb hole to the finger holes. There should be only enough space between the palm of the hand and the ball to insert a pencil. If the pencil fits too tightly, the fit is termed *overspanned*; if the pencil is inserted too freely, the fit is *underspanned*. Either one of these incorrect spans will cause undue strain to the hand and difficulty in releasing the ball.

The third point of importance in fitting the ball is the thumb hole. The thumb should be placed all the way into the hole. If you can rotate the thumb around the hole and still feel the sides of the hole against the thumb, the size is correct.

The last point of consideration in selecting a bowling ball is the size of the finger holes. The fingers are inserted in the holes up to the second joint. The fingers should fit as the thumb does —loose but with a minimum amount of space between the fingers and the sides of the finger holes (Fig. 2).

If you have been using bowling establishment shoes, you will notice that the soles of both shoes were made of leather, but when purchasing your own personal shoes it is important to inform the dealer as to which hand you use to bowl. For a

(2) Gripping the ball.

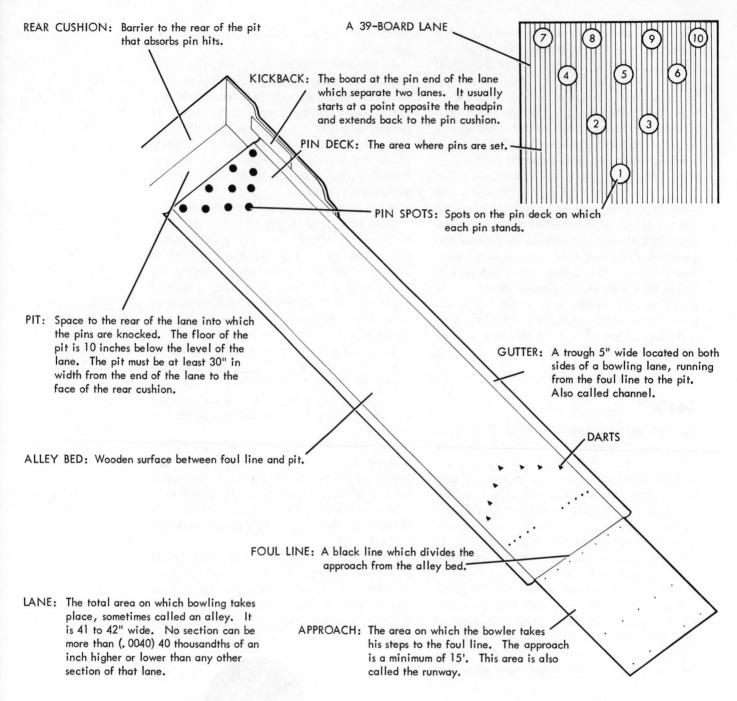

REAR CUSHION: Barrier to the rear of the pit that absorbs pin hits.

A 39-BOARD LANE

KICKBACK: The board at the pin end of the lane which separate two lanes. It usually starts at a point opposite the headpin and extends back to the pin cushion.

PIN DECK: The area where pins are set.

PIN SPOTS: Spots on the pin deck on which each pin stands.

PIT: Space to the rear of the lane into which the pins are knocked. The floor of the pit is 10 inches below the level of the lane. The pit must be at least 30" in width from the end of the lane to the face of the rear cushion.

GUTTER: A trough 5" wide located on both sides of a bowling lane, running from the foul line to the pit. Also called channel.

DARTS

ALLEY BED: Wooden surface between foul line and pit.

FOUL LINE: A black line which divides the approach from the alley bed.

LANE: The total area on which bowling takes place, sometimes called an alley. It is 41 to 42" wide. No section can be more than (.0040) 40 thousandths of an inch higher or lower than any other section of that lane.

APPROACH: The area on which the bowler takes his steps to the foul line. The approach is a minimum of 15'. This area is also called the runway.

(3) The lane.

right-handed bowler, the left sole of the bowling shoes will be made of leather to increase sliding ability, and the shoe for the right foot will have a rubber sole to increase traction. A left-handed bowler should simply reverse these directions. Bowlers should take extreme care to ensure the cleanliness of the soles of their shoes for safety reasons as well as for skill in execution.

Etiquette, Good Sportsmanship, and Safety

All sports have an unwritten code of ethics, courtesy, and sportsmanship that respects the privileges and rights of the contestants. The bowling rules of etiquette are designed to speed up the game and to make it more enjoyable. For maximum enjoyment of the game for yourself and bowlers on adjacent lanes, follow this basic suggested code:

1. *Be ready to bowl when it is your turn.* After bowling, move away from the approach and remain at the end of the alley while waiting to roll your second ball. Be seated when you are not bowling. Do not wander off between frames.
2. Bowling is not a timed sport; take your time, but do not waste it by useless posing or waiting until everyone else is off the approaches.
3. Allow the person on your right to bowl first only if you are ready at the same time. This applies only to the person on your immediate right. Never bowl at the same time with the player on either your left or right.
4. Do not pick your ball off the rack just as a bowler on the other lane is about to bowl or while she is making her delivery.
5. Never speak to a bowler after she has assumed her stance; to do so or to make remarks or undue noise with the intention of disturbing the player is a serious violation of bowling etiquette.
6. Remember to stay back of the foul line.
7. Confine "*body english*" *to your own lane.* Twisting, turning, jumping, and hopping disturbs bowlers on either side of you.
8. Do not use another player's ball, except with permission. This applies to a house ball chosen by another player or to one which someone has brought to the lane.
9. Use proper equipment, particularly shoes. Keep the approaches clean. Approaches covered with candy, water, or litter can cause serious physical injury. Be sure to check that your shoes are dry and clean and will not spoil the approaches for you or for others. Never put powder or chalk on the approaches. If adjustments need to be made notify the manager of the establishment.
10. Respect the lane. Getting the ball out on the lane is good bowling, but "lofting" hurts your game and damages the alley bed.
11. Refrain from loud noise. Save kidding for the bench or locker room. Concentration is vital for good bowling.
12. Do not roll your ball before the pinboy or automatic pinsetter is ready or you may damage the ball or machine.

13. Control your temper; strikes, spares, splits, taps, and misses are all part of the game.
14. Take practice swings only on the approach. It is dangerous to swing your ball any other place.
15. When you have finished bowling, return house balls and shoes to their proper places.
16. Above all, show good sportsmanship—be a gracious winner and loser and try to be courteous at all times.

These rules of etiquette function to protect you from injury and to insure your enjoyment of the sport.

Skills

PICKING UP THE BALL

The first skill a bowler learns is the proper way to pick up the ball from the ball return. The bowler should always face in the direction of returning balls. Pick the ball up *with both hands*, rather than by the finger holes. *Place one hand on either side of the ball*, taking care not to put the hands in line with the returning balls. This method is recommended to provide complete control and to eliminate the possibility of the ball slipping and dropping onto the approach or on the bowler's toes. It also relieves undue strain on the bowling hand (Fig. 4).

(4) Removing the ball from the return.

(5) Stance.

(6) First step.

(7) Second step.

(8) Third step.

(9) Fourth step or slide.

(10) Follow-through.

(5–11) Four-step approach.

(11) Completion of follow-through.

GRIPPING THE BALL

Place the two middle fingers in the holes first; next, slip the thumb into the thumb hole all the way. Do not squeeze the ball with the ends of the fingers, but rather maintain contact by attempting to press slightly the palm side of the fingers and thumb toward the center of the ball. The weight of the ball will be greater on the thumb on the backswing and on the fingers in the forward swing. The little finger and index finger should be relaxed and flat on the ball.

STANCE

Stance is the preparation the bowler makes before he moves toward the pins. The proper stance is essential in order to produce the best results in bowling. Proper stance does not mean that all bowlers assume an identical position, but refers to the bowling position best suited for each individual within restrictions of body structure and movement. It should be a position comfortable for the bowler to assume. To take the proper stance, one should stand erect with feet together, or with the left foot slightly forward if the bowler is right-handed. Weight should be on the left foot. Stand with knees slightly bent. The head should be up and over your knees; the shoulders are level (Fig. 5).

Even though the stance should be of your own creation and comfort, the ball should be held at about waist level. If the ball is held much higher than the waist, it may throw you sideways and off balance on the arm swing. The ball should be positioned to the right of the body so that the arm is straight from shoulder to wrist. This will enable the bowler to push the ball straight ahead and to swing the ball directly below the shoulder. The wrist should be straight and stiff; there is no wrist action in bowling.

In assuming the proper stance, the elbow should be allowed to move back along the side and not braced on the hips. The arms remain close to the body. The majority of the weight of the ball should be supported by the nonbowling hand. At this stage, the bowling fingers should be in the ball but without muscle tension gripping the ball. The shoulders, hips, feet, and toes should be square with the target during the stance and throughout the delivery. The moment you take your stance, complete concentration is necessary. Do not take your eyes off the target or permit your mind to wander until after releasing the ball.

AIMING

The two general methods of aiming are pin bowling and spot bowling (Fig. 12). In pin bowling, the bowler uses the pins as the "point of aim." In spot bowling, a particular spot or dart on the alley located between 12 and 15 feet from the foul line is used as the point of aim. The majority of bowlers prefer the spot method of bowling because they feel they can more accurately hit a target 14 feet away rather than one 60 feet away.

The aiming point is the only phase of bowling technique that changes from delivery to delivery. To simplify aiming, three basic angles are recommended to knock down any pins left on the alleys. The three angles are strike position (5 pin angle), left to right (10 pin angle), and right to left (7 pin angle).

At least 50 per cent of your bowling will be devoted to aiming at all ten pins. This is referred to as the strike position or five pin angle. This position is also used to pick up any spares that include the 1-2-3-5 pins. The bowler (right-handed) should start with the left foot in line with the first dot on the lane right of center and use the second arrow from the right channel as the point of aim.

The left to right 10 pin angle is used for spare shooting of the 6, 9, or 10 pins. The bowler should position the left foot in line with the last dot on the left side of the lane, toes pointed to the pin that is nearest to her.

Spares consisting of one or more of the 4–7–8 pins are played from the right to left or 7 pin angle. The bowler should position her left foot on the last dot on the right and point her toes to the nearest pin on the lane.

In calculating all spares, the following three points must be considered: (1) point of origin, (2) point of aim, and (3) lead pin. At the point of origin, the inside of the left foot should be used to mark the starting position. The bowler should attempt to roll the center of the ball over the point of aim. If the bowler rolls a hook ball, the point of aim must be calculated in order to compensate for the amount of break in the hook (Fig. 17). For further information see later section "Release."

APPROACH

The approach is the footwork of bowling. As speed is not desirable in bowling footwork, the approach should be thought of as a walk rather

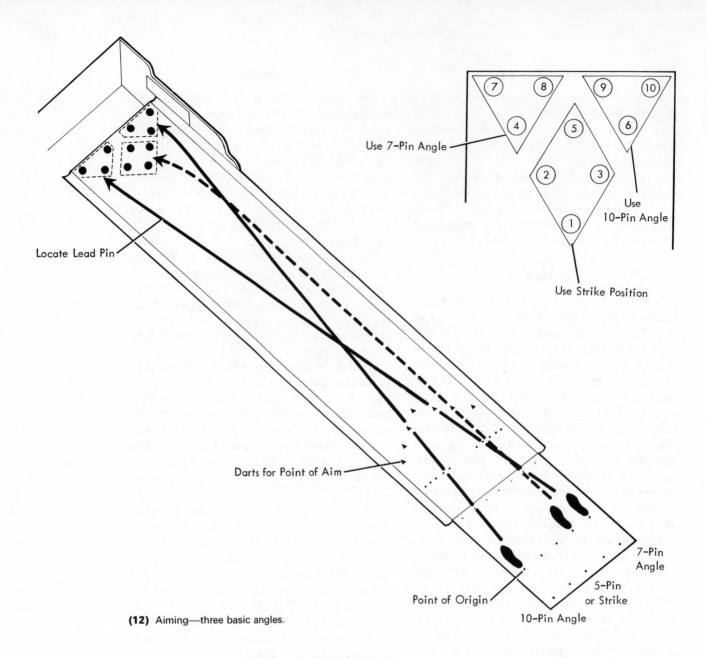

Locate Lead Pin

Use 7-Pin Angle

Use 10-Pin Angle

Use Strike Position

Darts for Point of Aim

7-Pin Angle

5-Pin or Strike

Point of Origin

10-Pin Angle

(12) Aiming—three basic angles.

than a run; however, reasonable ball speed is necessary. The ideal time for women from release of the ball to arrival at the head pin area should be $2\frac{1}{2}$ to $2\frac{3}{4}$ seconds.[1]

The bowling approach may be made in any number of steps; the four-step approach, however, is recommended. The stance is assumed at the point of origin for the approach. Rarely is the point of origin farther than 12 feet from the foul line. The beginner, with her back to the pins, can walk off $4\frac{1}{2}$ steps from the foul line to determine her starting point the first time that she bowls.

[1] Donald Casady and Marie Liba, *Beginning Bowling* (Belmont, Calif.: Wadsworth Publishing Co., Inc., 1962), p. 36.

The *first step* is taken with the right foot, if right-handed. The step should be approximately the distance of one half of a walking step. This is the most important step of the entire approach because hand position and arm swing are determined with it (Fig. 6, page 80).

The *second step* is taken on the left foot as the body is bent slightly at the waist, but care should be taken to keep the back straight and shoulders parallel to the target. The shoulder position on the second step is extremely important; the body should not pivot at the waist by allowing the right shoulder to follow the ball as it starts its backswing. The knees should be slightly bent throughout the approach (Fig. 7, page 80).

The *third step* is taken on the right foot. With each progressive step, increased bend in the

(13) Third step.

(14) Fourth step—beginning of slide.

(15) Ball released—continuing slide.

(16) Completion of follow-through.

(13–16) An experienced bowler slides. (Mrs. Lois Grant has won many honors in bowling. She has been one of the top women bowlers in Oklahoma for the last eight years. She was a member of the state championship teams for three years and was Oklahoma All-Star Match Game Champion for 1967. A member of the Oklahoma City "700" Club, Mrs. Grant uses a $15\frac{1}{2}$ pound ball.)

knees allows the body to be lowered into a more crouched position (Fig. 8, page 80, and Fig. 13).

The final step, the *fourth* one, is a combination of a one half step and a slide. The left foot should be drawn to the side of the right foot and then allowed to slide forward, while keeping the knees bent with the body weight forward and falling over the left knee. The left foot should complete the slide with the toe 2 to 6 inches behind the foul line and the foot pointing directly to the target (Figs. 9, 10, 14, 15, and 16).

The footwork from the point of origin as it progresses to the target must be in a straight line. Do not hesitate between steps after taking the first step; continue to move smoothly and continuously until the completion of the slide.

ARM SWING

The arm swing is started with the push-away. The ball should be pushed away from the body directing it toward the point of aim on a down-

ward angle. The ball should be pushed away with both hands in a slow, steady, push. The initial movement, however, should be with the heel of the bowling hand.

After the push-away, the supporting hand leaves the ball. This free arm then proceeds horizontally to the side for balance as the second step is taken. The bowling arm straightens and swings down and back, remaining close to the body. The arm should swing free from the shoulder, allowing the ball to swing under its own acceleration freely and easily, just like the pendulum of a clock. Care must be taken

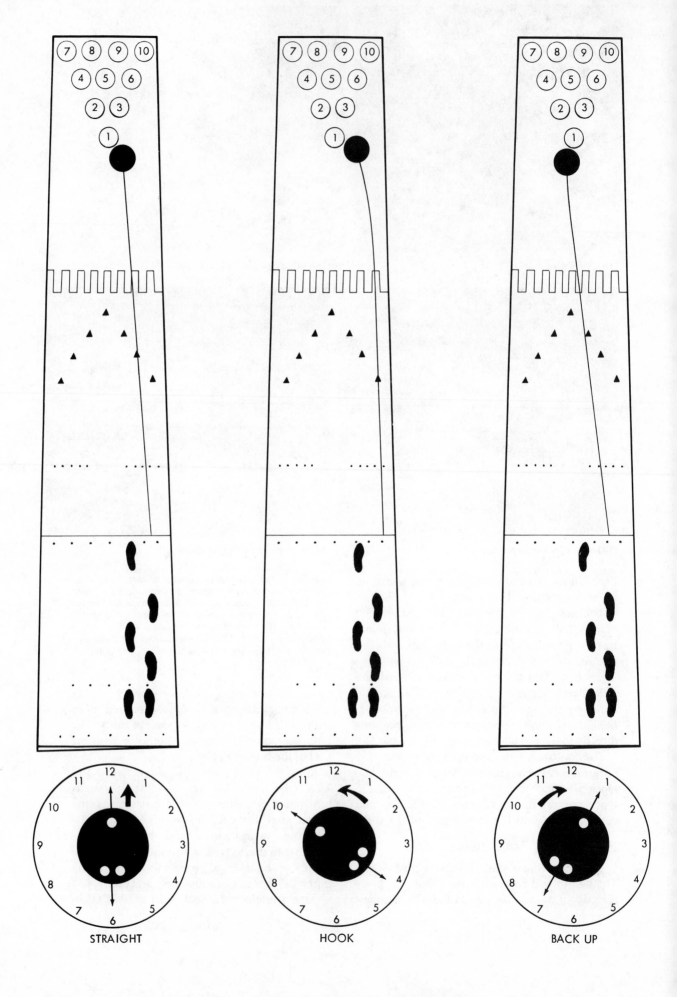

STRAIGHT   HOOK   BACK UP

to keep the shoulders square to the target and not to allow the elbow of the bowling arm to bend. The ball reaches the top of the backswing during the third step (Fig. 8, page 80, and Fig. 13, page 83). The backswing should never be higher than the shoulder and rarely is the backswing even that high. If the backswing is too high, it may result in too much ball speed. It is crucial that on the backswing the wrist remain straight. The forward swing completes the pendulum motion. Do not force the forward swing, but allow the ball to come through naturally.

RELEASE

On the fourth step, or the slide, the arm reaches the forward position to release or deliver the ball. The ball rolls out of the hand on the lane rather than being pitched or thrown. The hand should extend over the foul line to release the ball. In the correct release, the thumb should leave the ball first. The fingers lift the ball as it rolls from the palm of the hand. It is in the split second between the release of the thumb and the fingers that counterclockwise lift or roll is applied to the ball. The fingers should be firm as the ball rolls from the hand (Figs. 9 and 10, page 80; 14 and 15, page 83).

A straight-arm, follow-through motion will contribute greatly to the speed and accuracy of the ball. The position of the thumb and fingers at the point of release will determine the direction of the roll of the ball.

Hand position on the release makes a big difference in the way the ball rolls. To reduce the margin of error, it is best to assume the desired hand position before the bowler holds the ball in the stance. The three basic types of deliveries or releases are straight ball, hook, and back-up (Fig. 17).

To roll the straight ball, the thumb must be held at 12 o'clock and the fingers held at 6 o'clock with the lift given with the palm side of the fingers creating forward momentum and forward spin.

The hook ball has two advantages over other types of deliveries—forward momentum and counterclockwise spin. The hook ball may approach the pins with more angle than a straight ball, thereby decreasing the amount of deflection and increasing the potential carrying power of the ball. To roll a hook ball, the right-hander holds the thumb at 10 o'clock and the

fingers at 4 o'clock. As the fingers come out of the ball, they lift toward the index finger, thus creating the counterclockwise spin.

The back-up ball is the least desirable form of delivery, as it creates an unnatural rotation of the arm and usually proves to be inconsistent. To roll this delivery, the thumb must leave the ball at a 1 o'clock position and the fingers at 7 o'clock. The fingers lift to the little finger side of the hand with the arm rotating outward. The back-up bowler usually aims for the 1–2 pocket and bowls a little farther to the left than for a straight ball. A slow ball with much counterclockwise spin can become a curve-ball delivery. This type of delivery makes a wide arc or curve for the entire length of the lane. It is difficult to control this delivery; it is not recommended for beginners.

FOLLOW-THROUGH

The follow-through or finish position is as essential in bowling as it is in any sport. The importance of the follow-through lies in the fact that the precise second the ball is released cannot be pinpointed; it is necessary, therefore, to continue the pattern of the movement in an effort to perform the desired act. In the follow-through the bowling hand reaches out toward the point of aim and continues to swing in a circle until the hand swings up through the line of vision to the target. Arm, wrist, and hand should be in a straight line reaching toward the target.

Perfect balance is essential at the point of release if one is going to hit her target successfully. The sliding leg should be bent, weight balanced over the knee, toes of the sliding foot pointed toward the target, hips down, head up, shoulders parallel to the target and inclined toward the pins, and body bent forward at the waist. This position should be maintained until the ball has rolled over the point of aim and the bowler has checked her position and the accuracy of her release and follow-through (Figs. 11 and 16).

Consistency

Ball delivery must be consistent. Five sets of markings on each lane serve as guides for consistency (Fig. 18). On the approach to the lane there are two sets of starting markers of either five or seven dots each. One set is 12 feet behind the foul line and the other 15. When seven

(17) Basic deliveries rolled by beginners (page 84).

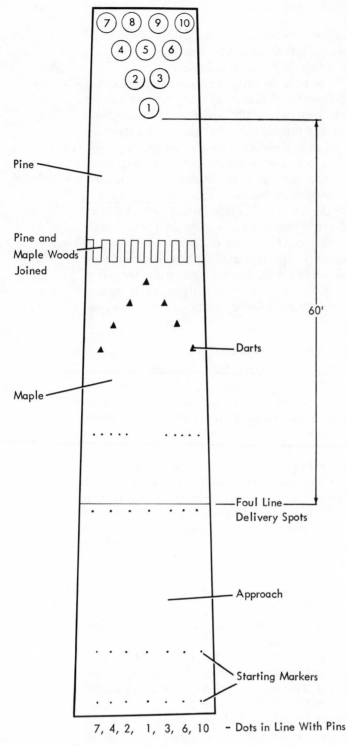

Pine

Pine and
Maple Woods
Joined

60'

Maple

Darts

Foul Line
Delivery Spots

Approach

Starting Markers

7, 4, 2, 1, 3, 6, 10 — Dots in Line With Pins

(18) Lane markings.

just in front of the foul line, are seven delivery spots that enable the bowler to check foot position and accuracy of release. Ten spots located 7 feet beyond the foul line serve as a guide for ball angle; and seven darts, 14 feet beyond the foul line and arranged in an inverted *V* pointing toward the pit, are used for point of aim in spot bowling. The bowler's height, length of stride, and speed of the ball are all factors that enter into determining the correct point of aim for the bowler.

Rules

The official rules governing bowling are established by the American Bowling Congress and the Women's International Bowling Congress. The rules of the game of bowling are few in number but they are essential to enjoyment of the sport. Nothing is more basic in bowling than knowing how to score the game.

SCORING

A game consists of ten frames. A bowler is allowed to roll two balls in each frame in an attempt to knock down all ten pins. However, if a bowler knocks down all ten pins with the first ball of a frame, it is termed a *strike*. If a bowler successfully knocks down all ten pins using both balls in a frame, it is called a *spare*. Failing to knock down all the pins in a frame is referred to as a miss, error, or blow.

A number of symbols are used in scorekeeping to describe what happens during the game. The scoring symbols (Fig. 19) include *foul*—touching or going beyond the foul line in delivery of the ball; *frame*—one tenth of a game; *gutter*—ball rolls into gutter (channel) on delivery; *miss*—failure to convert a spare leave when no split exists; *spare*—all pins down on two balls in a frame; *split*—two or more pins remain standing with intermediate pins knocked down in front and between; *converted split*—becomes a spare; and *strike*—all pins down on first ball of frame.

In order to keep score it is necessary to remember three basic rules and apply the proper one at the correct time. A bowler receives a bonus if she makes a strike or spare but does not receive a bonus if she misses. If she strikes, the bowler receives ten points for the strike plus the number of pins she knocks down with the next two balls rolled. If the bowler spares, she receives ten points for the spare plus the number

dots are used, they are on the boards on which the number 7, 4, 2, 1, 3, 6, and 10 pins are located. The markers enable the bowler to judge distance from the foul line and sideline for the starting position and also help in determining angle for spare conversion. On the approach,

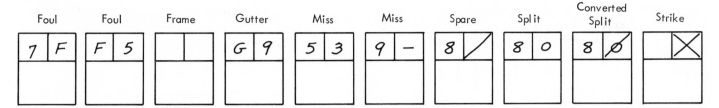

Foul	Foul	Frame	Gutter	Miss	Miss	Spare	Split	Converted Split	Strike
7 F	F 5		G 9	5 3	9 −	8 /	8 0	8 ∅	✕

(19) Scoring symbols.

of pins knocked down with the next ball rolled. If she misses, she receives no bonus but just the number of pins knocked down in that frame (Fig. 20).

The bottom portion of the score is the accumulation of points maintained progressively from frame to frame. Thirty points is the maximum that can be scored in one frame (Fig. 21). In the tenth frame, if a bowler marks (spares or strikes), she will roll a total of three balls in order to calculate bonus points. If the bowler misses, she will roll only two balls (Fig. 22).

FOULS

A foul occurs when the ball has been legally delivered and any part of the bowler's person comes in contact with any part of the bowling establishment on or beyond the foul line. A bowler does not foul when an object falls from

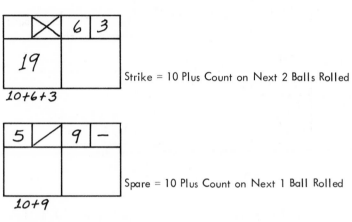

Strike = 10 Plus Count on Next 2 Balls Rolled

Spare = 10 Plus Count on Next 1 Ball Rolled

Miss = No Bonus

(20) Strike—spare—miss.

(21) Scoring the line.

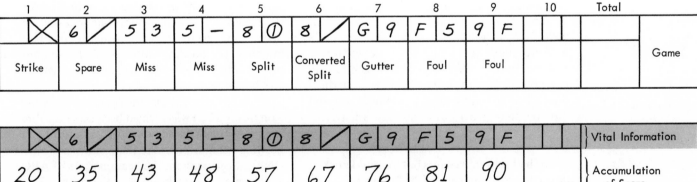

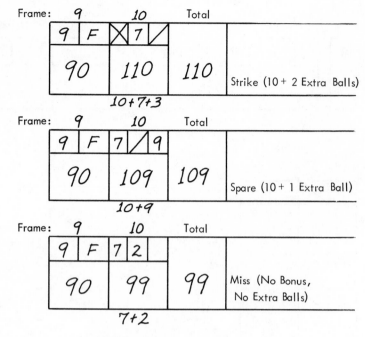

Frame:	9	10	Total	
	9 F	X 7 /		Strike (10 + 2 Extra Balls)
	90	110	110	
		10+7+3		

Frame:	9	10	Total	
	9 F	7 / 9		Spare (10 + 1 Extra Ball)
	90	109	109	
		10+9		

Frame:	9	10	Total	
	9 F	7 2		Miss (No Bonus, No Extra Balls)
	90	99	99	
		7+2		

(22) Tenth-frame scoring.

the person and lands on or beyond the foul line. The penalty for a foul is the loss of pins knocked down with a foul ball. If the bowler fouls on the first ball rolled in a frame, all ten pins are reset and the bowler has one ball in an attempt to try to make a spare. If a bowler fouls on the second ball in a frame, she forfeits any pins knocked down on that delivery.

LEGAL PIN FALL

Every delivery of the ball shall count unless the ball is ruled dead. Pins shall be counted as down if knocked down by another pin or pins rebounding from the kick-back or rear cushion or other portions of the lane. It will be the player's responsibility to determine if she is rolling at the correct set-up before delivering the ball. All pins knocked down but which remain lying on the lane or in the channels are termed *dead wood* and are counted as pins down and must be removed before the next ball is delivered.

ILLEGAL PINFALL

The ball delivered counts but the pins knocked down do not count if any of the following occurs: (1) pins hit by a delivery that goes into the channel prior to hitting the pins or by a delivery that rebounds from the rear cushion; (2) the pins hit any part of the pinsetter's body and rebound; (3) a standing pin falls or is knocked down by the pinsetter; it is considered a standing

pin and must be replaced; (4) pins that are bowled off the lane but rebound and remain standing must be counted as standing pins.

DEAD BALL

A dead ball does not count as a ball rolled. A delivered ball shall be declared dead under any one of the following conditions: (1) as the bowler delivers her ball, attention is called to the fact that one or more pins were missing from the set-up; (2) a bowler bowls out of turn or on the wrong alley; (3) a player is interfered with by a spectator, a bowler, a pinsetter, or a moving object as the ball is delivered and before delivery is complete; the bowler may either accept the pinfall or request that the pins be respotted; (4) any pins at which the bowler is bowling are moved or knocked down in any manner as the player delivers the ball and before it reaches the pins; (5) a bowler's ball comes in contact with any foreign object.

AVERAGE

A bowler's average is determined by dividing the number of games bowled into the total number of pins credited to the bowler. Fractions or extra pins are disregarded when using averages for the purpose of figuring handicaps or for classification purposes.

Organizations Promoting and Aiding in the Development of Bowling

The Bowling Proprietors Association of America (BPAA) is a cooperative, nonprofit organization of bowling establishments fostering the best interests of bowling through a continuous program of customer service, accommodation, and public relations.

On September 9, 1895, the American Bowling Congress (ABC) was formed because of the dire need to regulate the standards of equipment and bowling conditions. A nonprofit, noncommercial organization, the headquarters of ABC are located in Milwaukee, Wisconsin. This group has conducted an annual championship tournament for men since 1901.

The Women's International Bowling Congress, Inc. (WIBC) is the feminine counterpart of the ABC and was organized in 1916. Its main aim and purpose is to foster and to encourage sanctioned competition for women. *The Woman Bowler*, a popular monthly magazine, is the official voice of the group. The WIBC conducts an annual championship tournament in an attempt to popularize and increase interest in bowling among women.

The American Junior Bowling Congress (AJBC) was founded by Milton Raymer, a Chicago schoolteacher, in 1935. In 1940, with the help of the ABC and WIBC, it was extended to a national program. The AJBC program was suspended during World War II, but the movement was revived in 1945 by Raymer under the sponsorship of the National Bowling Council. The rules of the AJBC require good environmental conditions for the participation of its members; its program provides wholesome competition and encourages good fellowship and sportsmanship. National Championships are an important feature of the AJBC program.

Evaluation

The bowler can analyze her game more completely if she evaluates factors other than just her total score. Attention should be given to the average count knocked down with the first ball in a frame. After the initial learning stages of the game, the bowler should strive to average at least seven pins with her first ball. Another evaluation is the analysis of the number of marks made in a game. Particular attention should be given to the number of spares, especially those requiring a one-pin conversion.

Form in itself is not important, but the outcome derived in increased score from sincere concentration on the basic fundamentals of skills is important. The following checklist can be used to evaluate bowling form:

1. Stance:
   Body square to target
   Opposite foot forward
   Weight on forward foot
   Knees bent
   Shoulders parallel to target
   Ball held waist high
   Bowling arm parallel to floor
   Shoulders level
   Ball held to the side in line with shoulder
   Elbow back and into side
   Bowling wrist straight

2. Aim:
   Approach pins from correct point of origin
   Path of ball goes into the pins
   Ball hits lead pin first
   Eyes on point of aim

3. Approach:
   Start on proper foot
   Small first step
   Steps taken in a straight line
   Four steps
   Knees bent
   Slide on proper foot

4. Arm Swing:
   Push-away, down, and toward point of aim
   Free arm swing horizontal to the side
   Pendulum swing—arm straight from shoulder
   Backswing shoulder height or lower
   Release smooth
   Wrist straight
   Thumb released first
   Thumb in proper position on release

5. Follow-through:
   Balanced on sliding foot, knee bent
   Bowling hand extends through eye level
   Shoulders level and parallel to target
   Toes pointing to point of aim
   Body weight inclined toward target
   Hold position for two counts

Terminology

Anchor man: Person who bowls last in a team lineup.

Baby-split: A 2–7 or the 3–10 pin combination after the first ball is delivered.

Back-up ball: A ball that fades toward the side of the bowling hand; for a right-handed bowler it turns to the right, for a left-handed person it curves left.

Big four (double pinochle): 4–6–7–10 split.

Blow (error, miss): Failure to knock down the remaining pins with the second ball in a frame when a split does not exist.

Brooklyn (cross-over, Jersey): A hit to the left side of the head pin.

Channels: Areas running parallel to each side of the lane (sometimes called *gutters*).

Chop (cherry): To knock down, with the second ball of a frame, only the front pin or pins of a leave combination.

Count: The number of pins knocked down with the first ball.

Curve ball: A ball that works away from the bowling side from the moment it contacts the lane.

Double: Two strikes in a row.

Dutch 200: A score of 200 made by alternating strikes and spares for ten frames.

Error (miss, blow): Failure to knock down all pins after two attempts.

Foul: Touching or going beyond the foul line as the player delivers the ball.

Frame: One tenth of a game.

Full hit: Ball that hits the center of the target pin.

Grip: Means of holding the ball with the bowling hand.

Gutter ball: A ball that goes into the gutter (channel) on delivery.

Handicap: Means of equalizing competition.

Head pin (lead pin): Number one pin.

Hook: A ball that breaks away from the bowler's bowling side. (Breaks to left for right-hander; breaks to right for left-hander.)

Kegler: A bowler.

Lead-off: The first man in the lineup on a team.

Leave (set up): Pins remaining after the first ball is thrown.

Lift: Giving the ball an upward motion with the two middle fingers at the point of release.

Line: A game or ten frames.

Loft (lofting): Throwing the ball out on the lane too far beyond the foul line.

Mark: Making a strike or a spare in a frame.

Open frame: A frame without a strike or a spare.

Perfect game: Twelve successive strikes and a game that totals 300.

Pitch: Angle at which finger holes are bored in a ball.

Pocket: Area between 1–3 pins for right-handers and area between 1–2 pins for left-handers.

Pin bowler: A bowler who uses the pins as his point of aim.

Reverse: A ball that intentionally is rolled to break toward the bowler's side of release (right-hander's ball breaks to the right).

Scratch: Actual score without handicap added.

Series: Generally three games rolled in competition.

Sleeper (tandem): A pin hidden by another pin: 1–5; 2–8; 3–9.

Span: Distance between finger and thumb holes.

Spare: All ten pins knocked down on two balls in a frame.

Split (railroad): Two or more pins that remain standing with intermediate pins knocked down in front and between.

Spot: A place on the lane at which a bowler is aiming, referred to as *point of aim*.

Spot bowler: A bowler who uses a spot on the alley at which to aim.

Straight ball: Ball travels a straight line from the point of release to the 1–3 pocket or pin selected as target.

Strike: All pins down with the first ball in a frame.

Strike out: Three successive 10 pin counts in the tenth frame or striking to the end of a game.

Tap: An apparent good strike that leaves one pin standing. Normally leaving the 8 pin is the only one considered a tap.

Tenpins: Another name for the game of bowling.

Turkey: Three strikes in a row.

Washout: The 1–2–4–10 leave for a right-hander or the 1–3–6–7 leave for a left-hander.

Working ball: A ball with great spin that produces a lot of action among the pins.

DUCKPINS

Duckpin bowling is popular in some parts of the United States. The same bowling lanes can be used, but the balls and pins are smaller than those used in tenpin bowling. Duckpins are $9\frac{3}{8}$ inches high with a $1\frac{3}{8}$ inch base compared to the regulation tenpin of fifteen inches with a $2\frac{1}{4}$ inch base. The maximum weight for a tenpin ball is 16 pounds. A duckpin ball can weigh no more than 3 pounds, 12 ounces with a maximum diameter of 5 inches. Without finger holes, this smaller ball does not rest in the palm of the hand, but is gripped with the fingers and thumb.

Scoring for duckpins is the same as for tenpins, but three balls may be used for each frame. A strike is made on the first ball if all the pins are knocked down, or a spare on the second ball. If all ten pins are knocked down with the third ball, it is not scored as a spare. Theoretically, a

perfect game of 300 can be bowled, but it does not actually occur with these smaller pins and smaller ball.

The four-step delivery is used for the approach and a straight, cross lane shot is recommended for beginners.

Selected References

Bellisimo, Lou. *The Bowler's Manual.* Englewood Cliffs, N.J.: Prentice-Hall, 1965.

Casady, Donald, and Marie Liba. *Beginning Bowling.* Belmont, Calif.: Wadsworth Publishing Co., 1962.

DGWS Bowling, Fencing, Golf Guide, current edition. Washington, D.C. American Assoc. for Health, Physical Education, and Recreation.

Martin, Joan. *Bowling.* Dubuque, Iowa: William C. Brown, 1966.

Chapter 6

Equitation *Betty Lou Brunson*

Styles of Riding. Goals. Equipment. Mounting. The Aids. Gaits. The Saddle Seat Rider. Trail Riding. Care of the Horse. Terminology.

Throughout the ages the horse has been recognized as one of the animals most useful to man. In earlier times he was essential as a beast of burden and as a means of transportation. Today machines have replaced the horse for most utilitarian purposes, but he is still appreciated and used by much of mankind. Many people are riding today for recreation. Some ride for exercise, some for thrills, some to be in the out-of-doors; but many ride just because they like horses. There is satisfaction in working with and training this animal. Whether one enjoys the pleasures of trail riding, hacking, showing, or hunting, there is always the challenge of more to be learned.

The rider must have an understanding and appreciation of the horse, and rider and horse must be trained to work together. This is a sport in which your partner does not understand your language, but he does have a sure instinct and an excellent memory. The beginner learns to know the horse and to acquire the skills of riding; and with sympathetic handling, the horse will learn to respond to the rider's wishes.

Miss Betty Lou Brunson, riding instructor for Duke University, has her own stables. During the summer she teaches a riding instructor's course and is youth social director at High Hampton Country Club, Cashiers, N.C. Each year Miss Brunson sponsors a horse show at her stables. She judges for other shows, and also shows her own American Saddlebred and Arabian horses with both English and Western saddles.

A mutual understanding must exist between horse and rider so that they will perform as a team.

Styles of Riding

With such a large number of people enjoying riding, it is not surprising that there are a number of styles of riding; the most commonly used styles in the United States are the western seat, the forward seat, and the saddle seat.

The *western* or *stock seat* has taken the country by storm, and with it the Quarter Horse. This little horse with the quick take-off was so named because he can run a quarter of a mile faster than any other horse on earth. This type of riding is done with a loose rein. The reins are held in one hand in order to neck rein and thus turn the horse in the direction given with this hand through the pressure of the rein against the horse's neck. The hand holding the reins stays as near the pommel, or front of the saddle, as possible, while the other hand is resting on the leg. The western seat rider is erect in the middle of the saddle, uses long stirrups, and keeps heels slightly down.

The *forward seat* is often used in hunting and jumping. The rider shifts the weight of her trunk forward as the horse progresses from the walk into the trot and gallop. Both hands are on the reins, and stirrups are short so that the rider's knees and ankles are bent. When approaching a jump the rider assumes an extreme forward position with her weight centered on her inner thighs, head forward, and hands low. In this style of riding leg signals are used more than hands and the rider is taught to grip with knees and inner thighs. The hunt rider strives to be the perfect passenger so that she in no way interferes with the extended movement of her mount.

The *saddle seat* style of riding is frequently used with the American Saddlebred, the Morgan and the Arabian, and any other horse trained to this style. The saddle seat is recommended for its elegance and grace, for its poise and balance. It enables the horse and rider to perform with beautiful carriage and motion. The saddle seat rider is erect in the center of the saddle in all gaits. She never stands in the stirrups, but in posting with the trot the rider uses her knees and inner thighs to rise forward–upward in rhythm with the horse. Both hands are held above the pommel with their height being determined by the position of the horse's head. A straight line should be formed from the rider's elbow to the bit. The rider's head is erect. Legs are slightly bent at the knee, and feet are placed well into the stirrup with the ball of the foot on the stirrup. The rider's legs are in a natural hanging position with feet neither away from nor under the horse's body. In the canter the rider's knees and inner thighs lie close to the saddle with the waist absorbing the shock.

Goals

Styles of riding vary, but all riders must learn position and control of the horse. The beginner must learn position, or how to sit on a moving horse, and must also learn how to control the horse while riding. The advanced rider, in order to better understand the horse, will want to assist in the schooling or training of the horse. Regardless of style, the basic riding position must (1) enable the rider to be in balance with the moving horse; (2) avoid interference with the horse's balance and movement; (3) provide security for the rider through correct leg position and distribution of weight; and (4) allow effective use of the rider's hands and legs for guidance of the horse.

To become a proficient rider, the beginner must achieve a number of objectives:

1. Learn to mount and dismount.
2. Be able to ride correctly in one style of riding, and be aware of other styles.
3. Learn the proper use of aids and correct riding in the various gaits.
4. Know and observe the rules of safety in the ring and on the trail and practice trail etiquette.
5. Recognize that different horses require different degrees of forcefulness in handling. The good horsewoman learns to work with the horse.
6. Learn the terminology of horsemanship.
7. Learn care of the horse.

Equipment

WHAT TO WEAR

Clothing for riding varies with the style of riding. The chief concern for the beginner is leg and foot protection. Slacks or jeans are appropriate, and sturdy tie shoes or boots should be worn. The western rider may copy the cowboy's attire and wear ranch pants or jeans, a colorful shirt, boots, and even a bandanna and ten-gallon hat. Some of the riders in the show ring these days are wearing very gay colors, especially riders of the Tennessee Walking Horse; ladies showing this breed do not wear hats. Riders of Arabian horses, in another class for the show ring, dress in the elaborate and flowing robes of ancient Arabia. Both saddle seat and hunt riders have appropriate formal and informal attire.

Informal clothes for the *saddle seat rider* (Fig. 1) include *jodphurs*—"Kentucky jodphurs," high waist, form fitting all the way to the lower calf, flaring from there to the bottom, of any material or color; *shirt*—white or colored with a mannish collar; *tie*—bow tie or four-in-hand of any color; *coat*—about 6 inches longer than the hunt coat, vented in back or sides with an inverted pleat, of any material or color; *gloves*—leather or string; *boots*—jodphur boots with elastic sides or strap; and *hat*—soft felt pork pie with snap brim or hard crown derby.

Formal clothes for the *saddle seat rider* comprise *jodphurs*—any dark color with silk braid down the side; *shirt*—tuxedo style, winged collar, white formal front; *tie*—bow tie, preferably white; *coat*—extra long tuxedo coat with satin lapels, of any dark color and matching the jodphurs in a complete habit, including a boutonniere; *gloves*—white or dark color, leather, matching the habit; *boots*—jodphur style, black patent leather; and *hat*—high top silk (ladies' and girls' hair should be in a net and off the face).

Informal clothes for the *hunt rider* are *jodphurs* —cuffed with no flare at the bottom, solid color; *breeches*—flared at hips, snug at knee with buttons, also solid color; *shirt*—mannish collar or ratcatcher type, colored or white; *tie*—colored stock or four-in-hand; *coat*—flared at bottom with vent in back, of plain or checked salt sack or linen material; *gloves*—leather or string; *boots*—short jodphur type or high top (knee-length) boots worn with breeches; and *hat*—derby.

Formal clothes for the *hunt rider* are *breeches* —red brick or yellow in color; *shirt*—white, with neckband; *tie*—white stock; *coat*—black jacket with flared vent; *gloves*—pigskin; *boots* —plain black; and *hat*—black derby with hat guard.

HORSES

In learning to ride, it is important to be mounted on a horse that suits you as an individual. This is essential in a class or in buying your own horse. A skilled rider interested in doing some quick turning in a western saddle would get no pleasure from riding the docile mount a beginner may find is the answer to her prayers. The behavior of a horse is determined by his breed, his own individual nature, training, the weather, and even the amount of exercise he has had recently. When renting a horse at an unfamiliar stable, ask for a gentle horse. It is far better to underestimate your ability than to find yourself on an animal you cannot control.

Breeds

The purebred horse is one with no alien blood; in other words, both parents are of the same breed. This should not be confused with the "Thoroughbred," which is a specific breed of horse. Some of the better known pure breeds are the *American Saddlebred*—a horse bred for beauty, animation, and adaptability to collection and gait; *Arabian*—the oldest known pure breed; considered the foundation strain for the light horse breeds. This horse is small, yet noted for stamina, intelligence, an affectionate disposition, and spirit; *Quarter Horse*—a breed with pronounced muscular development of the hindquarters, noted for stability of disposition and

(1) Informal attire for the saddle seat rider.

the ability to move quickly. Bred to be a fast quarter mile racer. Very adaptable to stock work; and *Thoroughbred*—a specific pure breed of horse founded and developed by the British for speed and endurance. Now known and bred world-wide as a race horse; also used extensively as a hunter and jumper.

The main colors of the horse include *Bay*—red brown with black points; *Brown*—black brown with black points; *Sorrel*—reddish color with mane and tail of same, or lighter shade; *Gray*— mixture of black and white hairs giving gray look (at birth the gray horse is almost black, gradually lightens each year until almost pure white); *Black*; *White*; *Pinto*—two colors, white and another, arranged in patches on the body; *Roan*—basic coat of one color but having other colored hairs mixed (strawberry roan is sorrel with white flecks; blue roan is gray with black flecks giving a blue appearance); *Chestnut*—a tannish, nut brown color with mane and tail of same or lighter color (a liver chestnut resembles color of raw liver with mane and tail the same or lighter); *Palomino*—golden color with all white mane and tail; and *Buckskin*—light beige or cream with black points.

The face markings of the horse include *blaze*—a broad white strip down face; *strip*—a white strip down center of face; *snip*—a white mark between nostrils; *star*—a white mark on forehead; and *bald face*—practically whole face is white. The leg markings are *stocking*—white extending up leg to knee or above and *sock*—white extending up leg to or just above ankle.

TACK

All objects used in clothing the horse in the stables or at work are called tack. For riding this includes saddle, saddle pad or blanket, bridle with bit, breast-plate, girth, and martingale. The tack used in the stables includes halter, halter ropes, and blankets.

Saddle

Several types of saddles are in common use. The *western saddle* is designed for stock work; thus it is heavier, larger, and more sturdy than other saddles. It is a deep saddle with a prominent pommel and a saddle horn that is used in roping and holding stock. The *forward seat saddle* is also deep seated, but lacks the horn. A flap of leather extends forward to protect the rider's knee, which is bent at a greater angle than in other seats. Knee rolls are used to provide security in jumping. The *park saddle* is neither deep seated nor very flat. It is used for pleasure riding and for the saddle seat riding style, except in showing the horse.

The *show saddle*, more like the park saddle than any other but with wider flaps and flatter, is used in the horse show. The shallow seat of this saddle shows off the horizontal top line of the American Saddlebred, while its pommel is often cut back to show off the horse's shoulders. The wide flaps protect the rider's attire. Some riders may prefer the *dressage saddle*, a moderately deep seated saddle with small knee rolls that are lower than on the forward seat saddle. This saddle aids the rider in sitting erect, rather than forward. The dressage saddle is designed to give the rider's legs support and facilitate their use in collection.

Whichever saddle is used, it is imperative that it fits the particular horse using it. Each horse in a stable should have its own tack. A low pommeled saddle on a high withered horse can cause a fistula, an infection of the withers almost impossible to eradicate. A saddle too high off the horse's withers may slide out of place while it is being used in riding.

A *saddle pad* shaped like the saddle, or a blanket that extends beyond the saddle for ornamentation, is often used for protection of the horse's back. This must of course be kept impeccably clean.

(2) Ready to bridle the horse.

The *bridle*, the horse's headgear, may have single or double reins (Fig. 2). This is determined by the type of bit used, and bits vary in style and in the amount of pressure they create on the horse's mouth. Horses should be bitted with tack that gives the rider control and yet is as light as possible on the horse's mouth (Fig. 3).

The *snaffle bit* is a mouthpiece, jointed in the middle, with a ring on each end where the reins and cheek-pieces buckle on to connect it with the bridle. This bit has no shanks or chain; hence, most of the pressure is placed on the lips rather than on the bars of the mouth. It is a mild bit that is used primarily with colts and hunters.

The *curb bit* has reasonably long shanks and a half circle rise in the mouthpiece, which acts on the bars rather than the corners of the lips. The curb bit is used in combination with a curb chain so that pressure is exerted on both the chin and bars of the mouth, making this a rather severe bit. Working on a lever system, the curb bit is proportionately stronger than the action of the hands on the reins.

The *pelham bit* is in between the snaffle and curb in design and severity. With a solid and usually straight mouthpiece, and with rings on the shanks for two pairs of reins, this bit gives

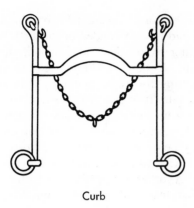

Curb

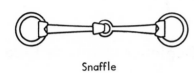

Snaffle

Pelham

(3) Bits.

both snaffle and curb action. It suits many horses inasmuch as it is mild and yet gives control.

Bridles

The three types of *bridles* most frequently used are the snaffle, the pelham, and the full bridle. The *snaffle bridle*, with snaffle bit and one set of reins, and the *pelham bridle*, with pelham bit and two sets of reins (curb and snaffle) are satisfactory for most riding. The *full bridle*, consisting of both curb and snaffle bit, are often used for showing horses, because the purpose of the two bits is to set the horse's head in the position one wishes. The snaffle bit and reins are called the *bridoon*. The bridoon lifts the head while the curb reins duck the chin. The little finger is kept between the two reins in each hand with the less

severe and more used bridoon on the outside. The full bridle should not be used without careful study of each rein and its use.

The *hackamore* is a control device that fits around the horse's head just above the muzzle and controls by exerting pressure on the jaw and over the nose. The hackamore is usually made of braided rawhide; however, Mexican hackamores are made like bits with long shanks, a nose piece, and a chain or strap under the jaw. This type of bridle may be used on green horses and on horses with either very tough or very light mouths.

The martingale

The *martingale*, a strap from noseband to girth, is used to keep a horse from tossing his head or carrying it too high. This mechanical device is sometimes needed to encourage the horse to maintain the correct head position. There are two kinds: (1) *Standing martingale*—a single strap attached from girth to noseband; (2) *Running martingale*—from a single strap at the girth, it divides at the chest and ends in two rings through which the reins slide.

BRIDLING AND SADDLING

The correct procedure for bridling and saddling the horse cannot be emphasized too much (Figs. 4 and 5). If the rider, after approaching the horse from the left, will lift the reins over the horse's head, the horse may be steadied by holding the reins close under his neck. The bridle may be lifted toward the horse's head with the right hand on the crown and the left on the bit. Place left thumb in the corner of the horse's mouth so that he will open it. By gently raising the right hand, the bridle is brought over the ears, which should be put in one at a time. The throat latch should be buckled loosely to allow the horse to arch his neck more comfortably. The nose band should fit snugly, as its purpose is to keep the horse's mouth closed and thereby make the bit more effective. The curb chain should be loose enough to allow the insertion of three fingers, but this will vary according to the individual horse.

Ill-fitting tack can cause discomfort for the horse or can cause him to misbehave. The saddle should always be used with a pad to protect the horse's back except during very short intervals as in showing. Raise the saddle slowly up to the back, gently place it forward at the withers, then slide it back to the horse's middle (Fig. 6). Walk

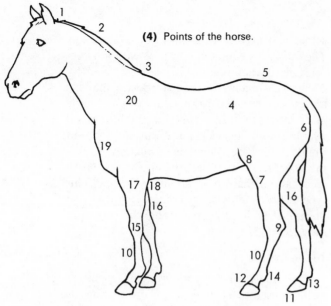

(4) Points of the horse.

1. Poll	11. Hoof
2. Crest	12. Coronet
3. Withers	13. Pastern
4. Flank	14. Fetlock
5. Croup	15. Knee
6. Point of Rump	16. Chestnut
7. Gaskin	17. Forearm
8. Stifle	18. Elbow
9. Hock	19. Point of Shoulder
10. Cannon	20. Shoulder

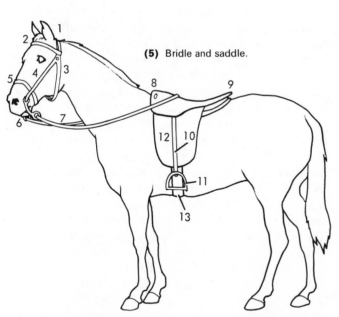

(5) Bridle and saddle.

BRIDLE	SADDLE
1. Crown Piece	8. Pommel
2. Brow Band	9. Cantle
3. Throat Latch	10. Stirrup Leather
4. Cheek Piece	11. Stirrup
5. Nose Cavesson	12. Flap
6. Bit	13. Girth
7. Reins	

around the horse, raising the flap to be sure the saddle pad is not wrinkled or the girth twisted. Returning to the left side, tighten the girth gradually. If the girth is tightened too quickly, the resulting discomfort might cause the horse to kick or bite. It might also give him the vice of "blowing up" when one begins to tighten the girth. Be careful not to pinch the skin under the girth by being sure to touch the horse on the pastern with your foot, causing him to extend his leg. Another way to check is to tighten the girth first, then walk in front of him and pick up his front legs, stretching each in turn as far forward as possible.

The Beginner Learns to Ride

One cannot overemphasize the importance of taking it easy when first beginning to ride. You may be surprised to find how much you can learn about a horse and how to ride from just walking.

A mistake commonly made by the beginner is to pull on the reins if anything goes wrong. For example, if one is mounted and at a standstill, the horse may take a few steps backward. Pulling on the reins in this instance only encourages him to keep on backing. If the rider then becomes panicky and jerks, this could cause the horse to rear. The correct procedure would be for the rider to use her legs to signal the horse to move forward as in a walk.

Work always on the theory of teamwork,

(6) Saddling the horse.

instead of mastery. Knowing full well your horse will never be perfect, learn to appreciate him for what he may be, for his is a dumb animal. Punish him for the bad and work hard on making him the best horse he can be, but be ever mindful of his limitations. Too many times an animal is punished for something he does not realize he has done, or for something you are attempting to teach him which he is incapable of learning. Every horse is an individual and you can ride no two exactly alike. Constantly remember that kindness, with a pat on the neck for a job well done, works wonders with animals. If you respect your horse, he in turn will respect you.

MOUNTING AND DISMOUNTING

Approach the horse slowly from the front with a stroke on the neck to let him know you are his friend. Before mounting, check the adjustment of the tack while standing on the left, or near, side. See that the bit is just high enough in the horse's mouth to fit snugly but not to wrinkle the lip. The width of the bit should be correct, and it should not be too low. Take the reins in hand just below the bit and signal the animal to back by applying slight pressure backward on the reins. If there is no response, you know the bit is not sufficient. On the other hand, should he toss his head high and jump back, he has been too severely bitted.

The adjustment of the girth should be checked by running your hand under it to make sure that it is snug. It should have to be forced slightly in order to get it fastened. If it is too loose, both the girth and saddle could slip. Of course this is dangerous and should be corrected before mounting. For jumping, the girth should be tighter than in any other types of riding.

When mounting, hold both reins in the left hand, which should be either on the withers of the horse or grasping a wisp of mane. This hand must be steady because an upward jerk on the reins could cause the horse to rear or suddenly move backwards. As you place your left foot in the stirrup, be sure it is all the way in to your heel with your toe pointing downward to the girth to avoid punching the horse in the stomach. Whether you mount facing the rear, front, or just facing the saddle depends entirely on your mount. If he tends to cowkick, or kick forward with his hind foot, it is sensible to be cautious and face the rear with the stirrup turned toward the front. If he has ever attempted to bite,

(7) Preparation for mounting.

mount facing the front with the right rein tight. On the other hand, if he tends to walk off, it is a good idea to keep the left rein tight to be able to turn him in a short circle. While holding the reins in the left hand, the rider should take hold of the far side of the stirrup with the right hand; then put the left foot in the stirrup while bracing the knee against the saddle (Fig. 7). As the rider is mounting, she should place her right hand across the cantle, spring onto the toes of the left foot which is in the stirrup, and swing the right leg over the horse. The right foot should not be dragged across the horse's rump. Pulling yourself up is hard on the horse's back, so avoid pounding his back as you first sit into the saddle. As the rider settles lightly into the saddle she should immediately find the right stirrup and assume the correct sitting position.

Check your girth after mounting, for it may still be loose. When saddling a horse, a good rider always tightens the girth by degrees, and some horses fool you by intentionally swelling their stomachs with air. This is their way of protecting themselves from the thoughtless person who buckles the girth too tightly. You may tighten or untighten a girth while mounted by putting the reins in the right hand (never dropping them), shifting the left leg forward without removing the foot from the stirrup, and raising the flap. Holding the billet strap in your left hand, use your index finger to push the buckle tongue in the desired hole.

(8) Dismounting.

When dismounting, hold the reins in the left hand and raise the body by placing the right hand on the pommel of the saddle. Extend the right leg over the horse's rump, and bring both legs together as you pause a second while leaning your body toward the saddle (Fig. 8). Kick the left foot free of the stirrup (this way you will not be hung in the stirrup should your horse move off), and slide gently to the ground to assume a position at the horse's side with the reins still in the left hand.

The length of the stirrup is usually adjusted to come to the ankle bone when the rider's leg is hanging free. In western and saddle seat a longer stirrup is used than in the hunt or forward seat. The forward seat rider places much more weight in the stirrup than is done in other styles of riding.

Only in western riding, when the horse has been trained to neck rein, are the reins held in one hand. All other seats require the use of both hands. To shorten the reins, reach over with one hand and catch the opposite rein with thumb and forefinger behind the other hand, then pull to desired length. To lengthen, simply let the reins slip through your hand until the desired length is reached. The reins must, of course, be held so that each side is the same length.

THE AIDS

Aids are the means used to control and direct the horse. Both natural and artificial aids are used in horseback riding. The natural aids most commonly used are the hands, legs, voice, and body weight. One always uses the natural aids before turning to the artificial. One should never apply artificial aids in collecting the horse or getting him mentally alert and ready to respond to command. Using a crop on an uncollected horse might cause him to bolt.

The hands are used to guide the horse, to slow him down, or stop him. One must learn to ride with steady, relaxed arms, for the reins should be taut but lightly held. When the horse feels the light pressure of the bit, his head will come into position. A steady, hard pressure on the reins irritates the horse and causes him to develop an insensitive mouth.

Never confuse light hands with riding on a loose rein. When you ride "on the buckle," or with very loose reins, your horse cannot be gotten under control quickly in case of shying or bolting—a circumstance that can be disastrous if riding in a group, or the forming of a bad habit if riding alone. Only after your horse has performed especially well should you ever drop your reins for a short period of walking.

The rider's legs are used to control the hind quarters of the horse. Because forward movement is initiated by the horse's hind legs, the rider can tap with the heel or press with the calf of the leg to increase speed; and she may use more sharp or resistant pressure to reprimand or restrain.

Kicking one's horse is an aid that is frequently overused; it can cause a horse to become stubborn, and makes a nervous horse more nervous. Always increase the severity of the aids by degree. For example, you need only to touch the horse lightly with your heels in rhythm with his stride to get him to walk faster. A more severe application would not be effective because it would probably cause the horse to break, that is change, his gait.

The body weight is of great importance in riding any horse, especially the western, in which shifts of body weight signal the horse to turn, change leads, and so on. The western rider carries the reins in one hand, and the other must be kept forward in order to prevent twisting the body, because an uneven distribution of weight will cause the horse to have a sore back.

The horse is very responsive to the rider's voice, even the tone of voice. The school horse trained to perform by voice (verbal commands having been gradually substituted for the other aids) is invaluable in any type of instruction.

However, incessantly urging your horse by voice can be annoying when riding in company.

Artificial aids are many, too many in fact. The crop, or short whip, is probably used most often. It should be used sparingly at first. Why give an animal a severe blow when frequently you need only to hold the crop in order to accomplish the same thing? The crop should be used on the shoulders because some horses tend to buck when hit behind the saddle. A long whip can be valuable in schooling, or in training a horse to collect. The long whip can be carried by the rider to touch the horse's back legs and thus encourage him to bring his feet up under his body. The canter that had previously been a jarring, uncomfortable gait can be changed into a rocking chair for the rider by this improved use of the horse's hind legs.

Spurs should be used only by the advanced rider in training a horse. They do serve to make the horse more responsive to leg aids, especially in controlling the direction of the hindquarters, but overuse of spurs could result in making the horse nervous or forming the vice of tail switching.

Martingales, both standing and running, also have their use. The standing martingale can help to correct the vice of head tossing or carrying the head too high. The running martingale can accomplish the same head carriage as the curb bit, but with less severity.

THE GAITS OF THE HORSE

A *walk* is a diagonal four beat gait; each foot strikes the ground separately and in an even rhythm. A *running walk* is a speeded-up fiat foot or ordinary walk involving the hind leg's over-stepping the stride of the front leg. A *trot* is a two beat gait in which the horse's feet move in diagonal pairs. A *canter* is a three beat gait with a period of suspension. The horse moves in this order: one hind foot, diagonal feet, remaining front foot. The lead foot is moved higher and farther forward than the other forefoot.

A *gallop* is a fast, ground consuming natural gait. Leg motion is essentially the same as in the canter but faster, and there is more suspension or floating action. A *slow gait* is a diagonal four beat gait with a slight hesitation. The hind foot strikes the ground just a little ahead of the lateral front foot. A *rack* is a diagonal four beat gait with one foot on the ground while three are off. A *pace* is a lateral two beat gait.

(9) The saddle seat rider in formal attire.

THE SADDLE SEAT RIDER

The saddle seat rider sits erect in the center of the saddle. The rider's legs are slightly bent with little weight in the stirrups, because the stirrups are relatively long in this style of riding (Fig. 9). In no seat does the rider sit on the cantle, or back of the saddle. This is harmful and hinders the horse's performance. The rider, out of balance with the horse, has difficulty posting and even more importantly, may damage her horse's kidneys.

After mounting, be sure your animal is collected and ready to move so that he will not be prone to stumble or suddenly wake up and shy at the appearance of a strange object (Fig. 10). When one is riding, the horse should know it is time to work. Relaxing and playing are done in pasture, in paddock, or in a stall. If one happens to be mounted on a horse that does not like to stand still, simply walk him in a short circle once or twice, and then try again to make him stand.

Collection for the saddle seat rider includes ducking the horse's chin. A slight pull of the reins brings the horse's chin back and raises his head. This also causes the horse to place his weight on his haunches or rear legs which is where it should be, because the horse propels himself by the motion of his hindquarters. There should be no slack in the reins at any time, but when the horse's head is in a neutral position, head movement should not be hindered. The rider attempts to feel the horse's mouth so that

COLLECTED

UNCOLLECTED

(10) Horses: collected and uncollected.

leg aids. From a standstill, one asks her mount to move off by applying leg pressure. Tightening the reins should be unnecessary, inasmuch as the good rider has no slack in the reins. The hands are held a bit forward of the pommel as a safety measure in order to allow the rider freedom of movement to pull slightly backward in case the horse becomes frightened. When the horse is doing his best, the aids should be relaxed. Never ask your horse to do more than he is capable of doing.

Although the saddle seat rider is constantly striving to follow the natural movement of the horse's head in all gaits, this should not be overdone. A loosening of the reins in attempting to follow the horse's head during the walk can result in too much bobbing of the head. Nevertheless, it is still sound advice to "let the horse lead you, not you the horse." A good walk should be done during a large portion of the riding period, thus teaching both you and the horse quite a bit, and giving you time to work on the correct position in the saddle.

Trotting and posting

The rider presses with her knees or, on less responsive animals, uses her heel behind the girth to move into the trot. When a horse trots, he uses his diagonal legs together, the right front and left hind. The diagonal pair leave the ground at the same moment and return to the ground together (Fig. 11). This gait is rougher than the canter, and the rider posts by briefly supporting her weight on her inner thighs and knees and by rising up in the saddle. In posting the trot, the rider follows one diagonal pair of legs, rising with one foreleg and sitting as that forefoot comes to the ground. The rider should not overdo her posting after she has learned the rhythm of the trot; posting too high is undesirable. This should be a smooth, graceful movement executed close to the saddle.

Diagonals

The rider rises at the trot, or posts, as one diagonal pair of legs move, and sits in the saddle as the other pair moves. This is known as a diagonal, and either right or left diagonal can be used on the straightaway. However, in order to avoid the overdevelopment of one shoulder in the horse, it is important to have the horse work in both diagonals.

When riding in a ring, the rider must post the correct diagonal for proper balance. To accom-

the horse and rider can act as one. With good hands and careful management of the reins, the saddle seat rider should be able to feel and anticipate the horse's breaking of gait or change of pace. The horse's mouth is sensitive and should always be handled with care and consideration.

Walking

Collection at the walk, as in all other gaits as well, is accomplished by using taut reins and the plish this the rider is sitting down when the outside front leg is resting on the ground, and she rises as that leg leaves the ground and moves forward in stride. A simple method of checking the diagonal is to observe the horse's point of shoulder on the outside of the curve. As it moves forward, one should be up in the posting. If incorrect, one should simply sit one or three strides and then begin to post again.

When bringing the horse back to a walk, apply lessening pressure on the reins and begin to sit the trot. Horses trained to the saddle seat style move when collected, and respond to the opposite type of signal, the relaxation of the rider's hands, by walking.

Canter and leads

The collected canter is the fastest gait used in saddle seat riding. In the canter the horse has a three beat movement. The rider does not post with the canter because there is no definite thrust to push one out of the saddle. Instead, one sits the canter and enjoys the rocking chair motion (Fig. 12).

When the horse canters, one front leg reaches out farther and hits the ground sooner than the other front leg. If the left front leg reaches out farthest the horse is said to be on the left lead. With a left lead, the horse's left front leg strikes the ground in front of his right front leg, and his left rear leg strikes in front of his right rear. Leading correctly is very important when the horse is circling, for his weight shifts to the side of his lead and when he goes around a corner he leans to that side. With an incorrect lead, the horse would be badly off balance and might even stumble and fall.

From the walk, the rider prepares to canter by shortening the reins slightly. The most popular canter departure or signal is to angle the horse's body away from the forefoot that is leading and then to apply the leg aid by pressing strongly about 3 inches behind the girth on the non-leading side. The horse must not be allowed to begin his gait until he is in the proper position. Releasing the inside rein, shifting the body weight toward the leading side, and using the toe on his elbow, or the crop on his leading shoulder, all are permissible.

In view of the fact that the horse's canter originates with the hindquarters, the use of leg aids is important. Leading improperly, or on one side in front and the other side in back, is termed *cross-cantering* and could cause the

(11) The trot.

(12) The canter.

Equitation   **101**

horse to fall. In case the horse should change leads (often caused by unskillful passing during which the rider has suddenly jerked the horse's head to one side) or should become disunited (cross-canter), the rider should be able to feel this in the saddle and immediately break gait and repeat the canter signal.

During the canter subtle wrist flexion will allow the hands to follow the movement of the horse's head with every stride and maintain an even tension on the reins until the rider wishes to slow down. Then, in order to slow down, tension on the reins is increased on the back stroke and the horse shortens his stride, thereby slowing. Pulling straight back only results in the horse's breaking into a trot, as the rider has interrupted the natural movement of the horse's head at the canter, and the horse does not move his head in a trot.

Backing

Skillful backing requires good hands and coordination of the aids. It is important for the horse to back in a straight line. Using the leg aids behind the girth will straighten the haunches in whichever direction is needed (for instance, the left leg moves the hindquarters to the right, and vice versa). It is helpful for the rider to move the horse forward a few steps before signaling him to back, because this encourages flexibility of the neck and prepares the horse for the actual backing steps. The stepping forward is also important with the parked show horse in order to get his legs up under him before he backs. Avoid using such rough hands that the horse slings his head up and opens his mouth in order to avoid abuse.

Avoiding Problems

The horse reflects the rider's nature. A nervous person should always ride a calm horse, one unlikely to be upset. Many problems can be avoided. Before condemning a horse for misbehavior, the rider should ask herself as a horsewoman:

Is he running because something has frightened him?

Is he biting and kicking when the girth is tightened because it is too tight and maybe twisted? Perhaps some other time it was, and the horse, having such a remarkable memory, expects discomfort again.

When has he been out of his stall for exercise? He should either be ridden, turned out in the paddock to play, or longed (exercised in a circle by means of a rope) daily.

Is the rider unsteady or heavy-handed? Are her toes turned out so that she is constantly jabbing her horse with her heels? Is she hanging on with her lower calves, thereby making her horse nervous?

Is the tack suitable for and adjusted to this particular horse?

Many times one blames the animal for misbehavior that was entirely one's own fault! A gentle but lazy horse may often stumble if not kept alert. This is not necessarily an indication of lameness.

All mounting, dismounting, tacking, and handling of the horse in any manner should be done from the near or left side. The right side is called the off side. The western horse, used for working cattle, is the exception to this rule because he is usually taught to be mounted and handled from either side, thus saving the cowhand from many hours of walking around to the correct side.

Rules for Trail Riding

The first of the rules for trail riding is always to walk the horse a good distance when leaving or returning to the stable. Walking tends to warm up the horse, promoting circulation of the blood and limbering of his muscles before he must trot, which, incidentally, should be done before he is cantered. This procedure will discourage the horse from bolting or bucking. Returning to the stable at a walk cools the horse off and also prevents the acquisition of the vice of running back home.

On a day when the wind is blowing, on a rather cold day, or maybe any day, some horses might buck. Bucking off into a canter by slightly lunging in the departure is no vice and should not be treated as one. The saddle seat rider's hands would be up off the neck with no slack in the reins and should remain there in order to prevent the horse's lowering his head, for if his head is low he is capable of giving a bad buck or jolt. Most horses will move out of these few playful bucks within several strides.

If you are ever mounted on a horse that rears, lean forward immediately, thus shifting your weight well on his forequarters. At the same

(13) Horses do not like to be crowded under saddle.

time anchor your hands in the horse's mane or on his neck. Never trust your balance and thus fail to do this. Even an experienced rider can easily pull a horse over backwards in such an emergency.

Runaways are almost always caused by the rider. Inattention, passive control, sloppy riding habits (heels in the side of the horse, hugging with lower calves)—all could unnerve an animal and cause a runaway. By riding on the bit, one should easily be able to anticipate the fact that the horse is getting out of control and should check him immediately with short, sharp pulls on the reins. A desperate, steady pull only results in freezing the mouth and making the horse unaware of any signals. If possible, turn the horse in small circles to bring him under control. If all else fails, seesaw on the bit as a last resort. Maintain a tight seat, use your voice constantly in low, soothing tones, and continue to give and take on the reins. Never run after another runaway horse, as this only makes him run faster. If a member of the party is having trouble with her horse, the others should stop and wait for her to get her mount under control.

Keep at least the length of one horse from the other horses, whether moving in pairs or in a line (Fig. 13). In this way the misbehavior of one

horse will not upset the others. If you are unfortunate enough to have a kicker in your party, always put him in the rear. It is a nuisance to have to worry about a horse of this kind in the group. Actually, the kicker should be punished severely for this vice and not ridden in groups until it is corrected.

The enjoyment and well-being of an entire group of riders is often affected by the rider in the lead. When breaking from a canter or a trot to a walk, she should hold up her hand to signal those behind of her intentions. This will prevent the abuse of their suddenly having to jerk on their horse's mouths. When a car is approaching, lady with an umbrella, baby carriage, or any of the numerous things for which a good horsewoman is always watching, the lead rider (or first one aware of these things) should warn the others.

If you approach a bridge, stream, or anything your horse may be frightened by, remember that the horse has a "one-track" mind. Speak to him in a normal tone of voice and use your legs quickly, but if he fails to pass the object after a reasonable length of time, do not frustrate him by continuing to demand obedience. Not all horses are willing to be leaders, so do not try to make something out of your horse that you

Equitation **103**

cannot. Pick instead the most stable horse in the group to lead, and nine times out of ten the group will follow. Remember that it is good to take a green colt and/or novice rider on the trail for the first few times with an old reliable horse from which confidence can be gained.

Occasionally a horse balks, not from fear, but as a vice. If this happens, after having used your legs or a crop, try turning him in a short circle and then suddenly asking him to move forward. This, or any other method, is of no value if the rider hesitates. She should anticipate the horse's reactions and think faster than her mount. In severe cases of balking it might be necessary for someone to assist by using a whip from the rear.

Do not allow your horse to drink from streams or eat while bridled. Unless you are on an endurance ride or planning on being out for several hours, drinking from streams is not necessary. It will only encourage your horse to paw in the water or perhaps lie down for a roll. Eating with the bridle on lends itself to the vice of continually eating surrounding grass and shrubbery and becomes very annoying.

Horses are naturally herd bound, so if you decide to go in the opposite direction you may expect your horse to be reluctant to leave his friends. With a little encouragement by use of leg aids, however, there shouldn't be too much trouble.

When riding up inclines, lean slightly forward as your horse pushes himself up with his hindquarters. When moving downhill, sit slightly forward in order to free the horse's hindquarters. However, in case the horse breaks into a jog, sitting back will encourage him to walk, as the weight is hard on his back.

It is unwise to change horses on the trail when you have been mounted by the owner before leaving the stable. He may have a definite idea about which one of your group would get along with a particular horse.

There are a few other items you should keep in mind when on a trail ride. In general, ride facing traffic with all riders on the same side of the road and allowing for as much room as possible for passing cars. On a curve, however, ride on the outside of the curve in order to be seen more clearly by oncoming cars. In crossing the road, all should cross at the same time. If passing becomes necessary, ask permission and then trot slowly by.

No matter how nervous you may become, never try to gain confidence by riding on too tight a rein. This will only relay your insecurity to your horse.

The Advanced Rider

The beginner looks forward to reaching the stage of not only riding correctly but being able to participate in the schooling of colts and the correction of vices in horses. A colt should be ridden regularly but only for short periods of time, thereby keeping his training interesting and pleasant, an experience to be anticipated. No training should be too advanced for his present state of mental or physical development. After initial training, the colt should be ridden in the company of other horses, because for the majority of his life he will be expected to perform with good manners in a group. However, correcting a horse of vices should be done alone if possible, depending on the vice, in order to avoid upsetting the group and to assure the animal's attention.

Many persons who work with horses lack the ability to stabilize the horse's gait. This is a must in advanced riding. The use of the cavaletti, a series of logs spaced on the ground a distance apart determined by the size of the horse, is beneficial in stabilizing a horse's trot, making him use his shoulders, and discouraging stumbling. This exercise should be done at a walk and a trot, but only for short intervals so as not to sour the horse.

The advanced rider will find small circles, figure eights, and serpentines (a series of half circles connected by an imaginary straight line) executed in all three gaits extremely beneficial to the horse, and fun as well as educational for herself. These exercises improve the horse's muscular development, balance, and flexibility. Do not forget the use of leg aids in these movements as well as correct use of the reins. The horse will naturally want to move in a straight line, so merely guiding him toward this center will result in his haunches being out of line. Therefore, as previously described in our discussion of backing, use the legs behind the girth to keep the haunches in line. Also helpful would be the raising of the outside rein to put pressure on the horse's neck. The advanced rider never forgets the individuality of each horse and therefore selects the best method by experimentation.

Riders of the different seats perform these exercises slightly differently. Forward seat riders and saddle seat riders are required to change diagonals in trotting the figure eight and serpentine; western riders would not be posting. Riders of the saddle seat halt in the center of the figure eight and between loops of the serpentine while cantering, whereas riders of the other seats perform the flying change (changing leads without breaking gait).

When selecting games for gymkhanas or activities for the advanced class, one should be sure the choices are not abusive to the horse. A good choice is the egg and spoon class, in which one performs all gaits while balancing an egg in a spoon, for this requires perfect balance and skillful maneuvering. The rough and ready chaos of the musical chairs type of activity as performed by lathered horses, ears flat back, head yanked back in the lap of the rider, is quite a contrast and should not be sanctioned by those who know better.

Another activity of value for the advanced student is bareback riding. The advanced student, having perfected riding in the saddle, continues to progress in her equitation without the saddle. This is not a skill for the beginner who has to hang on by clutching the horse in the belly with her heels. The benefits of bareback riding are many. The rider is able to sense every movement of the horse. Her balance must certainly be improved. She develops grace and becomes relaxed. The bareback rider learns to sit and trot and to maintain a correct position as if in the saddle. After having ridden bareback, the rider finds her posting more fluid, so that horse and rider truly become one.

General Information about Horses

The earliest known ancestor of the horse, the Bohippus was the size of a fox and had five toes instead of a hoof.

Horses are measured from their withers to the ground by a unit of measure called a hand and equal to 4 inches. An animal measuring 14.2 hands or less is a pony; one over 14.2 hands is a horse.

The gestation period in the mare is eleven months. A nursing foal is called a suckling; a foal no longer nursing is a weanling, then a yearling. A male foal is a colt until four years of age; then he is called a stallion. A female foal is a filly until age four, then is called a mare.

Care of the Horse

Many factors are involved in the proper care of the horse; one of the most important is grooming, necessary for good health as well as appearance. The horse should be groomed thoroughly every day. An electro groom for horses is, of course, ideal; but a good job can be done with a plastic curry comb and brushes. The entire body of the horse, with the exception of the lower legs and head, which are too sensitive for anything but a brush, should be curried in a circular motion. Then the body should be brushed vigorously and moving with the hair, followed by use of a finishing brush. A linen cloth is excellent for rubbing down the horse, but oils are of little value in making the coat shine; the resulting sheen is only temporary and dust soon sticks to the body. Manes and tails should be washed regularly and brushed, or picked out daily. They should never be combed, for this breaks the hair and pulls it out.

The hooves should be given daily attention. They should be cleaned with a hoof pick and periodically painted with a prepared hoof dressing, or one made from neat's-foot oil, pine tar, and so on. In cleaning the hooves, check to see if the horse needs to be shod. Incorrect shoeing can cause lameness, whereas proper shoeing can correct a faulty way of going as well as some forms of lameness. Be sure your blacksmith is a qualified one who heats the shoe in order to shape it to the individual foot.

If horses are to be stabled, they deserve box stalls about 12 feet by 12 feet. Horses need to be able to move around and lie down comfortably. Tie-in stalls are inhuman and tend to encourage vices in horses. Stalls should be cleaned three times a day, in the morning, early afternoon, and late afternoon. Any dry bedding such as oat or wheat straw, wood shavings, or pine needles used heavily will be fine. The stall should be well ventilated and admit plenty of light.

The amount of food required by each horse varies according to his build, temperament, and the work he is doing. It is of extreme importance that the horse be fed at the same time each day and the same quantities, unless of course he is being fattened or reduced. The small stomach of the horse makes great amounts of food dangerous. Colic may occur and can be fatal because of the horse's inability to vomit.

The average horse does well on three gallons of grain a day with approximately 15 pounds of hay if he is being worked regularly. Oats and bran are a good feed, with the possible addition of corn in the winter only. Alfalfa or pure clover hays are extremely rich and should be fed in small quantities. Timothy hay is excellent; lespedeza, orchard grass, clover, and coastal bermuda are also suitable for horses. Any hay selected must be free of mold or dust caused by improper curing. Hay that has been rained on, distinguished by its dryness and dark color, is not nutritious. As hay ages it also loses its food value. Unless the horse has access to water and salt, he will not maintain his weight regardless of the feeding program. Water should be kept before him at all times unless he is extremely hot, in which case a few swallows at a time are advisable.

Horses are prone to getting worms. Colts should be wormed about every three months, mature horses every six months. Tube worming, in December, will rid the horse of all types of worms; then in June a worm powder in the grain can be used.

Tack should be thoroughly cleaned at least once a week. It should be done with hot water (using very little water) and saddle soap. A light application of Lexol with a soft cloth is an excellent preservative and gets the leather soft and pliable, making reins easier to handle and preventing galls or saddle sores.

Remember the old saying, "one must be a friend to have one." This is true also in dealing with animals. Common sense should tell one that a horse well cared for and suffering no abuse from his rider will have no reason to kick or bite, rear or buck. When his association with people is pleasant, why wouldn't the average horse enjoy being taken out of his stall and ridden?

Terminology

Aids: The means used to control and direct the horse. The natural aids are the rider's hands, legs, body weight, and voice; the artificial aids include spurs, crops, and so on.

Bit: Metal part of the bridle, which goes into the horse's mouth and to which the reins are attached.

Boring on the bit: The horse lowers his head and pulls downward.

Bowed tendon: A lameness caused by strain in which the tendons become inflamed and bow outward.

Bridle: The horse's headgear, used when riding.

Collected: The horse is alert, moves with legs well under the body, takes shortened and energetic steps, and has an airy way of going with head held high and neck arched.

Conformation: Body build; not only is good conformation desirable for appearance, but it ensures more efficient, sound performance.

Cow hocks: A fault of hind leg conformation in which the hocks point inward.

Diagonals: The rider rises (posts) with the trot as one diagonal pair of legs moves, and sits in the saddle as the other pair moves.

Dressage: A method of riding and training to develop the horse's abilities and reactions so there is a high degree of understanding between horse and rider. Advanced dressage emphasizes the extreme collection of highly schooled horses proficient in many maneuvers.

Extended: The phase of a gait in which the stride is longer than in the regular or collected phase; may also refer to a lower, more outstretched head carriage.

Ewe neck: Fault of conformation in which the upper line of the neck dips downward at the withers (top of shoulder blades) instead of arching upward.

Fistula: A chronic, serious infection at the withers usually caused by the pressure of an ill-fitting saddle.

Floating the teeth: Filing off sharp points; the teeth should be checked once a year.

Founder: An inflammation of the internal hoof, the walls of which become ridged and the sole of the hoof drops; frequently caused by overfeeding.

Gelding: A male horse that has been castrated.

Glass eye: Lack of pigmentation in which the colored part of the horse's eye ranges from white to milky blue; visibility not affected.

Good hands: Implies the rider is able to ride on contact when desired, following the movement of the horse's head with no abuse of his mouth; does not mean "loose reins."

Green horse: An unschooled horse; often one accustomed to a rider on his back, but not well trained in gaits, and so on.

Hack: To ride for pleasure; originally the term referred to trail or cross-country riding.

Halter: Headgear used to lead or tie a horse.

Hard mouth: An insensitive mouth due to the temperament of the horse or, more often, one toughened by rough hands.

Heaves: A chronic respiratory condition in which air sacs of the lungs have broken down; horse exhales twice for each inhalation.

Longe: To exercise or school the horse in a circular path at the end of a long line.

Near side: The left side; we mount, dismount, lead, and tack a horse from the near side.

Off side: Right side.

Perfect horse: The ideal against which we measure the quality of individual animals.

Pig eyes: Small, unattractive eyes associated with poor breeding.

Pleasure horse: One ridden for his owner's pleasure; should have good gaits and manners.

School: To teach or train the horse.

Set tail: Setting the tail is a minor operation in which tendons at the base of the tail are severed, and the tail is then placed in a tail set harness and trained to rise in the desired fashion; note that the set tail has not been "broken."

Soured horse: One that has come to dislike and rebel against his work, probably through boredom or overwork; applied especially in regard to jumping.

Splint: A small bony enlargement on the lower leg caused by an injury; usually a blemish rather than serious unsoundness.

Thrush: A fungus disease of the hoof with discharge of a foul smelling black fluid; caused by moisture and dirty stalls.

Selected References

Crowell, Pers. *Cavalcade of American Horses*. New York: Bonanza Books, 1951.

Farshler, Earl. *Riding and Training*. New York: D. Van Nostrand, 1959.

Patten, John W. *The Light Horse Breeds*. New York: A. S. Barnes and Co., and London: Thomas Yoseliff, Ltd., 1960.

Wall, Sheila. *Young Sportsman's Guide to Horseback Riding*. New York: Thomas Nelson & Sons, 1961.

Wynmalen, Henry. *Equitation*. London: Country Life Ltd., 1964.

Chapter 7

Fencing *Evelyn F. Terhune*

History. Goals. Equipment. Etiquette. SKILLS: Grip, Salute, On Guard, Advance, and Retreat, Lines of Engagement and Target Areas, Attacks, Defense. Progression. Strategy. Basic Rules. Evaluation. Terminology.

Fencing is a combative sport that offers challenge and opportunities for competition for women as well as for men. The fundamentals of fencing can be acquired in a relatively short series of lessons, but one can spend a lifetime pursuing fencing as a recreational activity and learning and improving the skills and strategies of the sport.

The object of fencing is to hit or "touch" one's opponent without being touched. The foil, the weapon used by women, is theoretically a pointed sword, so the touch is made with the tip of the blade. In theory this is a puncture-type wound, but the tip of the blade is blunt and padded and the blade bends readily when the touch is made on the protective clothing that must be worn by all students of fencing. The valid target area is the entire torso or trunk on the front of the body and from the hips upward on the back (Figs. 2 and 3). Invalid target areas are the mask, bib, the arms, and the legs. There is no penalty for an invalid touch, but any touch stops the action so that the opponents must again assume the guard position before continuing the bout.

Men use three weapons in fencing: the foil, sabre, and/or épée (Fig. 4). The sabre has a triangular-shaped flexible blade and because, theoretically, the sabre has a cutting edge, both thrusting and cutting actions can be made with it. The head and arms are added as valid target areas for the sabre. The épée blade is heavier and stiffer than a foil blade, and touches with the point may be scored on any part of the body without any restrictions on order of play.

History

The sport of fencing has evolved from the combat duels that meant life or death in ancient days. It is said that the gladiator schools of Rome offered the first instruction in fencing. Up until the nineteenth century swordsmanship provided the solution to most arguments with France, Italy, and Spain leading the way in providing skilled duelists.

Facility with a sword was a necessity for soldiers, knights, and gentlemen during the period between heavy armor and the development of the rifle and hand guns. With the advent of guns, the practical value of fencing became negligible and the art of sword play developed into a sport.

Miss Evelyn F. Terhune coaches and participates in fencing. As a competitor she is current New Jersey state champion, has been a national finalist three times, was a member of the United States Olympic fencing team in 1960, and was a member of the United States World Championship Team, which toured Poland in 1963, and the team that went to Russia in 1966. Miss Terhune is an amateur coach at Fairleigh Dickinson University and Director of Development for the University. She has coached two intercollegiate championship teams as well as individual intercollegiate champions.

(1) A touch.

(2) Front target.

(3) Back target.

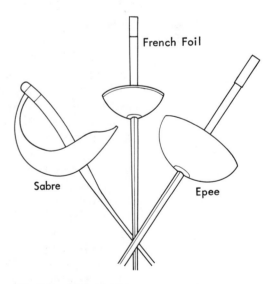

French Foil

Sabre

Epee

(4) Foil, sabre, and épée.

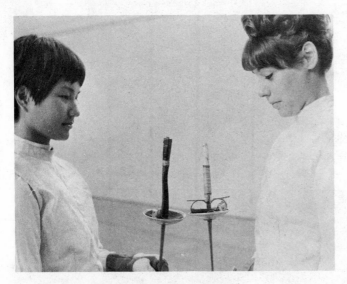

(5) French (left) and Italian grips.

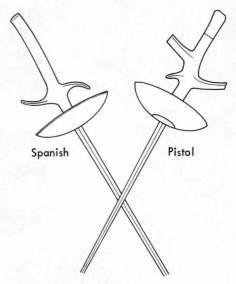

(6) Spanish and pistol grips.

The Amateur Fencers League of America was organized in 1891 to supervise the sport, and an American fencing team competed in the Olympic Games for the first time in 1912. In the last thirty years interest in fencing has grown so that it is now possible in most parts of the United States to follow up the fencing lessons of school or camp by joining a fencing club.

Goals

Fencing offers a combination of challenges for it is a test of one's own physical ability and reflexes and the matching of wits with opponents and, with only four touches needed to win, a test with a very small margin for error. The beginner finds that she is improving her agility, strength, endurance, and alertness as she becomes a skilled fencer.

Fencing offers women a chance to participate in a sport held in great esteem throughout the world, and for those who pay the price of time and effort, there are exciting opportunities for international competition and travel. Even if one's goals are not this high, fencing is good exercise in a sport in which one can participate throughout one's lifetime.

Specific goals for the beginner should include learning the following skills: the lunge; attacking methods, including the beat, disengage, one-two or double disengage, and cut-over; parries four, six, seven, and eight; and basic rules and strategy.

Equipment

FOILS

There are several styles of foils, but only the grip varies with the different weapons. The blade is 34 or 35 inches in length, rectangular in cross-section, and tapered toward the tip so that the blade is flexible. The bell guard in front of the grip protects the hand from being hit. The entire weapon from pommel to tip is 42 inches in length, and the pommel holds the handle and bell guard onto the blade. The tip should be blunted by covering the end with adhesive tape unless electrical equipment is used. When scoring bouts with electrical equipment the foil must have a blunted metal tip and a metallic cloth jacket is worn.

The handle of the foil is made of wood or metal and usually covered with leather or cord. The shape of the grip determines the style of the weapon (Figs. 5 and 6). The grip on the French foil is slightly curved and permits good finger and hand control. It is a more balanced foil than the other styles and therefore less tiring to hold. When the Italian grip is used, a strap is often placed around the pommel and wrist to hold the foil in position; the combination of strap and grip provides strength and power. The pistol grip, designed originally as an orthopedic grip for those who lacked power in their fingers and hand, is a grip that is held by all four fingers and thumb. The Spanish grip, still another variation, uses primarily the thumb and first two fingers and thus some fencers say that it offers a

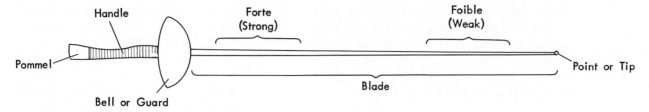

(7) Parts of the foil.

compromise between strength and finesse in the use of the arm and fingers.

The parts of the foil are shown in Figure 7. The strong half of the blade, the forte, is next to the handle; the foible is the weaker, more flexible half.

GLOVE

A fencing glove is padded on the back for protection of the hand. The fingers of the glove must be thin enough to allow for a "feel" of the weapon, and the cuff should be long enough to cover the jacket sleeve and to prevent opponent's weapon from sliding up the inside of the sleeve.

FENCING JACKET

Fencing jackets are made in a variety of styles. The half jacket, when worn by the right-handed fencer, has a full-length right sleeve and covers only the combat or right side of the body both front and back. The half jacket is adequate for skilled fencers, but not recommended for beginners because they are apt to fence too close to one another. The half jacket is less expensive than the full jacket, though perhaps not so attractive. The full jacket has a zipper in the back and long sleeves for both arms. Jackets are made of duck or gabardine cloth and must be well padded in the front; a good jacket has a quilted material between two layers of cloth. All jackets for women, regardless of type, should

be worn with breast protectors, which are made of a rigid plastic or metal.

MASK

The mask should fit snugly so that it stays in place with movements of the head. Masks are made in three sizes—small, medium, and large; the sides of the mask and the tongue of the mask, which fits over the back of the head, may be adjusted to better fit the individual. The wire mesh in a mask must be heavy enough to prevent the foil from penetrating the mask, and the bib, which covers and protects the neck, must be thick enough to stop a foil.

TROUSERS

White knickers are worn by women in competition and the thigh of the leading trouser leg is padded for protection. The knickers cover the knees and are worn with long white socks; for freedom of movement the trousers must be loose fitting or be made of a stretch material.

SHOES

Fencing shoes are made of canvas and have a heavily padded heel. If fencing shoes are not available, tennis shoes worn with heavy socks will suffice.

FENCING STRIP

The fencing strip designates the field of play for a bout. An official strip is 6 feet in width and

(8) The fencing strip.

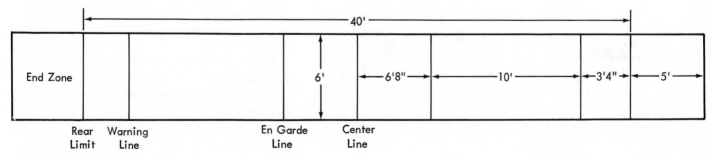

40 feet long (Fig. 8, page 111). The strip may consist of rubber matting, but when using electrical equipment for scoring it should be made of copper mesh wire. The beginner may simply mark off an area on the wooden floor with tape or chalk in order to designate the strip.

Etiquette

The following procedures should be understood and used by all fencers:

1. The salute is always used prior to a bout (see later section, "skills") to acknowledge the opponent and indicate readiness for the bout.
2. In a nonelectrical foil bout when one fencer has been touched twice, the fencers exchange ends of the fencing strip. They may salute and shake hands as they exchange places on the strip and again at the end of a bout.
3. The fencer should not speak except to ask questions, though she may acknowledge a touch against herself.
4. The fencer should not give indications of influencing the judgment of officials by any kind of gesturing.

Safety

Fencing is not a hazardous sport if safety procedures are followed:

1. One must always wear protective equipment including mask, glove, jacket, and trousers.
2. The jacket should be snug fitting on the torso. One is handicapped by a jacket that is either too large or too small.

3. The neck guard of the jacket should be fastened to prevent any possibility of the foil slipping inside the neckline of the jacket.
4. One must never remove the mask until a bout is completed.
5. Stamping the foot twice is a signal to stop play. Do not attack an opponent who signals she wishes to stop.

Skills

To learn specific fencing movements requires concentration, practice, and desire, which in turn lead to precision and speed. One must constantly repeat the basic moves until they can be quickly and correctly performed. The beginner's movements are often inaccurate and awkward but with practice they can become controlled and more precise.

THE GRIP

In order to assume the correct grip, first hold the foil in the nonfoil hand with the bend in the blade toward the floor. This should place the handle in a position with the broadest sides on the top and bottom, i.e., parallel to the floor. To take the proper grip extend the thumb of the foil hand along the top side of the grip close to the bell guard so that the convexity of the grip fits into the palm of the hand. The forefinger is then curled around the grip so the first knuckle is under the tip of the thumb (Fig. 9). The handle is gripped firmly by the thumb and forefinger for they provide much of the maneuverability of the foil. With the French foil the other three fingers should be placed comfortably around the handle. The fingers aid the thumb and forefinger in controlling the movement of the foil. With the Italian foil the third finger should be placed in the corner of the cross bar (Fig. 10). The wrist should be straight, and the pommel should be in line with the center of the wrist but not necessarily against the wrist. The arm and foil should form a straight line from elbow to tip of the foil.

One controls the weapon through the grip and must be able to tense and relax the grip as needed. Small manipulations can be made by the fingers or by the thumb and forefinger. Larger movements can be provided through wrist action.

(9) The grip—French foil.

(10) Gripping the French (left) and Italian foils.

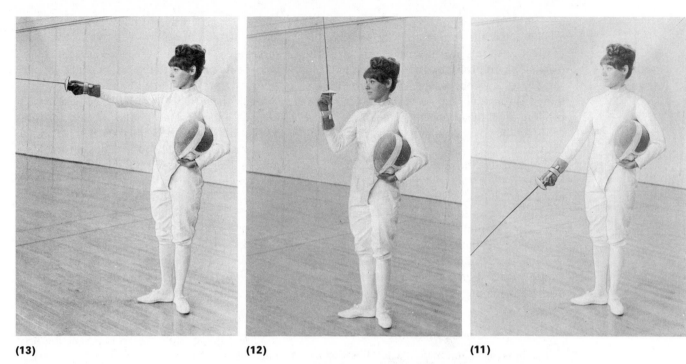

(13)　　　　　　　　　　　**(12)**　　　　　　　　　　　**(11)**

(11–13) The salute—fencer in standard clothing for competition.

THE SALUTE

The salute is a courtesy recognition of one's opponent and should be used prior to practice as well as for all competition. The fencers face each other with foil in weapon hand and mask in trailing hand and tucked under the trailing arm. One's heels should be together with the feet at right angles to each other and the leading foot pointing in the direction of the other fencer. The salute is comprised of three quick movements: first the foil arm is extended with the foil pointing toward the opponent's feet, then the foil is swung to a vertical position in front of the fencer's own face; and finally the foil is extended shoulder high toward the opponent (Figs. 11, 12, and 13). In a tournament the salute may be given to the officials and the audience as well as to the opponent.

After a quick salute, the fencer continues to hold the foil in the weapon hand and puts the mask on with the trailing hand by first resting the chin against the chin pad and then pulling the mask up over the top of the head.

ON GUARD

"On guard" is the position of readiness from which all other moves, both offensive and defensive, are taken. After the salute, with the feet still at right angles to each other, one takes a comfortable step forward with the leading foot to move into the guard position. The distance between the feet at this point should be approximately two times one's shoe size. One bends the hip and knee joints to about 45-degree angles. With the knees over the instep and the weight equally distributed on both feet, the torso should remain erect. Do not lean. The leading arm should be in line with the side of the body, with the elbow bent and about a hand span away from the body. The tip of the blade points toward the opponent's face. The trailing arm should be bent with the elbow held approximately shoulder high and the hand bent in a relaxed position with the fingers toward the head. The head should be turned so that one looks directly at the opponent (Figs. 14, 15, and 16).

ADVANCE AND RETREAT

The advance and retreat enable one to move closer to or away from the opponent. With each movement forward or backward one should resume the guard position.

To advance, lift the toes of the leading foot and extend the leg, then step out onto the heel while shifting the weight slightly forward and slapping the sole of the foot to the floor. Avoid rocking backward before moving forward by pushing forward with the inside edge of the back foot. As soon as the leading foot is on the floor quickly move the trailing foot forward so that the feet are the same distance apart as in the original guard position. The advance should be rapid and smooth. Balance should be maintained throughout the movement so that, depending upon the opponent's moves, the fencer can stop the advance action at any point along the way.

The retreat is the reverse of the advance. One lifts the trailing foot just enough to be able to move it back about 6 to 8 inches, then the leading foot follows to the original on guard distance and position.

Both the advance and retreat can be executed as even two-count movements, or an uneven tempo with a short second count can lead immediately into the next action.

THE LUNGE AND RECOVERY

The lunge is begun by first extending the arm smoothly, quickly, and completely in order to bring the point in line to be ready to hit the target area. The arm is extended as if the thumb were being pulled into a position slightly higher than the shoulder (Figs. 17 and 18).

Once the arm is extended the leading leg extends and the fencer takes a step forward. With this step, the heel lands first as in the advance. As the lead foot flattens on the floor and the knee bends, the trailing leg is extended. The trailing arm is flung down to a position where the arm is straight and approximately 6 inches from the thigh. The trailing arm should be in line with the trailing leg (Figs. 19 and 20).

The feet should be approximately 18 to 30 inches apart on the lunge—depending on one's height and flexibility. In the correct lunge position the leading knee is directly over the instep. If the foot is extended too great a distance one is not able to put the knee over the foot; if too short a step is taken, the bent knee will come to a position ahead of the instep.

To return to the guard position one shifts

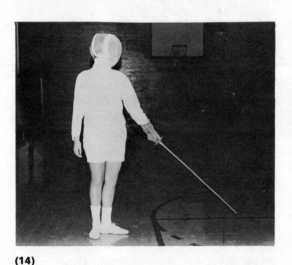

(14)

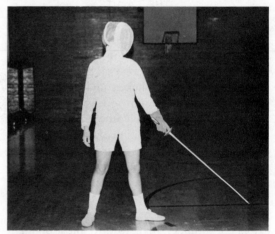

(15)

(16)

(14–16) Fencer assuming the guard position.

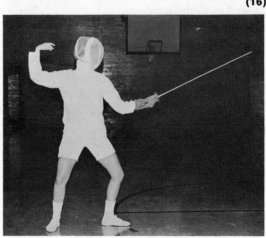

(17)

(18)

(17–18) Beginning of the lunge.

(20)

(19)

←

(19–20) Completion of the lunge.

the weight backward with a push-off from the leading heel while straightening the leading leg, bending the trailing knee, and swinging the trailing arm forcefully upward. The weapon arm is also drawn back to the original position. Another method of returning to the guard position is by moving the back foot forward to resume the guard stance and position. This recovery forward from a lunge enables one to press the attack if the opponent is retreating.

When practicing the lunge the shoulders must be relaxed and down so that one can respond quickly to the action of the opponent. Flexibility increases as the lunge is practiced so that one can assume a deeper and deeper lunge and therefore reach farther. The beginner should lunge a minimum of twenty-five times a day for the first few weeks of fencing and should increase this as time allows. Advances, retreats, and lunges should be combined in practice in order to prepare for quick changes and responses in the bouts.

LINES OF ENGAGEMENT AND TARGET AREAS

Engagement is the touching or crossing of the two opposing blades. The line of engagement is the position of the blades, which is assumed before an attack is initiated.

The target area, for the purposes of both offense and defense, is divided into four quadrants. The theoretical division into the four areas or lines of attack is determined from the on guard position (Fig. 21). A vertical line through the bell guard of the weapon divides the target into two sections called inside (in front of the fencer) and outside. A horizontal line through the bell guard divides the target area into high and low. Thus the four quadrants are high inside, low inside, low outside, and high outside.

For each line of the target there are two different guard positions for the hand and weapon. Only four of these, called positions 4, 6, 7, and 8, are generally used in foil fencing. In a bout, as

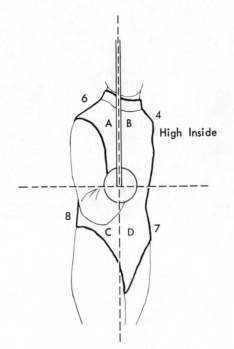

(21) Target areas.

a fencer assumes a position in preparation for the attack, the opponent will assume a position to defend herself by closing the line of attack that her opponent is attempting to take.

When one is in *sixth position* the high outside line of the target is involved (Fig. 22). To assume the sixth position from the basic grip and guard position one rotates the hand so that the fingers are on top (Fig. 23), and the hand and blade are moved slightly sideward (no more than the width of the opponent's neck). The point of the blade is at the opponent's eye level.

In *fourth position* the thumb is on top, the fingers and palm face sideways (Fig. 24), and the wrist is flexed slightly making the pommel move slightly away from the wrist. The hand and blade move sideways (no more than the width of the opponent's neck) to cover the high inside section of the target (Fig. 25). As in the sixth

(22) Parry 6.

(24) Parry 4 grip.

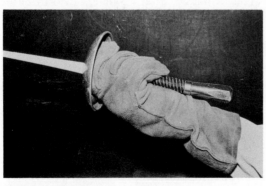

(23) Parry 6 grip.

(25) Parry 4.

position, the point of the blade is at the opponent's eye level.

In *eighth position* the low outside line is covered. The fingers are up as in the sixth position; however, with the hand and blade in line with one another, the blade is angled to point toward the opponent's knees.

The low inside line is covered when in *seventh position*. The fingers are on top, the point is lowered to knee level, and the hand and blade remain in line.

ATTACKS

In making an attack the fencer should have a specific area in mind. Attacks to the high outside are most frequently used for this is the closest area. Although many combinations of movements are possible in making the attack, one of the most effective actions is a simple attack made with speed and accuracy.

The simplest form of attack is a *straight thrust*, or extension of one's blade into an open line. However, because one's opponent is defending herself, the target area is seldom open to any direct attack; therefore most attacks are used with beat and/or feint combinations.

A *beat* is a sudden, short, sharp blow using the middle of the blade in order to deflect the opponent's blade out of the line of attack and yet keeping one's own blade in line. The beat action is started from the guard position and should be executed by a snap of the wrist while the index finger and thumb grip the handle. The beat should make a sharp, clear sound rather than a scraping down the blade. As soon as the beat is made it should be followed by an extension of the arm into a *thrust* and lunge along the same line as held prior to the beat. The beat-attack should be practiced on both the four and six target areas.

The *disengage-lunge* is a basic attack that involves moving the blade from one side of the opponent's blade to the other by passing under the opponent's weapon in a *V* path. This is done with the index finger and thumb. As one begins to disengage, the thumb lowers the blade slightly so that the blade passes under but as close as possible to the opponent's blade; then the blade is lifted by action of the index finger as the fencer goes into the thrust and lunge. The *V* should be as small as possible: it should only be as large as necessary to clear the opponent's blade.

The *beat-disengage* is another effective means of attack. This requires a beat action executed only to get a reaction from the opponent. Then when the opponent tries to block the blade the attack uses the disengage as described earlier to move into an open line or position for a hit.

A *feint* is a movement as if going into an attack without completing the action. The fencer extends her arm but does not lunge. As soon as the defender parries, the attack can disengage into a new line for the hit. The feint must be quickly made and decisive in order to draw a response from the opponent and thus clear a line for a hit.

The *one-two* attack consists of one disengage followed by another disengage that leads into the touch. The first disengage is a feint; then as the opponent's blade is drawn over to parry, the attack again disengages into a hit in the vacated area.

For the *cut-over* or coupé the attacking blade moves over rather than under the opponent's blade. The point of the blade is lifted by use of the fingers and wrist, just enough to allow it to pass over the other blade and into the thrust and lunge. The cut-over movement is used infrequently and only if the opponent is applying pressure to one's blade or if her blade is low.

DEFENSE

The parry is the defensive action that causes the opponent's blade to be deflected from her target area. The *block* is a type of parry, sometimes called opposition, in which pressure is maintained against the opponent's blade until her blade tip is out of line from the target area. The *beat* parry is a sharp tap against the opponent's blade as in the beat attack.

The parry may also be a combination of both block and beat. In all parries the defense should use the middle part of the blade to contact the opponent's blade and the tip of the foil should always remain directed toward the original target. The fingers and wrist only should be used in parrying. Parries may be executed in each of the lines of engagement and with the same hand placement as for attacking in each of the positions.

In the *counter parry* (or *circular parry*) the opponent's blade is moved out of her line of attack by first circling around the opponent's foil. Thus an attack to the line of four can be parried by a counter-six. In the high line the tip of the blade circles under the opponent's blade; in the low line it goes over the opponent's blade and is a more difficult movement to accomplish. Again, the circular movement should be as small as possible.

After a fencer has adequately defended herself with a parry she should immediately go into an attack. This thrust, delivered after a parry, is known as a *riposte*. It can be made with or without a lunge, but in any case the arm must be extended to reach the target. The riposting actions can be simple or complex inasmuch as the fencer may use the same actions that she uses in the attack.

Progression

One can learn the vocabulary of fencing by reading, but instruction and much practice are also needed. The fencer must have the skill, strength, and flexibility to execute strokes properly and must be able to correctly judge space and timing for each movement. The fencer must act quickly and respond to her opponent's actions with skill and dispatch in order to out-maneuver her opponent.

The lunge must be correctly learned and should be practiced regularly. The lunge can serve as a warm-up exercise, and the beginner who wants to progress in fencing skill would do well to practice the lunge twenty-five times every day.

Fencing requires fine manipulation of the foil with the thumb and fingers. The tip of the foil should be controlled by the hand in order to avoid superfluous movements. This action with the hand, the thrust with the arm, and the movement of the body requires use of the small and large muscles of the body and fine coordination.

One must learn to make a soft hit in the attack. The thrust toward the opponent should be firm, but not hard. The beginner can first thrust at a wall target, but should soon begin to practice with a partner. All footwork and hand actions require extensive drill, but as soon as one can move forward and back in a coordinated manner she is ready to begin informal bouts. The bouting interspersed with drills on combinations of the various movements will provide variety and challenge and lead one toward her own goals and desired level of accomplishment in fencing.

Strategy

Fencing requires strategy as well as skill. The fencer must be able to vary her attack, must react quickly to all actions on the part of her opponent, and should even strive to anticipate the moves that her opponent will make. The fencer should analyze the opponent's strengths and weaknesses and should try to set the pace rather than simply offering a response to the opponent.

The distance between the fencers must be correctly judged. The fencer must know the distance and type of movement needed to hit the opponent. Beginners frequently get too close together. Concentration is a most important factor in order to capitalize quickly on the opponent's errors and to maintain proper combat distance.

The fencer cannot be slow in making the attack, but neither should one always attack in the same rhythm. Change of tempo, as well as change in techniques, may catch the opponent off guard.

Rules for the Bout

When an individual initiates an attack she automatically has the right of way.

The person who has been attacked must parry the blade out of line in order to gain the right of way; and anytime the attacker misses the defender, the defender has the opportunity to assume the right of way.

An attack may be reestablished by withdrawing the arm back to the en garde position or by parrying a riposte.

The target area is the entire torso or trunk on the front of the body and from the hips upward on the back (Figs. 1 and 2).

A hit or touch is a puncturing action anywhere on the target area by a fencer who has the right of way.

Off-target touches are fouls. They carry no penalty but do stop the sequence of play.

A bout consists of four touches against one of the fencers, but no more than 5 minutes of actual fencing time. If time runs out before either fencer has four touches, the one who has the least number of touches against her wins. If there is a tie score at the end of 5 minutes of play, the next point wins the bout.

When officials assist with a meet, the President or Director oversees the bout and describes what happened immediately prior to a touch in order to determine who had the right of way or which point landed first.

Evaluation

The real test in fencing is the winning or losing of a bout, and one can learn much by fencing with an opponent who is more skilled than oneself.

Self-evaluation of form can be made by observing oneself in a mirror.

The fencer needs to constantly be conscious of the skills on which she is working. A check sheet of skills is helpful for practices as well as for review of performance in bouts.

Terminology

Abstain: A judge may refrain from voting because he is not certain about a valid hit (nonelectrical fencing).

Attack: The act of trying to score on the opponents; usually from the guard position while moving the weapon and/or the body forward.

Balestra: An advancing movement with a quick jump before the lunge.

Beat: A sharp hitting of the blades (usually in the middle of the blades) either for an attack or a defense.

Change of engagement: Moving the blade from one line of attack to another.

Closed line: The line the defense is protecting by the blade and the arm.

Compound attack: An attack involving two or more moves.

Corps-à-corps: Fencers get too close and the bell guards hit or lock. When this occurs the bout is stopped by the director.

Counter parry: A circular parry that may be made in either a clockwise or counterclockwise direction.

Coupé or **cut-over:** An attacking movement where the blade goes over the opponent's blade.

Engagement: The meeting of blades in a given line.

Envelopment: An attack that moves the opponent out of line with a circular movement of the weapon.

False attack: A movement made to look like a valid attack but without intent to score until the second attack.

Fencing time: The time it takes to make one simple attack. Each attack should be in one continuous move.

Lines: The area to defend or attack (4, 6, 7, or 8).

Off-target hit: A puncture that hits anywhere except the target, also called a *foul*.

Pass: An attack that does not foul or score is called a pass.

Phrase: The action before there is a pause, no matter how long or short. A phrase is reviewed by the director in determining the action.

Piste or **strip:** The fencing area, copper, rubber or wood, usually 40 feet by 6 feet.

President: The director of the bout who decides on right of way. He has one and one-half votes as opposed to one vote for each judge.

Right of way: In making an attack or parry one gains the right of way.

Touch: A hit in the target area that would theoretically puncture the opponent.

Selected References

Bower, Muriel and Torao Mori. *Fencing*. Dubuque, Iowa: William C. Brown Co., 1966.

Castello, Hugo and James. *Fencing*. New York: Ronald Press, 1962.

Crosnier, Roger. *Fencing with the Electrical Foil*. New York: A. S. Barnes and Co., 1961.

Crosnier, Roger. *Fencing with the Foil*. New York: Ronald Press, 1951.

Fencing Rules and Manual, Jose deCapriles, ed. Amateur Fencers League of America, Worcester, Mass.: Heffernan Press, Inc., 1965. (May be obtained from the Amateur Fencers League of America, Inc., 33–62 Street, West New York, N.J.)

Chapter **8**

Golf *Jane M. Lloyd*

History. Goals. Equipment. Etiquette. Swinging the Club. Position of Address. Analysis of the Swing. Wood Play and Iron Play. The Short Game. Playing the Course. Rules. Terminology.

Golf is a challenging outdoor game that can be played alone or with one to three people. With selected clubs, in as few strokes as possible, a small white ball is driven from a teeing ground, hit down a fairway to a green and into a cup $4\frac{1}{4}$ inches in diameter. A round of golf, or a game, usually consists of eighteen holes.

The golf course is made up of separate units or holes (Fig. 1). Each unit has a teeing area, a fairway, and a green with a cup. Included on all golf courses are man-made and natural hazards to challenge the player. Hazards such as sand bunkers are man-made; other parts of the course such as creeks and lakes form natural hazards. Woods, rough, and out-of-bounds areas also create a challenge for the golfer. Golf courses have nine to thirty-six holes, always in multiples of nine, but the majority are eighteen hole courses.

Each hole differs in the distance from tee to green, and par, a standard of excellence in play, is determined by the length of the hole. Any hole up to 210 yards in length is a par three for

women; par four is 211 to 400 yards; par five is 401 to 575 yards; and a hole with a distance greater than 575 yards is a par six.[1] An eighteen hole golf course usually has four par three holes, ten par fours, and four par fives, thus making the eighteen holes a par seventy-two.

History

There is controversy over who originated the game of golf. Some of golf's beginnings are found in Rome and France where the people had games in which a ball was hit with a mallet into holes dug in the ground. A golf type of game was also played in Holland many centuries ago.

Records show that golf was played in Scotland in the middle of the fifteenth century; then in the late fifteenth century laws were passed to prohibit the game. It had become so popular that it was a threat to national defense because it detracted from the practice of archery. When King James IV of Scotland became a golfer the game again began to grow in popularity. The most famous golf course in the world, the Royal and Ancient Golf Club of St. Andrews in Scotland, was founded in 1754 and is still in use as one of the most outstanding of courses.

Golf spread to New York in the late 1800's. John Reid, a Scotsman, built the first golf course in a cow pasture in Yonkers.

Golf has been an accepted game for women

Miss Jane Lloyd, an assistant professor in the Department of Physical Education for Women at Duke University, earned her bachelor's degree at Mary Washington College and her master's at the University of North Carolina, Chapel Hill. Miss Lloyd's graduate thesis pertained to the Women's Collegiate Golf Tournament, and she has taught golf in college and at country clubs. She was 1967 team champion of the Duke University Women's Interclub Tournament, and made a hole-in-one in May 1967 on the Duke University fifteenth hole—par 3, 178 yards—with a five wood. Miss Lloyd currently has a six handicap.

[1] United States Golf Association Standards.

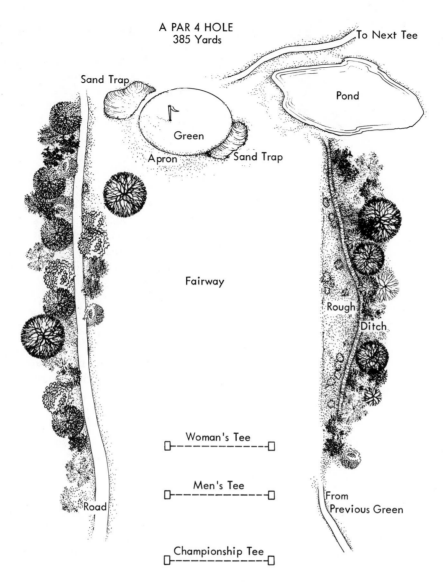

A PAR 4 HOLE
385 Yards

To Next Tee

Sand Trap

Pond

Green

Apron   Sand Trap

Fairway

Rough
Ditch

Woman's Tee

Men's Tee

Road

From
Previous Green

Championship Tee

(1) A par 4 hole.

for a long time. Mary Queen of Scots was the first skilled woman golfer. In this country the first national championship for women was held at the Meadow Brook Hunt Club, Long Island, in 1895. The first Women's Collegiate Golf Tournament was held at Ohio State University in 1941, a tournament that continues to be held annually.

have fun in a game of golf after six weeks of instruction. However, if one wishes to become a good golfer and to score consistently well, it will take several years of lessons and a great deal of practice. In a six-weeks' course one should gain an understanding of what constitutes a golf swing. This is a start toward pleasure with the game of golf.

Goals

Golf can provide pleasure, challenge, physical activity, and recreation in the out-of-doors throughout one's lifetime. Goals for the beginner in golf can differ. It is possible to go out and

Equipment

CLUBS

There are ten irons, numbered one to ten, and four woods, numbered one to four (Fig. 2). In addition to the standard clubs, other clubs such

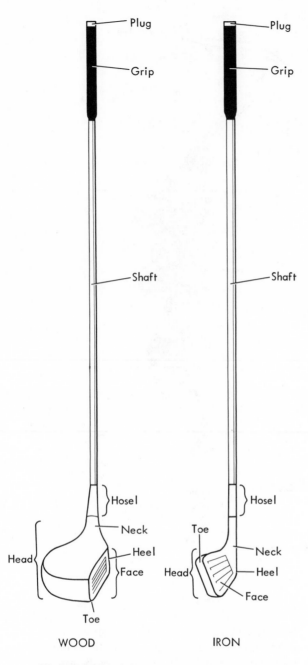

Plug

Grip

Shaft

Hosel

Neck

Heel

Face

Head

Toe

WOOD

Plug

Grip

Shaft

Hosel

Toe

Neck

Heel

Face

Head

IRON

(2) Parts of the club.

as the sand wedge, pitching wedge, and number five wood may be used for special play.

Golf clubs vary in length of shaft and angle of hitting surface. The number one wood (driver) has the longest shaft and a hitting surface or face that is almost perpendicular to the ground. The driver gives the greatest distance of any of the clubs because the greatest speed and lowest trajectory can be imparted to the ball with the swing of this club. As clubs increase in number,

the shaft is shorter and the club face has more backward slant or loft. The number two wood gives more height and a little less distance than the driver. The three wood and four wood send the ball higher yet achieve respectively less distance. The number five wood has the most loft of any of the woods.

Although the irons have names, they are more frequently referred to by number. The irons may be considered in groups: the numbers one, two, and three are called long irons; the four, five, and six, middle irons; and the seven, eight, and nine are the short irons. The number ten, the putter, is used to stroke the ball into the cup on the green.

In tournament play a golfer is limited to fourteen clubs by United States Golf Association rules. Men or women who frequently play in tournaments usually decide during their practice rounds which clubs they wish to use to make up the fourteen maximum.

A beginner does not need a full set of clubs to learn the game of golf. A starter set might consist of the driver, three wood, and the three, five, seven, nine irons and putter. Clubs vary in weight so it is necessary to select ones that are right for the golfer according to her height, weight, strength, and golf swing. The instructor can be of assistance to the golfer in her selection of clubs.

BAGS

Clubs are carried in a bag made of canvas, leather, vinyl or some other synthetic material. A lightweight combination bag-cart is now popular. Both the bag and the bag-cart contain pockets for balls, tees, and the other golf items one needs for playing.

BALLS

United States Golf Association regulations determine standards of size and weight for balls. When selecting a ball, the compression of the golf ball is important to consider. The ball is slightly flattened or compressed at the time of contact with the club head; this adds to the distance achieved. Many men choose high or medium compression balls for they have the strength and power in their golf swings to flatten even the more solid ball, but the average woman golfer is wise to use a low compression ball (about 80 per cent compression). Beginners should also use a ball with a tough cover—one that is not easily cut when the ball is topped.

GLOVE

A golf glove is used by most golfers. The right-handed golfer wears the glove on her left hand. This gives a firm left hand grip on the club and helps to avoid blisters. One may purchase either a full finger or half finger glove in a variety of colors and materials.

TEES

Small pegs called tees are used to elevate the ball above the ground. A tee may be used only at the teeing area, not for any other shot on the course.

SHOES

Golf shoes are a good investment if one wishes to play golf frequently. They are equipped with spikes, which aid in giving the golfer a firm footing and therefore contribute to better balance as one swings the club.

DRESS

The woman golfer should select clothes that fit properly, are in good taste, and will allow her freedom to execute her golf swing. Local custom often dictates the appropriate attire on a specific course.

Etiquette and Safety

When playing golf one must observe courtesy and safety procedures:

1. Each player must have her own bag and clubs, and must be able to identify her own ball by its markings.
2. Do not play until the group ahead is well out of range.
3. Refrain from talking, moving, or standing close to the ball when another player is swinging.
4. If the golfer's ball does accidentally go near others, shout, "fore", to warn the other players that a ball is coming their way.
5. If one hears a call of "fore" and does not immediately see the ball, turn the back to the direction from which the call came and duck the head.
6. Play without undue delay, and motion golfers behind to play through if one's group is slower or has lost a ball.
7. After swinging in a sand bunker, smooth over the sand with the rake that is provided, or with a club if no rake is available.
8. Replace divots made by the club on the fairway, and if the ball makes a pit mark on the green use a tee to lift and smooth the grass.
9. When putting on the green, leave the cart, bag and other clubs well away from the green on the side nearest the next tee.
10. While on the green, avoid letting one's shadow fall across the hole or on the path of another player's putting line.
11. Scores are recorded after leaving the green.
12. In case of thunderstorms with lightning, leave the clubs and go to a shelter. If no shelter is available stay close to the ground in an open area away from trees.

The Golf Stroke

SWINGING THE GOLF CLUB

The first step in learning golf is to get the feel of swinging the club (Figs. 16–23). The golf swing differs slightly from the movements of other sports for the golfer's body rotates without stepping or swaying from side to side. The body rotates on a central axis, the spine; and the swing of the club is on a path in front of the golfer. The body must coil and uncoil to build up speed and power to hit the ball—a small stationary object. Rhythm and timing are important. The golfer needs to establish a basic swing pattern and should understand the action of the club.

The swinging motion of a golf club can be compared to the action of a pendulum, for the club should be swung without any twisting or pressing motions. In order to feel this swinging motion, hold one of the short irons between the thumb and forefinger of one hand by gripping the top of the shaft; then let the head of the club swing like a pendulum. The weight of the head of the club helps it to swing with only a small amount of arm movement needed to initiate the action. The club will repeat the same path over and over again; but if one tries to control the movement by guiding the club or twisting or pressing, this interferes with and changes the path of the swing.

Swinging action should take place in the golf stroke. The arms provide the power to initiate movement, but the weight of the club should be allowed to expand the movement. In other words, the golfer who tries to guide the club is likely to miss the ball; by swinging the club, it

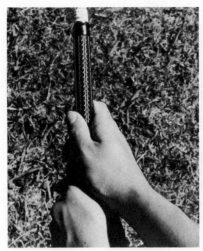

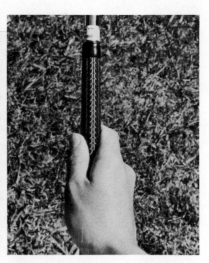

(3) The overlapping grip.   **(4)** Left-hand position for the grip.   **(5)** Right-hand position for the grip.

will remain in the desired path and contact the ball.

The beginner does not need to immediately analyze the parts of the swing; but she should observe the swing of a good golfer. Then, after learning to grip the club, she should try the golf swing. Assume the proper stance and grip, then swing the club back and forth several times in a repetitive swinging motion. This should be a relaxed easy swing back and forth, back and forth. It should be a rhythmic swing in waltz time: back, two, three; through, two, three. Arm action and body pivot come as a result of the swinging of the club. Let the club action and the weight of the head of the club set the pattern.

POSITION OF ADDRESS

The position one assumes prior to making a stroke is known as the position of address. This includes everything one does before hitting the ball: grip, lining up with the target, stance, and body position.

Grip

A good grip is essential for in the golf swing both hands must work together. A faulty grip can cause a poor swing pattern and inconsistency in direction of shots.

The *overlapping grip* (Fig. 3) is recommended for women, inasmuch as it encourages a firm, close contact with both hands working together as one unit.

LEFT-HAND POSITION. One should stand on a line parallel with the intended line of flight of the ball (Fig. 4). The feet are placed about shoulder width apart, allowing the arms to hang relaxed, palms facing each other, left elbow toward the hole, right elbow pointing toward the right hip. One shakes hands with the club using the left hand and gripping about ½ inch down on the grip of the club. The club face remains square to the line of flight.

The left palm should be placed diagonally along the club. The hand presses around the club until the left thumb is slightly right of center. The *V* formed by the thumb and forefinger should point between the chin and right shoulder. The first, second, and possibly third knuckles should be visible as one looks down at the grip. More pressure should be applied with the last three fingers than with the thumb and forefinger. The left hand and club shaft should be in line with the inside of the left leg, keeping the back of the left hand facing the target.

RIGHT-HAND POSITION. Because the right hand is below the left hand on the shaft of the club, posture must be adjusted by tilting the right shoulder slightly lower than the left (Fig. 5). It is also helpful to allow the right knee to bend in slightly toward the left knee. The right elbow should be close to the right hip. These adjustments permit the right hand to be lower than the left without turning the shoulders to the left. The right-hand grip is a finger grip in contrast to a palm grip with the left hand.

Check the following points: 1) the club rests in the fingers; 2) the thumb of the left hand fits into the pocket formed by the right palm; 3) the *V* formed by the thumb and forefinger of the right hand also points between the chin and right shoulder; 4) the thumb is slightly left of the center of the shaft of the club; 5) the thumb and forefinger should be slightly separated with the right forefinger gripping as one would to pull the trigger of a gun; 6) the little finger of the right hand overlaps the forefinger of the left hand and locks securely around the knuckle of the left forefinger or in between the first and second fingers; and 7) the right palm should be facing toward the hole.

In this grip the overlapping of the right little finger contributes firmness to the grip. The thumb of the left hand fits into the palm of the right hand throughout the swing. This helps to keep the hands together. One holds the club lightly but with control; the arms are relaxed. Be sure that the back of the left hand and the palm of the right are facing the hole. Also, the club face must be square to the intended line of flight for the ball. It is easy to make the error of changing the position of the club face without realizing it when taking the grip.

Stance

Stance, or foot position, changes according to the golf club used and the distance one hopes to achieve. Beginners should start with a square stance (Fig. 6).

SQUARE STANCE. Both feet and body are on a line parallel to the intended flight of the ball. The square stance should be used with all clubs when making a full swing to achieve the maximum distance which the club affords.

OPEN STANCE. The left foot is back from the line parallel to the intended flight of the ball. The right foot remains on the parallel line. This stance is used with a short backswing in order to make approach shots when the ball is near the green.

CLOSED STANCE. The left foot is placed in front of the line parallel to the intended flight of the ball. The right foot remains on the parallel line. This stance is used by highly skilled players when they want the ball to hook (curve to the left) while in flight.

Ball position

The placement of one's feet in relation to the ball depends on the club being used. Placement of the left foot is the same for all clubs (Fig. 7). The ball should be in line with the inside of the golfer's left heel. As the clubs increase in number and loft, the right foot moves progressively closer to the left foot. The ball is farthest

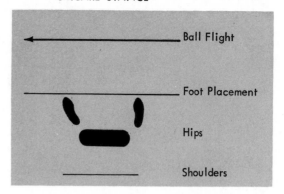

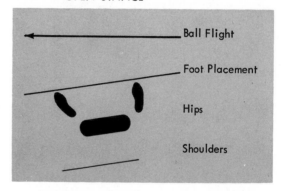

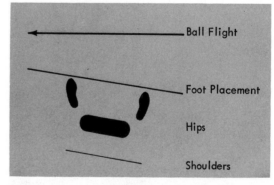

(6) Stance.

from the golfer's feet when using the woods and is moved closer to the player's feet as the clubs increase in number because the shaft of each successive club is shorter.

Golf posture

Golf posture, or the position of the body for the golf swing, must permit freedom of movement and must be consistent (Figs. 8 and 9). The following items need to be considered:

1. Bend forward from the hips, keeping a

Golf   **125**

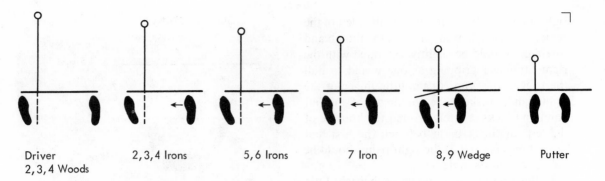

Driver
2,3,4 Woods

2,3,4 Irons

5,6 Irons

7 Iron

8,9 Wedge

Putter

Note width of stance and distance between ball and feet

(7) Ball position.

straight line from the tip of the spine to the top of the head.

2. The knees are slightly bent.
3. Use a square stance with the left foot slightly outward and the right foot either straight ahead or slightly outward.
4. The body weight is equally distributed on the insides of both feet and toward the heels to overcome the tendency to fall forward on the downswing. The inner leg muscles are tightened to feel a firm base of support.
5. The left arm is straight and the right elbow is bent slightly inward toward the right hip.
6. One looks at the ball by lowering the eyes, not the head.

Lining up

It is important to line up with the direction the ball is to go (Fig. 10). One takes the grip, walks behind the ball, and sights to the target. A spot is selected between the ball and the target over which the ball should travel—much as is done in spot bowling. The golfer then walks to the hitting position and places the club face behind the ball, square to the intended line of flight, and takes the appropriate stance, keeping in mind the spot over which the ball should travel. The shoulders and hips are parallel with the line of flight. This means that the left shoulder and hip should point slightly left of the flagstick when lining up for a straight shot. The

(8) Golf posture—side view.

(9) Golf posture—front view.

(10) Lining up—clubs on ground to show placement of head of club and feet in relation to the ball and line of flight.

left foot is pointed outward. This allows one to swing through the ball. The right foot should point straight ahead or slightly outward. It is essential, in order to maintain body position, to keep the eyes on the ball from the time the swing

(11–12) Body rotation.

(11) To the right.

is started until just after the ball has been contacted.

BODY ROTATION

The spine is a vertical axis about which the golfer's body rotates, and there should be no sway of the body either to the right or left. One achieves this coiling action by focusing the eyes on the back of the ball, keeping head position steady throughout the swing and making the correct shift of weight on the feet. In order to make the correct body rotation and weight shift, one might imagine rotating while standing in a barrel. To avoid touching the sides of the barrel one has to rotate the body without swaying.

Another way to get the feeling of this body rotation is to practice while holding a club behind the back. With the club parallel to the ground, one supports it with bent elbows while hands are clasped in front at the waist. With the grip end of the club extending beyond the right elbow, the body is rotated as in the backswing and the head of the club points toward the ball (Fig. 11). Then, with the turn for the downswing, the grip end of the club points toward the ball (Fig. 12). On the backswing rotation the weight rolls to the inside of the right foot. On the downswing, to the outside of the left foot.

To get the feel of maintaining the club and body turn as a unit, one may take the correct

(12) To the left.

(14) Body rotation for the backswing.

(13) Raise the clubhead straight upward.

(15) Body rotation for the follow-through.

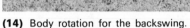

(13–15) Rotation.

grip and raise the club head straight upward with the grip end pointing to the ground and arms straight out in front chest high (Fig. 13). While the hands and arms remain shoulder high, the shoulders are turned to the right with the left shoulder moving under the chin; the right elbow bends and points down to the ground while the left arm remains straight. The wrists remain cocked as in the beginning of the exercise. This is the correct body rotation for the backswing when the club is at this position (Fig. 14). One returns to the starting position; then turns the shoulders to the left while the hands remain high; the right shoulder moving under the chin. The right arm remains straight and the left elbow bends, pointing down to the ground. This is the correct position after the hit (Fig. 15). Practicing this body rotation exercise may be of help to the beginner.

SHIFT OF WEIGHT

The body weight should be equally distributed on both feet at the position of address. As the club swings, the body turns to allow for an expanded or larger swing. This brings a shift of weight from left to right on the backswing, then a shift from right to left on the downswing and follow-through.

ANALYSIS OF THE SWING

The following should occur on the *backswing* part of the stroke (Figs. 16–39):

1. The head remains steady as the rest of the body rotates around the spine.
2. The backswing is slow and rhythmic and the initial movement of the club away from the ball must be a low, smooth movement. The hands, arms, shoulders, and hips turn together.
3. More than 50 per cent of the weight is transferred to the inside of the right foot by turning the left knee in toward the right knee and rolling the weight over from the ball of the left foot to the inside of the right foot.
4. The shoulders turn about 90 degrees compared to 45 degrees for the hip turn. In order to keep the left arm extended throughout the backswing, the shoulders must turn 90 degrees.
5. The right elbow remains close to the right hip until the hands reach waist high in the upward arc, then the elbow moves up and away from the body but continues to point downward.
6. The hands and club move in an arc to a position above the right shoulder. At the

top of the backswing, the left arm is straight but not locked. The wrists are bent back or "cocked" so that the club is parallel to the line of direction that the ball is to take.

7. The left heel may come off the ground about 1 inch as the weight is transferred to the inside of the right foot. Exception: left heel remains in contact with the ground with the short irons.

8. At the top of the backswing, the left shoulder should be turned until it points toward the ball, and the golfer's back is toward the hole. With the left shoulder low, the chin is over the shoulder and eyes are focused on the back of the ball.

In the *downswing* the uncoiling action begins with a shifting of body weight to the left (Figs. 16–39). Then the shoulders, arms, hands, and clubhead come into action in sequence.

1. The downswing starts with a shift of weight to the left heel by pushing off with the inside of the right foot while the right knee turns toward the hole. This gets the left hip out of the way.

2. The right elbow moves close to the right side as the right shoulder moves down and under the chin. This movement brings the path of the clubhead slightly inside the arc of the backswing.

3. The golfer gets added power by delaying the uncocking of the wrists until the last possible moment. One should pull down with the left hand as the grip end of the club comes down first.

4. Both arms are straight while the head of the club is in the hitting area. Then the right arm becomes the radius for the arc of the swing as it passes over the left arm; and the left elbow begins to bend downward.

5. Keep the head steady and look at the back of the ball on the swing through.

Golf is a game in which the *follow-through* is extremely important. When the club comes in contact with the ball, it maintains this contact for a short time as the ball begins to move. During contact with the ball, the clubhead must remain square and continue along the path the ball is to travel. Speed built up in the swing is dissipated in the follow-through. After the ball has been contacted, the club continues to swing out in the direction the ball is taking. The hands

turn over, and the swing continues until the hands are high and the club is behind the head.

At the completion of the follow-through the golfer's back is slightly arched. The left leg bears most of the body weight, and the right knee and right foot are pointing toward the hole. The player's right shoulder is lower than the left, and as the shoulders turn, the head turns and follows the flight of the ball. The golf stroke requires rhythm, coordination, and balance throughout the swing.

Wood Play and Iron Play

The swing is basically the same for all clubs. However, because the woods have longer shafts than the irons, it takes a little longer time to swing the wood back and through. With the longer swing of the club there is more opportunity to use the body; therefore there is more of a pivot, or coiling and uncoiling, of the body. If the wood is used effectively, one feels as if it is making a sweeping action in both the tee shot and on the fairway. Little or no divot is taken in a fairway shot with woods, and none at all with the driver from the tee.

The irons, with a shorter shaft, allow the player to hit down on the ball, thus contacting the ball first, then taking a divot. Downward movement of the club on the ball produces backspin, which imparts lift to the ball. The body pivot is not so great as with the woods, and it becomes progressively less as the clubs get shorter so that one depends mainly on shoulder turn with the eight and nine irons and wedge.

The Short Game

The average woman golfer is generally not a long hitter; she must depend on her short game to help in scoring well. The short game, in addition to putting, includes approaching the green by using the middle and short irons to chip and pitch. Inasmuch as many women cannot reach the green on a long Par 4 in two hits, they are faced with a possible pitch or chip shot from near the green.

PITCHING

The object of the pitch shot is to make the ball go up into the air in a high arc, then land and stop on the green near the hole (Figs. 40–43).

(16–23) Wood—front view.

(16–19) Backswing. (16) (17) (18) (19)

(24–31) Wood—side view.

(24–27) Backswing. (24) (25) (26) (27)

(32–39) Iron—side view.

(32–35) Backswing. (32) (33) (34) (35)

(20–23) Downswing.   **(20)**   **(21)**   **(22)**   **(23)**

(28–31) Downswing.   **(28)**   **(29)**   **(30)**   **(31)**

(36–39) Downswing.   **(36)**   **(37)**   **(38)**   **(39)**

(40) Address.

(41) Backswing.

(42) Contact.

(43) Follow-through.

This is the shot that must be used when it is necessary to clear obstacles such as a tree or sand trap in order to reach the green. The pitch is also good for distances up to about 100 yards from the green. Because the ball must go high, one uses a lofted club such as the nine iron or the pitching wedge. These clubs contact and compress the ball below its center of gravity; therefore, they impart backspin to the ball, which causes the ball to stop quickly when it lands. If one wishes to lift the ball high over an obstacle, and then have it run toward the cup after landing, a seven or eight iron should be used because these clubs have a little less loft than the nine and do not impart as much back-spin to the ball. The following adjustments must be made for a pitch:

1. One uses an open stance with the weight largely on the left foot. Both feet remain in contact with the ground throughout the backswing. There is no need to shift the body weight to the right and then back to the left because the shaft of the club is short and one is not able to make a full swing.
2. The golfer uses the normal grip, but shifts the shaft of the club so the hands are slightly ahead of the ball at the address position. The hands should lead as one swings down into the hitting area.

(44–47) Chipping.

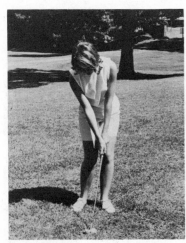

(44) Address.

(45) Backswing.

(46) Contact.

(47) Follow-through.

3. Take less than a full swing. Short swings are segments of the full swing and the feeling for the amount of swing needed for the distance desired comes only through practice. Swing the club straight away from the ball; keep a slow easy rhythm.
4. Pause at the height of the swing, then pull down with the left hand leading as the back of the left hand faces the hole.
5. Always hit down and through the ball, hitting the ball first, then taking a divot and following through toward the hole.

Common errors include allowing the right hand to take over and scoop the ball, and digging the club into the ground, thus stopping short on the follow-through. One should always use both hands and always follow-through.

CHIPPING

A chip shot is used when the ball is near the green—anywhere from right on the apron adjacent to the green up to 20 yards away (Figs. 44–47). Many golf pros describe chipping as an elongated putt made with a five, six, or seven iron. The ball is hit on a low trajectory so that it lands just over the fringe of the green and rolls to the cup. One should use only as much loft as needed to clear a small mound or fringe around the green. Regardless of the club used, the grip and the wrists should remain firm throughout the execution of the stroke. The following steps should be used for a chip shot:

1. Grip down on the club several inches lower than on the normal grip. This gives the golfer more feel for the shot. The grip should remain firm. Hold the club with a little more pressure in the last three fingers of the left hand. The left hand controls the chip.
2. The hands are placed slightly ahead of the ball at the address position as in the pitch shot; thus the hands lead the clubhead into the ball.
3. Use an open stance with the feet very close together and more weight on the left foot. The weight remains here throughout the chipping stroke. The body turns slightly toward the hole, head steady.
4. The right elbow should be in close to the right side; the left arm should be straight.
5. Take the club straight away from the ball in a low smooth backswing and only as much backswing as needed for the shot. The wrists

are firm and the club is taken back and through by a turning of arms and shoulders.
6. With the left hand leading, one hits down and through the ball and follows through toward the hole. Good chippers always finish their swing with the clubhead pointing toward the hole.
7. Keep the head down until after the club contacts the ball and the ball is on the way to the cup.

Common errors include looking up to see where the ball is going and therefore topping the ball; collapsing the left hand and letting the right take over with the result of digging into the ground or scooping the ball; or making a big backswing and stopping at the ball.

PUTTING

Putting is a different and separate skill from the rest of the game of golf. Through practice and feel one establishes a putting stroke. Basic fundamentals are needed to become a good putter: first, the clubhead must be square to the hole and stay square—this is accomplished with a good grip; the stroke must have rhythm; and there should be no body movement. In putting use only hands and wrists; the more body, the more chance for error.

Besides the stroke itself, one must learn to "read the greens": to judge distance; to see the contour of the green and know how this will affect the roll of the ball; and to see the type of grass, thickness, length, and grain of the grass. All these things should be considered in putting.

Basic points to remember in putting are first, the *grip*. Any grip is effective if it aligns the back of the left hand and the palm of the right hand to the line of one's putt. Both hands should work together. A common putting grip is the *reverse overlapping* grip. One takes the regular overlapping grip, then removes the left forefinger from the club, and places the right little finger in its place. The left forefinger is extended along the knuckles of the right hand.

Next, remember to use whatever stance (wide or narrow) is comfortable, but keep more weight on the left foot than the right. There is no weight shift nor movement of the body or head. The right elbow is close to or touching the right hip throughout the putt.

The ball is played from a point in front of the left foot. The eyes and hands should be directly over the ball. The stroke should be short, and

(48) Sidehill lie with ball lower than feet.

(49) Sidehill lie with ball higher than feet.

think she will make the putt, then she usually does not. Concentration and positive thinking are essential in putting.

Playing the Course

DIFFICULT LIES

Many golf courses are hilly, thus presenting the golfer with various types of lies. The ball may be resting on a sidehill or downhill slope. One has to adjust the swing slightly with these lies in order to hit the ball straight. The following situations are common. To play a sidehill lie where the ball is below one's feet (Fig. 48), 1) use the normal grip; 2) play the ball near the center of the stance and aim slightly left because the tendency is for the ball to go to the right; 3) stand a little closer to the ball; 4) shorten the backswing to maintain balance; and 5) stay down through the shot to avoid topping the ball.

To play a sidehill lie where the ball is above the feet (Fig. 49), 1) grip down on the club about 2 inches from the top of the normal grip; 2) play the ball near the center of the stance and aim slightly right inasmuch as the tendency is for the ball to go left; 3) to be in a balanced position, keep the weight on the whole of both feet, rather than just the heels, and bend the knees slightly; and 4) shorten the backswing to maintain balance.

the backswing low and slow. One hits through the ball, keeping the club face square to the line. Two accepted methods of putting are 1) wrist putting in which the wrists act as a hinge; 2) stroke putting where the hands and arms go back and through in one piece with no wrist break.

Many professionals say that once a stroke pattern for putting has been established, the problem is purely psychological. If one does not

(50) Uphill lie.

(51) Downhill lie.

(52) Sand trap.

To play an uphill lie (Fig. 50), 1) use a less lofted club than normal for the distance required as the loft of the hill will elevate the ball approximately one club more; 2) place more weight on the left foot than the right in order to maintain balance. Shorten the backswing; 3) play the ball forward off the higher foot so the club will follow the contour of the land; and 4) aim slightly to the right as the tendency is for the ball to go left.

To play a downhill lie (Fig. 51), 1) use a more lofted club than usual for the distance because the angle of the downhill slope will not elevate the ball as much; 2) distribute the body weight evenly on both feet; 3) play the ball from the center of the stance or toward the right foot so the club will follow the contour of the land; 4) aim slightly to the left as the tendency is for the ball to go to the right; and 5) shorten the backswing to maintain balance.

SAND TRAPS

It is very important to know golf rules pertaining to the sand trap. The golfer is not permitted to ground the club in a trap or hazard (Fig. 52). At address one must hold the club above the ball and must not make contact with the hazard until the club is on the downswing and coming into contact with the ball.

To play the ball out of a sand trap, use an open stance and play the ball toward the left foot. Both feet are firmly dug into the sand to avoid slipping, and the feet remain firmly planted throughout the hit. The object is to hit the sand about 1½ to 2 inches behind the ball. The impact of the club against the sand will help lift the ball into the air and out of the trap. Do not look at the ball during this shot; instead, focus the eyes on the sand just behind the ball where the club is to make contact on the downswing. It is important to follow-through toward the hole. If one only digs into the sand and stops short on the follow-through, the ball will still be in the trap!

The best club to use in the sand trap is a sand wedge. This club is especially designed with a thick phlange or head to force the sand toward the ball, thus causing the ball to be lifted more easily. If one opens the face of the club, she will get the maximum loft of the club and get the ball into the air very quickly. Rhythm is essential. A nice slow backswing, almost lazy in appearance, with a full follow-through will make this an easy shot.

DISTANCES FOR BEGINNERS

A beginner may hit only 100 to 120 yards with the five iron. Different players hit varying distances with the same club. A professional may hit 160 to 170 yards with a five iron whereas a skilled woman golfer may get 145 to 150 yards with the five. The distance one can achieve is known only after much practice and watching the distance one gets from each club after becoming consistent in the use of that club.

There is a simple formula for distance to be expected with the various clubs. This can be determined because of the relative difference in angle of face and length of shaft of each successive club. Working with the number nine iron down to the two iron, the golfer who has developed a consistent swing pattern will get approximately 10 yards more with each successive club. Thus, the beginner who gets 120 yards with the five iron should also begin to get 130 yards with the four iron, if she uses one, and about 140 yards with the three iron (Fig. 53).

A BEGINNER PLAYS THE COURSE

Let us assume that, as a beginner, one has the number one and number three woods, number three, five, seven and nine irons, and a putter. Nine holes, or even less, will be enough for the first round of golf. Because a beginner will be slower than experienced golfers, it is better to select a weekday time to play when the course is not so crowded. In order to accommodate more players, only foursomes are allowed to play most courses on weekends. One will do better on her first round to play by herself or with a sympathetic, but quiet, friend. Do not try to take a golf lesson while playing; simply concentrate on the swing and enjoy the game.

Suppose that the first hole is a Par 5 hole with a distance of 410 yards. In order to make par with that distance, the golfer should get on the green in three hits, then two putt for a score of five. If, as a beginner, one scores a seven or eight on the hole, one is making a fair start. Improvement will come with practice and playing.

The golfer will find two sets of markers on the teeing area. The markers giving the greater distance are for men, and the markers allowing the shorter distance on the hole are for women. Before starting to play, leave the bag outside the teeing area. Then take a few practice swings to get the feel of the swing and to relax the muscles. Take a tee, ball, and driver or number three

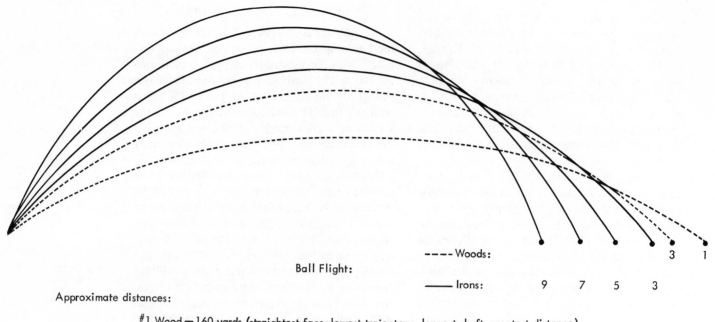

Ball Flight:

---- Woods: 3   1

—— Irons: 9   7   5   3

Approximate distances:

#1 Wood — 160 yards (straightest face–lowest trajectory; longest shaft–greatest distance)
#3 Wood — 140 yards
#3 Iron — 130 yards
#5 Iron — 110 yards
#7 Iron — 90 yards
#9 Iron — 70 yards

(53) Ball flight and approximate distances achieved by novices.

wood, depending on one's preference and ability to use the clubs, onto the teeing ground. Tee the ball up inside the women's markers or within two club lengths behind the markers. The golf stance is taken and one lines up the clubface for the middle of the fairway. On the swing, the golfer should feel as though she is going to sweep the ball off the tee.

Assuming that the hit is a very good drive of about 150 yards down the middle of the fairway, one has a remaining distance of 260 yards to the green. For this second shot the beginner would use the three wood. A good hit of 145 yards with the three wood leaves 115 yards distance to the green.

On the next stroke the player hopes to reach the green. If the flag and cup are located at the back of the green, the five iron is used, because it imparts a forward roll for the ball to roll toward the cup. The number seven iron is used if the cup is nearer the front of the green. One does not try to go for the flagstick, but aims for the center of the green.

If the ball makes the green, then one walks around to the back and leaves her bag off the

surface of the green on the side toward the next tee. When using the putter on the green, one tries to go for the distance needed in order to get close enough to make the second putt go into the cup.

Par 4 holes, like the Par 5's, require a wood shot for the first stroke. However, it is not always necessary to use a wood when playing a Par 3 hole. Depending on the distance one can hit with the club, a five or seven iron would be appropriate for the first stroke on a hole 120 yards in length. With a Par 3 hole the first stroke, the drive, is supposed to land on the green and thus allow two strokes for putting.

The distance a beginner achieves with her clubs after six weeks of lessons differs considerably depending on her size, strength, skill, and ground and weather conditions. One does not try to force the swing to get additional distance. This only causes the ball to go off in various unpredictable directions. The beginner should alternate practice with playing the course. On the course the golfer learns to judge distance and to swing effectively with a variety of lies, but one develops a consistent swing only through repeated practice. Enjoy a round of golf, then go back and practice some more.

Rules

The United States Golf Association (USGA) is the governing body for golf in this country and the rules set by this organization should be followed by all players. The golfer must also abide by local regulations pertaining to boundaries, hazards, and so on, on the course which she is playing.

Some of the rules a beginner must know to get started are

1. The first stroke of each hole is started by teeing the ball between the tee markers or within two club lengths back of the markers. If the ball accidentally rolls off the tee, it may be replaced without penalty. Each swing at the ball counts as a stroke even if the ball is missed.

2. The honor, or privilege, of hitting first from the tee goes to the player with the lowest score on the previous hole. Honor is determined by lot on the first tee.

3. The player who is "away", or farthest from the hole, plays first. This rule is followed throughout play, except of course for the tee shots.

4. If a ball is lost or goes out-of-bounds, there is a penalty of one stroke. If one cannot find her ball within five minutes, she must take another ball to continue play and consider the first ball lost. A provisional or second ball may be played from the same spot where the first ball was hit. This saves the time of walking back if the first ball is actually lost or out-of-bounds. If the provisional ball is not needed, it is picked up without penalty.

5. If a ball enters a water hazard and is unplayable, the player may drop another ball in back of the hazard keeping in line with the spot where the first ball crossed the edge of the hazard. Penalty one stroke.

6. If a ball is in an unplayable position, it may be dropped within two club lengths to either side or behind the spot, but no closer to the hole. Penalty one stroke.

7. To drop a ball, the golfer stands facing the hole and drops the ball back over her right shoulder. The ball must not be dropped nearer the hole than it had previously rested.

8. A player may not improve the lie of her ball. Penalty two strokes. Note: local rules may permit moving one's ball to improve the lie because of the local ground condition (winter rule), but this is not a USGA ruling.

9. When a ball is in a hazard, the club must not touch the hazard until the downswing of the club. This rule applies to both sand traps and water hazards.

10. Loose impediments, such as leaves and twigs, may be moved without penalty except when they are in a hazard.

11. If a ball is within two club lengths of an artificial obstruction such as a bench, the ball may be lifted and dropped (no closer to the hole) without penalty.

12. If a ball is in casual water caused by hose watering or rain, it may be lifted and dropped (no closer to the hole) without penalty.

Terminology

Apron or fringe: The area, about 5 feet in width, immediately surrounding the green. The grass is short on the apron, but not so short as the green.

Away: The player farthest from the hole. This person always has the first hit.

Birdie: One under par.

Bogey: One over par.

Bunker or sand trap: A depression in the fairway or a large hole filled with sand. These may be located on the fairway or at the edge of the green.

Casual water: Water standing on the golf course because of rain or excessive sprinkling. Not considered a hazard. Ball can be moved—but not closer to the hole—without penalty.

Divot: Turf taken by the club after contacting the ball on the hit. This should always be replaced by the player.

Double bogey: Two over par.

Eagle: Two under par.

Fairway: The cut (mowed) area from the tee to the putting green.

Fat: Taking too much divot by hitting the ball and the ground at the same time or hitting behind the ball and taking just turf.

Flagstick: A stick with a flag attached to designate the position of the hole on the putting green.

Green: The closely cut grass area with the cup for putting at the end of the fairway.

Gross: The total number of strokes it takes a player to play a round of golf.

Handicap: The method used to determine a player's ability based on the following: the best ten of the last twenty, eighteen-hole scores are averaged. Par for the course is subtracted from the golfer's average score. Then approximately 85 per cent of the difference is taken. This is the player's handicap. Example: Ten best scores average eighty-two. Par is seventy-five. The difference is seven. Eighty-five per cent of seven is 5.9 or a six handicap. Differential charts which take into consideration the degree of difficulty of the various courses played are now frequently used in figuring handicaps.

Hole-in-one or **an ace:** The ball goes into the cup on the hit from the tee.

Hole out: Getting the ball in the cup.

Honor: The first player to tee off. Except for the first hole where there is a toss for honor, the player who wins the hole has the honor on the next tee.

Hook: The ball starts out straight and curves to the left of the intended line.

Mark: Placing a ball marker where the ball was located on the green in order to allow other players to putt over this same line before you putt.

Match play: Two players playing hole by hole. The winner of the match is the person who wins the most holes.

Medal play: Also called stroke play. The player who has the fewest total number of strokes for the round is the winner.

Net: The total number of strokes it takes to play a round of golf minus the handicap of the player equals the net score. Example: a player shoots 85. Her handicap is 6. Her net score is 79.

Out-of-bounds: Outside the boundary markers of the course.

Par: Standard of excellence in scoring based on the length of the hole and allowing two strokes for putting.

Pull: The ball travels to the left of the intended line without curving.

Push: The ball travels to the right of the intended line without curving.

Rough: The uncut area on either side of the fairway.

Shank: Hitting the ball on the neck of the club and making it veer off sharply to the right.

Slice: The ball starts out straight and curves to the right of the intended line.

Tee or teeing area: The starting place for a hole. Two markers designate the area. A tee is also a cone-shaped piece of wood on which the ball is elevated for the first hit.

Top: The club head contacts the ball above the center and therefore the ball will travel low or on the ground.

Water hazard: A lake or stream.

Selected References

Bell, Peggy Kirk. *A Woman's Way to Better Golf*. Norwalk, Conn.: Golf Digest Book Service, 1966.

Hogan, Ben. *Modern Fundamentals of Golf*. Norwalk, Conn.: Golf Digest Book Service, 1957.

National Golf Foundation. *How to Improve Your Golf*. Chicago: The Athletic Institute, 1965.

Sports Illustrated. *Golf Tips from the Top Professionals*. Louisville, Ky.: Fawcett-Haynes, 1966.

United States Golf Association. *The Rules of Golf*. (published annually). New York: the Association.

Wright, Mickey. *Play Golf the Wright Way*. Garden City, N.Y.: Doubleday, 1962.

Chapter 9

Gymnastics *Rita Narcisian*

History. Goals. Safety. SKILLS: TUMBLING. FLOOR EXERCISE: Standing Positions, Positions in the Air, Low Level Positions. UNEVEN PARALLEL BARS: Mounts, Held Positions, Swinging Movements, Dismounts. BALANCE BEAM: Mounts, Locomotor Moves, Turns, Aerial Movements, Tumbling, Stationary Positions, Dismounts. SIDE HORSE VAULTING: Elements of Vaulting, Mounts, Vaults.

Gymnastic activities are thrilling to perform and beautiful to observe. The participant develops poise, balance, flexibility, and rhythm. Opportunities for competition in gymnastics challenge the highly skilled, and the satisfactions gained from recreational participation appeal to the novice. The four Olympic events for women are balance beam, floor exercise, uneven parallel bars, and vaulting. Tumbling and trampolining as well as ball and hoop routines are sometimes included in a gymnastics program for women.

History

Primitive man, in moments of play, was probably the creator of a crude kind of gymnastics. The first written record of gymnastics, as found in ancient Chinese history, indicates that the activity was used for medicinal and military purposes. Evidence of gymnastic activities has also been found in the early civilizations of Egypt, Japan, Persia, and India. Later the Greeks and Romans sponsored highly developed gymnastic programs aimed at preparing men for war. The Cretans held tumbling demonstrations prior to their bull fights.

There is little evidence of organized gymnastics in medieval Europe, but at about the time of the American colonization, gymnastic exercises were becoming popular. In 1774, in his school in Germany, Johann Basedow was the first to include gymnastics as part of the curriculum. Beginning in 1785, Johann Guts-Muths taught gymnastics at the Schnepfenthal Educational Institute for fifty years, which together with his literary contributions on the subject, earned him the title of "grandfather" of German gymnastics. Much of his philosophy is contained in his *Gymnastics for the Young*, the first published text on gymnastics. Rope ladders, climbing ropes, balancing skills, and a great variety of stunts were included in his program.

Friedrich Jahn of Germany, Per Henrik Ling of Sweden, and Franz Nachtegall of Denmark, younger contemporaries of GutsMuths, were fathers of gymnastics for their respective countries. Jahn founded the Turnverein, developed this organization's system of gymnastics, and is credited with designing the first balance beams

Rita Narcisian earned her bachelor's degree at South Dakota State University and her master's degree at the University of Colorado. She is presently teaching in the Jefferson County Public School System in Colorado. In addition to teaching gymnastics, Mrs. Narcisian has served on the DGWS State Gymnastics Committee and assists in judging gymnastic competition at local, state, and regional meets.

and vaulting bucks. Ling invented much of the Swedish apparatus and stressed group activities which were performed on command. Nachtegall was instrumental in establishing the teaching of gymnastics in the schools of Denmark and was the first Director of Gymnastics for all Denmark.

European immigrants, especially those from Germany and the Scandinavian countries, brought their gymnastic systems with them to the United States. In 1865 the American Turners organized a gymnastic college, which is now affiliated with the University of Indiana.

In the past, the term *gymnastics* was used to denote almost any kind of physical activity; today the scope is clearly defined with specific events for men and women. As a sport for women, the activity continues to increase in popularity, and since the early 1960's opportunities for competition among women have rapidly multiplied. Gymnastics is included in most school programs today.

Goals

Gymnastics offers a never ending challenge ranging from elementary skills to Olympic competition. Simple stunts and tumbling form the basis for many gymnastic skills. Ballet movements, which are also among the fundamentals of gymnastics, contribute to the grace and beauty of movement in floor exercise events.

The goals for a beginner are limitless. She enjoys the exhilaration and satisfaction gained from increasing control and agility while she works toward more advanced skills. The beginner can appreciate her own progress if she remembers that simple stunts well performed are beautiful. For example, the backward roll becomes polished as part of a routine when a leap and backward fall lead into the backward roll and rise into a toe stand.

After mastering a stunt one should add a variation of that stunt, or a different stunt, until a routine is developed. After learning the straddle backward roll, for example, one may perform in sequence (1) a backward roll, (2) a straddle backward roll, and (3) a backward roll. This makes all three rolls appear more interesting.

One should think, know, and feel the way a stunt is performed. The gymnast must have control of her body and its parts at all times, whether moving or holding a pose. Balance and control are significant elements of form. The toes should be pointed every time that the leg is extended. The legs should be together and straight unless the stunt requires a bending or a separation. The trunk should be straight with the head up. The arms should be straight when used for support.

Practice is of paramount importance, and the basic stunts for each area are the foundation for more advanced skills. When a stunt is performed, practice will be a determining factor in the level of skill of that performance.

Costume

Leotards are the accepted costume for gymnastics. Ankle length tights may also be worn. The performer may work either barefooted or with gymnastic slippers. Ballet slippers should not be used, because they do not give sufficient traction.

Safety

The performer should make a routine check of all equipment that she will use. The balance beam, horse, and bars must be adjusted to the proper height for each performer and must be properly stationed on the floor. The lock nuts on the bars should be checked frequently, because constant vibration can loosen them. Areas surrounding the pieces of equipment must be sufficiently padded. Tumbling mats must be thick enough, firmly anchored to prevent slipping, and joined together so that there is no floor space between mats. The performer must remove all jewelry, and the hands should be chalked to prevent slipping. If footwear is slippery, rosin can be dusted on the soles to give proper traction.

To ensure safety, the performer must be aided by persons who act as spotters; knowing when she needs assistance and arranging for spotters is her obligation. Never perform unless there is adequate assistance from competent spotters. The performer must know specific spotting techniques for each stunt and should be able to assist others. There is often more than one way to spot for the various stunts, but certain fundamental principles apply to all methods: a) The spotter must know the stunt, know the correct method for spotting the particular stunt, and focus her entire attention on the performer; b) The spotter must assume a wide base of support in order to ensure stability; c) The spotter must bend the knees and use the strong muscles of the thighs to provide the strength needed to help the performer and to avoid straining her own back; and d) for most stunts the spotter needs to be the same size or larger than the performer. The performer should always warm up before performing difficult stunts and stunts that involve considerable stretching.

Skills

TUMBLING

Tumbling, the performance of a sequence of stunts on a mat, is a basic skill requirement for the gymnast inasmuch as many of the same types of movements are used on apparatus. Tumbling can also be included as a special event in gymnastic competition.

It is customary to follow a progression or series in learning stunts, but no single progression of stunts would be satisfactory for all individuals. The degree of difficulty of the various stunts will differ according to the performer's experience, body build, and interest and motivation. However, the forward roll, backward roll, handstand, and kip are fundamental stunts that should be learned prior to attempts at more advanced tumbling. The forward and backward rolls are not only stunts in themselves but also serve as safety measures. Falling backward out of a handstand can be prevented by tucking the head and doing a forward roll. The handstand should be learned early because many other tumbling stunts also require the performer to support her own weight with her arms while in the inverted position. The kip is an important fundamental skill because it is used with other stunts and from it one learns control of body parts and transfer of energy.

Forward roll

Squat with the knees between the hands, which are placed on the mat with the fingers pointing forward (Fig. 1). Tuck the head to the chest; then bring the head down to the mat as the hips rise. Bend the arms until the shoulders

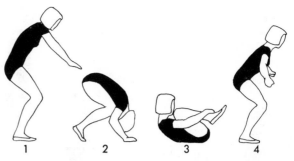

(1) Forward roll.

and upper back touch the mat. Push with the feet and hands and roll over to a stand.

SPOTTING. Stand beside the performer, facing opposite to the direction of her roll. Tuck performer's head and lift her hips if needed.

Coaching tips include

1. Round things roll easily. Keep the head and knees tucked to the chest and the back rounded.
2. Pushing with the hands enables one to roll past the neck without putting undue pressure on it.
3. Failure to roll in a straight line may be caused by pushing harder with one hand or foot than with the other.

The *variations* are

1. Stand—forward roll—stand.
2. Run—forward roll—stand.
3. Straight leg forward roll. In the starting position keep the legs straight; tuck them only when coming to a stand.
4. Running dive—forward roll. After the run, spring from the floor and take the force of the dive with the arms. Pike the legs (hips bent with knees straight) and roll, bend knees to come to stand. Diving over a rolled mat is helpful for the beginner.
5. Straddle forward roll. Stand in a wide straddle position and, bending forward, place the hands on the mat close to the shoulders. Tuck and roll while keeping the legs in spread position. Push hard to come to a stand.

Backward roll

Start in a squat position and roll backward onto the back and up to the shoulders while keeping the knees close to the chest (Fig. 2).

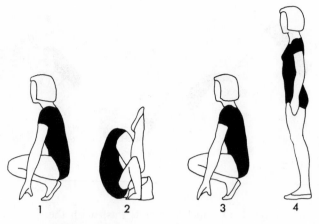

(2) Backward roll.

(3) Tip-up.

(4) Tripod.

(5) Headstand

Then push hard with the hands and rock back to the feet. After the beginner has rocked back and forth several times she is ready to try the complete roll. Assuming the squat position with knees to chest, continue to roll backward while placing the palms flat on the mat with fingers pointing toward the shoulders. Keeping tucked, roll onto the shoulders and push hard with the hands over to the feet into a stand.

SPOTTING. Stand facing the same direction as the performer. As the hips roll off the mat, assist by lifting them to get the body weight off the neck and head.

Coaching tips include

1. The beginner may try a backward roll downhill on an inclined board covered with a mat.
2. Keep the body round by tucking the knees and chin close to the chest.
3. Push hard with the hands to lift the weight off the neck.

The *variations* are

1. Long sit—backward roll—squat stand.
2. Straddle stand—backward roll—squat stand.
3. Straddle stand—backward roll—straddle stand.
4. Straight stand—backward roll—straight stand.

From a standing position, keep the knees straight and round the upper back while lowering the hips backward to sit on the floor. Place the hands beside the knees, arms extended with hands ready to touch flat on the floor to cushion the fall. As the hips touch the mat, quickly shift the hands above the shoulders for a push-off. Keep the legs straight and roll backward to the shoulders and on around to land on the feet.

Tip-up

The Tip-up is a lead-up for the headstand (Fig. 3). Place the hands on the mat shoulder-width apart. Put the knees on the elbows and tip forward until balance is gained. Keep the head up.

SPOTTING. Kneel at the performer's side and spot at the shoulder with a hand ready to keep her from falling forward.

Tripod

The *Tripod* is another lead-up skill for the headstand (Fig. 4). Place the forehead on the

(6) Handstand.

mat with the hands shoulder-width apart forming a triangle. Place the knees on the elbows, toes pointed.

SPOTTING. Same as for tip-up.

Headstand

From the tripod position, pull the bent legs close to the body and maintain balance (Fig. 5). After balancing in the tuck position, slowly extend the legs upward.

SPOTTING. Kneel at the performer's side and spot at the hip to help her find balance; then as she extends to a full headstand spot at the thigh.

Coaching tips include

1. Keep the weight on the forehead, not on the top of the head; keep the neck rigid.
2. The hips must be in a vertical line above the head.
3. Only a very slight arching of the back is needed.

The *variations* are

1. Headstand into forward roll.
2. Layout headstand. Lie face down on the mat. Place the hands shoulder-width apart and put the forehead on the mat to form a triangle with the hands. Push with the hands and draw the hips up and over the shoulders, keeping the body in a piked position. When the hips are over the shoulders, begin to extend the legs to a straight position. As the legs straighten, the hips must move back over the triangle formed by the hands and head.
3. Headstand with a toe to knee touch. After

(7) Handstand.

maintaining a momentary headstand, slide the right foot down until the toes touch the left knee.

4. Headstand—scissors. From a headstand position, straddle the legs forward and backward or from side to side.

Handstand

Place the hands on the mat shoulder-width apart with the shoulders over the hands (Figs. 6 and 7). The legs are in a forward stride position. The front leg (the pushing leg) is slightly

(8) Kip.

bent and close to the body. The rear or throwing leg is straight. The beginner should kick the throwing leg up and push hard against the floor with the other leg to achieve a momentary handstand, then lower one leg at a time. The hips must be lifted for the handstand, and the back is slightly arched. After the push-off the head is raised to check body rotation. With experience the performer will be able to hold the handstand for some time.

SPOTTING. A beginner needs two spotters, one on either side, facing her. The assistant on the right places her right hand under the performer's right shoulder while the assistant to the left uses her left hand. As the performer kicks up, they reach for her legs at about the knee joint. After the beginner has improved, just one spotter can stand in front of her to catch her legs and help her find her balance.

Coaching tips include

1. The performer must be able to support her own weight on her arms; and back and abdominal muscles must be firm during the handstand.
2. The kick-up must not be too vigorous or the legs will go beyond the head, causing loss of balance.
3. If there is a tendency for the legs to overthrow, lift the head.

The *variations* are

1. Straight stand—handstand—forward roll.
2. Backward roll—handstand (back extension). Start the backward roll, but as the legs come over the head in a piked position, extend them into the air, at the same time extending the elbows and pushing hard with the hands into a handstand.

   Spotting: Stand on either side of the performer. As she begins to extend her legs, grasp the leg near the knee and lift upward.
3. Handstand push up. Do a handstand against the wall and bend the arms slightly. Then extend the entire body fully, stretching as tall as possible. This exercise will aid the performer in improving arm thrust and push from the floor for stunts such as the kip, handsprings, and headspring.

Kip or snap-up

The performer rises from a sitting position to the feet by rolling backward to a pike position and snapping the legs through and under while arching the whole body (Fig. 8). From a long sit, roll backward to a candle stick (hips, knees, and feet in line above the shoulders); place the hands on the mat near the shoulders. Then drop the legs into a pike position over the head while keeping the knees straight and hips high. Snap the legs forward and down toward the mat while arching the back and pushing hard against the mat with the hands, head, and shoulders. Bring the feet under the body and snap the upper body forward to a slight squat, then stand.

SPOTTING. Two spotters are needed for the beginner, one kneeling on each side. The spotters place one hand under the performer's shoulder and the other hand under her hip. As the performer begins to snap her legs over, the spotters lift straight up first at the hip, then at the shoulder.

Coaching tips include

1. This stunt must be done with a quick start from the legs and hips while the head remains back.
2. The leg snap forward and the push from the mat must be well timed.
3. The feet must drop well under the body for a successful landing.

Cartwheel

Stand with the left side to the mat for a cartwheel to the left (Fig. 9). Lift the left leg, then place the left foot on the mat while swinging the right leg sideward-upward. Bend to the side and place the left hand down. Lift the right leg up forcefully and put the right hand on the mat. The right leg continues to swing over as the left leg pushes away from the mat. The legs remain split in the air and the right foot lands first, followed by the left. End facing the same direction as in the beginning.

SPOTTING. Stand at the performer's back with the left hand crossed over the right to grasp the right side of the performer's waist. The right hand grasps the left side of the waist. Assist by lifting at the waist so that the hips are over the shoulders.

Coaching tips include

1. The rhythm of the cartwheel is an even four count beat. The left hand is 1; the right, 2; the right foot, 3; the left foot, 4.
2. Arms and back should be straight and the head high; legs should stretch upward with toes pointed.
3. The hands and feet are placed in a straight line, approximately the same distance apart on the mat.
4. The cartwheel should be learned so that it may be performed both to the right and to the left.

The *variations* are

1. Cartwheel from a run.
2. Star cartwheel. As the right leg reaches a position straight over the body, bring the left up to it, tapping the toes together. Bring the right leg down first and finish as in a regular cartwheel.

Round-off

The round-off is used to change direction from forward into backward motion in order to do backward stunts (Fig. 10). The round-off should not be attempted until the participant can perform the handstand with a snap-down (legs together coming down) and the cartwheel.

Take a run and skip on the right foot while lifting the left leg. The weight shifts to the left foot and the left hand is placed on the mat as in a cartwheel. Then the right hand is placed in front and across the left hand as the body makes a quarter turn. The legs are held overhead in a handstand position for an instant before the legs snap down into another quarter turn to end facing the opposite direction from the starting position.

SPOTTING. None is required, because it is not really possible to assist with this stunt.

Coaching tips include

1. In this stunt the skip is needed with the take-off in order to increase forward momentum.
2. Keep the head up and elbows straight.
3. The round-off may be executed either to the right or to the left.

(9) Cartwheel.

1   2   3   4   5   6   7

(10) Round-off.

The *variations* are

1. The round-off is often followed by a back handspring.
2. The round-off can also be done with only one hand on the mat.

Front limber

The front limber is a lead-up skill needed for learning the springs; the prerequisite for this skill is the ability to do a backbend (Fig. 11). The front limber is a handstand with a drop forward into the backbend, followed by a push-off with the hands to come to standing position.

SPOTTING. It is well to have two spotters for the first few times. Assist the performer's

(11) Front limber.

descent into the backbend by placing a hand under the hips, then aid her to the standing position by lifting her shoulders.

Coaching tips include ,

1. Keep the head back. The arms and head should be the last to come up.
2. If the momentum is not broken it is easier to come to a stand. As soon as the feet touch the mat the performer should immediately push with her hands in order to come up.

Headspring

The headspring is a turn over from a head-stand to land on the feet (Fig. 12A and 12B). It is best to begin learning this skill from a rolled mat before working directly on the flat mat.

Place the hands and head on the mat and, with a two foot take-off, push to a piked position, balancing momentarily. As the hips begin to move forward, whip the legs over the head, giving a strong push-off with the hands at the same time. Land on the feet in a squat position.

SPOTTING. A spotter should be on each side of the mat to assist by lifting the shoulders and hips.

Coaching tips include

1. The hips lead up.
2. Keep the head back. The ears are covered by the arms as the body rises.
3. The pike position is essential. The knees should not bend prior to landing.

The *variations* are

(12A) Headspring.

(12B) Headspring.

1. Running headspring over a rolled mat.
2. Headspring on a flat mat. When doing this stunt on the flat mat, the body is supported primarily by the arms; the head barely touches the mat.
3. Running headspring on a flat mat.

Front walkover

Place the hands on the mat as for a handstand (Fig. 13). Kick up, assuming a forward-backward split with the legs. As the first foot comes around to the floor, push off the mat with the hands and remain slightly arched, then reach forward with the second leg. Push hard with the foot that landed first to return to a stand.

SPOTTING. Place one hand under the back and the other under the leading leg. Help to lift the leg up and over. A second spotter could be used to grasp the second leg, hold it up, and pull it forward. This will force the performer to use this leg in pulling up. The hands should leave the mat before the second leg is three quarters of the way over.

Coaching tips include

1. Keep the head back.
2. The arms remain stretched over the head until the movement is completed.
3. The legs must remain split, with the last leg coming over to touch the floor after the arms have pushed off the mat.
4. The movement must be continuous. Do not stop when the first foot lands.
5. The hips lead in coming up.

(13) Front walkover.

The *variations* are

1. Running walkover.
2. Scissors walkover. From the split, both legs meet in the handstand position. The leading leg then remains stationary as the second leg touches the mat first. Continue as a regular walkover.

Front handspring

The front handspring is a combination of run, to a handstand, and around to a straight stand (Fig. 14). Little back arch or joint bending is needed. A short run and skip into the handstand initiates the circular motion, which must be continuous. After taking a hop with the right foot, the left foot contacts the mat and the right

Part 1

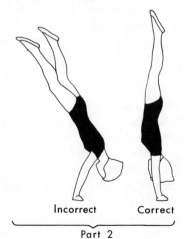

Incorrect   Correct

Part 2

(14) Front handspring.

1   2   3   4

(15) Back walkover.

leg is swung upward. Then the hands touch the mat and the left leg is thrust vigorously off the mat. As the body reaches the handstand position the legs continue swinging on around. If the motion has been continuous throughout, the momentum of the over-throw of the legs and hips as they swing past the shoulders rotates the body around to the standing position. The hands are on the mat very briefly in conjunction with this over-throw and shift of balance.

In order to achieve forceful rotation of the body in the momentary handstand of this stunt, it is essential to keep the arms straight, the shoulders above the hands, and the head down. This can be practiced with an approach, handstand with pause, and return back to a stand in the starting direction if a spotter is ready to catch the back of the performer's thighs and push her back to her feet.

SPOTTING. A spotter is needed on either side of the mat. Both spotters must stand close to the performer and, as she is in her handstand, must grasp her upper arm and reach under her back to aid her in the turnover.

Back walkover

Stand with the feet in a forward stride position with the weight on the back leg (Fig. 15). Leading with the arms and head, arch into a back bend. As the hands touch the mat, the rear foot pushes forcefully against the mat and the head is raised. The legs remain in an open split. Land first with one leg, then the other.

SPOTTING. Kneel at the performer's side and place one hand under the shoulder and the other

under the thigh. If there is only one spotter, she should kneel on the side of the leg that lifts first and assist in lifting that leg up and over while the other hand lifts at the small of the back.

Coaching tips include

1. Keep the head back.
2. Keep the movement continuous. Start to lift the forward leg before the hands touch.

Back handspring

Start in a standing position with the feet slightly apart (Fig. 16). The first movement is a bending of the hips and knees, as if sinking into a chair, while swinging the arms down and back. There is approximately a 90-degree angle at the knee and hip joints; then the arms swing vigorously forward and up overhead and the legs push forcefully up and back. As the hands touch the mat, the body comes to a momentary handstand. Then the snap-down is made to a standing position.

SPOTTING. It is best to learn this advanced stunt with the use of an overhead safety belt or a hand belt. If a belt is not available, two spotters must work with the performer until the stunt has been learned. The spotters may either kneel or squat while they grasp the performer's suit at the waist with one hand and reach under the thigh with the other. The hand at the waist provides support, while the hand at the thigh assists the leg whip. After the stunt is partially learned, the two spotters may grasp a rolled towel placed at the performer's lower back, thus assisting with the upward spring. Before using this method,

(16) Back handspring.

the spotters must be certain that the performer's arms will not collapse.

Coaching tips include

1. If the performer is having difficulty moving backward into the spring, put a piece of tape on the mat and tell her to keep pulling her head back until she sees the tape.
2. Once the stunt has been learned, the motion should be continuous; there should be no pause at the handstand position.

FLOOR EXERCISE

Floor exercise is a part of gymnastic competition for women and can include both a compulsory and an optional composition. This

(17) Floor exercise pose.

event is made up of balancing, tumbling and dance movements, and agility exercises. The competitor chooses her own routine for the optional composition. The four factors to be considered in a composition are floor area, time, music, and the elements of movement used in the composition.

The floor area for the event is limited to a space of about 40 feet square (12 meters). The surface may be a wooden floor or an area covered with a thin mat. The performer must, at some time during the routine, cover all parts of the floor, i.e., the four corners and the center. Figure 18 shows some simple examples of floor designs.

A floor exercise routine must not be shorter than one minute or longer than one minute and a half. The performer's score is penalized if her routine does not take place within these time limits.

Music must accompany the floor exercise routine. At the national competitive level the music must be performed by one instrument only. If possible, a routine should be composed, then music written especially to complement the particular routine. However, because this is often not feasible, a routine may be composed and music chosen afterward, or the performer may choose her music first and design a routine to accompany it. It is important for the routine and music to fit together harmoniously. Many recordings are now available with musical selections arranged especially for floor exercise routines.

The beginner derives satisfaction from learning separate skill movements that can later be used in floor exercise compositions. She can also learn to perform routines that have been planned for her own level of ability.[1] Later, however, she may enjoy creating and performing a composition of her own.

To design a floor exercise composition, the performer should use variety in direction, level, and pattern. A routine should have contrast in quality and range of movement, as well as smooth transitions, in order to be pleasing in appearance. Directional change should appear to flow out of a movement and create the impression of developmental sequence. Movement can vary from flowing to staccato, from light to forceful. Level, too, may be varied, with positions ranging from lying on the floor, sitting, kneeling or standing, to positions off the floor. A performer will not immediately find the best combination of skills, but after experimentation a logical composition will result.

Range of movement in a composition can vary from small to expansive. As the performer increases her flexibility through gradual stretching and regularity of practice, a greater range of movement or amplitude is possible in performance. Certain skills require great flexibility, although all are enhanced by it. A simple arabesque, for example, is more beautiful if full amplitude is used; the raised leg should be very high with the upper trunk arched and steady.

After an individual acquires a repertoire of skills she can create sequences according to her interest and ability. She draws on her knowledge of tumbling skills and dance, continuing to develop new skills and combinations of movements. The new skills should first be practiced and perfected on a mat; then they may be combined with other movements and used in a floor exercise composition.

Movements used in floor exercises may be classified in a variety of ways. Floor exercise composition includes locomotor movements, tumbling, dance, and floor exercise movements. These divisions overlap, the latter being largely an outgrowth of the first three. For the beginner, awareness of these categories can highlight the possibilities of movement as it is used in floor exercise. The locomotor movements—walk, run, skip, hop, jump, slide, and gallop—are used in many different ways for the floor pattern of a routine. Tumbling stunts presented in the previous section, especially the cartwheel, walk-

[1] For examples of floor exercise combinations and routines see the 1965–67 DGWS *Gymnastics Guide*. Washington, D.C.: AAHPER, 1201 Sixteenth St., N.W.

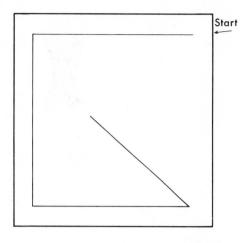

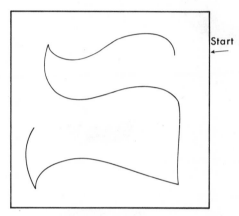

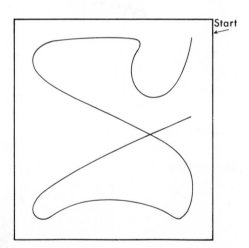

(18) Floor designs.

over, front handspring, back walkover, and forward and backward rolls, are used in a variety of combinations and can involve variations of each of the stunts. Dance movements also contribute much to the routines. As used in floor exercise compositions, tumbling and dance can complement each other. Such combinations

(19) Toe stand.

(20) Swedish fall.

(21) Scale or arabesque.

(22) Body wave.

1   2   3   4

make a pleasing presentation through the harmonious blending of varied elements. Floor exercise positions are often static positions, most of them to be held only momentarily and never longer than three seconds; they lend variety and beauty to the composition.

One way to classify floor exercise positions is by the level in which they are performed, such as low level, standing, and aerial positions. To give the beginner some understanding of this type of movement the following examples are presented.

Floor exercise in standing positions

Toe stand. From standing position rise to toes and extend the arms outward at shoulder height with palms down (Fig. 19).

Swedish fall (forward drop). From a standing position, fall forward and land on the hands, which are placed in line with the shoulders. The hands are brought forward with arms straight, then the elbows are bent to take up the force of the fall. One leg is lifted as the fall is executed (Fig. 20).

Scale or arabesque. From a standing position, one arm is extended forward and the other sideward. The trunk is bent forward at the hips while the leg opposite the forward arm is back and high (Fig. 21).

Body wave. From standing with feet together, bend the knees and hips and swing arms forward, then swing arms backward, arch the back, and straighten the legs; continue the arm swing to sideward-upward while rising on the toes (Fig. 22).

Floor exercise positions in the air

The performer leaves the floor in a leap or a jump (pushing from the floor with one or both feet) for the following skills.

Stag leap. While in the air the right leg is extended and the left knee is bent so that the left foot touches the right knee. The left arm is overhead and the right arm is extended sideward (Fig. 23).

Cat leap. While in the air, bend the knees sideward so that the soles of the feet are together under the body (Fig. 24).

Tuck leap. In the air assume a tuck position with head forward and knees bent while extending the arms backward and upward (Fig. 25).

Back arch leap. Jump and arch the entire body. Arm positions may vary. One arm can swing backward while the other is extended upward or to the side (Fig. 26).

Low level positions

Knee scale. Kneel on one knee with arm on the same side extended forward; extend the other leg backward and upward as high as possible (Fig. 27).

Split. From a front stride, slide forward until both legs are completely extended, with the weight supported by the entire length of both legs. Trunk is erect with arms extended sideward or in some combination of forward, sideward, or backward (Fig. 28).

V seat. From a long sitting position, the legs are raised upward while the trunk leans backward into a V or pike position. The weight is on the seat and the arms are extended sideward or upward (Fig. 29).

Bridge. From a lying position on the back, place hands on floor near shoulders while placing the feet on the floor with knees bent. Push upward with the arms and hips, straighten the arms, and arch the back. The body forms a bridge (Fig. 30).

Valdez. Must first be able to do back walkover. From a long sit, bend left knee and place foot close to buttock. Right hand is on floor near hip and left arm is forward. Push hard with right hand and left foot as left arm and right foot are thrown up and over the head, leading into a back handstand (Fig. 31).

Dance in floor exercise

Dance movements contribute much to the gymnast's performance, particularly in free exercises and on the balance beam. The person who is well trained in dance will exhibit correct posture and fluid movement. The increased balance, flexibility, and poise resulting from the use of dance movements is a definite asset.

Modern dance movements, such as the contraction and release of the trunk muscles as the impetus radiates outward from the hips and trunk, will assist the gymnast in the quality of her movements through space. The freedom of the body gained from trunk swinging movements, falls, and high leaps lends variety in the use of levels.

Ballet training helps one to have precision in the complete extension of legs and trunk as well as finesse in the controlled movement of the arms. Because many of the movements in

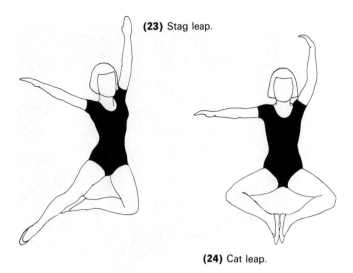

(23) Stag leap.

(24) Cat leap.

(25) Tuck leap.

(26) Back arch leap.

(27) Knee scale.

(28) Split.

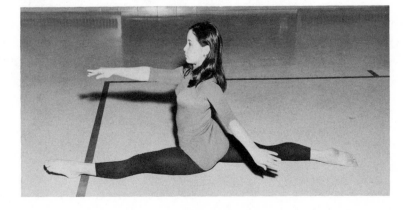

(29) V-seat.

(30) Bridge.

(31) Valdez.

1

2   3

gymnastics employ ballet positions and terms, the performer who lacks ballet training needs to acquire an understanding of the ballet terms that are commonly used.[2] This study will lend insight into the many possibilities for composing routines as well as developing a greater awareness useful in effective performance.

UNEVEN PARALLEL BARS

It is thrilling to swing from one height to another—this is what one does on the uneven parallel bars. A routine on the uneven parallels consists of swinging movements combined with grasps and regrasps as the performer swings from one bar to the other. The high bar is $7\frac{1}{2}$ feet from the floor and the low bar is at 5 feet. The distance between the bars can be adjusted for individual students.

The unevens did not come into general use until after they had been used in the 1952 Olympics. Events on the unevens are designed specifically for women; they require strength, balance, timing, and courage, but do not require as much strength as the even parallel bars, or as much flexibility and grace as the floor exercises. The uneven parallel bars do, however, require more arm, shoulder, and abdominal strength than most of the women's events.

It is important first of all to get used to this piece of apparatus, particularly the high bar. The beginner can start with holding briefly such positions as easy one bar movements, later combining them with a mount and a dismount. After learning several variations, one goes on to short sequences in order to get the feeling of continuous movement that should accompany performance on the unevens. One must be able to perform the simple movements well before advancing to more complicated skills.

Safety

1. Before mounting, the equipment should be checked to see that supports are secure and that mats completely surround and cover the base of the bars.
2. The hands should always be chalked to prevent slipping.
3. If a beat board is used for mounting, it should

---

[2] See Blance Jessen Drury and Andrea Bodo Schmid, "Dance for Gymnasts," *Gymnastics for Women* (Palo Alto, Calif.: The National Press, 1966), Chap. 2; and Ernestine Russell Carter "Ballet in Gymnastics," DGWS *Gymnastics Guide*, 1963–65 (Washington, D.C.: AAHPER, 1201 Sixteenth St., N.W.).

be removed immediately following the mount.

4. If a new skill is being learned, two spotters should be on hand. The spotter should check the elbow and the arm at a point just above the wrist to keep the supporting arm straight. Other details on spotting for specific skills will be mentioned with the individual skills.

The ultimate goal with work on the uneven parallel bars is the development of a routine. Although there is no time limit for the performance of the routine, most are from one to two minutes in duration. Movements on the uneven bars consist of mounts, swings involving the low and high bars with grasp changes, momentarily held positions, and dismounts. Only poses unique to the parallel bars should be used, and these should be held very briefly unless they precede a difficult sequence, in which case the performer may pause slightly longer to prepare mentally for the movements to follow. Also, when developing a routine, change of direction is important.

The *hand grasps* and some of the most frequently used mounts, held positions, swinging movements, and dismounts will be described. As soon as a new skill is learned, it should be worked into a combination of movements. There are four basic hand grasps for the unevens (Fig. 32):

1. The regular or over-grip. The palms are on top of the bar and are turned away from the performer. The thumbs may wrap around the bar or remain beside the fingers.
2. Reverse or under-grip. The palms are under the bar turned toward the performer. The thumbs may wrap around the bar or remain beside the fingers.
3. Mixed grip. One hand assumes a regular grip, the other a reverse grip. This grip is used for turns.
4. Dislocate. Stand with back to the low bar. Reach back and around the bar with fingers on top. Thumbs may wrap around the bar or remain beside the fingers. This grip is used for a few specific stunts.

Mounts

There are many ways to mount or get on the uneven parallel bars. One may mount either the low or high bar from the front, side, or diagonal position; from between the bars; from a stand-

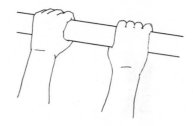

1. Regular or Overgrip

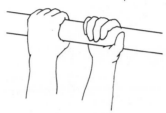

2. Reverse or Undergrip

3. Mixed Grip

4. Dislocate

(32) Hand grasps for uneven parallel bars.

(33) Straight arm support.

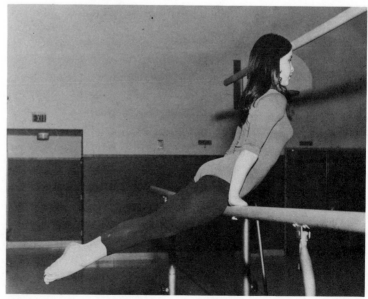

(34) Long hang on high bar.

(35) Long hang with wide straddle.

(36) Back pull-over mount.

ing position; following a run; or by means of a spring from a Reuther board.

Straight arm support. Stand facing the low bar (or the high bar) and use a regular grip with hands shoulder-width apart. Jump up while pushing down with the arms so that the upper thighs rest on the bar. Make sure the elbows are straight. Arch the body slightly (Fig. 33).

Spotting. Two spotters, one on either side of the performer, grasp her at the hip and below the elbow to aid in lifting and to make sure that the elbows remain straight.

Coaching tips include

1. Coordination of the leg and arm push is important and comes with practice.
2. Keep the head up.

Long hang on the high bar. Stand under the high bar facing the low bar (Fig. 34). Jump up and grasp the high bar with a regular grip. Arch the body slightly. A wide straddle position can be assumed with the legs (Fig. 35).

Spotting. A spotter at each side of the performer grasps her at the waist to aid in lifting her to the bar.

Coaching tips include

1. After positioning oneself, jump without looking at the high bar. Simply know that it is there.
2. Use a Reuther board if necessary.
3. Do not swing with the mount.

Back pull-over. Stand close to and facing the low bar (or high bar) with the hands in a

1   2   3   4

regular grip. Start the motion by swinging one leg forward and upward, immediately following with the other leg. Assume a pike position, head erect, and circle the bar feet first with the body finishing in a straight arm support (Fig. 36).

Coaching tips include

1. The kick must swing the hips up close to the bar. If the hips fall away from the bar, the performer will not be able to swing around and over the bar.
2. When going into the straight arm support, the legs should extend and the body arch. It is bad form to let the legs swing forward and then back into the arch position.

Cross seat mount. Stand between the bars facing their length and jump to a hang with one hand in over-grip on the high bar, the other on the low bar. With the arms supporting the weight, pike the legs over the low bar, and make a one-quarter turn into the cross seat mount with back to the high bar (Fig. 37).

Spotting. If spotters are located on either side of the performer, the spotter standing next to the low bar can aid the performer in keeping her elbow straight, while the other spotter aids in lifting the legs over the bar.

Coaching tips include

1. The hand on the low bar should be directly under the shoulder with the elbow straight. The hand on the high bar should be slightly ahead of the other hand.
2. The pike should be from the hips with knees straight and toes pointed.

Held positions

Held positions should be only momentary pauses between swinging movements. However, when practicing a new position, it is well for the beginner to hold the position for a longer period of time in order to develop a feeling of balance and stability. Held positions are preceded by a mount or some appropriate swinging movement that will lead smoothly into the held position.

V seat. Sit on the low bar facing the length of the bars, grasping the high bar with one hand and the low bar with the other. Raise the legs to a *V* position. As skill increases, let go of the low bar and extend that arm to the side (Fig. 38).

Spotting. Stand outside the low bar and grasp the elbow of the arm on the low bar to aid in stability.

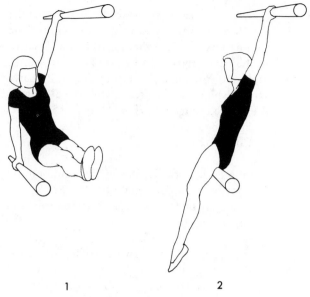

1   2

(37) Cross seat mount.

(38) V-seat.

(39) One-leg squat.

(40) Scale.

One-leg squat. Stand on the low bar facing the length of the bar. Squat with the weight on one foot and extend the other leg (the one closer to the high bar) and hold above the bar. Grasp both high and low bars in learning this skill. Later only the high bar is grasped, while the other arm is extended to the side (Fig. 39, page 157).

Spotting. Same as for *V* seat.

Coaching tips include

1. One should practice the one-leg squat on the floor before attempting it on the bar.
2. The body must be balanced directly over the supporting foot.

Scale. Stand on the low bar facing the length of the bar. Grasp the high bar with the closer hand and extend the leg on the same side backward. The entire body should be arched. Position of the free arm may vary (Fig. 40).

Spotting. None is needed. The performer, with her hand on the high bar, has control of her position.

Coaching tip. Line and form are important.

The performer must extend and arch the whole body.

Back pull-away. Stand on the low bar facing the high bar. Both hands grasp the high bar in a regular grip. Extend one leg to the rear in a scale (Fig. 41).

Spotting. None is needed.

Coaching tip. The weight should be on the ball of the foot and the arms should extend quickly to grasp the high bar at the same time that the leg is extended.

Thigh rest. From a straight arm support on the high bar, drop forward and grasp the low bar with both hands. Keep the arms extended, thighs resting on the high bar, and lift the legs to arch the body (Fig. 42).

Spotting. Stand in front of the low bar and give the arm support at the elbow.

Swan. The swan may be performed while facing in either direction on the high or low bar. From a straight arm support remove the hands from the bar, extend the arms sideways, and balance in an arched position. The point of balance is near the hip joint (Fig. 43).

(41) Back pull-away.

(43) The swan balance.

(42) Thigh rest.

1

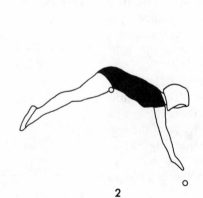

2

3

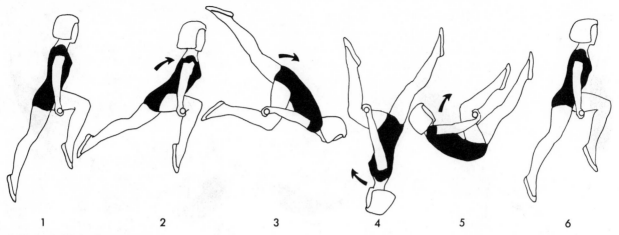

(44) Single knee circle forward.

Spotting. Spotter stands to one side and assists in balance with the hands at the waist; for the high bar one may spot by holding the legs.

Swinging movements

Great freedom and variety of movement is possible with the uneven parallel bars. The performer can go over, under, and between the bars in many different ways with variations in rotating, turning, and changing positions. Most of the movements can be performed facing inward or outward on either the high or low bar. One should work for continuous motion and flow of movement with only occasional use of held positions.

If a stunt is performed on only one bar, which may be either high or low, the beginner who uses the low bar while she is learning is easier to spot for.

Single-knee circle forward. The performer sits on the bar (one should start with the low bar) with the weight resting on the upper thigh of the forward leg, while the rear leg is behind the bar in an extended position (Fig. 44). This stunt consists of circling forward around the bar and returning to the starting position. The hands are in a reverse grip. The forward leg is bent at the knee, and the performer lifts herself from the bar by straightening the elbows. The upper back should be arched. The performer pumps backward with the rear leg, and drops forward while keeping the head back and leading with the chest. The bar is circled with a return to the starting position.

Spotting. Two spotters are needed. Stand outside the low bar and reach under the bar to grasp the wrist of the performer. With the free hand, one spotter grasps the extended leg to aid in the lift. The other spotter lifts the upper back on the return to the starting position.

Coaching tips include

(45) Single knee circle backward.

1   2   3   4   5

(46) Knee drop regrasp.

(47) Split sit on unevens—beginning position for mill circle forward.

1. The elbows must not bend.
2. The upper thigh must remain against the bar.

Single-knee circle backward. With the same starting position as for the single-knee circle forward, but with a regular grip, the performer circles backward over the bar (Fig. 45). The weight is lifted from the bar by the arms. Keeping the back and head arched, the trunk drops to the rear as the extended leg swings forward and upward. Continue to circle around, returning to the starting position.

Spotting. One spotter is located on either side of the performer; the spotters stand between the bars. Reach under the bar to grasp the wrist, then with the free hand push up on the

(48) Mill circle forward.

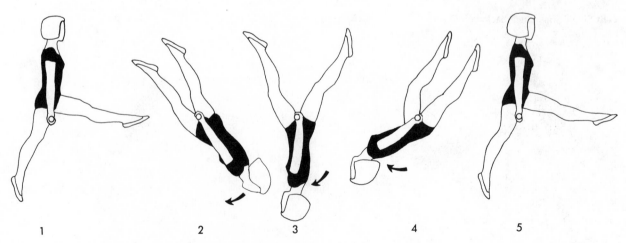

1   2   3   4   5

shoulder as the performer starts the upward swing of the return to the starting position.

Coaching tips include

1. Do not bend the elbows or relax the body.
2. The upper thigh should remain against the bar.

Knee drop regrasp. From a long hang on the high bar lift one leg and bend the knee over the low bar (Fig. 46). Release the hands from the high bar and grasp the low bar while swinging into a single-knee circle backward. As the performer swings under the low bar and starts to move upward she regrasps the high bar with both hands. The extended rear leg pumps forward to aid the swing back to the high bar.

Spotting. A spotter on either side of the performer places a hand at the back of the shoulder and the other hand at the knee. As the performer swings back toward the high bar the spotters aid in lifting the shoulders. The hand at the knee is needed only for the first few trials.

Coaching tip. Reach for the high bar with both hands at the same time.

Mill circle forward. The performer is sitting in a crotch position with a reverse grip (Figs. 47 and 48). She lifts the weight off the bar by straightening the elbows. Keeping the legs rigid, the trunk is arched with head back. Lead forward with the chest while the front leg thrusts downward. Circle the bar and return to starting position.

Spotting. Spotters stand outside the low bar on either side of the performer and reach under the bar to grasp the wrist. As the performer

swings downward, the spotters are ready to push at the shoulder to aid the upward movement to return to the starting position.

Coaching tips include

1. Hold the arched position and remain close to the bar throughout.
2. The arms must remain straight.
3. The beginner may at first wish to practice hanging in the upside down position.

Mill circle backward. The action in this stunt is the reverse of the mill circle forward (Fig. 49). From a crotch position with a regular grip, the performer lifts her weight off the bar. After swinging her rear leg a short distance backward, she whips it down and forward under the bar while keeping the crotch close to the bar. Keep the body arched, lean backward, and circle the bar, then return to the starting position.

Spotting. Stand in front of the low bar and lift the rear leg with one hand. The performer must remain firm for this to be helpful. As the performer swings under the bar, push upward on the front of the shoulder.

Basket. Sit on the low bar facing the high bar with hands in the regular grip on the high bar (Fig. 50). Swing the legs upward in a pike position and circle through the hands. On the swing-through, touch the right foot to the low bar, let go of the high bar with the right hand, make a one-quarter turn to the right, and end in a one-leg squat with the left leg extended forward. This stunt may also be performed on the other side.

Spotting. Stand between the bars and beside the performer. Help to push the hips upward and

(49) Mill circle backward.

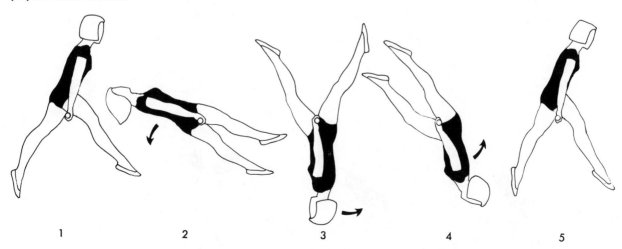

1   2   3   4   5

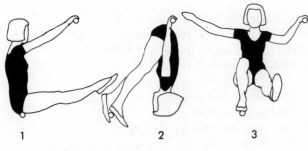

(50) Basket.

then assist the foot to the low bar. Stand to the left side of the performer if she is going to make her quarter-turn to the right.

Kick over or pull over. Sit on the low bar with back to the high bar and grasp the high bar with both hands (Fig. 51). Squat stand on one foot on the low bar and extend the other leg forward-upward. Push upward from the low bar while swinging the straight leg up and over the high bar and bending the elbows to bring the chest close to the bar. Swing up and over the high bar and come to a straight arm support on the high bar.

Spotting. Stand between the bars and assist in pushing the hips up and over the high bar.

Coaching tips include

1. The push from the low bar, kick-up with the straight leg, and pull with the arms must occur together in order to initiate the swinging action for going over the high bar.
2. The elbows must be bent when going over the bar; they do not extend until the legs are over the bar.

Stem rise. Starting position is the same as for the kick-over (Fig. 52). From the squat position on the low bar, lift the free foot upward until the

toes are near the high bar; then whip down with the leg while pushing up with the foot on the low bar and bending the elbows to pull the body close to the high bar. Swing backward and up into a rear mount of the high bar, ending in a straight arm support.

Spotting. Stand between the bars and aid in lifting the hips up and behind the high bar.

Coaching tips include

1. Keep the hand grip loose until the front support is reached.
2. The push against the low bar, the downward whip with the straight leg, and the pull with the arms must occur at the same time to produce the strong backward-upward movement that is needed.

Dismounts

The dismount can be performed over the high or low bar in a forward, backward, or sidewise position. As soon as the dismount has been learned, it should be practiced in conjunction with the movements of a preceding routine. There must be a smooth transition into the dismount and the difficulty of the dismount should conform to the difficulty of the routine. As the finale, it is essential that the dismount be a coordinated and appropriate part of the routine. Careful spotting and an adequate number of mats must be provided.

Cast off. This dismount takes the performer backward from the low bar and may be performed with the back to the high bar or facing it (Fig. 53). From a straight arm support, swing the legs forward and backward, then push up with the arms and jump backward to a standing position on the mat. The knees should bend to absorb the jar one receives on landing.

Spotting. Stand at the side of the performer,

(51) Kick over or pull over.

1   2   3   4

face to face with her. Assist in pushing the shoulder and hip back and up, away from the bar. If the performer should lose her grip too soon, the spotter must be prepared to catch her.

Underswing from the high bar. Stand on the low bar, facing the high bar with hands in the regular grip on the high bar (Fig. 54). Jump to a pike position on the high bar, continue to swing the legs forward under the high bar, and swing into an underswing dismount, landing on the mat with the high bar behind the performer. When dropping off the high bar the arms should be extended overhead and the body arched.

Spotting. Stand between the bars and be ready to move in back of the performer to grasp her at the waist if needed.

Forward roll. From a straight arm support on either bar, drop the upper trunk forward (Fig. 55). Control the leg descent over the bar, keeping the knees straight. Move into a long hang with a slight whip of the legs in order to snap outward to a standing position on the mat.

Spotting. Stand to the side of the performer, ready to grasp her, if needed, at the wrist and thigh as the roll is completed.

BALANCE BEAM

The balance beam, one of the pieces of apparatus in women's gymnastics, requires balance, grace, precision, and courage. Yet the

(52) Stem rise.

(53) Cast off.

(54) Underswing from high bar.

(55) Forward roll dismount.

beginner can quickly learn elementary skills and derive satisfaction from the performance of a simple routine. The standard dimensions of the balance beam are 5 meters by 10 centimeters and 120 centimeters high, or approximately 16 feet by 4 inches at a height of 4 feet. Commercially made beams are adjustable in height and can be lowered for the safety and convenience of the beginner. Skills should be practiced on the floor before they are tried on the beam.

This piece of equipment allows the performer to use creativity in the choice of movements and their sequence. Many of the movements of dance, tumbling, and floor exercise can be adapted for use on the balance beam. In AAU competition the optional balance beam routine is one minute and twenty seconds to one minute and forty-five seconds in length and must not contain more than three stationary or held positions. The quality of a routine depends on the skill of the performer and the continuity of movement in the routine. All movements should be performed with precision and control. For balance and beauty of movement, it is essential that good postural alignment be maintained in all performances on the balance beam. The center of gravity must be in the correct position, and movements should radiate out to all parts of the body.

Safety

Mats should be placed under the beam and on the floor around it. At least one spotter should be on each side of the beam and should know the movement being performed and how to spot for it.

Skills

Skills for the balance beam can be classified in a variety of ways. A routine involves a mount onto the beam, a series of movements back and forth along the beam, a few stationary positions that must not dominate the routine, and a dismount. The movement on the beam can be further divided into locomotor moves, turns, movement in the air, and stunts derived from tumbling skills. Examples of the various skill categories will be presented, but they need not prevent the performer from devising her own movements for the beam.

Hand grips

There is no standardization for the placement of the hands on the beam. Hand position depends on the strength, skill, and preference of the performer; the hands may be moved and the grip changed according to the demands of the performer's other movements. Four commonly used grips are

1. Over-grip the length of the beam—the thumbs are on top with the fingers gripping the sides of the beam.
2. Under-grip—the thumbs point up the sides of the beam and the fingers grasp under the beam.
3. Over-grip the width of the beam—the thumbs grip the side of the beam and the fingers grasp across the top of the beam.
4. Mixed-grip—one hand is in an over-grip and the other is in the under-grip.

Mounts

The mount from the floor onto the balance beam should be precise, made with the body erect and the head high. One may approach the beam straight on or at a diagonal from a standing position, short run, or a Reuther board. The beam can be mounted at either end or at the center. From a mount, one should immediately go into movement on the beam.

All mounts require an upward spring. The following mounts begin with a standing position adjacent to the beam. They may be performed by starting with a short run or with the run and a take-off from a Reuther board. If the Reuther board is used, it should be removed from the padded area as soon as the performer has mounted the beam.

Crotch seat mount. Stand facing the side of the beam and jump to a straight arm support with the fingers in an over-grip the width of the beam. (Fig. 56). Immediately make a one-quarter turn with the body while changing the hands to an over-grip the length of the beam and swing the leg over the beam into the crotch seat position with the hands supporting in the rear.

Spotting. Stand beside the performer, opposite the leg that will be lifted. Place one hand at the hip and the other at the shoulder to aid in balance.

Squat mount. Stand at the side facing the beam and place the hands in an over-grip the width of the beam (Fig. 57). Spring up while straightening the elbows; land with the feet on the beam between the hands, and the body in a deep squat.

Spotting. Two spotters are needed for the beginner. One stands at the performer's side and

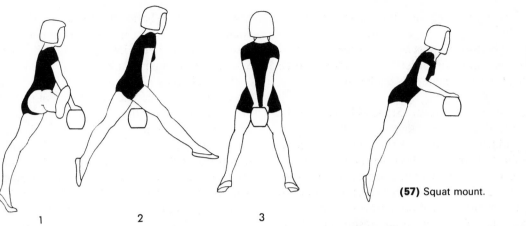

1   2   3

(56) Crotch seat mount.

(57) Squat mount.

(58) One knee mount.

(59) Wolf mount.

(60) Straddle mount.

lifts her hip, while the other stands on the opposite side of the beam and places her hands at the performer's shoulders to keep her from over-balancing.

Coaching tips include

1. The performer should focus on an object in front of her rather than looking down at the beam.
2. Springing to a tuck is a good lead-up for this mount. Only when the performer gets her hips up and her feet level with the beam should she try for the mount.

One knee mount. Stand facing the side of the beam with hands in an over-grip (Fig. 58). Jump to a straight arm support and at the same time bend one knee, placing it on the beam between the hands. The other leg is extended to the rear and the body is arched with head up.

Spotting. Same as for squat mount.

Wolf mount. This is the same as the squat mount except that in the final position of the mount one leg is extended to the side, parallel with the bar (Fig. 59).

Spotting. Same as for crotch seat mount.

Straddle mount. Stand facing the side of the beam with hands in an over-grip (Fig. 60). Jump to a wide stride or straddle stand on the beam.

Spotting. Stand at the opposite side of the beam and place hands at performer's shoulders to keep her from over-balancing.

Coaching tips include

1. One must be able to perform the squat mount prior to attempting this mount.

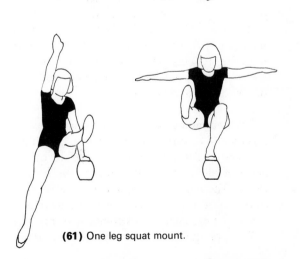

(61) One leg squat mount.

2. Flexibility is required for the straddle position.
3. The performer must be able to achieve height on her spring in order to raise her hips high and balance them over the beam.

One-leg squat mount. Stand sideways to the beam and place the closer hand on the beam (Fig. 61). Spring up and assume a squat position on the foot that has been closer to the beam while extending the other leg forward. After using the hand that was placed on the beam to help in the lift, extend both arms sideward.

Spotting. Stand on the opposite side of the beam ready to grasp the performer's hand if assistance is needed in balancing.

Movement on the beam

As soon as the gymnast learns to mount the balance beam, she should simultaneously learn a few of the movements that can be done on the beam so that she will immediately begin to perform short routines.

Even the beginner should work toward using the entire length of the beam, turning to face in different directions, and employing different levels and planes of movement. It is essential to blend one movement into the next, always working for continuity or flow of movement with sufficient contrast in the quality of movement to give variety.

One cannot move beautifully unless the arms are part of the total movement. The use of the arms adds to over-all appearance and aids in balance and stability. The beginner can rely on arm positions used in ballet, but can also begin experimenting with her own arm movements.

The focus should always be on the end of the beam. The performer may be seeing most of the rest of the beam, but she should not look down at her feet. Although this procedure prevents the performer from seeing the area that she will next be moving into, it also prevents the lowered head from destroying the line and grace of movement and balance.

The **locomotor moves** of various types tie together the turns, aerial moves, tumbling, and stationary positions, and enable one to perform along the entire area of the balance beam. The performer should be able to move smoothly along the beam without having to "feel" for the beam. This comes with practice.

To spot the locomotor moves, the spotter walks on the mat beside the performer with one hand stretched out to her. The performer catches the spotter's hand only if she needs help in maintaining balance.

Walk. The walk—forward, backward, or with variations—can become part of a routine. As one takes a step on the balance beam, the free foot, with toes pointed, slides along the side of the beam until the leg is extended; then another step is taken. A plié on the support leg or high lift of the extended leg between each step are two possible variations for the walk.

Step hop. With each step a hop is also taken. The hop should lift the performer several inches above the beam. As the step and hop are being taken on one foot, the other knee can be bent and raised high with toes pointed.

Skip. A dance skip, with the knees lifted high in front of the body, is particularly effective. In the skip one may move in long strides, in short strides, lifting the body high, or devise some other variation.

Glissade. While facing the length of the beam, slide the right foot forward, close the left to it, and slide the right forward again. Repeat, sliding forward with the left. The movement is lively and graceful.

Turns should be fast, but smooth. It is important to keep the body erect and the weight centered over the balance beam. All turns should be done on the half toe (ball of the foot).

Spotting. A spotter should stand, with arms outstretched, on either side of the beam beside the performer for the learning of all turns.

Tip-toe turn. With the feet close together, one in front of the other, rise onto the toes and pivot around to face in the opposite direction.

To do a full turn, one foot can be swung across in front and on around the other foot for a half turn before placing it back on the beam. Then one continues with the pivot half turn to complete the circle. The full turn, with practice, should become a smooth, continuous movement.

Squat turn. Assume a squat position and remain low while pivoting around on the balls of the feet. Do a half turn and end the turn facing in the opposite direction. A full turn can be made by swinging one leg around in a half turn, then completing the other half with a pivot as in the tip-toe turn.

Battement tourney. Face the length of the beam with the weight supported on one foot

(62) Battement tourney.

(Fig. 62). Swing the other leg back, then forward, parallel to the beam, while pivoting a half turn on the ball of the weight-bearing foot. End in a scale facing opposite to the direction of the starting position.

Scissors seat turn. From a *V* seat facing the length of the beam, swing one leg down to the side of the beam as the body makes a quarter turn toward that leg. Then swing the same leg up and out into another quarter turn of the body while the other leg swings down. Finally, assume the *V* seat facing the opposite direction.

Knee scale turn. In a knee scale position, one makes a half turn while remaining on the same knee (Fig. 63). When starting in a knee scale on the right knee, turn to the right by swinging the left leg down, bringing the trunk to an erect position, and continuing the turn on around into the knee scale facing the opposite direction.

For **aerial movements**, the feet should leave the beam completely. The beginner should work gradually toward achieving more height.

Spotting. For the learning of all aerial movements, a spotter should stand, with arms outstretched, on either side of the beam beside the performer. She moves along the side of the

beam as needed to stay in line with the performer.

Squat jump. Facing the length of the beam in a squat position, spring into the air while drawing the knees to the chest (Fig. 64). As the feet return to the beam, resume the squat position again. The arms may swing upward to give added height to the jump.

Changement. Stand facing the length of the beam with one foot in front of the other. Spring into the air to reverse the foot position, placing in front the foot that had previously been behind (Fig. 65). While in the air, the toes should be pointed.

Stationary leaps. These should be done while facing the length of the beam (Fig. 66). The performer springs from one foot (jump) into the air, assumes the desired position, and then, landing on both feet, bends the knees to take up the force of the impact. Possible positions in the air are split, stag (forward leg bent with toes touching the knee of extended rear leg), or attitude (split with knee of rear leg bent).

Tumbling stunts can be used on the balance beam. This part of the balance beam routine is the most difficult. Stunts are not performed

(63) Knee scale turn.

(64) Squat jump.

consecutively but are spaced throughout a routine.

Grips for the rolls. Four different grips can be used for the rolls on the balance beam: 1) over-grip the length of the beam, 2) under-grip, 3) a change from over-grip to under- during the stunt, and 4) a mixed grip with one hand in an over-grip and one in an under-grip.

Using a towel when practicing rolls provides more comfort and serves as a precautionary measure. A rolled towel, fastened diagonally on the back from the performer's shoulder to the waist will prevent bruising of the spine.

Back shoulder roll. Lie back on the beam, and reach overhead to grasp the beam in an under-grip (Fig. 67). The elbows should be together with the head dropped backward to one side of the beam. The legs are piked and drawn up over the body. As the feet are lowered overhead, one knee is placed on the beam, going into a knee scale upon completing the roll. The leg on the same side on which the head is placed is usually the one used for kneeling. As the knee touches, the grip is changed to an over-grip.

Spotting. A spotter should stand on either side of the beam to aid in lifting the performer's

(65) Changement.

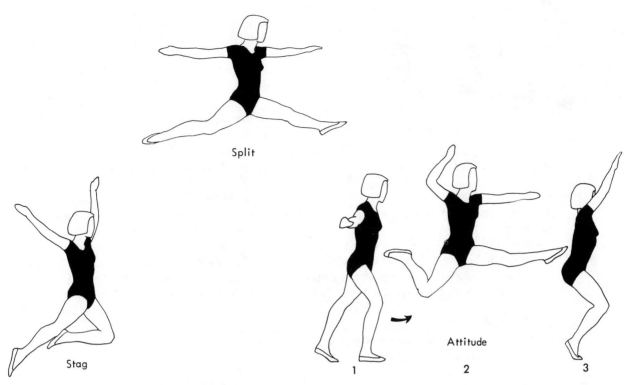

Split

Stag

Attitude

1   2   3

(66) Stationary leaps: split, stag, and attitude.

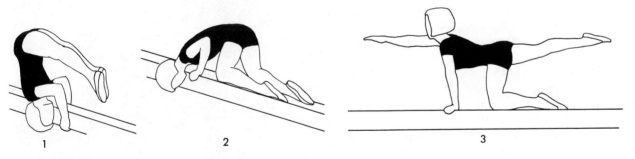

1   2   3

(67) Back shoulder roll.

1   2   3

(68) Front shoulder roll.

(69) Backward roll.

hips and shoulders around and to guide in placement of the knee.

Front shoulder roll. Kneel and place one shoulder on the beam, with the head to the side of the beam (Fig. 68). The hands are in an under-grip or mixed grip. Keep the elbows in close to the body, draw the hips up in a piked position, and slowly lower the back over onto the beam. As the lower back touches the beam, the hands change into an over-grip. The legs swing down to hang vertically, or go into some other position.

Spotting. A spotter on either side of the performer aids in guiding her hips and helping with the change of hand position.

Backward roll. Lie back on the beam and reach overhead for an under grip, keeping the elbows close to the beam (Fig. 69). Bend the knees and lift the hips backward into a tucked roll. As the knees and hips go overhead, quickly shift to an over-grip and push off with the hands in order to complete the roll. Continue over into a knee scale or squat stand.

Spotting. Same as for back shoulder roll.

Forward roll. Bend forward with the hands in an over-grip and the head forward with chin on chest (Figs. 70 and 71). Lift the hips in a pike position and roll over. As the hips are overhead, shift the hands to an under-grip in order to

control the return of the hips to the beam. If the roll is crooked, the hands and arms can pull until the hips are square with the beam. Keep the legs tightly piked throughout the turn to aid in control.

Spotting. Same as for forward shoulder roll.

Cartwheel. The performer must first be able to execute a very straight and controlled cartwheel on the floor (Fig. 72). The sequence is the same on the beam and the timing must be smooth. The hips must stay over the beam.

Spotting. The spotter stands on a bench beside the beam and places her hands at the performer's hips to aid in balance.

The **stationary positions** category includes different forms of standing, kneeling, sitting, and lying. The positions are held only long enough to demonstrate proper form before proceeding into the next movement.

(71) Preparing for forward roll.

(70) Forward roll.

1 2 3 4 5

(72) Cartwheel.

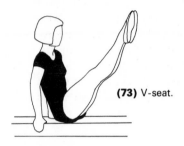

(73) V-seat.

Spotting. The spotter does not touch the performer, but stands ready to assist if needed.

V seat. Sit lengthwise on the beam and grasp the beam in back of and close to the hips (Fig. 73). Lift the legs to form a *V* position with the upper body. After balance is achieved, the arms can be lifted sideward.

Knee scale. Kneel and place one hand on the beam in an over-grip (Fig. 74). Extend the other arm forward while the leg on the same side as the extended arm is stretched backward, and the body is arched.

Arabesque. Stand facing the length of the beam and lift one leg backward as high as possible with the toes pointed (Fig. 75). The knees should be straight, back arched, and head held high. Arm positions may vary.

Croisé. Stand on one foot facing the length of the beam (Fig. 76). Lift the other foot forward and across the supporting leg with knee bent and toes pointed. Arm positions may vary.

One-leg squat. Stand facing the length of the beam, bend one knee, and slide the other foot

(74) Knee scale.

(75) Arabesque.

Gymnastics **171**

(76) Croisé.

(77) One-leg squat.

(78) English handstand.

(79) Side handstand.

forward on the beam until the squat position is achieved (Fig. 77). Extend the forward leg above the beam in the final position. With practice, one should be able to keep the forward leg above the beam while bending the other knee to lower the body. Arm positions may vary.

Spotting. It is well for the performer to hold the hand of the spotter while learning this pose.

English handstand. Face the length of the beam and place the hands in an over-grip with the thumbs on top of the beam (Fig. 78). Kick to a handstand.

Spotting. A spotter is needed on either side of the beam. One places her hand at the performer's shoulder, while the other stands on a stool, ready to grasp the performer at her hip and leg to aid in balancing.

Side handstand. From a straddle position, place the hands on the beam in an over-grip, thumbs to the rear and fingers reaching over the top of the beam (Fig. 79). Lift the hips up over the hands, bring the legs together, and slowly raise to a handstand. Many different returns are possible; an easy one is to lower the legs into a squat position.

Dismounts

The dismount from the apparatus to the mat should be a smooth outgrowth of the moves preceding it.

Jumps. Jumps may be done off the side or end of the beam (Fig. 80). One should lean forward, and then spring upward into all jumps. The hips, knees, and ankles should bend to take up the impact of landing. Variety can be added to all jumps by making a quarter or half turn in either direction before landing.

Spotting. One spotter should stand on each side of the beam ready to assist.

Straddle jump. Jump high into a straddle leg position and touch the toes with the hands, then land with the legs together.

Pike jump. Jump high, pike the legs, and touch the toes with the hands.

Swan or arch jump. Jump high and arch the back. Come to an erect standing position after landing.

Front vault dismount. Push up with the arms from a prone position with the hands in an over-grip (Fig. 81). Swing one leg upward, followed immediately by the other, and shift both legs over to the side and off the beam. Drop to a standing position at the side of the beam. One must work for a high kick-off.

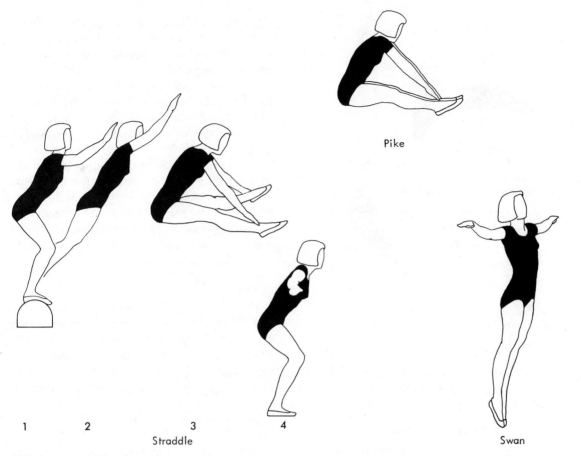

Pike

Swan

Straddle

1 2 3 4

(80) Jumps: straddle, pike, and swan.

SPOTTING. Stand on the side opposite the dismount and place hands on performer's elbow and shoulder to aid in controlling the dismount.

English handstand dismount. From an English handstand drop the legs down to the side of the beam and come to a stand (Fig. 82). This should not be attempted until a handstand can be performed on the beam in good form.

SPOTTING. Stand on the opposite side of the beam to control the supporting arm and to push the performer farther away if she comes too close to the beam on the drop.

Cartwheel dismount. This dismount begins as a cartwheel with the performer going off the end of the beam (Fig. 83). One must judge the amount of space needed on the balance beam so that the second hand down in the cartwheel is only an inch from the end of the beam. The hands are placed and the legs kick up as in a cartwheel; then the legs come together over the body so that the performer continues on over to land on both feet. The movement is similar to a round-off.

(81) Front vault dismount.

1

2

3

(82) English handstand dismount.

SPOTTING. Stand behind the performer and be ready to grasp the elbow of the second arm to go down in order to prevent it from bending.

SIDE HORSE VAULTING

Vaulting consists of a run with a take-off from both feet, a preflight, momentary touching of the hands on the horse, a postflight, and landing.

Vaulting competition for women involves movement over the side of a horse, but practice in vaulting can also be gained by the use of other pieces of apparatus.

A Reuther board, horse, and mats are needed for side horse vaulting. The Reuther board is standardized as to size and specifications, and it gives a better spring than a solid board. The horse is 63 inches long, approximately 14 inches wide (35 to 37 mm.), and set at a height of $43\frac{3}{8}$ inches from the floor to the top of the horse at the saddle. The women's side horse has no pommels or handles on the top. The area on the landing side of the horse should be padded with a double thickness of mats to aid in cushioning the landing.

Safety

The beginning vaulter needs four spotters for most vaults. Two spotters stand on the approach side of the horse and two on the landing side. They stand with side to the horse, facing each other and the performer. The spotters should know which vault is to be performed and how to spot for it. As a general rule, the spotters on the approach side grasp the performer's upper arm with one hand and lift at the hip with the other. The spotters on the landing side grasp the performer's arm near the shoulder and spot the waist or hip with the other hand. A few of the

(83) Cartwheel dismount.

1   2   3   4

vaults require special spotting methods. These special cases will be covered as the vaults are described.

Pommels are not used in vaulting competition for women. If the men's side horse with pommels is used, the pommels should be removed and the holes should be covered with wooden pegs and tape.

Elements of Vaulting

The various parts of the vault need to be considered separately for consideration of common elements and for a better understanding of techniques. However, the vault itself must be carried out as a continuous movement; any hesitation or stop in the movement is a serious break in form.

Run. The first thing to work on in preparing for vaulting is the run. There should be a slight forward lean with the total body in the run, and the performer should always start at the same distance from the Reuther board. Good vaulters use a run of 25 to 50 feet. Start at the take-off point on the Reuther board and pace back the distance that you want to use. One should always take the same number of running steps and the running steps themselves should be equal in length. Speed can increase, but not the length of the step.

Take-off. The run takes the performer directly into the second part of vaulting—the take-off. The last step of the run, a low hurdle onto the Reuther board, is slightly longer than the preceding strides. After the hurdle from one foot, the performer lands on two feet on the Reuther board in preparation for the take-off from the board with two feet. The Reuther board must be hit at the crown, which is about 8 to 10 inches back from the front edge of the board. Most boards have a mark at this point.

One lands and takes off from the board primarily on the balls of the feet. The heels do not touch the board and the knees should not bend. The direction of the bounce is up and forward, which raises the body before it gets to the horse. The Reuther board should not be watched on the approach; instead, the focus should be on the horse or beyond it for most of the vaults.

Preflight. The preflight begins as the feet leave the Reuther board and ends as the hands touch the horse. The preflight should be accomplished in good form: head up, legs straight and together, and toes pointed. For a

vault the Reuther board should never be closer to the horse than 3 feet. As the performer acquires more skill, the board should gradually be moved farther away from the horse.

During the take-off and preflight, in order to achieve height, the performer should feel that she is jumping over something to get to the horse. One way to instill this feeling is to practice vaulting while a rope is loosely held by two extra spotters. The rope should be between the Reuther board and the horse, about 6 inches lower than the horse and 2 feet away from it.

Contact with the horse. The touch of the hands to the horse is momentary and directly on top of the horse. There should be no bend at the elbow; the arms should remain straight. The touch is made when the shoulders are almost directly above the hands and the push-off should be a strong hand and finger movement with wrist extension.

Postflight and landing. The postflight begins as the hands leave the horse and ends as the feet touch the floor. It should cover about the same distance as is covered in the preflight. Good form is important.

In its function as the ending for the vault, the landing should be light and in good balance. One must bend the ankles, knees, and hips to absorb the force of the landing; the arms may also be used in a sideward or forward position to assist with balance. An erect standing position must be assumed as quickly as possible. However, if necessary, a hop or step forward may be taken after landing as long as it appears to be an integral part of the movement.

Mounts

A mount in vaulting means that parts of the body other than the hands rest momentarily on the horse.

Preliminary mount. To begin vaulting, an easy progression should be used. Following is the lead-up for an elementary or preliminary mount:

1. The performer stands facing the horse and places her hands on the saddle of the horse with the fingers pointed forward. Jump to a straight arm position with the shoulders over the hands, thighs touching the horse, and the back slightly arched. Dismount backward by pushing up with the hands and wrists.
2. Take several consecutive bounces on the

Reuther board before taking off forward and upward to land on the mat.

3. Take an approach of several steps onto the Reuther board, then spring from the board to a squat position on a vaulting table or some other low object placed near the Reuther board.

4. Move the Reuther board as close to the horse as possible. Bounce three times on the board and tuck the knees to the chest on the third bounce. After the performer has accustomed herself to bouncing and getting her hips high, she is ready to bounce and land with her feet on the horse in a squat position.

Spotting. As the performer springs from the Reuther board to the horse, the spotters on the approach side aid in lifting at the hips. The spotters on the landing side grasp the performer's wrist and shoulder to keep her from over-balancing.

Squat mount. Begin this skill with the Reuther board positioned not more than 3 feet away from the horse (Fig. 84). On the spring from the board the hips must rise high enough to let the feet come to rest on the horse. After the spring, place the hands on the horse shoulder-width apart with fingers pointed forward and the feet on the horse between the hands. From this squat position, stand and jump down. Absorb the force on the dismount to the mat by bending the ankles, knees, and hips while the arms swing down to the sides, then stand erect.

Spotting. Same as for the preliminary mount.

Wolf mount. After the spring from the board,

1　　2　　3　　4

(84) Squat mount.

the hands are placed shoulder-width apart on the horse (Fig. 85). One leg is tucked so that the foot lands on the horse between the hands. The other leg is fully extended to the side and parallel to the horse. Then bring the feet under the body to come to an erect stand before jumping off.

Spotting. Only two spotters are needed, one on either side of the horse on the end opposite the extended leg. Spot at the hip and arm.

Straddle mount. Prior to attempting this mount, the performer must have enough flexibility to be able to assume a straddle position (wide stride) standing on the floor with the hands flat on the floor (Fig. 86).

Practicing an exercise on the floor prepares one for this mount: Assume a prone (face down) position with body fully extended; then push up with the arms until they are straight, with the weight supported on hands and toes. Keep the hands on the floor while springing to a straddle position by lifting the hips and sliding the feet outside of the hands.

For the straddle mount, the legs should remain straight. Place the hands shoulder-width apart on the horse while the legs assume a wide stride position with the feet in a straddle stand. The feet should be out toward the edges of the horse, head up and focus forward. To dismount, push off with the hands and feet while

(85) Wolf mount.

1　　　　2　　　　3

swinging the arms overhead, and then come to a straight stand.

Spotting. One spotter should stand on the landing side of the horse facing the performer. She grasps the performer at the shoulders. Another spotter stands on the approach side out of the way and steps in behind the performer to help if she fails to get enough height or begins to lean backward.

Vaults

In a vault only the hands touch the horse. If any other part of the body touches, no credit is given. Unless otherwise stated, the hands are always shoulder-width apart, the elbows straight, and the ascent during the preflight with a bent hip. This means that there is slight flexion at the hip joints, but no bend in the knees.

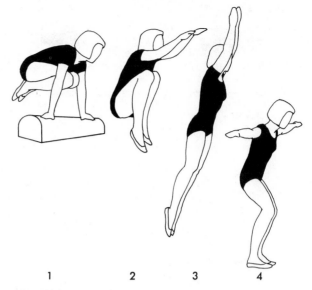

(86) Straddle mount.

1   2   3

(88) Flank vault.

(A straight body ascent is learned by advanced performers.)

Squat vault. After the preflight, place the hands on the horse, tuck the legs, and swing them through the hands (Fig. 87). Extend the legs as soon as they swing through; the feet do not touch the horse. Push off with the hands and come to a stand.

Spotting. Same as for preliminary mount.

Coaching tip. Get the hips as high as possible so that the hands need only barely touch the horse.

Wolf vault. After the preflight, tuck one leg to the chest as in the squat vault, extend the other leg to the side parallel to the horse, and place the hands on the horse (See Fig. 85, Wolf mount). The extended leg should not bend, nor should the legs or feet touch the horse. Push off with the hands and come to a stand.

Spotting. One spotter should be on the approach side and one on the landing side at the end of the horse opposite the extended leg. Spot at the arm and hip.

Flank vault. This vault may be done to either side (Fig. 88). For the right flank vault, as the hands are placed on the horse, both legs are swung up and to the right so that the performer

(87) Squat vault.

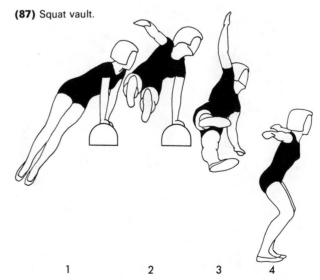

1   2   3   4

(89) Face vault.

goes over the horse with the left side, or flank, to the horse. The hips are extended after the preflight so that the body is straight as it crosses the horse. On the take-off, both feet leave the board at the same time; then contact is made with both hands on the saddle. As soon as the spring has been taken, the legs begin to swing to the side; the top arm is removed from the horse to allow the legs to swing through, and the shoulders should be over the supporting hand.

Spotting. A spotter stands at either side of the horse on the end away from the outstretched legs. Spot at the arm and shoulder.

Face or front vault. This vault may be done to either side (Fig. 89). From a 2-foot take-off, place the hands close together over the left pommel mark of the horse (pommel holes should

be covered) for a face vault over the right end. Swing the legs up and over the horse while facing it. The hips and heels should be as high as the shoulders on the touch. As soon as the body is directly over the horse, throw the right arm up while the legs continue to swing over into a landing with the left side to the horse.

Spotting. Same as for the flank vault.

Straddle vault. The straddle mount should be learned prior to attempting this vault, in which the legs are in a straddle position outside the arms (Fig. 90).

Spotting. Same as for the straddle mount.

Stoop vault. The stoop vault is performed with the legs straight, together and directly under the body in the pike position (Fig. 91). For this vault the hips must be lifted high on the take-off,

(90) Straddle vault.　　　　　　　　　**(91)** Stoop vault.

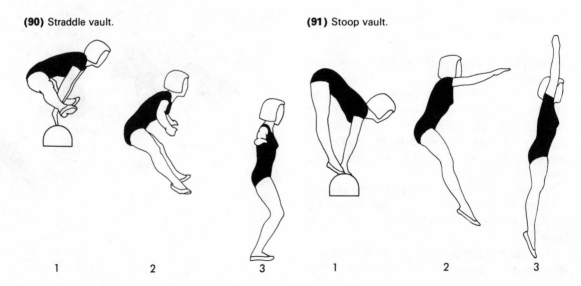

the head is up, and the focus is several feet beyond the horse. After the take-off, the performer pikes the legs and swings them between the hands as the hips come over the shoulders and the hands push off the horse.

Spotting. Two spotters on the approach side grasp the performer's wrist and push up at the thigh. Two spotters on the landing side stand about 4 feet from the horse and catch the performer at the waist and shoulders to keep her from falling forward.

Coaching tips. The performer must work for flexibility in bending forward before attempting the stoop vault. She should be able to do the following:

1. Stand and place the hands on the floor. Hold this position.
2. In a long sit position on the floor, point the toes, grasp the ankles, and place the elbows on the floor.
3. From a push-up position on the floor, spring to a stand by leaving the hands on the floor and putting the feet between them. Learn to do this without bending the knees.

Headspring vault. The headspring is a lead-up to the handspring (Fig. 92). It is not a competitive vault. Prior to doing the headspring vault, the performer should master the headspring from a rolled mat.

(92) Headspring vault.

For the headspring vault the hands should be placed shoulder-width apart on the horse with the head barely touching the horse. The legs come to a pike and, after the hips have passed over the shoulders, are whipped over the head as the hands give a strong push-off.

Spotting. The first time this vault is attempted, as many as six spotters can assist. The approach side spotters grasp the performer's wrist and push up at the thigh. The landing side spotters next to the horse place one hand at the hip and the other at the back of the shoulder to

(93) Bent hip handspring vault.

aid in lifting. The two extra spotters on the landing side stand about 4 feet back from the horse; each places a hand at the performer's waist and shoulder to aid in stopping her forward movement.

Bent hip handspring. The headspring vault should be learned before attempting this advanced vault (Fig. 93). With a bent hip ascent (pike position), the hips are raised high as the straight arms are placed on the horse. Only a three-quarter or partial handstand is assumed, because as the hips pass the shoulders, the legs whip overhead and the hands push off.

Spotting. Same as for the headspring vault.

Selected References

Amateur Athletic Union of the United States, current edition. *Gymnastics—Official Rules Guide*. New York: Amateur Athletic Union.

Athletic Institute. *Gymnastics for Girls and Women*. Chicago: Athletic Institute.

Babbitt, Diane H., and Werner Haas. *Gymnastic Apparatus Exercises for Girls*. New York: Ronald Press, 1964.

DGWS Gymnastics Guide, current edition. Washington, D.C.: American Assoc. for Health, Physical Education, and Recreation. (Examples of routines in floor exercise, uneven parallel bars and balance beam for beginners and intermediates are given in the 1967–69 publication.)

Drury, Blanche Jessen, and Andera Bodo Schmid. *Gymnastics for Women*. Palo Alto, Calif.: National Press, 1965.

Frederick, A. Bruce. *Women's Gymnastics*. Dubuque, Iowa: William C. Brown, 1966.

Hughes, Eric. *Gymnastics for Girls*. New York: Ronald Press, 1963.

Loken, Newton C., and Robert J. Willoughby. *Complete Book of Gymnastics*. Englewood Cliffs, N.J.: Prentice-Hall, 1967.

Chapter 10

Tennis *Ruth B. Eddy*

History. Goals. Equipment. Etiquette. Ground Strokes and Ball Spin. Forehand and Backhand Drives. Service. Volley. Lob. Smash. Rules. Strategy. Mechanics of Movement. Evaluation. Terminology.

Tennis is a very popular racket game that is played by two players opposing each other (singles) or by two teams of two players opposing each other (doubles). The object of the game is to hit the ball with the racket over the 3-foot high net into the opponent's court so that she will have difficulty in returning it.

An inexpensive sport, tennis can be played indoors or out; it is enjoyed by all ages at any tempo, and is an excellent activity for developing sportsmanship, lifelong friendships, and physical well-being. It is considered by many to be an ideal co-recreational game.

History

The beginnings of tennis date from ancient Persia and Egypt where a primitive form of handball was played some five hundred years before the Christian era. Gradually, spreading westward to Greece, the game was later played in England and France. In the Middle Ages the game changed from batting a ball against a wall to batting it between two opponents. Originally

---

Miss Eddy is an associate professor in the Department of Physical Education for Women at Duke University. An enthusiastic instructor of tennis, Miss Eddy teaches semester-long tennis classes out of doors in North Carolina and then in the summer is able to enjoy the grass courts of her home town of Newport, Rhode Island.

---

the ball was hit with the bare hand; later gloves were worn for protection, and finally rackets replaced the gloves. The early balls were made of leather stuffed with hair; later, rubber balls were used. The game was played on an indoor court with no boundaries and later, on a court shaped like an hourglass with a line drawn across the narrow middle portion.

In 1873 Major Walter Wingfield, a British cavalry officer, published a pamphlet in which he simplified the scoring and serving rules and actively promoted the game, which was played outdoors on a lawn. The hourglass-court game became known as lawn tennis, and was especially popular in England and her colonies.

In 1874 Miss Mary Outerbridge, who had seen the game played in Bermuda, introduced it in the United States at the Cricket and Baseball Club at Staten Island, New York. The popularity of lawn tennis spread quickly through the Eastern seaboard and in 1881 the United States Lawn Tennis Association (USLTA) was formed. This organization became responsible for standardizing the game, regardless of the type of playing surface—grass, clay, cement, asphalt, and so on. The USLTA is still the official governing body for amateur tennis in the United States.

The first official championship games under the sponsorship of the USLTA were played at Newport, Rhode Island, in 1881 on rectangular courts with the same dimensions as today's courts. For these games the USLTA followed

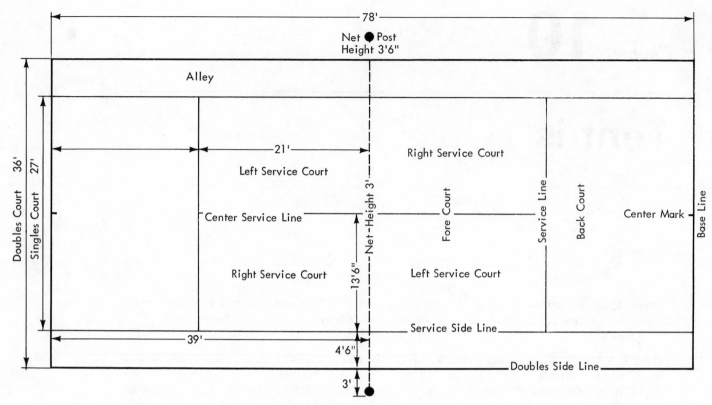

(1) Tennis court.

the official rules which England had adopted for the first all-England championship games at Wimbledon four years earlier. It was not until 1884 that the height of the net was established at its present official height of 3 feet 6 inches at the posts and 3 feet at the center.

In 1915 the nationals were moved from Newport to the West Side Tennis Club at Forest Hills, New York, where the championship singles matches are still played. Although the doubles championships are played in Brookline, Massachusetts, Forest Hills is considered the tennis capital of the United States.

In 1900 Dwight Davis, then an undergraduate at Harvard, donated a cup for international competition for men. The Davis cup, one of the most famous of international sports trophies, is contested annually today, as it was originally, with four singles and one doubles match.

In 1919 Mrs. Hazel Hotchkiss Wightman offered a cup for annual competition for women between the United States and England. The Wightman Cup matches, first contested at Forest Hills in 1923, are played alternately in the two countries with five singles and two doubles matches.

In 1963, to commemorate its fiftieth anniversary, the International Lawn Tennis Federation (ILTF) presented a Federation Cup for women's international competition for which all member nations, totalling almost one hundred, may compete.

The rules of tennis are basically the same as they were at the beginning of the twentieth century. There have been suggestions (mainly relative to changing the method of scoring and to increasing the difficulty of service), which have been tried out in several professional tournaments, but are not official with the USLTA.

Goals

What does one hope to accomplish in six or seven weeks of tennis instruction? What one gets out of any course depends on one's interest, experience, and motivation. It takes more than six weeks to play well, but the following is typical of progress to be expected:

1. After dropping the ball to self, ability to

stroke with forehand from the base line to the opposite back court in good form while using the Eastern forehand grip.

2. Backhand stroke using Eastern backhand grip (as in 1).
3. Ability to serve with fair form either a slice serve or flat serve.
4. Ability to use the block volley from position near the net.
5. Knowledge of the basic playing rules for singles and doubles.
6. Ability to play the singles and doubles game.

Equipment and Facilities

COURTS

Tennis courts are made of a variety of surfaces. Grass courts are considered best, but are expensive to build and difficult to maintain. Composition courts can be played on shortly after rain but require continual upkeep as does clay; concrete and asphalt require little maintenance.

Many of the big tournaments are played on grass, such as those at Wimbledon, Forest Hills, and Brookline, but the majority of games are played on other surfaces. The main distinction in the various surfaces is the difference in the speed of the bounce of the ball, which in turn affects the strategy of the game.

RACKET

It is important to select a good quality racket that feels right when swung. The most common grip sizes are $4\frac{1}{2}$ inches to $4\frac{5}{8}$ inches. The racket should be light to medium in weight: $12\frac{1}{2}$ ounces for slight women, 13 ounces for those of average build, and never heavier than $13\frac{1}{2}$ ounces. Most rackets are evenly balanced. A racket that is heavy in the head will be slow. A well-made laminated frame or a frame of first quality cold bent ash is best. Split sheep's gut stringing provides the most resilient surface, but is the most expensive and is subject to moisture damage. Nylon or other artificial stringing is used by the average player. The racket should be kept in a press and waterproof case when it is not in use. The newest tennis racket, recently used in some of the top tournaments, is made of a tubular steel alloy. The racket has an open throat and is slightly shorter than the average wooden frame.

The combined length of the racket (27 inches) and the width of the head (9 inches) serve as a handy means of measuring the height of the center of the net, which should be 36 inches from the court surface.

BALLS

New balls have a true bounce and flight; their use will facilitate improvement for all players regardless of skill. When the fuzz on the felt cover is worn off, the reduced air resistance makes it difficult for the player to control the ball. If the ball is old or has been wet, it loses its bounce. When balls have been played on asphalt or composition courts, they darken in color and cannot be readily seen. Balls should be firm (not easily dented with the thumb) and have a good white felt cover. Only balls that

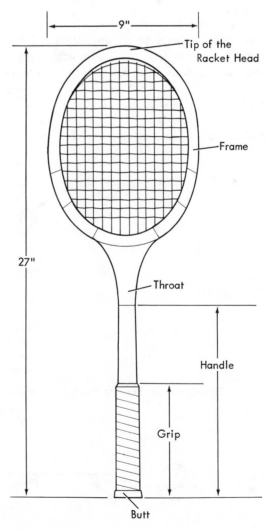

(2) Tennis racket.

are stamped "Approved by USLTA" should be purchased.

COSTUME

The traditional correct tennis attire is white. For women, either a tennis dress or shorts outfit that allows freedom of movement is appropriate. Flat-soled tennis shoes should be worn over heavy socks. A visor is helpful against sunshine.

Etiquette

Inherent in the game of tennis are the traditional attitudes of good sportsmanship as shown by respect of oneself and one's opponents, regardless of the intensity of the competition. Knowledge of the rules of the game as well as the rules of etiquette adds greatly to the enjoyment of playing.

As a player, one should always be courteous, controlling feelings about an unfair call, an unpleasant opponent, or, more often, one's own inadequacies. The server should be sure the receiver is ready, whereas the receiver should not return the first service if it is an obvious fault. She should try not to interrupt the delivery of the second service. The receiver

should keep the server supplied with balls. The server should have two (or three) balls in her hand before starting service. The server should call the score after each point. If the score cannot be agreed upon, the server offers to play the point over. In doubles, the receiver's partner calls service faults.

Balls from neighboring courts should be sent back near the fence. Instead of retrieving one's own ball from a neighboring court, one should ask between plays that the ball be returned. No one should walk behind any court while the ball is in play. A ball that is going out should never be returned before it bounces. It is customary to shake hands and to thank the opponent for the game.

After a play is completed a spectator may applaud winning shots, but never applaud errors. One should not distract players by moving or talking during a point.

Skills

Directions for strokes will be given for right-handed players; left-handed players should reverse directions.

GROUND STROKES AND BALL SPIN

The term *ground strokes* applies to shots that bounce once before they are hit back across the net. They are hit with a forehand on the right side of the body or a backhand on the left side. Beginners stand well behind the base line, use a swing that is slightly uphill (backswing lower than follow-through) and hit the ball as it descends, making contact with the ball at waist height with the racket face perpendicular (or very slightly open) throughout the swing.

Height of the ball at contact

Power and control in stroking is most effective when the ball is contacted at waist height or slightly lower. Experts and beginners alike contact the ball at this height. The difference is that the expert with excellent timing is able to hit the ball as it ascends, or "on the rise," and the beginner waits until the ball bounces up to its peak and descends to the proper height. Therefore, the expert stands on the base line or sometimes within the court for ground strokes, whereas the beginner should stay well behind the base line (Fig. 3).

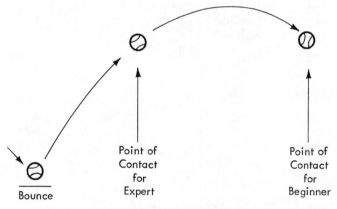

(3) Height of ball at contact for ground strokes.

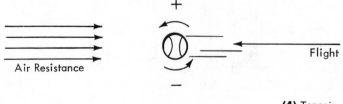

(4) Topspin.

The uphill swing

The beginner who is interested in becoming a good player and in having good form should swing the racket slightly uphill as the expert does. The reasons for the upward swing are 1) the ball hit at waist height must be hit up to overcome the force of gravity and clear the net; and 2) the only way to hit hard and still keep the ball within the boundaries of the court is to apply top spin. Topspin can be applied when the racket moves forward and upward.

Topspin

Topspin is imparted to the ball when hit with an uphill swing (Fig. 4, p. 184). The ball with topspin describes a long arc in the air. Air resistance is greatest on the top part toward which the ball is spinning, thus pressing the ball down. When the spinning ball contacts the ground, the spin and speed result in a fast, deep bounce.

The experts apply additional topspin by turning the face of the racket over the top of the ball (closing the face) while swinging forward and upward. This movement requires a strong wrist and excellent timing and is not recommended for beginners. Because wrist action is beyond the control of the average player, it is suggested that the wrist remain firm and fixed throughout the entire stroke. Enough forward or topspin is imparted to the ball by hitting uphill with a perpendicular racket face.

The angle of the racket face

A very slight variation from perpendicular angle of the racket face results in a pronounced difference in ball flight. The beginner may have to open the racket face a little more than the expert does. The exact angle for different shots can be determined only by experimenting. For purposes of the text, the perpendicular racket face will be used throughout the stroke for forehand and backhand drives (Fig. 5).

The exact angle of the racket face for ground strokes depends on several factors: 1) the distance of the ball from the net and the desired distance of the hit; 2) the vertical height of the ball from the court when it is hit; 3) the angle of the trajectory of the oncoming ball and its spin; and 4) whether the ball is ascending or descending. With the same swing, a ball that is ascending can be hit with a slightly more closed face than a ball that is descending as shown by the angle of rebound in Figure 6.

Backspin

Backspin is produced by chopping action of the racket coming down and under the back of the ball with an open face (Fig. 7). In backspin, the opposite of topspin, the ball spins backwards while traveling forward. Air resistance is greatest on the under part of the ball causing the ball to slow down and float. On bouncing, the backspin, which is a turning away from the direction of the flight, cuts down on the forward momentum of the ball so that it bounces lifelessly.

The forehand and backhand drives with topspin are the most dependable strokes for general use. The chop and slice, which are strokes imparting backspin or cut, are used less frequently. They can be learned readily after the ground strokes are well grooved. They are considered accessory strokes to add variation and change of pace to one's basic tennis strokes.

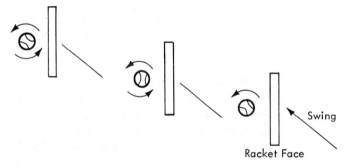

(5) Angle of racket face.

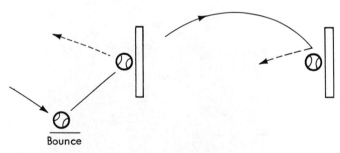

(6) Angle of rebound from racket.

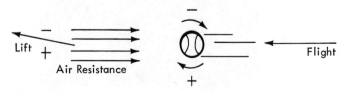

(7) Backspin.

The step

Although the tennis swing, especially for the ground strokes, is relatively simple, tennis is nevertheless a difficult sport to play well. Its great challenge comes from the fact that hitting a moving object requires the player to move fast enough to be in the correct place to make contact. Few beginners, in fact only a few players who are very strong, have enough power to make forceful hits with arm swing alone. Most players, especially women, need to *step forward* as they hit in order to bring the force of the whole body into action. In tennis the swings are relatively slow and easy; the feet must move fast.

THE FOREHAND DRIVE

The forehand drive is used to return ground strokes that bounce on the racket side of the body.

Forehand grip

The Eastern forehand grip is the most orthodox and popular grip. Holding the racket head perpendicular to the ground with the left hand at the throat of the racket, the player uses the right hand to "shake hands" with the racket handle. In this position the palm is in the same plane as the perpendicular face of the racket. As the player looks at her grip she sees that the *V* formed by the thumb and index finger is in the center of the top surface of the handle (Fig. 8).

The fingers, especially the index and middle finger, are spread somewhat apart and point diagonally up and around the handle. The thumb points about 45 degrees up the other side of the handle. The hand is in a strong position, because the palm is on the side of the handle opposite the ball, so that the player feels she is hitting the ball with her palm. The racket head is slightly elevated. The wrist is in its strongest position when the racket is not allowed to drop below the wrist level. For low shots, the player bends her knees and maintains this strong wrist position.

Ready position

The ready position is the alert stance taken by the player prior to receiving a ball. The feet are apart, with the weight on the balls of feet. The racket is held up with the left hand at the racket throat, racket head pointed toward the net. The crouched body is facing the net and almost off balance so the player can move quickly in any direction (Fig.9).

Stroke

The analysis of the stroke will be divided into three parts: the backswing, the forward swing and contact, and the follow-through.

BACKSWING. To execute a forehand drive, the racket is held with the forehand grip and the body is turned sideways so that it faces the right side line with the left shoulder toward the net.

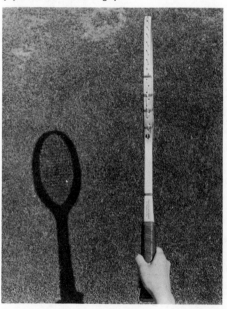

(8) Eastern forehand grip.

(9) Ready position.

(10) Backswing.   **(11)** Contact.   **(12)** Follow-through.

(10–12) Forehand drive.

The right foot points directly toward the side line at a right angle to it. Well before the bounce, the racket is taken back until the tip of the racket head points toward the back fence. The face of the racket is perpendicular to the court surface and should remain in this almost straight-up-and-down position throughout the stroke. The body weight is on the back (right) foot so that it can be transferred forward as the hit is made. The right elbow is slightly bent. The wrist is straight and should remain firm and straight throughout the stroke. The racket head is slightly higher than the wrist and is never allowed to drop below the hand level or to lag behind the hand. The knees are bent so the body can move slightly upward on the forward swing. The eyes watch the approaching ball (Fig. 10).

FORWARD SWING AND CONTACT. The toes of both feet are on an imaginary line that runs parallel with the direction in which the ball is to be hit. The forward swing is initiated by stepping forward onto the left foot. The left foot points diagonally forward about 45 degrees to the net and is firmly planted. Most of the weight goes to the left foot. As the body turns forward or counterclockwise, the inside of the back (right) foot pushes back and down against the ground. Knees are bent. Contact with the ball is made at a point just forward of the forward foot and far enough away from the body to reach comfortably (Fig. 11).

For most players the comfortable and effective point of contact is achieved with the arm very slightly bent. The ball should not be so close to the body that the arm swing is restricted, nor so far to the side that the arm must be rigidly extended. A rigidly extended arm does not absorb the shock of an oncoming ball, and could therefore be a source of strain and fatigue.

The most effective impact point is just forward of the forward foot. The stroke loses its force if the ball is allowed to travel back until it is even with the body or, worse still, back behind the body. The overcorrection (hitting when the ball is too far forward) results in the ball going too far to the left, but many more tennis errors are caused by hitting too late rather than too soon. The player should try to keep the ball between herself and the net and *never* let it get behind her.

At impact the player should have the feeling that she is keeping the ball on the strings of her racket for about a foot, and that she is applying a firm, slow, prolonged thrust through the ball in the direction of the target. The wrist must be firm as the ball is carried forward on the racket. By a combination of weight transference forward while reaching and extending the arm, the arc of the swing is flattened and the racket moves straight forward and slightly up with the ball.

FOLLOW-THROUGH. The racket continues moving forward toward the target, as far as the player can comfortably reach, until the tip of the racket head points slightly above the target with the racket face still perpendicular to the ground (Fig. 12). Fundamentally this 180-

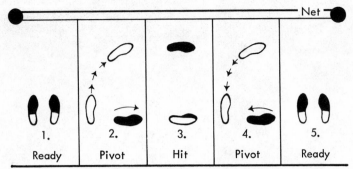

(Shaded Areas Show Weight Distribution)

(13) Forehand drive footwork.

degree swing, from back fence to net, is all that is necessary. But when the ball is hit hard, momentum carries the racket up and around beyond this point. Some players may even follow-through so far that the right hand approaches a point high on the left side of the head. The action should not be stopped abruptly but allowed to continue until the momentum of the racket gradually ceases. Where the racket eventually ends up is not so important as the accuracy with which the racket pointed toward the target on the forward swing. The follow-through is longer and higher than the backswing.

To recover after the forehand shot, the weight simply returns to the right foot and the left foot is replaced beside it, both feet pointing straight ahead. Thus the ready position is reassumed (Fig. 13).

BACKHAND DRIVE

The backhand drive is used when the ball comes to the nonracket side of the player. The swing is freer than the forehand because it is away from the body instead of across the front. Any difficulty the player may encounter stems from the relative lack of support provided by the grip. This can be compensated for to a large extent by an assist with the left hand, which may be placed high on the handle at or near the throat. The two-handed stroke may be helpful for the beginner, but it must not impede the follow-through.

Backhand grip

Because the Eastern forehand grip does not offer enough resistance, the Eastern backhand grip must be used. The hand is moved very slightly to the left on the handle with the thumb pointing 45 degrees up the handle. The *V* of thumb and forefinger is on the bevel between the top and the surface to the left of the top (Fig. 14). It is important that the hand not be moved too far to the left on the handle as this tends to hinder the follow-through of the swing. If the backhand grip feels weak, it is better to assist with the left hand rather than use an incorrect grip.

The change of the grip from forehand to backhand is easiest with the left hand steadying the racket and the right hand moving on the handle. This change must be practiced so both grips have the right feel without the player having to look. The opposite face of the racket is used for the backhand.

Backswing

The backhand involves a more complete turn of the shoulders away from the net on the backswing than does the forehand. The body is turned away from the net until it faces a point between the left side line and the base line. The left foot points diagonally back from the base line, and the weight is on the left foot. The right elbow is close to the body; the firm right wrist holds the racket head above the wrist. The tip of the racket points toward the back fence. The face of the racket is vertical and will remain almost vertical throughout the stroke. The body is lowered by bending the knees and the eyes are focused on the ball over the lowered right shoulder (Fig. 15).

(14) Eastern backhand grip.

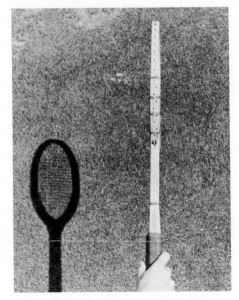

(17) Follow-through

(16) Contact with ball.

(15) Backswing.

(15–17) Backhand.

Forward swing and contact

The forward swing is initiated by stepping diagonally forward toward the left net post with the forward (right) foot. The body turns forward clockwise while the inside of the back (left) foot pushes back and down against the ground. The left hand can give impetus to the forward swing by a slight push and is removed just before the racket contacts the ball. Ball contact is made at a point just forward of the forward foot and far enough sideways to be reached comfortably (Fig. 16).

Follow-through

The racket moves straight forward after the hit until the tip of the racket points toward the target with the racket face still straight up and down. If the left hand has aided in the hit, it may follow the right or point somewhere toward the side for balance (Fig. 17). As on the forehand, if the ball has been hit hard, the player may continue the follow-through up and around until the hitting hand is high and slightly to the right. On the recovery and preparation for the next shot, the weight goes back to the back (left) foot, and the forward (right) foot is brought even with the back foot. Feet and body face the net in the ready position.

FOOTWORK

Tennis strokes are relatively simple; getting into the right place fast enough is the real challenge. The player must have excellent timing, alertness, speed, and agility, for tennis

is a game of perpetual motion from beginning to end of every point.

The receiver in the ready position is poised for a quick start. As soon as the server hits the ball, the receiver bounces on her feet to get her body in motion even before she knows whether it will come to the forehand or backhand (Fig. 18).

Seldom in a tennis game does the player find that the ball is hit to her so that all she has to do is pivot and step forward into the shot. Not very often is she in a position to hit the ideal shot with perfect form. However, she should always

(18) Bouncing when receiving.

Tennis **189**

try to move as the ball comes to her side of the net so that she can take a step forward into the stroke. No matter how far she has to run or how fast, her goal should be to arrive in time with the weight on the right foot for the forehand and the left for the backhand.

If the player must move sideways for the forehand, she should use a slide step, concentrating on keeping the weight on the right foot. If the ball comes out of reach to her right, her left foot pushes off sideways, the right foot receives the weight, and the left foot comes up to the right and pushes off again. This sideways sliding action helps to keep the weight mainly on the right foot until the step into the shot is taken on the left foot. The reverse action is true for the backhand, i.e., push with the right, land on the left, and step forward into the shot on the right foot. As this sliding, two-step action is occurring, the racket is being drawn back. When the hitting position on the court is reached, the body pivots on the back foot and the backswing is completed.

The beginner's impulse is to run toward the bounce. The footwork should be taking her well behind and a little to the side of the bounce so that there is plenty of room for the forward step into the shot.

Immediately after hitting each shot, the player must get back to her ready position at the center of the width of the court. The area between the base line and the service line is called *no man's land*. Inasmuch as most balls bounce in this area and it is extremely difficult to handle a ball that bounces near one's feet, one should never stay in this area. The two best court positions are 1) just back of the center service mark of the baseline, or 2) about the center of the forecourt. Footwork involves not only getting into the best possible position for making the shot, but also in returning quickly to one of these two court positions. The recovery is immediate.

SERVICE

The three basic types of serves are the flat serve, which is a fast ball with no spin; the slice serve, in which the racket face is turned slightly to the left and the ball is contacted at about two o'clock (the ball bounces to the right of a right-handed receiver); and the American twist serve, in which the racket crosses over the top of the ball from left to right (the ball bounces

to the left of a right-handed receiver). The latter is recommended only for men.

The flat serve and the slice serve are the standard serves for women. The flat serve, made with the racket face squared to the desired flight of the ball, can be hit hard; the slice serve, with the racket face turned slightly to the left so that it hits at two o'clock on the ball's surface, imparts slight sideways and topspin to the ball.

The serve gives the server the opportunity to execute a strong attacking play that will put the receiver on the defensive. A good service has 1) placement, 2) speed, and 3) spin. Each player will develop her own individual mixture of these three factors by experimentation. The service is a difficult stroke to learn, because it involves the coordination of two separate movements—ball toss and swing.

Anyone who can throw a baseball overhand can learn to serve, for the movements are similar. For those who have not done much throwing, time is well spent in practicing the throw first. For an effective throw the body should turn away from the target with the weight on the back (right) foot. The arm bends to about a right angle, the elbow is high and points away from the target, and the wrist bends (Fig. 19).

The throwing action is merely an unwinding, starting with the center of the body. First, the hips turn and the weight is transferred to the forward (left) foot. Then the hand travels up, over, and forward toward the target with complete extension of shoulder, elbow, and then wrist in that order and the fingers release the ball (Fig. 20). The hand travels out toward the target as far as it can reach. Then, if the action is strong, a step forward onto the right foot is taken to regain balance. The throwing hand continues down to the left side of the body (Fig. 21).

Service grip and stance

Beginners can start with the Eastern forehand grip, but as soon as possible, the Continental grip (halfway between the Eastern forehand and backhand) should be used. The Continental grip allows more wrist action, which is especially important in the serve, and also imparts more spin to the ball.

The player assumes her stance behind the base line, on the proper side of the center mark, with her feet comfortably apart and her toes

| (19) Backswing. | (20) About to release ball. | (21) Follow-through. |

(19–21) Overhead throw.

on an imaginary line that points diagonally toward the center of the service court. Her racket tip also points toward the target. (Figure 22 shows the server aiming to the left service court from the left side of her court.)

Backswing

The racket swings easily down close to the body with the stroking face toward the body (Fig. 23). As the hand passes the thigh, the weight shifts to the back (right) foot; the body turns to the right away from the net and the arm starts to rotate outward. At the peak of the backswing the right shoulder is well back, the elbow high and bent at a right angle, the wrist bent, and the racket points down behind the back. On this wind-up, the server is poised, ready to make the overhead swinging action, which feels as if the racket itself were to be thrown into the service court (Fig. 24).

Forward swing

The forward swing starts with the body un-winding; the weight shifts to the toes of both feet as the body inclines forward. The elbow extends, bringing the arm and racket straight above the shoulder; the wrist straightens at the last minute, releasing the built-up power as the racket face contacts the ball squarely (or at the two o'clock surface for the slice) (Fig. 25).

Follow-through

Nothing should impede the follow-through. The extended arm continues out toward the target and then down and around until the hitting hand is at the left side of the left knee with the hitting surface of the racket facing in toward the body. Balance is maintained by stepping forward into the court with the right foot (Fig. 26).

(22) Ready to serve to left service court.

(23) Starting backswing.   **(24)** Continuing backswing.   **(25)** Ball contact (flat).   **(26)** Follow-through.

(23–26) Service.

The ball toss

The toss with the nondominant hand is a skill that needs much practice. It is best controlled by holding the ball in the thumb and first two fingers. The arm is kept straight, goes down to the thigh and then *slowly* up as far as it can reach. At the height of the reach the ball is released, followed by a holding of the follow-through of tossing arm and fingers. The toss of the ball should be high enough so the ball will be hit with the arm and racket fully extended. It should be to the right and forward and if the unhit ball were allowed to drop, it would land on the court slightly forward and to the right of the left toe.

After practicing the swing and toss separately, the two movements are put together. The racket arm starts its downward swing and the moment it passes the thigh (the racket arm continuing in its pendulum swing backward), the left arm begins its forward-upward lift for the toss. Inasmuch as this coordination is difficult for some, it is possible to simplify the serve by starting with the racket behind the shoulder, racket tip pointing down toward the ground, and holding it there while the ball is tossed (Fig. 24). The racket is then swung forward for the hit. For those who are accustomed to throwing, this lead-up skill may not be needed at all; for others it may require considerable practice before the coordinated swing and toss can be executed. The satisfaction of a well-controlled rhythmical stroke is worth working for.

VOLLEY

The volley (stroke made before the ball bounces) is a strategic stroke that may give the player a distinct advantage. It is played from a position about half way between the net and the service line. If the player can advance to the net and take the shot before the bounce, she has gained the advantage of quickness of return, as well as the possibility of placing the ball out of the opponent's reach.

By comparing the angle (Fig. 27) of A with B, B is seen to be wider than A, showing the advantage the net player gains over the base line player when she is aiming for back court. However, by comparing angle C with D, the increase of D is seen to be even greater, showing the wide angle available to the net player when aiming to either side of the forecourt. In addition to the greater choice of placement for the net player, the closer one is to the net the greater the possibility that the ball will not be netted. A third advantage is gained by the net player from the shortness of time the opponent has to get in position to return a ball hit from the net.

The Continental grip (halfway between the

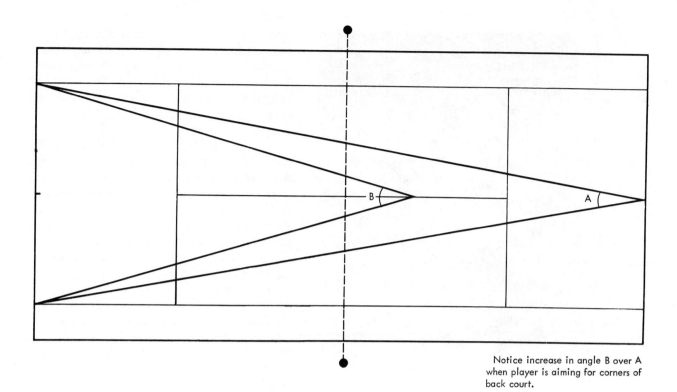

Notice increase in angle B over A when player is aiming for corners of back court.

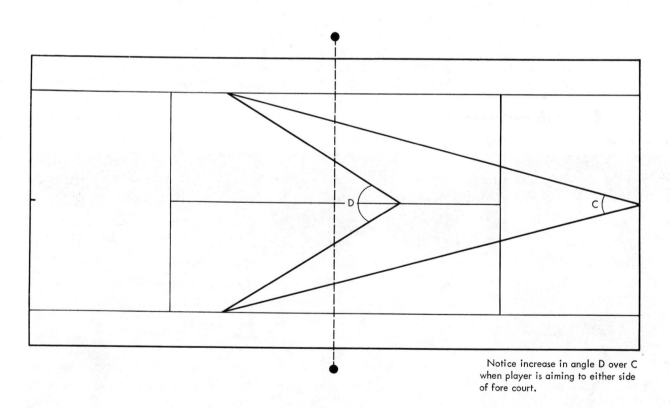

Notice increase in angle D over C when player is aiming to either side of fore court.

(27) Comparison of stroke placement from baseline and net.

(28) Volley—backswing for forehand.

Eastern forehand and backhand) is used for both the forehand and backhand volleys because often there is not time to change. It is important to have a grip that is strong on the backhand side because more shots at net are taken on that side, for strokes hit directly at a player are returned with the backhand. The Continental grip works well on the forehand, except for a high forehand volley. This stroke may necessitate an Eastern forehand grip. To compensate for the beginner's weakness of wrist and forearm, it is sometimes advisable to choke the handle (grip it near the top of the leather rather than near the end).

Opposite faces of the racket are used for the forehand and backhand volleys. Because this is the only difference in the volley between the forehand and backhand, no separate discussion will be given.

The volley stroke requires more turning than arm swinging. Ideally one should step into the shot as with ground strokes, but often because of lack of time a shoulder turn is all that can be accomplished. To prepare to hit the volley, the weight goes to the foot on that side (right for forehand), and the shoulders turn to that side until the racket tip points at the side line. The racket is not taken any farther back than parallel to the net (Figs. 28 and 29). The hit is made by stepping forward on the opposite foot (right for backhand), and meeting the ball forward of the body (Fig. 30). Often there is little follow-through, but if there is a follow-through the tip of the racket points at the target (Fig. 31).

As with the ground strokes there is no wrist action, but rather a firming up of the wrist to withstand the force of impact with the ball. The

(29–31) Backhand volley.

(31) Follow-through. (30) Contact. ← (29) Backswing.

racket is kept in line with the forearm by a straight, very firm wrist. The head of the racket should never be allowed to lag or get behind the wrist.

If the ball goes to the right out of reach of the player, she steps across with her left foot for a forehand volley (Fig. 32), and across with the right for a backhand. If the ball is very low, the player bends her knees and body and opens the face of her racket (turns the stroking face upward) so the ball will clear the net. The angle of the face of the racket varies with the height at which the volley is made. When the volleyer reaches up high to meet the ball, she must close the racket face (slant face downward).

The volley can be practiced by two or four players up at the net, in the centers of the four service courts. They endeavor to keep continuously volleys going as long as possible. Caution should be taken not to hit the ball hard, but rather to punch it with a shoulder turn. The footwork must be extremely fast.

(32) Stepping into a low volley.

LOB

A lob is a stroke in which the ball is hit in a high arc over the head of a net-playing opponent so it will land near base line. Lobs are used to drive net players back from the net, or they may be used by a player to gain time for herself.

The grip is the same as for the drives. On the backswing the face is slightly open, the racket is swung under the ball, and the ball is hit upward with the whole arm lifting the racket. One should aim for the high point in the trajectory. One should learn to hit a lob on both the forehand and backhand. This stroke requires great finesse. It must not be too high, for that would give the opponents time to recover. It also must land near base line where its high bounce will be difficult to handle. If the lob falls short, it is a set-up for the opponents to make an overhead smash.

OVERHEAD SMASH

The overhead smash is used to return a short lob coming into the forecourt. Such a ball can be taken in the air before it bounces, or by the easier method of taking it after the bounce. The grip on the racket is usually the Continental, the regular service grip. However, because the ball is hit with the *flat* face, the Eastern forehand grip can be used effectively.

The swing is similar to the serve, yet is much more difficult because the ball is moving through the air in an arc, and is traveling much faster than it is in the service. For the smash, the player takes a short backswing to get the racket and arm well back while moving to a spot slightly back of the expected point of contact and waits, fully poised (making small shuffling movements to correct the body position), until the ball drops to her reach. Highly skilled players often jump in the air but this greatly increases the difficulty of timing. Because of the possibility of error in the stroke, the overhead smash is best taken when the ball is close to the net, or at most, no farther back than the service line. The ball is sent downward into the opponent's court with such speed that it is usually unreturnable. Because the overhead smash is similar to the serve, it is not attempted on the backhand. If a player does not have time to run around the ball to put it on her forehand, she is forced to play it as a backhand volley, a much weaker stroke. For this reason the lob is usually aimed for the backhand.

Brief Rules of the Game[1]

Play is started by the server who projects the ball by hand into the air, and before it bounces, hits it with her racket. The service, struck from

[1] Complete rules may be secured from the United States Lawn Tennis Association, *Umpire's Manual*, published by USLTA, 51 E. 42nd St., New York, N.Y. 10005. Rules may also be secured from the American Association of Health, Physical Education and Recreation, *Tennis-Badminton Guide*, published by the Division for Girls and Women's Sports, 1201 Sixteenth St., N.W., Washington, D.C. 20036.

behind the base line and to the right of the center mark must bounce in the opponent's right service court (or on its boundary lines), and from left of center to left service court. The server has two chances to serve the ball into the correct service court, with the ball being in play if the first serve is successful. After service the ball can be sent to any part of the court and may be hit after one bounce or may be volleyed (hitting the ball before it has touched the court surface).

A point is made after each rally when one of the players fails to return the ball within the court boundaries. The server then serves from the base line to the left of the center mark into the opponent's left service court. After each point the server continues to serve alternately from the right and left until the game is completed. The receiver then serves the next game.

In doubles play, a 4½ foot "alley" is added to each side of the court that is in bounds for the rally following the service. The service court is the same in singles and doubles. Serving in doubles alternates between the two teams in regular rotation, so a person on team A serves for the first game, then a person on team B, and so on. The same serving order is maintained throughout the set.

Scoring consists of points, games, sets, and matches. Each rally results in a point for either server or receiver. Scoring is "love" (no points), 15 (1 point), 30 (2 points), 40 (3 points), and game. A minimum of four points for one side with at least a two-point margin is necessary for game. If the score is tied at 40-all, it is called "deuce," and then two consecutive points must be won for game. The first point after deuce is called "advantage." The next point is either game or deuce. The server calls the score giving the score for her side first.

A set consists of a minimum of six games for one side with at least a two-game margin, for example, 6-4, 7-5, 12-10, and so on. A match consists of two out of three sets for women and three out of five sets for men.

Strategy

GENERAL

As soon as the beginning player has learned the rudiments of the game, the serve, the forehand and backhand drives, she is ready to learn how she can best cover her own court, as well as what tactics she can use to make it difficult for her opponent to do the same. The challenge of trying to outthink and outplay an opponent is usually the essence of enjoyment in tennis.

Playing a steady game is more important than trying to play a flashy one. The latter approach will cause one to make needless errors; such a player beats herself. Having a steady, dependable serve in which speed is balanced with control is a psychological asset. Two equal serves are better than a fast one that often goes out, and a soft shot which the receiver can place too advantageously. The service should always hit deep in the court to keep the opponent from rushing up to the net position.

The player soon realizes that usually the harder she hits the ball, the harder and faster it returns to her. And yet if she gently pats the ball to her opponent, it may be returned too fast for her to reach. Therefore, she should strive to achieve well-paced shots that land near her opponent's base line and also the ability to change the pace and vary the game.

Besides how hard and deep she hits the ball, there is the all important factor of angles. One learns to look ahead to the possible angles of return as well as the direction in which the shot is made. For example, what may appear to be a brilliant shot to the far side line opens up the possibility of a wide angle of return both cross court and down the line; whereas, a drive down the center of the court limits somewhat the angle of return.

The player must analyze the opponent's weaknesses and then send her the kind of shots she has difficulty in handling. She must realize that consistently playing to the opponent's weakness gives the opponent the opportunity of practicing and overcoming that weakness. Also the opponent is presumably analyzing the weakness of the opposition.

Anticipating the opponent's shots comes from carefully watching how she moves and the position of her racket as she hits. Then, as soon as one sees the direction of the returning ball, one must switch from watching the opponent to watching the oncoming ball and continue to watch it carefully until the shot is completed.

SINGLES STRATEGY

Even the three-stroke game of beginners—serve, forehand and backhand drives—presents the possibility of planning the attack and playing to the opponent's weaknesses.

Side line drives are very effective in singles (in doubles one aims for the center between the players). If the drives are sent alternately to the forehand and backhand corners, the opponent will be forced to run and eventually to make an error. This alternation should occasionally be varied by sending two drives to the same side. The opponent, in trying to get back to her center position, will find it difficult to change direction quickly. An oft-used tactic is to send several balls deep to the backhand; when the opponent stays there, leaving the forehand area wide open, a cross court shot can be sent to the forehand. The cross court shot is very effective, because the opponent is forced out of court to return it. If the opponent has little confidence in her backhand, she may stand on her backhand side. This is an open invitation for a cross court drive to her forehand.

In service, the beginning player tries merely to get the balls in the correct service court. With practice, however, she will learn to serve balls deep near the lines, thus keeping the receiver guessing. The tactics for the two service courts vary somewhat. In the right service court a forehand (for a right-handed player) draws the player over toward the side of the court, thus leaving her backhand unprotected for the next shot. In the left service court, a service to the opponent's backhand is especially effective, as her opponent is forced to the side of the court. Being a backhand, it may be a weak return. The server then has a chance to drive a cross court to her forehand.

After the volley and lob have been practiced, the five-stroke game offers the opportunity of going to net to volley when the opponent makes a weak return. On the other hand, if the opponent goes to net, she can be driven back either by a lob or a well-aimed drive. Because the drive has maximum speed as it crosses the net, it makes an excellent passing shot. The decision in singles is always: *when* is the opportune time to go to net. This will depend in a measure on the skill of the player in volleying, and on her ability to recover if the ball is lobbed over her head.

DOUBLES STRATEGY

Success in doubles depends on team play. Partners must have an understanding as to who will take shots landing between them, a willingness to let the partner do her share, and a readiness to back up her partner if she is passed.

In the three-stroke game of doubles, drives will be the basis of the rally. Drives down the center are especially effective in doubles, as there may be a moment's hesitation as to who will take it, especially if it travels somewhat diagonally. Usually the person takes the shot who has it on her forehand, i.e., the player on the left for two right-handed players. The stronger player usually chooses to receive in the left court for an additional reason: she has the opportunity of "saving" the game, because game point is decided when receiving in the left court in all cases except when the score is 40-15.

In the beginners' game of doubles, both server and her partner can play back. As soon as the players learn to volley, they try to take the net position. The side-by-side, or parallel, team work is the strongest defense and offense. If the server's partner assumes the net position for return of service, either the server should immediately come up to the net, or if this move is impossible, the server's partner should run back to be parallel with the server. The one-up-and-one-back position is extremely weak after the return of service, because there is a diagonal opening between them which neither one can defend. In Figure 33, if receiver's partner D gets the ball, she can send a low fast drive between A and B. There is not time for B to go back or for A to go to the side. Hence, as soon as the ball gets in D's territory, the one-up-and-one-back position is not feasible. The common positioning of the server's partner at net presupposes that the server will run up after the serve. But until both players have some skill in the volley and overhead smash, the net position immediately following service is untenable. Beginning players will be drawn to the net by short shots requiring the net position, and once there may be able to "finish off" the point.

In high-level tennis, the strategy is to see which team can get to net first. The plan to get to net starts with the service. The server will send a deep, well-placed ball with considerable spin that does not travel so fast (due to air resistance), but is difficult to return. The faster the serve is hit, the faster it will come back (the same as hitting a fast ball against a wall). Immediately after the follow-through of the service, the server will dash toward the net, trying to get as far as possible. In most cases, she will be in "no man's land" when the return comes aimed at her feet. She must momentarily pause to adjust her footwork for the return. She then continues

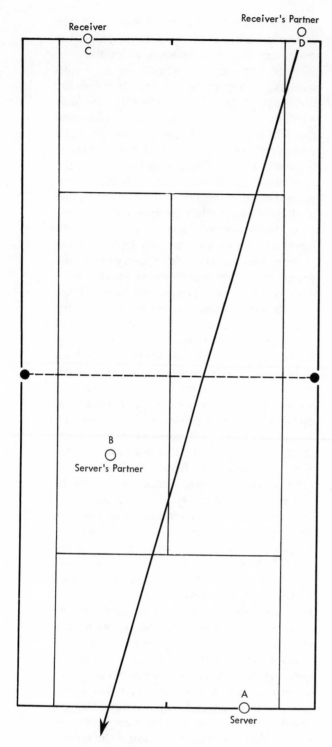

(33) Weakness of up and back play in doubles.

The position of the receivers is also planned to aid them to get to net. The receiver's partner will start out on the service line and either advance or retreat, depending on the strength of her partner's return of the service. If she was not able to handle the spin of the service agressively, both will play back waiting for a weak return of the opponents, at which time they will go to the net.

Because doubles consists in seeing which team can get to net first, the lob is used much more than in singles as an essential tactic. The arc in the air must be out of reach of the opponents' rackets, yet not so high that they will have time to recover, and the ball must drop just inside the base line.

Mechanics of Movement in Tennis

Every action has an equal and opposite action. As one steps forward for ground strokes, one also pushes back with the back foot.

The wider the base of support, the more stable the body will be, and the lower the center of gravity, the more stability. These principles are important in hitting ground strokes. When the player is in position to hit the ball, she stabilizes herself by widening the base of support with a long step and by bending her knees.

The principle that the center of gravity must fall within the base of support for balance applies to the ready position. However, in waiting for the ball, the player does not want too much stability. The center of gravity falls within the base but is advanced forward of the center of the base so that one can move quickly.

A body at rest tends to remain at rest and a body in motion tends to continue in motion. This is the underlying reason for staying on the balls of the feet and maintaining a slight springing action while waiting for the ball.

The flatter the arc of a swing, the greater the accuracy will be. The ball goes off the racket in a tangent to the arc of the swing. If the swing is circular there can be great variation in the direction of the tangent that the ball takes. The arc should be lengthened and flattened by stepping forward as the hit is made, and by swinging in a long flat arc. The hand should travel in as straight a path as possible.

The longer the radius in a swinging motion, the greater the speed and force will be. A straight

her dash to be parallel with her partner, who is one half to two thirds of the way back from the net in the service court. In this position, they both can go back if a lob is sent over their heads, or move somewhat closer to the net for a "kill" if the opponents send a weak return.

arm swing in a circular path gives a long swing and allows for increase in momentum; thus force is gained, but control is lessened. It should be noted that both the previous and this principle require modifications of the swing pattern. Accuracy should not be sacrificed for force. The player must decide how much force she can use and still control the shot.

Accomplishment—Improvement —Evaluation

If the beginning player assesses her weaknesses and strengths, she can continue in her progress toward learning and enjoying the game of tennis. Self-testing activities can give one an evaluation of one's accomplishments by comparing results with others. (Many of the following skill tests can be done when practicing alone.)

Improvement comes from practice, so practice alone or with others is a must. Increased enjoyment will be experienced as one is able to control one's body and racket as desired. To match one's best efforts with another's in friendly rivalry makes the game of tennis an exciting experience.

The beginning player can strengthen the arm, wrist, and hand muscles, as well as develop eye-hand coordination, by the following three simple daily exercises.

1. Ball tapping upward. Holding the racket with the stroking face upward, bounce the ball upward on the racket from 6 to 8 inches. The object is to bounce the ball in the center of the strings. The individual counts the number of times up to 100 she can bounce the ball continuously without moving more than one step.
2. Ball tapping from racket to floor. The object is to tap the ball downward from the center of the racket to the floor. The individual counts the number of continuous bounces up to 100.
3. Alternate ball tapping. The ball is tapped downward against the floor five continuous times, then tapped upward for five continuous times, continuing in this alternating pattern. The individual counts the number of times up to 100 she can tap continuously.

The beginning player should practice dropping and hitting forehand and backhand drives

until the stroke is rhythmical and fairly well grooved in relation to the height of the ball at contact, as well as the distance sideways and forward from the ball.

An excellent test for measuring achievement in the placement of forehand and backhand drives into the back court area is the Broer and Miller test.[2] A rope is stretched 4 feet above the net. The individual stands behind the base line, drops the ball to self, and drives it over the net and under the rope to land as near as possible to the opposite base line. One practice and fourteen trials are given for forehand drives, and the same number for the backhand drives. The scoring system gives highest scores to balls that land within 9 feet of the base line, scores diminishing progressively for balls that land in front of or beyond the target area. Balls going over the rope score one half the value of the area in which they land.

If a backboard is available, one can have excellent practice in returning shots, as the balls always come back. The player has the opportunity of controlling the height of the ball and can hit as hard as she wishes. Improvement in backboard practice can be measured by counting the number of continuous strokes in which the ball is hit above the net line by either a forehand or backhand drive after one bounce of the ball. Practice in changing the grip from forehand to backhand is secured by driving at the backboard alternate forehands and backhands after one bounce, working for ten or more consecutive strokes.

Dyer's Playing Ability Test is a standard test that has been scientifically validated. The player stands behind a restraining line 27.5 feet from the backboard, drops the ball, and hits it after the first bounce. The individual counts the number of strokes in which the ball lands above the 3-foot net line, having been hit after any number of bounces or by a volley, when the individual is back of the restraining line. Any number of balls may be used. The starting drop and hit does not count. The score for three 30-second periods is totaled. This is an excellent test for beginners to take at the end of the season to measure their accomplishment. For intermediates, it can be taken at the beginning and end of the season to show improvement.

The backboard is also useful for practicing

[2] Marion R. Broer and Donna M. Miller, "Achievement Tests for Beginning and Intermediate Tennis," *Research Quarterly*, October, 1950.

the serve and volley. For the serve, a line 39 feet from the board is marked. The server counts the number of serves out of ten trials that land above the 3-foot net line. For the Volley Test, a restraining line is drawn 6 feet from the backboard. The ball is put in play by hitting the ball against the backboard either with or without a bounce. The player counts the number of times she can volley the ball without crossing the restraining line in three 30-second periods. Balls may be hit after a bounce, but such a stroke does not count. Any number of balls may be used. The starting stroke does not count.

If a ball-throwing machine is available, the consistency of ball placement helps the beginner to practice the same shot over and over. Practice of a wide range of strokes is possible because the machine can be adjusted to vary angle and pace of the shots. Volleys can be practiced as well as ground strokes.

A simple serving test for beginners consists of counting the number of serves that land in court out of ten trials served to each of the service courts. If the foot fault rule is broken, the serve does not count.

To improve placement in the service for intermediates, the service court can be marked into areas giving higher scores to the area just in front of the service line and to the corners. A restraining rope stretched above the net is helpful to encourage forceful serves. The rope is also good for practicing lobs.

Tournaments are an excellent index of a person's ability to apply the skills and tactics she has learned.

Terminology

Ace: A good service which opponent is unable to touch.

Advantage: The first point after deuce (40-40). Advantage server or advantage in (shortened to ad-in) if the server wins the point; advantage receiver, or advantage out (ad-out) if the receiver wins the point.

American twist: An advanced service stroke in which the racket strikes the ball upward from left to right causing the ball to spin and bounce high to the receiver's left or backhand.

Back court: The area between the service line and the baseline; referred to as *no man's land*.

Back spin: A backward spin imparted to the ball by striking downward and under the back of the ball with an open racket face. The ball spins away from

the direction in which it is moving (underspin, chop, or slice).

Base line: The end boundary line of the court.

Break a serve: To win a game served by the opponent.

Chop: A stroke made by drawing the racket down and under the ball, imparting back spin.

Closed racket face: Hitting surface of the racket slanting down.

Continental grip: The grip with the *V* formed by thumb and index finger on the bevel to the left of center. Sometimes called the service grip. This grip is used by some players for all strokes with no change needed for forehand and backhand.

Cross-court: A shot hit diagonally across the court.

Deuce: Even score when each side has won three or more points.

Double fault: Two consecutive failures to make the service good, resulting in loss of point by the server.

Down-the-line: A shot hit parallel with the side lines, i.e., from a spot on one side to a spot directly opposite.

Earned point: A point actually won by good playing rather than lost by error.

Eastern grips: Eastern forehand—the "shake hands" grip in which the *V* is on the top when the racket is perpendicular to the ground. Eastern backhand—the grip in which the *V* is on the top left bevel.

Fault: An error in service.

Flat racket face: Hitting surface of racket at right angle to the ground.

Foot-fault: A violation of Rule 7, which states that the server shall not change his position by walking or running, and shall not touch with either foot any area other than that behind the base line between an imaginary extension of the center mark and the appropriate side line, singles or doubles.

Forecourt: The area between the service line and the net.

Half-volley: A short stroke hitting the ball immediately after it has bounced.

Let: Replay of a service or a point. A service is a let if the ball hits the net and is otherwise good, or after touching the net, hits the receiver before it hits the ground. Other lets are replay of points because of outside interference.

Lob: A stroke that sends the ball in a high arc, usually over the opponent's head into the back court.

Love: Zero or no score.

Open racket face: Hitting surface of the racket slanting upward.

Rally: A series of shots hit after the bounce back and forth across the net.

Referee: Person in charge of running a tournament.

Set: A score of at least six games for one side with at least a two-game margin, i.e., 6-0, 6-4, 7-5, 16-14.

Slice: A stroke made by drawing the racket across, down and under the ball, imparting back spin and side spin to the ball.

Slice service: A service hit with side spin, which causes the ball to bounce toward the receiver's right or forehand.

Top spin: A forward spin imparted to the ball by striking up and over the top of the ball with a flat or closed racket face. The ball spins in the same direction as its flight and is caused to bounce deep and fast.

Toss: a) Spin of the racket before play to determine choice of serving or receiving, or side of court; b) Projection of the ball into the air by hand preparatory to hitting it with a service stroke.

Umpire: The official in charge of calling the score of a match.

Volley: A shot hit before the ball bounces (other than service).

Selected References

The Book of Tennis, by Editors of *World Tennis Magazine* and Cornel Lumiere. New York: Grosset and Dunlap, 1965.

Cummings, Parke. *American Tennis*. Boston: Little, Brown and Co., 1957.

DGWS Tennis-Badminton Guide, current edition. Washington, D.C.: American Assoc. for Health, Physical Education, and Recreation.

Johnson, Joan D., and Paul J. Xanthos. *Tennis*. Dubuque, Iowa: William C. Brown, 1967.

Kenfield, John F., Jr. *Teaching and Coaching Tennis*. Dubuque, Iowa: William C. Brown, 1964.

Murphy, Bill and Chet. *Tennis for Beginners*. New York: Ronald Press, 1958.

Chapter 11

Track and Field *Nell C. Jackson*

Equipment. Safety. Goals. Running—Relays. Hurdling. **HIGH JUMP:** *Western Roll, Straddle Roll.* **LONG JUMP:** *Sail, Hitch Kick, Hang. Throwing the Discus. Putting the Shot. Throwing the Javelin. Evaluation. Terminology.*

The skills involved in track and field—running, jumping, and throwing—are basic to man. Many years ago, men were using these skills for human survival. Today, these same skills are basic to most physical activities. Regardless of the circumstances, girls find tremendous satisfaction from participating in activities using these skills.

Track and field is a sport that is enjoyed by most people either as spectators or as participants. The program is so varied that it offers a place for almost every girl regardless of her size, shape, or age. For example, a girl endowed with endurance may find pleasure running long distances, whereas large girls who cannot compete successfully in running events may find pleasure in throwing implements of different sizes and weights.

The track and field program is divided into three major categories: running, jumping, and throwing. Each of these categories may be sub-

divided into the following groups: running includes sprinting, hurdling, middle distances, distances, and relays; jumping includes the long jump and high jump; and throwing includes putting the shot, throwing the discus, javelin, and balls of various sizes.

Equipment and Facilities

Personal equipment for track and field involves a pair of shorts, a blouse, socks (to prevent blisters), shoes (warm-up and spikes), and a warm-up suit. General equipment consists of starting blocks, batons, disci, javelins, shots, balls, high jump standards, and a cross-bar.

The track is a quarter mile oval (440 yards). It is generally located around the football field. Usually it has six lanes that vary in width from 32 to 48 inches. The over-all width of the track determines the size of the lanes. Located within the oval are the high jump and long jump pits. Adjacent to the track is sufficient throwing space for the shot, discus, javelin, and other implements.

Today many schools are using an all-weather composition on their tracks and runways as well as cement circles for putting the shot and throwing the discus. Although the initial outlay for this material is relatively expensive, the upkeep of the facilities is minimal compared to cinders.

Dr. Nell Jackson has been a member of the U.S. Women's Olympic Track and Field Team and has also served as manager for the U.S. Women's National Track and Field Teams on three European tours. Miss Jackson has conducted workshops in many universities throughout the United States and has written numerous articles on track and field, particularly in the areas of training and conditioning. She earned her bachelor's degree at Tuskegee Institute, her master's degree at Springfield College, and her doctorate at the University of Iowa. Dr. Jackson is presently an assistant professor at the University of Illinois.

Safety

A sense of alertness should be emphasized at all times around the track. Listed here are a few general safety precautions that should be observed by everyone: 1) Always run around the track in a counterclockwise direction (left arm to the inside). 2) Learn to stay in your own lane to avoid running in the path of another person. 3) For efficiency and speed, learn to run in a straight line. 4) Practice all throwing events away from the running area. 5) Avoid wandering in the areas designated as throwing sectors.

Goals

Within a period of six to eight weeks, three general goals may be achieved: improvement of individual skills, development of an appreciation of the sport, and development of an understanding of the basic principles involved in the various events.

Skills

RUNNING

Basic principles

For a given force, a short lever will move faster than a longer lever of the same weight.

Any off-centered force that is applied to the body will impart a turning effect to it.

Speed depends upon the rate and length of one's stride. The use of the arms and legs as well as the position of the trunk will contribute to both the length and rate of one's stride.

To every action there is an opposite and equal reaction.

Techniques of running

ARM ACTION. The arms swing in opposition to the legs. They are carried in a bent position with the forearm and upper arm forming almost a right angle. The hands are relaxed in a semi-closed position. A comfortable position can be assumed by having the thumb and second finger lightly touching each other.

The arms should swing in a forward and backward direction. They swing up on a line even with the shoulder, and *back* toward a line even with the hips. Often, the arms will swing toward

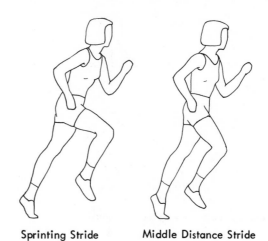

Sprinting Stride   Middle Distance Stride

(1) Sprinting stride and middle distance stride. Knee lift is higher in sprinting. Trunk is more vertical in middle distance running.

the midline of the body rather than in a straight forward and backward direction. It is permissible to do this as long as they do not swing across the midline. Swinging the arms across the midline of the body tends to encourage a great deal of lateral rotation or twisting of the trunk causing an additional amount of effort to be distributed.

TRUNK POSITION. The purpose of a slight forward trunk position is to place the center of gravity just ahead of the driving foot. The extent of the lean depends upon the speed and the amount of resistance encountered by the runner. Sprinters will adapt a forward lean varying up to 15 degrees from the vertical whereas middle distance runners will have a more vertical trunk position (Fig. 1). An exaggerated lean of the body restricts the amount of knee lift in sprinting, and it will also cause the runner to fall forward because of an inability to maintain any degree of balance because her center of gravity falls outside her base of support.

LEG ACTION. The action of the legs is divided into three phases:

1. Supportive phase. When the body rotates over the foot it is in its supportive phase. There is a momentary letdown of the heel. For a second, the foot is relatively flat on the ground.
2. Driving phase. As the body passes over the foot it is driven forward by a thrust from the leg through the foot to the ground. The amount of drive depends upon one's speed

(2) Sprinting—driving phase of stride.

(Fig. 2). Sprinters push with their driving leg until the knee, ankle, and foot are in full extension.

3. Recovery phase. At the completion of the drive, the foot is pulled forward as quickly as feasible. The leg lifts up and forward with the knee leading in a flexed position. The amount of knee lift depends upon the speed of the

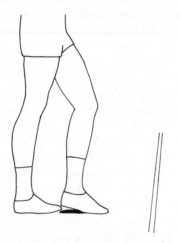

Heel of power (forward) foot is in line with toes of other foot

(3) Bunch start

(4–5) Bunch start.

(4) "Take your mark"—eyes focus 3′ in front of body.

(5) "Set"—hips slightly higher than shoulders.

runner. A high knee lift puts the leg in a more desirable position for sprinting. This is preceded by bringing the heel close to the buttocks. Sprinters, therefore, will have a high and powerful forward drive of the knee and thigh, whereas middle distance runners have a lower and less powerful drive of the knee and thigh.

FOOT ACTION. The feet should move in a forward and backward direction accompanying the action of the legs. Toeing-out in running, as in walking, puts the foot in a potentially weak position causing a reduction of the driving power. Contrary to walking, the ball of one's foot touches the ground first. As the weight is transferred over the foot, there is a momentary letdown to the heel. Then the foot extends causing the weight to move forward over the ball of the foot.

Starting

The bunch and medium starts are the most popular starting positions used today. The bunch start will put one out of the starting position the fastest. However, the medium starting will put one into his running stride the quickest. In sprinting, the important thing is to get into the running stride as soon as possible. Determine which foot is the "power foot." This is the forward foot in the starting position. As a rule, if one is right-handed the left foot is the "power" foot.

BUNCH START. The toe of the power foot is placed approximately 2 feet (2 measured foot steps) away from the starting line (Figs. 3, 4, and 5). The toe of the other foot is placed 2 inches opposite the heel of the power foot.

MEDIUM START. The toe of the power foot is placed approximately $1\frac{1}{2}$ footsteps away from the starting line (Figs. 6, 7, and 8). The knee of the other leg is placed opposite the toe of the power foot.

Elements common to both positions: The arms,

(6) Medium start: shoulders over hands; knees opposite toe.

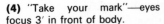

relatively straight, are placed approximately shoulder-width apart with the shoulders over the hands. The hands form a high bridge with the thumb separated from the fingers. The fingers are held closely together. The head should be in natural alignment with the shoulders and trunk. The eyes are focused on a spot approximately 1 to 3 feet ahead of the starting line.

Starting commands

Take your marks. The runner stands behind her starting blocks. On the command, "take your marks," she walks forward, in front of the blocks. Putting her hands on the track, she backs into the blocks making sure that the front foot is lined up firmly against the block with just the toes touching the ground before placing the rear foot against the block. The hands are then placed up to, but not on or over the starting line.

Points to check include the knees and feet should form a straight line; the heel should be over the toes; the arms are relatively straight; the shoulders are over the hands; the hands form a bridge; and the eyes are focused approximately 1 to 3 feet ahead.

"Set!" After the runner has settled down, the command, "set," is given by the starter. The runner then elevates her hips until they are even with or slightly higher than the shoulders. At the same time she shifts forward until the shoulders are just ahead of the hands.

Points to check. Eyes are focused 1 to 3 feet down track. Head is in line with trunk. Shoulders remain just in front of hands. Hips are slightly higher than shoulders. Rear leg is bent slightly more than forward leg.

"Go!" The command "Go" is given when the runner is steady in the "set" position. Generally it is given within 1.5 to 2.0 seconds of the previous command. The runner drives out of the starting position pushing both feet against the

(7–8) Medium start.

(7) "Take your mark."

(8) "Set"—hips slightly higher than shoulders.

starting blocks. While keeping the body low, shoulders parallel to the ground, the arms lift first, followed very closely by the forward drive of the rear foot. While the rear leg is driving forward the arms complete their initial drive. The arm opposite the driving leg swings forward and the arm on the same side as the driving leg swings to the rear. Both arms are flexed at the elbow. The forward leg drives against the block. The sprinter accelerates out of the blocks and into her full running stride.

Setting the blocks. In races that start on the straightaway, all blocks should be set in the middle of their respective lanes. In races that start on the curve, the blocks should be set at an angle, near the outside of the lane.

Coaching tips

Sprinters will reach their maximum acceleration approximately 50 to 60 yards from the start of the race. The trained runner learns to maintain her maximum acceleration throughout the latter part of the race, whereas the untrained runner tends to decrease in speed during this phase of the race. Sprinters should learn to run in a straight line and drive through the finish of the race.

In distances such as the 220 yard dash, the runner will find it difficult to maintain her maximum acceleration over the latter half of the distance. She, therefore, learns to distribute

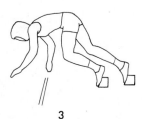   

4   3   2   1

(9) Driving from the start using starting blocks.

her energy over the distance. First, she will accelerate for about 60 yards, "float" through the middle of the race, and then drive through the latter part of the race. The "float" may be described as maintaining a fast pace with relaxed hips and arm action. This change may be difficult for the observer to notice. The floating period will be reduced when the runner becomes stronger as a result of training. Eventually, the accelerating phase of the run will blend with the driving finish.

In the 440 yard run, speed and pace are very important. First, the runner must learn to distribute her energy throughout the race instead of starting fast and fading in the end or starting too slow and finishing with a lot of reserve unused.

Pacing is very important in running the middle and long distances (440 yards or more). Good pacing is a product of speed and stamina. The runner must learn to feel the pace in order that she may properly distribute her energy evenly throughout the entire distance.

The basic principles of running the 440 are the same as for the shorter distance sprinting; however, the arm action is less vigorous. The arms are used more to balance the body than to drive it. The length of the stride is very important. It is shorter and less demanding than the sprinting stride. The length of one's stride should be natural. Overstriding is a common fault among beginners. However, if one needs to increase the stride length she should do so by developing more flexibility in the area of the hips.

Relays

Relays are fun to run! However, even though the over-all distance of a relay may vary, the basic problem remains the same—passing the baton. Relays are composed of four runners, each one running a designated distance. In some relays, all runners cover the same distance (i.e., 440 yard relay: 4 × 110), whereas in medley relays different distances are covered by the runners (i.e., 880 yard medley: 220—110—110—440).

In a pursuit relay (all participants run the same direction around oval track) the baton must be exchanged in a passing zone that is 22 yards long. The problem in all relays of this nature is to keep the baton moving as fast as possible throughout the race including the passing zone. The baton is generally passed from left to right. That is, the incoming runner carries it in her left hand and passes to right hand of the out-going runner; however, a right to left exchange may also be used by runners.

Teamwork is very important for the members of each relay team. To help the outgoing runner determine when to start running in the passing zone, she puts a mark on the track approximately 5 to 7 yards to the rear of the passing zone. When the incoming runner reaches this mark, the outgoing runner turns and starts sprinting from a semicrouched position.

BATON EXCHANGES. There are two general classifications of baton exchanges: blind or nonvisual exchange, and visual exchange.

Blind or non-visual exchange is used in sprint relays, i.e., 440 yards (4 × 110) and 880 yards (4 × 220). The incoming runner passes to the outgoing runner, who is accelerating to top speed and looking forward in the direction of the run. Ideally, the exchange should take place within the last 5 yards of the passing zone. This allows the outgoing runner to gain as much momentum as possible before receiving the baton. At the same time, the baton will be

(10) Hand position for underhand baton exchange.

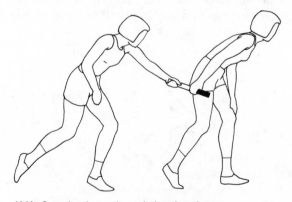

(11) Grasping baton in underhand exchange.

exchanged at a faster rate of speed. Therefore, the momentum of both runners will be maintained throughout the exchange.

There are two types of Blind or non-visual exchanges: underhand and overhand. In the *underhand* the outgoing runner extends her right arm back with the palm facing the rear (Figs. 10 and 11). The fingers are extended with the thumb separated from the other fingers forming a reverse *V*. The four fingers are held very close together. The incoming runner carries the baton in her left hand. With an upward and forward swinging motion, she passes the baton to the right hand of the receiver. It is placed between the thumb and first finger of the right hand. The incoming runner is expected to reach forward to complete the pass. As soon as the outgoing runner receives the baton in her hand, she swings it forward and immediately transfers it to the other hand.

In the *overhand exchange* the right arm of the receiver is extended backward with the palm turned up by flexing the wrist (Figs. 12 and 13). The thumb is on the inside toward the body. With the baton in the left hand, the incoming runner swings the arm forward and down placing the baton across the palm of the receiver's hand. The baton is immediately changed to the receiver's left hand, or it may remain in the right hand for a right to left exchange.

A more advanced technique may be used by the outgoing runner. When the incoming runner reaches the checkmark, the receiver starts running by using both arms in a pumping action to help her accelerate faster. When the incoming runner is close enough to pass the baton she will give a verbal command, such as, "Reach," to the receiver, who will respond by extending the right arm down and back to receive the baton.

The *visual exchange* is used in longer relays. The incoming runner may be tired and uncertain in her speed and precision of hand-eye coordination. In these relays the receiver must keep her attention on the baton until it is in her hand. She judges her pace by the speed of the approaching runner.

In the actual exchange the outgoing runner extends her right arm back with the palm up similar to the position for the nonvisual exchange (Fig. 14). At the same time her trunk is rotated toward the right to enable her to see the oncoming runner. If the oncoming runner is very tired, the baton exchange should occur in the rear half of the zone. However, if she is not too

(12) Hand position for baton overhand exchange.

(13) Overhand exchange—Grasping the baton.

(14) Baton visual exchange.

Track and Field   **207**

tired the exchange should occur in the forward half of the zone.

COACHING TIPS. If a left to right exchange is being used, the receiver should start running on the left side of the lane. In a right to left exchange she starts on the right side. All runners should learn to slow down and remain in their own lanes until all exchanges are complete at their station. If the relay starts on a curve, the starting block should be placed on an angle to permit a straight run into the curve.

Runners differ in ability and temperament, characteristics that should be kept in mind when placing the girls on the team. It is not a simple matter of starting with the second fastest runner and finishing with the fastest runner. It is wise to consider some of the following factors: ability to work together; ability to run the curves and straightaways; need for a reliable starter in the lead-off position; and best placement for each person (does the individual run best in front or from behind?). Also consider the over-all distance to be run by each leg of the relay (first runner covers approximately 118 yards, second and third approximately 128 yards, and fourth approximately 120 yards) in the 440.

Hurdling

Hurdling is a form of sprinting. It is a modification of the normal sprinting form. The height of hurdles used by girls and women is the standard 2 foot 6 inch hurdle. However, there are several recognized distances for hurdle races, as listed here.

(15) Hurdling form.

Distance of Race	Number of Hurdles	Distance from Start to first Hurdle	Distance between Hurdles	Distance from last Hurdle to Finish
50 yards	4	39′ 4½″	26′ 3″	31′ 10½″
70 yards	6	39′ 4½″	26′ 3″	45′ 9″
50 meters	4	39′ 4½″	26′ 3″	39′ 4½″
80 meters	8	39′ 4½″	26′ 3″	39′ 4½″
100 meters	10	13 m.	8.5 m.	10.5 m.
200 meters	10	16 m.	19 m. (9 strides)	13 m.

HURDLE CLEARANCE. The leg that goes over the hurdle first is called the lead leg (Fig. 15). The other leg is referred to as the rear or trailing leg.

The thigh of the *lead leg* is pulled up toward the trunk until the lower leg is level with the top of the hurdle. At this moment, the heel of the leg extends toward the top of the hurdle. As the leg clears the hurdle, it is pulled as close

as feasible to the other side of the hurdle taking the weight on the ball of the foot.

The *trunk* moves forward ahead of the supporting foot as the thigh is pulled toward the chest. The *arms* are used as in sprinting to balance the trunk and to prevent lateral rotation. If the left leg is leading over the hurdle, the right arm is extended forward while the left arm is moving back.

The *rear leg* is left behind as long as possible on the take-off. The purpose is to encourage a wide split between the legs so the hurdler will skim close to the top of the hurdle. The rear leg, in a continuous motion, pulls forward and sideways over the hurdle with the leg flexed to the side. The inside of the leg and foot pass over the hurdle in a relatively flat position. The foot is held in a flexed position.

LANDING. The lead leg will touch down first with the toes pointed straight ahead approximately 2 to 3 feet from the hurdle. The weight should be taken on the ball of the foot, then transferred to the other part of the foot as in sprinting. As the rear leg continues to pivot around the top of the hurdle, the knee is pulled up slightly in order to place the leg in a good position to drive forward. The first step forward is taken with the rear leg; therefore, it should be a full running stride.

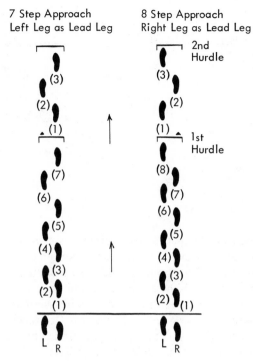

7 Step Approach
Left Leg as Lead Leg

8 Step Approach
Right Leg as Lead Leg

2nd Hurdle

(3)   (3)
(2)   (2)
(1)   (1) 1st Hurdle

(7)   (8)
(6)   (7)
(5)   (6)
(4)   (5)
(3)   (4)
(2)   (3)
(1)   (2) (1)

L R   L R

(16) Approach to hurdle.

While running between hurdles, sprinting form is used with the arms and legs. An odd number of steps are taken between hurdles to insure the use of the same lead leg each time. For example, in distances up to 80 meters, three strides are used between hurdles.

THE START. Hurdlers use the same type of start as sprinters because they want to accelerate as quickly as possible into their sprinting stride. Usually, they will take 7, 8, or 9 strides to the first hurdle. If the left leg is the lead leg in the starting position and it is also the lead leg over the hurdle, 7 or 9 strides are used by the hurdler. If the right leg is the lead leg in the starting position and the left leg is the lead leg over the hurdle, 8 strides are used by the hurdler.

BEGINNER'S PROGRESSION. Run over a low barrier, such as a long jump rope or a crossbar. The barrier is stretched 6 inches high across the track. If a jump rope is used, it should be held by two people, and if a runner touches the rope, those holding it should release it immediately.

Increase the height of the barrier gradually until it is approximately 20 inches high. The beginner should lift the lead leg to clear the barrier instead of lifting the body as in jumping. If the leg is lifted properly, the over-all height of the body's center of gravity will not vary in the run.

As the barrier is raised higher, the rear leg begins to assume hurdling form in order to miss the obstacle. The knee of this leg rotates out to the side while the lower leg folds sideways and pivots over the barrier.

Practice swinging the trail leg along the side of the hurdle. Gradually, add a walk and jog to the swing.

COACHING TIPS. Stress that hurdling is sprinting. Speed is gained by being on the ground, not floating in the air.

Encourage a good "split" by lifting and driving the lead leg forward.

Do not encourage overstriding between hurdles. Instead, develop more hip flexibility.

Do not rush the rear leg into action too soon. This will cause the hurdler to land with the feet too close together and sit on top of the hurdle.

Stress keeping the foot of the rear leg flexed to the side as it crosses the hurdle to prevent tripping over the barrier.

Stress arm opposition as the body crosses the hurdle.

JUMPING

High jump

Among the basic principles in the high jump, two key factors are spring and layout. Spring can account for almost 90 per cent of the height of the jump; however, it should be pointed out that one may be obtained at the expense of the other. The importance of speed in the approach increases as the bar is raised and as the take-off angle becomes smaller.

The jumper should impart maximum vertical velocity to the center of gravity along with sufficient body rotation for a layout. Any movement originating in the air causes an equal and opposite reaction. For example, in the western roll, reaching into the pit with the hands at the height of the jump causes an elevation of the hips.

Two popular *styles* of jumping are the *western roll* and the *straddle roll*. Both of these styles will enable the jumper to clear the bar with an economy of effort. Using maximum spring, they will also enable the jumper to clear the bar very close to the height to which she is capable of lifting her center of gravity. In other words, there will be less body surface between the center of gravity and the bar.

The approach and take-off are basically the same for both styles of jumping. The take-off for the *western roll* is made with the foot nearest

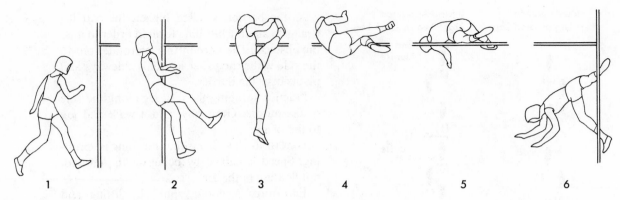

1	2	3	4	5	6

(17) High jump—western roll.

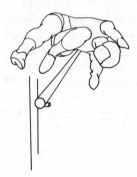

(18) Western roll—over the bar.

the crossbar (Figs. 17 and 18). In this style, the bar is cleared with the side of the body next to it.

The lead or free leg, head, and shoulders cross the bar first. The head drops toward the shoulder nearest the bar while the arms reach for the pit. The general idea is to have some parts of the body over the bar before other parts have risen to its level. As the arms reach toward the pit, the hips are lifted away from the crossbar. After a strong push-off, the take-off leg tucks under the body with the knee pulled toward the chest. The jumper lands on the take-off leg and both hands, a three-point landing.

The leg nearest the crossbar is also used as the take-off leg in the *straddle roll*; however, with this technique, the body rotates around the bar in a face down position (Figs. 19 and 20). The free leg drives up toward the bar as the take-off leg pushes against the ground. The leg may be extended or it may be flexed at the knee.

The arms drive upward also. At the height of the jump the outside arm swings across the bar, toward the pit. When the head and shoulders clear the bar they are dropped toward the pit. The legs remain apart as the body rotates around

the bar. In fact, a *V* is formed as they pivot around the bar. To clear the take-off leg, the knee and foot should rotate away from the bar, or they should be extended up and back as they cross the bar. A three-point landing should be used if landing in a sawdust pit; however, if landing in a soft pit, such as foam rubber, the jumper may land on her back or side.

THE APPROACH. Generally, the approach is long enough to allow the jumper to gather sufficient speed to clear the bar and to have maximum control of the limbs at take-off (Fig. 21). This is usually accomplished with five, six, or seven smooth strides. A long fast run is not needed because speed is not important. The approach should be made from a 40 to 45-degree angle to the crossbar.

The last stride in the approach is slightly longer than the other strides. This will enable the jumper to place the center of gravity just behind the take-off foot in order to get a good layout and a long swing of the free leg. The jumper approaches from the left side if springing from the left foot or right side if springing from the right foot.

THE TAKE-OFF. The take-off spot should be approximately an arm's distance from the center of the crossbar (Fig. 22). This spot may vary a little but not very much.

In the last stride up to the bar, the heel of the take-off foot hits first. It is followed by a rocking-up to the ball of the foot for a strong push-off. The jumper must extend the take-off leg and push the body off the ground as high as possible before going into the layout position. As the weight is transferred to the ball of the foot, the free leg swings forward vigorously, either partially bent or extended, to assist with the upward thrust and beginning layout position. Actually, the take-off is a combination of

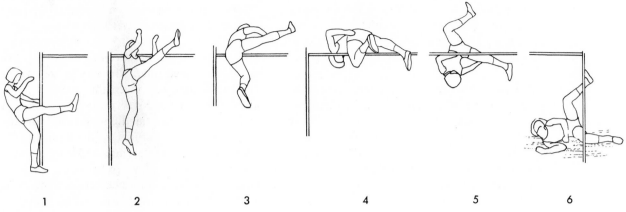

1   2   3   4   5   6

(19) High jump—straddle roll.

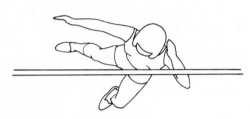

(20) Straddle roll—over the bar.

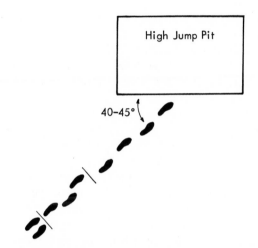

High Jump Pit

40–45°

(21) Seven stride approach to high jump: approach from left side for spring from left foot.

kicking and springing instead of springing and then kicking. If maximum spring and layout are to be obtained, the timing of this movement is very important.

The arms are used to help lift the body by extending them upward as the take-off leg extends.

COACHING TIPS. The western roll is generally taught first because the performer learns to jump over the bar, whereas with the straddle roll the jumper is encouraged to roll over the bar. For the western roll, determine the take-off foot by taking three running strides and pop up into the air off one foot. Repeat this several times to see if the same foot is used each time. Generally, right-handed jumpers will use the left foot and vice versa.

Place the crossbar 1 foot above the pit. Standing in front of the bar, take three strides up to it, spring over the bar and land on the same foot. Those who wish to take off from the left foot form a line on the left and those using the right foot form a line on the right. Both groups will approach the bar between a 40 to 45-degree angle from their respective sides.

Each person jogs up to the bar, kicks the free leg up toward a standard, and then springs over the bar, landing on the take-off foot.

(22) High jump take-off.

The foregoing step is repeated, kicking the free leg up, followed closely by a spring off the other leg. This should emphasise the kick then spring sequence.

Track and Field   **211**

Raise the bar to 2 feet. Repeat the foregoing movement. This time emphasize pulling the take-off leg as close as possible to the chest as the body passes the bar. Land on the take-off foot.

Place a small piece of foam rubber in the pit to the right or left of the center of the bar depending upon the take-off foot (to the left for those taking off with the left foot). Jump over the bar—kick then spring. At the height of the jump, the jumper reaches into the pit with the inside hand to pick up the foam rubber. At the same time, she drops her head toward the same shoulder. This initiates a layout across the bar and it helps to raise the hips over the bar. To every action there is an equal and opposite reaction. Land on the take-off foot.

Jump over the bar—kick, spring, tuck the take-off leg, and reach into the pit with both hands. Land on the hands and take-off foot for a three-point landing.

For the straddle roll, determine the take-off foot and review the kick and spring sequence. Place the bar at 2 feet. Take off from the leg that is nearer the bar; land on the opposite foot and both hands. Drop the head and shoulders toward the pit as the body crosses the bar. Kick the take-off leg up and away from the bar.

POINTS TO REMEMBER. The take-off spot is approximately an arm's distance from the center of the bar. On the take-off, swing the lead leg high and vigorously. It should rise higher than the crossbar. Remember to kick (swing the leg), then spring. Push the foot against the ground and extend the take-off leg.

In the western roll, tuck the take-off leg tight under the body in mid-air. In the straddle roll, kick the take-off leg up, or rotate the knee and foot out as the body crosses the bar. The head may be rotated toward the bar as the body passes over it for a side or back landing. If the take-off spot is too close, the bar will be dislodged on the upward part of the jump. If the spot is too far from the bar, it will be dislodged as the body starts on its downward flight. Turning the trunk too soon and/or leaning into the bar on take-off will cause the shoulder to dislodge the bar.

Long jump

The basic principles of the long jump include the following. Maximum vertical velocity should be imparted to the jumper's center of gravity during the take-off. Greater distance can be obtained in the jump when the initial velocity contains an upward as well as a forward component.

The flight path of the center of gravity has been determined once the body leaves the ground; therefore, movements made by the body in the air are concerned with an efficient landing. The ideal landing position for the jumper is one that permits the flight path of the center of gravity to continue as far as possible and at the same time provide the greatest possible horizontal distance between the heels and the center of gravity. In practice, however, these actions interfere with one another, so there has to be a compromise between the two.

THE APPROACH. In general, a jumper reaches approximately 75 to 80 per cent of her top speed in the approach. Maximum acceleration is not obtained because she would have trouble converting the horizontal speed to an upward lift. The average run-up is approximately 90 to 120 feet. Depending upon the length of one's stride, this distance is covered in 17 to 19 strides.

The speed of the run permits the jumper to accelerate, then "gather" herself in the last three or four strides before reaching the board. The jumper runs with smooth and even strides, not short and choppy strides. The approach, therefore, should be practiced often.

Check-marks are used to establish a stride pattern to the take-off board. Usually, two check-marks are used by the jumper: the first being four strides from the starting mark; the second, approximately six strides from the first mark. The advantage of the check-marks is to let the jumper know if she will hit the take-off board with the proper foot without having to alter her speed or stride length. For convenience in the run, the first step in the approach should be the same foot used for the take-off.

THE TAKE-OFF. The take-off is a continuous movement; that is, the jumper runs off the take-off board rather than running up to the board, stopping or slowing down, and then taking off.

As the jumper "settles" into the last three strides, she relaxes and prepares herself for the jump. The trunk is in a relatively upright position to enable the take-off foot to drive off the board and to enable the free leg to reach up and forward on take-off. Some jumpers tend to shorten their strides 4 to 8 inches in the last three steps, whereas others shorten only the last stride.

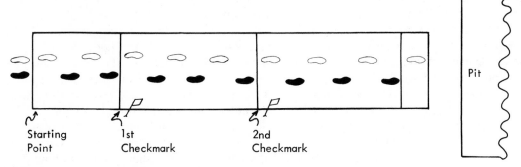

(23) Long jump stride pattern.

When the foot touches the take-off board, the body rotates forward over the heel and pushes off with a strong action from the ball of the foot. The take-off leg extends as it begins to lift the body forward and upward. The head, chest, and shoulders are carried high to assist with the vertical lift. At the same time, the arms continue their driving movement to assist with the upward lift of the body. The free leg drives up and out with the knee in a flexed position.

STYLES. The three styles used by jumpers today are the sail, the hitch kick or run in the air, and the hang. The *sail* is the easiest style to learn (Fig. 24). Once the body leaves the ground, the free leg drives up and reaches forward. The take-off leg pulls forward as soon as possible. Both legs are carried in a partially bent position while the body is in the air. In an effort to keep both feet up as long as possible, the jumper tries to keep the heels on a line even with the hips, well ahead of the trunk. The trunk is carried in an upright position with a minimum amount of forward rotation. The head, chest, and arms are carried high.

(24) The sail.

(25) The hitch kick.

(26) The hang.

(24–26) Styles of the long jump.

(27) Hitch kick action sequence.

Most of the better jumpers use the *hitch kick* or *run in the air* (Figs. 25 and 27). It is performed by taking one complete step in the air. The free leg drives up and forward as the jumper leaves the board. The leg continues to straighten out; then it sweeps down and back. The foot is pulled very close to the hips as it continues its circular movement to the front. In the meantime, the heel of the take-off foot folds up toward the hips as it swings forward. It remains partially extended in front of the body until the other leg completes its stepping action. Both legs are held as high as possible. Upon landing, the jumper reaches forward into the pit with the feet. The arms counterbalance the body, moving in opposition to the legs, by swinging back, then around the shoulders, and then forward as both legs extend forward for landing.

The *hang* is the most difficult style to learn because of the need for tremendous strength in the abdominal muscles and hip flexors (Fig. 26). After the free leg drives up, it swings back to join the take-off leg, which is flexed at the knee. Both legs trail the body. The arms, moving together, swing backward over the shoulders, then forward. As the arms swing forward, the legs reach out for landing.

LANDING. The various jumping styles are designed to get the feet as far ahead of the center of gravity as possible before landing. The trunk, head, and arms contribute to proper landing if they do not rotate too much in either direction—forward or backward. As the feet drop to the pit, the arms swing forward and back while the trunk is leaning slightly forward.

COACHING TIPS. For the sail, determine the take-off foot. Using a short approach, five or seven strides, take off by pushing against the ground and extending the take-off leg. Swing the free leg up and forward and then land on it with the other leg trailing the body. Repeat the foregoing movement, and bring both legs forward in the landing position. Try to lift the heels to the height of the hips. Land on both feet. Carry the chest high throughout the movement.

For the hitch kick, determine the take-off foot. Using five strides, run up to the pit, take off on one foot, and swing the free leg up and forward. Land on the free leg. Repeat the foregoing movement; however, while in the air, the free leg drops and swings toward the rear. The take-off leg swings to the front. Land on the take-off leg with the other leg trailing. Repeat the latter movement. This time continue the

action of the free leg until it returns to the front. Land on both feet.

In the hang, after the take-off, the free leg straightens out under the body. It swings to the rear flexed at the knee. This leg is joined by the take-off leg, which is also flexed at the knee. The trunk is in an extended position along with the arms. Both legs are brought forward flexed then extended for the landing. Land on both feet.

GENERAL COACHING TIPS FOR ALL JUMPING. An approach that is too short does not allow time to build up speed, whereas an approach that is too long will tire the jumper. The approach should be smooth, not a series of short choppy steps. The arms should swing up vigorously at the take-off and reach forward on landing. The chest and head should be kept up as the body leaves the take-off board. Too much forward rotation of the trunk will cause the feet to drop too soon. Too much backward bending of the trunk will cause the hips to drop too low and the jumper will probably fall backward in the pit.

THROWING

Basic principles common to all throws

All throws are rotational events. The discus rotates in a horizontal plane, whereas the javelin and shot rotate in a vertical plane.

The body is moving forward over the ground at the moment of release in all throws. The feet may be stationary, but the upper body continues to move forward in the direction of the throw.

In order for the speed of the body to complement the speed of the throwing arm, the path of the implement (when released) should be parallel to the path of the body during the acceleration period.

The longer the radius of rotation, the faster the angular velocity for the same turning speed. This means that the thrower should try to keep the implement away from the body. The arm is extended sideways on the discus and backward in the javelin. In the javelin throw, there is a strong hinge movement caused by the body whipping forward braced against the forward foot.

Acceleration of the movement depends upon the length of time force is exerted on the implement. This may be noticed in the shot put when the performer leans over the rear edge of the 7 foot circle. The discus thrower rotates in the

8 foot circle and the javelin thrower extends the javelin well back in the throwing stance.

To impart maximum speed to the implement used, the feet should remain in contact with the ground to offer resistance to the thrower's movements.

SEQUENTIAL BODY MOVEMENTS OF THE THROW. The basic movement pattern of the body in the throwing stance is similar for all throwing events; therefore, this movement pattern should be stressed first.

The body is in a forward stride position with the weight on the rear leg, which is usually the right leg. The rear leg is flexed at the knee and the trunk is turned toward the right side. The direction of the foot and knee of this leg will vary with the event.

The rear foot pushes against the ground causing a lifting and forward rotation of the right hip. This movement is followed very closely by a forward rotation of the trunk and an arching of the back. At the completion of this movement, the chest is high, back is arched, and trunk and stomach are facing the direction of the throw.

Throwing the discus

The discus is thrown from a circle that has a diameter of 8 feet, $2\frac{1}{2}$ inches (Fig. 28). Because of the limited space, the thrower takes a one and a half step turn in the circle to gain momentum, which is imparted to the discus. At the end of the turn, the discus is released in the front part of the circle. It should land in a throwing sector, which is a 60 degree arc of the circle.

SPECIFICATIONS OF IMPLEMENT. An official discus is made of wood or of some suitable material with metal plates set flush into the sides. The weight is 2 pounds, $3\frac{1}{4}$ ounces. The outer diameter of rim is a minimum of $7\frac{3}{32}$ inches and a maximum of $7\frac{5}{32}$ inches.

THE GRIP. The discus is held in the hand with the fingers spread comfortably apart (Fig. 29). Only the flesh part of the first joints of the fingers should overlap the edge of the discus. It is important to have the fleshy part of the first joint of the first finger over the edge in order to obtain the proper release of the discus. The thumb is relaxed on the discus and forms an extension of the forearm. The hand is cocked toward the rear of the discus.

THROWING PATTERN. The beginner should first learn to throw the discus from a stationary position with feet spread shoulder-width apart and left shoulder (for right-handed thrower)

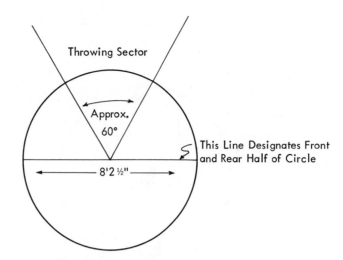

(28) Discus throwing circle.

pointed in the direction of the intended throw. This is the same release position used by the more skilled performer as she gains power by making a one and three-quarter turn into the throw.

In preparation for the throw, the right arm is held about chest high and extended away from the body while the left arm is flexed across the chest. Using a horizontal swinging pattern around the body, the discus is released at the side of the body with a final roll off the index finger. A palm down position of the hand is maintained at all times.

THE TURN. The thrower stands near the rear edge of the circle (Fig. 30). Experienced throwers stand with their back to the throwing sector; beginners, however, may have trouble starting

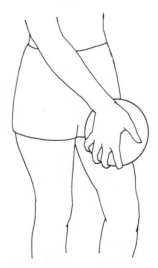

(29) Grip for discus throw.

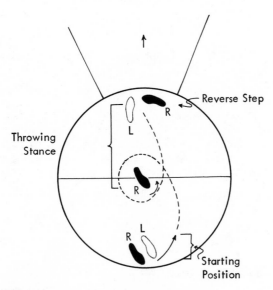

Throwing
Stance

Reverse Step

R

L

R

R

R L

Starting
Position

(30) Rotating in circle for throwing discus.

in this position, so they often begin a quarter turn to the left of this position

With the knees slightly flexed, and trunk upright, the thrower turns or coils to the right as far as possible, shifting the weight from the left foot to right foot. The discus is carried as far as possible behind the shoulder in its coiled position so that it trails the trunk as it uncoils. The head and eyes focus on some distant object in the intended direction of the spin.

At the end of a preliminary back swing, the thrower starts to pivot to the left on the left foot making a 360-degree turn. The right leg drives across the circle, toward the front, touching down near the center of the circle. The thrower is actually turning 360 degrees, but stepping toward the center of the circle.

(31) Releasing discus.

The thrower spins on the ball of the right foot, trying not to interrupt the forward flow of the body. Continuing the spinning action, the left foot is placed close to the forward edge of the circle just behind a line even with the right foot.

THE RELEASE. The body has completed a one and a half step-turn. The extended right arm continues to trail the body. As the left foot is planted, the right foot begins to push against the ground causing an elevation and forward rotation of the right hip. This is followed very closely by an arching of the trunk and elevation of the chest. The left arm is used to help pull the trunk around.

Following the action of the trunk, the right arm whips around the body with the palm facing the ground. The discus is released when the arm is almost level with the shoulder and parallel to the trunk. It is released at an angle of approximately 30 to 35 degrees in relation to the ground (Fig. 31). The index finger is the last to leave the discus. The pull of this finger causes the discus to spin clockwise as it floats in the air.

After the discus leaves the hand, a follow-through takes place. This is accomplished by transferring the body's weight to the right foot, which becomes the forward foot. A follow-through should not be taught. Instead, it should be a natural movement caused by the speed and power of the throw.

COACHING TIPS. As control of the release improves, the driving action of the leg, hip, and trunk are added to the movement. Try to cross the circle in a relatively straight line. Pressure of the thumb on the discus will affect the delivery angle and it will cause the discus to wobble in the air. Keep the discus and arm trailing the body as it moves across the circle. To prevent dizziness, focus on a distant object when moving across the circle instead of looking at the ground.

Putting the shot

The put is made from a circle 7 feet in diameter. A stop board is placed in the middle of the circumference in the front half of the circle (Fig. 32). The shot should be put from the shoulder with one hand. At no time should it be permitted to drop behind the line of the shoulder.

The "O'Brian technique" of putting the shot is the most popular style used by performers today. This style permits the shot to travel through the greatest possible distance before it is released, thereby giving extra distance to the put.

SPECIFICATIONS OF IMPLEMENT. The shot is made of solid iron, brass, or any metal not softer than brass. It is spherical in shape and the surface is smooth. It should conform to the following specifications. The weight should be a maximum of 4 kilograms (8 lbs. 13 oz.) and a minimum of 8 pounds. Its diameter should measure a maximum of $4\frac{11}{32}$ inches and a minimum of $3\frac{3}{4}$ inches.

THE GRIP. Rest the shot in the left hand, and then place the right hand loosely on top (Fig. 33). For small hands, a four-finger grip should be used. All four fingers are spread comfortably behind the implement for a better grip. The thumb offers lateral support. For a larger hand, a three-finger grip is used. The thumb and fourth finger give lateral support to the shot whereas the other fingers are spread behind the implement. In either case, the shot is held by the fingers and cushioned at the base of the fingers; it is not resting on palm of the hand. It is desirable to have a well-balanced grip.

STARTING POSITION—O'BRIAN STYLE. Stand at the rear of the circle facing the outer edge. The shot is nestled under the jaw, on the right side of the neck for support. The elbow is under the shot; however, the arm is held midway between the shoulder and side of the body. The line extending from the shot to the elbow along the forearm should be an extension of the line of flight of the implement as it leaves the hand. The eyes are focused on an object about 5 yards away.

THE GLIDE. The glide is initiated by a vigorous swing of the left leg (Fig. 34). It moves up and back toward the front part of the circle. At the same time, the trunk drops toward the rear of the circle. Following this movement, the right leg flexes, then extends, pushing the body across the circle. As soon as the right leg completes its thrusting action, the left leg drops to the ground near the toe board. The right leg remains partially bent.

The left arm started the movement in an extended position above the head; however, when the trunk bends forward, the arm also follows the same movement of the trunk.

At the completion of the glide, the body's weight is over the right leg, which is near the center of the circle. The left leg is near the toe board. The momentum initiated by the glide continues its forward movement even though the feet are remaining stationary. The shot

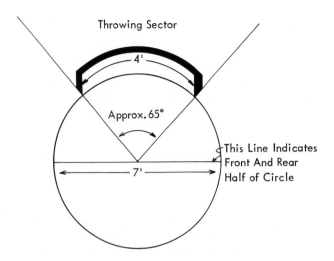

(32) Shot put throwing circle

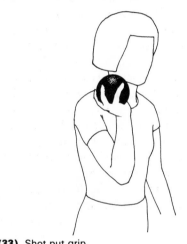

(33) Shot put grip.

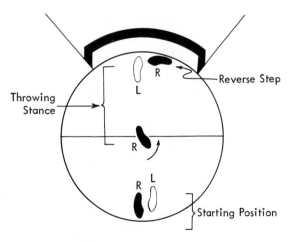

(34) Steps in circle for shot put.

(35) Putting the shot.

putter is now in the throwing position; however, she is still facing the rear of the circle.

THE RELEASE. The large muscles continue to act upon the movement. As in the other throwing events, the body begins to uncoil. The right leg thrusts against the ground lifting and rotating the right hip toward the front. This is followed closely by a rotation and lifting of the trunk and shoulders. The left arm, with the elbow bent, assists in the trunk rotation by its forceful pulling action.

As the trunk completes its movement, the force initiated by the thrusting of the right leg moves through the arm. The elbow remains away from the body while the hand pushes up and away from the shoulder. The fingers, being the last to leave the implement, impart a forward flicking action (Fig. 36).

THE FOLLOW-THROUGH. The follow-through is used to maintain balance after the implement leaves the hand. This consists of shifting the weight from the left foot to the right foot. Often this is accomplished by switching the position of the feet after the shot leaves the hand.

(36) About to release the shot put.

BEGINNER'S PROGRESSION. Stand with the feet about 8 inches apart, facing the direction of the put. Raise the left arm above the head. Hold the shot in the right hand, but keep the arm midway between the shoulder and side of the body. Using just the arm, push the shot up and away from the body.

Using the foregoing stance, bend the knees, then extend the legs and push the shot away. Again, using the foregoing stance, bend the knees and rotate the body to the right as far as possible without moving the feet. Extend the legs and uncoil the body, then push up and out with the arm.

With the shot under the jaw, stand in a forward stride position with the feet 18 inches apart. The left foot is closer to toe board. Turn the feet so that the back is facing the direction of the put. Drop into the putting position by bending the knees and trunk. The body's weight is over the right foot. The shot is carried near the edge of the base of support or just outside the edge depending upon the strength of the individual. From this position, the force is exerted through the foot, knee, hip, trunk, shoulder, arm, and hand as the body uncoils. The left arm pulls down and back in an automatic response.

After this phase has been done correctly, move into the glide. Draw a line 7 feet long. Stand near the end of this line and practice the glide trying to cover two to three feet with the thrusting movement. Combine the glide with the uncoiling movement.

COACHING TIPS. Move across the circle in a relatively straight line. Blend the glide with the put in order to utilize the speed in the gliding action. Grip the shot with the fingers, not with the palm of the hand. The desirable position of the elbow is between 40 to 45 degrees away from the body.

Keep the shot nestled close to the neck as long

as possible as the body uncoils to permit the shot to travel the greatest distance before leaving the hand. Ideally, keep both feet in contact with the ground, in the throwing stance, until the shot leaves the hand. Use the entire body in the put instead of just the arm and hand.

Throwing the javelin

The javelin consists of three parts: a metal head, a shaft, and a cord grip. The shaft is constructed of wood or metal. Attached to the shaft is a metal head that forms a sharp point. The cord is located at the center of gravity of the implement.

The javelin is thrown from behind an arc of a circle drawn with a radius of 26 feet, 3 inches. Parallel lines 13 feet, $1\frac{1}{2}$ inches apart, extend from the extremities of the arc marking the runway or javelin approach. The javelin is thrown into a sector of approximately 28 degrees (Fig. 37).

SPECIFICATIONS OF IMPLEMENT. The weight is 1 pound, $5\frac{1}{4}$ ounces. The overall length is 7 feet, $2\frac{5}{8}$ inches (minimum) and 7 feet, $6\frac{1}{2}$ inches (maximum). The diameter on shaft at thickest point is $\frac{13}{16}$ inches (minimum) and 1 inch (maximum). The distance from tip of metal head to center of gravity measures 2 feet, $7\frac{1}{2}$ inches (minimum) and 3 feet, $1\frac{3}{8}$ inches (maximum).

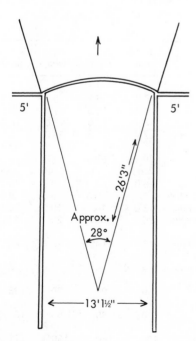

(37) Javelin approach.

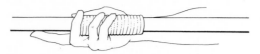

(38) Javelin grip.

THE GRIP. The javelin lies diagonally across the palm with the tip of the thumb resting on the top of the binding (Fig. 38). The second finger is also curled around the top of the binding, while the index finger is curled lightly around the shaft. The other fingers are curled around the binding.

THE APPROACH. Approximately fifteen to seventeen running strides are used in the approach. The speed of the run varies with the individual; however, the javelin is thrown on the run. Therefore, the speed of the run must be under control. Usually, it is a run with easy strides after a smooth acceleration.

The javelin is carried over the shoulder near the top of the head. The point is held slightly up while the javelin is parallel to the line of the run.

The last five strides of the run are very important because they put the body in position for the throw while continuing the forward momentum.

THE LAST FIVE STRIDES (starting with left foot). During the first, second, and third steps, the right arm is extended back and carefully aligned so that the tip of the javelin is parallel with the hair line (Fig. 39). The arm remains about shoulder level. The feet turn slightly to the right with each step to permit the trunk to rotate in this direction while extending the right arm.

On the fourth step, a "cross step" is executed by placing the right foot across the left to enable the hips and trunk to turn sideways in order to extend the arm over the greatest possible distance. On the fifth step, the left leg quickly reaches forward to act as a brake. This also begins a hinge movement of the rest of the body. Throughout these steps, the arm stays relatively relaxed and straight. The palm is carried up.

The throwing stance is assumed when the left foot reaches forward and the back is arched. In a sequence of movements, the legs, hips, and trunk elevate and rotate to the front. The right shoulder, followed by the elbow and hand, whips forward and upward. The elbow should be carried higher than the shoulder.

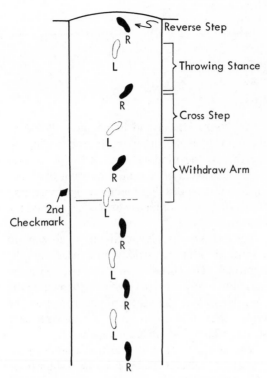

(39) Foot pattern in approach for javelin throw.

Because the fingers are the last to leave, they impart a rotation to the javelin (Fig. 40).

BEGINNER'S PROGRESSION. First, learn the grip. Then, hold the javelin over the shoulder and spear it in the ground. Aim for an object about 10 feet away. Point the javelin downward when working on short distances. Gradually lengthen the throwing distance. At the same time, start pointing the javelin up about 30 to 40 degrees from the horizontal.

Extend the arm back and rotate the trunk to the side. Then pull the trunk and arm forward, concentrating on the shoulder, elbow, and hand coming into the movement in that order. Practice the five-step approach emphasizing the "cross-step." Combine the five steps with the arm extending back and trunk rotation. Gradually combine the running approach with the complete throw.

COACHING TIPS. Keep a firm grip with the fingers on the javelin so it will not wiggle in the hand. Learn to throw on the run instead of running up, stopping, then throwing. Keep the javelin parallel to the path of the run, so the point will not move away from the body during the approach.

An approach that is too fast will be difficult to control. The thrower, therefore, will have difficulty converting the run into a throw. An approach that is too slow will have an insufficient amount of speed to impart to the delivery. Failure to use the hip, trunk, and shoulder in the delivery limits the distance of the throw.

Rules

Copies of the rules governing track and field for girls and women are published by the Amateur Athletic Union (AAU) of the United States, 231 West 58th Street, New York, N.Y.; and Division for Girls and Women's Sports, American Association for Health, Physical Education and Recreation, 1201 Sixteenth Street, N.W., Washington, D.C.

Evaluation

It is difficult to evaluate objectively performances in track and field. Many teachers have found a great deal of satisfaction comparing performances at the beginning of the unit with those at the end of the unit. Others have set up predetermined standards that must be achieved by the performers. Listed here is a guide that may be used to evaluate performances. These standards are based on data collected over a period of five years.

Events	Excel- lent	Good	Average	National Record
50 yd. dash	6.6	7.1	8.1	5.7
60 yd. dash	7.6	8.1	9.1	6.7
75 yd. dash	9.0	10.0	11.0	8.1
100 yd. dash	12.0	13.0	15.0	10.5
220 yd. dash	27.0	31.0	36.0	23.4
440 yd. run	1:10 (70 sec)	1:20 (80)	1:30 (90)	53.4
880 yd. run	2:40	3:10	3:40	2:04.6
440 yd. relay	55.0	60.0	70.0	45.4
50 yd. hurdles	7.8	8.5	9.5	6.4
80 m. hurdles	13.0	14.0	15.0	10.7
8 lb. Shot Put	35′	30′	25′	47′ 9″
Running Long Jump	16′	14′	12′	21′ 10½″
Running High Jump	4′ 10″	4′ 4″	3′ 8″	5′ 10″
Javelin Throw	130′	90′	70′	188′ 11″
Discus Throw	120′	80′	60′	189′ 5″
Baseball Throw	200′	160′	130′	271′

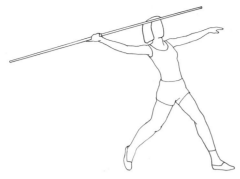

(40) Throwing stance with javelin.

Terminology

Anchor: The fourth runner of a relay.

Baton: A metal or wooden tube that is used in a relay race. It is passed from one runner to another.

Circle: A metal rim (restraining area) that encloses the area in which the shot put and discus are released.

Crossbar: A metal or wooden bar used in the high jump.

Curb: The inside edge (border) of the track.

Cut down: The snapping down of the lead leg in hurdle clearance.

Exchange zone: The area in which the baton must be exchanged during a relay race. The distance is 22 yards.

False start: Leaving the starting position after the command "set" has been given, but before the gun has been fired.

Inside lane: The lane that is next to the curb of the track.

Jog: A very slow, relaxed run that is used during the warm-up.

Lane: Guide-lines on a track that indicate the path a runner must follow in specific races.

Lap: One trip around the track.

Lead leg: The forward leg in the high jump and the first leg over a hurdle.

Lead-off runner: The first runner of a relay team.

Leg of a relay: One position of a relay team. Also refers to the distance one must run.

Medley relay: A relay race in which the runners run different distances.

Nonvisual exchange: A technique used to pass the baton. The outgoing runner does not look back while receiving the baton.

Pace: The rate of speed used by runners of middle and long distances to conserve their energy.

Passer: The incoming runner on a relay team who gives the baton to the next runner.

Pursuit relay: A relay in which all four runners run in the same direction (counterclockwise) around the oval track.

Put: The action of pushing the shot away from the body.

Runway: The approach area used in the long jump and javelin throw.

Sector lines: Boundary lines for good throws in all throwing events.

Staggered start: The marking on the track designating the starting position of runners in races which must extend around one or more curves. The runners in all lanes run the same distance.

Starting blocks: An implement used by runners to get a faster start.

Straddle position: A technique used in high jumping to clear the bar. The stomach of the jumper passes next to the bar.

Straightaway: The straight area on the track. It is generally referred to as the distances between curves; however, some tracks have an area of 220 yards on one side of the track.

Take-off board: A board at the end of the approach of the long jump from which the jumper makes her jump.

Toeboard: A curved piece of wood used on the front edge of the shot put circle.

Trail leg: The take-off leg (rear leg) in hurdling.

Visual exchange: A technique used to pass the baton in which the receiver watches the incoming runner throughout the exchange.

Western roll: A technique used in high jumping in which the side of the jumper's body passes next to the bar.

Selected References

Canham, Don. *How to Improve Your Track and Field.* Chicago: The Athletic Institute, n.d.

Foreman, Kenneth, and Virginia Husted. *Track and Field for Women.* Dubuque, Iowa: William C. Brown, 1964.

Scott, Phebe M., and Virginia R. Crafts. *Track and Field for Girls and Women.* New York: Appleton-Century-Crofts, 1964.

Wakefield, Frances, and Dorothy Hawkins. *Track and Field for Girls.* St. Louis: C. V. Mosby, 1966.

Chapter 12

Trampolining *Mary J. Culhane*

History. Equipment. Safety. Goals. SKILLS: *Foot Bounce, Basic Drops, Swivel Hips, Roller, Half Turntable, Lead-Up to Forward Somersault. Mechanics of Movement. Evaluation.*

Trampolining permits one to bounce on a rebounding surface and perform stunts of varying levels of skill. Besides affording enjoyment, the trampoline is a means of conditioning for the beginner as well as for the expert. It can be a most vigorous activity in a very short period of time. It provides an excellent opportunity for the performer, as well as the observer, to acquire a better understanding of the principles underlying movement. As one acquires proficiency in the skills, creativity in planning routines adds to the enjoyment of the activity.

History

Court jesters were the first to use equipment to allow the individual more time in the air for performance of acrobatic skills. The job of entertaining the king and his court through skill in acrobatics demanded variety to maintain interest and approval. It was discovered that by supporting a resilient plank above the ground and bouncing on it, greater height could be obtained on jumps into the air, and thus more

intricate actions could be performed. The next step in the origin of the trampoline was come upon by chance. An aerialist's mistake in timing as he performed on a trapeze over a safety net caused him to fall, and upon rebounding from the net, he performed a somersault. The audience looked favorably upon this maneuver and the mistake evolved into an act of its own. The safety net became a rebounding surface for a bouncing and tumbling routine. The actual piece of equipment that we now use was devised in the 1930's by George Nissen. It became very popular during World War II, for at that time it was found that the trampoline was an excellent piece of equipment for use in the training of pilots for development of spatial relationships and sense of balance. Today there is widespread use of the trampoline in school physical education programs from elementary through college levels as well as in recreational programs.

Equipment

The trampoline is rectangular in shape, and about table high, with a canvas or nylon surface tightly drawn to the sides of the frame. It is a costly item in the initial outlay, but if properly cared for will withstand much usage for years.

The costume worn may be gym outfit—shirt and shorts or leotard. Some performers prefer to wear a covering on the arms and legs to prevent any possibility of skin abrasions in the

Miss Culhane received her bachelor's and master's degrees at the University of Iowa and has done graduate work at the University of Colorado and the University of Southern California. She was formerly an assistant professor at Oberlin College where she taught classes in trampolining. Miss Culhane is now teaching in the Riverside, California public schools.

initial learning stages of stunts such as the knee drop and front drop. Socks should be worn when the trampoline has a web bed.

Safety

Anyone taking part in this activity must constantly keep safety in mind. The very nature of the equipment, with its bounding reaction to the body weight, combined with the feeling of freedom and fun, can be a hazard if not properly supervised. For the promotion of safety the following precautions must be stressed:

1. No use of trampoline without supervision.
2. Equipment should be kept folded and locked when not in use.
3. Class members should learn the proper manner of folding and unfolding the equipment.
4. Instruction should be given in the correct way to mount and leave the trampoline: by using the metal frame instead of the suspension system to support the body weight; by holding the frame and stepping from the apparatus when dismounting. Precaution must be taken when leaving the apparatus in order to avoid a hard landing and to prevent slipping on the floor, especially for those in stocking feet.
5. Performers should wear socks to protect the toes from being injured in a trampoline with a webbed bed.
6. Glasses may be worn for the basic skills but are not recommended with the more advanced figures involving somersaults. If glasses are worn they must fit securely.
7. When a class is in session the trampoline should be properly "spotted" by at least two persons on each side of the trampoline and one on each end. The responsibility of spotters is to watch the performer at all times and to direct the individual toward the center of the bed if she moves toward a side of the trampoline.
8. The beginner should remain on the trampoline for very short periods of time in order to avoid lack of control caused by fatigue.
9. Instructor and students must know the logical sequence in difficulty of skills. Performers must warm up and carefully lead into each new movement pattern.
10. The back somersault and other more advanced stunts must not be attempted until the instructor says the student is prepared for them. A safety belt should be used when learning advanced twisting movements and advanced routines.

Goals

One participates in this activity in order to, among other things, acquire a fair degree of skill and understanding of the basic drops: seat, knee, hands and knees, front and back, and the foot bounce; develop large and small muscle groups, to stimulate the cardiovascular system, and to aid in the over-all body coordination; develop an increasing sense of balance and spatial awareness; help build confidence and courage in learning new movement patterns; develop the ability to make quick decisions in order to make changes in body position; realize the enjoyment possible in the performance of the skills; and experience the creative aspects inherent in the activity.

It is surprising how many skills one can learn in the short amount of time that is actually spent by an individual in activity on the trampoline. For example, the total activity per person for a session usually amounts to about three minutes. This amount of time might represent four turns with progressive time increases from thirty seconds to one minute. Learning also occurs, of course, in the observation of others as they are performing.

Skills

The bed is marked with colored lines midpoint along its length and width and an individual endeavors to center on and over the area where these two divisions bisect. During all activity upon the trampoline bed the performer focuses the eyes on a designated area, usually the end frame. Focusing the eyes is known as *spotting* and is essential for maintaining balance as well as aiding in the centering of activity. Stunts on the trampoline are performed in the air above the center of the bed with a return to the same center spot for every bounce. One should not travel forward or backward as in tumbling stunts.

FOOT BOUNCE

The first fundamental skill to be learned is the foot bounce. One has to acquire good body balance over the base of support in the upright position in order to work the bed correctly. The following correct technique should be learned. At the beginning of the foot bounce the feet are spread about shoulder-width apart and knees bent while the body weight depresses the bed of the trampoline. The knees straighten and arms lift as the bed rebounds. The feet and legs come together with toes pointed during the upward movement of the body. The arms lift to shoulder height or higher at the height of the jump; then a slight pause, termed *floating*, precedes the drop back to the bed of the trampoline (Fig. 1).

As the body drops, the arms move downward and the feet and legs open or spread again in order to maintain balance. The contact on the bed is made with slight flexion in the hips, knees, and ankles. There is some tension in the body in order to increase the downward depression of the bed, followed quickly by extension into the repetition of the lift if this is desired.

Controlling the bounce

Upon landing, the bounce may be stopped by increasing hip, knee, and ankle flexion in order to absorb the rebound action of the bed. Checking the bounce with this "kill spring" must be practiced so that the performer has control of her bounce and can stop at any time. Also, one has the tendency to increase the height of succeeding bounces. It is best for the beginner to maintain a moderate height until balance and control are assured.

Twists

The basic twists can be learned along with the foot bounce. These are the half and full twist done in the vertical position. The twist is initiated, after the feet leave the bed, by a quick turn of the head and shoulders in the intended direction. At the same time the arm on the side of the turn swings across the body at chest height, and the opposite arm swings above the shoulder and overhead (Fig. 2). The half twist should be learned first, and one should be capable of performing this twist in either direction. With a higher jump and more vigorous arm action, a full twist can be accomplished. All skills should be mastered progressively, with the initial emphasis on control; working on form and increasing height can be emphasized later.

(1) Foot bounce: rebound in air.

(2) Vertical half twist to the left with head turned to "spot."

(3) Knee drop: arms ready for lift action.

(4) Seat drop: about to land.

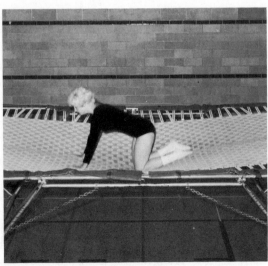

(5) Hands and knees drop.

After sufficient control has been acquired with the foot bounce and twists, the basic drops may be attempted. These are known by the body parts which make contact with the bed: knee drop, seat drop, hands and knees drop, back drop, and front drop.

Knee drop

The knees are bent so the legs and extended feet are parallel to the bed with the actual touch being made by the knees, front of the legs, and top of the insteps. The rest of the body is in good alignment, maintaining tension, with the hip joint fixed, back and head erect, and arms ready to assist in lifting the body from the rebound (Fig. 3).

Seat drop

The contact with the bed is made in a long sitting position (Fig. 4). At the height of the bounce the legs and feet are extended forward and held parallel to the bed with the arms being brought down to the sides. The hands should be close to the hips with the palms parallel to the bed and fingers extended forward. The backs of the legs, seat, and palms of the hands touch the bed while the eyes are on the focus spot. The back and head are erect. The body maintains tension upon contact so that a live rebound will result. The hands and arms press harder at the time of greatest bed depression to add to the rebound.

Hands and knees drop

At the height of a bounce the body assumes a table-like position with the back parallel to the bed, knees bent and directly under the hip joint, and hands with palms parallel to the bed and under the shoulder joint. The focus for the eyes changes to the lengthwise colored strip, i.e., to a spot just ahead of bed contact. The touch upon the bed is made by the knees and palms of the hands, hence the other name for this stunt: *four point* (Fig. 5). The body is held firm, with tension in hip, shoulder, elbow, and wrist, in order to acquire the most rebound action. The hands should give added press action at the moment of greatest bed depression to aid in rebound backward for the upper trunk.

Back drop

For this stunt the back, from the shoulder blades to just below the waist, makes contact

Trampolining   **225**

(6) On the mat.

(7) At height of rebound.

(8) About to land on feet after rebound.

(6–8) Back drop.

with the bed. The knees are bent slightly and brought almost over the hip joint. The shoulders and head are brought forward and held firm when contact is made to prevent whip back of the head. The hands may hold the legs above the knee joint and thus prevent elbow abrasions (Fig. 6). During the rebound the legs are extended and the body arched in a layout position above the bed (Fig. 7). The descent is a curved path toward the pointed feet (Fig. 8).

Front drop

The front drop is best learned after the four point drop has been mastered so that the forward descent can be controlled. Starting with a foot bounce, the back is brought parallel to the

bed at the height of the bounce. A quick touch of the hands to slightly bent knees is followed by extension of legs and body with elbows half bent and palms down (Figs. 9 and 10). The contact is made by the lower chest, abdomen, thighs, forearms, and palms. The head is held up and back with the upper chest raised and eyes focused upon the bed ahead of the contact area (Fig. 11). Body tension is maintained to secure the necessary rebound and to prevent injury.

FOOT BOUNCE VARIATIONS

Several stunts may be performed on the rebound from the foot bounce to provide variations for this basic skill. The positions for these figures are taken at the height of the rebound,

(9–11) Front drop.

(9) Partial pike in air with back parallel to bed.

(10) Beginning of stretch to horizontal.

(11) Body parallel to bed just before contact.

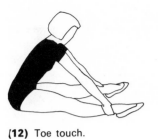

(12) Toe touch.

(13) Tight tuck or cannonball.

and then the performer immediately returns to the vertical position to land on the feet. As control and ability in performance improve, one may land in other positions from these stunts.

Toe touch

At the height of a foot bounce the long sitting position is taken with the legs spread apart, toes pointed, and hands touching as far down the legs as possible while keeping the legs straight (Fig. 12). The quick action for this stunt comes at the floating stage following the foot bounce.

Tight tuck or cannonball

The knees are pulled up to the chest and held by the arms while keeping the back straight (Fig. 13). As the various stunts are learned, they may be combined and performed in sequence (also termed *swingtime*). An example would be toe touch, seat drop, knee drop, foot bounce. The vertical twist can be combined with either the knee drop or seat drop as follows: knee drop or seat drop; one-half vertical twist to feet, or one-half vertical twist to knee or seat drop.

STUNT COMBINATIONS

Some of the more popular stunt combinations are swivel hips, roller, half turntable, and somersault lead-ups. The *swivel hips* stunt combines a seat drop with a vertical half twist, followed by another seat drop in the reverse direction. It is best learned after one has control of the seat drop from some height in order to obtain more time in the air for the twist in the vertical position. The quick turning of the head and hips, with the arms lifting over the head in the opposite direction when in the vertical position, gives impetus for this twist (Figs. 14, 15, and 16).

The *roller* is a combination of the seat drop, a full twist (or roll) in the horizontal position, and landing in another seat drop. One faces the same direction throughout the stunt. Height is needed on the rebound from the first seat drop. As one begins the rebound, the body is straightened and nearly parallel to the bed. This is accomplished by lifting the midsection up,

(14–16) Swivel hips.

(14) Begins with seat drop.

(15) Hip twist in vertical position: arms swing overhead and to the right (reaction aids shoulder and hip twist to the left).

(16) Ends with seat drop and facing opposite direction.

Trampolining   **227**

(17) Starts with front drop.

(18) Tuck position for turntable: back remains parallel to bed.

(19) Reverse position front drop for turntable.

(17–19) Half turntable.

(20) Forward somersault take-off.

followed immediately by the twist initiated by the hips and a quick head turn to focus on the spot after the completed twist. After the full twist the body assumes the seat drop position for landing. The stunt should be practiced at first in two separate stages: (1) seat drop with horizontal twist to front drop; (2) front drop with horizontal twist to seat drop.

The *half turntable* stunt is a combination of the front drop with a one-half turn in a tucked position and landing in the opposite direction in a front drop (Figs. 17, 18, and 19). A good lead-up sequence, divided into two stages, is (1) A four point drop, a push by the hands in order to turn on the rebound, then into a front drop. A tucked position is assumed on the turn while keeping the back parallel to the bed. The

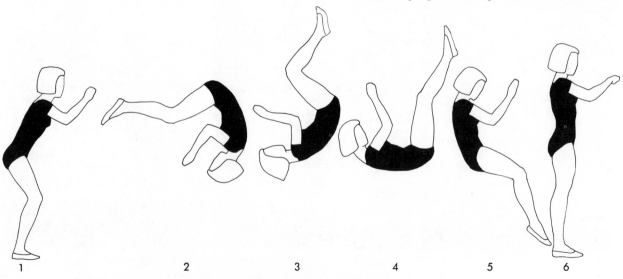

1 2 3 4 5 6

(21) Forward somersault—sketches shown across page to illustrate turn. Somersault on trampoline is up and down without forward traveling.

head leads in the turn and the eyes quickly spot on the reverse side; then the body is extended and lands in the front drop. (2) Reverse the procedure and begin with a front drop, tuck tight on the rebound, turn head and shoulders, and land in a four point position in the opposite direction. When these two stunts are under good control, one may begin and end with the front drop.

The *somersault* is one of the more difficult stunts on the trampoline and should be attempted only when one has acquired good skill and control in the basic landing positions. For the forward somersault one must change up-and-down motion into forward rotation. The hips must be lifted first, then the tuck position is taken, in order to avoid any forward travel (Fig. 20).

Through the *lead-up* stunts for the somersault one gains confidence and ability to perform with forward rotation of the body. The stunts to be progressively mastered are (1) four point, tuck turnover, seat drop; (2) foot bounce, tuck turnover, seat drop. An important factor to keep in mind throughout each of these stunts is that there should be no traveling. This is accomplished by keeping the body weight directly over the points of bed contact so that the rebound direction will be straight up from the bed. The turnover action is initiated after the rebound action has started. As the body rebounds from the bed the performer assumes a tucked position and quickly pulls the head forward and down while rounding the shoulders. The tuck position is held until the back is parallel to the bed, then the landing position for the seat drop is taken. Keep the knees apart so that the nose is not bumped on the knees.

The finished form for the forward somersault, with the take-off from an upright position, requires bending the body at the hips at the moment of take-off. The feet push downward, then the hips move backward and upward (Fig. 21). It is best, in the early stages, to avoid a tight tuck because this can give too much spin and possible loss of control. Lift the head before landing and extend the body to check spin; arms in front of the body provide balance.

Skill Synchronization

After a fair degree of proficiency has been attained in the fundamentals, one may practice

(22) Alternate bouncing on one trampoline.

some of the other variations such as partner alternate bouncing, synchronization of routines on separate trampolines, and synchronization of bouncing with music.

Partner alternate bouncing involves two people bouncing alternately so that one is at the top of a bounce while the other is at the bottom of a bounce (Fig. 22). In alternate bouncing the trampoline is shared so that performers are in the center of one-quarter section of the bed diagonally opposite each other. The partners should be approximately the same body build and weight in order to produce similar reactions on the trampoline bed. There are, of course, increased problems of balance, timing, and spotting. One is soon aware of the keen sense of timing that is demanded in this type of activity. For best results, moderately high bouncing is necessary in order to allow one's partner adequate time for her rebound and to keep the bounces equal. One performer acts as leader and cues in the partner during a foot bounce preliminary to the start of the routine. It is essential

(23) Synchronization of foot bounce on two trampolines.

that the simple routine be fixed well in mind for the sake of coordination and cooperation.

Synchronization of skills on separate trampolines is possible when two or more trampolines are available. Individuals of similar weight may team up, beginning with foot bounce practice in the same rhythm, progressing to the basic drops and later to simple routines (Fig. 23).

Synchronization of skills on one trampoline is also possible in the following positions: facing each other with hands clasped, or side by side facing opposite directions with inside forearms together and inside hands clasped at partner's elbow. Low bouncing is recommended, because this minimizes the uneven rebound action that results from error in timing between performers and avoids placing undue stress on the spring cables. Performers working in unison on the same equipment will find it more difficult than when each works on a separate trampoline because errors in timing can be felt by the participants. Unison work demands great accuracy in timing and coordination to produce pleasurable results.

Synchronization of bouncing with music can also be accomplished. It will soon be noticed, as one performs or observes, that the work on the trampoline has an inherent rhythmic pattern. It is possible to impose a rhythm for performance by the use of music in the background. The music makes an interesting variation for practice to improve form and control, as well as to gain increasing height. Recommended rhythms are marches and fox trots.

Mechanics of Movement

Several principles of movement relate to performance on the trampoline. These mechanical principles should be understood, for they are essential for skilled performance and for safety.

For every action there is an equal and opposite reaction. The pressing of the body weight downward into the bed of the trampoline initiates the rebound reaction of the bed, which is springy by virtue of its construction. Increased downward pressure on the bed results in an equal and opposite reaction, thus giving greater rebound and more height.

Body balance is proportional to the base of support. A small base means less stability. This

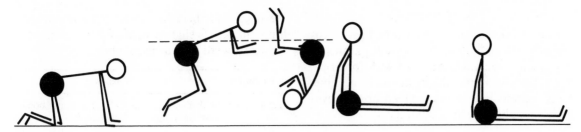

(24) Performer rotating around center of gravity.

principle is important in the foot bounce where the feet should be shoulder width apart and thus provide a base equal in width to the structure above.

The path that the body travels depends upon the relation of its center of gravity to its base of support. The center of gravity must be kept over the base of support and directed vertically upward in order for the body to return to the same spot.

When a performer is free of support in the air, no body movement will raise or lower the center of gravity, but the body can rotate around its center of gravity. This principle applies to the turnover stunts and the somersault. For example, on the rebound from a knee drop, the hips (center of gravity) are pulled back and the upper body leans slightly forward. The center of gravity does not rise from this position, but as the arms press down and forward lean increases, the body rotates around its center of gravity (Fig. 24).

The body may be put in motion by transfer of momentum from a part to the whole. This principle is used in turning the body around its long axis as in the vertical twist or the half twist. The turn is initiated with the arms, shoulders, and head. The action of these parts causes the body as a whole to turn around its long axis as a result of transfer of momentum from parts to the whole.

Evaluation

Analysis of performance and understanding of mechanical principles involved can be gained through observation of the performance of others on the trampoline. The following information covers the foot bounce and the five basic drop positions with reference to good form and some of the more common results of faulty form.

FOOT BOUNCE

Good form: Head, shoulders, hips, knees, and ankles are in a straight line. Upon landing, the feet are shoulder-width apart. When in the air, the feet and legs are together with toes pointed. Arms lift up to at least shoulder height as individual goes up on rebound, and drop to sides upon descent. Eyes are focused directly ahead on bed frame.

Faulty Form	Results
Head forward and body lean	Forward travel
Back arched	Backward travel
Ankles not extended on rebound	Little or no push-off from bed; less height
Feet together when landing	Unstable position
Eye focus wanders	Traveling

SEAT DROP

Good form: Legs together, straight, and parallel to bed with toes pointed. Hands near hips with fingers pointing toward toes. Back straight, and eyes focused on bed frame ahead.

Faulty Form	Results
Body lean forward	Forward travel
Back arched	May strain back
Knees bent at more than right angle	Uneven landing
Little or no arm action	Less rebound action

HANDS AND KNEES DROP

Good form: Shoulders over hands and hips over knees with back parallel to bed. Change focus to spot slightly ahead of landing.

Faulty Form	Results
Back not parallel to bed with the shoulders high	Knees rebound before hands; hands land heavily
Sitting back on heels	Same as foregoing entry

FRONT DROP

Good form : Forearms, shoulders, hips, knees are in a straight line so that body is parallel to bed upon contact. Contact bed with forearms, chest, abdomen, and thighs at the same time. Legs together and pointed. Head up and eyes focused on bed ahead of landing.

Faulty Form	Results
Body parts not parallel before contact	Part of body landing first will rebound first and could cause strain in the back muscles
Diving approach instead of a stretching action	Traveling forward with elbows contacting first, possibly resulting in a mat burn

BACK DROP

Good form : Contact the bed on the back from the shoulder blades to just below the waist. Keep legs together, making a right angle at the hip joint, knees slightly bent and toes pointed. Reach forward with arms and head.

Faulty Form	Results
Make contact with bed low on back—waist and hip area	Snap back of upper body and shoulders
Neck muscles not set	Snap back of head
Knees greatly bent as in a tuck	Rebound straight up or tendency to rebound over backwards

Selected References

Griswold, Larry. *Trampoline Tumbling*. New York: A. S. Barnes and Co., 1962.

Keeney, Chuck. *Trampoline Illustrated*. New York: Ronald Press, 1961.

Ladue, Frank, and J. Norman. *This is Trampolining*. Cedar Rapids, Iowa: Nissen Trampoline Company, 1960.

Chapter **13**

Skiing *Ruth Elvedt*

Skiing in the United States. Systems of Teaching. Equipment. Safety. Preseason Activities. Orientation to Skis. Finished Forms—The Skills in American Technique. Mechanical Principles. Use of Ski Lift. Terminology.

Skiing is a beautiful outdoor sport that provides for a wide range of activity and develops coordination, rhythm, balance, and agility. It is a national phenomenon that is here to stay and grow!

History

Although skis did not reach the Atlantic shores until the middle of the eighteenth century, the art of skiing is almost as old as man himself. Ethnological records have traced it back to the Stone Age. According to Charles Dudley, in his *60 Centuries of Skiing,*

Skiing as a sport is of comparatively recent origin, but skiing as a means of travel or transportation dates

Miss Ruth Elvedt is an Associate Professor of Physical Education at Mount Holyoke College. Miss Elvedt has been a student of most of the various systems for the teaching of skiing and has assisted with the certification of teachers for the United States Eastern Amateur Ski Association. She is faculty advisor to the Mount Holyoke Ski Team, which competes in the Women's Intercollegiate Ski Conference, a league of eleven colleges sponsoring racing for those of novice and intermediate ability. Miss Elvedt has given numerous lecture-demonstrations on dry skiing, and while on sabbatical observed and participated in skiing throughout the Eastern United States and Canada as well as Colorado. During 1968 Miss Elvedt attended the Winter Olympics in Grenoble, France.

(1) Skiers in action.

(2) Skiing at night—snow guns for man-made snow in background.

back of written history. . . . Throughout the ages we can trace the history of the ski along with man's travels from the time of his earliest migrations to those which occurred as late as the ninth and tenth centuries.[1]

At this early date, equipment consisted of barrel staves with toe straps. With all the advancements in equipment and technique, it is evident that the evolution and adoption of skiing has resulted from constant adaptation and testing.

Today skiing is highly specialized and undoubtedly one of the most popular of the winter sports. There is extensive publicity and literature for the skier. The sport has been highly glamorized and has reached epidemic proportions in both spectator interest and mass participation. Skiing is fun, thrilling, and adventuresome for both novice and advanced skiers. Skiiing is for everyone from the toddler to the golden-ager, regardless of an individual's height, weight, occupation, sex, or experience. During the past decade, no skiable region has escaped the invasion of ski facilities and skiers. As a result, mammoth resorts as well as more unpretentious ski areas have sprouted up all over the country. Automation has brought manicured slopes, lifts, and even snow-making machines. Skiing has rapidly taken an important place in school and adult life as a weekend and vacation sport.

THE DEVELOPMENT OF SKIING IN THE UNITED STATES

In 1904, the National Ski Association was organized at Ishpeming, Michigan. It largely controlled the development of skiing until the 1920's when divisions started to organize. Forming of these divisions reflected the rapid growth of interest in skiing. The United States *Eastern* Amateur Ski Association was organized in 1922, initiated by Fred Harris of Dartmouth College. This was the first divisional unit of the National Ski Association. Others followed until now there are seven.

Otto Schneibs, ski coach at Dartmouth College, brought the Arlberg technique to this country in 1927 and stimulated interest in having skiing as a part of the physical education program. Mass enthusiasm and interest in all winter sports was stimulated when the Winter Olympic Games were held for the first time in the United States at Lake Placid in 1932. The

National Ski Patrol System was organized by Charles Minot Dole in 1938.

In 1958, the American Ski Technique was initiated at NSA and a certification committee meeting was formed at Alta, Utah. The PSIA. (Professional Ski Instructors of America) was organized and gained approval of NSA (National Ski Association) in 1961. A year later, the PSIA., working with NSA, took over certification of instructors and an International Ski Instructors Association was formed. The American Technique was announced in October, 1962 by the PSIA.

Technique or Systems of Teaching

Through the years, skiing has progressed through various systems of teaching—from the early Arlberg to the present widely accepted American Technique. In this country, the change included Arlberg, Swiss Interassociation, French or Allais, and Austrian. The Canadian and Natur-Teknik systems are also used by some skiers. All of these systems involve weight-shifting from one ski to the other. A few of the high points of each system follow.

Arlberg was the first modern system that had graded classes, and it involved techniques for control of speed. Turns were executed by the use of a wide base with ski tips together in a *V* position, and by free body swing or rotation involving extreme vorlage (forward lean from the ankles and knees). This system was introduced in the Arlberg Mountains of Austria as recently as 1907 by Hannes Schneider. In 1927 Otto Schneibs brought the Arlberg System to this country. During the 1950's, it became modified and stressed the use of a "delayed shoulder" on the follow-through.

The *Swiss Interassociation Technique* was formulated in 1932 with a basic concept of having the body pivot with the ski rather than ahead of it; thus the skier "stayed square" with the skis. The weight was taken off the heels so that turning of the skis was done on the tips. Side-slipping (sliding downhill with skis at right angle to the slope) was used, and unweighting or lifting one's weight off the ski was an up-down movement.

The *French or Allais Technique* was formulated in 1937. It discarded the stem or *V* position of the skis and used side-slipping. The hip

---

[1] C. M. Dudley, *60 Centuries of Skiing* (Brattleboro, Vermont: Stephen Day Press, 1935), p. 17.

Skiing   **235**

blocking that developed was initiated by upper body rotation, which aided in turning the skis, and the weight was fairly evenly distributed between the skis although the outer ski became gradually weighted. Unweighting was done with a down movement or bending of the body.

The *Austrian Technique* involved a fairly exaggerated comma or flexed position of the body with considerable weight on the downhill ski and with the uphill shoulder leading.

The *American Technique* employs a modified reverse shoulder, weighting of the uphill ski in a stem turn and resetting the edges of the skis with a down motion to complete the turn. This method of skiing is concerned with three components of skiing:

1. The execution of finished technical forms or skills.
2. Methods of teaching including progressions, learning the terrain, and so on.
3. The theory or bio-mechanics of skiing.

The American Ski Technique is based on seven principles:

1. Forward Lean—The skier's center of gravity is ahead of the ball of the foot.
2. Total Motion—When maneuvering and turning, the action is continuous until completed.
3. Up-Unweighting—Action is initiated by a quick upward extension of the body that momentarily eliminates body weight on the ski.
4. Counter Rotation—One part of the body acts against another part in turning.
5. Weight Transfer—Shifting the weight to one ski aids in changing direction and providing force.
6. Natural Position—The skier should be relaxed with the weight of the body being supported by the skeletal structure rather than the leg muscles.
7. Angulation—With a bend at the hips, the upper body tilts outward while the hips are angled in toward the hill.

The *Canadian Technique* is similar to the Austrian but introduces considerable hopping and pole planting even at the beginning stages. This presents no problem for the child but frequently becomes difficult for the adult or poorly coordinated individual.

The *Natur-Teknik* was introduced in the United States about 1957. It is based on the natural body and muscular movements used in other sports. Walter Foeger, the founder, keeps the skis parallel throughout and uses the same skills and progressions for the beginners as for the advanced skiers. He claims therefore to progress more rapidly by introducing only one new element—the varying pitch and contour of progressively more difficult terrain. As in the Canadian System, the use of poles and hops is occasionally a problem.

Equipment

Although there are certain guideposts about quality and cost of items to be purchased, many decisions will be based on individual preferences, particularly for the experienced skier. If the skier is unsure of his love and ability for the sport, it is often best to rent equipment the first few times prior to undertaking the substantial investment involved in purchasing equipment. When buying equipment, the novice should seek advice at a reliable ski shop.

BOOTS

Because boots are the contact point for the communication of the body with the skis, they are a most important piece of equipment. The boot should be comfortable and fit snugly over one heavy sock and a light one, or a light one and an inner sole. The heel must *not* slip when the boot is tightly laced, and one must be able to wiggle the toes and have each in contact with the boot.

The boots should be kept well polished with ordinary shoe polish (oil softens leather too much and is therefore harmful), should always be kept away from heat, and one should walk in them as little as possible (to maintain stiffness of the sole). Whenever boots are not in use, shoe trees should be used in them, particularly when damp and drying.

BINDINGS

A simple release type binding with a taut Arlberg safety strap attached to the heel piece or cable is a necessity. The Arlberg strap attaches the ski to the boot and, in case of a fall, prevents a runaway ski. To be sure of proper placement, the binding should be mounted at the ski shop.

This is usually done in such a way that the toe of the boot will be located at the center of the ski. In any case, the bindings must be set to release under the stress of impact with an object and with the torsion or twisting caused by a fall. For the proper setting the individual's size, weight, strength, and skiing experience must all be taken into consideration. The skier should understand the method of adjustment so that the safety bindings that release the boot from the ski under undue stress can be checked periodically.

Because of a slight difference in the last of the boot, the ski binding must be set for the right or left boot, and therefore one must know the right ski from the left. A small *R* and *L* marked on the ski is helpful.

SKIS

For the novice, length and flexibility are more important than a particular name brand.

Length

A safe suggestion is that a ski be equal to one's own height, or a bit taller for the experienced skier. The short ski may seem more manageable, but it is hard to handle in some kinds of snow and its use makes it difficult for the skier to change to the normal length ski.

Material

Both the metal and epoxy (similar to fiberglas) skis have assets, but a good wooden ski should be entirely satisfactory for the novice. The first two kinds take little or no care, maintain durable sharp edges, and are registered so that one ski can be replaced or matched if the other is damaged. The quality of the wooden ski is based largely on the number of laminations, which in turn determine flexibility, strength, and cost.

Points to look for when buying or renting wooden skis

INTERLOCKED, FULL-LENGTH, OFF-SET EDGES. An off-set edge is a metal strip placed along the bottom of the ski in such a way that it protrudes a fraction of an inch downwards and thus grips hard surfaces to prevent the skis from slipping when trying to traverse, slow down, or change direction. If the edge is full length it extends up over the bend of the ski a bit (but not the tip) to protect the ski. The edge is more likely to be ripped off the ski with use if it is shorter. Inter-

(3) Checking the camber of skis.

locked edges fit into one another and are more secure than ones that are only placed adjacent to one another piece by piece.

CAMBER. The skis are curved, but should be flexible enough to flatten with pressure. To test the curve of the skis, the bottoms of the skis should be placed together. With one hand, at the footplate, the skier should be able to press the skis together so that they touch (Fig. 3). Otherwise, the skis are too stiff and the skier will be skiing on only the tips and heels of the skis and thus lack the support of the groove and the whole ski.

Avoid using warped skis. When a pair of skis is placed flat on the floor they should have equal camber. One can also test for warping by looking down the groove on the bottom of the ski.

Protective base

Most skis today have a carefully prepared durable base (such as ebonite, kofix, plastic, and so on). If not, a protective base *must* be applied. The skis must be clean and dry, and wooden skis should first be sandpapered, then the dust completely wiped off, before applying the base as per the manufacturer's instructions. For convenience, lacquer is durable, quick-drying, and easy to reapply. If used, it must be spread evenly in a series of *thin* layers with a soft brush. A second coat cannot be applied until the first is thoroughly dry.

Wax for skis

Wax may be used on skis and many kinds of waxes are available for the varying snow conditions. For the experienced skier, waxing is a matter of personal preference. Usually, after the skis have a good protective base, the only wax one needs to apply will be a silver "surface" wax for wet conditions.

Storing skis

Skis should be dried after use, strapped together, and then stored in a cool, dry place. A 1-inch block of wood placed under the toe plate offers sufficient spread between the skis.

POLES

The poles are an item of equipment where one can cut down on expense. Kind and height is largely a matter of preference. A length commonly used is to the base of the armpit. The ring, or basket, should be securely attached at the point of contact on the lower end of the pole and should not be too large or heavy. Hardened aluminium poles will serve as a good starter. Steel, fiberglas, and the ultra light, strong, and "balanced" poles are lovely, but very expensive and unnecessary for the novice skier.

SKI WEAR

The clothing must be warm and comfortable, but not restricting or cumbersome: *pants or knickers*—tightly woven and water repellent; *long underwear*—a two-layer "thermal" type is best to keep the skin warm and dry and allow for circulation of air; *parka*—a hooded nylon shell or quilted jacket is recommended. These are light in weight, retain body heat, and keep the wind out. Dacron or down are recommended fillers. *Mittens*—although most people believe it is easier to grasp a pole while wearing gloves, it is generally agreed that mittens are warmer. In either case, the leather thermal type is the most acceptable. For added warmth, one may also wear a silk glove (available at ski shops); *socks*—one thin lightweight wool or silk pair under a heavy wool pair is sufficient; the foot too must be free to move and breathe. *Sun glasses or visor*—needed to protect the eyes from glare and storms; *head gear*—cap, hood, head band, or ear muffs may be worn to protect the head and ears from extreme cold.

Safety

Ideas for several of these statements were drawn from Frank Elkins' very useful text.[2]

Never ski alone.

Never ski when tired or ill.

Check your bindings regularly and be sure they are properly adjusted. All attachments should be secure. A safety strap is essential.

Never step on the slope without skis on unless it is icy or hard packed.

Always ski "under control" and on slopes you can handle and enjoy. This means you should have the ability to stop and/or turn quickly.

Consider others as well as yourself and recognize your limitations; otherwise, you are a menace to others.

If the slope is too big for you to handle safely, take lift down or traverse and side-slip down.

Never stand in the path of a runaway ski.

On a crowded slope or trail take a glance "uphill" before setting out. Likewise, when turning, take a quick glance over the shoulder first.

When overtaking another skier, call, "Passing on your right (or left)," not "track." It is the responsibility of the overtaking skier to avoid those below him.

After a fall stay still at first so others can dodge you. Then move out of the way as soon as possible.

Stand still; don't dodge an oncoming skier.

Keep to the sides of the slope and to the right of the trail on ascent. When standing still, have tips away from the trail.

Mark any dangerous spots and fill in any ruts or bathtubs (sitzmarks) you see.

Before ascent, always check kind of snow, degree of difficulty of the trail or slope, and ability to control self on the particular slope.

Before entering a slope or intersection, check for approaching downhill skiers.

Acquaint yourself with the various kinds of snow and learn to recognize and handle them.

Check speed (slow down) above and below an icy spot, not on it.

Eat well and dress properly.

Skiing does not have a high accident rate in proportion to the number of skiers but, like airplane crashes, they are spectacular and receive much publicity. To protect oneself, fully

[2] Frank Elkins, *The Complete Ski Guide* (New York: Doubleday Doran and Co., Inc., 1940), pp. 248–251.

enjoy the sport, and give it a worthy reputation, it is vital to heed these tips before skiing on unknown terrain: 1) stay within your own ability group, 2) stay on the size slope which you can control, and 3) continue taking lessons in order to improve your skill and become oriented to varied conditions. Minot Dole tells us:

Seventy-eight percent of the accidents happen to novices. . . . Inexperience, lack of control, fatigue and skiing on terrain or in snow beyond one's ability to handle are the chief causes.[3]

Otto Schneibs gives wise counsel:

It is advisable, too, that one get into condition before winter arrives. . . . I stress the importance of learning to ski through the proper channels. Don't try to be a champion overnight. . . . Begin on the practice slopes. Then when you have improved sufficiently, attempt the steeper inclines. But be sure that you have learned the fundamentals before trying advanced trails.[4]

SKI FIRST AID

The following are minimum essentials every skier should know in order to assist if needed at the scene of an accident:

Keep the victim warm and immobile and send for the Ski Patrol. Place crossed ski poles sufficiently far above the accident to allow oncoming skiers to slow down and avoid another accident or collision with the victim. Do *not* remove the boot. It serves to splint and protect the joint from further injury and from frostbite. Be very careful when removing skis to avoid twisting the leg and thus risk further injuring joints.

THE NATIONAL SKI PATROL SYSTEM

Recognition should be given to a branch of the National Ski Association, the National Ski Patrol System. This country-wide volunteer organization was first organized in March 1938 by Charles Minot Dole. The Ski Patrol aim is to promote safety, develop first aid improvements, equip areas with first aid supplies, encourage the formation of additional patrol systems, and raise the standard of patrolman requirements. Education in safe skiing and first aid improvements have been developed and

informative materials disseminated to all sections of the country.

The Ski Patrol System deserves much praise for the attention, service, and care it gives the carefree skier who seldom thinks he will need help and takes it for granted that he will be cared for by the Ski Patrol if he is in trouble. The Ski Patrol merits the respect and obedience of all skiers.

Conditioning and Preseason Activities

Exercises do not make a skier, but they do make actual skiing easier through good body conditioning and toning of muscles that will be under great stress. Preseason conditioning also helps one to become acquainted with ski terms and positions prior to maneuvers attempted on the slippery snow while exposed to climatic elements.

To ski one needs to be as strong, agile (knees, ankles, legs, and upper trunk), and as relaxed (free from undue tension, which merely builds up fatigue) as possible. Speed must be regulated and controlled over a constantly changing terrain, thus necessitating smooth actions and split-second decisions.

The preseason program is divided into four parts: 1) warm-up suggestions, 2) ski conditioning exercises without skis (that can be done indoors or out, preferably with boots on), 3) basic orientation to skis, and 4) ski conditioning exercises on skis.

WARM-UP SUGGESTIONS

Prior to strenuous exercises, simple warm-up activity should take place. For example: runs in place—obtaining lots of ankle action and high knee lifting; shoulder hunching and circling; jumping jack exercise; arm and leg swings; trunk springing forward and sideward; trunk twisting and arm flinging; and modified push-ups.

SKI CONDITIONING EXERCISES WITHOUT SKIS

Rope skipping, for flexibility and strengthening of the wrists, knees, and ankles (Fig. 4). Movement: Jump rope springing high enough to get complete extension of the knees and ankles. Start slowly, but gradually increase the speed and, after much practice, the amount. Heart and

---

[3] C. M. Dole, "The National Ski Patrol System in the Winter 1946–47," *American Ski Annual*, 1948, p. 180.

[4] Elkins, *op. cit.*, p. 76.

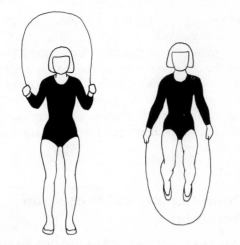

(4) Rope skipping for flexibility and to strengthen wrists, knees, and ankles.

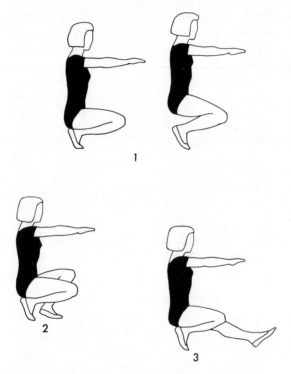

(5) For balance and to strengthen legs and ankles.

(6) For balance and to strengthen abdominal, back, and thigh muscles.

lung performance are speeded up with this activity so it can also be used to build up one's endurance.

For balance and strengthening the legs and ankles (Fig. 5). Take a squat position, arms raised forward about shoulder height. Movement: (1) Alternately flex and extend the ankles by springing up, keeping the back flat and erect. The knees should be kept well bent throughout. (2) Walk in this squat position. (3) After the foregoing have been mastered, spring and alternately extend the leg forward to touch the heel lightly to the floor with the knee straight. (4) The same as 3, but extend the leg to the side. This may be done holding hands with a partner in order to balance more easily.

For balance and strengthening the abdominal, back, and thigh muscles (Fig. 6). Sit on the floor with the knees bent to the chest. Movement: Lean slightly back and alternately flex and extend the legs from the chest to the floor.

For balance and strengthening the legs (Fig. 7). Stand with the feet together, toes pointed straight ahead. Movement: (1) Deep knee bending and stretching, weight as far forward as possible with the heels flat. (2) Balance on one foot with the other leg out in front. Slowly lower to a squat and return to a stand without touching the free foot or hands to the ground.[5]

For strengthening the abdominal muscles (Fig. 8). Lie flat on back with the knees bent to the chest. Movement: Alternately flex and extend the legs in bicycle fashion, making wide circles but not quite touching the floor. Keep the back in contact with the floor. (See footnote 5.)

For balance and strengthening the lateral trunk muscles (Fig. 9). Take a knee-stand position with the arms raised at the side. Movement: Alternately sit to the left and right without using the hands. Come to the starting position between times.

For strengthening the abdominal muscles (Fig. 10). Sit at a 45-degree angle with the legs straight and the body resting against the arms, which are extended behind for support. Movement: (1) Without any assistance from the hands, come to an erect sitting position, lean forward and bounce over the knees as you reach for the toes. Uncurl and return to the starting position. (2) Once the foregoing is mastered, the sit-up and bounce may be done from a lying position.

[5] It is preferable to do these exercises with boots on for added resistance.

(7) For balance and to strengthen legs.

For strengthening the thighs (Fig. 11). With the hips, knees, and ankles at a 90-degree angle, lean the back against a wall and hold this position as long as possible. Begin with a period of twenty seconds and each time try to hold the position longer.

Stride stand (Fig. 12). With the arms out to the side, feet about 8 inches apart, and shoulders relaxed, alternately swing one leg across so that the toe touches the opposite hand. Keep the body erect and the arms and head stationary.

BASIC ORIENTATION TO SKIS

It is helpful for beginners to use their skis in basic techniques before actually being on the snow. Ideally, one would participate in this phase of the program outdoors on the grass prior to the start of the ski season. The beginner should practice such basic skills as: walk, step turn, side step, herringbone, kick turns, falls,

(8) To strengthen abdominal muscles.

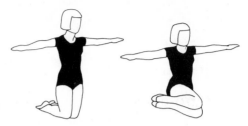

(9) For balance and to strengthen lateral trunk muscles.

and recoveries (from all positions) both on the flat and on the slope (see later section on skill descriptions). For this, skis must have a good protective base and be thoroughly dried off afterward just as during the ski season.

Regardless of whether this program is carried on indoors or outdoors, it is conducive to the development of body control and gives one a working knowledge of ski vocabulary. The following words must be put into practice (see terminology): *fall line; uphill and downhill*—ski, knee, shoulder edge, and so on; *inner and outer edge; stemming; inside and outside ski;* and *schussing.*

One also needs to handle the equipment frequently enough to be well acquainted with it: knowing the right ski from the left, how to adjust bindings, and how to properly grip and use the poles.

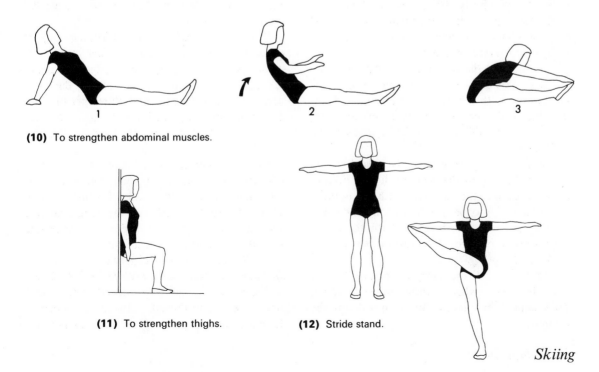

(10) To strengthen abdominal muscles.

(11) To strengthen thighs.

(12) Stride stand.

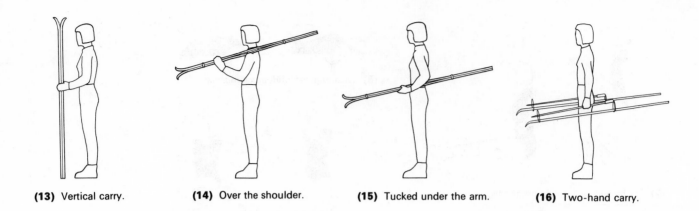

(13) Vertical carry.   **(14)** Over the shoulder.   **(15)** Tucked under the arm.   **(16)** Two-hand carry.

Ways to carry skis

Vertical carry (Fig. 13): In order to lift the skis, it is necessary to squeeze the midpoints together with their running surfaces facing one another. From the vertical position skis may be shifted to any other carrying position, and this position is useful in crowded areas and in going through a door.

Over the shoulder (Fig. 14): When there is sufficient space, this carry is the most useful. The skis are swung over the shoulder with the running surfaces together, preferably the tips facing forward. This position is efficient because the shorter part of the skis is behind the body resulting in better balance; the risk of hitting someone in the face with the tips is minimized; the toe plate keeps the skis from slipping forward on one's shoulder; and the skis do not come apart as easily when the tips are together in front of the body. The poles may be carried in the same hand, the other hand, or over the other shoulder and under the skis to relieve the weight on the one shoulder.

Tucked under the arm (Fig. 15): Another way to carry skis is with the weight of the skis partially on the hip, the running surfaces together with the tips pointed forward and down. This is seldom used for it tends to be awkward.

Two-hand carry (Fig. 16): This is done by keeping the ring of the pole on the ski tip and the handle under the toe strap. With tips pointed down, one ski may be carried in each hand while holding the pole just in front of the toe irons. This is useful only for short distances when the walking is good.

Irrespective of the carrying position, care must be taken when setting the skis down. They should be placed, not dropped, on the ground.

SKI CONDITIONING EXERCISES ON SKIS

Although these exercises can be done without skis, it is much better to do them with skis on so that one can gradually develop the necessary "feel" for the skis before the slippery element of snow is added. Simultaneously, the muscles are gradually being trained and strengthened by the weight of the skis. The orientation and fitness gained through exercise develops confidence and contributes toward greater enjoyment of the sport during the snow season.

To be in condition, one needs to develop flexibility and strength in various parts of the body. The sport involves a considerable amount of bending, twisting, coordination, and knee-action. Conditioning exercises are presented with the understanding that it is necessary to establish order of performance and number of repetitions according to one's present ability. It may be advisable to lead up to these suggested exercises with even simpler gymnastics.

For flexibility and stretching of the legs and the spine (Fig. 17): Start with the feet in a slight stride position, hands stretched over head. Movement: With the heels flat on the skis, stretch from the toes through the finger tips and then relax, drop forward, and bounce. Balance may be challenged more by keeping the feet together.

For stretching the lateral trunk muscles (Fig. 18): Start with the feet together, one arm at the side, the other over the head. Movement: With no twist, bend directly to the side reaching toward the feet on the side opposite the extended arm. Bounce and come to a stand.

For flexibility of the neck and strengthening of the back and abdominal muscles (Fig. 19): Lying on the back with the knees raised to the chest, arms extended to the side. Movement: Keeping the hands and as much of the back as possible

(17) For flexibility and to stretch legs and spine.

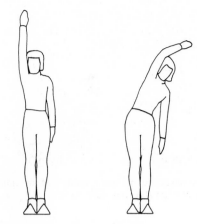

(18) To stretch lateral trunk muscles.

on the ground, roll to one side and touch the knees to the ground. At the same time turn the head in the opposite direction. Return to the starting position, repeat to the other side, and then continue.

For flexibility of the trunk, stretching of the legs, and strengthening of the abdominal muscles (Fig. 20): Start in a snowplow stand with the knees straight, arms raised at the side. Movement: Bend forward and twist down alternately touching the back of the diagonally opposite heel. Come to an erect stand between times.

For stretching the back of one leg and strengthening the thigh of the other (Fig. 21): Start in a forward lunge position, arms hanging at the side with the body erect, weight on the forward leg, toes pointing straight ahead, heels flat on the skis and the back leg straight. Movement: Tuck the hips under by contracting the gluteal muscles (the ones you sit on) and force the hips forward while bending the forward knee. In so doing, the back leg is being stretched.

For flexibility of the upper trunk and strengthening the muscles of the thigh and shoulders (Fig. 22): Stand in a snowplow position with the arms bent forward at shoulder height on the chest. Movement: Fling one arm to the side and twist as far around to the same side as possible; then bend that arm to the chest and fling the other arm to the side as the trunk twists to that side.

For flexibility and strengthening of the extensors of the ankles and knees (Fig. 23): Start with the arms by the sides in a deep knee bend (crouch) position, knees together, heels as flat on the skis as possible. Movement: Fling the arms over the head and spring up as high as possible with the knees and ankles together and

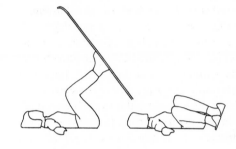

(19) For flexibility of neck and to strengthen back and abdominal muscles.

(20) For flexibility of trunk and to stretch legs and strengthen abdominal muscles.

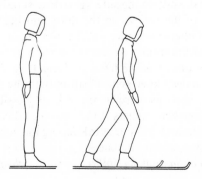

(21) To stretch back of one leg and strengthen thigh of the other.

(22) For flexibility of upper trunk and to strengthen muscles of thigh and shoulders.

(23) For flexibility and to strengthen extensors of ankles and knees.

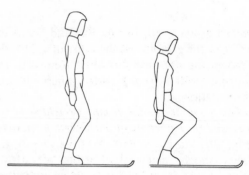

(24) To stretch back of legs, strengthen front muscles of thigh, and make ankles flexible.

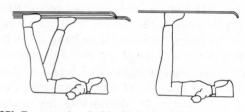

(25) To strengthen inside thigh muscles.

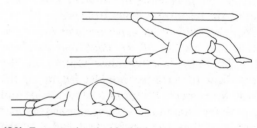

(26) To strengthen inside thigh muscles.

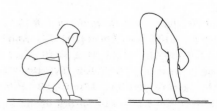

(27) For flexibility of trunk and legs.

fully extended. In landing, bend the knees and ankles using them as shock absorbers.

For stretching the back of the legs, strengthening the muscles on the front of the thigh, and flexibility of the ankles (Fig. 24): Start with the feet together, toes pointed straight ahead, and the arms hanging at the side. To assume a crouch position, bend the knees forward while keeping the heels flat on the skis. Movement: Bounce in this position, each time trying to get a bit deeper. Keep the knees together and forward, hips tucked under by contracting the gluteal muscles. One may increase the difficulty by alternately springing enough to slide one ski forward, and then after a few bounces, the other.

For strengthening the inside thigh muscles (Fig. 25): Lie on the back, arms extended to the side, hips bent at right angles, and the legs stretched over head with the knees straight. Movement: Drop the legs apart to the side as far as possible and slowly recover, keeping them in a stretched position.

For strengthening the inside thigh muscles (Fig. 26): Start in side lying position on the ground, bottom hand extended over the head, top hand supporting the body with the hand on the ground in front of the chest. Movement: With the knee and body straight so there is no bend at the hips, the top leg is raised and lowered directly to the side. A partner stands at the feet of the person on the floor and behind her, and offers resistance to the lower leg on the downward motion.

For flexibility of the trunk and legs (Fig. 27): Start in a deep knee bend position with the feet parallel, heels as close to the skis as possible, knees together, fingers touching the skis in front of the toes. Movement: Keeping the fingers on the skis, stretch the knees.

For coordination, flexibility, and strengthening

(28) For coordination and flexibility and to strengthen ankle muscles.

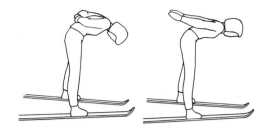

(29) To strengthen back and shoulder blade muscles and to stretch front shoulder muscles.

(30) For balance and agility.

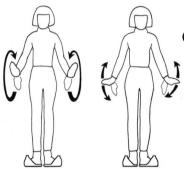

(31) For flexibility of wrists.

(32) To strengthen wrists.

of the ankle muscles (Fig. 28): Without poles, stand with the feet together, arms at sides. Movement: Jump to a snowplow position and clap the hands over the head and then jump the feet together and clap hands behind the back.

For strengthening the back and shoulder blade muscles and stretching the front shoulder muscles (Fig. 29): Stand in a snowplow position with the trunk relaxed forward, hands clasped behind the back. Movement: Raise the trunk enough to flatten the back. To pull the shoulder blades together, straighten the elbows by thrusting the clasped hands up and back. Keep the chin down and in. This can also be done with skis parallel.

For balance and agility (Fig. 30): Stand with the arms bent sideways, fingers touching the shoulders. Movement: (1) Hop and extend one arm to the side as the opposite leg is extended to the other side. Hop and return to the starting position to continue in succession from there. (2) Do the same exercise but displace one foot with the other so there is no pause between extensions.

For flexibility of the wrists (Fig. 31): Start with the arms hanging at the side. Movement: Forcibly flex and extend the wrists in every possible direction and then combine this action in a circular motion.

For strengthening the wrists (Fig. 32): Start with one arm at waist height across the front of the body so that the fingers are straight, palm facing the skis. The other hand offers resistance to the desired motion. Movement: Forcing the hand toward and away from the body as well as up and down, all against resistance.

For adjustment to the snowplow technique (Fig. 33): Stand with the feet together in a running position. Movement: Jump to a snowplow

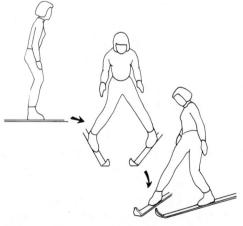

(33) For adjustment to snowplow technique.

position by springing and force the knees forward over the toes. Then roll from one ski to the other, always keeping the knee of the unweighted ski bent, and shift the weight as if making a turn. Jump the feet together and continue. Never allow the body weight to go beyond the outside edge of the weighted ski.

USE OF POLES

It is wise to become acquainted with the ski poles prior to actual skiing. The beginner learns to grip the pole by first inserting her hand through the pole strap from underneath. Then one grasps the pole with the strap pressed between the palm of the hand and the pole. When not in use the poles are held with the hands about waist high and pole tips to the rear of the body.

To build up endurance and help orient one to the use of the poles, a short cross-country trip without skis may be taken. This might include walking, running, and the geländesprung, which is a means of jumping upward and forward with the use of the ski poles and the momentum of the spring. With arms extended, the poles are planted in front of the body and the skier swings through the poles; this action requires arm and shoulder strength and coordination. It is an advanced skill, but can be practiced over a tiny stream or bump by even a beginner. The skier uses this skill to go over an object rather than around it.

Skills

ORIENTATION TO SKIS ON SNOW

One should apply what has been practiced in the preseason program. It is advisable to begin on level terrain before trying the slope. Knees and ankles should always be relaxed, never stiff. Relaxation is extremely important for the performance of all skills.

Walking: Alternately slide the skis, keeping them close together and pointing them straight ahead. The body should lean slightly forward over each ski as it slides ahead. Forward motion comes from knee pressure and from pushing with the poles, which are used with the natural arm movement.

Step turns: Turning from a stationary position on level terrain can be done with a series of small steps to one side. Only one end of the ski

(34) Fall and recovery.

(heel or tip) is raised slightly off the ground in order to pivot about. To turn to the right the right ski moves to the side and so does that pole; then the left ski is moved beside and parallel to the first ski. It is important to pivot each ski. Lifting the whole ski upsets balance and complicates the simple turn.

Falls: One should practice falling by relaxing and sitting above and in back of the uphill side of the skis. The legs should be kept together and extended forward. To then get up one must have the skis horizontal to the slope and below the body. Roll onto the back if necessary in order to get the skis below the body. One assumes a sitting position beside the skis with the poles together on the uphill side of the body and, by placing one hand at the top and the other hand at the bottom of the poles, pushes to get up. This is the correct recovery position regardless of the initial fall position (Fig. 34).

Side step: This technique is used to ascend or descend a steep hill by keeping the skis parallel to one another and at right angles to the fall line. One ski is moved uphill or downhill and edged into the slope; then the other ski is moved close to the first one. Pressure is used on alternate poles when transferring the weight (Fig. 35).

Traverse: This is used to go across a slope and for linking turns together. With the body relaxed, the uphill ski, knee, hip, and shoulder remain advanced and the weight is almost entirely on the downhill ski. The skis are kept close together with the uphill ski one-half boot length ahead. The upper body is slightly angled over the weighted ski, consequently, the hips are "into the hill" (Fig. 36).

Step into the slope: This turn is a basic one used to move into the downhill run from the side of a slope or from the top of the hill. The poles are used as extended arms and placed on the downhill side of the skis about shoulder width apart. With the weight on the arms and

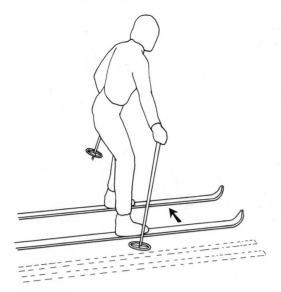

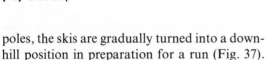

(35) Side step.

(36) Traverse.

poles, the skis are gradually turned into a downhill position in preparation for a run (Fig. 37).

Downhill running (Fig. 38): Keep the ankles and knees bent directly forward over the skis and keep the hips tucked under. The angle of lean depends on the slope and snow conditions but it should occur at the ankle and knee, not the waist. One should not lead with the chin, but should stay as completely relaxed as possible and go with the skis. The hands should lift the poles only enough to keep them from dragging. Let the skis come to a gradual stop at the bottom of the slope by keeping the knees and ankles bent and pressing down on the skis. Later the step turn can be learned and used just before coming to a stop at the bottom of the hill.

Herringbone (Fig. 39): This technique enables one to go straight uphill. It is quicker than sidestepping but is used primarily for short distances because it requires much energy. Steps are taken alternately in a diagonally forward manner so that all the weight shifts from one ski and pole to the other. To maintain the edge, and thus prevent slipping, it is essential to press the knees toward the tips of the skis and lean forward into the hill. One must have the feeling of "edges" before trying this on the slope. The weight is carried entirely on the inside edge; the outer edge hardly touches the ground.

Step turn into the hill while in motion: This can be used as a way of stopping. With continuous steps and edging, one can easily stop by stepping into the hill from a running or traverse position.

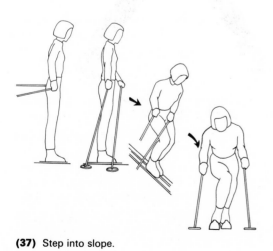

(37) Step into slope.

(38) Downhill run.

(39) Herringbone.

Skiing   **247**

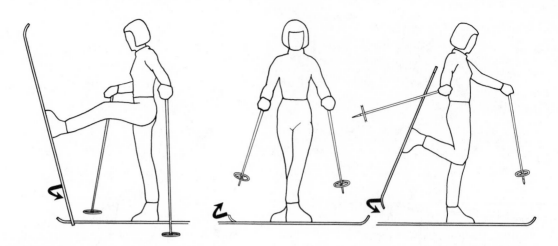

(40) Kick turn.

(41) Snowplow.

Kick turn (Fig. 40): This is a way of making a 90-degree stationary turn either on the flat or on the slope. The poles have to be planted behind the body for support, then the turn is made. Put all the weight on one ski (uphill if on a slope) and plant the poles behind the body. Slide the other ski forward into a vertical position so that the heel end of the ski is adjacent to the tip of the weighted ski. From this position, (1) let gravity swing the ski downward next to the other ski and (2) step on it immediately (edged if on a hill). Complete the turn by letting the other ski and poles follow (3). This is a fast way of turning but requires balance and timing.

Snowplow (Fig. 41): This is an elementary way to reduce speed in going downhill (over the fall line) by placing the skis in a *V* position. The heels push outward, and knee pressure is forward. The knees should remain over the skis, not rotated inward. The tails of the skis must be moved out from the center line equally and the weight distributed evenly on the skis with slight extra pressure along the inside edges. The snowplow is not effective at a high speed.

Adjustment to terrain: To develop balance and adjust to varying terrain and snow textures it is necessary to experience bumps of all sizes. This can be done on the slope or by cross-country skiing (touring).

The skier should take the top of a bump in a crouched position with knees bent. The knees should straighten with a dip in the terrain and then bend again for any further bumps.

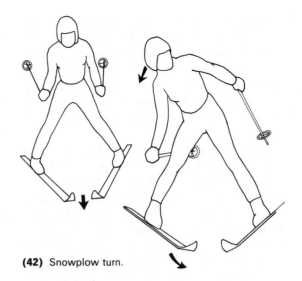

(42) Snowplow turn.

FINISHED FORMS (THE SKILLS TO BE ACQUIRED IN AMERICAN TECHNIQUE CLASSES)

Snowplow turn (Fig. 42): From the snowplow position, shift the weight to one ski (the right one to turn left and vice versa) and this will bring about a turn. Keep the knees and ankles "easy" and the uphill ski flat. To make several successive turns, shift the body weight alternately from one ski to the other, always flattening the uphill ski throughout the turn.

Stem turn (Fig. 43): From the traverse, open the uphill ski in preparation for the turn itself. With an up motion, transfer the weight to that opened ski which turns into and across the fall

(43) Stem turn.

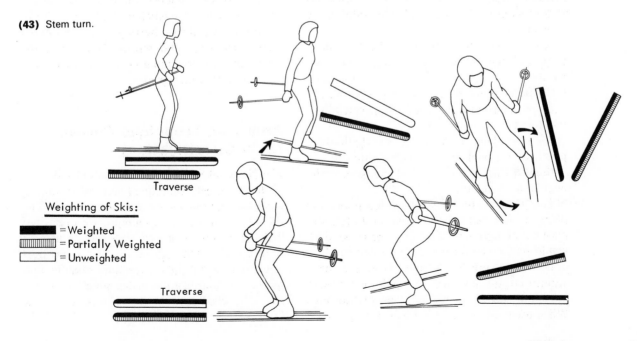

Traverse

Weighting of Skis:

█████ = Weighted
▦▦▦▦▦ = Partially Weighted
▭▭▭▭▭ = Unweighted

Traverse

line. (While on the fall line one is actually doing a snowplow turn.) Right after crossing the fall line the uphill ski is pressed forward and next to the downhill ski to return to a traverse position. The progression involves: traverse, open into a snowplow, shift the weight to the outside ski for the turn itself, which is a snowplow, and return to a traverse.

Side-slipping: This skill is used for traveling directly sideways down the slope or forward-sideways. With the weight on both skies, one simultaneously releases the edges by pressing the ankles away from the slope and thus flattening the skis on the snow. To stop or control the slip, the skis are again edged by pressing the ankles toward the slope.

Uphill christie: The christie or christiana is a skid turn. From the traverse, the skis remain parallel for the uphill christie but the weight is shifted forward. As a result of unweighting, the uphill edges cause the tips of the skis to swing uphill or into the hill and the tails of the skis skid slightly downhill.

Stem christie: This is a speeded up stem turn. With the skier moving at a greater speed, more heel thrust is needed to cross the fall line. This causes the tails of the skis to skid halfway through the turn—sliding out of the *V* position into a parallel position.

Parallel christie (Fig. 44): This most advanced christiana technique is a fast stem christie without the *V* position. Throughout the turn the skis remain parallel, but as the outside ski takes the body weight on an up-motion, the inside ski slides forward. This is immediately followed by a heel thrust.

Short swing: This is done by a series of sharp turns with the use of "edge setting" and "pole planting" just before reaching the fall line. The turn is accomplished by a speedy, even weight shift, pushing on the pole, and lifting (extending) the knees.

Wedeln: This is a series of rhythmical, parallel turns back and forth across the fall line without a traverse. The end of one turn is the beginning of the next.

Pole planting: In the American technique, the poles are not planted for turns until after the mastery of parallel turns. It is believed they would only be confusing, cause actual trouble, or become too much of a crutch. However, some authorities do endorse the pole plant and introduce this at an earlier stage of learning. When used, the planting is a light touch, rather

(44) Parallel christie.

than a vaulting type placement. At the time of the "planting" the downhill elbow remains relaxed and close to the body as the forearm swings forward to plant the pole about a foot in front of the downhill boot. Then the pole is quickly withdrawn as the turn is being made.

SKILL TESTS FOR SELF-ANALYSIS AND PRACTICE

For motivation and self-analysis, a test course may be set up by using flags to designate the area. The course should be explained and diagrammed on a blackboard or mimeographed sheet so that skiers can practice on their own. Skills covered could be *climbing:* walk, step turn, traverse, kick turns, herringbone; *snowplow:* start, turn, stop, and repeat; and *stem turn:* start, turn, traverse and go under crossed poles, traverse, turn, and repeat.

American Technique Classes (Skill Classification)

The National Ski Association endorses the use of the American technique and most of the ski areas throughout the country are using it. The ski schools using this technique are organized with progressions in six different "classes": A through F. Through an instructor certification program of clinics, teaching sessions and ratings, standardization of teaching has occurred. The classes or ability groupings are as follows:

Class A: The end product is the straight snowplow, but one covers the basic elements also: walking, sidestepping, falls and recovery, step turns and straight running.

Class B: The end product is the traverse, but one also learns the kick-turn and the snowplow turn.

Class C: The end product is the uphill christie but in progression one learns the stem turn and sideslipping first.

Class D: The end product is the stem christie but in progression one also learns the snowplow christie and other lead-up techniques in preparation for the finished technical form of the stem christie.

Class E: Works entirely in parallel turns in progression from a christie from the fall line to parallel christie and parallel christie with a check.

Class F: Short swing and/or wedeln.

At a glance, the accomplishment of such a multitude of skills may seem insurmountable. However, one is simply learning to maneuver from a wide base (as with the snowplow) to a smaller and smaller platform (from stem turn to parallel). Much of this is accomplished through mastery of basic skills on small to longer and longer hills and through the speeding up of basic movements and weight shift. For the safest and best results, it is important to progress through the various stages under the discipline of an instructor.

Skiing is not only fun, but a way of life. However, it can be dangerous if approached without careful supervision as one climbs the ladder of skills to be mastered. The safest and best way to success is by attending formal ski school classes. Thus one can avoid the formation of bad habits and casualties resulting from ignorance. Ideally, it is best to devote several days at a time to just skiing. A long week end or a week of lessons, intermingled with practice sessions, is far superior to lessons taken once or twice a week. In all cases, relaxation and a minimum energy expenditure in ski performance are essential for progress and enjoyment.

Mechanical Principles

Simplicity of performance and skill come only through an understanding and analysis of principles that relate to basic movement. For the skier, these principles include leverage, equilibrium, motion, inertia, gravity, application of force, friction, and acceleration. All factors are interrelated; it is difficult to even partially isolate these principles, but for discussion purposes an attempt follows.

LEVERAGE

The skier on his skis forms a lever. The skis and snow offer the resistance, the ankles serve as the fulcrum, and the body provides the force. The body, which is composed of many levers, serves as the source of power or force transmitted through the skis, to act on the snow and affect the skis. With proper manipulation of the skis less energy will be expended. The body should exert only the minimum amount of force and energy required to do the job. Careful consideration must also be given to the physiological position of the joints in order to avoid undue strain or stress.

EQUILIBRIUM

Instability or lack of balance is one of the skier's biggest problems because it is difficult to keep his weight directly over his base of support, the skis. If one stands in good alignment, the body segments (each having its own center of gravity) approach the vertical line of the body and offer a stabilizing effect to the force of gravity. While standing, neither the skis or poles affect this alignment. However, when a body part is moved sideways from the center of gravity, either the base must change or another part of the body must shift in an opposite direction if one is to maintain balance.

The novice skier finds it difficult to maintain balance and has trouble in controlling momentum in order to remain upright. Consequently, to adjust to varying terrain, the novice reverts to the use of a wide base (frequently the snowplow or wide running position) in order to stabilize himself. Because the more highly skilled skier has learned to counterbalance slight lateral forces, he finds that momentum helps him keep his equilibrium.

Even when close together, the length of the skis provides a stable base in the direction that the force is being applied, and as long as this force is in the same direction as the length of the base, the skier remains stable from front to back.

INERTIA

A body will remain in its present state of rest or uniform motion unless there is interference by an outside force. Numerous forces act upon a skier in motion on a slope.

Gravity

A downward as well as a forward-downward force. This is the main source of movement for the skier because of the incline and the fact that his weight is applied vertically to the earth itself. His center of gravity is in the hip area and force is applied perpendicularly to the slope from the center of gravity. A tendency to lean backwards forces the skis forward and results in a backward fall; to counteract this, the skier must lean forward. It is equally important to keep the knees and ankles bent. This not only lowers the center of gravity and increases stability but makes it possible for these joints to absorb the bumpy effects of the terrain.

Friction and air resistance

These work against the acceleration of the skier, but can be minimized. The greatest resistance offered is friction on the edges of the skis, particularly if any snow sticks to them and freezes. To apply force other than that supplied by gravity, one needs to build up a ledge under the ski. By using the edges to build snow under the skis, friction is increased. This is an asset for such skills as sideslipping, herringbone, uphill traverse, and turns.

Momentum

Newton's law of inertia also indicates that once a body is in motion, it takes less effort to maintain a given speed than to change it. It is important for the skier to use momentum as a means of conserving energy and executing skills. In skiing, there is a gliding action similar to that in canoeing and swimming. Consequently, less energy is expended if turns are timed so that the rhythm and momentum from the previous turn is not lost prior to the next turn. The end of one turn is also the start of another.

ACCELERATION (INCREASE IN SPEED)

Change of speed is proportional to the force that caused it. An example of this is the racing start.

ACTION AND REACTION

For every force there is an equal and opposite reaction. Two objects must be involved—one to exert the force and one to receive it. To walk on the level on skis force is applied by use of the arms and shoulders through contact of the poles in the snow. This contact point is made close to the skis behind the center of gravity (behind the foot). To avoid rotation or turning, the skier tries to coordinate the push of an arm and opposite foot.

CENTRIFUGAL FORCE

When turns are made, centrifugal (outward) force is created by the body deviating from its original path. As the skier's speed increases and the turn becomes sharper, this centrifugal force also increases. To counterbalance this force, the skier leans into the hill. This is called the *comma position* or *angulation*. The more of the body that is used in this angulation, the more effective is the counterbalancing of centrifugal force.

SPEED

Speed is determined by the skier's weight, snow texture, and the type of terrain, steepness, and length of the slope. Readjustment of body position is needed as these factors change. It is essential to keep slightly ahead or at least have the body at a 90-degree angle to each slope or pitch of the ski run; otherwise the skis will be forced out from under the skier because the center of gravity has shifted to a point behind the feet. Consequently, it is advisable for the novice to avoid skiing on slopes of changing conditions.

Control of speed is maintained by the angle of traverse and by the use of edges during turns that link the traverses. To change direction, thus turn the skis, involves several changes: weight shift, edging, and the lead of the inside ski—all of which relate to the skier's speed, momentum, the kind of turn employed and the proper application of muscular force.

In high speed skiing, there is a specific change of tactics. Instead of turning by creating a ledge and pushing on it, the skis are rotated by turning the upper part of the body in the opposite direction to the turn. This is particularly true in wedeln.

TURNING

When making a gradual turn, linear or straight motion changes to curvilinear (moving on a curved path). In a quick turn the movement is rotatory (moving about a fixed axis). In this latter case, the weight is shifted to the tips of the skis and gravity pulls the heels around.

The Use of a Ski Lift

If the novice skier is well informed prior to using a lift, it will mean less tension and/or falls in the learning process as well as real enjoyment throughout. Lack of knowledge on proper dress is a basic cause of numerous unfortunate and unnecessary experiences.

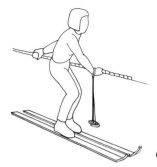

(45) Rope tow.

GENERAL HINTS FOR ALL LIFTS

Never wear clothing or dangling items susceptible to entanglement with the lift equipment. Observe others before trying the lift yourself. Tell the attendant you have never tried this type lift, or any at all if this is the case. Prior to contact with the lift, stand in the tracks with the *skis flat and parallel and knees relaxed.* The weight should be evenly distributed on both skis and it is often helpful to ride with the ski closest to the rope slightly advanced. At the top, *immediately* ski away from the lift line. Never readjust poles or clothing near the take-off point.

HINTS ON SPECIFIC KINDS OF LIFTS

For the *rope tow* wear leather palm mittens or gloves; dangle both poles by the strap over the outside wrist; place hands loosely over the rope; and *gradually* tighten the grasp (Fig. 45).

The weight should be centered or slightly back when starting on the tow. This counteracts any sudden forward motion that may occur as the rope is grasped. Then a slightly forward lean is appropriate after the skier is in motion. This helps one to maintain balance if the tow stops on the way up the slope.

If you fall, let go of the rope and move off the track immediately; then go back to the start to get on. If someone falls in front of you, temporarily loosen your grip in order to remain stationary and avoid going into him, or ski around him. Skiers often find it comfortable to have the outside hand behind the back instead of both in front.

For the *T, J,* or *L* Bar (shape of bar conforms to letter after which it is named), hold the poles in the outside hand; don't dangle them on the wrists. Step into line immediately after the person or persons in front of you, but not before. Keep an eye on the approaching bar by looking over the inside shoulder. Hold it loosely and lean the thighs against it. *Do not sit.*

For a *T* bar (Fig. 46), stand next to your partner but leave some space between the two

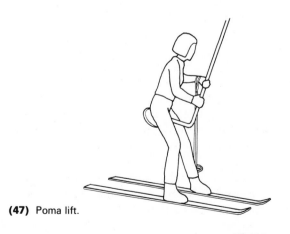

(46) *T* bar—left incorrect, right correct technique.

(47) Poma lift.

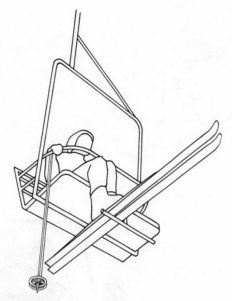

(48) Chair lift.

inside skis to avoid catching or tripping. It is very helpful to balance and steady the bar by putting the outside hand on the outside end of the bar.

At the take-off point, first one skier presses down on the bar and pushes away, and then the other skier. If you fall, let go and get out of the way. If is very difficult and even dangerous to you and your partner to try to recover. Release the bar gently and avoid making it swing for this is the cause of many accidents.

For the *poma lift*, hang both poles over one wrist (Fig. 47). Be ready to receive the bar from the attendant, and pull down on it to place the disc or platter between the legs to *lean* against. *Do not sit*. To get off, apply slight downward pressure and separate the legs slightly. At the top, release the bar gently and step well off to the side to avoid being hit by any oncoming swinging bar.

For the *chair lift* watch for the chair, sit back in it, and *lift ski tips up* (Fig. 48). Steady the chair a bit with your free hand. If the chair is very low, squat down a bit to avoid being hit in the calf of the legs. Once seated, close the gate and hang up poles if a hook is provided. Watch the line and raise ski tips whenever the chair is close to the ground or approaches a take-off ramp.

To get off, simply stand, push the chair back, and ski off. It is advisable to duck down if one is descending at a ramp. *Never* jump off a lift.

Get well off the track before depositing robes or coats with the attendant. Take special notice of the type chair and how people hold their poles. In some cases the poles are held in the outside hand and for others in the inside hand. In either case, hold them about the middle of the pole so they do not catch in the ground as you sit. Also be careful not to hit yourself or your partner with them.

For the *gondola* or *tramway* remove skis. Hold poles in one hand and skis in the other. The skis should be held vertically with the bottom surfaces facing one another. Hand both to attendant and board the lift. *Never* open doors or jump out while in transit.

Highlights on Rules

The recreational skier is concerned only with rules and scoring pertaining to races from a spectator viewpoint. The regulations she needs to observe are covered under safety. However, for racing, specific regulations have been established.

Rules are formulated by the National Ski Association and the *Fédération Internationale de Ski*. The Division for Girls' and Women's Sports also has similar regulations. The rules designate required officials and their duties, equipment, events, running order, starting, timing, the finish, disqualifications, and computation of results.

KINDS OF RACES

Downhill involves going straight down a mountain course, preferably dotted with some "control gates." The race has only one run. *Giant slalom* is a controlled downhill type of race shorter than the above and is slowed down by the use of 30 to 40 gates (*see* Terminology). The race has only one run. *Slalom* is a test of one's ability to make time between tight gates. The course is much shorter and has 40 to 60 different type gates (open, closed, hairpin, and flush) to test the skier's ability on difficult terrain.

Cross country racing, covering distances of eight miles or more on natural terrain including uphill, downhill, and flat sections, is a test of endurance, technique, and knowledge. Waxing is extremely important for this type of skiing. *Jumping* is a challenge to advanced skiers.

Terminology

Angulation: The body is curved. The knees and hips remain pressed into the hill in order to get a good bite with the edges of the skis, but the shoulders remain away from the slope and over the downhill ski.

Arlberg: The region of the Austrian Alps where the Arlberg techniques were developed.

Arlberg strap: A safety strap that attaches the ski to the boot, and, in case of a fall, releases but prevents a runaway ski.

Breakable crust: A thin crunchy surface that will not support a skier but tends to catch the edges instead. It is the result of either sleet or a thaw and quick freeze.

Check: A movement used to reduce and/or control speed.

Christie or **christiana:** A means of turning by keeping the skis parallel and skidding around.

Comma: The body position formed by angulation.

Corn snow: A texture of snow found in the spring as a result of cold nights and warm days (freezing and melting). It is somewhat heavy and very fast and delightful.

Counter rotation: A preliminary wind-up prior to a turn.

Downhill ski or **outside ski:** The ski that is on the downhill side of the body (nearest to the bottom of the hill) at a given time.

Edges: The metal strip along the outside of the bottom of the ski.

Edging: The setting of the metal running surface of the ski at an angle with the slope for control of the amount of gripping or sliding action desired.

Fall line: The line of gravity straight down the hill.

Gate: A colored pair of flags used on a racing course to indicate the course and to control speed.

Heel thrust: Lateral displacement of the heel of the skis sideways.

Herringbone: A method of climbing. The skis are kept with the tips out in a *V* shape and the weight is shifted diagonally forward upward from one ski and pole to the other.

Inside edge: The metal strip at the bottom of the long side of the ski closest to the mid-line of the body.

Inside or **uphill ski:** *See* Uphill ski.

Kick turn: A stationary turn used on the flat or on the slope. One ski is kicked up to a 90-degree angle with the ground, turned around and stepped on and then the other follows.

Mogul: A bump or mound formed by many skiers turning at the same spot (thus throwing snow to one area and wearing down another).

NSA: The National Ski Association, the parent organization of the country.

NSPS: The National Ski Patrol System, which is the First Aid branch of the NSA.

Outside or **downhill ski:** *See* Downhill ski.

Outside edge: The metal strip at the bottom of the long side of the ski farthest from the mid-line of the body.

Platform: The base made by the skier for preparatory motion of a turn.

Pole plant: The brief placement and light touch of the pole into the snow as used in short swing and wedeln.

Powder snow: A dry, fluffy type of snow that is a skier's dream.

Schuss: A straight run downhill on the fall line.

Sidestep: A simple method of ascent (or descent). Gradual steps upward (or downward) with the skis parallel to each other and horizontal to the slope.

Sitzmark (or **bathtub**): A hole made in the snow when a skier falls. (For the safety of other skiers, these must be smoothed over and filled in.)

Ski lift: The uphill transportation provided (poma, T-bar, chair, gondola, and so on).

Stem: Preparation for a wide turn by opening the tail of the uphill ski.

Track on: A call for "right of way" used particularly on blind corners.

Traverse: A means of going across a slope, which can be used with sidestepping in a diagonally upward fashion so as to zigzag across the slope to the top. When used in descent, it is a means of controlling speed and of linking turns.

Unweighting: Temporary removal of weight from the ski. Types include *up-weighting*—a quick upward extension of the body (used in American Technique) and *down-weighting*—a quick dropping of the body (used in Austrian Technique).

Uphill ski: The ski that is on the uphill side of the body (nearest to the top of the hill) at a given time.

Vorlage: The forward lean of the body when the center of gravity is ahead of the binding. This angle occurs at the ankle and knee joints, *not* at the hips or waist.

Wedeln: An advanced skill consisting of continuous, short, parallel turns down the fall-line. The end of one turn is the beginning of the next.

Weighting: The application of one's weight to one or both skis according to the demands of the particular skill involved.

Selected References

Dole, C. M., ed. *The National Ski Patrol System.* New York: National Ski Patrol System, 1941.

Elkins, Frank. *The Complete Ski Guide.* New York: Doubleday, Doran and Company, 1940.

Lash, Bill. *An Outline of Ski Teaching Methods.* Salt Lake City, Utah: Elbert Kirkham, 1959.

Schaeffler, Willy, and Ezra Bowen. *Sports Illustrated Book of Skiing.* Philadelphia: J. B. Lippincott, 1960.

The Official American Ski Technique. Salt Lake City, Utah: Professional Ski Instructors of America, 1966.

Chapter 14

Swimming *Janet Moldenhauer*

Goals. Equipment. Safety. Mechanics of Movement. Skills for the Beginner. Swimming Strokes. Diving—From the Board, Back Dive. Synchronized Swimming. Skin and Scuba Diving.

"His hands went out to stroke, and he gave a swimmer's kick." A quote from another swimming textbook? A new way to perform the breast stroke? No, merely Odysseus, in Homer's *Odyssey*, making his way to the island home of Circe in one of the early classical references to swimming. Inasmuch as 75 per cent of the world is covered with water, man has been concerned with ways to move over it, through it, and under it. The fascination of water has been with man since the beginning of time, and has inspired art, inventiveness, and above all, a desire to subdue this element that is foreign to him.

Swimming, or propelling one's body through the water without mechanical aids, is the concern of this chapter. It is an activity that can be enjoyed by young and old alike. Once thoroughly learned, it is never unlearned, and can be returned to after years of no practice. In its competitive form, it is a vigorous and demanding sport with an emphasis on speed and endurance. In its recreational form, it provides the body with relaxation, gently stretching and easing tension in almost all muscles. Basic swimming opens the door to summer fun at the shore with friends. It is a necessary prerequisite to such water sports as fishing, boating, sailing, and water skiing, none of which can be done in complete safety without a sound knowledge of swimming. To the interested performer, basic swimming is the first step toward such specialized sports as diving, synchronized swimming, scuba diving, and competitive swimming.

Swimming is one activity where the body approaches weightlessness. The buoyancy of the body in the water counteracts the pull of gravity and allows the performer a new freedom of movement. This buoyancy creates new experiences and sensations as one moves in new and different patterns.

There has been widespread increase of knowledge and skill in swimming during recent years. Much of the credit must go to the American Red Cross and its nationwide "learn to swim" programs, the YMCA's and their swimming programs, and to competitive swimmers and coaches. The basic strokes and principles have been taught to a wide variety of age groups through standardized courses provided by the Red Cross and the YMCA, and schools, colleges and community pools have all played an important role in improving and dispersing knowledge about the science and sport of swimming.

It is from the competitors that we have learned the strokes as they are today. As specialists in their area they have studied every possible source and used many mechanical

Miss Moldenhauer, an assistant professor at Wisconsin State University in Oshkosh, is aquatic director and advisor for the Synchronized Swimming Club and Girl's Swimming Team. Miss Moldenhauer has been waterfront director at summer camps and an aquatic school water safety instructor-trainer for the American Red Cross.

devices to determine what will make the body move faster and more efficiently through the water. Application of this knowledge has brought about modifications in strokes over the years, thus increasing interest and enjoyment of the sport.

Goals

The person who wants to learn to swim must realize that performance is often directly proportional to desire. It is also apparent that one enjoys that activity which one performs with ease, grace, and confidence. To gain this, one must first adjust to the water; then strokes and stunts follow along with endurance and satisfaction.

Before learning strokes, one must learn how to breathe in water, how to use the water's support to advantage, and how to feel relaxed in this medium. Learn to breathe in through the mouth and, when the head is under water, out through the nose or both nose and mouth. Learn to walk in the water, to jump and splash, to duck under water while keeping the eyes open, and to float in shallow water. With the help of a teacher, try out the various strokes and master at least one for recreational swimming. Learn to tread, bob, and change position in order to be safe in deep water. Learn a simple dive for entry into the water. If you want to swim one length of the pool, two or ten lengths, or a half mile, you will need to learn to apply force effectively, to glide and relax with the strokes, and to develop endurance by swimming a little farther with each practice period.

Many studies show that swimming is the one sport that most college women participate in throughout their lifetime. Don't be a social drop-out because you can't swim.

Equipment

"Bring a swim suit and a smile" certainly describes the equipment needed for swimming. A swimming cap is also desirable. The cap helps the performer by keeping hair out of the face, thus making it easier to see and breathe, and helps the pool operator, as well, by keeping hair out of the filter system. When choosing a suit for recreational swimming, one should put the suit on and try stretching one's hands directly overhead to test the length and comfort of the suit. There are suits that are meant to be worn only on the beach, and others that are just as attractive and suitable in or out of the water.

Nose clips were probably invented by a sinus sufferer, but they can be a decided boon to the beginning swimmer who has not yet adjusted to inhaling through the mouth. All the other accessories seen at the shore or pool, such as swim fins, kick boards, air mattresses, beach balls, can be used for fun or practice. However, they are not essential equipment, and are in fact outlawed at many of the more crowded beaches.

Safety

Swimming is fun—when safely done! Never swim alone and know your own limitations: simple advice that covers a multitude of situations. A distance that could be covered with ease after a summer of swimming appears much longer the first day of the next season. Remember that water is a changeable medium, distances over water are deceptive, and water temperatures vary widely. A hundred yards in a temperature controlled pool is easier swimming than from the boat to the dock in a wave-whipped lake with warm and cold spots. Cold water may be brisk and refreshing for a short time, but quickly exhausts the performer in any prolonged effort. The warmer waters around islands such as Bermuda may prove very inviting, but also have a peculiarly enervating effect on the swimmer. Build toward endurance and swim within your competence.

Swimming naturally brings to mind sun, sand, and shore. In these elements your body may be in a position much like a piece of meat on a griddle because the sun provides heat and burning rays, and the water and sand serve as a reflector. Many a vacationer has spoiled his holiday by turning a bright lobster red the first day in the sun, and suffering the rest of the time in the shade. There are many sun tanning lotions available; pick one that works for you, use it wisely, and enjoy the out-of-doors with good sense and judgment.

Although the statement, "never swim for an hour after eating" is an empirical one, it stands to reason that one should not indulge in a strenuous activity immediately after eating. An athlete does not compete on a full stomach because much of his body would be concentrating on digestion rather than championship performance. When you go for a dip, a championship performance may not be what you have in mind; but it is always wise to use good judgment and avoid excessive physical activity immediately following a large meal.

It was mentioned earlier that 75 per cent of the earth is covered with water. Man has increased this percentage by creating lakes in deserts, and pools in backyards. Not every body of water is safe or has a life guard. We fight an ever-increasing battle against pollution and just plain trash in the water. One should choose a safe place to go swimming; a good bottom, a lack of current or undertow, and preferably a life guard.

The regulations protecting a public swimming area are for everyone's benefit and should be followed. For example, it is important to observe the "no running" rule because surfaces around water are often slippery and may cause falls. Playing around may be fun to a point, but what is play to one may be potentially dangerous to another person.

When swimming in a lake it is important to stay near shore because visibility is diminished by glare and reflection from the water. A white swimming hat can easily be mistaken for the crest of a wave or the wake of a boat.

A bleak picture? Not really, when one considers that true fun is the result of confidence in oneself—the feeling of "being at home" in the water. This at-homeness is built up by being aware of the dangers involved, by knowledge and practice of safety rules and precautions, by the use of common sense, and by gradually building up one's skills and endurance in the water.

Mechanics of Movement

Before entering the water, let us briefly examine some of the mechanical principles that are important to the swimmer.

For every action there is an equal and opposite reaction. In accordance with this law of motion, the body moves in the direction opposite to that in which the force is applied. Pressure toward the feet results in movement toward the head; and if in a kick or arm stroke one presses down on the water, the body will rise up. Thus pressing toward the bottom results in bobbing up and

down and impairs progress through the water. One should apply force horizontally (opposite to the direction in which one wishes to move), rather than vertically, for an effective swimming stroke.

Resistance is proportional to the greatest cross-sectional area of the body. The swimmer's cross-sectional area is determined by size of the body and position in the water as well as the spread of the arms and legs in stroking. To keep resistance to a minimum, the recovery movement should be made with as small a cross-sectional area as possible. In the breast stroke, for example, the hands come together under the body for the recovery, then the fingers lead in the forward reach of the arms.

Streamlining the body enables one to move a greater distance with each stroke. The body should be stretched and streamlined to reduce resistance to the water, and the glide should be maintained so long as the body is still moving with the impetus gained from the power phase of the stroke.

Body position affects buoyancy. Because the body is buoyant and free moving in water, the total body reacts to the movement of any segment. If an arm or leg is raised out of water, the rest of the body sinks in response unless the propulsive force of a swimming stroke compensates. A change in head position causes the body to rise or sink in the opposite direction to movement of the head. The beginner should avoid lifting the head high above the surface of the water because this causes unnecessary sinking of the rest of the body.

Skills for the Beginner

With the foregoing information in mind, let us take that first step into the water. The water may feel cold but jumping and kicking will soon help one to adjust. It also has a heavy feeling around the body, especially noticeable when one submerges to the neck. This can be easily explained: water is heavier than air, and the muscles must become accustomed to it before one will be able to breathe easily. The feet must definitely push off the bottom to make any forward progress. The legs bend, just as they do when walking on land. Remember this walking, because it is closely allied to the first kick to be learned.

The second step, so to speak, is just as easy. Hold on to the gutter or a partner, take a breath in through the mouth, close it, and submerge the face in the water while holding the breath. Open the eyes and notice how things are magnified by the water. It is important to start opening the eyes at once, so that you know where you are and do not run into things.

BREATHING

In all swimming it is important to remember that inhalation is done through the mouth, and so is most of the exhalation. Develop the habit of always taking the air in through the mouth. Then, after learning to hold the breath while the face is in the water, practice exhaling under water. One must "blow out" through the mouth or mouth and nose. More force is required to exhale underwater than in air. It is easy to observe the amount of air expelled by watching for bubbles. As one exhales underwater the bubbles should come in a steady stream rather than a few at a time. Beginners often fail to exhale enough to be prepared for the next inhalation.

Inasmuch as swimming is done in a horizontal position, it is best to practice breathing in the same position. Hold onto the gutter and rest the face on the water. Exhale, then roll the face to the side. One ear should still be in the water as the face breaks the surface. Take a breath in through the mouth and, keeping the eyes open, roll the face back into the water. Exhale. This should be practiced until one can continue it indefinitely without a feeling of breathlessness. The air must be pushed out when exhaling, otherwise after about five breaths there will be a tight feeling in the chest from over inflation. Often a little water will be taken into the mouth with the air; push this out along with the air on the exhalation. Roll, do not lift, the head to the side. Practice in a slow rhythmic pattern.

To prevent water from entering the nose while the face is in the water, one must maintain a slight exhalation pressure. If this is not quickly learned, it is better to use a nose clip than to have the discomfort of getting water in the nose.

FACE FLOAT

Floating is best learned in water that is about chest high (Fig. 1). Bend the knees until the water comes up to the chin, take a breath through the mouth, and stretch the arms forward slightly under the water. Lean forward on the water, placing the face into the water. Keep stretching forward and the feet will normally lift

(1) Face float.

(2) Recovery from face float.

up off the bottom. This is a face or front float. To regain the feet, simply curl the legs under, press down with the hands, lift the head, and stand up (Fig. 2). Move slowly and surely and success will be attained.

FLUTTER KICK

To move through the water, a propelling force must be added. The flutter kick is easy because it is much like walking in a horizontal position. Walk in the water, noticing how the thighs pass each other as one steps, the legs are relatively close together, and the toes push off for each step. The flutter kick is done with similar leg action. To determine the depth of the kick, place the heel of one foot in line with the toes of the other foot—this is the depth of *your* kick. Get the body in a horizontal position by holding onto something, and kick vigorously up and down with pointed toes turned slightly inward (pigeon-toed). The feet remain underwater; only the heels break the surface of the water so there is little splashing. Both up and down motions of the legs provide power, but emphasis should be on the up part for added power. Movement for the kick originates in the hip with easy action from the knee and ankle, and a final whip-like motion of the foot.

ARM STROKE

The arm movements for the human stroke can be practiced while the beginner stands in waist deep water and bends forward at the waist in order to put the shoulders in a more nearly horizontal, or swimming, position. The arms pull back toward the waist alternately; one arm is pulling while the other is recovering. One arm is in the power phase while the other is in the recovery phase. To prepare for the power phase, the arm is extended forward. The pull with hand and arm is down and back. It is a pulling motion in front of the body that brings the hand in to the chest. The water is pressed back with the palm of the hand and inside of the forearm. The recovery is made by reaching forward, fingertips first, until the arm is again extended. In the human stroke the arm circle is small and recovery is made underwater. In the crawl the recovery is above the water with a full reach forward for maximum power.

HUMAN STROKE

The human stroke, sometimes called *dog paddle*, is started with a face float and flutter kick. As previously suggested, the arm stroke is a short pull with an underwater recovery. In this stroke the head may be raised so that the face is out of water with chin resting on the water. Because the face is above water breathing is no problem, but one should inhale through the mouth only.

Check *body position*: stretched out as near horizontal as possible; *kick*: alternating up and down movement with pointed toes; only the heels should break the surface of the water; *arms*: alternately pressing the water back with broad hand and forearm surface, recovering fingertips first to a comfortable stretch position in front of shoulder; and *breathe*: inhale through the mouth. This simple stroke will keep one moving through the water without much effort. Remember to keep the body as streamlined as possible at all times.

BACK FLOAT

A back float must be learned before a stroke can be started (Fig. 3). Begin in chest deep water, bend the knees until the water is up to the chin, and extend the arms straight out from the shoulders just under the surface of the water. Look up and gently place the ears underwater while keeping the chest and palms up. This requires a bit of arching in the back. Take a deep breath in through the mouth. The feet should normally rise off the bottom. If they do not, slowly move the hands overhead toward each other, still underwater, until the feet do rise. Each person has a slightly different specific gravity, or degree of buoyancy, which means the back float will vary from a nearly vertical to a perfectly horizontal position in relation to the surface of the water. To recover from this position, slowly bring the head forward until the chin comes near the chest, at the same time curling the legs. When the body is in a sitting position, simply press the feet and arms down and stand up. A partner may help you get into the back float position by standing to one side and extending an arm under the waist until you feel secure in the float position. Experiment with different arm positions until you find the one that balances the body most perfectiy.

BACKSTROKE FOR BEGINNERS

After the back float position is comfortable, start using the same flutter kick that was used on the front. In the up and down leg movement on the back, emphasis should be placed on the lift; but there is drive or power in both parts of the kick. The hips, knees, and ankles all assist in the action and the toes may break the surface of the water.

The hands are used in a finning motion for this stroke, starting with arms extended along the sides of the body. Hands are drawn up to waist height, then the wrists bend and fingertips turn outward. Fingers are together as the palms of the hands press downward toward the feet with a thrust that provides power and returns the hands to the starting position. The hands always remain underwater.

Check *body position*: as near horizontal as possible with the nose straight up; *kick*: flutter kick with the legs and keep the toes pointed; *arms*: press the water down with both forearms and palms, then recover hands close to body up to the waist; and *breathe*: through the mouth.

TURNING OVER

The learning of strokes enables one to travel in a straight line through the water on the face or back. In order to change from a back stroke

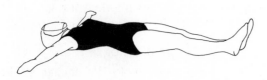

(3) Back float.

to a front float, one may roll over by turning the head and shoulders in the direction one wishes to turn. The rest of the body will follow the lead of the head. In rolling from back to face, as the body begins the turn and is on the side, the top arm can reach across the body to aid in turning over. The arm that comes under the body should reach out and scoop the water in toward the body. The legs can also aid in the roll over. By crossing the ankles and reaching out in the direction of the turn with the top foot, leg action complements arm, shoulder, and head action.

To roll from face to back one turns the head and shoulders, reaches across with the arm that comes under the body, and scoops toward the body with the opposite arm.

TURNING AROUND

One must be able to change direction when swimming. To turn from one direction to another in the water, press forcefully against the water opposite to the direction you wish to turn, and minimize the action of the other hand. This enables the body to make a gradual turn and will require several arm strokes. It is also possible, with the same arm action, to draw the legs up under the body and pivot around them for a faster turn.

TREADING

Sometimes it is necessary to get into a vertical position with head upright to survey a situation, or to make a decision about swimming farther or turning around. Treading water then becomes a needed skill. Treading water can be done with the legs alone, but to begin with, the arms may be used. Get into chest deep water, keeping the arms underwater, and move the hands in toward the chest and out beyond the shoulders in a smooth paddling motion. Palms should be facing the bottom. Do this slowly. Move out a little deeper, until the water is up to the chin. Continue the arm movement, and add the legs. The legs can do almost anything as long as it is done slowly and easily. To tread water is to rest. Some leg movements that are used are the bicycle, which is like pedaling; a scissors kick; or a breast stroke kick. The last two will be explained later.

BOBBING

Bobbing can be used to progress through the water or as a practice drill for rhythmical breathing and increasing the strength of the chest muscles. Bobbing starts in a vertical position in water over the head. Press down vigorously on the water with the hands, and give a strong kick. This drives the body upwards, then gravity pushes it down. Streamline the body as much as possible during descent by keeping the legs together and the arms at the sides. If the speed of descent slows, push the arms up overhead slowly, and continue pushing with the hands until the toes touch the bottom. Upon reaching the bottom, bend the knees while the arms are coming in close to the body near the head and shoulders. Push off the bottom by forcefully straightening the legs and pointing the toes. If you desire to progress forward, push off on a forward angle; if you wish to stay in place, push straight up.

These are skills and terms that every beginner should have in her movement vocabulary as well as speaking vocabulary. It might be good to add a word of encouragement here. Swimming is an individual sport, and each individual learns at her own pace. Desire and determination, as well as knowledge, certainly will increase the learning pace. Try to understand what is being performed, and think the movements through before entering the water and before attempting something new.

Swimming Strokes

Although you can now move through the water with some ease, this hardly looks like the swimming you have seen in movies or at a swimming meet. Bona fide swimming strokes are next in order.

THE ELEMENTARY BACKSTROKE

The elementary backstroke introduces a new kick and arm pattern. It is primarily a resting and gliding stroke, which should be kept in mind during its performance. The arms and legs move together, then the body glides before another stroke is taken. Keep the body in a streamlined position during the glide, and much space may be covered with little effort.

Body position: Back float with the nose pointed directly up.

Arms: The starting position is with the arms at the sides touching the thighs. To begin stroking draw both hands up the sides of the suit until they reach the waist. Then, with the fingertips leading, reach out underwater until the arms

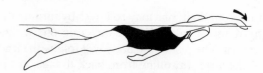

(5) Front crawl.

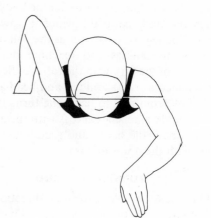

(4) Elementary back stroke: power phase.

are straight and the hands are at shoulder height or higher. Keep the elbows straight while pressing the arms toward the feet until the hands again come in contact with the thighs. Glide.

Breast stroke kick: The legs bend at the knees and the feet drop down and to the *outside of the knees*. The feet are rotating outward at this time, with the toes cocked up toward the knees. The knees may be kept together or they may fall apart a comfortable distance. The important part of the kick is to keep the feet wider than the knees. Because the feet are rotated out, the push comes from the inside of the ankles and calves of the legs. The resistance of the water makes the legs go through a small circular movement as they are pressed back, and inward pressure with the feet brings the legs straight and together near the surface of the water.

Coordination: The legs and arms start at the same time (Fig. 4). Inasmuch as the arms are going through a longer arc than the legs, the leg stroke will be completed first. Hold the streamlined position for about three counts. The breath is taken either on the power phase of the stroke or during the glide.

THE CRAWL

The crawl, known as *freestyle* in competitive swimming, is a stroke for speed, but can also be used for long distance swimming after it has been mastered (Fig. 5). Arm and leg action is

(6) Front crawl: arm pull.

continuous; the arms pull and recover alternately while the legs aid in propulsion with a steady up and down or "flutter" motion. The crawl is performed in a front float position with the head resting in the water so the surface of the water is just above the eyebrows. The waterline location will vary slightly with the buoyancy of the individual.

Flutter kick: The flutter kick is an up and down movement from the hips with the knees and ankles relaxed and toes turned in. The whip-like leg action provides continuous power throughout the kick, but the upward motion should be a little more forceful than the downward kick. There can be as many as eight kicks per arm cycle although most people use four or six. (Also see, earlier section, "Flutter Kick," for the beginner).

Arms: The arm stroke is an alternate pressing and recovery as in the human stroke, but now the recovery is over the surface of the water and slightly out to the side (Fig. 6). A relaxed, rounded arm position is best on the recovery. Reach out in front of the shoulder until the arm is straight, elbow remaining slightly higher than the hand. After the hand enters the water, pull back and under the body, and then continue with a pushing motion as the hand comes under the chest. On the pull the water is pressed back with the hand and inside of the forearm; the push part of the power phase continues until the

(7) Head position for breathing—side of face and ear in water.

(8) Side float.

(9) Scissors kick.

arm passes the end of the suit, and then the arm relaxes and elbow bends as the shoulder muscles swing the arm forward. One arm is starting the power phase as the other is starting the recovery.

If speed is desired, the power action of the arm stroke begins immediately upon entry of the hand into the water. If speed is not the prime purpose of the stroke, the hand and arm may glide or ride the water briefly.

Breathing: Breathe in through the mouth and out through mouth or mouth and nose (Fig. 7). Exhalation is done with the face in the water and the head turns to the side for inhalation. Either side can be used for breathing, but one should not alternate sides. The head rolls sideward as the pull or power phase of the arm stroke begins, and the face turns back into the water as that same arm is in the recovery phase. Turning the head away from the stronger arm is favored by some swimmers. The head may be lifted a little higher on the water by the preferred or stronger arm, thus making the head turn easier on that side. Keep the ear in the water as the head rolls to the side. Breathe on every cycle, but take small breaths. Too much air can be as fatiguing as too little.

SIDE STROKE

The side stroke is a favorite stroke in recreational swimming. Because the body position is on the side with the back of the head in the water the swimmer can see to the back, side, and even to the front without too much difficulty. It is an easy, restful stroke when correctly performed, and has a powerful kick that also makes it an important stroke for life saving skill. Life savers must be able to perform the stroke on both sides, but beginners may prefer one side to the other.

Body position: A side float position with the arm closest to the bottom extended overhead and

under the water, and the other arm resting on the side of the body (Fig. 8). The ear or back of the head rests on the arm that is extended overhead, and the face remains out of water. This is a very streamlined and stretched position.

Arms: The extended or overhead arm initiates the action by scooping water toward the chest with a bent arm. As this is being done, the arm close to the body slides up the side and extends out from the chest, crossing the first arm at this point. The extended arm recovers by returning, fingertips first, to the original position as the other arm goes through its power phase of pushing the water down to the thigh. This is an alternate pull-push action with the two arms. When both arms have returned to the starting position, they rest in a glide position.

Scissors kick: This kick is known as the scissors kick because of the opening and closing action (Fig. 9). Feet separate, with top leg forward and bottom leg back, while both knees bend until there is almost a 90-degree angle between the thighs and the body. The upper leg continues bending and extending forward from this position while the lower leg extends backwards. When the legs are nearly straight in a wide *V*, they are squeezed forcefully down and in, bringing the legs together in straight alignment with the hips. Glide.

Coordination: The action of the upper arm and upper leg is the same and is done simultaneously. The legs draw up as the arm draws up, extend as the arm extends; then both arms and legs return to the original glide position at the same time. The glide and rest on the side should be held until speed is lost; then the cycle of the stroke is repeated.

THE BACKSTROKE

The backstroke is similar to the beginner's backstroke, except for the arm movement, which becomes an alternate stroking movement with recovery over the water rather than a simultaneous one with an underwater recovery (Fig. 10).

Body position: Back float, with head resting in the water so that the ears are covered. The nose should be pointed up. When seeking the correct body position, it is easier to think of the nose position than to just look up. One can look up while the head is nearly vertical, but if the nose is up, the head is horizontal.

Arms: This is an alternate press and recovery of each arm, with one arm starting the power phase as the other is starting the recovery. The reach is overhead and slightly to the side with the fingers and little finger side of the hand making the catch. The first part of the power phase is a pulling motion with the hand relatively close to the surface of the water. As the hand passes the shoulder, the elbow bends and points toward the bottom, and the hand and forearm push the water until the hand touches the thigh (Fig. 11). The recovery phase starts as the hand lifts out of the water. With elbow straight, the arm swings outward and upward, wrist relaxed ready for the catch with the fingers.

Flutter kick: Alternate up and down movement from the hip with the toes pointed and knees and ankles easy. Most swimmers use a six-beat rhythm with three kicks on each arm pull.

(10) Backstroke.

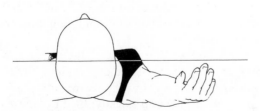

(11) Backstroke: pulling phase with arm.

Breathing: Take a breath in through the mouth on each complete arm cycle.

THE BREAST STROKE

The breast stroke may be a fast and powerful one or a relaxing one. Inasmuch as we are interested in a recreational stroke, a glide is added at the completion of the stroke. To make it a competitive stroke, the glide is eliminated.

Body position: The front float position with the arms extended overhead and the thumbs touching (Fig. 12). The hands are just below the surface of the water; the face is resting in the water as in the front crawl.

Arms: The arm pull is to shoulder level only, with the hands pressing down and back and the arms bending at the elbow (Fig. 13). As the hands come in line with the ears on the pull, they start the recovery by coming together almost under the chin and extend to the starting position, fingertips first. Glide.

Breast stroke kick: The breast stroke kick, as previously described, except that the knees drop down toward the bottom as the heels are drawn up toward the sides of the hips. The feet are rotated out, and the toes cocked toward the knees. Press the feet out and bring them back forcefully in a small circular motion until the legs are together and straight near the surface of the water. Think of pressing with the inside of the ankles and soles of the feet.

Breathing: As the arms press down and back the head is lifted until just the chin remains in the water. Inhale through the mouth and return face to water. Exhale through the mouth underwater.

Coordination: From the glide position the arm pull starts the stroke. The legs should begin the recovery phase, knees dropping down, just before the arms finish their cycle. As soon as the knees are bent, the pressing or forceful action of the feet and legs follow. Glide and exhale.

THE TRUDGEN CRAWL

In many scientific studies of strokes there is mention of ratios, or percentile ratings, of power. It is commonly known that most of the power in the crawl stroke, when performed by championship swimmers, comes from the arms in a nine to one ratio. In the breast stroke the power ratio is reversed with the greater drive coming from the legs in a three to seven ratio. Championship swimmers have much arm

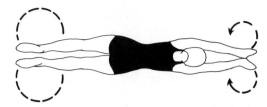

(12) Breast stroke: glide.

(13) Breast stroke: arm pull.

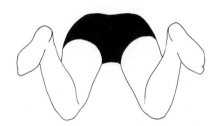

(14) Breast stroke: kick.

power, but most swimmers are not physically capable of supplying great power with the arms. The trudgen crawl is a hybrid stroke, which enables the swimmer of average skill to gain power in stroking through the use of a modified kick. This stroke is performed much like the front crawl but with the addition of a small scissors kick in a vertical position on the breathing arm side.

Body position: Front float, same as the front crawl.

Arms: Same as the front crawl.

Legs: About three flutter kicks, then a small scissors kick on same side as the strong arm. As the recovering arm leaves the water the legs draw up, extend, and squeeze. This kick has to be much faster than in the side stroke, so the kick must be considerably smaller. With a little practice this combined flutter and scissors kick soon becomes automatic. The small scissors kick adds power and lifts the body to make breathing easier.

Breathing: On the strong arm side, as in the front crawl.

Entering the Water

FEET FIRST ENTRY

An easy way to enter the water is to jump feet first. After first ascertaining the temperature with a wary big toe, and boldly splashing a little water on the body, a slow and cautious descent of a ladder can be pure torture. *Jump* in and get it over with! The jump should be forward and upward with the body in a straight line while looking straight ahead. Bring the legs together in the air, and, if in shallow water, descend to the bottom with the arms fairly close to the body. Ankles, knees, and hips must bend upon touching the bottom. Then shove off with the feet and return to the surface.

Before jumping into water over the head one should take a breath. Then, if the swimmer is not using a nose clip, she should exhale through the nose on the descent in order to counteract pressure against the nose. This soon becomes automatic, but at first one needs to think about it. After a complete exhalation there is a feeling of being ready to inhale; therefore, it is best to exhale only a small amount of air in a steady pressure on the way down with the completion of the exhalation on the ascent.

On the first jump into deep water, the bottom may seem a long way off. The body should be firm and streamlined while descending; then one can push hard from the bottom with the feet. Extending the arms overhead at this time puts them in a position to pull and thus level off to a horizontal position after returning to the surface of the water.

DIVING

A head first entry, or dive, is a more sophisticated entry, and one that should be learned by every swimmer. To do this correctly a few facts must be taken into consideration. The water will buoy the body up. Because there is surface tension on the water, the greater the amount of body surface hitting the water at one time, the more shallow the resulting dive. Unless the body cuts through the surface tension swiftly, the water resists and slaps the body. This is often referred to as a belly flop. To eliminate this, one cuts a hole in the surface of the water with the hands, and makes the rest of the body enter through that hole. In the air the body is subject to the laws of gravity and will fall. Because the body has no stabilized position in the air, it will follow the lead of the head and shoulders.

Certain procedures are common to all dives. A breath is taken prior to entry, is held while entering the water, then exhaled on the way up. The body must be in alignment when entering the water; firm back and abdominal muscles maintain the entry position until one touches the bottom, then the head is raised, legs curl under the body, and the feet push off for the return to the surface.

SITTING DIVE

Sit on the edge of the pool, and separate the legs while the feet rest on the gutter. Stretch the arms overhead, pressing the sides of the head and ears with them while interlocking the thumbs. Then lower the arms between the legs while looking at the hands and lean forward until the body falls into the water. The eyes remain open until contacting the water, close momentarily in a reflex action, then open underwater. Keep the head between the arms.

STANDING DIVE

The first standing dive or "fall-in" should be taken from a forward stride stance at the edge of the pool while curling the toes of the forward foot over the edge. The arms are stretched overhead, pressing against the head and ears, with hands together. Look at the palm side of the fingertips, bend forward at the hips, and fall into the water. Hands enter the water first, then head and shoulders. The hips roll forward until they are above the shoulders. As soon as the entire body is in the water, lift the head toward the surface, pull down with the arms, and kick to the surface. In the standing position on the deck, bring the feet closer together on each successive dive. With the feet together the dive is still a fall into the water, and the hips roll to a nearly vertical position above the shoulders in the air. Keep the body firm and in alignment while entering the water.

STANDING DIVE WITH SPRING

The diver stands erect on the edge of the pool with feet together. For this dive the whole foot is on the deck in order to get a spring. The arms are stretched overhead. Focus on the point of entry, which should be about 3 feet from the side. Bend the knees a little, lean slightly forward from the ankles, then forcefully push off with the feet as the legs extend. The body describes an arc in the air and the hips roll above the shoulders as one enters the water.

STANDING DIVE WITH SPRING AND ARM PRESS

Arms are raised sideward, shoulder high, as one assumes an erect standing position. The slight body lean comes with the arm action to bring the body forward on this dive. Arm action starts with a sideward-downward or lateral press, and is followed by a forward-upward or vertical lift. The knees bend to prepare for the spring while the arms press downward. A forceful extension of the knees and feet occurs while the arms are close to the thighs. Then the arm lift and stretch lead into the position of body extension in the air. Eyes focus on the point of entry and, as the body moves through an arc in the air, back and abdominal muscles must remain firm to keep the body in alignment. At the time of entry into the water the hands must be together with the head tucked between the arms.

DIVING FROM A SPRINGBOARD

After initial diving skills are established, the springboard can be approached. The low or one meter board is comfortably wide, 14 to 16 feet long, and rests on a fulcrum. The board slants slightly upward from the fixed end to the free end with the free end approximately one meter from the surface of the water (about $3\frac{1}{3}$ feet). The depth of the water under a one meter board should be 10 feet to meet safety standards.

FALL-IN DIVE FROM BOARD

With the feet together, arms stretched overhead and legs straight, bend forward at the hips. Focus the eyes and point the hands toward a spot for entry about 3 feet out from the end of the board, then fall in. The height of the board enables the body to assume nearly vertical entry. There should be no spring and the body position should remain constant until the bottom is reached.

A true vertical entry *of the hands* would result in an overthrow of the body, because the body continues to move in an arc until it is underwater. What looks like a vertical entry of the hands is just slightly short of vertical inasmuch as the body rides over to a vertical position.

STANDING DIVE FROM BOARD

A standing dive from the board is performed in the same way as the spring from the side, but the action of the board will give added force to the push-off. Both the arm press and the spring from the board provide power to propel the body into an arc in the air. One must not lower the head during the push-off, because this action would increase body rotation in the air and could cause the legs to overthrow upon entry into the water. The spring is upward, and the push-off with the feet, accompanied by a slight body lean, provides the needed forward-upward thrust. The body should be in a stretched position for entry: arms extended, ears touching arms, back and abdominal muscles firm and legs straight.

The approach

Competitive rules state that the forward approach in diving must consist of at least three steps plus a hurdle (Fig. 15). It has been found that three steps allow for a maximum of momentum with a minimum of loss of balance. On the last step the knee of the free leg is raised for the hurdle. This aids in giving lift to the body and places one in a more vertical position. Both feet

then come down together quite near the end of the board, toes touching first. As the knees bend, the feet roll back so the heels are touching. The body presses down and continues off much like the standing dive. For the take-off, the legs and feet extend; the toes are the last to leave the board. The hurdle leg is the one you would most likely kick with; it is usually on the same side as the handedness. Start the approach with the leg opposite the hurdle leg. Take three normal smooth steps, swing the hurdle knee forcefully upward, land on both feet on the end of the board, and take off into a foot first entry. Judgment of where to start on the board can be achieved by estimating the distance to be covered, or by going to the free end of the board and taking four normal steps toward the fixed end. This distance will change with conditions and confidence. No hard and fast rule can be applied. Try to make the approach about the length of four normal steps. During the approach, without bending the head forward, the eyes should focus on the tip of the board.

While the foot pattern is being established it is foolish to worry about the arms. However, as soon as the footwork can be performed, it is time to add the arms in order to make a finished approach to a dive. Standing with both feet together and the arms down at the sides is the correct starting position. The hands remain comfortably at the sides through the first three

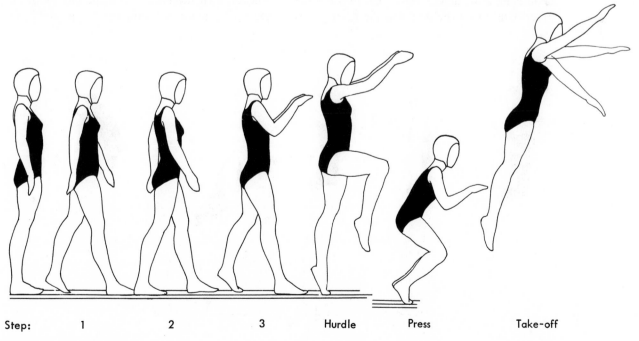

| Step: | 1 | 2 | 3 | Hurdle | Press | Take-off |

(15) Approach and hurdle.

steps, trailing slightly behind the body. As the knee is brought up in the hurdle action, the arms swing forward and overhead helping the lifting motion of the hurdle leg. As the feet return to the end of the board, the arms press down to the sides, slightly to the front. When the body leaves the board for the dive, the hands meet overhead in the stretch position described earlier. The body goes up into the air, moving in an arc, and enters slightly short of vertical. This should all be done smoothly without break, hesitation, or exaggerated movements.

BACK DIVE

A back dive is the next logical step in diving because it is the other basic direction that must be learned by the diver. It is helpful to go through some lead-up dives. Many divers will meet with immediate success; others will have to become accustomed to this new position.

Back fall-in dive

The back fall-in dive is an assisted dive. The performer stands with weight on the balls of the feet and with heels just over the edge of the board while facing the fixed end of the board. An assistant can steady the diver while she is assuming this position. The diver arches backward in the upper back and must reach back for the water with arms overhead and head back. The knees do not bend. The assistant holds one hand behind the diver's waist, and may use the other hand to lift the thighs as the diver leaves the board. When done correctly the diver falls no closer to the board than the length of the legs. The head stays in line with the arms and the diver must reach with hands toward the point of entry. The entry position is continued into a back layout somersault underwater.

Back dive with spring

The starting position is the same as for the back fall-in dive. There is a slight backward lean while the entire body is kept in its stretched position. As the loss of balance is felt, the diver bends the knees and pushes off. As this occurs the head falls back and the hands reach for the water. Focus is on the point of entry.

Back dive with spring and arm press

The feet are over the edge of the board so that only the ball of the foot remains on the board (Fig. 16). Many divers form a V with their toes out and the heels together for better balance. The arms are straight ahead at shoulder height until one is in a balanced position with the ball of the foot on the board and heels off. Lower arms to sides and pause. Then lift the arms sideward-upward slightly above shoulder height while also lifting the heels. Without pause press down with the hands to the sides while the knees, hips, and ankles bend. Swing the arms up and slightly back as the body stretches and leaves the board. It is important to maintain contact with the board until the last phase of the spring action is completed. Focus and head

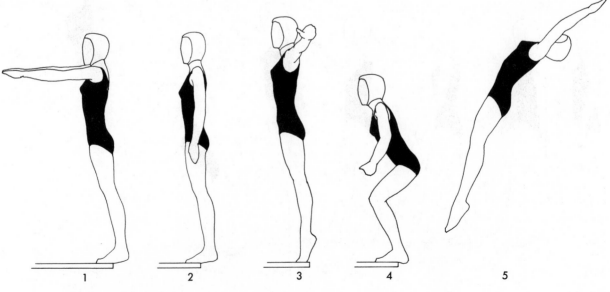

(16) Take-off for back dive.

position are the same as on previous back dives. Lift the chin, tilt the head backward, and look at the water.

Diving positions and groupings

Dives are performed in three basic positions: lay-out or straight body position; tuck or clasping the bent knees to the chest; and pike, where the body is flexed to a 90-degree angle at the hips with the legs straight. There are five possible directions in which the diver may go: forward; backward; reverse or rotation backward following the forward approach; inward or a start from the backward position followed by forward rotation; and twisting or rotation around a longitudinal axis. The five dive groups for competition are derived from the five possible directions that a diver may go.

A good approach and take-off is important to all diving and must be thoroughly practiced and learned. One should develop the kinesthetic feel and a mental image of each dive before attempting it. Follow progressions and learn one step well before proceeding to the next.

Synchronized Swimming

Perhaps the most creative and interesting phase of swimming is synchronized swimming. It can be done either individually or in a group. It can be either highly taxing physically when performed for competition, or intensely pleasing and relaxing when done just for the fun of it with friends. Even in beginning stunts it stresses those things which are important to most young women: beauty, grace, and poise. The rhythm that is inherent in swimming naturally accommodates itself to the sound of music and makes it a pleasant experience on any level.

Synchronized swimming is truly an American sport, and one that is relatively young, so we may still talk and correspond with those who first recognized its possibilities and challenge. Kay Curtis, Gertrude Goss, Fern Yates, and Theresa Anderson are names that are familiar to most serious students of synchronized swimming, and all are still involved with this activity. Three major groups in the country promote the sport and dispense information. The International Academy of Aquatic Art headed by Beulah and Henry Gundling stresses the artistic and aesthetic potential of synchronized swimming. The Amateur Athletic Union stresses competitive synchronized swimming, and the Association of Synchronized Swimming for College Women tries to combine the advantages of each for the sake of better college water shows.

An understanding and mastery of the basic strokes is essential to synchronized swimming. One may then use the known as a point of departure for experimentation in order to create new forms. Knowing and being able to hold the three basic body positions in and under the water is also important. Ability to hold one's breath and endurance to perform underwater stunts increase with practice and may be facilitated by the use of nose clips.

STROKING

Almost all strokes or variations (hybrids) of strokes are used in synchronized swimming. The chief difference in the stroking is the body and the head position. It is easier to synchronize a stroke with another swimmer's when one can see, so the head is most often carried rather high—and smiling, please. This means that the legs sink, and the entire body is often at about a 45-degree angle in the water. Swimming is always done with as smooth a motion as possible and paced to the ability of the weakest swimmer. Both of these factors tend to slow the stroking to the point where sculling is necessary somewhere during the stroke to maintain body position.

Try side-by-side stroking with the front and back crawl. It is a rule of thumb to "guide right" in this situation. When stroking with a partner is mastered, try variations of the stroke, experimenting with pauses, arm positions, and so on. Enjoyment can come from experimentation and creativity.

MUSIC

An element that increases enjoyment in synchronized swimming, music gives direction and rhythm to the stroking. For the beginner, it is wise to have music that has a definite and even beat, not too slow or too fast. Although competitive swimmers will have underwater speakers dangling in the water all around the pool, a good loud record player will suffice in most situations. The beat of the music should almost vibrate in the water. It might be blaring to those out of water, but by the time it gets through the cap, water in the ears, and the swimming sounds, it is a bare whisper. Syncopated rhythms seem to lend themselves to hybrid variations of strokes; as soon as rhythmic stroking is established, experiment with different rhythms.

SCULLING

Sculling is one skill that must be learned and practiced over and over to get the smooth and fluid motion of the accomplished synchronized swimmer. Sculling can be done over the head, at the side propelling the body head or feet first, or under the waist when the body is in a prone position. It is also used during many of the hybrid stroking movements that are found in this sport. Although the hands may be in almost any position, it must be remembered that the body will go in the direction opposite to the palms of the hands.

Sit on the pool deck with the legs in the water and the hands resting comfortably on the deck, palms down, near the sides of the hips. The fingertips should be forward. Lift the little fingers while maintaining contact with the deck with the thumb portion of the hands. Push the hands away from the sides with the fingertips describing an arc until the fingertips are pointing directly to the sides. This should be a distance of a little over one foot. Bring the hands back to the sides, again describing an arc, this time letting the little fingers maintain contact with the deck, and the thumb portion of the hands raising just a bit.

Get into the water and assume a strong back layout position. Stretch and point the toes. Lift the legs so that the thighs and toes break the surface of the water. Then try the sculling motion that was learned on the deck. The hands execute a figure-eight and push the water toward the feet with palms facing the feet. Make sure the hands are always underwater, and stay relatively close to the body and the hips. This action will move the body slowly through the water toward the head. To go foot first, simply reverse the hands so the palms are facing the head. There is more emphasis on the outward motion, away from the body, in the reverse scull.

STUNTS

In addition to modification of strokes and swimming to music, synchronized swimming also involves stunts. The stunts are of course used as a part of swimming routines, but are also performed separately for competition.

Many variations exist within stunt groupings, and there are five basic categories of synchronized swimming stunts: 1) ballet leg group, 2) dolphin, head first group, 3) dolphin, foot first group, 4) somersault group, front and back, and 5) a diverse group including such stunts as corkscrew, crane, swordalina, and so on. All this adds up to challenging creative expression that can be enjoyed for the rest of one's life.

Skin and Scuba Diving

The last and perhaps most fascinating phase of swimming is also the most recent. Although man has explored the depths of the sea for centuries in all sorts of bells, diving suits, and submarines, it was not until World War II that free diving to the depths was made feasible. Jacques Cousteau of France is generally given credit for perfecting a regulator or breathing apparatus that allowed man to descend below the surface with only a tank on the back, and no umbilical cords back to the surface to impede him. Since 1943 perfection of equipment has progressed at a fantastic pace. In fact, it seems to have completed a circle in some respects. One of the newest developments has a flexible air tube extending down approximately 50 feet from a small raft that supplies oxygen to the diver. This same device was used many years ago, before a flexible tube had been invented—the diver walking around with a 20- or 30-foot pipe of tin extending from his mouth. One would assume that this was not very comfortable, nor did it allow much freedom of head movement.

The beauty of the depths fascinates man, and today even a novice can enjoy snorkeling around reefs and exploring familiar lakes with a minimum outlay of money for equipment. Skin diving, or snorkeling, is a definite lead-up to Scuba diving, and should be mastered first. The word *Scuba* is an abbreviation for self-contained underwater breathing apparatus. Neither sport should be attempted until one feels completely at home in the water in all positions, and has mastered all basic swimming skills. This cannot be overemphasized.

EQUIPMENT

The mask is the most important part and must be fitted directly to the diver's face. Although many sporting goods stores have a large variety of masks with nozzles extending from the face plate, huge wrap-around face plates, and masks with double horns extending from them, the mask should have a shatterproof glass for a face plate, and the part that touches the face should be of a soft, molding material. The best type is normally made of a neoprene composition. The less chrome on the mask the better, for bright objects underwater attract fish, sometimes undesirable ones. To try on the mask, take it in both hands, bend the sides down, and place the bottom of the mask directly under the nose. The top of the mask normally has a mechanism that holds the face plate in place. Press the mask up against the face, releasing the sides slowly. Be sure the hair is away from the face so a complete seal can be made. Take a breath through the nose and remove the hands. If the mask stays on the face a seal has been made and the mask fits. Adjust the head strap to fit comfortably around the widest part of the head.

Snorkels can be made of plastic or hard rubber or a combination of both. They can be in a stiff *J* form, or have a flexible bottom to adjust to the head and mouth conformation. Each diver seems to have a definite preference for one or the other, but either will serve the purpose so long as it is comfortable. The mouthpiece should have some form of bite plate and guard that fits between the lips and the teeth to keep water from entering the mouth. There should be no ball or other contraption on top of the snorkel. Breathing should be controlled by the diver, not by a mechanical contrivance.

Fins for the feet are available in plastic and rubber with a molded heel or with a strap around the heel. At the present time the plastic fins have not been developed to a point where they are more than toys. The fin should fit comfortably over the bare foot, not rubbing at the toe or heel. The stiffness of the fin is directly proportional to the power that may be attained with it. Unless the legs and feet are very strong, a fin of medium stiffness will suffice. If much ocean snorkeling is anticipated, the fin with a molded heel may be best because it allows the diver to put the foot down on reefs or coral without danger of cutting or scratching the heel. The molded heel aids but does not give complete protection against sea urchins or other underwater life.

USE OF THE FINS

The kick that is most often used with fins is a modified flutter kick. Because the fins supply so much added power, the kick becomes deeper and much slower. Most of the power is applied on the up stroke of the kick, with a very relaxed knee on the recovery or down stroke. A scissors kick, in a modified form, may also be used with fins. Drop the hips a bit so that the fins remain underwater at all times. When putting on fins, it is easiest to first wet the fins and feet. On a beach, go into knee deep water, rinse any sand out of the fins and off the feet; once the fins are on, it is easier to walk backwards until the water is of swimming depth.

USE OF THE MASK

Before putting on the mask, dip it into the water and rinse it out. With the hand, spread some saliva on the inner side of the face plate until the glass squeaks all over. This takes care of fogging in the water. There are many antifogging devices, but this is the handiest one. Rinse it once again, and put it on as explained earlier.

USE OF THE SNORKEL

Rinse out the snorkel by running water through it; little animals sometimes get in these pipes while they are stored. Insert the pipe between the straps of the mask and the temple, fit the mouthpiece into the mouth and breathe. Work the equipment around until it feels comfortable. It is much easier to do this on land or in shallow water than in deep water with a rolling surf. To prevent fogging of the mask, all breathing from now on is done through the snorkel. First lower the face into the water and breathe a few times while looking through the face mask at the bottom. Adjust the height of the pipe so that it extends a few inches above the surface of the water when lying in a face float position. Still in shallow water, and preferably holding on to something, take a deep breath through the snorkel, put the tongue in the mouthpiece, sealing it, and lower the entire head and body underwater. There will be pressure against the mouthpiece as the snorkel fills with water. Slowly raise the head until the pressure lessens, but keep the mask in the water. Remove the tongue from the mouthpiece and blow out the snorkel, or clear the water from it by saying "TWO" very forcefully. If there is still some water in the curve of the snorkel, blow it out again. A little water in the snorkel can be tolerated because it keeps the inside of the mouth moist.

Now is the time to experiment with breathing while swimming. Swim with one arm out in front to protect the head. Sight is limited in the mask unless the head is continually rolled from side to side, and this becomes very tiring. Watch the ever changing panorama of the bottom, take a breath, insert the tongue in the mouthpiece, dive by lowering the head and the extended arm and rolling the hips over the head. Come up before it is absolutely necessary, and clear the snorkel without lifting the head out of water. Practice this in known water until confident. Experiment with rolling in the water with just enough air escaping through the snorkel to keep it clear.

Everything is magnified by water and the face mask, so the first encounter with a fish or plant may be a terrifying one. A perch can turn into a barracuda in a fresh water lake, and a lily pad stem seems like a jungle vine. It takes a while to accustom the eyes to these sights. Depth is also very deceptive. What seems to be within an arm's reach may be 20 feet down. Go slowly, and keep within sight of a partner at all times. This distance varies with the clarity of the water. Much of the plant life in open bodies of water is well within the reach of the skin diver, and many hours of enjoyment can be derived from moving very slowly over it.

To progress from skin diving to scuba is a step that can be handled only by a professional teacher or a very accomplished amateur. Because one is dealing with highly sophisticated equipment and depth pressures, it is necessary to be aware of possible hazards. Death can result in an error in only 10 feet of water. Take lessons and follow instructions. This sophisticated sport demands knowledge, skill, fitness, and caution, but the reward is boundless.

Selected References

Counsilman, James and Barbara Drinkwater. *Beginning Skin and Scuba Diving*. Belmont, Calif.; Wadsworth Publishing Co., 1965.

Fairbanks, Ann. *Teaching Springboard Diving*. Englewood Cliffs, N.J.; Prentice-Hall, 1963.

Mackenzie, M. M. and Betty Spears. *Beginning Swimming*. Belmont, Calif.; Wadsworth Publishing Co., 1965.

Vickers, Betty. *Teaching Synchronized Swimming*. Englewood Cliffs, N.J.; Prentice-Hall, 1965.

Yates, Fern and Theresa W. Anderson, *Synchronized Swimming*, 2nd ed. New York; Ronald Press, 1958.

PART THREE

Team Sports

Chapter **15**

Basketball *Betty G. Hartman*

History. Goals. Equipment. Etiquette. Passing. Shooting. Catching. Free Throw. Dribble. Pivot. Feinting. Cutting. Screening. Strategy. Guarding Systems. Rebounding. Evaluation. Terminology.

Basketball is a game played by two teams of six players each. The object of the game is to pass, throw, or "shoot" a ball through baskets that are suspended from flat-surfaced back-boards 10 feet above the floor at the ends of a rectangular-shaped court. Each team attempts to gain possession of the ball in order to throw the ball up and through the hoop. The team that does not have the ball tries to prevent the other team from shooting and tries to intercept the ball.

The court is divided into two halves by a division line (Fig. 1). At the start of the game, three of the six players of one team are in one half of the court. One of the remaining three is in the center circle and the other two players are in the opposite half of the court. The opposing team takes similar positions. The game is started by a jump ball between two of the opponents in the center circle. An official throws the ball into the air between the two opponents who jump and attempt to tap the ball to a team-mate.

Dr. Hartman, Coordinator of Women's Physical Educa-tion at Kent State University, Ohio, earned her A.B. and M.S. degrees at MacMurray College and her Ph.D. at Ohio State University. She has served as a state basket-ball chairman for the Division for Girls and Women's Sports and is currently on the national executive council as publications chairman. As a student, Miss Hartman was an enthusiastic participant in basketball for women, and since then has taught and officiated basketball in her various teaching positions.

After one team gains possession of the ball, teammates try to pass the ball close enough to the basket at their end of the court to be able to shoot and score a *field goal*, a value of two points. The half of the court in which one team shoots is called the *front court*; the other half of the court is their *back court*. The reverse is true for halves of the court for the opposing team. When a team scores a field goal, a member of the opposing team takes the ball out-of-bounds at the end line beneath the basket where the goal was scored. This team then attempts to pass the ball up to their front court and to score.

If a team succeeds in passing the ball to their front court, a fourth player, called a *rover*, may come into that court; the remaining two team-mates stay in the back court. The opposing team may balance the court by having a fourth player cross the division line to guard their opponents' roving player. When the ball moves to the other half of the court each team may again bring a rover across the line into that half-court. The game continues in this manner for four quarters of eight minutes each.

In passing, shooting, and maneuvering to receive the ball, players may not shove, push, trip, or use body contact; such actions are called *fouls*. The player who fouls is penalized, and the opponent who was fouled against is awarded a free throw. The free throw is an unguarded shot taken in the fouled player's front court while the other players in this half-court remain outside the free throw area. One point is scored if the free throw goes through the basket.

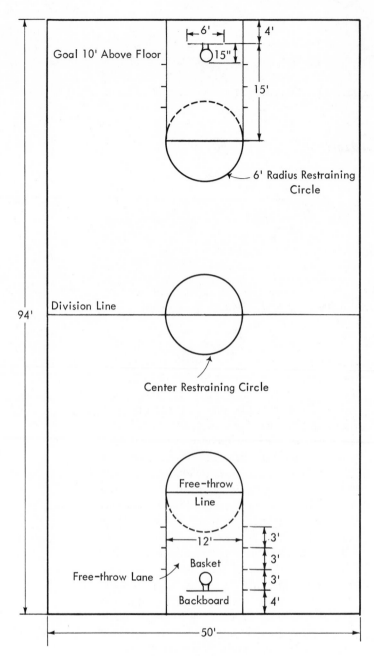

Goal 10' Above Floor

6'

15"

4'

15'

6' Radius Restraining Circle

Division Line

94'

Center Restraining Circle

Free-throw Line

12'

3'

3'

3'

4'

Free-throw Lane

Basket

Backboard

50'

(1) Basketball court.

Players who run with the ball commit a violation called *traveling*; one is allowed to take only two steps after catching the ball on the move. The ball may be advanced by a series of bounces to oneself called *dribbling*, and by passing to teammates. Players not in possession of the ball may move freely within the court boundaries. Traveling and stepping on the boundary lines are examples of violations, and carry the penalty of loss of the ball. An opponent is awarded the ball outside the boundaries;

she passes the ball into the court to one of her teammates for play to continue.

The game is controlled by two officials, a referee and an umpire. The major duties of these officials are starting the game by a jump ball and stopping the game for fouls and violations in order to administer penalties. Timekeepers and scorekeepers assist the two officials.

The basic basketball skills are catching; passing; shooting; basic moves for receiving and shooting as well as moves to try to prevent opponents from receiving and shooting; and teamwork involving the elements of both offense and defense. Offense is defined as play by the team in possession of the ball. Defense is defined as the attempt of the team not in possession of the ball to prevent their opponents' shots and passes and to intercept the ball.

History

The game of basketball was invented in 1891 by Dr. James Naismith and his physical education class at Springfield College in Massachusetts. In 1892 the first rules were established for women. Mrs. Senda Berenson Abbott, first editor of the *Women's Basketball Guide*, made adaptations of the game for women.

The American Association for Health, Physical Education, and Recreation appointed a subcommittee for women's basketball rules in 1899. Since 1916, yearly meetings have been held to discuss and revise the rules. The Division of Girls' and Women's Sports, now involved with many aspects of a great variety of girls' and women's sports, is an outgrowth of the early concern for appropriate rules of basketball for women. Officiating standards, rules revisions, and the publication of rule books are today part of the Division's responsibilities in relation to basketball. Recently, the Amateur Athletic Union and the DGWS have cooperatively established basketball rules.

Basketball rules for women have gone through a number of major changes. The original change from rules for men divided the playing court into three sections, supposedly to guard against extreme physical exertion. Players were assigned to these parts of the court and could not move from one to the other. Snatching and batting the ball were prohibited. Dribbling was limited to three bounces, and a player could keep the ball for only three seconds.

Until 1923 players could guard only in a vertical plane in attempting to prevent an opponent from passing or shooting. In 1923 the rules were changed to allow guarding in any plane; personal contact, however, was prohibited. In 1938 the number of sections of a court was changed from three to two. This was followed by a rule change allowing "brush contact" during the guarding process. The means of starting the game has also changed through the years. In 1932 the game could be started by a center throw, but the jump was optional; the center throw became official in 1936 but was later dropped. In 1962 another major change was made when the roving player opportunity was added.

At the present time the game is started at each quarter with a jump ball. A player who has the ball may not hold it for longer than five seconds. A "tie" ball is called when a player places one or both hands firmly on a ball held by an opponent, or when a player takes the ball or taps it away from an opponent. Personal contact, except for the hands, is not permitted. A 1966–1967 rule change allows an unlimited dribble—the ball may be bounced as many times in succession as the player wishes.

Goals

In six or seven weeks one should be able to learn to play a game of basketball with some degree of satisfaction and success. One's skill in ball handling will improve with passing, catching, and shooting practice. Teamwork, both offensive and defensive, will be attained to a modest degree. More practice is needed if games are to be played with experienced opponents.

Short, fast passes should be the first to be attempted. Passing and catching on the move is essential, and should be practiced from the beginning, for the ability to get rid of the ball without "traveling" is an important skill. Ball handling skills involve intercepting opponents' passes and retrieving shots that miss the basket (rebounding). As the players' skills develop, the ability to avoid contact with other players and to position oneself strategically for receiving passes and rebounds will be acquired. Skill in dribbling, pivoting, feinting, running, stopping, changing direction, and jumping with and without the ball is also needed.

Shooting accuracy is developed through practice. A beginner usually starts with the chest shot, the one-hand push shot, and the one-hand lay-up; she then moves to the two-hand overhead and one-hand set shots. Hook shots and jump shots may also be explored. Short shots close to the basket are best because they are more accurate. Practice should be concentrated on shooting from the free-throw area into the basket. Long shots from farther away can be practiced later as strength and accuracy develop.

Guarding and positioning to prevent opponents' shooting and passing need to be learned, and offensive tactics are also essential. Out-of-bounds plays and full-court plays may be tried, and quick, evasive movements should be practiced.

Some girls and women will discover that they have a knack for accurate shooting and may wish to concentrate on forward positions; others may wish to work especially on defensive or guarding roles. However, all players should be able to run, pass, and shoot. In today's game with a roving player, each player may find herself playing the forward's shooting role at one time or another, and all players will have to know how to guard opponents. The roving-player game necessitates all-around skill for all players.

Equipment and Facilities

The basketball court is a hard-surfaced rectangle. Indoor courts are usually constructed of hardwood, whereas outdoor courts are often surfaced with asphalt or concrete. The maximum size of the rectangular court is 94 by 50 feet, with a minimum of 74 by 42 feet. The court is marked by boundary lines, a circle in the center, a center dividing-line parallel to the end lines, and two free-throw areas.

Two white wooden or plate glass backboards are suspended above the court, one at either end. The backboards, located 4 feet inside the court and parallel to the end lines, are 9 feet above the floor. A ring or basket 18 inches in diameter is attached to each backboard. The ring is 10 feet from the floor and extends 6 inches from the face of the backboard. Suspended from the rings are goal nets.

The free-throw lines are 15 feet from the face of each backboard. The free-throw lane, perpendicular to the end lines, consists of two parallel lines extending into the basketball court and placed 6 feet to each side of the midpoint of both end lines. The two parallel lines connect to the free-throw line. A free-throw circle, with the free-throw line as its diameter, is also marked on the floor (Fig. 1).

The basketball is ordinarily covered with leather or synthetic material. It must weigh between 20 and 22 ounces and is approximately 30 inches in diameter.

Players' costumes usually consist of shorts, blouse, and rubber-soled shoes. The soles of the shoes should be designed to prevent slipping on smooth, hard surfaces.

(2) Basketball grip for pass or shot.

Etiquette

Cooperation with teammates and officials is expected in basketball. Players should learn the rules in order to understand the officials' role. A player should indicate when she violates a rule, and should not question the decision of the officials. Distracting opponents or using delaying tactics are inappropriate in women's basketball. Players should respond quickly and quietly to the officials' directions and should confine conversation to quiet encouragement and compliments.

Basketball is defined by the rules as a noncontact game. Successful skill execution and safe play depend upon avoiding contact with teammates and opponents. Skillful play thus eliminates danger to self and opponents.

Skills

PASSING

Skill in passing is a prerequisite for playing basketball. The basic passes are the chest pass, two- and one-hand underhand passes, two-hand overhead and overarm passes, the bounce pass, and the hook pass. These passes can be used to send the ball in the air to a teammate, or with a bounce pass, in which the ball is thrown to the floor so that it rebounds to a teammate.

Chest pass

The chest pass can be the most accurate and forceful of all the passes. The ball is held about 10 to 12 inches away from the body at chest height. The elbows are held close to the body in a relaxed manner, and both hands contact the ball with the fingers spread comfortably apart. The ball is gripped gently but firmly, and the thumbs are positioned somewhat behind the ball, pointing toward each other. The ball should not be touched by the palms of the hands (Fig. 2).

Two types of footwork may be used with the chest pass; one pattern is the side-by-side foot position, the other a forward stride. The latter position enables the player to move quickly after the pass. In the side stride position, the weight of the body is balanced on both feet and evenly distributed over the heels and balls of the feet. Players may choose the more comfortable position, but both types should be explored. In either foot position, the knees are bent with the hips slightly flexed. The shoulders should be squared in the direction of the pass, and the head balanced over the shoulders. The eyes should focus over the ball and sight at the place where the pass is to be thrown.

The pass is started by pushing from the feet, then the knees. The ball is dropped slightly downward and toward the chest, then lifted upward and forward. As this action takes place, the elbows, wrists, and fingers extend, pushing the ball toward the target. The ball should roll off the fingertips as a result of the thrusting action of the arms, wrists, and hands. Good wrist snap and finger control is essential.

Follow-through is needed after the release. The body is extended in the direction of the pass. If the side stride position is used, the follow-through requires a step forward in the direction of the pass in order to dissipate the force generated in the thrusting action of the release. The knees, body, and arms extend forward and the hands should finish with the fingers pointing outward.

COACHING HINTS. Most beginners have difficulty in achieving the proper elbow and hand-finger position in the chest pass. There is a tendency to push the elbows away from the sides. This causes the hands to roll backward to a position behind the ball rather than remaining on the sides of the ball, and the fingers end up pointing toward each other; palm contact may also result. Hampered by these faults in form, the ball will not spin, the thrusting force will be inhibited, and inaccuracy may result.

Two-hand underhand pass

The two-hand underhand pass can be used to avoid the outstretched arms of a guarding opponent. The player passes below her own waist and below the guard's arms. It is accurate and can be thrown with a great deal of force.

The ball is held with the hands on the sides of the ball, fingertips contacting the ball firmly but not tensely, and the thumbs pointing toward each other. This pass may be thrown from the right or left side; the only change of body position involves the feet. If the pass is to be started from the right, the feet should be in a forward stride with the left foot forward. The reverse is true for a pass from the left side. Because the body rotates and bends from waist and hips as the ball is swung to the side, weight must be balanced over the bent knees and feet.

The passing action begins with the transfer of weight onto the back foot as the ball is swung down and backward. The body rotates and the knees bend as the ball is brought back. The elbow on the side of the ball is bent and turned out to the side, while the other arm is as straight as possible (Fig. 3).

The release of the ball starts with the arms swinging the ball forward in the direction of the target. The arms and wrists straighten as they swing forward. The weight shifts from the back foot to the forward foot, and the knees straighten as the hips and shoulders rotate forward in the direction of the pass. The release comes in front of the body with the ball touched last by the fingertips.

During the follow-through the body weight is shifted to the forward foot. An additional step may be taken after the ball is released if the force of the throw is strong. The arms extend, the fingers point forward and outward, and the thumbs point upward.

(3) Two-hand underhand pass: start of pass.

COACHING HINTS. The point in front of the body where the ball is released will determine its trajectory. The arms swing forward and then upward. If the ball is not released before this upward action begins, the ball will arch upward. However, if the ball is released too soon, that is, before the arms swing toward the target, the trajectory will be low.

Body action also determines the action of the ball. The more the knees are bent, the lower the ball will be swung. Beginners tend to fail to twist to the side in order to bring the ball as far back as possible. This cuts down on speed, because the body weight cannot then be added to the arm swing. Placing the right foot forward when swinging the ball to the right side also inhibits body rotation.

The feet should point in the direction of the pass. Turning the feet when the ball is rotated to the side will cause the ball to be directed sideward. If the forward stride is not maintained, the player limits the force she is trying to develop and may even lose her balance.

One-hand underhand pass

Like the two-hand variety, the one-hand underhand pass can be used to launch the ball beneath the opponent's arms. The ball is balanced on the fingers and fingertips of one hand, with the hand under the ball, thumb pointing away from the body. The other hand touches the top of the ball to steady it. The ball is swung down to one side of the body and as far back as possible. The feet should be in a forward stride with the left foot forward if the ball is swung to the right.

The body position, balance, and rotation are the same as for the two-hand underhand pass. As the body and shoulders rotate, the throwing arm swings backward and sideward, and the top hand is removed. The ball remains balanced on the fingers and thumb of the hand as the throwing arm swings backward to an extended position.

The release is started by the arm swinging forward. The elbow and wrist straighten along with a shift of weight to the front foot. The knees straighten as the hips and shoulders rotate forward until they are at right angles to the direction of the pass. The release comes in front of the body with the ball rolling off the fingertips.

The follow-through involves a weight shift to the forward foot, and an additional step for balance if needed. The throwing arm and hand are extended in the direction of the pass, with the thumb out to the side at the finish of the pass.

COACHING HINTS. Beginners may fail to take the top or supporting hand from the ball soon enough. This inhibits body rotation and shortens the backswing so that force and accuracy are lost. Stepping on the same foot on the side to which the ball is swung also limits body rotation.

Two-hand overhead pass

The two-hand overhead pass can be used to project a ball over the arms and head of the opponent. It can be an accurate and forceful pass. The ball is held in both hands, using the fingertips in the manner described for the chest pass. The pass is started from a position over the head, with wrists bent toward the top of the head. The elbows are bent so they point almost directly toward the target. The body is positioned as in the chest pass except that the weight is balanced slightly farther backward because the ball is held overhead for this pass.

The thrusting action for the release begins with the feet and moves through the knees, hips, trunk, and shoulders. On the throw, the arms move forward and the elbows, wrists, and fingers straighten.

The follow-through involves complete extension of the whole body. If the pass is sufficiently forceful, the feet may leave the floor. This is especially true if the side stride foot position is used. If the forward stride foot position is used, weight transfer from the back to the forward foot may occur. The finish of the follow-through is the same as for the chest pass. The hands turn outward, and the head and eyes focus on the spot to which the pass is being thrown.

COACHING HINTS. The two-hand overhead pass is not so forceful as the chest pass. The path of the arm swing is not large, so greater knee flexion and body force are needed. Beginners may have trouble generating force until strength is increased. Because this pass is slower than the chest pass, it is more easily guarded.

The timing of the release of the ball may be difficult to achieve. The same principles are involved as in the two-hand underhand pass. Loss of balance may be caused by taking the ball too far back at the beginning of the pass.

It is difficult to change the ball from this pass position to a dribble; once the overhead pass position is assumed, one must move quickly. Palm contact, which inhibits power and ball spin, is another fault.

One-hand overhand pass

The one-hand overhand pass is similar to a baseball or softball throw, but both hands are used to balance the larger ball at the beginning of the backswing. This is the most powerful of all the passes. The feet are in a forward stride with the foot opposite the throwing arm forward, the knees flexed, and the body upright. The ball is held in both hands, but balanced on the spread fingers and fingertips of the throwing hand. The elbow of the throwing arm is bent and held close to the side of the body. The wrist is bent back and the back of the hand is over the shoulder. As the throwing arm swings back, up, and behind the head, the supporting hand is removed; the shoulders and hips rotate backward with the arm action, and the weight is transferred to the back foot.

First the elbow of the throwing arm begins to straighten and the shoulders and hips start rotating forward. The body weight shifts from back foot to both feet and then to the forward foot as the knees straighten.

The release of the ball is in front and above head height. The throwing arm swings forward, up, and over the shoulder with the forearm and hand ahead of the elbow. The arm extends, the wrist snaps forward, and the ball rolls forward off the fingertips. The shoulders and hips stop rotating at a position at right angles to the direction of the pass.

The follow-through ends with the weight on the forward foot. The throwing arm, hand, and fingers are extended and the palm of the hand is down. The throwing arm continues in a downward arc toward the opposite side of the body. An additional step may be taken after the release of the ball in order to maintain balance.

COACHING HINTS. Beginners may experience the same faults in timing the release as with the other passes. Releasing the ball at too high a point over the head may cause it to go too high into the air. Releasing the ball as the throwing arm starts downward will direct the ball toward the floor.

If the elbow is not straightened as the throwing arm is brought forward, the shoulder and body rotation are restricted and the path of the arm through the air is shortened, resulting in limitation of force.

Stepping on the foot on the same side of the throwing arm prevents body rotation. This results in poor balance, inaccuracy, and loss of power. Girls and women are apt to throw the ball without using body rotation.

Hook pass

For the hook pass the ball is swung up and over the head with the body sideways to the direction the ball is to be thrown. It is a pass that is difficult to direct; but it is also difficult to guard, because the passer's body is kept between the opponent and the ball. The pass starts with the feet in a side stride position. The wrist is bent to a right angle so that the ball may rest on the fingertips and the forearm. The shoulders and hips rotate backward while the throwing arm, completely extended, is swung back, away from the body, and upward. The arm swing must be rapid enough that centrifugal force keeps the ball against the forearm.

As the ball is swung away from the body, the weight shifts to the back foot; as the ball is brought up over the head, the weight transfers to both feet. On the release, the wrist straightens and the ball rolls off the extended fingertips. The hips and shoulders remain sideways to the direction of the pass to gain power and to keep an opponent from preventing the pass. The whole body straightens during the arm swing,

and if enough force is generated with the swing, both feet may leave the floor. The elbow bends slightly and the fingers point in the direction of the pass on the follow-through.

COACHING HINTS. Failure to keep the arm straight or stopping the throwing arm at any point in the arc of the swing will cause the ball to drop from the forearm and hand. The ball may also be dropped, or go to the right or left, if the throwing arm does not swing back, upward, and over the head in a full arm swing with the release at the top of the swing.

Straightening the wrist too soon during the arc of the swing will cause the ball to fly high into the air. Releasing the ball too late, going downward from the overhead position, will cause the ball to go too low.

Bounce pass

The bounce pass is a short one, used when a player is closely guarded. It is so named because the ball is directed at the floor so that it will rebound to a teammate. The passing action can be the same as the chest, overhead, or overarm throw; however, the chest pass is the best because the other passes start the ball release from a high position that makes it easier for opponents to intercept.

The flight of the ball on the bounce pass is lower than a ball thrown through the air; otherwise, hand, arm, and body positions are essentially the same.

SHOOTING SKILLS

Shooting the ball through the basket is the major purpose of the game of basketball. Outscoring the opponents is essential to winning the game. The two major shooting skills are set shots and moving shots. Set shots are those executed from a stationary position; moving shots are those with ball release while the player is moving. Set shots may be done from a spot on the floor or by jumping and releasing the ball at the height of the jump. This latter type of set, the jump shot, requires precise timing.

Shots may be classified as short, medium, and long. Short shots are those released from a 10-foot radius of the basket; medium shots are from 10 to 20 feet away; long shots are 20 feet or farther from the basket. The shorter shots are more accurate than medium or long shots, though this varies with the individual. Beginners should start with the shorter shots, practicing them until strength and accuracy increase. Being able to shoot and score from any spot on the floor is the ultimate goal. Players will find, however, that they are more accurate from certain spots and will develop skill in some shots and not in others. A good team is composed of players who can make a variety of shots from various distances.

Certain general principles should be applied to all types of shots to the basket. The important principles involve height of the shot, spin, and sighting or aiming. A high, arched shot is usually the most accurate. This shot, often called a *soft shot*, drops straight through the basket or, if it hits the rim, usually bounces through the hoop. Flatter shots with less height tend to spin out of the basket. Ball spin, which is extremely important, is imparted by proper hand and finger action during the release and follow-through. The spin imparted is called *backspin*, because the ball rotates backward toward the shooter. Sighting or aiming the ball is essential for accuracy. Focusing on the basket before, during, and after the release of

the shot increases accuracy. If the basket is approached from the front, the focus is at the rim of the basket; if the shot is angled, the focus is at a spot above and slightly to the side of the rim.

Set shots

The major set shots are the chest shot, the two-hand overhead shot, and the one-hand set. Any of the standard set shots may be used for free-throw shooting. The hook shot may be done from a stationary or moving position.

The chest shot

The chest shot is the most common shot in basketball. It can be used at any distance from the basket and as a free throw. It is executed in the same way as the chest pass. The major differences between the chest pass and the chest shot are in the release and follow-through. At the finish the hands point upward and outward with the arms extended overhead for the chest shot. The body also stretches upward and the feet leave the floor if the thrust and release action are sufficiently powerful (Fig. 4).

COACHING HINTS. The same faults encountered in the pass may be experienced with the chest shot. Attention should be given to proper hand, finger, and elbow positions. The hands are kept on the sides of the ball and should not roll under and back of the ball at the beginning of the shot.

The two-hand overhead set shot

The two-hand overhead set shot is more useful to tall players because the ball is started from a position over the head. Short players have difficulty guarding the shot. It may be used as a free throw and may also be adapted to a jump shot.

The action of the shot is the same as for the pass, but the release differs; the ball is arched higher for a shot than for a pass. The release is made from a point over the head rather than in front and the follow-through is upward rather than forward.

COACHING HINTS. Varying the release point and bringing the ball too far back over the head are common errors. The same errors associated with the chest pass may also affect the two-hand overhead shot.

The one-hand set shot

Considered by many to be the strongest and most accurate shot, the one-hand set shot is

(4) Follow-through: hand, arm, and body position following a shot.

(5) One-hand overhead shot: start of shot.

often used for a free throw as well as during floor play. The ball is held close to the body at about shoulder height with the back of the right, or shooting, hand toward the body. The ball rests on the fingertips of the shooting hand. The left hand, placed against the front of the ball, supports the ball at the start of the shot and is removed as the right hand pushes the ball forward.

At the start of the shot the right wrist is slightly cocked. The shooter concentrates on the basket, lifts the elbow of the right arm, and pushes forward with the forearm. Just before the push and release of the ball, the wrist bends as much as possible (Fig. 5).

The feet are separated about the width of the hips, with the right foot several inches ahead of the left and pointing to the right at about a 45-degree angle from the target. The knees are bent, hips flexed, and the weight balanced comfortably over both feet.

When releasing the ball, the knees, hips, body, flexed elbow, and wrist all straighten to give force; the follow-through involves extending the entire body. The complete extension of the wrist is essential and the ball is touched last by the fingertips. Eye focus continues on the basket rim after the release of the ball. (Left-handed players reverse the foot and hand positions.)

COACHING HINTS. Beginners often throw, rather than push, the ball. A good starting position will help to correct this tendency, but the bad habit of throwing the ball may result if the player lacks the strength to execute the push. Strength and power will develop with practice. The beginner should start with the two-hand set, and should be close to the basket when first trying both the two-hand and one-hand set shots. It is well for beginners to start learning the one-hand set shot because it leads to more advanced styles of shooting.

Jumping and jump shooting

A good jump should be developed because it is used for rebounds, jump shots, lay-ups, catching passes, and the tie or jump ball. The one-hand set shot and the two-hand overhead shot are more effective with a jump. The higher one can get into the air, the more one can avoid interference by an opponent.

JUMPING ELEMENTS. To prepare for a jump, the feet should be in a stride position with ankles, knees, and hips flexed and the weight balanced over the balls of the feet. An explosive push from the feet with extension through the legs and body gives height. At the height of the jump, the legs and ankles are completely extended, with the toes pointing down toward the floor. If the arms and hands are free, as in trying to catch the ball or attempting to tap the ball on a jump ball, the arms should also swing strongly upward. Good jumping for basketball involves complete upward stretching of the body. Jumping forward instead of upward expends the energy in the wrong direction.

JUMP SHOOTING. If a shot is to be combined with a jump, the release of the ball comes at the height of the jump while the person is momentarily suspended in the air. This might be described as jump—height—release—descent; the timing is very important. Shooting while in the process of jumping upward, or on the descent, is not a true jump shot. If a player jumps and shoots, or jumps and passes, other than at the height of the jump the force of the pass or shot is restricted.

Jump shots are usually executed while facing the basket on the jump and the release. However, it is possible to start with the back to the basket, then jump into a turn and shoot, or to move into a position for the jump shot by dribbling. In this latter instance forward momentum must be translated into vertical force. The player stops with the weight on both feet, catches the ball as it rebounds from the floor, and then jumps and shoots. The jump should be straight up; the player should be on the same spot after the jump has been completed.

Moving shots

Moving shots involve releasing the ball without pausing. They may be combined with a leap, hop, or run. Moving shots are difficult for an opponent to prevent. All players should learn to shoot on the move.

LAY-UP SHOT. The lay-up shot is one in which the ball is released by one hand at the height of a jump. It is an effective shot for moving in to the basket and, with practice, results in great accuracy because the player is nearer to the basket rim than with other shots. The lay-up may be taken from the front or from either side of the basket. Shots from the left side are usually taken with the left hand, so beginners should first practice the shot from the right or front, if right-handed.

In a lay-up from the right side the ball is held with both hands and moved to the right side and

(6) One-hand lay-up shot.

(7) Hook shot.

overhead (Fig. 6). The left hand supports the ball in front and is removed after the ball has been balanced on the fingers and fingertips of the shooting hand. The right wrist is cocked and elbow bent. The movement of the ball is combined with a forceful push from the left foot. On this take-off, the forward momentum of the preparatory run or leap is checked by bringing the right leg forward-upward, thus forcing the weight backward onto the left leg for a stronger push-off.

The legs, hips, trunk, shooting arm, and wrist completely extend, pushing the ball into the air at the height of the jump. The ball rolls off the fingertips, directed over the rim of the basket by wrist extension. After the jump, the landing on both feet is cushioned by bending hips, knees, and ankles.

The lay-up shot involves a pushing motion. Lay-ups may be done with a one- or two-hand

underhand motion similar to the arm action described in the underhand passes. However, because of the forward body movement, body rotation is not needed. The underhand lay-ups are, of course, more easily blocked by opponents.

HOOK SHOT. Hook shots may be done on the move or from a stationary position with the side or back to the basket. The shot is executed the same as the hook pass except that it has a higher release point and a higher arc in the air (Fig. 7). The same advantages and disadvantages of a hook pass apply to the hook shot.

If the ball is released on the move, the take-off foot is opposite to the shooting hand, and the take-off should be a vertical jump as described in the lay-up shot. The landing after the shot should be on both feet with the force being absorbed by bending knees and ankles. Hook shots are often combined with a pivot (movement of one foot with the other foot stationary).

CATCHING

Due to the size of a basketball, two hands should be used to catch. A ball caught above the waist is caught with the fingers pointing upward; a ball caught below the waist is caught with the fingers pointing downward. Players should move to align themselves with the path of the ball. The feet are placed in a forward stride position, the knees and hips are flexed, and the body weight is balanced over the balls of the feet. The shoulders are squared in the direction of the ball with eyes focusing on the flight of the ball. The arms and hands are away from the body, reaching in the direction of the ball, with fingers relaxed. To catch balls dropping straight down, the hands are held straight out with palms up in a cupped position.

As the oncoming ball strikes the outstretched hands, the fingers and thumbs make contact. The player immediately allows the ball to push her hands and arms toward her body. This absorbs the impact of the ball and is called *giving with the ball*. If a forceful throw is caught, the whole body "gives" by shifting the weight to the back foot and bending the wrists, arms, and shoulders.

Coaching hints

Effort should be made to be in a balanced position when catching a ball. It is sometimes necessary to jump into the air to catch high rebounding balls or to intercept passes, but these may be dropped because the player's feet are off the floor in an off-balance position. The same is true if a player reaches out to the side to catch a ball. Bending at the hips and knees when landing or reaching helps the player to maintain her balance and absorb the force of the ball.

The fingers should not point toward the oncoming ball for they may be injured; but finger and thumb, rather than palm, contact with the ball is necessary. The ball may rebound from the player's grasp if caught in the palms.

FREE THROWS

Free throws are shots at the basket taken from the free-throw line. They are awarded to players who have been fouled during play and are not guarded so a player has a chance to aim carefully. Any of the set shots are appropriate;

players should use their most successful shot. Free throws require much practice for accuracy.

BASIC BASKETBALL MOVEMENTS

The dribble, feint, pivot, cut, and screen are basic moves used by players to position themselves for shooting or passing and are designed to outmaneuver guarding opponents.

Dribble

The dribble is a series of bounces that enable the player to move in any direction and still retain possession of the ball. According to basketball rules, the dribble must be done with one hand at a time, but players may alternate hands. The dribble may be combined with a pass or shot.

The ball, resting against the fingers and fingertips of the hand, is started in the bounce from waist high or lower (Fig. 8). The back of the hand is toward the player with wrist cocked; the elbow is bent and close to the side of the body. The body is in a slightly crouched position and the free hand supports the ball until the dribble is begun. The dribbling action starts by pushing the ball forward and downward, straightening the bent elbow, then the wrist, and finally the fingers. The body inclines forward, taking a step or two as the ball hits and rebounds from the floor. Directing the ball to the side and forward as it is pushed to the floor assures ball control. At this point the ball may

(8) Dribbling.

be bounced again by the same hand or by the other one.

The speed of the bounce should be varied, and players should be able to dribble the ball with either hand or change hands during the dribble. They should be able to move left, right, forward, and backward while dribbling. The ball should be bounced at the side so it is away from a closely guarding opponent. As skill develops, players should be able to focus their gaze on the opposing players, not on the bouncing ball.

COACHING HINTS. The angle of the bounce must be controlled so that the player can move and still retain possession of the ball. Too extreme an angle will allow the ball to rebound too far away from the player, whereas bouncing the ball straight down will not allow a player to progress.

The height of the bounce must be low. Too high a bounce may allow an opponent to intercept. To keep the dribble low the knees and hips are flexed; starting the ball low helps to maintain a low bounce.

Players must not dribble the ball too often. A dribble is slow and does not involve teammates; it limits opportunities if players continually dribble instead of passing.

Pivot

Players may remain stationary and retain possession of the ball for not more than five seconds. A pivot is used to keep the ball away from an opponent or to pull an opponent out of the way for a shot or pass, thus avoiding holding the ball too long. A player may take a step in any direction while in possession of the ball, but one foot must maintain contact with the floor. A player may combine forward, backward, and sideward placements of one foot, providing the other foot keeps its initial contact with the floor.

COACHING HINTS. Establishing the proper pivot foot is essential. While running or moving, a player may take two steps after catching the ball; but if two steps are taken, the back foot must become the pivot foot. Players should be able to pivot from either foot and from a forward or side stride position.

Pivoting forward into a closely guarding opponent may result in body contact, which is a foul; a backward pivot should be used in this situation whereas a forward pivot should be used if a player is closely guarded from behind.

Dragging the pivot foot should be avoided for this too is a violation of the rules.

Faking or feinting

Standing in a sideways position, a player pretends to pass the ball in a certain direction, then quickly shifts her arms and body to pass in the opposite direction. Deception is aided if the player rotates her shoulders and head as she makes the initial movement with the ball; when she shifts, she must not look in the direction of the pass.

COACHING HINTS. A pivot can be added to a feint by stepping quickly backward on the moving foot if guarded from the front. A player should practice a feint, both with and without a pivot, followed by a bounce, dribble, pass, or shot to the basket.

Cutting

Cutting is a quick movement by an offensive player to free herself to receive a pass; it can result in a quick shot at the goal. A player may cut outside or inside. For the outside cut the player moves quickly toward the side line and around her opponent. For the inside cut, the player tries to move toward the free-throw lane or middle of the court and around the opponent. The movement for the cut is a quick elongated step, followed by a run. The cut may be preceded by a feint or fake. It may also be started either facing the opponent or with the player's back to the opponent.

COACHING HINTS. Good balance, body control, and timing are needed. The player must determine when to start the cut in relation to the teammate who has the ball, because the ball must be passed after she has moved around her opponent. Players must find an opening for both the cut and the pass; and the quick movement of the cut around an opponent must be skillfully executed to avoid body contact.

If several opponents are in the player's path, the cut may not work. Having passed one opponent, a second opponent may be able to intercept the pass. Teammates can help to create openings by getting their opponents to move with them away from the path of the intended cut.

Screening

Screening is a deliberate movement of a player to place herself between a teammate and her guard. Her teammate may or may not have the ball for this movement gives the team-mate time to pass, cut, or shoot, or to receive a pass before the guard can get around the screening player.

The body position used for the screen involves some modification of the basic guarding position described in the section on defense. The screening player should cover as much floor space as possible but still maintain balance; the arms are held out and up, the feet are separated in a forward stride, and the player bends forward from the waist and hips. The screening player may face the guard or have her back toward her; the bent body position keeps the guard away from the teammate.

COACHING HINTS. Beginners may wish to screen by placing their back to the guard because this allows the screener to keep her eyes on the ball and her teammate. Successful screening depends on proper timing and teamwork.

Personal contact must be avoided. The screening player must have enough space to set up the screen without contacting the guard. Screens are more successful when guards are not guarding closely. The establishment of the screen must be done quickly before the guard realizes what is going to happen.

STRATEGY

In the roving player game one player may change from one court to the other. If in the front court she shoots; in the back court she is a guard. Any of the six players on a team may be the roving player; therefore all players should be able to guard and shoot, and should work toward enough speed and endurance to be able to play in both halves of the court. In the learning stages some players may discover they have the ability to be good rovers. Others may not have the stamina to play the whole court and therefore should remain in one half of the court. In addition, some players may prefer to concentrate on defense or guarding; others may prefer to remain in the front court as shooters or offensive players. As teamwork develops, the specialty roles of offensive, defensive, or roving players become established.

Basic offensive and defensive maneuvers and strategy need to be explored. Inasmuch as a team gains possession of the ball in the back court after the opponents score, the offense begins from there. In fact, the offense begins from any place on the court as soon as a team

gains ball possession; defense begins as soon as the opposing team gets the ball.

The offense should attempt to get the ball to the forecourt by fast, quick passes. Moving the passes up the sides of the court is basically the best strategy. Passing across the court or using high, long passes should be avoided. Once the ball is maneuvered into the front court, certain systems of offense may be used by the four teammates in that court. These systems are designed to get the ball close to the basket for the shot. More than one shot is often needed to score; hence, offensive players must be able to position themselves to regain possession of the ball (rebounding) for a second or third shot.

Beginners may start by exploring systems of offense—ways to get the ball to the basket for a shot. Some of the systems are the fast break, the screen, a two-two system, and a one-two-one offense. The type of offense used depends upon the opponents' defense. Other offensive systems exist and may be learned as players reach intermediate or advanced play.

Fast break

The fast break is an attempt by the offense to move the ball quickly up the floor and across the division line to the basket before the defense can get between them and the basket. Depending upon the number of opposing defensive players between the offense and the basket, the fast break becomes one-on-one, two-on-one, and so on. One offensive player against a defensive player is a one-on-one, two offense against one defense becomes a two-on-one.

An offense that does not move quickly enough for the fast break will be faced with four defensive players ready to prevent the shots. Then the offense to be used depends upon the defensive system opposing them.

Two-two offense

The offense is arranged in a square formation with two players at the edge of the free throw circle and the other players closer to the basket. If any one player moves out of her position, she is replaced by one of the other three; all four players interchange with one another.

Movement from any of these positions to get free to shoot is called *cutting*. A player runs, stops, starts, or fakes a move toward the basket trying to lose the defensive player, and then runs toward the basket. The player with the ball tries to pass in front of this moving or cutting player. If the cut is unsuccessful, because of the opponent remaining close, the player returns to any one of the positions of the square formation. Exchanges, cross-overs, and the direction of cuts may vary and can consist of as many combinations as the skills of the players allow. This two-two offense is often used against zone style defense. It allows time to pass to the inside or outside, to feint or to cut.

One-two-one offense

The one-two-one offense is used with a tall player or with a player who can shoot well when close to the basket. One player is stationed at the free-throw circle edge farthest from the basket and two others at either side of the outer edge of the free-throw circle. With the fourth player at the basket, the positions form a diamond, one point at the basket and the others just outside the free-throw circle.

There are variations of the one-two-one and the two-two systems. For example, in the double post offense, a modification of the two-two, the two inside players (closest to the basket) move closer to the center of the free-throw lane. These players are in a position to pivot and shoot and the system can be very effective with two good inside shooters.

DEFENSE-GUARDING

The object of the defense is to stay between the opponents and the basket to prevent them from shooting and to gain possession of the ball. In order to achieve these goals every player must be able to guard both the player who has the ball and those without the ball. Guarding requires good footwork and effective use of the hands and arms.

The basic guarding position, with a forward stride and the weight balanced on the balls of the feet, requires flexion of the hips, knees, and ankles for balance and readiness to move. The arms are away from the body; one arm is usually up and the other held out to the side. As the opponent moves, the guard slides her feet sideward, forward, or backward in reaction to the opponent's movements (Fig. 9).

If a guard has her left side to the side line, with left foot sideward and right arm and hand held upward, this may invite her opponent to try to move past her right side. Positioning in guarding is important and much of the guard's positioning is on a moving basis. In order to stay between an opponent and the goal, the guard must use

(9) Guarding position.

quick movements. Sideward slides and running backward are two footwork skills that need to be learned.

Quick movements of the hand are needed, because guards try to block shots, intercept or deflect passes, and deflect or stop dribbles. They may also be able to grab or "tie up" a ball held by an opponent.

A player guards her opponent closely when she is near the basket ready to shoot; she will guard farther away when the player does not have the ball or is farther away from the basket.

Guarding systems—man-to-man and zone

Man-to-man guarding is the simplest system; one defensive player is responsible for one offensive player. Where the offensive player goes, the guard must follow, trying to stay between her opponent and the basket. As guards become more proficient, they may exchange opponents; if two guards are near the basket and one of their opponents cuts toward the basket, one guard may leave her opponent to follow, while the other guard covers the the second opponent. This is a form of interchange.

Zone guarding is more complex than man-to-man, but may be attempted as soon as guarding fundamentals are understood. It is not so fatiguing as man-to-man guarding and often results in pass interception.

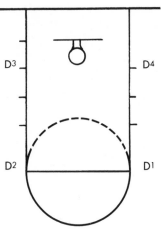

(10) Box zone diagram.

(11) Box zone defense.

Two zone systems may be tried by beginners: the box zone and the diamond. The box zone is the same pattern as used in the two-two offense; the diamond zone involves the same pattern used in the one-two-one offense; however, the positions are taken by guards, not forwards.

In the *box zone*, the two players outside the free-throw circle (Fig. 10—D^1 and D^2) shift to the right or left as the ball moves. If the ball is on the left, the left outside player guards the opponent with the ball, the other guard moves toward the left of the court into the free-throw circle, and the other two defense players who are close to the basket shift to the left in the same relationship as the outside guards. If the

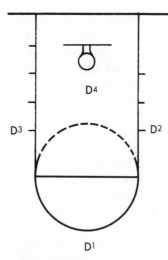

D4

D3 — — D2

D1

(12) Diamond zone diagram.

D4

'D3 — D2

D1   O1

(13) Diamond zone—shift.

(14) Diamond zone defense.

ball goes to the right, the four guards take the same position on the right. The box zone is one of the best defenses against an offense that tries to send players cutting through the middle of the court. It is not effective against good outside shooting.

In the *diamond zone*, one guard is out beyond the free-throw circle to guard the opponent who has the ball (Fig. 12—D¹). If the ball goes to the right of the court, she shifts right; if the ball goes to the left, she shifts left. Behind her are two other guards on either side of the free throw lane. If one guard shifts right, the other guard moves into the free-throw lane. If the ball moves to the left side of the court, the fourth guard remains close to but slightly in front of the basket. She moves right or left maintaining the diamond relationship, but never leaves the basket area—she always stays between the ball and the basket (Fig. 13).

The diamond or one-two-one zone is effective against outside shooting, because the person guarding can move quickly to guard the outside shooter (Fig. 14).

Rebounding

As soon as a shot is taken the guards should position themselves for the rebounding ball. If the guards are between the opponent and the basket, they should maintain that position; the zone guarding can be continued during the rebound. The guards, keeping their eyes on the ball, need to be able to cover all angles involved as the ball comes off the backboard. Jumping is important in rebounding; the player who jumps highest has the best chance to get the ball.

Rules

The official rules of the game of basketball for women are published by the Division for Girls' and Women's Sports of the American Association for Health, Physical Education and Recreation.

Evaluation

The most effective means of determining success in basketball is in the game situation: Did we win or lose? Why or why not?

Individual players should ask themselves such questions as: Did I play well in the game and did my teammates play well with me? Did I pass at the right time? Was I in a position to receive passes? Did I shoot when someone else might have been in a better position to shoot? Did I try all the time, or did I loaf? Could I keep up with the rest of my team? Was I able to guard effectively? If my passing and shooting were ineffective, why? How can I improve? Do I know the rules?

The team should evaluate together, asking such questions as: Did we work together or as individuals? Who shot or passed the best and why? Did we position ourselves and move quickly? Were we getting the rebounds and if not, why not? Did we shoot enough or spend too much time passing? Were we protecting against fast breaks and did our guarding system work effectively? Were we effective in passing up the floor? Did the movers know when to cross the center line? What fouls or violations are we consistently making and why? Did we win or lose gracefully? Did we play in a sportswoman-like manner?

Positive answers to these questions bring success to individual players and teams.

Terminology

Backboard: Flat-surfaced rectangle from which the basket is hung.

Back court: The opponents' half of the court.

Basket, goal, or hoop: The metal ring through which the basketball is thrown.

Blocking: A foul involving personal contact impeding an opponent's progress.

Court: The entire playing area.

Dead ball: A ball that is out-of-play.

Dribble: A series of bounces caused by directing the ball to the floor and giving it impetus each time it rebounds.

Foul: A rule infraction for which the opponents get one or two free throws.

Free throw: An unguarded shot for the goal. It is shot from behind the free-throw line in the free-throw circle. It scores one point.

Front court: The half of the court in which a team's basket is located.

Halftime: A ten-minute intermission between second and third quarters of the game.

Jump ball: A ball tossed by an official between two opponents and taken in one of the three circles on the court.

Officials: A referee and umpire who are in charge of the game.

Pivot: Movements of a player in any direction around one stationary foot.

Rover: A forward or guard who crosses the center line to oppose the fourth guard or forward.

Substitute: A player who replaces another player in the game.

Tie ball: A simultaneous catch or deliberate ball grab with one or two hands.

Time out: A time interval taken from the playing time for rest, substitution, free throw, and so on.

Timers and scorers: These officials keep track of game time, time outs, substitutions, goals, free throws, and fouls.

Traveling: Running, walking, or jumping while holding the ball.

Unbalanced court: More than three players of one team in one half of the court as the result of the movement of the rover.

Violations: Infractions of the rules that result in the ball being awarded out-of-bounds to an opponent. Violations are not fouls. Simultaneous violations by opponents result in jump balls.

Selected References

Bell, Mary M. *Women's Basketball*. Dubuque, Iowa: William C. Brown, 1964.

DGWS Basketball Guide current edition. Washington, D.C.: American Assoc. for Health, Physical Education, and Recreation.

Neal, Patsy. *Basketball Techniques for Women*. New York: Ronald Press, 1966.

Teague, Bertha Frank. *Basketball for Girls*. New York: Ronald Press, 1962.

Chapter **16**

Field Hockey and Lacrosse *Verna Klye and Dorothy A. Richardson*

FIELD HOCKEY: *Goals. Opportunities for Play. Equipment. Etiquette. Preparation for Play. Stickwork. Fielding the Ball. Tackling. Positional Play. Special Plays. Team Tactics. Rules. Evaluation. Terminology.* LACROSSE: *Equipment. Game. Techniques.*

FIELD HOCKEY *Verna Klye*

Women's field hockey is a thrilling game to play; a team game that provides great satisfaction to all players. With twenty-two players pitted against each other for two thirty-five

minute halves, this game offers a challenge to the individual to show speed, skill, and thought, and a challenge to eleven players to combine together to score more goals than their opponents. The time for a match may be less for school or club games if agreed upon by respective captains.

Hockey requires energy, skill initiative, and team spirit. Ten players of each team, pitted against their respective opponents, endeavor, with the use of a stick only, to move a ball from teammate to teammate, or by individual effort, down the field and score more goals than their opponents. The eleventh player, the goalkeeper, may use her legs as well as her stick to defend her team's goal. The only times a player may use her hand is to stop a ball or to roll the ball back into play when it has gone out of bounds over the side line. Outside boundaries are defined and lines are placed on the field of play to indicate different sections, but no marks within the outside lines restrict the movements of a player. However, it is usual for each player and her opponent to play a particular position and therefore confine their movements to a certain

Miss Verna Klye is presently head of the Physical Education Department at Presbyterian Ladies College, Melbourne, Australia. Born in Tasmania, Miss Klye was a member of the Tasmanian State Hockey team from 1957–1960. She served as a United States Field Hockey Association coach in Pennsylvania and the Midwest in 1963 and also coached for three summers at the Hockey Camp in the Poconos. Miss Klye was a member of the international hockey team that played in the world hockey tournament at Goucher College, Maryland in 1963; then her team made a playing tour of Kenya in 1964. Miss Klye has played A-grade hockey in New Zealand and England, and in 1965 was Vice Captain of the Tasmanian Hockey Team.

Miss Dorothy Richardson was born and educated in England. She is a graduate of I. M. Marsh College of Physical Education in Liverpool. Miss Richardson earned her master's degree at the University of North Carolina, Greensboro and is now an assistant professor at the University of Massachusetts. She has played lacrosse with the Philadelphia Association, and has coached junior high through college levels in schools and hockey and lacrosse camps in Pennsylvania, New Jersey, Virginia, and California.

area, playing up and down the length of the field in a section approximately 15 yards in width.

The eleven players are usually divided into (a) five forwards, whose objective is to move the ball forward into the attacking goal circle and shoot goals. This may be done by passing the ball between each other or by an individual player "dribbling" the ball forward; (b) three halfbacks, whose job it is to support their forwards in attack and to defend against a particular opposing forward; (c) two fullbacks, who combine with the halfbacks to prevent the opposing forwards from shooting at the goal; (d) one goalkeeper, who endeavors to prevent the ball from passing between the goal posts.

Field hockey is the only game where players must be exclusively right handed. The stick has a flat side and a rounded side, and the ball must only be played with the flat surface. No left-handed sticks are made. Apart from the first awkwardness of playing the ball on the right side of the body, the left hander has an advantage over right-handed players inasmuch as the stick is controlled with the left hand and a player with a strong left wrist will have better natural control.

Goals

A beginner will find a challenge confronting her the minute she takes the field. But what does a player hope to achieve, what goals does she have in front of her?

Many people play the game for the exhilarating feeling of movement coupled with a knowledge that through this medium she will gradually build up her fitness and stamina. Hockey encourages a keen sense of team spirit and cooperation and as this understanding and confidence grows, friendships will develop, which may continue throughout the years.

All players should aim to learn the rules of the game immediately. To read the rule book is not sufficient; players should discuss the various fouls and penalties and develop an early understanding.

The ability to run and to stop and hit a ball are the only skills necessary for a girl to commence playing. But it will soon become obvious that until the various techniques are mastered, the game will mean very little. Therefore players will begin to practice stickwork exercise and running to help develop a higher degree of fitness. When these goals are reached the way is open to delve into the ever-widening circle of questions of how best to use this stickwork to outplay the most difficult opponents.

Opportunities for Play

The cry of "Hockey is a running game!" has resounded over the playing fields of many schools, colleges, and camps over the past sixty years. The person responsible for those emphatic words is Miss Constance M. Applebee and it was she who first introduced the game of field hockey to a few women's colleges in the Eastern United States. From that beginning at the turn of the century, hockey has steadily grown in popularity and the sport now boasts a following in most sections of the country.

The United States Field Hockey Association, founded in 1922, sponsors the game through affiliated clubs. It is possible for a girl to be introduced to the game in her physical education program as early as the upper grades in elementary school. From there she can progress through junior high, varsity, club, association, and sectional teams to the annual National Tournament where the All-American team is selected.

The opportunities to learn more about the game through extracurricular coaching or through watching high caliber games are numerous. In the past few years there has been a dramatic increase in the number of inexpensive camps organized specifically to give both experienced and novice players intensified instruction in skills and tactics, and to improve the standard of coaching. Over and above the actual participation, a hockey enthusiast has the opportunity to see first class competitive and exhibition games, played by the most talented players from this country and from abroad, during the frequent tours sponsored by the United States Field Hockey Association.

With the growth of the game has come a widening of the horizon for the aspiring player. The dream of representing one's country and traveling abroad to play against foreign teams is one that every young player should strive to bring to reality for it is within the reach of those willing to aim that high.

Equipment

THE HOCKEY FIELD

In most countries where hockey is played, the surface used is grass. However, in some countries (India, Kenya) conditions are so dry that a hard dirt surface called *murrum* is used. As the ball travels on the ground for most of the game, it is extremely important to have a smooth surface with the grass cut very short. The standard of the game usually deteriorates if the surface is uneven or the grass too long.

The maximum dimensions of the field are 100 yards by 60 yards. Minimum distances should be 85 by 50 yards. The field is divided in two by a center line, and then divided in two again by two dotted 25-yard lines. It is important to note that when marking a field that is shorter than 100 yards, the 25-yard line is always marked 25 yards from the back line, rather than half way between the center and back lines. A "5-yard line" is marked parallel with and 5 yards from the side line. The striking circle has a radius of 15 yards and when an attacking player is shooting for goal, she must hit the ball from within the circle. The goal posts must be 4 yards apart and 7 feet high. Flag posts 4 feet high should be placed at each end of the 25-yard lines and center line (Fig. 1).

THE STICK

The choice of a good stick is all important for good stickwork. Although the weight may vary from 16 ozs. to 23 ozs., it is best to use an 18 or 19 oz. stick. A good test for appropriate weight is to hold the top of the stick in your left hand, and from there it should be possible to move the stick easily and to control the movement. The stick should be flexible. If you lean on it you can feel it spring. One can see, at the top end of the stick, two or three parallel strips of rubber or fiberglas running through the handle. This provides flexibility and prevents the stick from jarring when stopping or hitting the ball. The handle should be covered with either towelling or rubber, to ensure a good grip.

In selecting the length, hold the stick in both hands, left hand at the top of the handle, right hand close up to the left; stand upright with your arms comfortably straight; and then swing the hockey stick in front of your feet. The stick should just skim the surface of the ground. Another method of determining the hockey stick best suited to your height is to rest it against

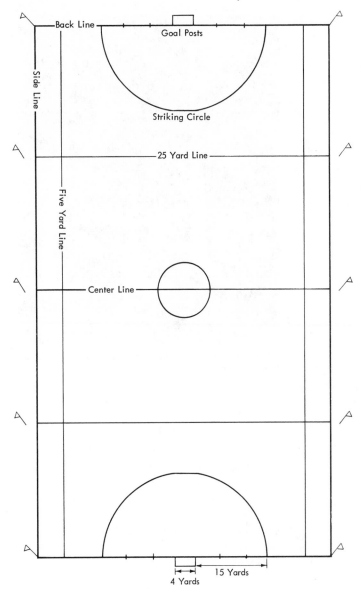

(1) Hockey field.

the side of your leg. The top of the handle should just reach your hip joint.

It is extremely important to check the grain in the wood of the stick you select. When examining the flat surface, select a stick that has parallel grain running around the curved area, rather than a grain that runs out half way round. Today, sticks are divided into two main categories: those with an English head and those with an Indian head. The trend seems to be towards the use of an Indian head stick where the stick presents a more solid, condensed surface for stopping the ball, and a player can achieve more controlled stickwork, especially for reverse stick play.

(2) Hockey sticks. Left to right: English head, combined Indian and English head, Indian head.

THE BALL

Three types of hockey balls are available for use. The leather ball is expensive and mainly used in match play. The plastic ball is used extensively when the grounds are wet, but can rise dangerously from the ground if used in dry conditions. The white-painted composition ball is inexpensive and entirely suited for practicing stickwork.

FOOTWEAR

Players may wear ordinary sneakers, but it is preferable to have leather-topped shoes with bars or studs to give added grip for fast acceleration and quick turns and to help prevent falling on wet grounds. The studs may be made of plastic, rubber, or leather, but not of any metal.

SHIN GUARDS

As the stick and ball are hard, it is obvious that the players' shins require some protection. There are two types of shin guards: the small, light pads, which fit inside long socks, and the heavier ones with ankle padding worn outside the socks. Players should get into the habit of wearing the shin guards; they will protect them from knocks. Most colleges insist they be worn, particularly by beginners.

GOALKEEPER'S EQUIPMENT

As in most sports requiring a goalkeeper, this member of the hockey team wears special protective equipment. This gives her confidence when standing up to a barrage of attacking forwards. The goalkeeper should always wear sturdy leather boots or shoes. The leg pads reach from above the knee to the top of the shoe, and kickers strap over the shoe, particularly covering the toe and instep. As the goalkeeper uses mostly her legs and feet to defend the goal, this additional protection is essential.

UNIFORM

The usual uniform is a blouse and tunic or blouse with skirt or culottes. The tunic or skirt must be of regulation length, measuring 6 inches from the ground when the player is kneeling. The goalkeeper may wear either the regulation uniform or track suit.

Etiquette, Good Sportsmanship, and Safety

Although anyone who participates in a competitive game likes to win, to quote Grantland Rice: "He marks not that you won or lost—but how you played the game." In hockey this is seen at school games and up to international competition where no trophies are given to winning teams. The joy of playing and of making friends gives the players the incentive they need.

Before the game commences, it is customary to wish your opponent good luck and at the end of the game, to congratulate and thank the players. Don't let poor play or bad sportsmanship prevent you from always showing this courtesy. It is usual to congratulate a player who has scored a goal. A "well done" or "good goal" never goes amiss.

During the game, have consideration for a player who has left the field to retrieve a ball. Do not continue the game until the player has returned to her normal position.

While on the field, every player is tempted to call out to teammates—but the captain is the only person who should give directions. As a member of the team, play your own position and control the urge to coach a teammate or goad an opponent.

It is possible that your team may come up against a team that is playing roughly or resorting to unfair tactics. It is important at all times that your team retain the high standards of play and sportsmanship and not resort to the rough play of the other team.

Rules of the game cover any play that may be dangerous, but accidents can occur if a player swings her stick in an uncontrolled manner, hits the ball straight at an oncoming player, or uses her body to push through opponents. A good player has control of stick and body and avoids injuring other players.

There is a tendency these days, in many types of games, for the umpire to be criticized for some decisions. Always take the umpire's decision as final and do not contradict her. If you find that a decision has been made for you and you know that this is incorrect, you should tell the umpire who may then reverse her decision. However, if a player appeals for a ruling against her own team, the umpire will probably not alter her decision. If an umpire is lax and seems to be permitting rules to be broken, do not take advantage of this and play roughly or unfairly. For unintentionally broken rules, play on; but do not deliberately start breaking rules because you feel you will not be penalized. Always play fairly with consideration for your teammates and opponents and you will leave the field with a feeling of exhilaration and well-being.

Preparation for Play

If skills are to be used at top speed it is essential that a certain degree of physical fitness and stamina be acquired. A player must be able to move freely and to maintain her speed for the full game. It is not sufficient to stand and wait for the ball to be hit to you. You must run at top speed to meet the ball, chase an opponent, or recover to your correct position. There are many ways to improve fitness. It is up to the individual to try various methods and adopt the way that helps most.

Running: (1) Commence by running twice around the field prior to stickwork practice. Increase this by one lap each session until reaching at least six laps. Remember you need endurance to keep going for a game that lasts at least 60 minutes. (2) Intersperse 25-yard and 50-yard sprints with 25-yard jogs, changing direction for some sprints and jogging backwards for some rest periods. Spend 5 minutes on this each day.

Footwork: Balance and quick footwork are essential for good stickwork. Unless a player positions herself correctly in relation to the ball, the execution of the strokes will be poor and she will continually be penalized for blocking or obstructing an opponent. When running to meet the ball, the feet should be in such a position that the following stroke may be played immediately, that is, with the ball about 18 inches ahead and to the right of the right foot. Suggestions for footwork practice are

1. Run straight ahead at top speed, swerve quickly to the left then continue running forward.
2. Zigzag through obstacles placed in a straight line.
3. Face any one direction and move as fast as possible to the four corners of a 3-yard square. This requires movement forward, sideways, and backwards.

Exercises: By spending about 5 minutes each session on various exercises, with emphasis placed on speed of execution, players should strengthen the whole body, but particularly legs and wrists. Suggested exercises include

1. With back to the wall, bend to touch the floor (back straight) then stand, stretching above head to touch the wall (20 times).
2. Lift a heavy object in one hand, arm outstretched, and rotate the wrist to left and right. Change hands. Increase the number of times as the wrists strengthen.
3. Single step up onto a bench, single step down (10 times).
4. Make a figure of eight with stick in left hand four times, right hand, then both (repeat 5 times).
5. Double knee jumps up to chest (20 times).
6. Dribble with stick held in one hand; hit single handed.
7. Skip rope 100 times lifting knees high and holding arms high while turning the rope with a wrist movement.

Stickwork

A player's grasp of the handle of the stick is of paramount importance. To gain maximum control take a "shake hands" grip with the left hand at the top of the handle and retain this for the execution of all strokes except a scoop. The right hand, with a similar grip, moves up and down the handle depending on the stroke to be used. Remember always that the left hand controls the position of the hockey stick. There will be occasions when a player moves up and down the field without actually playing the ball. In order to be ready to receive the ball at any time the stick should be held in both hands, right hand a few inches down the handle, with the blade of the stick close to the ground. The stick is of no use, carried at waist height. The following strokes should be practiced and mastered by all players.

THE DRIBBLE

When dribbling (taking the ball along the ground at the end of the stick while running), it is essential to have the ball positioned to enable you to see the area of field ahead, see any oncoming opponents, dodge an opponent, or pass the ball to a teammate at any given moment. Therefore, the ball must be kept well out in front and a little to the right of the body. The right hand should be held about 9 inches down the stick for good control and the stick held practically at right angles to the ground. The left forearm and the back of the left hand

(3) Dribbling (left wrist flexion somewhat exaggerated by camera angle).

should lead the movement with the elbow of the left arm held away from the body. The player should keep her head well over the ball, but she should remember to keep upright enough to enable her to see where she is going at all times.

Many players tend to hit the ball 2 or 3 yards ahead of them and then run on to it again. It is obvious that if an opponent is near, this will give her the chance to cut in quickly and take the ball away. If a forward is completely free, then the easiest and quickest method of dribbling will be a series of short taps, putting the ball a few feet ahead, and then collecting it again (loose dribble). But if an opponent is near, these short taps should change so that the stick is in constant contact with the ball (close dribbling).

Many beginners tend to dribble the ball too much, forgetting that this is a team game. This is a good rule to remember: draw an opponent towards you, then pass to a team mate *before* your opponent can tackle. But if you can gain ground more quickly by passing, then do not dribble at all.

THE DRIVE OR HIT

The simplest method of passing the ball to another player is to hit it. Whether driving from a stationary or running position, the correct grasp of the handle will assist in keeping the ball on the ground while giving control of direction and distance.

As the stick is swung back, the right hand slides up the handle to fit directly below the left hand. The thumb and first finger make a *V* on the top of the stick. The stick must remain below the level of a player's shoulder at all times. Failure to observe this is known as *sticks*, and is a foul. Thus it is essential to have a short back swing and a low follow-through. To prevent giving "sticks" on the backswing, the left wrist should be kept straight and firm, the right hand grip also should be kept firm, and the elbow of the right arm should be at right angles. The stick is swung straight back, not back around the body, when hitting. Keep the right hand "behind" the stroke, not under it. To prevent "sticks" at the follow-through, swing out toward the ball with arms and wrists straight.

Unless a player positions herself correctly in relation to the ball, a poor drive will be executed. This again shows the importance of good footwork. A player should position herself so that the ball is about 18 inches away from and a

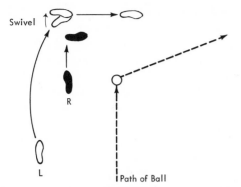

(4) Position of feet for pass to right.

little ahead of her left foot, with her left shoulder pointing in the direction of the proposed hit. With feet apart for good balance, the weight is taken back onto the right foot with the back swing and transferred onto the left foot as the stick is swung forward. The ball should be hit smoothly with the face of the blade at the bottom of the swing (Fig. 4). This will ensure that the ball travels safely along the ground and not dangerously in the air. When the ball has been hit, the stick follows through in the direction the ball is travelling. The transfer of weight from back to front foot is an essential part of a well-executed drive. Even with a stationary hit, it is advisable to step forward onto the left foot, stepping in the direction of the hit.

Once the fundamentals of the stationary drive have been mastered, the player must learn to combine dribbling and driving the ball: (1) forward, (2) to the left, and (3) to the right. Prepare yourself for disposing of the ball by seeing that your feet and the ball are in the correct hitting position. To direct the hit it will be necessary to glance up quickly before striking the ball.

Dribble and drive forward. Allow the ball to roll freely while the stick is taken back, slip the right hand up the stick, and turn the body at right angles to the running direction for the drive.

Dribble and drive to the left. This is the natural way of hitting and should present little trouble. Give the ball a small tap so that it is in front of the left foot (not to the right of the body as for the dribble) before taking the stick out to the right and swinging across your body to the left.

Dribble and drive to the right. This can be done well only by moving the body and feet around

the ball so that they are at right angles to the desired direction of the hit. Leave the ball in the dribbling position, take a long step forward with the left foot while pointing that foot to the right, and, while commencing to slide the right hand up the stick, take a short back swing. Pivot to the right on the left foot as the right foot is brought up to it. Then step out on the left foot in the direction of the hit as the stick is swung through. Think of a polka step; the rhythm of the the footwork would be left slow, right quick, left quick.

A faster but more difficult way to hit to the right is to continue running forward, getting ahead of the ball and turning at the waist to bring the shoulders around so that you are facing the right. At the same time take the stick back and then swing forward to the right. This can be done with either the left or right foot forward, but the ball should be opposite the right foot for a hit off the left foot or behind the right foot for a hit off the right foot.

THE PUSH

The push is used 1) to execute a pass or shot for goal quickly when there is no time for the backswing used in a drive; 2) to provide an easier method of passing to the right, as the feet do not have to move "around" the ball. This is not as effective as the drive when a hard pass is required; 3) to give better control in speed and direction; and 4) to disguise the direction of the

(5) The push: wrists firm with stick upright behind ball; body weight moving through to front foot.

pass. To gain the control necessary for this stroke, the right hand should be about 15 inches down the stick, and the ball farther away from the body than for a drive. There is no back swing as the stick rests flat against the ball at the beginning of the stroke. Although the push can be executed with either foot forward, it is best to learn first with the left foot forward. When this is mastered, try the same stroke with the right foot forward.

The whole flat side of the stick faces at a right angle to the direction of the push with the top of the stick as far forward as the blade. The stroke is initiated by the right hand and the whole body leans well into the stroke as you step forward onto the left foot (knees bent) and push the stick forward (blade always flat) (Fig. 5, page 299). By turning the wrists as the stick is pushed forward, the direction of the stroke may be altered.

The push is an ideal stroke to use for a pass because the ball has good direction and travels along the ground; thus it is easy for the receiving player to control.

THE FLICK

The flick is similar in execution to a push stroke, but by a quick flick of the wrist the blade of the stick is brought slightly under the ball so that the ball is lifted and pushed forward at the same time. Because the ball is lifted in the air about knee height, this is not a good stroke to use if passing directly to a team mate. It is used to get the ball clear of opponents' sticks and

through to a teammate. It is also an excellent stroke to use for shooting for goal.

When learning this stroke, place the flat blade of the stick around in front of the ball and, without allowing the stick to lose contact with the ball, bring the blade around the right of the ball, to the back and slightly underneath, and then push forward. When the knack of pushing and lifting has been learned, this preparatory movement from the front of the ball can be stopped. It is essential to have the body weight right behind the movement and to step well forward into the movement with the front foot. The ball *must* be well ahead of the player before commencing the stroke.

THE SCOOP

Providing the scoop is used in a controlled manner and not dangerously (e.g., lifting into an oncoming player), it is an effective way for 1) a forward to dodge a tackle from in front, 2) a defense player to keep the ball from an onrushing forward player, 3) a forward to shoot goal, 4) a player to pass the ball when opponents are close, and 5) all players to dodge opponents when the ground is very wet or muddy.

For an effective scoop, the left-hand grip is changed by turning the flat surface of the stick upwards. The round part of the stick is held in in the palm of the right hand about 18 inches from the top. With the ball well out in front of the body, place the blade of the stick under the ball and scoop it off the ground. To prevent "sticks" when attempting a high scoop,

(6–8) The flick.

(6) Contact.

(7) Lift (knees bent; weight behind and under ball).

(8) Stick follows ball; knees must be bent.

concentrate on pushing down quickly with the left hand, rather than lifting up with the right hand. It is essential for a player to bend the knees, so that the stick is low and may be placed well under the ball.

THE JAB OR JOB

As the names suggest, the jab or job stroke is played by simply jabbing the stick under the ball so that it jumps forward slightly. It may be used effectively by both forward and defense players. A stick is lifted to hit the ball, or a player plays at the ball in a tackle, a quick jab will push the ball momentarily out of position. The jab is usually made with the stick held in one hand and the arm fully extended. This is only used when it is impossible to use a two-handed stroke.

A forward, dribbling the ball, may jab quickly as a defender tackles thus placing the ball in a different position, or a defense player may jab the ball away just as a forward is swinging her stick back to take a shot at goal.

Fielding the Ball

All players other than the goalkeeper (goal-keepers' privileges are discussed later) may stop the ball either with the stick or with the hand.

STICK STOP ON THE RIGHT (STICK SIDE)

A player must at all times move quickly to meet the ball if she does not wish to see her opponent reach it first. She must also endeavor to receive the ball on her stick side. This quite often means moving very quickly to the left so that the ball will be on her right by the time she reaches it.

The ball is generally moving along the ground; therefore the stick should always be kept low. As it is important to completely control the ball when stopping it, the right hand should be down the stick about 12 inches, and the left forearm extended so that the back of the left hand leads the movement. If the left hand is held back near the body, the stick slopes backwards and the ball may travel over the stick or up the stick into the player's body or face. Therefore, keep the stick in a vertical position. As the ball comes onto the stick, relax the grip and "give" with the arms so that the ball will remain on the stick and not bounce away uncontrolled. If extra practice is required, try using a golf ball.

(9) Jabbing ball away as opponent dribbles; note use of right hand.

The ball should not be stopped in front of the body. Many players think that if the ball is missed it can be stopped on the legs. Apart from possible injury, this is a foul, and the player will be penalized. Even if the ball is stopped successfully in front of a player, then it would be necessary to move the feet into a position suitable for hitting. The feet *must* be moved into position before the ball arrives.

The player should keep her head well over the toe of the stick and watch the ball right onto the blade. If the ball lifts off the ground, then just raise the stick sufficiently to catch it on the blade, making sure that neither end of the stick is raised above the shoulder making the foul of "sticks."

STICK STOP ON THE LEFT (NONSTICK SIDE)

Never get into the habit of allowing a ball to come on the nonstick side if it can be avoided. There are occasions when it is impossible to move round the ball every time (*Getting your feet around* is the common term). In this case the player must reverse her stick so that it is always the flat side of the blade that comes in contact with the ball. (It is against the rules to use the rounded side of the blade.) To gain this position, move the stick across the body from the right to the left side, keeping the face of the stick always to the front. As the stick is moved across, it moves around slightly in the left hand and the right-hand grip is loosened momentarily so that the stick may slip completely around. The ball should be stopped on the toe of the stick and, as the area is small, special care must be taken to watch the ball as contact is made. When the ball has been stopped, it should be pulled across to the right side or the feet moved quickly around, before attempting to play on. If the ball is travelling very wide on the left side then it can be stopped by taking the stick across while holding it only in the left hand and reaching out. The stick would have slipped around in the hand 180 degrees.

HAND STOP

If the ball is at such a height that "sticks" would be given in order to stop it, then a player may use her hand. The right hand should be used as the left hand is rarely taken off the stick. The ball may not rebound from the hand. To prevent this, catch the ball and then release it immediately so that it drops vertically to the ground. A player may also use her hand to stop a ball travelling along the ground. This is done for speed at corners when one player stops the ball and a second player hits it. Providing the ball is stopped dead, no foul is called.

RECEIVING A PASS

One must always take into account the fact that the ball may come, not only from in front of a player, but also from the right or the left.

Receiving a pass from the left. If no opponent is near, then allow the ball to run across in front of the body. Have the stick held out in front at right angles to the path of the ball, controlling its movement from this direction before turning the stick to dribble it forward. If an opponent is close, then the player must reach across her body to trap the ball (the blade still held at right angles to the path of the ball) and retain this position while quickly moving the feet to the left.

Receiving a pass from the right. It is important to keep the left foot and the left shoulder pointing toward the goal and to swivel from the waist to face the ball. The face of the blade is turned at right angles to the path of the ball, and the right elbow is held in close proximity to the body with the left elbow quite high and in front of the body. After the speed of the ball has been controlled, the blade of the stick is turned and the player resumes a dribbling position.

Receiving a pass from behind. If the ball is coming through very quickly, turn the blade of

(10) Receiving pass from the right—stick turned to control ball before playing forward.

the stick around so that the ball is trapped when it comes opposite the left foot; then quickly bring the stick around behind the ball and play on. If the ball is coming slowly, then the movement is similar to that for receiving from the left or right but with a more exaggerated turn of the wrist and upper body or a quicker and greater movement of the feet around the ball.

Tackling

Although it may appear at first that tackling is done only by defense players, you will soon see that if the eleven players are to work as a team, then the forwards will be required to use tackling as well as the defenses.

TACKLING AN ONCOMING PLAYER— A TWO-HANDED TACKLE

Defense players tackling a forward. Never wait for the player to come to you. Move toward the player who has the ball with as much speed as possible but still maintaining balance in order to change direction quickly or stop suddenly if the need arises. Then make her play the ball. Your object is to get the ball yourself, or to make your opponent get rid of it hastily so that another of your own team can gain possession.

Always keep your eye on the ball *and* the blade of the opponent's stick as this will give you a clue as to the type of dodge or pass about to be used by her. Your anticipation will help you to cut off the attempted stroke.

Keep your stick in *both hands* and close to the ground. It is best to have the right hand slightly down the stick for better control.

The ideal moment to tackle is when the opponent has lifted her stick for a hit, or allowed the ball to move away from her stick while dribbling. Therefore, it sometimes pays to hesitate before committing yourself to the attack. Keep the wrists firm when meeting the ball if the forward still has control of it. Your firmly held stick may stop the ball as she moves past.

If the ball is trapped between the sticks of the attacker and defense player, then, with a quick pressing upward movement of the stick, you should be able to lift the ball over your opponent's stick. Or place your stick to the right of the ball and then pull the ball quickly towards you, moving your feet back so that the ball remains in front of you. Once a successful tackle is made, immediately pass the ball, or the opposing player will surely "tackle back."

A forward tackling a defense player. In this case the player with the ball will be standing still and the attacker will be running in to try and take the ball away. Again, there must be control in the run and knowledge that the defense will do one of the following four things with the ball: pass to another player before you can reach her, pull the ball to the left, push the ball to the right, scoop the ball over your stick. If the attacker can anticipate the intended dodge, keep her eyes on the ball, her stick on the ground, and retain good balance, she will probably gain possession of the ball.

TACKLE FROM BEHIND

When the ball is taken from a player, she should immediately "tackle back." There are three main tackles to be considered: two-handed tackle for close play (covered in previous section), the left hand lunge, and the circular tackle.

Left hand lunge: This is used when a player finds herself behind and to the right of the player with the ball and *not close enough to make a two-handed tackle.* Set out after the player with both hands on the stick. When you are "stick-and-arm" length away from the ball, lunge

(11) Left hand lunge: play the ball, then catch up and put right hand on stick.

forward with a straight left arm, letting the right hand drop. Your intent is for the blade of your stick to either trap the ball so that the forward continues to run on, leaving the ball behind her, or to knock the ball to the left of the player. You would then quickly replace your right hand on the stick and pass the ball.

Even if a lunge is not successful, continued attempts will disturb the player and perhaps cause her to give a hurried, poorly directed pass. Be sure that all attempts to tackle are directed at the ball, thus avoiding stick interference, which is a foul.

Learning to execute a lunge and to follow it with a pass to the right, or a scoop or pull to the left is an advantage because this will allow the player to keep the ball away from the opposing forward long enough to make a pass. *It is very important* to get the right hand back onto the stick as quickly as possible after lunging.

Circular tackle: This is used when a player finds herself behind and to the left of the opponent who has the ball, i.e., on her nonstick side. Before making the tackle it is essential to run ahead of the player with the ball as it is against the rules to place oneself between an opponent and the ball. Once ahead of the player, reach out and place the stick on the ball, and attempt to tap it away to the opponent's right side away from her stick. The left elbow leads the movement around in front of the opponent, and the right shoulder should be kept as far away as possible. If the opponent is faced throughout

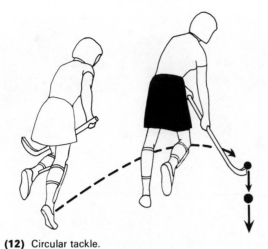

(12) Circular tackle.

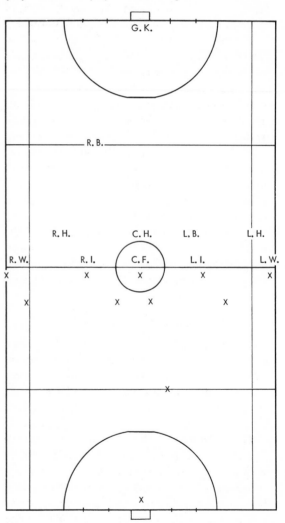

(13) Circular tackle: move quickly around and keep away from opponent.

the tackle and the ball is kept between the players, then no foul occurs.

When the forward movement of the ball is stopped, the feet should be brought around quickly so that the tackler is now facing her own goal and has the ball on her stick side. The attacker should keep both hands on her stick unless the tackle is commenced with a well-timed jab. Care must always be taken to avoid body contact as this will be deemed obstruction.

Positional Play

The eleven players are divided into 4 sections: 5 forwards, 3 halfbacks, 2 fullbacks, and 1 goalkeeper.

Each player must learn the strokes already mentioned. Even though a player may learn about her position, it is also important for her to comprehend the basic ideas of all other positions. This enables a player to be placed anywhere on the field in an emergency, and to gain understanding of the difficulties facing other players. But all players should at all times:

1. Keep their sticks down near the ground,
2. Know where they are standing in relation to their goal and their opponents,
3. Move to meet the ball, unless they are completely free of an opponent, when it is best to wait for it,
4. Have good stickwork, which can be used effectively and at top speed at any moment during the game,

(14) Positions of players at start of game.

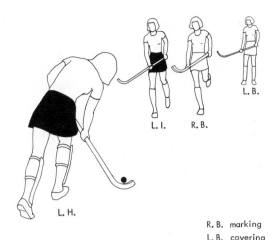

(15) Defense covering and marking.

R. B. marking
L. B. covering

5. Be in a position to see the ball when waiting for a pass and also be able to see the goal which she is attacking.

Most of the points that are to be discussed are a general guide to positional play, but it must be realized that there is always the exception to the rule. This is one of the wonderful things about hockey. It is not a stereotype game where set plans are always used. Variation and unexpected moves make this an ever-changing and interesting game.

TERMS USED FOR POSITIONAL AND TEAM PLAY

Marking: When told to "mark" an opponent, a player is required to position herself either between the opponent and the ball or the opponent and her attacking goal, in order to prevent the player from gaining possession of the ball. Play "stick to stick." A player may also be asked to mark a *space.* This would necessitate standing farther away from the opponent and thus preventing the ball from passing between two opponents.

Covering: In this instance a player must position herself to cut off a pass that might be played through a gap ahead of the opposing players. Always cover the space on the left side of the opponents, not in the center, as this keeps the play on your stick side.

Types of passes

The *diagonal pass* is used when a teammate is closely marked. Your aim is to angle the ball ahead of your teammate, but behind her

opponent. Your teammate is able to run forward onto the ball, whereas her opponent must turn and chase after it. A general directive for a diagonal pass is "aim for the corner flag."

The *through pass* is made almost straight up field. The ball is generally pushed or flicked (greater control of speed and length) through a gap on the nonstick side of the opposing player. The receiving player must anticipate the pass if she is going to reach the ball before a covering defense player.

The *square pass* is used when the opposing player is not marking your teammate closely, but is covering the gap to prevent a diagonal pass. The ball is hit or pushed straight across the field directly onto the player's stick.

The *triangular pass* is a combination of the square and through passes, or two diagonal passes used when trying to eliminate one defense player. As an opposing player moves in to tackle, a controlled square pass is made to a free player who immediately makes a through pass back to the first player (Fig. 16).

Types of dodges

A player must decide upon the dodge to be used and be prepared before her opponent's stick reaches the ball.

Right dodge: Push the ball to the nonstick side of the opponent and run around her stick side to

(16) Triangular pass.

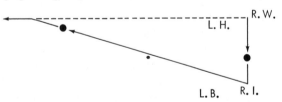

a) A square pass and a through pass

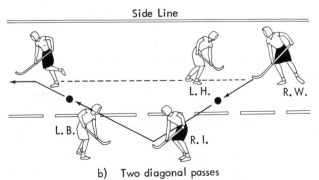

b) Two diagonal passes

Field Hockey and Lacrosse   **305**

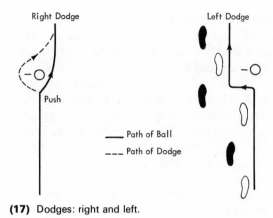

Right Dodge   Left Dodge

Push

_____ Path of Ball
_ _ _ Path of Dodge

(17) Dodges: right and left.

retrieve the ball. This prevents obstruction. (See rules.)

Left dodge: As the opponent reaches forward to tackle, quickly sidestep to the left, pulling the ball after you. When the opponent's stick has been dodged, continue in dribbling position.

Scoop dodge: Knees must be bent quickly, and by using a small controlled scoop, the ball is lifted over the opponent's stick.

FORWARD PLAY

The five forwards are left wing (L.W.) and right wing (R.W.), who play well out in the alley, center forward (C.F.), who occupies the center length of the field keeping goal posts as a guide; left inner (L.I.) and right inner (R.I.), who play in·the areas between the center and wings.

If the five forwards spread across the field (which is 50 to 60 yards wide) in a line, then theoretically each forward has a strip of field 10 yards wide in which to work. This varies in the attacking and defense areas (Fig. 18).

Remember this is just a general guide, but beginners are advised to try to maintain their area at all times. Interchange of areas comes only after much practice. If you move too close to another forward, then you are not creating spaces through which the defense can pass to you, and you are making it possible for one opposing defense player to mark both forwards. A team cannot win unless the forwards score more goals than the opposition. Therefore, the task of a forward "line" is to take the ball up the field into the attacking circle, by passing from one to the other, to score. If the ball is passed across your path, do not run after it and crowd the next forward. Let the ball go on and retain your position in the line. All efforts made by players in midfield should be carried through

by the forwards in the circle, whose determined and constructive play should result in goals.

Some coaches prefer the forward line to stretch straight across the field, whereas others advocate the *W* formation, with wings and the center staying up the field and inners dropping back more into defense. Once the team is in attack, the inner must make every effort to catch up with the line in order to make five determined forwards who are forcing the ball towards goal.

All good forwards need:

Speed and anticipation: A forward must always be looking for the opportunity to make a quick dash for a loose ball so that she can force the play forward into the circle. This demands split-second acceleration and good footwork for when she reaches the ball she must dispose of it successfully without any hesitation. Remember, good stickwork depends on good footwork.

Concentration and thought: Continual planning and thinking are paramount at all times and

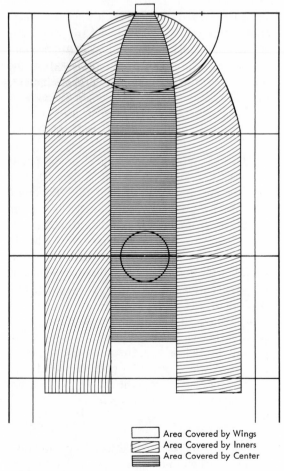

☐ Area Covered by Wings
▨ Area Covered by Inners
▤ Area Covered by Center

(18) Areas for forwards.

this calls for undivided concentration on the task at hand.

What does a forward do before she receives the ball?

1. Be sure of her position with relation to her other forwards and opposition, with the correct shoulder and foot facing her goal so that she will be able to play the ball correctly the moment she receives it.
2. Keep on the move at all times and make the task of marking difficult for the opposition. Continually try to be in the clear.
3. If a forward is being closely marked, then she must make spaces by drawing her opponent away from other forwards.

What does a forward do when she receives the ball?

1. If there is another forward in a better position to use the ball, the forward with the ball must pass immediately, for holding onto the ball will give the defense time to reposition themselves.
2. At all times show consideration for your fellow forwards and give sympathetic passes according to their placing and ability.
3. Show variety in the types of passes used and the direction in which they are sent. A defense player will soon take control if the same pass is continually made.
4. You will make it more difficult for the goalie by varying the speed with which you shoot for goal.

Know and remember the offside rule: This rule is basic to the whole forward play and must be understood by forwards immediately. You are *not* offside if, when the ball is hit or rolled in, you; are in your own half of the field, are behind the player with the ball, have three opponents nearer their own goal line than yourself. Quite often a forward will appear to be in an offside position when she receives a pass, but, providing she complied with one of the three sections of the rule as just listed *when the ball was hit,* then she is not offside. Many attacking moves are spoiled because of the thoughtlessness of forwards with regard to this rule.

Shooting for goal: The main error made by most forwards when taking the ball into the circle is to take an extra tap to position the ball before shooting. This "teeing-up" generally costs the forward the strong accurate hit she

could have made for she has given the defense the extra seconds needed to get into position to tackle. Preparation for the hit should be made before going into the circle so that the shot can be taken immediately. (A shot from outside the circle is not counted as a goal.)

When the shot is taken, it should be immediately followed up in a controlled run (not a mad dash straight at the goalie) in anticipation of a rebound from the goalie's pads. More goals are scored by playing the rebound from the goalie's pads than a direct shot at goal.

When the ball is in the circle, keep your stick down, and don't attempt to hit unless you are sure you have time. Quick pushes, flicks, and scoops, with no time wasted on a backswing, are better. Know where the goalie is, and try to aim the ball into the other side of the goal.

Forwards in defense: It is not possible for forwards to remain in the attacking half of the field and wait for the ball to come to them. If a forward is robbed of the ball, she must immediately tackle back and try to regain possession. The forwards must drop back and position themselves to receive passes from their defense. But care should be taken not to go so far back that the defense is hindered by your closeness. Be in a position for a quick push out (inners), or a long hit out to the side lines (wingers).

When free hits are being taken, the three forwards nearest the ball should make a semicircle around the hitter and 5 yards away from the ball (see rule on free hits). This makes it difficult for the defense to find a gap to send the ball through.

If a free hit is taken in the attacking area, then the forwards must move around in order to make spaces and opportunities for effective use of the pass.

Specific positions

Left and right wing responsibilities include the following.

To create maximum space in which the forwards may work, the wings should position themselves out on the side lines. The L.W. will find it easier to pick up passes if she runs *outside* the side line. Providing the ball is not off the field, play may continue. Be prepared to come in from the side line to meet a slow pass. Never let the opposing half intercept a pass; instead make a quick pass to your inner, and then be off down the wing for the long through pass (triangular pass).

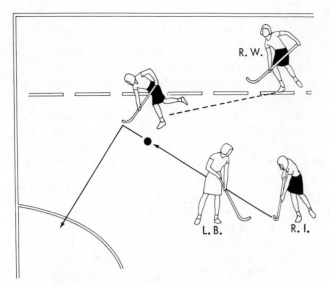

(19) Occasion when right wing takes ball into circle.

Wings must be very speedy, running to pick up long diagonal or through passes directed toward the corner flag.

Don't dribble the ball right down to the goal line before passing. A good general rule to follow is to pass after the center line and before the 25-yard line, but this need not always be followed. As a wing learns more about her position, she will find there are times when she will take the ball in towards the goal circle and either shoot for goal, or draw a defense and then pass. This latter alternative is the exception that is used only occasionally. A quick look before centering will ensure that the ball goes to a team mate. By varying the angle of the pass and the place at which the pass is made, the defense will be kept guessing.

Tackle back on the half back.

Drop back when your team is in defense (a little behind the 25-yard line) so that your back or half back may use you for a quick pass. But be ready to sprint forward for a long pass.

Be ready for the through pass or the square pass from your inner. Inner and wing cooperation is extremely important.

When the play is in your attacking circle it is best for the wings to stay out on the edge of the circle waiting to pounce on defense clearances. A hard hit for the opposite corner of the goal is then required. Let the three inside forwards move in on the goalie—if you go as well, play will become too congested. If you find yourself with the ball near the goal line, remember the three possibilities: a flick or drive at goal, a hard hit across goal for inside forwards to convert, or a controlled hit back to the top edge of the circle to the waiting center half.

Left wings will find that they have more difficulty in centering than right wings. It is essential that they make their pass before the half catches up to them as they need more time to get their feet around to make a firm hit. (See "hitting to right.") Some left wings wait until the half is just about to tackle, then trap the ball by turning their stick in front of it, stop quickly, allowing the half to run on, then center. This can be used effectively but only occasionally, as the whole forward movement has been stopped and the advancing forward line may be put offside.

Right wings will find centering very easy but as they are hitting onto the stick side of the defense, they will have to be especially careful about the angle and timing of the pass. Develop an understanding with the left inner to drop back and receive a hard square pass behind the R.I. and C.F. Right wings will probably find it more difficult to receive passes. If you are clear, allow the ball to come to you but if an opponent is near you must run to meet the ball. When the ball is received you will have to run on with it in a small circle, clockwise around your opponent, in order to pass her. Remember to take the ball out towards the side line once you have run in to collect it. Do not continue to run in, for this crowds the inner. When cooperation between the inner and wing has been established, then it is possible for the wing to continue to run into the inner position while the inner runs out to the wing area.

Specific tasks for wings include corner hits and roll ins.

Corner hits (also see section on Corner): It is not necessary for the wing to have her feet outside the goal line or side line. Make sure the ball is on the line and position your feet so that the left shoulder is facing the direction in which the ball is to travel. Have the stick back so that the defense players do not know when or where you are going to hit. A push may also be used. Once you have decided to whom you are hitting, keep your head down and swing the stick straight through. To give your forward the opportunity to stop the ball dead, make sure that the ball travels along the ground. The hit must be quite strong. If you make a soft hit, the defense will catch up to the ball before it can reach the forwards. Direct the ball about a yard ahead of the player on her stick side, not at her feet. She wants to be able to stop and hit in two quick movements. Do not use the same forward each time; vary your choice of player to confuse the defense. As soon as you have hit the ball move quickly onto the field in order to avoid off side. Remember at "long" corners (not penalty corners) you may take the hit from either the goal line or the side line.

Roll-ins: When the ball goes over the side line from a player's stick, the opposing team is awarded a roll-in. (See more detailed treatment in later section, "Roll-ins.") When this occurs in the attacking 25-yard area, it is the wing's task to roll in thus allowing the halfback, who usually takes roll-ins, to be free to position herself in readiness should her opponent get the ball. You will usually try to roll to the inner, but if she is not free, a hard roll parallel to the goal line can be quite effective.

Left and right inner responsibilities include the following.

As the inners are relatively free in midfield, they are generally used by the defense to put their team into attack. Consequently, maintain your position and keep clear so that your defenders can quickly find you when clearing. This means dropping back farther than the other forwards, but never back behind the halves. You should tackle back on your opposing inner and mark her on free hits until the play is near the edge of the defending circle. This is where you will pull away and make yourself ready to receive a pass.

The inner must realize that as soon as she has received the ball, the opposing back will come to tackle. She must therefore gain control quickly (see receiving passes from left, right and behind) and make accurate passes to the other forwards.

In attack, the inners are in line with the other forwards and ready to grasp any opportunity to score; either direct hits at a goal or rebounds from the goalie's pads.

Although inners will pass to all forwards, it is important for each one to develop a special understanding with the wing on her side of the field. A wing depends mainly on her inner for passes.

There will be occasions when the inner must be prepared to take the ball through by herself. This will occur when a through pass has eliminated her opponent.

If a back doesn't immediately tackle, the inner should dribble the ball, draw the player, then pass.

Left inners must concentrate on receiving passes from the right, then getting their feet around quickly to hit or push to the right. When shooting for goal, the flick and push are used perhaps more than the hit. It is useless attempting to play this position unless you can "get your feet around."

Right inners will find that they use the drive for goal more than the L.I. but the use of a push or flick should not be discounted.

Center forward responsibilities include the following.

The C.F. is the spearhead of the attack, but as she is watched more closely in midfield than the inners, she must be exceptionally quick off the mark and ready to take advantage of any opportunities that may occur. By continually moving around, she should be able to worry her opposing C.H., but she must be careful not to crowd either inner. When her team is in defense, the C.F. usually places herself nearer her goal than the other forwards, and is often in a good position to make a quick dash upfield and shoot for goal.

It is the C.F.'s task to make constructive passes in either direction; she should not favor one side. If the opposing C.H. has the ball, then it is up to the C.F. to tackle her. This is especially true at a defending corner. The foreknowledge that a C.F. might tackle back will make the C.H. get rid of the ball more quickly. The C.F. also takes the center bully.

HALFBACK PLAY

Unless you are prepared to become fit and be very energetic, it is no use considering the halfback positions. Halves have two main functions: to support their forwards in attack, and to combine with the backs when the team is defending. The halfbacks cover their respective forwards. Outside halves mark wings, and the center half marks the center forward. This means a great deal of movement back and forth up the field, so speed and stamina are essential.

There are general rules that apply to all halves:

1. Show good distribution of the ball in feeding forwards and initiating attacks.
2. Follow up about 5 yards behind forwards in order to support their attack and cut off

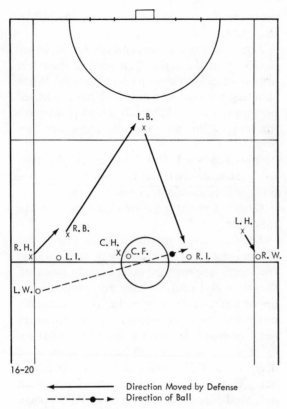

16-20

←―――――― Direction Moved by Defense
– – – ●― ► Direction of Ball

(20) Movement of defense when ball swings from left side of field to right.

passes made by the opposing defense to their forwards.

3. Generally, do not dribble the ball as this may force your forwards upfield into an offside position.

4. Remain marking your opposing player, and don't try to cover all forwards.

5. Remain around the edge of the circle when your forwards are attacking, and be ready to pounce on loose balls and shoot. Yes, halves *do* score goals.

6. Take all free hits that occur in the attacking half of the field and take them as quickly as possible. Wings, rather than the outside halves, should take free hits that are within 10 yards of the attacking goal line.

Center half

At all times the center half is responsible for the opposing C.F. A wandering C.H. creates uncertainty and upsets the entire defensive system of a team. Always position yourself between the opposing C.F. and the ball and keep your eye on her as she will probably move around

continually to evade you. When your team is in attack, you must leave your opposing C.F. to back up your own C.F., but always be conscious of where your opponent is, so that if your team does lose the attack, you will be able to move back quickly and mark her.

The center half acts as a pivot, distributing the ball to each forward of her team and giving all an opportunity to join in the play. Therefore it is necessary to be able to hit or push the ball accurately to left or right. When near the circle, the diagonal pass is best to the L.I. and a through pass to the R.I. or C.F. Remember, an occasional controlled pass to either wing may bring about a score if play is very congested in front of goal.

Back up both the inner and center at an attacking corner as the outside half will be covering the gap out to the wing. Watch for cross passes made by the opposing defense through the middle of the field. Try to anticipate and cut off these passes. Do not be drawn too far from the center of the field. Play up and down the center and about 10 yards either side of this.

Do not leave your opposing forward in order to tackle her C.H. This is a task for your C.F. But if the C.H. is about to shoot for goal, you must tackle her and your left back will mark your opponent. Tackle back quickly if your opposing C.F. breaks free with the ball and is close enough to shoot for a goal. However, have an understanding with your backs if this situation should arise. Generally the left back (player on her stick side) will tackle, and you must quickly recover behind her to complete the defense covering.

Outside halves (L.H. and R.H.)

When in attack, the left and right halves will back up their respective left and right wings, and join with the C.H. to try to block any hits out by the opposing defense. For example, at an attacking corner taken on the left, the left half will cover the gap between the L.I. and the side line and the R.H. will back up the R.I. (vice versa from the right).

Each outside half is responsible for her opposing wing. When positioning, the *right half* will find it easier to position herself about the 5-yard line as this will mean that most of the play will be on her stick side. The *left half*, however, should move out near the side line, to eliminate play on her nonstick side.

When the team is defending, and the ball is

on the right, the right half will be marking the opposing L.W. very closely. But the L.H., realizing that the R.W. has little chance of gaining possession of the ball, will move to cover the R.I. Normally this is done by the L.B., but she should have dropped back to cover the area behind the right back. If the play switches to the left, then the L.H. will move back to mark the R.W., and the R.H. will move in to mark the L.I. This is a basic system employed by most defense to gain extra support against ever-pressing forwards.

In defense, the wing halves will generally use a long pass down the wing, or a short pass onto the inner's stick if she is clear. But in midfield, halves should always consider the possibility of passing across the field to the opposite inner; this quite often gives openings for a scoring opportunity.

If the back is finding it difficult to clear when hard-pressed in defense, the half on her side of the field can be very helpful by positioning herself near the side line for a quick square pass.

When the ball travels out over the side line from an opponent's stick, then the half on that side of the field will take the roll-in (see Roll-in). The wing will take the roll if the ball is in the attacking 25-yard area. The L.H. should roll with her right hand and the R.H. should develop a controlled roll with her left hand.

FULLBACK PLAY

A fullback must have complete confidence in her ability to make a strong tackle. She must always feel that she can win the ball from her opponent and put her team into attack. To do this, a back should have a good eye, anticipation, speed, good stickwork, and a good clearing hit. But she must also have confidence in her other defense players and show this by only tackling the player for whom she is responsible—the opposing inner. Although you may feel that you should tackle another forward, don't be drawn into play unless your opponent joins in. Especially in the circle, your inner must not be left free to shoot.

At the beginning of the game it is best for one back (usually the L.B. who will stand on the nonstick side of the C.H.) to position herself 5 or 6 yards from the center bully. The other, or covering, back should place herself between the ball and the goal, about the 25-yard line. As soon as the game has commenced, the left back would be in a position to cut off a pass made in

her direction and put her team immediately into attack. But if the ball is passed to the opposing team's L.I. then the R.B. moves up quickly to tackle and the L.B. drops back as fast as possible into the covering position. As you move, *do not turn your back on the ball.*

The change-over between backs must be done as quickly as possible, otherwise they will be caught "square on" and a through pass by the opposing forwards will eliminate both backs simultaneously.

Never clear the ball across the goal circle, as it is easy for an onrushing forward to cut in and shoot for goal. There will only be a rare occasion when this "rule" is broken. When clearing in defense, the ball must be passed to the halfback, wing or inner (i.e., away from the circle).

Don't go out and tackle the wing. It is a great temptation if you see a free wing running up the field with your halfback completely beaten. But remember that if you go out to tackle the wing, you leave your inner free—and she is the more dangerous player as she is closer to goal. Continue to mark your inner, watching for the pass that may come across. If the wing continues dribbling the ball in to the edge of the circle, and the half still isn't in a position to tackle back, before she shoots for goal you will be forced to tackle, while the covering back watches your inner.

Do not wait for your opponent to come to you. The only way to defend is to attack (see "Tackling").

A question asked by fullbacks is, "How far up the field may I go?" This will depend largely on the individual—her speed in recovering, and her confidence in tackling. As a general rule, you should not go further up the field than the attacking 25-yard line.

Have an understanding with the C.H. concerning a break-away C.F. Usually the L.B. will tackle as the player will be on her stick side.

Do not get in the goalie's way. The goalie has command in the circle and if she calls that she is unsighted or coming out to kick the ball, then move out of the way. Take all free hits in your half of the field, except in the alleys, and take them as quickly as possible.

GOALKEEPING (G.K.)

Do not have the opinion that the slowest player should be given the goalkeeping position. This person needs agility, anticipation, quick reflexes, and the courage to stand up to a hard

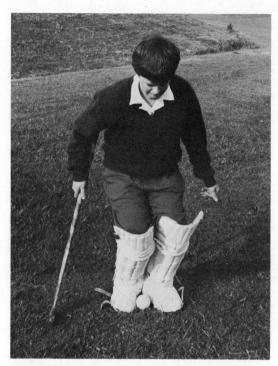

(21) Goalkeeper: stopping ball on pads; knees bent.

ball being hit at her from all angles and heights.

Goalkeepers are given special privileges that are valid while she plays within the striking circle. (These privileges do not apply if the G.K. takes part in a penalty bully.)

Privileges for goalkeepers include

1. The use of protective pads and kickers.
2. Using legs and feet to stop and kick the ball.
3. A more lenient attitude on the umpire's part to the rule concerning a ball stopped by the hand. If it appears that the ball merely rebounds off the hand, no foul is called; but

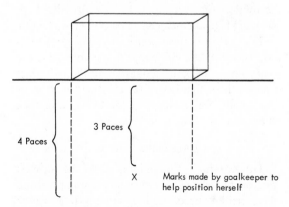

(22) Marks made by goalkeeper to position herself.

the G.K. may not strike at the ball with her hand.

Suggestions for goalkeepers include the following.

Never turn your back on the ball, move backwards instead. To enable a G.K. to know her exact position in relation to the goal posts at all times, it is necessary for her to put identification marks of her own, on the ground in front of the goal. This is usually done with the end of the stick, or toe of the shoe (Fig. 22).

Hold the stick in your right hand (about half way down), thus allowing maximum reach to the right with the stick and stretch to the left with the left hand. Use the stick only in an emergency, to push or flick the ball away, or to stop a shot at goal which is coming wide on the right side. The stick may also be used to pull the ball back into position before a kick, if it has bounced too far away from the pads.

Keep your legs together. When moving across goal, use small side steps, keeping knees close together.

To stop the ball, use the inside of the kicker rather than the rounded toe section. If the ball is off the ground, then the pads are used. Position yourself squarely behind the ball and by bending slightly forward at the knees, the ball should drop near the feet. Direct kicks at the ball are to be discouraged, unless there is absolutely no time to control the ball first. A G.K. must develop quick reflexes in order to move and stop a ball, then to kick away to the sides in two swift movements.

A G.K. must learn to kick equally well with the left and right foot, in order to clear to either side. *Never clear in front of the goal or across the goal* as this will give the attacking forwards another chance to score. To ensure a flat kick (a lifted kick is usually termed dangerous play), the body weight must be forward and the follow-through should be out, more than up, transferring the weight onto the kicking foot. For good balance, the head is kept down with eyes on the ball, and the arms are held out, slightly away from the body.

Defense play in the circle must be controlled by the G.K. She should call to her backs when coming out to clear and she should tell the defense players to move if they are obstructing her view or trying to play a shot which is her responsibility. If a direct hit at goal has been made, it is the goalkeeper's task to stop it. Do not

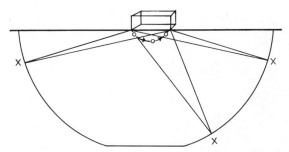

(23) Movement of goalkeeper as position of ball changes.

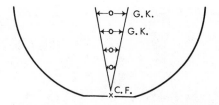

The further out the goalkeeper comes, the less distance on each side of her she has to cover

(24) Goalkeeper and lone forward.

allow backs to attempt a stop as the ball may deflect off their stick and go into goal.

If a lone forward is dribbling into the circle, the G.K. should go out to meet her near the edge of the circle. This limits the space on either side of the goalie (see diagram) and possibly delays the shot at goal sufficiently for a quickly moving back to drop back and cover.

At corners, take one step out from the goal line and be alert for a shot to either corner of the goal. *Never stand behind or on* the goal line. Good positioning is essential if a G.K. is to adequately cover the 4 yards between each goal post.

When the attack is coming from the center of the circle, it is obvious that the G.K. will stand in the center of the goal. As the attack shifts to the left or the right, the G.K. must move to the corresponding side. If you study Figure 23 you will see the angle in which the forward must shoot if she is to score. If the G.K. remains in the center of this angle, she should be able to prevent a goal.

Special Forms of Play

BULLIES

A game is started by a bully. Both teams must be "onside," that is, in their own defending half of the field (Fig. 25). Play begins with a *center* bully after the umpire has blown her whistle. This takes place between the two opposing center forwards in the middle of the center line. They stand facing each other squarely, left shoulder pointed towards the opposition goal, the ball between the blades of the two sticks. The players tap the ground with the blades of their sticks; then they strike the face of the opponent's stick. Do this three times, then try to gain control of the ball, and pass. After each

consequent goal and at the beginning of the second half, play is recommenced with a center bully.

An "*onside*" bully (teams standing on their defending side of the ball) will also be taken on a spot where two people simultaneously foul, or to recommence the game after an accident has occurred. (Note: If this spot is less than 5 yards from the goal line, then the ball must be moved to a position 5 yards from the line.)

A *penalty bully* is awarded against a member of the defending team who willfully fouls within the striking circle or who, by fouling, prevents a certain goal.

The bully is taken by the offending defense player and any member of the attacking team. The ball is placed 5 yards out from the center of of the goal line. All other players must wait behind the 25-yard line until the bully is completed. There is no time allowed for a goalie to remove her pads if she is the offending player,

(25) Bully.

Field Hockey and Lacrosse   313

(26) Left dodge after bully.

and she is not allowed to use them as she usually does (see section, "goalkeeper").

The bully is retaken if the defense player hits the ball over the goal line not between the goal posts, or if both players foul simultaneously. A goal is scored and the game recommenced at the center if the ball passes over the goal line between the goal posts, or if the defending player fouls again. The game is restarted at the 25-yard line with a center bully if the defender clears the ball out of the circle, or the attacking player fouls.

Rules for all bullies

1. The ground and opponent's stick must each be hit three times.
2. The blades of the sticks must be vertical with the ground (no turned sticks).
3. All other players must remain 5 yards away until completion of the bully (except penalty bully).
4. Only before the center bully must the whistle be blown. If any point is not carried out correctly, the bully must be taken again.

Points to be noted for a bully

1. Keep the right hand down the stick in a dribbling position. Have feet apart, and knees slightly bent.
2. Keep the stick as close to the ball as possible on the ground, and in the air when tapping opponent's stick.
3. Do not hit the opponent's stick hard; keep the movement small so that you are in a position to get your stick to the ball immediately following the completion of the third ground-stick sequence.
4. Make sure that you retain your "square-on" position with the opposing player throughout the bully—do not turn your shoulder so that you obstruct your opponent (see rule on obstruction).
5. Know which of the bullies you are going to attempt before you start.

Methods of bulleying

1. Perhaps the simplest method to gain the ball is to quickly place your stick against the ball and wait for your opponent to lift her blade to hit, then use a push or flick pass.
2. If both centers employ this measure and the ball is held between the sticks, a quick upward jerk of the stick should allow the ball to roll over the opponent's stick.
3. Bring the stick quickly to ball and flick or push to the right inner.
4. Pull the ball towards your feet while moving backwards, keeping the ball between you and your opponent. You may then pass quietly to either your left or right inner.

5. If you notice that your opponent always strikes at the ball at the completion of the bully, then by keeping your stick above the ball, she will unwittingly hit straight ahead to your waiting C.H.

There are other methods, but if those cited can be mastered and used with variety, then you should have success with your bullies.

FIFTEEN-YARD HIT

If the ball is hit over the goal line by a player of the attacking team and a goal is not scored, or the ball comes off the stick of a defender who is beyond the 25-yard line, then the game is restarted by a defending player taking a free hit 15 yards in from the goal line and directly opposite the spot where the ball crossed this line.

ROLL-INS

When the ball is hit over the side line, a player from the opposing side is awarded a roll-in, which is to be taken at the spot where the ball crossed the line. Hold the ball in the hand closest to the side line. The stick must be held in the other hand and the player's feet and/or stick must not come over the side line until the roll-in is completed. If rolling with the right hand, swing the right arm back and step forward onto the left foot while bending both knees, and swing the arm down and forward so that the fingers brush the ground as the ball is released. This will ensure that the ball touches the ground within one yard of crossing the line, and does not bounce. The ball must be *rolled* underarm, not thrown. Until the roll-in is taken, all players must remain outside the 5-yard line and the player rolling in may not play the ball again until someone else has touched it. If the roll-in is not taken correctly, then a player from the opposing team will roll-in.

Types of roll-in

When in defense there is only one roll-in to use. This should be a hard roll down the sideline for the wing to run onto.

When the roll-in takes place farther down field, then other rolls should be considered: to the inner, through a gap to the center forward, or straight to the waiting back providing she is free. Special care must be taken with this last type. It should *never* be used in defense.

(27) Roll in.

Corners

Penalty corners, or short corners, are awarded to an attacking team when a defending player fouls in the striking circle or deliberately hits the ball over the goal line.

A penalty corner may be taken on whichever side of the field the attacking team prefers and the ball is placed on the goal line, no less than 10 yards from the nearer goal post. Generally the wing on that side of the field will take the hit or push (no other stroke is allowed), and the remaining forwards stand with feet and sticks outside the striking circle. The attacking halves support their forwards as shown in Figure 28.

All six defense players of the opposing team stand with feet and sticks behind the goal line and may not enter the field until the ball has been hit. The five forwards of the opposing team must remain beyond the 25-yard line until the ball has been played by a second player or it has passed out of the circle.

When an attacking forward receives the hit from the wing, she must stop the ball before shooting for goal. The ball may be played from one player to another before stopping the ball, providing a shot at goal has not been made.

Each opposing defense player must run out as quickly as possible onto her opposing player remembering that the halfback on the side of

Field Hockey and Lacrosse   **315**

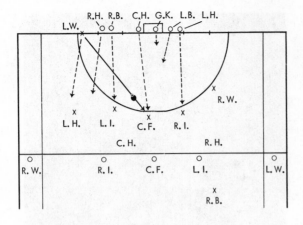

R.H. R.B. C.H. G.K. L.B. L.H.

L.W.

R. W.

x
L. H.　　L. I.　　C.F.　　R. I.
C. H.　　　　　　R. H.

R. W.　　　R. I.　　C.F.　　L. I.　　L.W.

x
R. B.

Defense opposite the forward they will mark

← — — — — — Movement of Players

←——————— Movement of Ball

(28) Position of forwards and defense at penalty corner.

the field away from the ball will mark the inner, not the wing, thus allowing the fullback on that side to cover the space to the side and behind the goalie. If the defense players run out before the ball is hit, then the corner is taken again. If the ball is not controlled by the attackers before shooting, then the defense will be awarded a free hit.

A *corner* (or long corner) is awarded to an attacking team when the ball is unintentionally hit over the goal line by a defense player. The corner hit is taken on the side of the field nearer the corner flag and the ball is placed either on the side line or the goal line no further than 5 yards from the corner flag. Other details are similar to those for a penalty corner.

FREE HITS

A team receives a free hit for a breach of the rules by a member of the opposing side unless the foul is committed by an attacking player in the striking circle. The free hit is taken at the spot where the foul occurred. In the striking circle the hit may be taken anywhere, but it is advisable to take the ball to the edge of the circle and away from the center of the field, thus allowing a clearing hit to the wing.

Points to be noted at a free hit:

1. The ball must be stationary before being hit.
2. The ball must go along the ground, i.e., a hit or a push.

3. All other players must be 5 yards away.
4. The player taking the free hit may not play the ball again until someone else has touched it.
5. If the player taking the hit misses the ball, unless she gives "sticks," she may take the hit again.
6. The player taking the free hit should take it quickly so as not to allow her opponents time to recover.

Team Positions and Tactics

Hockey is essentially a team game. Individual efforts may be required at some stage of any game, but basically this is a game where co-operation between the members is essential if the team is to do well. Eleven brilliant individuals can be defeated by a group of players who work together thinking of the end result rather than their own performance.

Sometimes, within a team, there may be a member who is not so strong as the other players. It is up to the stronger players to encourage the weaker. Give her the opportunity to play and improve her position.

Rules

Each player should have her own rule book and thoroughly study the contents. It is necessary not only to know the rules and fouls, and their penalties, but to completely understand how they are applied in the game. A player must position herself to avoid fouling and be able to recognize situations that may lead to fouls.

With the more difficult offside, obstruction, and blocking fouls, it is necessary not only to discuss these rules, but to walk slowly through situations, learning how to prevent the fouls.

Never stop when a foul occurs until the umpire has blown her whistle. An umpire will not blow if she feels that the team who should receive the free hit has gained an advantage by "playing on."

FOULS AND PENALTIES

The following actions constitute a foul:

1. Sticks—raising any part of the stick above one's shoulder.
2. Using the rounded side of the stick.

3. Interfering with opponent's stick.
4. Body contact—rough play.
5. Obstruction—moving between opponent and ball.
6. Dangerous hitting, e.g., undercutting ball.
7. Stopping the ball with the body—exceptions: hand stop and goalkeeper.

The penalty for any of the foregoing fouls is

1. Outside circles—free hit where foul occurred.
2. Inside circles,
   a. attackers—penalty corner
   b. defenders—free hit anywhere within the circle.

See "Penalty bully" for special cases.

BALL OUT OF BOUNDS

1. Over side line—roll-in for opposing team.
2. Over goal line
   a. hit by attacker, 15-yard hit
   b. hit by defender
      (1) Penalty corner (deliberate hit)
      (2) Long corner (unintentional hit).

ACCIDENTS

The game may be stopped for 5 minutes (time added on at end of half). In official games there is no substitution or replacement.

Evaluation

How can skills be improved?

It is useless to think about evaluation unless one completely understands what is required, the technique and use of each stroke, and a knowledge of the game as a whole. It is also essential for players to be able to accept constructive criticism from others. Watch other players—their stickwork, tactics, and team work.

Through discussions, demonstrations, and films, it is possible to build up a knowledge and understanding of the game. With this information you should then experiment, try different suggestions, and develop your own techniques. Remember that there are a variety of ways to perform in any given situation and continued thought must be given to the strokes and strategy used.

Select situations that occur during a game between two or three players (e.g., triangular

(29) Obstruction: running between opponent and the ball.

(30) Avoiding obstruction.

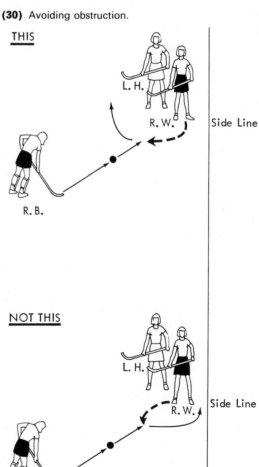

THIS

NOT THIS

pass), discuss the moves to be made, then practice them slowly, gradually building up the speed.

To be effective, a player must continually practice her strokes and learn to know when and how to use these strokes in a game. Aimless hitting at practice is useless. Use practice time to develop instinctive execution of all strokes at top speed with accuracy and control of pace and direction.

Continual thought, discussion, and practice will improve a player's game and she will experience the great thrill of enjoying a game to its full.

Remember, practice, speed, and thought make the player!

Terminology

Advancing (foul): When player stops the ball with any part of her body (exception—hand stop and goalkeeper).

Alley: Area of field between side line and 5-yard line.

Bully: Method used to commence and restart game. Two players hit ground and opponent's stick alternately, three times (facing each other) before attempting to gain possession of the ball (also see Penalty bully).

Circle (striking circle or goal circle): Area included in semicircle and backline at either end of field.

Circular tackle: Method employed by player to prevent obstruction when trying to gain possession of the ball from an opponent who is on her right (nonstick side).

Corner: Used to recommence game when ball has passed over the backline, off the stick of a defending player. Defending backs behind the back line, defending forwards beyond the nearer 25-yard line, and attacking players outside the striking circle. (See Long corner, and Penalty or Short corner).

Covering: Action of player in backing up of teammate to give additional defense (cover a space as opposed to marking a player).

Diagonal pass: When ball is passed ahead of player who is possibly marked closely. She must run forward to intercept it.

Dodge: Method used by player to carry ball up to and beyond an opponent, while retaining control of the ball. (See Right, Left, and Scoop dodge.)

Dribble: 1) A continuous pushing action that moves the ball along the ground, with the stick always in contact with the ball (close dribble). 2) A series of short taps that move the ball forward. This does not give complete control.

Drive: The action of hitting the ball with a controlled backward and forward swing.

Fielding: Trapping and controlling a moving ball. May be done with stick or hand. (See Hand stop.)

Fifteen-yard hit: Method used to recommence game, when the ball is hit over the goal line by an attacking player and no goal is scored.

Flick: By using a wrist action, the ball is sent spinning forward clear of the ground.

Foul: An infringement of the rules. (*See* Obstruction, Sticks, Advancing, Offside.)

Free hit: Awarded to opponent of player who fouled. Taken when foul occurred except when in striking circle. (*See* Short corner.)

Goal: Is scored when the ball, hit by an attacking player when in the circle, passes over the goal line between the goal posts, whether or not it has touched another player's stick or person.

Hand stop: Method used to stop a ball, either in the air or on the ground, in such a way, that the ball drops perpendicular to ground, and the hand is removed immediately.

Holding the whistle: Judgment shown by the umpire in allowing the game to continue if foul occurs, but a member of the opposing team gains an advantage by playing on.

Left dodge: Pulling ball to the left around the stick of opponent without placing body between opponent and the ball.

Left-hand lunge (Lunge): Method used to tackle with left hand only on stick, when player approaching opponent from stick side and is too far away to reach ball with two hands on her stick.

Long corner (Corner): Awarded to the attacking team, when a defending player unintentionally hits ball over the goal line (not between goal posts). Hit is taken on goal line or side line, not more than 5 yards from corner flag (taken on side of field, ball went out).

Marking: Player positioning herself closely between opponent and ball to prevent opponent gaining possession of the ball. As opposed to covering a space.

Non-stick side: The left-hand side of player.

Obstruction (Foul): Placing of stick or body in such a way that opponent is not permitted to move freely to the ball.

Offside (Foul): Illegal position of attacking player in relation to the number of defense players between her and the goal when the ball is hit or rolled in.

Own half: The half of the field between center line and the defending goal.

Pass: To propel the ball to another member of the team.

Penalty bully: Awarded to attacking team when defense player deliberately fouls, preventing a sure goal. Taken by the defense player concerned and any attacking player, 5 yards in from center of goal line.

Penalty corner (Short corner): Awarded to the attacking team when a defending player fouls within the striking circle or deliberately passes the ball over the goal line. Taken on the goal line no less than 10 yards from either goal post.

Push: Stroke used to advance ball quickly and with great accuracy along the ground. There is no backswing.

Reverse sticks: Turning the stick so that the flat side of the stick may be used to control the ball on the left side of the player.

Right dodge: Pushing the ball to the right (nonstick side) of an advancing opponent, with such control that it may be recovered when the opponent continues forward.

Roll-in: Method used to recommence play when the ball goes out over side line.

Scoop: Stroke used to lift the ball off the ground. The ball may be advanced as well as lifted.

Scoop dodge: Lifting the ball over an opponent's stick.

Shoot (shooting): Attacking player aims the ball at the area between the goal post from within the striking circle.

Square pass: When the ball is passed directly onto the stick of a teammate who is in line with the hitter.

Sticks (foul): Lifting the stick above the shoulder at any time.

Tackle: Any attempt to take the ball from an opponent.

Tackle back: Quick recovery to regain the ball after you have lost possession.

Through pass: When the ball is passed directly forward through a gap between any two players.

LACROSSE *Dorothy A. Richardson*

Lacrosse is an exciting team sport that involves manipulating a ball through the air by means of a stick. The game demands the ability to think and act quickly; basic skills include control of the ball in the stick, and throwing and catching passes that advance the ball toward the goal.

The North American Indian game of Baggataway is thought to be the origin of the sport presently known as lacrosse. Early settlers named the game *la crosse* because the stick used by the Indians resembled a bishop's crozier. The game was adapted by the French Canadians around the middle of the nineteenth century and soon developed into a national sport.

In 1876 a visiting Canadian team impressed spectators in England and the game became popular in that country, even being introduced into some school physical education programs. By the late 1890's, several girls' schools were playing lacrosse, and during the early part of the twentieth century adult clubs were formed throughout Great Britain. The All-England Ladies' Lacrosse Association was founded in 1912 and international tournaments were instituted at that time.

English coaches were instrumental in introducing the modified game to school and college programs in the United States and since the early 1920's there has been a steady development in the women's game. The United States Women's Lacrosse Association, founded in 1931, has promoted interest and participation in many parts of the country. The playing season in this country runs from March to the latter part of May, terminating in a National Tournament, a competition among teams chosen to represent the various associations from different geographical areas; from these players the All-American team is selected. Although few international games are scheduled, there are occasions when Great Britain sends a touring team to this country or the United States team tours Britain. As a result of these competitive opportunities both the standard of play and the interest in playing have increased dramatically over the past few years.

Equipment

THE GROUND

An area of approximately 120 × 80 yards is the approved size of a lacrosse field but there are no measured boundaries. The only markings on the field are the center circle, a center line, and the goal creases. Unlike sports played predominantly on the ground, lacrosse does not require a perfectly smooth playing surface, although such a surface would be ideal (Fig. 31).

GOALS

From goal line to goal line measures approximately 100 yards; each goal is 6 feet high and 6 feet wide (Fig. 32).

STICK

Most sticks are constructed out of hickory, the wood being bent at an angle to form the top edge. It is best to select a stick in which the

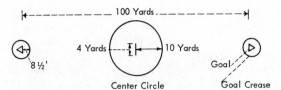

(31) The ground.

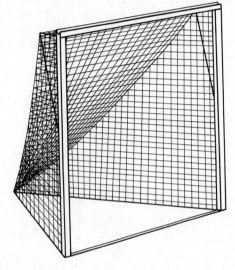

(32) The goal.

grain of the wood follows the curve of the angle, thereby lessening the chance of splintering. The net is made of leather thongs and gut or twine. The bridge, extending between the wood and the guard, should be firm and upright, thus preventing the ball from lodging in the net. The stick may be any length but the head of the crosse may be no more than 12 inches wide. Because the rules dictate that the wood must be on the right-hand side of the bridge, both right- and left-handed players must use similar sticks. In choosing a stick the individual should select one in which the handle is approximately the same length as her arm (Fig. 33).

BALL

The ball is made of solid rubber and has a circumference of $7\frac{3}{4}$ to 8 inches.

GOALKEEPER'S EQUIPMENT

The goalkeeper is the only player who needs additional equipment. For protection against hard shots she wears a face mask, as well as leg and body pads. These should be lightweight, comfortable, and should not hamper her movements.

The Game

The principles governing the game of lacrosse are similar to many other sports. The object of the game is to score goals by carrying or passing the ball through the air from one player to another by means of the stick or crosse, and attempting to shoot the ball past the goalkeeper into the net. Lacrosse is largely an aerial game and, with the lack of restricting boundaries and the absence of an offsides rule, it has the potential of being a very fast, open, and exciting game. A team consists of twelve players spaced from one goal to another, and apart from the goalkeepers, each player is marked closely by an opponent. The elements of man-to-man marking dictate quick changes of direction when dodging or moving for a pass and the challenge to the defense is in quick reactions and good body balance, which are required for players to keep up with their opponents.

Although the whole team should be on attack when they have possession of the ball, the initial lineup consists of six attack and six defense players. The main function of the designated attack players is to maneuver the ball into a position from which one of them may attempt a shot at goal. The defense players are primarily responsible for making their opponents

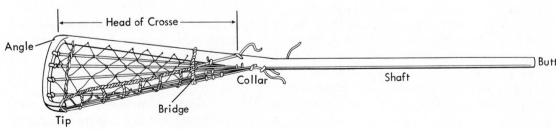

(33) Lacrosse stick.

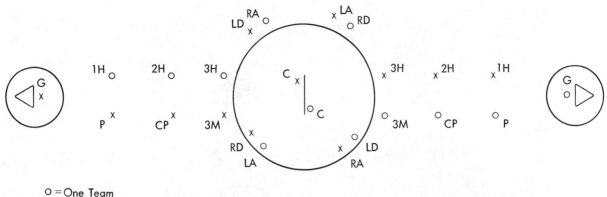

O = One Team
x = Other Team

Positions:

Defenses	Attacks
G = Goalkeeper	C = Center
P = Point	LA = Left Attack
CP = Cover Point	RA = Right Attack
3M = Third Man	3H = Third Home
LD = Left Defense	2H = Second Home
RD = Right Defense	1H = First Home

(34) Positions of players at center draw.

so closely that the possibility of the opposing attacks passing the ball to each other is eliminated, or that a chance to intercept the pass is likely to present itself. If the opponents do get possession of the ball it is the defense's job to slow down the ball carrier's progress toward goal by body checking, or to force her to drop the ball or pass hurriedly or inaccurately by stick checking. Any player may initiate an attack movement. Similarly, any player may attempt to break up a play by the opposing team.

The few rules governing the game are operative primarily to control any elements of rough play and, as no body contact is allowed, the skills involved in gaining possession of the ball, maneuvering it around opponents, and angling it past the goalkeeper demand great control of the body and the stick. Each player is called upon to move at top speed much of the time, and even the goalkeeper may have to move out of her area quickly to pick up a loose ball and initiate an attack play. There are no restrictions as to where any player may move, other than the goal crease, and this presents the possibility of interchanging positions or faking and cutting, as skill and understanding of the game increase.[1]

Lacrosse calls for stamina, technical skill, and

a quick mind. There is a freedom and a grace about the game that makes it a thrilling sport both for the player and for the spectator.

The game is started by a draw between the two centers. The players toe the center line with their sticks held back-to-back and the ball resting between the netting. The sticks are aligned wood to wood, angle to collar, and parallel to the center line, so that they are between the ball and your defending goal. The action of the draw is a strong upward and outward lever of the sticks, which lifts the ball into the air in the general direction of Left Attack . . . Right Defense position. The draw occurs on the command, "Ready, draw," from the umpire and is used to restart the game after each goal as well as at the beginning of each half.

Once the ball is in play each player attempts to get free from her opponent so that she is in a position to receive a pass and either run with it or pass it again unhindered. By moving in one direction and then suddenly reversing that direction you can pull your opponent off-balance and, with your stick, ask for the ball going away from her. Having received a pass you may be checked by one of the opposing team and it is important that you know how to dodge. The first essential is an increase in speed as you begin your dodge so that your opponent's

[1] For complete rules, see the current *Field Hockey–Lacrosse Guide* published by DGWS, Washington, D.C.

(35) The draw.

timing of her tackle is disrupted. Secondly, the pull of the stick to the side away from your opponent should be increased by an exaggerated shoulder pull and body twist. The cradling action continues but your body is between opponent and stick throughout, and the running pattern is obliquely forward. It may be necessary to do several dodges with quick diagonal changes of direction before your opponent is beaten.

When the opposing team has possession of the ball the defending players should place themselves between their opponents and the goal being attacked. From this position you can maneuver your opponent off a direct path to goal by forcing her to twist away from you. This is known as body checking and requires neat footwork and control of body balance to avoid incurring the rules penalty for body contact. The defense player's movements should duplicate those of her opponent's as her body and stick match the evasive tactics.

From the moment the ball is put into play at the center draw each player is involved. The team on attack has to use speed and ingenuity to outmaneuver the opponents. Good stickwork is needed to keep possession of the ball while running at top speed, dodging the defense, and shooting for goal. Although the basic skills of

cradling, throwing, and catching are initially complicated, they soon become graceful and effective; once mastered, they are the tools for putting into effect the short, quick passing game that keeps the defense off-balance. The defending team meanwhile must place themselves in such a way as to allow their opponents a minimum of space in which to move for the ball. The pressure of close marking may well deter an attack player from involving herself in the play. By positioning herself between her opponent and the goal a defense player can have the advantage of being able to see both the play that is developing and her own opponent's position in relation to it. You must be ready to move forward quickly for an interception or back-up to body and stick check, so good footwork and balance are essential. Defensively, movements of the stick should be firm and controlled. Once your opponent has the ball your objective is to check the head of her stick with a series of short, sharp taps to dislodge the ball and, ideally, retrieve it yourself while it is still in the air. No body contact is allowed, so there is a considerable degree of skill needed to keep close enough to your opponent to be able to stick check and yet not touch her. Rough checking is illegal and usually results from slipping the top hand down the handle and reaching across your opponent or swinging your stick in too wide an arc.

Those players not immediately involved in the play are nevertheless involved in the game. The attacking team should be looking for any openings left by the defense, while the defenders are continually trying to force the attacks into errors. Even the players at the opposite end of the field to the ball should be repositioning in anticipation of a quick shift in attack.

The sport of lacrosse is unhampered by rules that restrict the essential flow and speed of the game, but in the event of a foul or the ball going out of bounds, the umpire blows her whistle and all players must stand where they were positioned when the infractions occurred. If the ball goes out of bounds the nearest player to it gets possession and the game resumes on the word, "Play," from the umpire. If two opponents are equally close to the ball they stand 1 yard apart and 5 yards within the field from the spot where the ball went out. The umpire, from a distance of not less than 10 yards, throws the ball to them and the game restarts.

A free position is the penalty for any foul. The rules are designed to eliminate rough play or the gaining of an unfair advantage. A player may not swing or strike her opponent's crosse roughly or recklessly. She may not reach over her opponent's shoulder from behind with her crosse. Holding down the ball carrier's crosse either in the air or on the ground is illegal. Checking a stick when the player does not have possession of the ball or using body contact to detain or push her are infractions. The ball may not intentionally be moved with the hand or feet except to block a shot within the goal crease. Certain other rules also pertain to the goal crease. No attack player may have any part of her body or crosse over the crease during or after a shot, although any player may run through the crease to field a wide ball. The goalkeeper may not be checked while she is standing within the crease but she is not allowed to hold the ball there indefinitely.

For any infraction of these rules the whistle blows, all players "stand," and a free position is awarded against the offending team. The player taking the free position is given possession of the ball and on the word, "Play," she may shoot, pass, or run with the ball. No other player may stand within 5 yards of her before this. If the foul is by the defense and is closer than 10 yards

to the goal the free position is taken by the attacking team at a spot determined by the umpire on a 10-yard radius from the goal. In the event of the game being stopped for any other reason, or two opponents fouling simultaneously, the game is restarted with a draw.

Techniques

GRIP

Having decided which hand will be placed at the collar of the stick, usually your natural throwing hand, you must make certain that your grip is correct. Although the power for most of the basic techniques comes from the lower hand the position of the top hand dictates the accuracy and ease with which these techniques are performed. With the open part of the crosse facing you, grip the collar so that the V of the thumb and first finger corresponds to the V of the guard and the wood. Your lower hand should grasp the butt of the stick on the same line. The bottom hand holds the butt firmly at waist level while the top hand supports the stick lightly in a vertical position. The grip of both hands should remain constant except for the overarm throw, in which instance your top hand moves around slightly behind the stick. Allow the elbow of your top arm to relax letting the forearm drop down close to the handle. Your lower elbow should be bent and close to your hip. From this position a rhythmical swing of the stick from side to side is initiated by a pivoting action of your lower arm at the elbow. The top hand follows the path of the butt hand, thus keeping the crosse upright. The arc can be extended even farther by flexing and extending the wrists.

CRADLING

A rhythmical swing, or cradling action, is used to prevent the ball from bouncing out of the net as you run. It is timed to fit in with the cadence of running, and the smooth swing of the arms and stick across the body counterbalances each step. The crosse should be maneuvered through a semicircular arc, the main power coming from the bottom hand rather than a "waving the flag" action of the top hand. The rotation of the stick to the left should correspond to the step forward on the left foot. The main concept to be grasped in cradling is the idea of the crosse encircling the ball rather than the ball being rolled from side to side as the stick swings across your body. The pivot from

(36)

(37)

(36–37) Cradling.

the lower elbow and the strong wrist action at both extremes of the swing will help to press the ball into the netting, just as centrifugal force acts on water in a swinging pail. Once the basic rhythm has been learned you should practice running at top speed, which will enhance the arm action rather than increase the difficulty of the skill.

(38) Catching.

CATCHING

Catching is simply an extension of cradling. By exaggerating the action of both wrists, while still gripping the crosse correctly, the head of your stick should be turned to face the path of the ball, and the top arm should extend the stick ahead of your body. As the ball enters the net the arms give toward and across your body in a cradling movement while the head of the stick is wrapped around the ball by use of a strong wrist action. The momentum of the ball as it enters the stick may be considerable, and the length of the swing across your body can be increased by twisting the body slightly in the same line as the stick, thus helping to absorb the force. Relaxation and timing are the keys to success in this skill and the link between the moment of contact and the beginning of the cradling action is the critical point. You should practice increasing your speed as the ball is caught because in the game of lacrosse, passes should be caught without having to break stride.

OVERARM PASS

Again there is a link with cradling. In the overarm pass the swing of the stick to the right (for right-handed players) is exaggerated by pulling back your right shoulder and elbow as the stick rotates. The head of the crosse is angled back, the top hand sliding around behind the stick, and the bottom hand lifts the butt to

(39)

(40)

(39–40) The overarm pass.

point in the direction of the pass. The ball is levered out of the stick by pulling the butt forcefully in toward your armpit while snapping the top hand upwards and forwards. Your stick should finish pointing to a spot some distance above the receiver, with the handle extended in line with your arm. As soon as the pass is completed the correct *V* grip of the top hand should be resumed.

PICKING UP

The relationship of the stick, the ball, and your feet is the point to be noted in this skill. In picking up a stationary ball or one rolling away from you, you must position your stick to the side of your lower hand, with the opposite shoulder pushed well forward and the head of the stick dropped forward and down. Your left foot (for right-handed players) must step level with the ball as the knees are bent and the crosse is pushed strongly under the ball. Front foot, stick, and ball should all be in close proximity as the pickup is made and a cradling action initiated immediately to bring the stick from the horizontal to the vertical position.

These are the basic techniques used in the game, and with an understanding of the principles involved and a willingness to practice diligently, any beginner should be able to perform them well enough to enjoy a game situation fairly soon.

(41) Picking up.

Terminology

Body checking: When an opponent has the ball, the defending player places herself between that opponent and her goal. The defense's body and stick movements should try to match those of her opponent in order to make her pass or force her off her direct path to the goal. This must be done without touching an opponent.

Cradling: A technique used for keeping the ball in the crosse while running.

Draw: Used to begin the game, after every goal, after half-time and when two players have fouled simultaneously (see Fig. 35).

Free position: The penalty for a foul. The umpire shows the player taking the free position where to stand, and other players must be 5 yards away. When the umpire calls, "Play," the player awarded the free position may run, pass, or shoot.

Goal crease: A circle $8\frac{1}{2}$ inches in radius surrounding the goal. A player may not have any part of her stick or body over the crease during or after a shot or pass.

Stand: On seeing a foul, the umpire blows her whistle and calls, "Stand." No player may move after this.

Stick checking: Using one's stick to give a series of short sharp taps against the head of the opponent's stick in order to dislodge the ball. A player may not reach across her opponent's shoulder to stick check from behind, nor may she hamper her opponent's movements with her body as she stick checks.

Selected References

FIELD HOCKEY

Hickey, Melvyn. *Hockey for Women.* London: Nichols Kay, Ltd., 1962. (Available from Gertrude Hooper, 242 Highland St., Milton, Mass.)

Meyer, Margaret H. and Marguerite M. Schwarz. *Team Sports for Girls and Women.* Philadelphia: W. B. Saunders, 1965.

Pollard, Marjorie. *Know the Game—Women's Hockey.* London: Educational Productions, Ltd., 1957. (Available from Gertrude Hooper, 242 Highland St., Milton, Mass.)

LACROSSE

Boyd, Margaret. *Lacrosse Playing and Coaching.* Cranberry, N.J.: A. S. Barnes and Co., 1959.

Reeson, Joan, and All England Ladies' Lacrosse Assoc. *Know the Game—Lacrosse.* London: Educational Productions, Ltd., 1964. (Available from Gertrude Hooper, 242 Highland St., Milton, Mass.)

FIELD HOCKEY AND LACROSSE

DGWS Field Hockey—Lacrosse Guide, current edition. Washington, D.C.: American Assoc. for Health, Physical Education, and Recreation.

Richey, Betty, ed. *Selected Field Hockey and Lacrosse Articles.* Washington, D.C.: American Assoc. for Health, Physical Education, and Recreation, 1963.

Chapter **17**

Soccer and Speedball *Jo Anne Thorpe*

SOCCER: *History, Goals. Equipment. Etiquette. Individual Skills. Team Strategy. Rules. Mechanics of Movement. Evaluation. Terminology.* SPEEDBALL.

SOCCER

Soccer is a popular game in every country of the world, and in most countries it occupies the same place of prominence among spectator sports as that of football in the United States. It has been said that the sun never sets on a game of soccer, for as one game is ending another is beginning somewhere else in the world.[1]

Soccer has the distinction of being the only organized team game in existence today that requires ball play predominantly with the feet. Only the goalkeeper may legally play the ball with the hands, and all other players must train diligently to avoid the natural tendency to use the hands in catching a ball, which is flying through the air and is therefore difficult to stop by another means.

[1] Florence L. Hupprich, *Soccer and Speedball for Girls* (New York: A. S. Barnes and Co., 1942), p. 1.

Dr. Thorpe did her undergraduate work at Florida State University, Tallahassee, received her master's degree at the University of North Carolina at Greensboro, and her doctorate from Texas Women's University, Denton. She played on the soccer team at Florida State, has taught soccer theory for a number of years, and was editor of the DGWS Soccer Guide 1966–1968. Dr. Thorpe is currently assistant professor of physical education at Southern Illinois University, Carbondale.

Soccer is played by two teams of eleven players each. The field diagram is presented in Figure 1. Players include the following: five forwards—center forward, right inner, left inner, right wing, and left wing; three halfbacks—center, right, and left; two fullbacks—right and left; and a goalkeeper.

THE GAME

The game begins with a kick-off by the center forward of one team. This kick-off is a pass to one's own team, and the object is to control the ball following the kick-off so that possession is retained. The rules state that the ball must travel at least 27 inches and that all players must remain 5 yards away until the ball is kicked.

After the kick-off, forwards should attempt to move the ball downfield and to score by kicking the ball between the goal posts and under the crossbar. Halfbacks and fullbacks have the dual role of backing up their own forwards when they have the ball and of tackling when the opposing forwards have the ball. The fullbacks are the last line of defense other than the goalkeeper. One fullback may move downfield and assume the same duties as the halfbacks, but the other fullback should

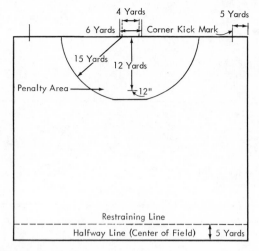

(1) Playing field.

remain in her own half of the field in a covering position.

The game is divided into quarters of eight minutes each with a two-minute rest period between the first and second quarters and between the third and fourth quarters, as well as a ten-minute intermission between the halves.

SCORING

A team may score by means of a field goal (two points) or a penalty goal (one point). A field goal is scored when, during regular play, a player kicks or otherwise legally gives impetus to a ball and causes it to pass wholly beneath the crossbar, between the goal posts, and over the goal line. The penalty goal is scored as a result of a successful penalty kick that is awarded for various serious infractions of the rules.

OUT-OF-BOUNDS

When the ball passes wholly over the sideline, a throw-in is awarded. When the ball passes wholly over the end line outside of the goal posts or over the crossbar, a defense kick is awarded if the attacking team caused the ball to go out-of-bounds, or a corner kick if the defending team caused the ball to go out-of-bounds.

FOULS

Players may not trip, kick, strike, hold, push, handle the ball, be unnecessarily rough, or jump at an opponent.

VALUES OF SOCCER

A most important value of soccer is undoubtedly the fact that the ball must be largely manipulated with the feet and body without the use of the hands. Because in all other games objects are caught, thrown, or held in the hands, soccer is unique in its contribution to the development of fine manipulation and coordination of skills by the lower extremities.

One has only to play a regulation game of soccer to realize that the demands for endurance, agility, speed, and strength place it among those sports which are the greatest contributors to the physical fitness of the participants.

History

Accounts of the history of soccer are conflicting; however, most sources agree that the game is probably derived from an ancient Grecian and Roman game called *harpaston* or *harpastum*. A form of soccer is also reported to have existed in China in A.D. 112. The ball originally consisted of a skull, a bag filled with moss, or, in later times, an inflated bladder.[2]

In the Middle Ages, kings of England suppressed the rapidly increasing popularity of soccer by forbidding it in order that young men would have more time for practicing archery, which was a skill necessary for fighting and war. When the bow and arrow was no longer used for military purposes, the kings began to allow the playing of soccer once again; and the game achieved great popularity in the seventeenth and eighteenth centuries.[3]

In the United States soccer was played in the 1820's, barred in the 1830's by Yale and Harvard because of its roughness, and revived again in the 1860's. Princeton and Rutgers played the first college game in 1869.[4]

The first rules for women appeared in 1927 and contained some alterations, which consisted mainly of eliminating some of the roughness that was legal in the men's rules.[5] Some differences between men's and women's rules, particularly relative to amount of body contact allowed, still remain; for example, charging (pushing one's opponent with the body) is legal in men's rules but is a definite foul in women's rules.[6]

[2] *Encyclopedia Americana*, International Edition (New York: Americana Corporation, 1966), p. 158.

[3] Florence L. Hupprich, *op. cit.*, p. 2.

[4] *Ibid.*

[5] *Ibid.*

[6] V-Fine Association of America, *Soccer* (Annapolis, Md.: United States Naval Institute, 1950), p. 51.

In the United States the play today is mostly by amateurs, and soccer is, for the most part, considered a minor sport. In England and other countries it is a major sport, and the fact that it is the only football-type game played in the Olympics is some indication of its prominence all over the world.[7]

Goals

Goals or objectives for soccer may be divided into those appropriate for individuals and those appropriate for teams. The section on evaluation contains levels of attainment relative to some of the individual and team goals suggested here. The following goals are stated in general terms.

GOALS FOR INDIVIDUALS

1. Dribble the ball effectively, using both feet at a good rate of speed while focusing predominantly on one's teammates and opponents.
2. Place kick from a moving approach for good distance, lifting the ball high into the air on the kick.
3. Block a ball that is approaching in the air without handling the ball and maintain possession.
4. Dribble toward an oncoming would-be tackler, evade or dodge around her, and maintain possession of the ball.
5. Trap a moving ball and maintain possession of it.
6. Volley (by several methods) an oncoming ball to a teammate so that possession is maintained.
7. Goalies should be able to punt a ball quickly, with good distance, and with good height.
8. Run continually for ten minutes with sudden stops and starts without becoming overly tired.
9. Be able to play effectively more than one position, i.e., forward or back.
10. While moving at top speed, pass a ball so that it goes directly to the teammate for whom it was intended.
11. Tackle a ball from an opponent and maintain possession of it.

GOALS FOR TEAMS

1. Work the ball downfield as a unit with forwards moving the ball, backs backing up

the forwards, and backs reintercepting and returning the ball to the forwards when opponents successfully tackle.
2. Score at least once every fifteen minutes.
3. Rush every time the ball is in the penalty area.
4. Convert at least two thirds of all corner kicks into goals.
5. Score on every penalty kick.
6. Discourage fouling by encouraging a policy of not more than one foul per team member per game.
7. Permit the goalie to be alone in defending the goal not more than once in an entire game.
8. Interchange (both forwards and backs) at every natural opportunity and avoid crowding on the ball.
9. Cover for teammates at every opportunity.
10. Tackle back immediately (forwards), but allow your own backs to take over if the dueling persists.
11. Judge the timing of passes so that an opponent is drawn to the play before the pass is made.
12. Keep a ball as long as no tackler challenges.
13. Center a ball by the time the penalty area is reached (forwards).
14. Dribble the ball to the forwards rather than directing long kicks to them (backs).
15. Employ triangular passing when at all possible (forwards).
16. Cover spaces on free kicks and throw-ins.

Equipment

Equipment for soccer is not elaborate. It includes a ball, which may be leather or rubber-covered, pinnies of contrasting colors, and glasses guards for those who need them. Women's field hockey shoes with reinforced toes are extremely useful for soccer. Players may wear shin guards if they wish, although they are not absolutely essential.

Etiquette and Good Sportsmanship

Players of soccer have an opportunity to display proper etiquette and good sportsmanship by retrieving and placing balls for throw-ins, free

[7] *Encyclopedia Americana*, International Edition (New York: Americana Corporation, 1966), p. 158.

kicks, or defense kicks for teammates and opponents. Good sportsmanship in soccer includes avoiding fouls, admitting when one has touched the ball with the hands, and admitting when one has been responsible for hitting the ball out-of-bounds. Accepting officials' decisions graciously is also the mark of a good sportsman. Some mistakes in calls may occur, but it all evens out in the long run!

Skills

The skills of soccer may be divided into two categories: individual skills and team skills or strategies. Individual skills include all of the methods by which a person manipulates the ball toward the ultimate objective—scoring. Team skills include all of the formations and plays used by the team in order ultimately to score.

INDIVIDUAL SKILLS

Dribbling is the skill used by an individual to move down the field while maintaining possession of the ball. The ball should be tapped alternately with first one foot, then the other, while the player maintains a running jog. Approximately three steps are taken between each tap, and it is extremely important that the ball be kept close to the dribbler. Sending the ball too far ahead (more than 2 or 3 yards) will make interceptions more likely. Players must learn to use both feet with equal facility and

must develop the ability to control the ball at great speed while dribbling.

Passing involves sending the ball to a teammate who is in a more advantageous position, and it is most often used when a defensive player approaches to take the ball. The ball should not be passed until a defensive player is drawn to the play. Players may pass with the toe, the inside of the foot, the outside of the foot, or the top of the instep. The outside or inside of the foot offers the possibility for greater control than does the toe, because a ball rebounding off the toe may glance at odd angles. The ball should be passed diagonally ahead of the receiver so that she may receive the ball without breaking her running stride. The ability to pass with either foot, outside or inside, should be developed. Short passes are more effective than long ones because opportunities for interceptions are minimized. Players attempting to receive passes should move toward the ball and should try to cut off the defensive opponent from the pass as they do so.

Trapping, a method of stopping a ball that is bouncing close to the ground or is on the ground, is usually used to get the ball under control before changing its direction. Methods of trapping include using the sole of the foot, the front(s) of one or both legs (Fig. 2), the inside of one leg (Fig. 3), or the heel. Very tall players will find using the fronts of both legs less satisfactory than other methods because these players have a disadvantage in leverage when attempting to rise quickly to play the ball after trapping it. Players should practice trapping the ball, then moving immediately to play the ball by means of dribbling or passing. Opponents will find it quite easy to tackle a stationary ball; therefore the trapping should involve only a momentary stopping of the ball.

Blocking the ball is a method used to intercept the progress of a ball that is in the air as it approaches. The arms should be folded across the chest in order to prevent fouling with the hands (Fig. 4). The ball may be met with the chest, hips, thighs, or abdomen. As the oncoming ball is contacted, the player must give (Fig. 5) so that the force of the ball is absorbed; the ball will roll down the player's body (Fig. 6), and should be kept under the player's control and in her possession. Failing to give as the ball is received will usually cause the ball to rebound out of control.

Volleying is a skill used to intercept and

(2) Trapping—fronts of both legs.

(3) Trapping—inside of one leg.

(6) Ball rolling down player's body.   **(5)** Giving on impact.   **(4)** Position for receiving.

(4–6) Blocking the ball.

redirect an oncoming ball. The sharper, bonier protuberances of the body, which offer the greatest rebounding potential—the hip, knee (Fig. 7), shoulder (Fig. 8), heel, toe, and head— are used for volleying. Although heading the ball is an acceptable method for volleying and is used by many skilled players, it is questionable whether or not it should be employed, because some potential danger surrounds its use. Players might play more safely by positioning themselves to use a shoulder volley instead. When folded across the chest and held in contact with the body, the arms also may be used to volley the ball. Folding the arms is both a safety precaution and a precaution against fouling by handling the ball; therefore, during attempts to block and volley the ball the arms should always be folded across and held against the chest provided the upper portions of the body are those used during the play.

Blocking with the body is a technique used to shield the ball from an opponent who is a potential tackler or intercepter. This skill is most often used after trapping or intercepting the ball. The player using the body block simply moves between her opponent and the ball and protects the ball until she can get in position to make her next move. The body block is referred to as an obstruction in field hockey and is illegal in that sport. Soccer players will find that the body block is an effective skill that may be used frequently.

Tackling is the technique employed to intercept the ball from an opponent. Four commonly used tackles are the following: (1) Front tackle —the tackler approaches the ball from a position directly in front of the opponent and reaches forward with one foot to make the tackle (Fig. 9); (2) Hook tackle—the tackler approaches the opponent from in front but to the side, reaches in with one foot, and scoops the ball away from the opponent (Fig. 10); (3) Side tackle—the tackler runs along side-by-side with the opponent, then overtakes and circles in front of her, making the tackle as she does so (Fig. 11); and

(7) Knee volley.   **(8)** Shoulder volley.

(9) Front tackle.

(10) Hook tackle.

(11) Side tackle.

(12) Split tackle.

(4) Split tackle—the tackler is not in position to execute one of the other recommended tackles so she drops to one knee and reaches for the ball with the opposite outstretched leg in an attempt to spoil or momentarily detain the play of her opponent (Fig. 12). Of the four types of tackles described, the hook tackle is probably the safest and most widely used. The side tackle is the correlate of the circular tackle in field hockey. Players should always tackle back immediately in an effort to regain possession of the ball.

The *dodge* is a technique used to evade a tackler and maintain possession and control of the ball. The dodge is performed by waiting until the precise moment when the tackler commits herself and extends one leg to make the tackle; then the ball is tapped slightly beyond her reach. The dodge may be performed to either side. It is most important that a long kick be avoided when dodging, because possession of the ball will usually be lost when a long kick is used. As soon as a player makes a successful dodge she must follow up and continue dribbling and passing. Players should avoid dodging before the tackler commits herself, thus allowing the tackler time to adjust her position and make the interception. A forward who alternates pauses with attempts to dodge will leave some indecision with the tackler so that she can never be sure which maneuver the forward will attempt.

Specific types of *kicks* include passes (short kicks), place kicks, punts, and drop-kicks. Passing was described earlier and drop-kicks are rarely used in soccer; therefore, only the punt and the place kick are described here.

The *place kick* is used to send a ball kicked from a stationary position a great distance downfield. The player executing the place kick should stand back, run, and get the toe well under the ball when making contact. The ball should travel high over the heads of any opponents who are standing between the kicker and her own teammates. The kicker's own team should move well downfield in anticipation that the kick will be a good one. The place kick is used for all free kicks, defense kicks, and corner kicks; therefore, goalies, fullbacks, and halfbacks must develop this skill particularly. Although a place kick may be used on the kick-off, it is customary for the center forward to pass rather than to make a long kick.

The *punt* is a kick that may be used legally only by the goalkeeper because the ball is kicked after it is dropped from the hands, and the goalkeeper is the only player who has the special privilege of playing the ball with the hands. The punter may, and usually does, take two steps preceding the kick. The foot pattern for a right-footed kicker would therefore be "right, left, and kick," and the ball should be dropped on the "and." The goalkeeper should use a means other than punting for clearing the ball when the penalty area is congested and opponents are rushing the goal.

The methods, known as clearing, by which the goalkeeper may clear the ball from the goal include kicking, passing, punting, volleying, and throwing the ball. If a throw is used, a one-hand overhead throw gives the greatest distance with accuracy. The other methods that may be used for clearing have been described previously. Goalkeepers should avoid using the punt when the penalty area is congested and should use instead one of the other methods suggested.

TEAM SKILLS OR STRATEGIES

Triangular passing consists of a series of diagonal passes made between any two adjacent forwards. The forward with the ball should draw an opponent, pass the ball, evade the tackler, and position herself to receive the ball again after her teammate executes the same pattern. The pass should be made behind the teammate's opposing defensive player as indicated in Figure 13.

Interchange involves the changing of positions by two forwards, two backs, or a forward

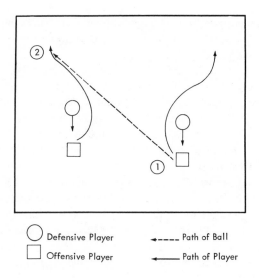

○ Defensive Player   ●----- Path of Ball
□ Offensive Player   ●——— Path of Player

(13) Triangular passing.

and a back. The necessity for interchange by forwards usually arises when one forward moves to meet a pass that does not completely come into her area of the field. The forward whose area it was should move into the teammate's area. Another occasion for interchange arises when a wing takes a ball downfield, no tacklers approach, and she decides to take the ball in for the shot at the goal. In this situation her adjacent inner should interchange with her. Anytime a player is drawn into a teammate's area and an interchange would make play more effective, there should be no hesitation to use this technique.

It is customary for backs not only to defend when the opponents have the ball but also to support their own forward line when they have the ball. When the opponents clear the ball, the backs are then in a position to return the ball to their own forwards immediately. Occasionally a back who is supporting her forwards' attempt for a goal has an opportunity to continue with a shot for the goal. The shot should be taken rather than making a pass to a forward who is closely marked or in a less advantageous position to score. Thus, in this instance, the back continues the play and attempts the shot for the goal; and the forward should drop back to cover the back's position.

Two backs usually interchange when the opposing forward has succeeded in getting around one of them and is dangerously clear of any opposition. The two fullbacks are the backs who most often have the opportunity to interchange.

Covering implies anticipating where passes may be sent and filling the spaces that are potentially dangerous. Defensive forwards must use this technique to fill spaces during free kicks, throw-ins, and so on; and defensive backs must constantly use this technique to hinder forwards from passing into open spaces. Fullbacks most often use the system of covering. The fullback on the side of the field where the ball is in play positions herself upfield more than the other, and the one who plays back moves diagonally behind the other so that a quick interchange can be initiated if the first one is evaded.

It is extremely important that forwards learn when to *center* the ball for the shot at the goal. The speed at which the player with the ball is traveling, the position of defensive opponents, and so on affect the timing of sending the ball into the center of the field; however, in most situations the ball should be centered by the time the player is even with the circle bounding the penalty area. It is probably wise to begin centering at a distance of about 25 yards from the goal. The forward controlling the ball must use judgment as to whether she should dribble or pass the ball to center it. If she is unattended by a defensive opponent, she should dribble in to the center and interchange with a teammate as she does so. It is unwise to pass when an opponent has not been drawn to the play.

Undoubtedly the most vulnerable spots for aiming when *shooting for goal* are the corners, because the goalkeeper is forced to position herself in the center between the posts until she knows what directional approach the opponents will use. Forwards should get as close to the goal as possible before shooting, so that the goalkeeper will not be able to pick up the ball, punt it, or place kick it. She will, instead, be forced to use a less effective method of clearing —that of passing. Most often a kick is used, but a volley is an equally acceptable technique for use in making the shot at the goal.

As soon as the ball is near the penalty area the entire forward line should *rush*, i.e., converge as a unit, with one objective in mind—that of literally forcing the ball through the goal. If the ball rebounds from the posts or from the body of a defensive player, the rush should be repeated. It is completely acceptable for forwards to

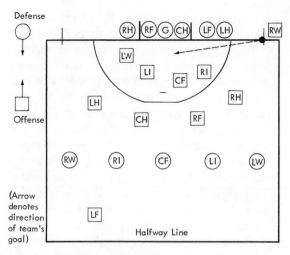

(14) Formation for corner kick.

crowd on the ball when rushing; and it is acceptable and mandatory that forwards play aggressively at this particular time in the game. Failure to score when the ball is within 5 yards of the goal is usually the result of the forwards' inability to rush aggressively and to follow up their shots for goal with second and third attempts.

The occasion for a *corner kick* arises when a defensive player sends the ball out behind her own endline. The ball is placed on the corner kick mark and it is usually kicked in by the attacking wing. The defensive halfbacks, fullbacks, and goalkeeper line up behind the end line; and they may be between the goalposts but may not step on the line until the ball is kicked. The player kicking the ball should attempt to center it, and her teammates should rush it through. Because attacking forwards may be within the penalty area when the ball is kicked, the defense is at a definite disadvantage, and a score should result from every corner kick. The defense should concentrate solely on the individuals they are marking rather than on guarding the goal and should try to prevent the opponents from having any opportunity first to get the ball and then to kick for goal (Fig. 14).

A *penalty kick* is awarded when a member of the defensive team fouls while inside her own penalty area. The center forward usually takes the penalty kick; however, any player may take it. Only the defensive goalkeeper may be between the goal posts. All other players except the one taking the kick must be outside the penalty area until the ball is kicked. If the

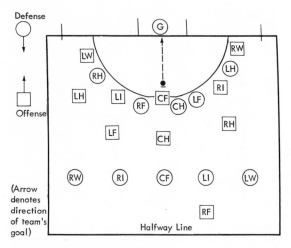

(15) Formation for penalty kick.

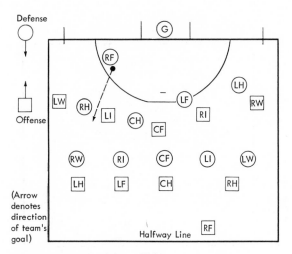

(16) Formation for defense kick.

attempt is unsuccessful, forwards should rush in an attempt to score a field goal. Defensive players must move quickly to mark their opponents should they attempt this follow-up shot for goal. The player taking the penalty kick will score most frequently by aiming for the high corners of the goal and kicking the ball over the goalkeeper's head at an angle that she cannot reach (Fig. 15).

A *defense kick* is awarded when a member of the attacking team sends the ball out over the opponent's end line. The defensive fullbacks and the goalkeeper should work together to retrieve the ball, place it anywhere on the circle marking the penalty area, and kick it with a place-kick. One may retrieve the ball, throw it to another to place, and the third may take the kick. It is important that the kick be taken quickly before the opponents have time to position themselves effectively (Fig. 16).

The game begins with a *kick-off*. The forwards of the team that kicks-off line up behind the halfway line, and the opposing forwards must line up behind the restraining line, which is 5 yards from the halfway line. Players may cross these lines as soon as the ball is kicked. A long place-kick may be used for this kick: however, it is customary for the center forward to use a short kick (a pass) instead so that her team may retain possession. A pass to the inner is safest. All players must remain 5 yards away from the ball until it is kicked; it must roll forward at least the distance of its circumference; and the player taking the kick may not play the ball again until another player has played it. Each

quarter is started by a kick-off, and a kick-off follows the scoring of any goal.

A *roll-in* is taken when members of each team simultaneously send the ball out or simultaneously foul. The two players involved stand 5 yards apart, face their opponents' goal, and move to play the ball as soon as the umpire rolls the ball and blows her whistle. All players must be 5 yards from the ball until it has been kicked. Both forward lines should be positioned toward their opponents' goal in anticipation that their teammate taking the roll-in will be successful.

Occasion for a *throw-in* arises when one team sends the ball wholly over the side line. The formation suggested for the throw-in is presented in Figure 17. In general, the offensive forward line should move as far downfield as the half-back (or fullback) can throw. The defensive forwards should cover spaces and try to intercept the ball should the thrower fail to get it high into the air and downfield. The offensive backs must position themselves so that they may mark their opposing forwards if the thrower succeeds in getting the ball far downfield. The throw-in should be taken as quickly as possible before the defense can position themselves adequately.

Free kicks are awarded for fouls by both teams outside the penalty area and for fouls by the attacking team inside the penalty area. The free kick is awarded for the following infringements: improperly taken kicks, off side, and violations of the goalkeeper's privileges. The same suggestions for the positioning of offensive and defensive players on throw-ins hold true for the positioning of players on free kicks (Fig. 18).

Soccer and Speedball **335**

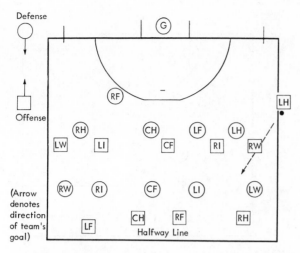

(17) Formation for throw-in.

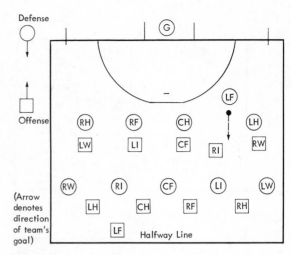

(18) Formation for free kick.

The free kick should be taken as quickly as possible.

Marking is the system of defense most frequently used in soccer. It is comparable to the player-to-player defense in basketball. Each player is responsible for guarding another player, but interchange is often necessary. The players are paired in the following manner: center forward—center halfback; right inner —left fullback; left inner—right fullback; right wing—left halfback; and left wing—right halfback.

Rules

The Soccer Committee of the Division for Girls' and Women's Sports of the American Association for Health, Physical Education, and Recreation formulates the official rules for women's soccer. The *Soccer-Speedball Guide* is published in even-numbered years and includes the rules. A summary of the rules follows.

The *field* should measure 60 yards × 100 yards (maximum) and 40 yards × 80 yards (minimum) (Fig. 1). The *length* of game comprises 4 eight-minute quarters, 2 minutes between quarters, and 10 minutes between halves. With regard to *substitution*, an unlimited number of entries are allowed each player and 30 seconds maximum time is permitted each team for a substitution. Two *time outs* (of 2 minutes each) are allowed each team for the entire game.

Scoring comprises field goal—2 points;

penalty goal—1 point; defaulted game—2-0; and tie game—score stands. The *officials* are two umpires, each responsible for one end line and one side line (a diagonal one half of the field); two scorekeepers; and two timekeepers. The *whistle* is used by the umpire to begin game, before each kick-off, when ball is out-of-bounds but players do not realize it, before a penalty kick, before a roll-in, after a goal, and after temporary suspension of play.

Serious offenses include pushing, tripping, striking, kicking, holding, handling ball (except goalies), jumping at opponent, and unnecessary roughness. A *direct free kick* results from any of the foregoing offenses. *Less serious offenses* include improperly taken kicks and throw-ins, infringement of goalie's privileges, illegal substitution, and off side. Any of the foregoing results in an *indirect free kick*.

Goal may be scored from corner kick, roll-in, and free kicks awarded for fouls (direct free kicks). Goals may *not* be scored from throw-in, defense kick, and free kicks awarded for infringements less serious than fouls (indirect free kicks).

Fouls and results. Free kick for foul or infringement committed by (1) either team outside penalty area, (2) attackers inside penalty area; and penalty kick for foul committed by defenders inside penalty area. An *out-of-bounds* ball, if over the end line, requires a corner kick if sent out by defenders and a defense kick if sent out by attackers; and if over the sideline a throw-in if sent out by either team and a roll-in if sent out by both teams.

Mechanics of Movement

Mechanical analyses of soccer skills are limited or nonexistent. Glassow and Mortimer[8], however, have analyzed kicking and have suggested the following for improving soccer techniques: 1) increase the force of the run; 2) take a longer step than usual with the foot that will support the body during the kick; 3) get at least 90 degrees of knee flexion prior to extending the knee during the actual kick (ask someone to check this for you); 4) contact the ball with the instep as well as the toe; 5) place the supporting foot by the side of the ball for better distance and height combined; 6) place the supporting foot more directly behind the ball for greater height; 7) contact the ball with great speed so that the leg will naturally follow through and the heel of the supporting foot will leave the ground.

The explanations for these suggestions reside in the application of mechanical principles (numbers correspond to suggestions): 1) the transfer of momentum from the whole to the part, 2) and 3) increased angular momentum of the pelvis and knee, 4) greater control as a result of greater area of contact, 5) and 6) contact of the object when the desired line of direction is at right angles to the limb, and 7) transfer of momentum from the part to the whole, as well as Newton's third law of motion —the law of reaction.

Evaluation

Certain standardized tests are available for assessing ability to perform the various skills of soccer. Some of the more popular tests listed here may be used both as tests and as practice devices.

VOLLEYING TEST[9]

The player begins in the center of a 30-foot square area and volleys the ball by any legal means to the wall on or above a wall line that is 8 inches from the floor. The player must remain within the 30-foot area. If a ball gets out of control, she may take one of the extra balls, which are placed on the boundary line. Three thirty-second trials are given on one day, and the score is the total for the three trials.[10] If possible, a second day of testing (three thirty-second trials) is desirable. If two days are utilized, the subject's total score is the total for the two days of testing. A foul on any hit voids the hit and it does not count in the final score. A restraining line placed 6 feet from the wall may improve the test.[11] Stepping on or over the line while making an otherwise good hit would constitute a foul if the restraining line were used.

FOOT PASS TO WALL TEST[12]

A floor target (Fig. 19) is utilized, and the player taking the test begins in area A. The object of the test is to hit the ball by a pass made with the foot to the wall from areas A, and B, and so on, alternately. A hit made while standing on any line or beyond the restraining line or one made from the neutral area does not count. The score is the total number of legal hits in three thirty-second trials taken on one day.[13]

[10] Revision suggested by writer.
[11] Revision suggested by writer.
[12] Scott and French, *op. cit.*, p. 213.
[13] Revision suggested by writer.

[8] Ruth B. Glassow and Elizabeth M. Mortimer, "Analysis of Kicking," *DGWS Soccer-Speedball Guide*, 1966–1968 (Washington, D.C.: AAHPER, 1966).

[9] M. Gladys Scott and Esther French, *Measurement and Evaluation in Physical Education* (Dubuque, Iowa: William C. Brown, 1959), p. 187.

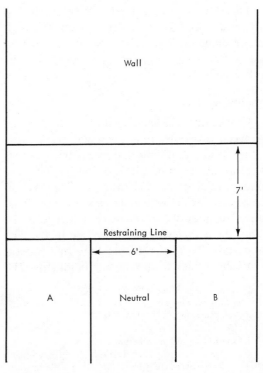

(19) Target for foot pass to wall test.

If two days are utilized, the subject's final score is the total for the two days of testing. A subject may cross the restraining line to retrieve a ball but must return behind the line before hitting again if the hit is to count.

KICK FOR DISTANCE[14]

A place-kick is used, and the player runs and kicks a stationary ball. The test is taken on a field containing markers or lines every 5 yards for 50 yards; and the ball must stay within a lane 25 yards in width. Three trials are given and the total of the three scores constitutes the final score. If a second day of testing is possible, the total of the scores on two days should be utilized as the total score.

OBSTACLE DRIBBLE[15]

A course with a starting line and five obstacles placed every 5 yards is utilized for the test. The player dribbles to the right of the first obstacle, to the left of the second, and so on, until she gets to the last obstacle, which she dribbles around, and continues in the same manner back to the starting line. The score is the time for the total of three trials.[16] If two days of testing are possible, the score would be the total of the trials for two days.

SKILLS CHART

Players may improve their skills by attempting to reach level III for each skill on the skills chart shown in Figure 20.[17] Some of the items are self-explanatory. Explanatory notes for the other skills follow.

Passing at clubs

Five clubs are arranged 10 yards apart between two restraining lines that are 5 yards apart. While dribbling, the player tries to pass the ball at the Indian Clubs, first from behind one restraining line, then the other. She may aim at any of the clubs as long as she passes from alternate lines. When she reaches the end of the lane, she dribbles to the other side of the lane and starts back, continuing the same process until she is back to the starting point (Fig. 21).

The player may go into the lane to retrieve a ball, but she must dribble to a point outside the lane before making her pass. Clubs knocked down do not count if any of the stated conditions are violated.

Tackle

One player dribbles within a lane 10 yards wide while another tries to tackle the ball. The third level involves not only tackling the ball in four out of five attempts but also maintaining control by keeping the ball within the 10-yard lane.

Dodge

The player dribbling within a lane 10 yards wide dodges a would-be tackler and maintains possession of the ball for two out of five trials (level I) and four out of five trials (level II). For level III the player must maintain possession for three out of five trials in a 5-yard wide lane.

Shoot for Goal

A bench is placed between the goal posts and the player must kick for goal to the left side of the bench and to the right side of the bench. The bench (2 yards long) is placed in the center, right of center, or left of center in between the goal posts. The player dribbles from 15 yards out and when she reaches a line 5 yards out, she kicks for goal. She may not step more than one step within the 5-yard line before shooting. The bench is placed in the exact center for level I, with the right leg on center for level II, and the left leg on center for level III (Fig. 22).

When the bench is placed left of center, the player approaches the goal from the right of center, and vice versa. In addition, each level requires kicking with both the left and the right foot.

The player scores one point for each level attained. The total for the chart is eighteen points for the six skills, three levels each.

Terminology

Attacking team: The team that has the ball.
Carrying: An infringement committed when the goalkeeper takes more than two steps while she holds the ball.
Direct free kick: A free kick from which a goal may be scored directly.
Goalkeeper's privileges: The privileges extended the goalkeeper within her own penalty area. She may

[14] Harold M. Barrow and Rosemary McGee, *A Practical Approach to Measurement in Physical Education* (Philadelphia: Lea and Febiger, 1964), p. 296.
[15] *Ibid.*, p. 297.
[16] Revision suggested by author.
[17] Jo Anne Thorpe, "Self-Testing in Soccer Skills," *DGWS Soccer-Speedball Guide*, 1966–1968 (Washington, D.C.: AAHPER, 1966).

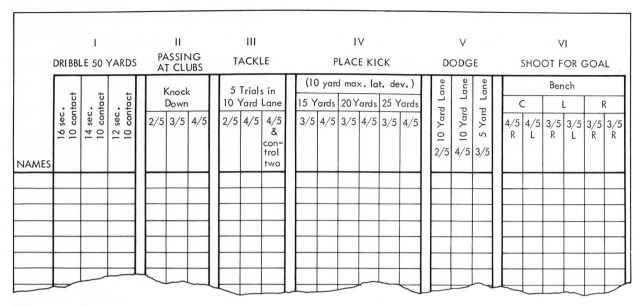

	I			II			III			IV						V			VI					
	DRIBBLE 50 YARDS			PASSING AT CLUBS			TACKLE			PLACE KICK						DODGE			SHOOT FOR GOAL					
				Knock Down			5 Trials in 10 Yard Lane			(10 yard max. lat. dev.)									Bench					
										15 Yards		20 Yards		25 Yards						C		L		R	
	16 sec. 10 contact	14 sec. 10 contact	12 sec. 10 contact	2/5	3/5	4/5	2/5	4/5	4/5 & control two	3/5	4/5	3/5	4/5	3/5	4/5	10 Yard Lane	10 Yard Lane	5 Yard Lane	4/5 R	4/5 L	3/5 R	3/5 L	3/5 R	3/5 R
NAMES																2/5	4/5	3/5						

(20) Soccer skills chart.

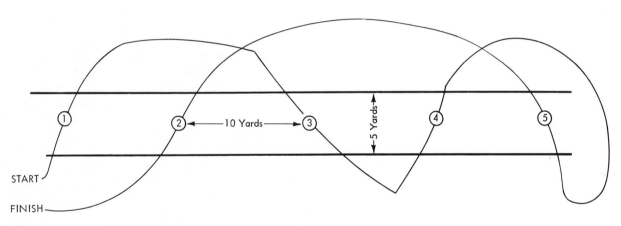

(21) Passing at clubs.

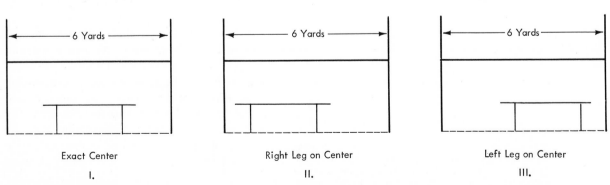

Exact Center   Right Leg on Center   Left Leg on Center

I.   II.   III.

(22) Placement of bench.

pick up the ball; bounce the ball once; punt; throw; drop-kick; combine a bounce with a punt, throw, or drop-kick; take two steps preceding a punt, drop-kick, or throw (if a bounce is not combined).

Handling: A foul called when a player who is not eligible to touch the ball with the hands or arms does so.

Indirect free kick: A free kick from which a goal may not be scored directly.

Off side: An illegal position called when a player is nearer the opponents' goal line than the ball when the ball is played unless she is in her own half of the field or there are at least three of her opponents nearer to their own goal line than she is.

Opponents' goal: The goal through which a team must send the ball in order to score.

Own goal: The goal a team is defending.

Penalty area: The area enclosed by the quarter circles and the goal line.

Unnecessary roughness: Kicking dangerously to gain possession or kicking into a player at close range without concern for safety.

SPEEDBALL

Lifting ball to a team-mate.

Lifting ball to self with one foot.

Lifting ball to self with two feet.

(23) Fundamentals unique to speedball. (From "Fundamentals Unique to Speedball," *1964–66 DGWS Soccer-Speedball Guide*, p. 83. By permission of the American Association for Health, Physical Education, and Recreation, Washington, D.C.)

The game of speedball, originated for men by Elmer D. Mitchell at the University of Michigan in 1921, is a combination of soccer and basketball.[18] When the ball is rolling on the ground or is dropped to the ground, the rules of soccer apply; when the ball has been legally converted to an aerial ball, basketball rules apply.

Legal means of converting a ground ball to an aerial ball include the following: (1) kicking up to oneself with one or both feet, (2) allowing the ball to roll up the foot and leg, (3) lifting the ball (with the foot) to a teammate, and (4) place-kicking or drop-kicking a ball into the air. A ball that is bouncing from the ground into the air may not be played as an aerial ball.

Positions and names of players are the same as for soccer, but scoring and out-of-bounds rules differ slightly. Scoring is as follows: (1) field goal, two points; (2) touchdown, two points; (3) penalty kick, one point; and (4) drop-kick, three points. The field goal is scored as in soccer. The touchdown is scored when a pass (with the hands) originating from behind the penalty area is completed to a player standing anywhere behind the goal line. The penalty area is that area which is parallel to the goal line and is bounded by the goal line, the 5-yard line, and the two side lines. The penalty kick is awarded and scored in the same manner as in soccer; however, in soccer a place kick must be used and in speedball a drop-kick must be used. The drop-kick as a method of scoring may be utilized by drop-kicking the ball over the crossbar and between the uprights. The kick must

[18] Hupprich, *op. cit.*, p. 435.

be made from outside the penalty area to be successful. The drop-kick is performed by dropping the ball to the ground and kicking it just as it rebounds.

When a player sends the ball out-of-bounds over the side line, a throw-in is utilized to begin play again. When the ball is sent out over the end line, a punt, drop-kick, place-kick, or throw-in may be used to start play again. Any ball sent out-of-bounds by members of both teams simultaneously results in a jump ball, which is taken 5 yards in from the boundary line.

Fouls in speedball include the fouls listed in the section on soccer as well as some fouls that are related to basketball. Blocking (not to be confused with blocking the ball and body blocking in soccer) is a foul that involves impeding the progress of another player by means of personal contact. Charging results from one player moving into and contacting another player whose position or path is established. Tagging (repeatedly touching), traveling (more than two steps) with the ball, holding the ball (more than five seconds if closely guarded), threatening the eyes, air dribbling more than once, touching a ground ball with the hands, and drop-kicking for a goal or attempting a touchdown while inside the penalty area are also fouls. Double fouls result in a jump ball. Individual fouls are penalized according to the location of their occurrence. A free kick or penalty kick is awarded for individual fouls. See the soccer section for details about the appropriate kick to be taken. It should be noted that the goalkeeper in speedball has no special privileges and must therefore avoid picking up a ground ball.

Strategy for playing the aerial game differs somewhat from the strategy for playing the ground game. In basketball short quick passes are preferable to long high passes. Whereas in soccer it is better for the forwards to remain spread out under most conditions, in speedball, as in basketball, it is acceptable and desirable for the forwards to play closer together to facilitate shorter passes, which invite fewer interceptions.

The game of speedball is a combination of two complex games—basketball and soccer. Players need a good basic understanding of and some degree of proficiency in both basketball and soccer in order to play speedball successfully.

Selected References

DGWS. Soccer-Speedball Guide, current edition. Washington, D.C.: American Assoc. for Health, Physical Education, and Recreation.

Meyer, Margaret H., and Marguerite M. Schwarz. *Team Sports for Girls and Women*. Philadelphia: W. B. Saunders, 1965.

Miller, Donna Mae, and Katherine L. Ley. *Individual and Team Sports for Women*. Englewood Cliffs, N.J.: Prentice-Hall, 1955.

Sevy, Ruth, ed. *Selected Soccer and Speedball Articles*. Washington, D.C.: American Assoc. for Health, Physical Education and Recreation, 1963.

Chapter 18

Softball *Betty G. Hartman*

History. Goals. Equipment. Etiquette. Fielding. Throwing. Pitcher. Catcher. Outfielders and Infielders.
Batting. Bunting. Baserunning. Play for Defense and Offense. Evaluation. Terminology.

Softball is a game played by two teams consisting of nine players each. The object of the game is for one team to score more runs than the other in seven innings of play.

Runs are scored by the team that is up at bat, the offense, while the defensive team tries to keep their opponents from scoring. The ball is pitched by a defensive player in an underhand motion to the batter, who attempts to hit the ball into the playing area. If successful, the batter becomes a baserunner. She runs from home plate to first, second, and third base and then back to home plate. If she completes running the bases in succession, either following her own hit, or aided by a teammate's hit, or by "stealing," she scores a run for her team.

The nine players on the defensive team are positioned in areas of the softball diamond as shown in Figure 1. They catch, or field, the batted ball and tag the runner with it, or throw the ball to the base ahead of the runner in attempting to force her out.

The pitcher, in pitching the ball to the batter, tries to deliver a ball, which is difficult to hit, or if hit, easy to catch. The batter is out if she swings

and misses three times; then the next batter takes her turn at bat. As soon as three offensive players have been put out at bat or in the field, the two teams exchange roles; the former defensive team comes up to bat, and the opponents go onto the field. After each team has completed its turn at batting, an inning is completed. If the game ends in a tie after the regulation seven innings, one or more additional complete innings are played until one team wins.

The game is officiated by two umpires: the plate and base umpires. The plate umpire stands behind the catcher and batter and judges the direction and delivery of pitched balls. The pitched ball must pass over home plate between the batter's armpits and knees (strike zone) in order to be called a "strike," and is so called whether the batter swings or not. Balls pitched outside the strike zone are called by the umpire; four "balls" allow the player at bat to walk to first base. If the batter swings at a pitched ball, it is considered a strike. The second official, or base umpire, watches baserunners to determine whether they touch the bases in succession, and whether baserunners arrive at bases before the defender throws the ball to the base.

Players must adapt the basic softball skills to the positions played in the game. The basic skills are throwing, catching, fielding, batting, and baserunning. In addition to these skills, players must learn the basic rules as well as strategy for offense and defense. Many softball skills can be

---

Dr. Hartman has been interested in all phases of sports for women as participant, teacher, official, scholar, and writer. At one time a skilled participant of a softball league, she has always worked toward increased opportunities for instruction and participation in sports for women at all skill levels and in a variety of sports.

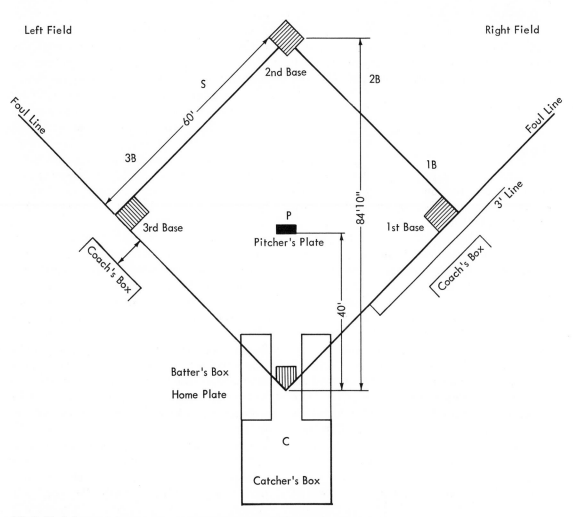

CF

LF   RF

Center Field

Left Field   Right Field

2nd Base

S

Foul Line   Foul Line

60'   2B

3B   1B

3' Line

P
Pitcher's Plate   1st Base

3rd Base

84'10"

Coach's Box   Coach's Box

40'

Batter's Box

Home Plate

C

Catcher's Box

(1) Softball diamond. Positions indicated by abbreviations: Catcher (C), pitcher (P), first baseman (1B), second baseman (2B), shortstop (S), third baseman (3B), left fielder (LF), center fielder (CF), and right fielder (RF).

practiced indoors, and the game can be played indoors with fleece or plastic balls on a diamond reduced in size to adjust to the space available.

History

Softball is a relatively recent adaptation of the game of baseball. Evidence has been found that a baseball type game was played in England as early at 1744. Similar types of games were played in the United States before 1839, but at that time Abner Doubleday of Cooperstown, N.Y. is credited with drawing up the basic rules of our present day game of baseball.

Different indoor and outdoor modifications of baseball developed, one favorite being "playground ball," which became popular in the early 1920's. The modified game began to be more commonly known as "softball," and, in 1926, Gladys Palmer of Ohio State University wrote the first girls' softball rules. These rules were published shortly afterwards by the Division for Girls' and Women's Sports of the American Association for Health, Physical Education, and Recreation.

The Amateur Softball Association established a rules committee in 1934. Today the International Joint Rules Committee on Softball determines the rules that govern play for both men and women.

Goals

Beginners cannot expect to become proficient in all aspects of the game with only six or seven weeks of softball instruction, but they can learn enough to enable them to enjoy the game. Skill should be developed in a variety of throws. The overhand and underhand throws are the easiest. Most beginners will also be able to use a sidearm throw. All beginners should be able to catch different types of thrown and batted balls. Batting against various types of pitches should also be learned. Most players will be able to bunt well enough to use the skill in the game.

The baserunning skills involved in running consecutive bases, stealing, and leading off are easily accomplished. Some beginners may wish to learn to slide and should experience little difficulty with this skill. Beginners will develop preferences for different defensive positions. They need to develop the special skills for a specific position so that they can better understand basic defensive strategy that involves backing-up or being ready to assist various teammates as they field offensive hits and receive throws by teammates.

Some experimentation with signals for offense can be attempted. Acting as first and third base coaches and inventing signals for "taking" (allowing the ball to go by without attempting to bat), bunting, and stealing adds to an appreciation of game complexities. Basic rules should be learned by the beginner.

Equipment

The playing area is called a softball diamond and consists of two parts, the infield and outfield

(Fig. 1). Home plate and the three bases form the diamond of the infield. Beyond the bases is the outfield, divided into right, center, and left field. The outfield is bounded by two base lines called foul lines. These lines are extensions of the first base and third base sides of the diamond. The outfield, or area between the foul lines, extends in a radius of at least 200 feet from home plate. A backstop should be placed 25 feet behind home plate. This is a barrier constructed of wood and wire used to stop pitched and thrown balls missed by the batter or catcher.

The pitcher's "box" is located 40 feet from home plate toward the center of the diamond. This 6-inch wooden or rubber plate used by the pitcher is level with the ground. The batter's box is an area on either side of and parallel to home plate from which the batter attempts to hit. The catcher's box, an area $8\frac{1}{2}$ by 10 feet, is behind the batter's box. The coaches' boxes, outside first and third bases, are for one coach at each of these bases for the purpose of assisting batters and baserunners.

The 3-foot line serves as a guide to first base, inasmuch as the baserunner may not run more than 3 feet from the base line. The baserunner may run outside the 3-foot line as she approaches first base only if necessary in order to avoid interference with a fielder who is attempting to field a ball. The pitcher's plate and home plate are made of wood or rubber. The bases are 15 inches square and are made of canvas stuffed with resilient material. The bases are fastened to the ground.

The bats are made of wood. One end of the bat, although no more than $2\frac{1}{8}$ inches in diameter, is thicker than the other end. The more narrow tapered end is called the grip; it is covered with nonslip material. Bats come in various weights, but must not be more than 34 inches in length. Players develop preferences for weights and styles of bats as their batting skill improves.

Defensive players use protective equipment. Gloves may be worn by any player, but mitts may be used only by the catcher and first baseman (Fig. 2). Women catchers must wear a mask and chest protector. The mask is made of bands of wire or steel mounted on a padded frame, which is worn over the face and suspended from the head by means of elastic webbing. The chest protector, suspended from the shoulders, is a padded, apron-like device covering chest and abdomen.

Shoes with canvas or leather uppers and smooth soles, or with rubber or $\frac{3}{4}$-inch metal cleats, may be worn. Blouses and slacks that do not restrict the player's movements should be worn. Slacks, rather than shorts, should be worn to avoid injury from sliding. A jacket or sweater should be worn by players waiting their turn to bat, as it is advisable to keep warm when inactive.

Etiquette, Good Sportsmanship, and Safety

Players frequently encourage teammates. Good sportsmanship dictates that players' comments be limited to encouragement rather than derogatory remarks directed at opponents and officials. The officials are in charge of the game. Players should accept the officials' judgments without question.

Softball is essentially a noncontact game. Instances occur in baserunning where there is body contact, but baserunners should try to avoid running into baseplayers because injury to both may result. Baseplayers should leave a path open to the base. Blocking of the base or base paths should be avoided. Players often attempt to slide into the base. A discussion of the sliding technique is found later in this chapter. If players intend to slide they should master the proper form through practice.

Although the ball used in this game is called a softball, it is not "soft," Gloves or mitts should be used. The use of gloves or mitts should be encouraged to avoid injury to the hands. Beginners often tend to let go of the bat following a swing or hit, which can be extremely dangerous. Players should learn to hold on to the bat when swinging at pitches. When the batter becomes a baserunner following a hit, she must drop, rather than throw, the bat.

Occasionally two defenders attempt to catch the ball simultaneously and in so doing may collide with one another. To prevent this, players should be designated to call out the name of the player who should make the catch. The player whose name is called should use a warning cry such as "I've got it," as she attempts the catch.

The catcher must always wear a mask and chest protector. This player, due to her position behind home plate, is in danger of being struck

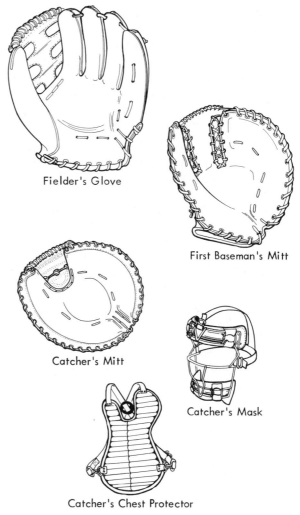

Fielder's Glove

First Baseman's Mitt

Catcher's Mitt

Catcher's Mask

Catcher's Chest Protector

(2) Gloves and mitts.

by misdirected pitches or balls "tipped" by the batter's bat.

Baserunners should avoid stepping on the center of the bases as they run. They should touch the corners of the bases, because stepping in the center of a base may cause a turned ankle. Runners need to anticipate and adjust before making a sudden stop. They should not jump, leap, or try to stop suddenly because they may be thrown off-stride and fall.

Experienced softball players advocate "warming up" by throwing and catching easily for ten to fifteen minutes before the start of the game. This seems to keep players' arms from becoming sore and also enhances throwing accuracy.

Proper skill development is one of the best safety factors. Incorrectly performed throws, catches, runs, and slides may cause injuries.

Skills for Defense

FIELDING

Fielding is the term used for catching grounders (balls caught after hitting the ground) or flies (balls caught before hitting the ground).

Ready position

Infielders and outfielders assume a "ready" position to enable them to move for catching. In the ready position the player stands with her feet in side-stride position facing home plate. The feet are parallel and about shoulder-width apart. The knees and hips are slightly bent; the weight is slightly forward and balanced on the balls of the feet. The hands rest on the knees or hang loosely in front of the body, and the head is up with eyes focused on the ball as it is pitched to the batter.

As the pitcher delivers the ball, the player shifts her weight farther forward to the balls of the feet. The player is ready to move in any direction if the ball is hit, and ready also to move to field a fly or a ground ball (Fig. 3).

Fielding grounders

The player moves forward a step or two from the basic ready position and into the position for fielding ground balls. The "set" position for grounders involves a foot placement of 45 degrees with the weight on the balls of the feet. The hips and knees are bent so that the player is in a squat position with the knees turned outward.

If a ground ball is hit directly at a player, she starts moving toward the ball with the body low and eyes focused on the ball. The player stays low.

To field *low grounders* the arms and hands reach down between the knees so that the hands can touch the ground. The right-handed player catches the ball in the gloved left hand.[1] For balls caught below the waist, the fingers of both hands point downward. The palm of the gloved left hand is perpendicular to the path of the ball. The right hand is placed at a 45-degree angle to the left hand. The little finger of the ungloved right hand touches the little finger side of the gloved hand and the thumb of the right hand is forward in the direction of the ball.

As the ball strikes the gloved hand, the right

(3) Ready position for fielders.

hand rolls over the ball to trap it. The hands and arms "give," moving backward at the time of the ball's impact to start into the backswing for a quick throw.

Ground balls often bounce into the air so that the ball has to be caught above the waist. In fielding *high grounders*, the player raises her body and reaches up for the ball. The hands and arms are held up and out from the body with the fingers pointing upward. The gloved hand is perpendicular to the path of the ball; the other hand is held at a 45-degree angle with the thumb touching the thumb of the gloved hand. The free hand traps the ball on impact, and the hands give, moving toward the body as the ball strikes the gloved hand.

On *hard-hit balls* that hug the ground, the player drops to the right knee to block the ball with the body. The left-handed player drops to her left knee.

Medium-hit balls may be fielded with the feet in a forward-backward stride. The left foot is ahead of the right foot with the back foot at right angles to the forward foot (Fig. 4).

For *ground balls hit to the left or right* of the fielder, the player moves accordingly. She turns and runs in as straight a line as possible, keeping low during the run. Players should maneuver into the set fielding position as soon as possible.

SUGGESTIONS FOR SKILL IMPROVEMENT WITH GROUNDERS. Beginners tend to thrust the hips

---

[1] Left-handed players reverse the hand positions described for right-handed players.

(4) Fielding a grounder.

(5) Position for fielding a fly ball.

too far backward in assuming the ready position. This may force the rest of the body too far forward and result in poor balance. Avoid trying to catch the ball on the bare hand. The previously described position of the gloved hand with bare hand at a right angle, should be used.

Players should avoid pointing the fingers at the ball. Fingers should point upward for balls caught above the waist, and downward for those caught below the waist. It is essential to allow the hands and arms to give with the impact of the ball. Stiff hands and arms cause the ball to rebound from the player's grasp. One should always move, lining up with the path of the ball, in order to avoid an off-balance position while fielding.

Fielding fly balls

To catch fly balls, players move from the ready position to a "set" catching position. They may move forward, backward, or to the right or left prior to the set.

The basic catching position involves a forward-backward stride with the back foot (right for right-handed player) pointing to the side and the toes of the forward foot pointing in the direction of the path of the ball. The knees and hips are slightly bent with the weight centered on the back foot. The body is upright with the head held up and the eyes following the ball's flight (Fig. 5).

The hands move from the sides to one of three positions according to the place where the ball is to be caught. To catch a fly ball coming straight down requires lifting hands and arms at elbow length from the body with the palms up and the hands cupped. The fingers point straight out with the little fingers touching. Balls caught at head or shoulder height involve reaching upward. The arms are held up so that the elbows are at shoulder height with the forearms pointing upward. The thumbs are together with fingers cupped and pointing upward. The ball may also be caught high over the head. In this case arms extend completely upward with the palms toward the ball.

When a player is fielding a fly, she runs with arms in the normal running position, then reaches for the catch at the last minute. For a long fly ball over the head, the player turns away from the ball and runs while watching the ball over one shoulder. Players should hurry to the spot where they think the ball will come. They should be waiting for the ball in the set position with the left foot forward (right-handed player), and should make the give of the catch become a part of the backswing of the throw.

SUGGESTIONS FOR SKILL IMPROVEMENT WITH FLY BALLS. The same errors occur in fielding flies as in catching grounders. Catching with the bare hands, pointing fingers at the ball, and stiffening arms and hands should be avoided.

Softball **347**

Judgment of the flight of fly balls needs to be developed and aligning the body needs to be practiced. Properly "set" players become dependable fielders. Players should not block their view of the path of the ball. Beginners tend to reach up for the fly ball and place their hands in front of their eyes. Players should throw the ball immediately after catching; avoid running and then throwing.

THROWING

The three basic throws are overhand, underhand, and sidearm. All players will use one or the other of the throws at some time in the game.

Grip

The ball is grasped with the tips of the first two fingers on one side of the ball and the thumb on the opposite side. The third and fourth fingers rest lightly against the ball. The grip is the same for all throws with the exception of pitching.

The overhand throw

Fielders must learn to use the overhand throw, the most accurate and powerful of all the throws. The feet are in a forward-backward stride with the backward foot on the side of the throwing arm. The toe of this foot points away from the thrower out to the side at a 45-degree angle, and the forward foot points in the throw direction. The weight is balanced over the balls of the feet with the knees and hips slightly flexed.

The hand gripping the ball is sent back at the wrist. The elbow is bent, with the forearm perpendicular to the ground, and the upper arm parallel to the ground. The ball is raised to a head-high position as the arm moves backward. The shoulders and hips rotate backward in the direction of the backswing. As the ball is brought back, the weight is transferred to the back foot.

The opposite arm moves forward as the throwing arm is brought back so that the player is in balance. As the throwing arm passes the shoulder in the forward swing, the elbow starts to straighten. The arm completely straightens, the wrist snaps forward, and the fingers release the ball. The weight transfers forward with the throwing action, and the arm follows through in the direction of the throw.

The throw can be combined with a step if greater power is needed. If the throw is started

(6) Overhand throw.

with the feet in a side-by-side position, the ball is brought back as the weight is transferred to the foot on the throwing side. As the arm snaps forward the player steps forward on the other foot (Fig. 6).

FACTORS AFFECTING THE OVERHAND THROW. If the weight is not transferred during the throw, the player loses throwing force. Failure to rotate hips and shoulders backward and forward with the arm swing also detracts from the force of the throw. Beginners tend to throw with only the arm.

The height of the ball release is important. The higher the release, the higher the flight of the ball. The later and lower the release, the lower the throw. Outfielders throw long distances; they release the ball at higher points than infielders. Height contributes to distance, but additional force is needed with a high release point.

The elbow is brought up, out, and away from the body at the start of the throw; if this is not done the arm cannot move freely and force will be lost. Players should avoid the tendency to throw with the forearm only. This may result if the elbow is kept close to the side of the body.

Wrist snap at the point of release is essential. Beginners tend to forget this forceful motion.

The path of the arm as it is swung forward

(7) Sidearm throw.

should be "over-the-head." Sideward motion, swinging the arm away from the head on the swing through, affects ball direction. The ball will not be accurately thrown if a combination overhand and sideward swing of the arm is used.

Sidearm throw

The sidearm throw is used by infielders when the throw must be hurried. The player, after fielding a low grounder, does not take the time to straighten up but instead bends the body toward the throwing side, swings the forearm back parallel to the ground, and cocks the wrist. The forearm then whips forward, the wrist snaps, and the ball is released. Body weight shifts forward on the throw. This can be a quick throw because less backswing is used than in other types of throwing.

The major difference between the overhand and sidearm throw is in the arm pattern. As the arm swings back for the sidearm throw, the hand and arm move parallel to the ground; this differs from the perpendicular position of the forearm in the backswing of the overhand throw. The shoulders and hips rotate in the same fashion as in the overhand throw and the weight transfer is also the same.

The forward arm swing of the sidearm throw is parallel to the ground with a fast whip-like

motion. The body weight shifts forward with the throw, and a wrist snap accompanies the release. The ball should be released immediately after the hand passes the body (Fig. 7); then, on the follow-through, the hand and wrist point in the direction of the throw.

Beginners should try to throw from the same forward-backward stride as is used in the overhand throw and should practice the sidearm throw immediately following the actual fielding of a grounder.

FACTORS AFFECTING THE SIDEARM THROW. The timing of the ball release affects direction in all throws, but because of the arc of the throw, timing is especially important in the sidearm throw. A right-handed player will find that the ball flies off to the right if released too soon, and if released too far in front of the body, the ball will go to the left.

The player should bend toward the side of the throwing arm, and the throwing hand should be kept lower than the shoulder. These actions aid in attaining the desired sidearm pattern.

Underhand throw

Whenever a short, quick throw is needed, the underhand throw is used. Infielders, when fielding balls close to a base, use this throw to get the ball quickly to a baseman.

Beginners find the underhand throw easy to master, but because it is difficult to generate much force by using it, this throw should not be attempted when distance is needed.

The body position and grip are the same as that used at the beginning of the overhand throw. The hand and arm swing down and backward from a position in front of the body. The arm straightens on the short backswing and the wrist cocks. In the forward swing, the arm is first perpendicular to the ground, then moves forward, the wrist snaps, and the ball is released in front of the body at about waist height. The arm follows through in the direction of the throw (Fig. 8). The weight transfers to the back foot as the arm swings backward and then to the forward foot on the forward arm swing.

INDIVIDUAL SKILLS FOR DEFENSE

The pitcher, catcher, and the third base players need to learn certain specialized skills.

Pitcher

The pitcher's skills contribute greatly to team success. According to the rules, she must throw

(8) Release of underhand throw or pitch.

(9) Catcher's position.

an underhand ball in which the hand shall be below the hip and the wrist not farther from the body than the elbow. Change of pace is achieved by varying the grip, backswing, and the speed of the throw.

In the *wind up and delivery*, the pitcher holds the ball in both hands while facing the batter and both feet contact some part of the pitcher's plate. The shoulders are squared toward home plate. The pitch must be underhanded and one step is allowed before the ball is released.

Windmill deliveries are often used. The throwing arm is started from a position in front of the body, and in this delivery the arm moves forward, up, back, and over the head, then continues downward and forward in making the underhand swing.

The pitcher's back foot is brought to a point parallel to the forward foot after the ball's release. This "sets" the pitcher and enables her to field batted balls.

The pitcher must develop *control*. The ball must be thrown over home plate at a level between the batter's armpits and top of her knees to be called a strike. The pitcher tries to pitch the ball into the strike zone, but avoids putting it "down the middle." She aims for the corners of home plate and tries to throw knee-high and chest-high balls. She tries to make the batter miss, or at least force her to hit a ball that is easily fielded.

Speed is also a pitching factor. Variation in the speed of pitched balls disconcerts the batter. Pitchers should practice slow and fast pitches. *Slow pitches* are delivered with a grip using all the fingers and contacting the ball with the palm of the hand. This causes the ball to spin and slows its flight. *Fast pitches* are achieved by throwing the ball with the standard grip but turning the palm inward at the moment of release. The ball is gripped with only the thumb and first two fingers of the throwing hand.

Clockwise and counterclockwise ball spins cause a *curve* in the flight of the ball. Curving balls are difficult for batters to hit. The *incurve spin* is clockwise and causes the ball to move away from a right-handed batter. The pitcher grips the ball with the thumb and first two fingers while the palm faces to the left. On the release the pitcher snaps the wrist to the right and the little finger leaves the ball last. Balls spinning counterclockwise, an *outcurve spin*, curve toward the batter. This spin is achieved by snapping the hand and turning the wrist forcefully to the left at the time of release.

Catcher

Two basic positions are used by catchers: a

squat position and a more upright or crouch position (Fig. 9). Comfort and the ability to throw better from one or the other position determine the choice. In the squat position the feet are side by side, shoulder-width apart, with hips and knees flexed and the weight balanced over the balls of both feet. In the crouch position the foot opposite the throwing arm is forward and the upper part of the body is bent slightly forward and balanced over hips and legs.

The catcher presents the glove as a target. both hands and arms are held up and out. The bare hand is clenched and held beside the glove until it moves over the ball to trap it on impact with the glove. When attempting to catch fouls or throws from the field, catchers should quickly remove masks for better visibility.

The catcher must be a strong player. She must catch and throw consistently and well to all bases. Fielding accuracy is also essential. She must catch all players' throws as well as all pitched balls.

Outfielders and infielders

The various fielding positions require special abilities. The *outfielders*—left, center and right—should be able to throw far and hard. They must also be able to run, inasmuch as they must cover a large amount of the playing area. The *infield* players are pitcher; catcher; first, second, and third basemen; and shortstop. The *shortstop* must be extremely quick and agile. She covers a great deal of territory for, when needed, she backs up second and third bases and the pitcher.

She must be able to field batted balls quickly and relay balls from the outfield.

The *baseplayer* stands facing the oncoming runner with one foot touching the inside edge of the base. As she waits for the runner to come to the base, the baseman must be prepared to stretch for poorly directed throws (Figs. 10 and 11). If a runner is forced to a base because a teammate has moved to her previous base, the runner is out when the base player catches the ball and tags the base, prior to the runner's touch on base. If the baserunner is not forced, the baseplayer must touch the runner with the ball before the latter touches the base. In this case the baseplayer catches the ball and assumes a straddle position with one foot on either side of the base (Fig. 12). The baseplayer, without obstructing the base, is in a good position to tag the runner inasmuch as the runner is forced to come straight to the base. The baseman must continue to hold the ball while touching the runner; if she drops the ball, the runner is safe.

The *first baseman* must be able to move quickly into position for fielding and to catch balls from every possible position. Teammates' throws may not be accurate, and her ability to catch poor throws enables her to put base-runners out at first. She must also be able to throw well and hard.

The *second baseman* must be able to move quickly. Inasmuch as she should assist the shortstop and first baseman, she must cover a large portion of the infield area. The discussion on backing up found in the section on defensive

(10–11) The baseplayer must be prepared to reach for throws.

(10)

(11)

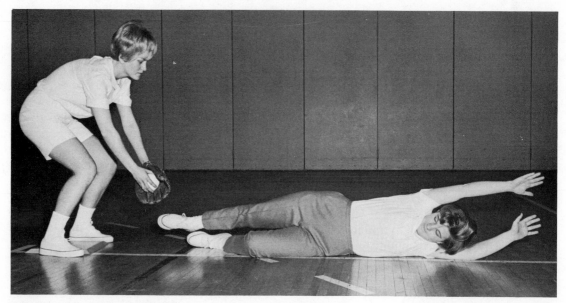

(12) Baseman receiving ball on slide.

strategy points up the need for this type of teamwork.

The *third baseman* should be quick and accurate as a fielder. She must have the ability to make long throws which frequently cover the greatest infield distance, the area from third to first base.

Skills for Offense

Offensive skills are divided into batting and baserunning. The strategy of baserunning requires learning how to lead off and steal. Batting includes power hits and bunting.

BATTING

Bats are selected according to weight and size of the grip. Heavier bats give greater power and distance, but require more strength than the lighter bats.

Grips

The bat is gripped firmly in both hands at the handle. The batter's right hand is above the left. Left-handed batters reverse the hand position.

The *three grip positions* are standard, choke, and long. As batting skills develop, grip variations may be explored. Beginners ordinarily use the *standard grip*, which involves placement of the hands 1 inch from the end of the bat. This grip provides control and power. The *choke grip*

is used against fast pitching. The hands are placed 3 or 4 inches from the end of the bat handle. This shortens the length of the bat and the arc of the swing, providing for a faster swing. Bat control is still maintained, but some power is lost. The *long grip* involves hand placement at the end of the handle. This grip develops power because the bat is swung in a larger arc. Strong hitters use this grip.

Stance

The batter stands in the batter's box, squarely facing home plate (Fig. 13). Her feet are placed side by side with the weight balanced on the balls of the feet. The foot toward the pitcher is opposite the center of home plate; the back foot is placed about a hip's width from the forward foot. The distance the batter stands from home plate depends on the length of the player's arms. The batter holds the bat out and over home plate with the tip end of the bat reaching the far edge of the plate. When the bat is swung, the heaviest part swings over the center of the plate. With head turned toward the pitcher, the batter focuses on the ball in the pitcher's hands, and the bat is held up, back, and away from the body. The hands are at shoulder level with the elbows flexed and away from the body. The wrists are cocked. The bat slants backward at a 35-degree angle. The tip or heavy end of the bat points up. The shoulders are partially rotated. They are swung backward only as far as the batter can

(13) Batting position: waiting for the pitch.

(14) Batter and catcher.

comfortably move them without changing her head position.

Swing

The swing starts as the pitched ball approaches home plate. The batter partially shifts the weight to the back foot and leg. The left arm starts the swing and pulls the bat around and forward; the right arm follows and controls the swing. The bat is swung parallel to the ground. As the bat contacts the ball, the wrists uncock or straighten. The arms and wrists become fully extended as the shoulders and hips start to rotate forward, and the weight is transferred from the back foot to both feet.

The swing continues into a follow-through as the ball rebounds from the bat. The wrists roll over after the ball is contacted; the right palm turns downward and the left upward as the bat swings around the player. The hips and shoulders continue to rotate forward, and the weight transfers to the forward foot with the back foot still remaining in contact with the ground. The follow-through is completed when the elbows bend with the force of the swing, left elbow in toward the body. The bat points backward and slightly upward.

SUGGESTIONS FOR SKILL IMPROVEMENT IN BATTING. Beginners tend to grip the bat too tightly. The grip should be firm, but not tense. Batters must keep the elbows away from the body at the start and during the forward swing. If a right-handed batter keeps the right elbow close to the body, the swing tends to direct the ball upward. The left arm kept against the side makes the batter hit down on the ball.

Beginners tend to swing the bat with just the arms. Power and force must be generated by weight transfer and hip rotation. Weight balanced on both feet is acceptable at the start of the swing, but the weight must be transferred to the back foot during the backswing. It takes time to transfer the weight to the back foot, and this may cause the beginning batter to swing too late. The shift toward the back foot must be started as the ball approaches.

Some batters step into the ball on the hit. This takes time and may not be possible if the pitcher throws fast balls. Against medium-speed pitches, the step action generates force because more body weight is put into the swing. The feet are together while waiting for the pitch; then the left foot slides forward during the swing. The weight transfers to this forward foot during the hit and on the follow-through.

BUNTING

A bunt is a short hit. Instead of swinging the bat, the batter lets the ball strike the bat, or "catches" the ball with the bat, so that the flight of the ball will be brief, causing it to land within the infield.

The bunter assumes the regular batting stance. As the ball approaches home plate, the batter shifts the weight to both feet. The bat position is suddenly changed with the upper hand sliding up the bat to the trademark while the lower hand remains in the original position. The upper hand grips the bat lightly with the fingers underneath and back of the bat and the thumb on top. The bat must be moved into position before the ball arrives if the bat is to block the ball (Fig. 15).

(15) Bunting position.

The body is slightly crouched with the weight forward on the balls of the feet. The bat is moved to a position parallel to the ground at right angles to the path of the ball. The arms are relaxed, slightly bent at the elbows, and held well away from the body. As the ball approaches, the body is raised or lowered by bending or straightening the knees and hips to adjust the bat to the level of the ball. Because balls that are too high or too low should not be bunted, the batter needs to make only minor adjustments.

The batter lets the bat give on contact with the ball, attempting to "deaden" the impact. The ball can be directed toward first base or third base. The right-handed batter moves the left hand forward to angle the bat toward first base. The reverse is true for a bunt directed toward third.

A bat held too tightly during the bunt causes the ball to rebound, making a fly ball likely.

Discussion of the use of the bunt is included in the section, "General Play for Offense."

BASERUNNING

The responsibilities of the baserunner, including the lead off and the steal, are essential offensive skills.

Run to first

The moment the batter hits or bunts she should run toward first, attempting to get to first before the defenders can throw to that base. If the runner decides she can make only one base, she goes full speed, touches first, and without breaking her stride over-runs the base. She then turns to the right to return to the base without liability of being put out.

The baserunner aims to touch the base line side of the first base. She avoids running over the center of the base or jumping or leaping onto it.

A batter should always run to first even though she feels the defenders may get the ball to the base before her arrival. Baserunners should never give up, for the defense may make a mistake.

Running to second base or beyond

If a baserunner thinks she can advance more than one base following her hit, her approach to first changes. The baserunner runs toward first by curving out to her right, then in toward first base and in the direction of second. She attempts to hit the inside edge of first base on the run. The inside edge of the base is the corner toward home plate. The baserunner does not break her stride but runs on toward second. If she feels she can run to another base she approaches each base in the same way. The run pathway curves out, then in toward the inside corner of the base and in the direction of the next base.

The steal and advance

Players advance from base to base on hits, pitches, or throws to other bases. The rules allow baserunners to advance from base to base when the ball is in play, i.e., whenever it is in the playing area. The rules do not allow a baserunner to advance when the pitcher is standing on the pitcher's plate with the ball.

If the baserunner's advance to another base is made without the aid of a hit, force-out, or put-out, it is called a steal. The speed of the runner is a factor in determining whether a steal should be attempted. Stealing may be accomplished when the catcher misses the pitch or when an overthrow is made to a base. Other opportunities for stealing include a slow throw from outfield, a long throw from a catcher with a weak throwing arm, or a play at another base.

First to second base is a frequently used steal, attempted as soon as the pitch leaves the pitcher's hand. Before she attempts a steal, the runner must be sure that no runner is on the next base unless a double steal is to be tried.

Lead-off

The baserunner faces home plate with the left foot touching the edge of the base. As soon as the pitcher releases the ball, the baserunner leads off toward the next base. A lead-off of one or two steps places the player in a position to advance to the next base or, if necessary, to return to the base she just left. It is used whether the baserunner advances on a hit, intentionally steals, or returns to the base.

Sliding

Sliding is a skill used by a baserunner attempting to touch base before being tagged. In addition to helping the runner evade the tag, the slide is a useful tactic to avoid over-running the bases. The player should wear slacks to protect her legs if she plans to slide. Two common slides are the straight-in and the hook; the hook slide is a skill for advanced players.

The *straight-in slide* is a foot-first body action (Fig. 10). The runner moves toward a base and takes off on either foot. She pushes from the take-off foot, raises the other leg off the ground, then bends the take-off leg as the upper part of the body is thrown backward. The upper leg and the thigh of the take-off leg absorb the force of the fall. The slide momentum moves the body toward the base. The top foot reaches for the edge of the base and the lower leg remains bent. The torso and arms stretch back from the slide direction and the body is extended and stretched until momentum is lost. The higher the elevation, the more impact force developed; therefore it is essential to keep the body low on the take-off to avoid hard impact. The hands are kept above the head until most of the sliding momentum is lost. This prevents jarring the arm and elbow.

Players develop a favorite sliding side but as their skill develops they should be able to slide on either side.

General Play for Defense

POSITION RESPONSIBILITIES

Each defensive player should assume responsibility for a specific territory on the softball diamond. The players move forward, backward, left, and right, fielding balls hit to their territory (Fig. 16). The dotted lines mark the areas of responsibility. The zones overlap in order to cover the entire playing area completely and allow players to assist each other.

BACKING UP

Backing up is the movement of a teammate to a position behind the player attempting to field a ball. When any ball is hit, the player closest to the hit moves to field it. The nearest player moves to back up the fielder if she misses. There should be two or three players lined up in the direction of the batted ball. For example, balls hit toward third base are fielded by the third baseman. The short stop moves behind her, and the left fielder in turn backs up the short stop. Hits to the short stop are backed up by the third baseman or second baseman depending on whether the hit is closest to second or to third. The center fielder backs up the player behind the short stop. Throws to base also involve backing up by those fielders nearest the bases. The catcher is backed up by the pitcher on

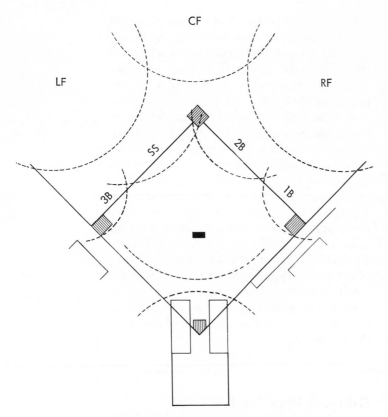

(16) Defense fielding zones or areas of responsibility.

field; fielders move closer to home plate when a weak hitter comes to bat.

Balls hit deep into the outfield may have to be relayed to a base. Fielders who can't throw long distances are assisted by an infielder. For example, a ball hit deep to centerfield is fielded by the center fielder. It is thrown part way to an infielder such as the short stop, who comes toward the outfield. She catches the fielder's throw and relays it to the appropriate spot in the infield. Throws coming great distances from outfielders are often affected by the wind. They also tend to slow down because they must be lofted. If throws are directed to home plate they should be aimed to take one bounce before reaching home plate. It is preferable to keep throws low so that the speed of the throw is preserved and wind effects minimized.

General Play for Offense

BATTING HINTS

Batters should swing only at good balls, but must be in position ready to swing on every pitch. If the pitch is bad, the batter must check her swing.

Batters have a better chance to hit curved balls if they move forward in the batter's box, because the pitcher tries to have curved balls "break" or curve over home plate. Moving forward enables batters to hit before the ball "breaks."

USE OF THE BUNT

A bunt is used to advance baserunners from one base to another. A bunt is also used as an element of surprise. This short hit may enable the bunter to get to first before the fielder's throw reaches the first baseman.

The baserunner's one- or two-step lead-off aids in the advance to the next base on a bunt. The defender must move into the ball and often has time enough only to throw to first base. In this case the bunter, if put out at first, has made a sacrifice hit. One of the best times to use a bunt is when first base is occupied by a runner and there are less than two outs. If the baserunner can advance to second base she is in a better position to score or get home. The next hit may bring her in to home plate.

PLACE HITTING

Place hitting is a bunting technique. Beginners

throws to home plate. The catcher backs up the first baseman on throws to first base if there is no runner on third base. Fielders also back each other up in the outfield.

Backing up demands teamwork and players need to practice this teamwork. With experience, the backing-up roles become automatic, and players know where they should move on every hit and throw to a base.

POSITION VARIATIONS

The positions of infielders and outfielders vary at times. The infielders ordinarily assume a ready position behind the base paths or base lines. However, when there are baserunners on second, third, or both, they play in front of the base line on the infield. This enables an infielder to field a ball more quickly because the hit does not travel as far before it is fielded.

Outfielders shift to the left or right on occasion. Left-handed batters tend to hit toward right field; therefore the outfielders move to the right. For right-handed batters, the outfielders move to the left. When a powerful hitter comes to bat, the outfielders move farther out into the may wish to explore this skill, but they cannot expect to become expert without a great deal of practice. Place hitting is accomplished by varying the foot position. Movement of the forward foot away from home plate causes the batter to meet the ball in front of the body. This directs the ball to the left side of the diamond. The reverse foot position causes the ball to be hit to right field.

COACHING

Players, acting as base coachers, can assist teammates by signaling for plays such as bunting and stealing. (Coaches' boxes are indicated in Figure 1.) Teams devise signals to indicate offensive plays to batters and base-runners. The base coach at first or third, in directing a steal, may signal the batter to bunt or to "take" (let the ball go by without an attempt to hit). An obvious place for the take signal would be when the batter has three "balls" (three bad pitches) to her credit. If the pitcher throws four "balls" before the batter is credited with three strikes, the batter walks to first.

Verbal directions and various subtle motions can be used for signaling baserunners and batters. Skill in designing and using signals contributes to the excitement of the game.

BATTING ORDER

Each batter has her turn at bat, in a pre-arranged lineup, until all players have batted. This batting order does not change. With each successive inning the same order is maintained, starting with the player next in the lineup. The order in which players bat can contribute to scoring runs. Careful selection of the first batter is important. She should be a girl to whom pitchers find it difficult to pitch. This is often a tall or short batter. The distance between arm-pits and knees is large or small depending on the batter's height. The pitcher may experience difficulty in making adjustments under these circumstances.

The second batter should be a good bunter and/or left-handed, and a good runner. If the first batter succeeds in becoming a baserunner, the next player may bunt. The purpose of the bunt is to advance the baserunner even at the expense of the batter. The left-handed batter stands closer to first base while batting, and may be able to get to first base on the bunt before the ball can be thrown.

The third batter should be a "sure-hitter." If the third batter has hit and the others have not scored but have advanced to the next base, a hit will bring at least one runner in. A solid hit may score more than one run.

The fifth batter should be similar to the first batter with the continuation of the foregoing order; or a variation of this batting order might alternate strong and weak batters after the first four have batted.

STRATEGY FOR OFFENSE

Two common strategy plays in softball are the hit and run and the squeeze play.

Hit and run

With a runner on first and no one out, the batter tries to hit into right field behind the base runner. The runner must start as the ball is pitched, and continue to second base, hoping to pull the second baseman toward second. This leaves an area for the hitter to place her hit. The batter attempts to hit, or at least swings at the ball, for even if she misses, her swing may slow the catcher's throw to second.

Squeeze play

The squeeze play is usually attempted late in a game when the score is close. It is used when a runner is on third and there are less than two outs. The batter bunts the ball and expects to be thrown out at first. The runner on third scores if the bunt is fielded and thrown to first.

If the runner waits to run until the ball is bunted, this play is called a safety squeeze. A perfect bunt is needed for the safety squeeze. If the runner runs as soon as the ball is pitched the play is called a running squeeze. A good bunt is not as necessary for the running squeeze but if the batter misses, the runner will undoubtedly be put out.

Rules

The Amateur Softball Association, through its International Joint Rules Committee, determines the rules of softball that govern play for both men and women. With the permission of this organization, the rules are printed in the *Softball Guide* published by the Division for Girls' and Women's Sports of the American Association for Health, Physical Education and Recreation.

Evaluation

The simplest evaluation procedure is to ask "did we win or lose, and why?" Individual players should ask themselves the following questions:

1. Did I play well with others? Did others play well with me?
2. Did I play my defensive position well? Field effectively? Throw effectively?
3. Did I hit well? Bunt well?
4. Did I run well? Steal when I could? Follow signals?
5. How can I improve my own skills?
6. Do I understand the rules?

A team should evaluate together asking such questions as these:

1. Did we play as a team, or as individuals?
2. Did we back each other up?
3. Did we throw to the proper place at the proper time?
4. Did we encourage each other?
5. Did we use the best batting order?
6. Did we hit, bunt, and respond to the coaches' signals?
7. What caused our errors?
8. How can we play together more effectively?
9. Did we lose or win gracefully and in a sportsmanlike manner?
10. Did we respond properly to the officials, and do we know the rules?

Terminology

Assist: Any defensive player who helps make an out is credited with an assist. For example, if a fielder throws to a baseplayer before the runner arrives, the baseplayer is credited with an assist.

Balk: If the pitcher starts to throw and stops, the batter is credited with a "ball," and baserunners advance one base without liability of being put out.

Ball: A pitched ball outside the strike zone not swung at by the batter.

Battery: The pitcher and catcher are called the battery.

Batting Average: The percentage calculated by dividing a batter's hits by the number of times at bat.

Double: A hit that allows the batter to run to second.

Double play: The defenders make two outs in succession as the result of continuous action.

Error: A misplay charged against a player which, with perfect play, would have resulted in an out for batter or baserunner.

Fair ball: A batted ball that settles or is touched by a player on fair ground between home and first, or between home and third; or falls in fair ground in the outfield.

Force out: A baserunner who must advance to the next base is forced out when the baseplayer catches the ball before her arrival. The baseplayer does not have to tag the runner but must touch the base.

Foul ball: A batted ball that settles outside home and first or home and third base lines, or passes outside these lines in the outfield.

Fungo hit: A ball batted by the batter, who tosses it into the air for her own hit (used in fielding practice).

Hot corner or **hot spot:** Third base, where the majority of balls are hit by right-handed hitters. Also so named because runners passing this base may score.

Illegal pitch: Improper wind-up, improper delivery such as a sidearm rather than underhand, and taking more than one step on delivery are examples of illegal pitches. The batter is credited with a ball.

Infield fly: A ball hit into the air in the infield that is, or could be, caught.

Inning: After each team has batted and made three outs the inning is completed. There are seven innings in a softball game.

Line drive: An aerial ball that is batted sharply and directly into the playing field.

No-hitter: One team is unable to make a safe hit during an entire game.

Overthrow: A throw that passes over the head of a defender into foul territory.

Passed ball: A pitched ball that should have been held or controlled by catcher.

Put out: Defensive action that makes batter or runner out.

Sacrifice: A hit that results in the batter being put out but advances a baserunner to the next base.

Singles: A hit that enables the batter to reach first base.

Slide: A baserunner's technique used to avoid being tagged when attempting to touch base.

Stolen base: An extra base taken legally and voluntarily by a runner.

Strike: A pitched ball thrown over home plate between the knees and shoulders of the batter. The ball may be struck at or not. A foul ball is a strike except on the third strike.

Texas leaguer: A fly ball, over the heads of infielders, which cannot be caught by outfielders.

Triple: A hit that enables the batter to reach third base.

Walk: The batter goes to first base as a result of four balls.

Wild pitch: Ball legally delivered so high, low, or wide of the plate that the catcher cannot handle it.

Selected References

DGWS Current Softball Guide. Washington, D.C.: American Assoc. for Health, Physical Education, and Recreation.

Kneer, Marian, ed. *Selected Softball Articles*. Washington, D.C.: American Assoc. for Health, Physical Education, and Recreation, 1962.

Meyer, Margaret, and Marguerite Schwartz. *Team Sports for Girls and Women*. Philadelphia: W. B. Saunders, 1965.

Paterson, Ann, ed. *Team Sports for Girls*. New York: Ronald Press, 1958.

Chapter 19

Volleyball *Calla Ann Raynor*

History. Goals. Equipment. Etiquette. Volley. Overhead Pass. Set-up. Two-Arm and One-Arm Bounce Pass. Serves. Spike. Block. Dig. Net Recovery. Practice Drills. Strategy. Rules. Mechanics of Movement. Evaluation. Terminology.

Volleyball is a team sport that provides an opportunity for participation and enjoyment by men and women, young and old. It can be a vigorous game requiring stamina, quick reaction time, strength, speed, and agility, or it can be a game played for its recreational values. The common denominator in all volleyball games is the enthusiasm of the players, whether they be novice or expert. The simplicity of the equipment (a net and a volleyball) and the modesty of the space requirements (any reasonably level area approximately 30 feet by 60 feet) make informal games a frequent occurrence on lawns, parks, beaches, playgrounds, and in recreational rooms as well as on athletic fields and in gymnasia.

The game consists of two teams of six players each. Modifications may be made to include as many as ten to twelve or as few as three to four on each side. The object of the game is to pass the ball over a net so that the opponents on the other side of the net cannot return it. This form of activity provides a wonderful opportunity to exercise as moderately or strenuously as desired while socializing with teammates and opponents. Volleyball can be played for a lifetime and can be a good coeducational activity.

History

After graduation from Springfield College in Massachusetts in 1895, William G. Morgan took a position as physical director of the Holyoke Young Men's Christian Association. The main activity was basketball, a relatively strenuous sport for the businessmen who used the facilities of the gymnasium. In 1896 at a YMCA Conference at Springfield College, Mr. Morgan publicized a new game. A net 6 feet, 6 inches was stretched across the gymnasium; for a ball, the bladder from a basketball was used. The main object of this new game was to hit the ball back and forth over the net with the hands. The game was started with a serve; the server was allowed three "outs," after which the opposite team was permitted to serve. To constitute an out, the ball had to land out-of-bounds or hit the floor on a second bounce. The game was introduced as "Mintonette"; but after watching the game, a faculty member of Springfield College, Dr. A. T. Halstead, recommended that the name be changed to volleyball. Shortly after the game's invention, Mr. Morgan drew up specifications for a special

Miss Raynor, an instructor in physical education at Duke University, received her bachelor's degree at the University of North Carolina at Greensboro and her master's degree at the University of North Carolina at Chapel Hill. Miss Raynor has been active in DGWS as State Coordinator of the Officiating Services Area and as Secretary-Treasurer of her area Officials Rating Board.

ball, and these specifications are still used for the official volleyball.

By 1912 several rule changes had been made. These included raising the net to 7 feet, 6 inches, eliminating the bounce and innings, setting the game at fifteen points, and rotating the players.

The game spread throughout the YMCA and also became very popular with schools, colleges, playgrounds, and the armed forces. In 1929, the United States Volleyball Association was formed. This organization determines the rules and sponsors competition for both men's and women's teams. Volleyball, in terms of the number of people participating throughout the world, ranks third among the team sports, and it is the leading competitive sport in at least twenty-five countries.

Goals

Much can be achieved in a game of volleyball. The average person can play the game for fun, relaxation, and exercise; the more active athlete can play for a strenuous workout. The desire to win need not stifle other objectives. The game requires skill, endurance, coordination, physical alertness, and muscular activity.

A spirit of self-reliance and discipline is expected in the game of volleyball. A player who barely touches the net without being seen by the official has a choice to make. This is a test of moral fiber. Admission of the foul may lose the game; but the standard of conduct is high in this sport and a hand should go up immediately, even though there is no rule requiring the player to admit this infraction.

In a volleyball class that lasts about seven weeks, one should be able to develop the following abilities:

1. Perform most skills of the game, including one or two methods of serving, overhead pass, set-up, volley, two-arm bounce pass, spike, block, dig, and recovery of the ball from the net.
2. Know the rules of the game.
3. Be a member of a team, always ready to assist teammates.
4. Be able to develop strategy for both offense and defense.
5. Understand mechanics of the movements involved in order to be able to analyze performance and work for self-improvement.

Skills are very important for providing enjoyment and effective play. When players are on the court, the only way to ensure control and skilled performance is to practice the fundamentals of the game. A few weeks of practice on basic skills and drills for teamwork can eliminate many errors and later provide many points for the team.

Equipment and Facilities

THE COURT

A volleyball court is a rectangle measuring 60 feet by 30 feet; it may be situated either indoors or out. Stretched across the center of the court from side line to side line is a net, with an official height of 7 feet $4\frac{1}{4}$ inches from top of net to floor. The net is made of heavy thread so that repeated contact of the ball on the net will not destroy the mesh.

The ideal out-of-doors court is smooth, level, and free from obstructions over the court; indoors it is often difficult to avoid hanging fixtures or equipment overhead. In such a case, ground rules should be established to take care of occasions when the ball hits the overhead obstructions.

THE BALL

The volleyball is a round ball with a standard weight and circumference. It should not be kicked, sat on, or hit onto rough surfaces.

CLOTHING

The wearing apparel of the participants needs to allow for free movement because much bending, stooping, reaching, jumping, and stretching is required in the game. When competing, members of a team usually wear the same type of costume.

Etiquette, Good Sportsmanship, and Safety

Volleyball is not so quiet and restrained as games such as tennis and golf. It is often necessary to talk to your team members during the course of play to tell them what you plan to do. Two players may need to decide quickly who is going to make a play on a ball coming over the net. A call of "mine" to your teammates signals that you will attempt to play the ball and for them to move out of the way. If you are attempting to set up a ball to a teammate, you can call her attention to this fact by calling her name. During a highly competitive game it is not unusual for the two teams to display their enthusiasm with cheering and clapping. This adds spirit and challenge to the game and contributes to a relaxed atmosphere.

A spirit of self-reliance and discipline is expected in a game of volleyball. It is an unwritten rule, but one regularly observed, that players call their own fouls. For example, a player who touches the net, or touches a ball going out of bounds, raises her hand to indicate a fault.

It is good etiquette to pass the ball under the net to the serving team and to compliment them on their good plays.

There is no excuse for a display of bad temper either on or off the court. The officials are placed on either side of the court to look for and call rule infractions. They should be competent, well trained, know the rules, and be able to handle a game with ease. Players should not argue with the officials over decisions. If there is a disagreement there are proper channels through which a protest is filed. Decisions of the officials are final in the interpretation of rules. If the captain of a team wishes to protest the decision involving an interpretation, she must immediately notify the official that a protest will be filed.

Running over into an adjacent court to retrieve a ball is not necessary and may interfere with another game. The players on that court will return the ball to you at their earliest convenience.

The following safety factors are important:

1. Warm-up before playing, as well as a daily routine of warm-up exercises, may help to eliminate jammed fingers, pulled muscles, and sprained ankles.
2. Before playing, all extra balls and any other equipment should be removed from the court.
3. When playing indoors all players should wear socks and rubber-soled shoes. Playing in bare feet can result in blisters, whereas playing in stocking feet causes one to slip.
4. While playing outdoors, tennis shoes should be worn as protection against rocks, broken glass, or any objects which might cause injury; the rubber soles will also reduce the likelihood of slipping.
5. Jewelry, pencils, pens, and other sharp objects should be removed from one's person.
6. Glasses guards should be worn by those who need them.

Skills

VOLLEY

To volley a ball is to hit it into the air without first letting it bounce. Because the rules of volleyball permit three contacts with the ball before sending it over the net, the ball should be volleyed to teammates for spiking and for strategic placement to the opponents. A pass or set-up should be high and controlled to allow one's teammate time to position herself for an effective play. Making a quick, low pass to a teammate is evidence that one was caught unprepared or needs to practice this skill.

Volleyball rules require that the ball must be clearly batted; it may not visibly come to rest at contact. Therefore, in volleying the ball, it must be hit; the player must avoid catching, holding, throwing, or lifting.

Overhead pass

The overhead pass is used when playing a ball above chest level. It is used to pass a ball from one teammate to another or as a set-up preceding a spike. The pass is used to move the ball from one place to another on the court, whereas the set-up is used to put the ball high and close to the net in the most advantageous position for a spike.

To execute an overhead pass the hands are held above the hairline and forward with palms up and thumbs and index fingers almost touching (Fig. 1). The hands form a diamond or window through which the ball may be seen. The fingers are spread, relaxed, and flexed. The wrists are bent slightly back, elbows are bent and raised to shoulder level. If the elbows are too far out or too close to the body, this causes the index fingers or thumbs to separate. The feet should be in a forward stride position, one foot in front of the other, and knees slightly bent. The ball should be contacted with the fleshy part of the fingers, not the palms. As the ball is contacted, force is applied by straightening the elbows and knees, snapping the wrists forward, and shifting the weight to the forward foot. This puts the body in a straight line, leaning in the direction of the pass (Fig. 2).

(1) Start.

(2) Follow-through.

(1–2) Overhead pass.

Set-up

The set-up is somewhat like the overhead pass, inasmuch as the ball is contacted with the hands in front of the face or higher, but it covers less distance and must be placed more accurately. A set-up precedes a spike; therefore on the set-up the ball must be placed above the level of the net but close to the net. Accuracy is very important. The player usually sets-up to the person on her left. This means that the spiker has the ball on her right side and does not have to reach across her body, whereas the player on the right would have to let the ball cross from the left side of her body to the right before she could execute the spike.

On a set-up the ball should be hit high enough to allow the spiker to get into position to play the ball. To make a good set-up, get under the ball with the palms of the hands forward, head bent back, knees and fingers flexed, and elbows away from the body. The player making the set-up should face in the direction toward which she is placing the ball (Fig. 3).

The set-up should simulate the effect of the ball being dropped from above. The ideal

(3) Set-up.

(6) The knees straighten as the ball rebounds from the surface of the arms. **(5)** Meeting the ball with the forearms. **(4)** Preparation.

(4–6) Two-arm bounce pass.

placement is about 5 feet above the top of the net and 16 inches away from it.

Two-arm bounce pass

The two-arm bounce pass is used to play balls that have dropped below shoulder level (such as serves) and balls that have been spiked or need to be recovered from the net (Figs. 4, 5, and 6). To execute this pass, the player must take a position in line with the ball to be received. The feet are in a side-stride position with the knees flexed. The hands are clasped, one within the other, and the thumbs are in the palm of the top hand. The elbows are extended, pointing toward the floor, and the inside surface of the arms rotated upward to obtain the flattest surface possible. The arms and elbows should be close together. On contact, the ball rebounds from the forearms at the same time that the knees straighten to give added impetus. The legs are most important to the action; they do most of the work. The ball merely rebounds from the arms.

One-arm bounce pass

The purpose of the one-arm bounce pass is to get low balls that go to one side of a player back into the air and passed to a teammate. This technique is not so easy to control as the two-arm bounce pass, and should be used only when it is impossible to get into position to use both arms. Occasionally there is not time to take the better position but one must be alert and ready to move.

For the one-arm bounce pass, the player must step toward the ball with the foot opposite the arm to be used for the pass. The knees are flexed to lower the body as much as is needed to retrieve the ball. Contact with the ball should be made by the wrist and cupped heel of the hand or fist so that the ball will rebound back to a teammate (Fig. 7).

SKILLS FOR OFFENSE

Serves

The game is started with a serve. Because this gives the team a chance to score points, the server should have some definite plan in mind to take advantage of the opportunity. The server, the person in the right back position, stands anywhere behind the end line provided she is no farther from the end line than 6 feet. Then she puts the ball into play by using one of the following serves.

UNDERHAND SERVE. The underhand serve,

(7) One-arm bounce pass.

similar to the underhand throw in softball, is the simplest and easiest serve to control and receive. This serve does not travel with great force. It usually goes over the net in a high looping arc. To get into position, the server stands behind the end line facing the net, the left foot ahead of the right (right-handed player) in a stride position, and the knees slightly bent. This allows for a shift in body weight, which is needed for added impetus. The ball is held in the left hand, about waist high, and toward the right side of the body. The

body is bent slightly forward so that when contact is made and the body straightens, this too will add impetus to the serve (Fig. 8). The right hand strikes the ball with the heel of the open hand or a closed fist. In either case the palm of the hand is toward the net. The right arm, fully extended for greater leverage, is taken back as the body is bent forward. The weight is transferred to the right foot during this movement. After the arm reaches the peak of the backswing, the arm and the body weight move forward. As contact is made the ball leaves the left hand in an arc great enough to carry the ball over the net into the opponents' court. On the follow-through, as the arm continues to swing forward-upward toward the point of aim, the server moves forward into her own court.

OVERHEAD SERVE. The overhead serve, which is much like a tennis serve, is more powerful than the underhand and more difficult to receive. With practice, the player should be able to control this serve and learn to impart top spin to the ball.

For the overhead serve the player positions herself behind the end line facing the net with the feet in a forward stride position. Coordination is very important because the left and right hands must work together for an effective serve. The left hand, holding the ball, tosses it up at arm's length in front of the right shoulder and

(8) Underhand serve.

(9) Overhead serve.

2 or 3 feet above the head as the weight shifts to the rear foot. At the same time, the right arm is swung back of the head with elbow bent and wrist cocked (in a position similar to throwing a ball overhand), ready to swing the arm forward into the ball. Accompanying the backward arm swing with a body pivot gives additional power. With the ball overhead, the weight is shifted to the forward foot and the serving arm is fully extended as contact is made by the heel of the hand or a flat fist (Fig. 9). On the follow-through the elbow is straight and wrist flexed. The player continues moving forward to return to her position in the court.

This serve should clear the net in a low trajectory with great speed. To add topspin to the ball, contact should be made with the heel of the hand and a wrist snap forward. Combined with the elbow extension, this enables the cupped hand to move, from initial contact at the back, up and over the top of the ball.

SIDEARM SERVE. Like the overhead serve, the sidearm serve is powerful and difficult to receive. This serve goes over the net into a downward trajectory.

The server positions herself behind the end line in a forward stride position with the left side toward the net. The ball is held in the left hand in front of the body and over or slightly ahead of the left foot. The body is not bent forward as much as in the underhand serve. The right arm, fully extended, is taken back to approximately shoulder level and there is a shift of weight to the rear foot. Then the right arm moves forward, as does the body weight, and contact is made with the ball with either the heel of the hand or a closed fist (Fig. 10). The follow-through is in the direction in which the ball is to travel, after which the player returns immediately to the court in position to play.

ROUNDHOUSE SERVE. For the roundhouse serve the player positions herself behind the end line in a forward stride with the left side toward the net. The ball is tossed into the air as the weight is shifted to the rear foot and the trunk twists to the right. The toss is slightly above and behind the right shoulder. As the ball begins to fall, the weight is shifted forward and contact is made with a cupped hand and straight arm (Fig. 11). The heel of the hand contacts the ball first, and topspin is added to this serve by having the fingers pass over the top of the ball. Topspin causes the ball to rotate or spin toward the net as it travels, and the spin governs the arc at which the ball passes over the net. The hips swing around and are parallel to the

(10) Sidearm serve.

(11) Roundhouse serve.

net on the follow-through. This serve requires much practice in order to get the needed amount of spin on the ball.

FLOATER OVERHEAD SERVE. The floater serve differs from the overhead serve in that the ball does not spin on the former. The left hand tosses the ball upward without spin as the right arm is brought backward slightly higher than shoulder level with the elbow bent; then the right arm is thrust forward to contact the ball. The elbow leads forward, as in throwing, until contacting the ball in front of the body; the arm is extended as the ball is hit. In order to have the ball float, it must be contacted squarely in a straight forward swing to the center of the ball. As the right arm is straightened, the body weight must be shifted forward to give power to the serve. Follow-through to a straight arm position.

This serve requires coordination and the use of the entire body for successful performance. The floater serve is difficult for opponents to pass because of its irregular flight.

Offensive volley

The offensive volley may be used as a lead-up to learning the spike, and it may be used in the game by the short player who will never be able to spike.

For this volley the forward stands with side to the net, approximately 3 feet from the net. The ball is sent low and fast over the net to the desired placement in the opponent's court. The forward may or may not jump for this volley, depending on her height and the height of the set-up. However, if the forward is short, she will probably have to jump to avoid sending the ball into the net.

The hand away from the net is used to hit the ball. A half circle is made as the arm is brought up from the side of the body and over the head to the position where contact is made (Fig. 12). The fingers or the heel of the hand may be used to direct the ball over the net. In either case there must be a clean hit, never letting the ball come to rest on the hand. The heel of the hand provides more power and less tendency to push the ball. The follow-through continues in the direction in which the ball is to travel, but the player must be careful to avoid touching the net.

Spike

In the spike the ball is hit forcefully at a sharp angle into the opponent's court. This offensive technique is a thrilling and effective

(12) Offensive volley.

play when skillfully done. To execute a spike, there must first be a high and well-placed set-up. The person making the set-up and the spiker must practice the timing together.

Two different court positions can be used in spiking. In the first position the forward stands about 3 feet from the net, facing the set-up player. Anticipating the spike, the player takes a crouch position with knees bent. In the second position for spiking, the forward stands near the side line and about 10 feet back from the net. The person on the left of the set-up player usually spikes the ball because this places the ball on the spiker's right side, thus the ball does not have to cross her body. The spiker starts her approach as the set-up is made. When the spiker is about 3 feet from the ball, she jumps with a push-off from both feet. Some players prefer to use a one-foot take-off, but using both feet allows more opportunity for change of direction with the body if this is needed at the last moment. In any event it is important to jump up instead of forward.

The movements of the spike are the same regardless of starting position. The spiker coordinates her jump with the set-up; as the ball starts to descend, she springs into the air and swings her spiking arm overhead and behind

(13) The spike.

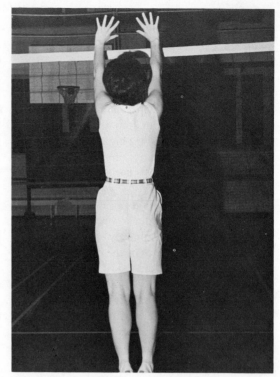

(14) Preparing for the block.

her shoulder as she rotates her body toward the net. The elbow is bent and wrist cocked; then, as the spiking hand contacts the ball, the arm straightens with a powerful thrust on the top of the ball. Contact is made with the heel of the cupped hand or a flat, firm hand rather than the fingertips (Fig. 13). The ball is forced downward at an angle into the opponent's court.

The spiking hand may follow through over the net so long as there is no contact of any part of the body or clothing with the net. When landing from a spike, the player should land on the toes, roll back on the heels, and flex the ankles and knees. This allows the body to absorb the shock.

SKILLS FOR DEFENSE

Block

The defensive skill used against the spike is the block. The objective is to block the spike at the top of the net immediately after it has been hit. If the blocker is to succeed with this technique, she must concentrate on timing. The blocker watches the spiker's movements and jumps just a split-second later than the spiker.

The blocker takes her position facing the net opposite the set-up for the spike. As she jumps, the elbows are straight and both arms are

extended overhead with palms and heels of hands thrust slightly forward, thumbs together, and fingers spread (Fig. 14). If the hands are in position and timing is correct, the ball should rebound to the opposite side of the net without use of any follow-through. The player who is blocking must not reach over the net to contact the ball. In order to be assured that the block is successful, it is not unusual for two adjacent players on the same team to attempt the jump and block at the same time. To coordinate their action, the two blockers should touch elbows or hips and then jump together.

Dig

The dig, sometimes referred to as the bump or bounce, is a useful defensive skill for recovery of the ball close to the floor. It is effective with a fast, hard driven ball such as a serve, offensive volley, or spike, because it enables one to "save" and gain control, usually by passing to a teammate. (Details of form are given under the section on one- and two-arm bounce passes.)

Net recovery

Recovering the ball from the net is an important volleyball skill, and timing and alertness are essential in performing this skill. Because the volleyball net is stretched tightly across the court, the ball rebounds when it hits the net. A ball hitting the top of the net slides down the net and will not rebound with as much force as one hitting a lower area of the net. The force and angle with which the ball hits the net also determine the amount of rebound. To retrieve a ball hitting near the top of the net, the player must move close to the net. With more rebound from the lower part of the net, the player may be several feet from the net and still make a good recovery.

After the ball drops free of the net, the player hits the ball upward with the heel of the hand, closed fist, or the one- or two-hand dig. The knees are bent to adjust body position to the height of the ball as it rebounds or drops free of the net; the feet are in a forward stride (Fig. 17).

In recovering a second contact ball from the net, the one-hand dig can be used to send the ball over the net if it has rebounded enough to be redirected up and over. The play is difficult. The ball has lost momentum, and arm movement into the ball is required to provide impetus. Care must be taken to avoid lifting or holding the ball.

(15) Preparing to meet the ball. **(16)** The ball rebounds from the fore-arms.

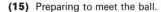

(15–16) The two-handed dig.

Drills

In all drills the principles of body mechanics must be observed in order to maintain control of the ball. The body must be balanced, in good alignment, and have a wide enough stance to permit freedom of movement.

Overhead pass: Player number 1 passes the ball to player 2, and so on down the line until it reaches player 6. Player 6 reverses the action by sending the ball back to player five and on up the line (Fig. 18).

1. Players get into a circle with player 0 in the center. Player 0 passes the ball to each player who must return the ball to the center player. Take turns in center position (Fig. 19).
2. Player 0 sets the ball straight into the air and moves back quickly so player 1 can come in and set the ball up high for player 2 to run in, and so on. This is a good drill for height and control.

Set-up:

1. See 2 under "Overhead pass."
2. Using the basketball goals in the gym, have

(17) Recovery from the net.

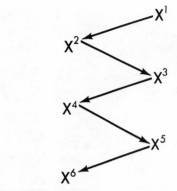

(18) Overhead pass drill.

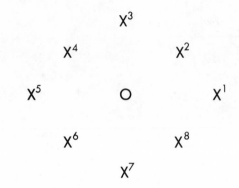

(19) Overhead pass in circle.

(20) Bounce pass drill.

the set-up players hit the ball up high enough to put the ball in the basket. Be sure the players stand to the side of the basket in the same position as they would for the set-up to a spiker.

Bounce pass:

1. Player 1 passes the ball to player 2 so that it is received below the waist. Player 2 uses a two-arm bounce pass, then moves to end of her line. Procedure repeated with players 3, 4, and so on. Players 6–9 retrieve the ball (Fig. 20).

2. Player 1 tosses to the left or right side of player 2 so that she can use a one-arm bounce pass. Players rotate positions.

Serve . . . and Receive: Players face each other behind the end lines and serve over the net using the different serves. Players should assist each other in analyzing form and technique (Fig. 21).

Players 0, the servers, serve to players 1, 2, and 3. The various serves may be practiced. The person receiving the ball makes a pass forward to another player, thus practicing receiving and passing. After five serves, the server and other players rotate positions (Fig. 22).

Spike: The spike drill should be done at the net, and space is needed for moving into the spike. Two or three other drills should be in progress in the gym so that players may rotate and take turns at the net. Players X set up and players 0 come in for the spike. The players on the other side retrieve the ball. After some skill is attained in the spike, let players Y come in and block. Rotate positions (Fig. 23).

Block: See foregoing spike drill.

Dig: Players X throw the ball forcefully toward the feet of players 0. Players 0 "dig" the ball back into play toward players X. Repeat and rotate positions (Fig. 24).

Net Recovery: Players X throw the ball into the net and players 0 make the net recovery. Watch the ball and work on timing. Rotate positions (Fig. 25).

Strength

The volleyball player needs strength in the fingers, forearms, and shoulders. It would be helpful to practice the following exercises daily:

1. Squeeze a tennis ball in the right hand, then the left.
2. Push away from a wall: stand about 18 inches from a wall and lean forward, placing the fingertips on the wall at shoulder level. Keep the body straight while bending the elbows so that the face is close to the wall, then give a strong thrust with the fingers in order to straighten the elbows. Gradually increase the number of repetitions, and move the feet farther away from the wall.
3. Do push-ups to the knees by pushing away from the floor with the weight on the fingertips rather than on the whole hand.

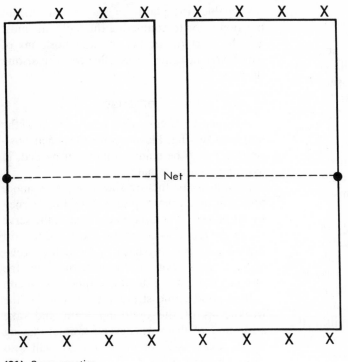

(21) Serve practice.

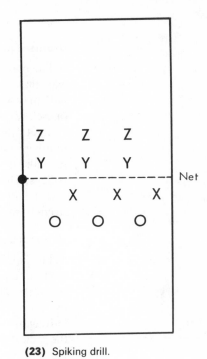

(23) Spiking drill.

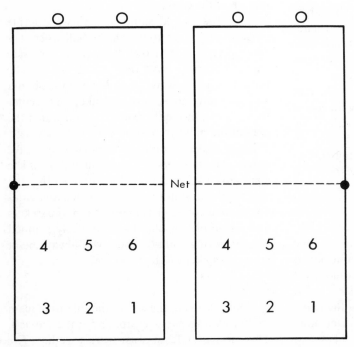

(22) Serve and pass.

O O O   O O O   O O O

X   X   X

(24) The dig.

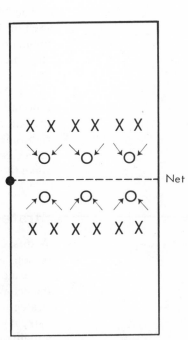

(25) Net recovery practice.

Overhead pass

The player volleys the ball above a line on the wall that is the height of a volleyball net. The ball may be put into motion by tossing it to oneself or tossing it against the wall; every contact after that should be a volley. Score the number of volleys accomplished in thirty seconds, or try to achieve 25 or 50 consecutive volleys. The same drill can be performed with a soccer ball or basketball to develop additional strength in the fingers, wrists, and arms.

Two-arm bounce pass

The ball is tossed against the wall and permitted to bounce on the floor after it rebounds from the wall. Then the player positions herself to use the two-hand bounce pass in volleying the ball against the wall. As the player gains skill, the same drill can be used without permitting the ball to bounce on the floor. Beginners may bounce-pass the ball to the wall at any height, but as practice continues, they should work toward getting the ball above the height of the net.

One-arm bounce pass

Use the same drill as for the two-arm bounce pass and practice using both right and left arms.

Spike

The correct technique for spiking should be used in this drill. Hold the ball in the left hand about eye level and in front of the right shoulder; then hit the ball on top with as much force as possible. The ball should be directed downward to hit the floor near the wall and, as the ball rebounds from the wall, the player again spikes the ball before it bounces. Keep the ball to the right side of the body and hit down from as high as one can reach. Practice toward being able to spike the ball twenty consecutive times.

Strategy

With six players on a volleyball team, no one person can win the game alone; everyone has to make a contribution. When the ball comes over the net, returning it immediately is seldom good strategy. Skill and thought in playing the game make it varied and challenging for all. One must anticipate ball action just before it happens;

this enables the player to start to move into position prior to contacting the ball. One must also be alert to the actions and positions of teammates in order to be effective in assisting them.

OFFENSE

A team is on offense when it has control of the ball or is serving. Players must play their positions and also be ready to move, if needed, in assisting their teammates.

Inasmuch as the overhead serve is more powerful than other types, it should be learned by all players. The best places to aim the serve are in the rear corners of the court and toward the sidelines midway back in the court. However, if these spots are well covered by the opponents, the serve should be aimed elsewhere.

It is good game strategy to watch for the weaknesses of the opposing team and take advantage of them whenever possible. Playing to the weaknesses of another team will also show up their faults so that they can benefit from further practice.

Positions on the court for offense

The forwards should position themselves about 3 feet back from the net. The players in the back court should play about halfway between the net and the end line with the center back playing a little farther forward to cover the middle of the court.

Forwards should stand in a forward stride position and pivot to watch the ball when it is being played in their own back court. The side forwards should have their backs to the side lines in order to watch the play of the ball and still be ready to set-up or spike. The center forward can face either side line and watch the play of the ball over a shoulder.

Every player should be a capable offensive player. The tall person has an advantage if she learns to spike, but this does not mean that the short person cannot become a skilled and valuable team member. The placement of the spikers and set-up players should be carefully planned so that during rotation there will always be at least one spiker on the front row.

Team play

Upon receiving the serve, the offensive team should plan to pass, set-up, and spike the ball. This means the team must work together. The set-up player should be situated on the right side of the spiker. The person who receives the ball should make her pass to the set-up player, and the pass must be high enough to give the set-up player time to get into position under the ball. Although the pass should be accurate, height will sometimes cover up inaccuracy because of the extra time it allows. Upon receiving a pass, a player should make the set-up for the spike. Then her teammate's effective placement of the spike depends on the abilities and location of members of the opposing team. Opponents known to be effective blockers should be avoided and, if possible, the ball should be sent to an open place.

DEFENSE

The team that is not making a play on the ball is on defense and each member of this team must react according to the actions of the team on offense. Each player has an area on the court for which she is responsible. If a teammate is pulled out of position, the closest player should shift to help cover that position.

Forwards should stay approximately 3 feet from the net and the center forward may move sideward to help a side forward defend a spike. One player may be able to handle a block, but it is safer for two players to cover together. The center forward is always one of the two players to cover; the players jump shoulder to shoulder to coordinate their efforts and angle their hands toward opposite side lines so that a greater angle of play is possible. However, a forward should not stray far from her position because she may interfere with the back line players and there is always danger that she will not be in position to receive a pass.

The players in the back line should move up to the middle of the court after receiving the serve. This will enable them to better recover spikes. Playing in midcourt forces the spiker to make more errors when trying to direct the ball away from these players.

Receiving the serve

A team may agree to have the forwards move back about 6 feet away from the net while the opponents are serving. This allows the backs to play deeper where serves frequently land. A forward should not attempt to receive a serve if it is over her head; instead, she should leave the play for her back line teammate.

BODY POSITIONING

The player should always be in a state of readiness. The feet should be in a forward stride position with knees flexed and weight on the balls of the feet. The arms should be up, moving toward the ball. The player in the best position to play the ball should let her teammates know of her intentions by simply saying "mine," and the other players should move aside, positioning themselves to be of assistance if needed.

Rules

Volleyball rules, determined by the United States Volleyball Association, are printed in the USVBA Guide and in the DGWS Volleyball Guide (see reference list). Some of the basic rules follow.

PLAYERS

1. Six players make up a volleyball team. A game may not begin or be continued if a team has less than six players.
2. The player who is to serve the ball must stand out-of-bounds behind the end line. All other players must stand inside the boundaries of the court and be in their own position when the ball is served.
3. A player may go outside the boundary lines of the court to play a ball.
4. Players must remain in the same rotation order throughout a game, but may change positions prior to the beginning of another game.

SUBSTITUTES

1. A player may enter the game twice. Starting the game counts as one entry.
2. A substitute must report to the scorer and referee before entering the game. Fifteen seconds is allowed for substitution.
3. The substitute must take the position of the player she is replacing.

THE GAME

1. Before the game begins, the captains from each team meet with the official, and a coin is tossed. The winner of the toss chooses the serve or the preferred side of the court. After the first game, the team that lost serves first.
2. After the first game and at the middle of the

third, the teams change sides of the net. The middle of the third game is determined by eight points or four minutes of play, whichever occurs first. The serving order may not be changed during the change of courts.

3. A match consists of winning two out of three games.

4. The game is started with a serve by the player in the right back position.

5. A team must serve to score. Failure of the receiving team to return the ball legally over the net results in a point.

6. A served ball must neither be assisted nor touch the net. Any ball except service, touching the net, remains in play unless it is the third contact of a team.

7. Each team must have a serving order. Rotating into the right back position begins a player's term of service. She continues to serve until side-out is called, then the service goes to the other team.

8. Teams rotate across the back line to the left and across the front line to the right. On the first service of a team there is no rotation, after that each team rotates when it regains the service.

9. A game consists of one team scoring fifteen points, or eight minutes of actual playing time, whichever occurs first. With either a time or score ending there must be a two-point advantage before the winner is declared, and the game continues until there is such a lead.

10. A ball may be played with the hands or forearms and must be clearly batted. Contact with any other part of the body is illegal (DGWS ruling).

11. A team is allowed three volleys; on the third contact, the ball must be sent over the net. Two successive hits by one player are not allowed.

12. Simultaneous contact of the ball by two or more players is counted as one hit and any player may make the second contact.

13. Simultaneous contact of the ball above the net by two or more players from opposing teams does not count as a volley for either team and any player may make the next contact. After the simultaneous contact each team is allowed three volleys before sending the ball over the net.

14. A play may be made on the ball as soon as any part of it crosses the net.

15. A ball touching any boundary line is considered in-bounds.

16. A ball is declared dead when:
    a. Side-out or point is called.
    b. It lands outside the boundaries of the court.
    c. It strikes the floor or any object within the boundaries of the court.

17. The player making the serve shall not step on or over the end line before contact is made with the ball. This is a foot fault.

18. A player may step on but not over the center line while the ball is in play.

19. A player may follow through over the net, but any contact of the body or clothing with the net when the ball is in play is a foul.

20. A time-out rest period consists of one minute. A team shall be allowed two such time-outs during a game. A third time-out may be requested but the team making the request is penalized by awarding side-out or point to the other team. Time-out may be requested by the captain of a team when the ball is dead.

21. Time-outs:
    a. Substitution—fifteen seconds
    b. Between games—three minutes
    c. Injury—five minutes

Mechanics of Movement

The body, a system of weights and levers, should be used correctly for mechanical efficiency and effective performance. Applying good body mechanics in drills and games produces skill and control. The following points involve principles of movement that should be considered in volleyball.

1. The "ready" position enables one to move quickly into a play on the ball. In this position the player should have the weight on the balls of the feet; ankles, knees, hips slightly bent; head up to watch the ball; and the arms up with hands moving toward the ball.

2. Greater height can be achieved on a jump to spike, block, or pass if the player first assumes a slight crouch. This places the extensor muscles on a slight stretch so that they will then contract with greater force and thus enable one to extend or jump higher.

3. In landing from a jump, one absorbs the shock in all the body parts if the landing is made on the toes with a roll back to the whole

foot while bending at the ankles, knees, and hips.

4. The longer the lever the greater the force; thus a straight-arm hit imparts more power to the ball than a hit made with the elbow bent.

5. The angle of the force as it approaches the ball is a determining factor in the direction of the flight of the ball. For example, the spiker should swing the arm down into the ball from above in order to direct the ball toward the floor.

6. The point at which a ball is contacted helps to determine the direction in which the ball will travel. Hitting underneath the ball on the underhand serve causes the ball to travel in a high arc. Hitting the ball in the center or slightly above on the overhead serve will cause the ball to travel almost straight forward.

Evaluation

A volleyball player needs to practice regularly the skills involved in the game. As the player practices she can watch for errors and make corrections for herself and her teammates. Some of the common errors and corrections are listed in the following table.

Error	Correction	Error	Correction
1. Overhead Pass		c. Ball going out-of-bounds at side lines	Adjust holding hand or ball toss so that contact and follow-through are made toward the net.
a. Contact with whole hand	Use only fingertips.		
b. Lack of control	Stay behind the ball. Face direction ball is to travel.	d. Ball missed	Watch the ball!
		5. Offensive Volley	
c. Ball going over head of passer	Stay behind the ball. Get in position so that if hands were removed ball would hit player on the forehead.	a. Ball going into net	Pass or contact is too low. Jump and hit slightly under the ball.
		b. Ball hit out of court	Practice hitting down on ball with heel of hand.
d. Spin on the ball	Make contact with the fingertips. Stay behind ball—do not pull hands down behind ball.	6. Spike	
		a. Ball hit upward	Contact top of ball. Jump higher and reach.
2. Set-up		b. Jumping too late	Jump so contact with ball is made above net level.
a. Set too close to net	Move close to the net and make set-up parallel to the net.	c. Ball into net	Jump and contact ball sooner.
b. Set too low	Practice high sets parallel to the net. For practice stand beside basketball goal and hit ball high enough to make a basket.	d. Hand touches net	Follow through over net. Jump upward—not forward.
		e. Player out of position	Face set-up player and watch her movements.
3. Bounce Passes		7. Block	
a. Loss of control	Contact ball with flat part of forearms. Force ball upward.	a. Missed block	Time jump with spiker.
		b. Net contact	Jump straight upward—not forward. No follow-through on the block.
b. Lack of direction	Get directly behind ball whenever possible. Contact in front of body.	8. Dig	
		a. Missed ball	Move quickly to get under ball.
4. Serving		b. Loss of control	Angle ball high and back to teammates.
a. Ball going into net	Underhand serve: hit under the ball and use a high follow-through. Overhead serve: contact the ball higher above the head.	9. Net Recovery	
		a. Missed ball	Watch the ball and work on timing.
b. Ball going too high over net	Underhand serve: lower the holding hand. Overhead serve: hit down on the ball—not under it.	b. Hit back into net	Bend knees, get under ball, and hit it high and about 3 feet behind net.
		c. Lifting	Hit ball clearly with forearms or heel of hand.

Terminology

Ball in play: Begins with the serve and continues until the ball is declared dead.

Block: A defensive skill where one or more players try to contact the ball as it crosses the net.

Body ball: A ball touching the player on any part of the body other than the hands or forearms. This is a foul.

Dead ball: A ball that is not in play; follows a side-out, point, or temporarily interrupted play.

Defensive player: A player on the team not in possession of the ball.

Dig: A defensive skill in which a player attempts to "save" a ball that is below waist level.

Double foul: A foul committed simultaneously by members of the two opposing teams.

Follow-through: The final, continuing motion of forearms and hands when contacting the ball.

Foot fault: Stepping on or over the end line before contact has been made on the serve.

Match: Best two out of three games.

Multiple block: An attempt by two or more players to contact the ball as it crosses the net.

Offensive player: A player on the team in possession of the ball.

Point: A unit of scoring.

Rotation: Refers to the clockwise shifting of players preceding a serve.

Service: Method by which the ball is put into play.

Set-up: Placing the ball into position for a spike.

Side-out: The loss of the right to serve.

Spike: Contacting the ball at an angle and with great force, directing it into the opponent's court.

Selected References

DGWS Volleyball—Fourth National Institute on Girls Sports. Washington, D.C.: American Assoc. for Health, Physical Education, and Recreation, 1966.

DGWS Volleyball Guide, current edition. Washington, D.C.: American Assoc. for Health, Physical Education, and Recreation.

Egstrom, Glen H., and Frances Schaafsma. *Volleyball.* Dubuque, Iowa: William C. Brown, 1966.

Lockhart, Aileene, ed. *Selected Volleyball Articles.* Washington, D.C.: American Assoc. for Health, Physical Education, and Recreation, 1960.

Thigpen, Janet. *Power Volleyball for Girls and Women.* Dubuque, Iowa: William C. Brown, 1967.

Tom, Marilynn C., and Margaret N. Luckman. *Coed Volleyball.* Palo Alto, Calif.: National Press, 1966.

Trotter, Betty Jane. *Volleyball for Girls and Women.* New York: Ronald Press, 1965.

Walters, Marshall L., ed. *Volleyball Official Guide* (published annually). Berne, Ind.: United States Volleyball Association.

PART FOUR

Dance

Chapter 20

Folk Dance *Helen E. Domonkos*

Goals. History. Dance Fundamentals. UNITED STATES FOLK DANCES: *Square, Progressive Circle, Contras, Round Dance, Mixers, Play Party. Dance Styling. Terminology. Classified Listing of International Dances. Source Books. Records.*

Folk dance encompasses that great body of dances evolved by the people and handed down from generation to generation. By a process of selectivity, these vignettes of life have developed regionally into characteristic rhythms and design; the time-honored patterns have been virtually unchanged through the years except as natural modifications have occurred in the transfer. These dances reflect a people's native pride in their heritage and facilitate cultural continuity.

In the United States square dancing is the most popular form of folk dancing; it is enjoyed in all sections of the country even though there are great regional variations in style. Other forms of Americana are progressive circle dances, contras, couple or round dances, mixers, and play party games. Some feel that the recently created American dances are not truly folk; but inasmuch as they are based on folkways, they will be included here in that category. A parallel instance is found in the recently composed dances of the Israeli people, whose dances, based on common experiences, must be regarded as expressions of the people.

Dance—whether it be folk, ethnic, social, modern, ballet, or other variation—satisfies the universal urge to move rhythmically, and each appeals in a different way and degree to man's creativity.

Folk dance, based upon the principle of group participation, is social dance in the broad meaning of that term; it is recreational dance as it is enjoyed for the pure pleasure of the activity. Creativity is expressed within the framework and rhythm of the specific dance. Variation in style permits individual expression, especially in such forms as the free polka and schottische.

Ethnic dance is prompted by pride in national origin and a desire to retain social customs. Such dances require a high level of execution and are associated with folk ballet or theatre dance.

Social dance, as synonymous with ballroom dance, is historically an outgrowth of folk dance and has in common with folk dance many social and recreational values. Such dances offer an opportunity to the individual for creative expression within the limits of accepted step idioms and the evershifting jazz forms.

Modern and ballet dance are creative expressions of emotional experiences transformed by thought and movement into an art form.

In addition to the dances indigenous to the United States, today's folk dancer enjoys the traditional gems from other countries, experiencing vicariously the exuberance and sociability of a different culture.

Mrs. Domonkos has taught folk dancing at Oberlin College for many years. She has conducted workshops for church and rural recreation leaders and for the last decade has sponsored an international folk dance festival at Oberlin.

(1) Folk dancing reflects a people's native pride in their heritage. (Courtesy of the Department of Physical Education for Women, Oberlin College.)

Goals

Folk dancing is first of all a joyous response to the rhythm of music. Folk music is enchanting. Through the insistence of its beat, self-consciousness is lost and confidence gained. The informal atmosphere encourages fellowship not only with a partner but with others in the group. Because pleasure aids the learning process, the folk dancer quickly gains the skills implicit in the efficient use of the body—coordination, balance, agility, endurance, strength. Folk dancing is healthful exercise, and it may relieve mental strain or emotional tension.

Folk dancing is an ideal medium for co-recreation and for mixing with people of all ages and walks of life. Desirable social attitudes are developed as one learns to adjust to a cross-section of people. Through folk dance one gains respect for one's own cultural heritage as well as that of other ethnic groups, and discovers that there are significant similarities.

Folk dance clubs or informal groups are an increasingly popular leisure-time pursuit. Participating regularly in such a group may enhance one's enjoyment of people and dancing, and provide a recreational hobby for a lifetime. Our pioneers, feeling the need for sociability, gathered for dancing in barns, kitchens, or on porches. Today the appeal may be to the sophisticated city dweller who, in home or community recreation rooms or in social organizations, finds in folk dancing a welcome combination of fun and fellowship, exercise and release of tension.

History

PRIMITIVE DANCE

Primitive man's first means of communication was the dance. Through it he expressed his hopes and fears, joys and sorrows, loves and animosities. His frenzied movement reflected his strong emotions, heightened by an accompaniment of hitting sticks together, beating drums, clapping hands, and chanting.

In the belief that he could control the supernatural world through movement, primitive man danced to celebrate fertility of self, animals, and vegetation. He supplicated, placated, and rewarded the mystic spirits governing rain and movements of sun, moon and stars. By rituals of sacrifice and thanksgiving, he celebrated births, initiated the youth of the tribe into adulthood, and escorted the spirits of the dead to their future animistic life. Believing in animal ancestry, he mimicked animals in dance in order to bring him closer to the animal's spirit, facilitate the hunt, and in turn appease the soul of the slain animal. Curative rites were widespread, the various cults having their specialized witch doctor or shaman who, dressed in animal skins and a mask, danced to dispel the evil spirits from the sick.

ANCIENT CIVILIZATION

As civilization developed, man found protection in communal organization and thus did not have to face a hostile world alone. Carvings in stone show that in ancient and medieval times the communal chain dance was universal throughout Europe and Egypt. Peasants, holding hands and singing as they moved, danced in a closed circle around a Maypole or bonfire, or in an open circle in a serpentine line. The chain, guided by one of the better dancers, would progress through the village, with additional participants joining the end of the line. In France this chain dance was called *carole*, meaning circle. From it is derived the Christian custom of caroling: a group moving from house to house to sing and bring good fortune to each household. In Yugoslavia the chain dance became known as the *kolo*, in Bulgaria *horo*, in Roumania *hora*, in Macedonia *oro*, all based on the Greek word *choros*. In Germany, where the chain dance was adopted later, it was called *reigen*.

The open circle or serpentine dance without partners is immensely popular with present-day folk dance groups.

Dancing was an important aspect of the early Christian Mass, but abuses crept in during the Middle Ages and dancing was banned by the church. Then, too, asceticism had become a dominant philosophy of the monastic leaders, and dance along with all artistic expression was considered worldly and pagan.

THE RENAISSANCE ERA

When social stratification began to develop at the beginning of the Renaissance, the new aristocracy, although fascinated by the hearty and uninhibited peasant dances, considered them improper for polite society. The nobles hired dancing masters who "tamed" the peasant dances into precise, stilted movements, and taught the courtiers ballroom etiquette along with finesse in the management of their elaborate costumes. The minuet is an example of this subduing, for it was originally a dance of "restrained sprightliness." Under the dancing masters' perfectionist approach, it lost all spontaneity and would have disappeared into oblivion were it not for the beautiful music written for it. Nor were the nobles the only ones to modify dances, the peasants were in turn influenced by the dignified couple dances of the courtiers.

During the Renaissance the humanistic approach to life brought renewed interest in secular dancing. As the new outlook spread across Europe and England, whole communities danced on the village green to celebrate festive occasions.

In England the chain or choral form of dance developed into a double line with partners called "Longways for as Many as Will." This democratic dance formation spread to France where it was given the name "Contredanse Anglaise." Its acceptance was immediate, due perhaps to the fortunate combination of a single-couple dance incorporated into the choral form. After gaining wide popularity on the Continent, it returned to its former home "by the back door," so to speak, and was now known as "Country Dance." In 1650 John Playford published *The English Dancing Master*, which was outstanding for its early recording of English country dances. This book had eighteen reprints with revisions, and it is still an important reference.

In France the closed circle for four couples developed into a square and this dance, known as the *cotillion*, was much enjoyed at the court of Louis XIV. An English variant of the square formation, called *quadrille* by the French, later supplanted the cotillion. Both the cotillion and the quadrille had so many figures that the dancing master would often remind the dancers by naming the next figure. Thus the cotillion and the quadrille are the forerunners of the "called" American square dance.

As the need for communal unity diminished in mid-eighteenth century, individualism began to flourish. At this time couple dances gained the spotlight: the schottische, polonaise, gavotte, polka, mazurka, two-step, and German and Viennese waltzes were danced in most western European countries, the complexity of steps and exuberance of performance varying with the social level of the dancers.

In the course of time, much of the original ritualistic meaning of folk dances has been lost, but traces of superstitions, customs, and emotions of an earlier age are still present. Even though only a vestige of the original significance remains, these traditional dances are rich in the suggestion that historically they were once meaningful. A study of the origins of folk dance involves the story of mankind, its migrations, conquests, cross fertilizations, religions, occupations, folk music, art, crafts, and climate.

FOLK DANCE IN THE UNITED STATES

The people who immigrated to this country in the pioneer days came from many lands, the largest percentage coming from the British Isles. They brought with them the dances that were popular in their homelands and so successfully have these dances blended into the American folk pattern that it is often difficult to discover the original source. The contagious enthusiasm which these early settlers had for folk music and dancing, in spite of religious objection and pioneer hardship, set the stamp for future generations in the United States. Inasmuch as nothing is transplanted without change, we have added our own expression to these imported folkways with the result that the American folk dance is both vigorous and varied.

The growth of folk dance in America into the present healthy movement is due in great part to one woman's foresight and leadership. Elizabeth Burchenal, in 1905, introduced folk dancing into the public schools of New York City; the folk festivals she instituted are still held annually in the city's public parks. She traveled extensively in Europe, the British Isles, and the United States, carefully recording music and directions for folk dances, and from 1909 to 1938 published a series of books including the authentic dances found in her research. As founder of the American Folk Dance Society and its first chairman, Elizabeth Burchenal worked through physical education associations conducting workshops and demonstrations and inspiring all with her philosophy of the educational value of folk dance.

Others deserving mention are Mary Wood Hinman, teacher, writer, researcher in folk dance and music, and leader at Hull House in Chicago; Frank Smith, originator of the Mountain Folk Festival and founder of the Christmas School at Berea, Kentucky for training of folk dance leaders; Lloyd Shaw, educator, author, and leader of the Cheyenne Mountain dancers of Colorado Springs, Colorado; Cecil Sharp, musicologist and author, who revived interest in traditional dances and festivities in England and America; May Gadd, who, after working with Cecil Sharp, became national director of the Country Dance Society of America and of the C.D.S. camp at Buzzards Bay, Massachusetts; Jane Farwell, who in 1941 organized at Oglebay Institute the first folk dance camp in the country, and who directs the Christmas Festival at Mount Horeb, Wisconsin; Vyts Beliajus, founder and editor of *Viltis*, folklore magazine, and outstanding folk dance workshop leader throughout the United States; Sarah Gertrude Knott, founder and director of the National Folk Festival in St. Louis, which draws participants and audience from the western part of the United States; Mary Ann and Michael Herman, outstanding teachers and folklorists, who direct Folk Dance House, New York City and Maine Folk Dance Camp; and Ralph Page, acknowledged leader and contra dance caller, who directs a New Hampshire Fall and a Year-End camp. All these and many more have contributed significantly to folk dance in the United States.

In addition to the human guidance, one mechanical aid should be mentioned. The public address system has made it possible for leaders to instruct large groups, hush noisy crowds, and even dispense with an orchestra by amplifying recorded music. Without this aid the folk dance movement would not have attained its present scope.

Dance Fundamentals

FORMATIONS FOR FOLK DANCING

The following figures show commonly used dance formations:

→ the arrow indicates the direction one faces

○ Girl

□ Boy

1. Nonpartner Formations (Figs. 2–5).
2. Circle Formations (Figs. 6–11).
3. Contra Formations (Figs. 12–16).
4. Square of Four Couples (Fig. 17).

DANCE POSITIONS

Closed (Fig. 18): Partners face each other. The man's left hand is held out at his left side approximately shoulder high, and his right hand is placed just below his partner's left shoulder blade, giving support to her back. The lady's right hand is placed on the man's left hand, and her left hand on the back of the man's right shoulder. The lady's left arm should be in definite contact with the man's right arm, but must not drag down on her partner. The lead is generally initiated by the man's shoulder, right arm, and hand.

Butterfly (Fig. 19): Two dancers face and join hands out to the sides, palm to palm, elbows slightly bent.

Facing (Fig. 20): Partners face and join both hands.

Open (Fig. 21): Partners stand side by side and join inside hands, generally facing in line of direction.

Promenade (Fig. 22): Partners stand side by side with the girl on the right. Hands are joined right to right, left to left with right arms above.

Semiclosed (Fig. 23): From a closed position, both dancers turn to face forward around the room, maintaining the same arm and hand positions. Also called "conversation" position.

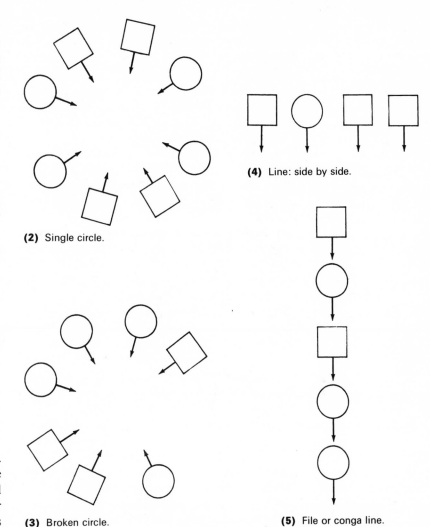

(2) Single circle.

(3) Broken circle.

(4) Line: side by side.

(5) File or conga line.

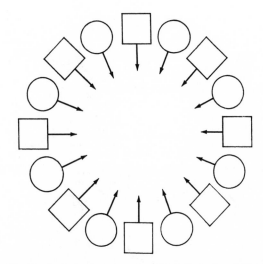

(6) Single circle; facing center with lady to the right of her partner.

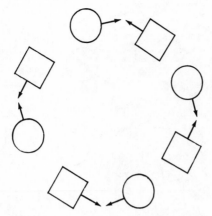

(7) Single circle; man facing line of direction, lady facing reverse line of direction.

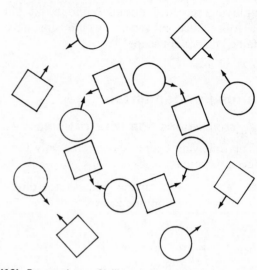

(10) Progressive or Sicilian circle: two facing two with the lady on the right.

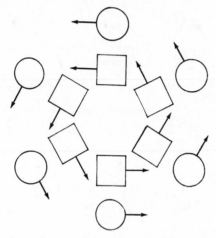

(8) Double circle: couples facing line of direction.

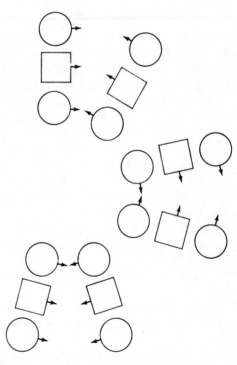

(11) Progressive circle with three facing three.

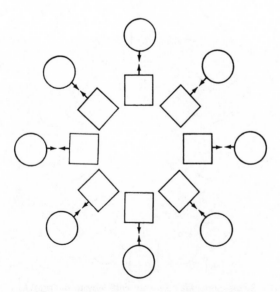

(9) Double circle; partners facing, man's back to center.

384 *Dance*

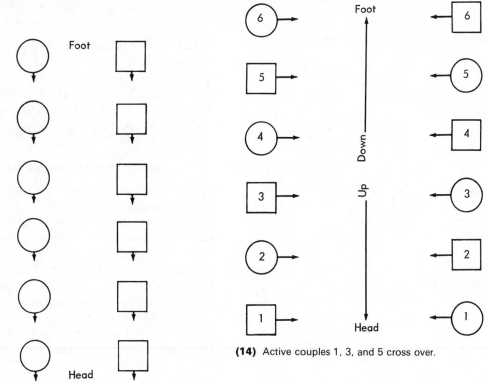

(14) Active couples 1, 3, and 5 cross over.

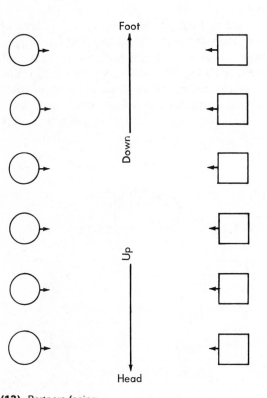

(12) Couples facing head—lady on the right.

(13) Partners facing.

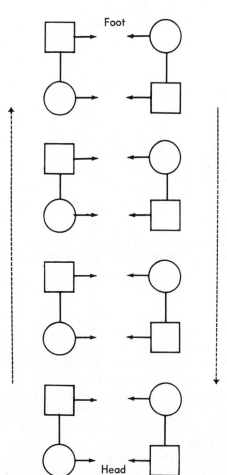

(15) Couples side by side facing center progress laterally.

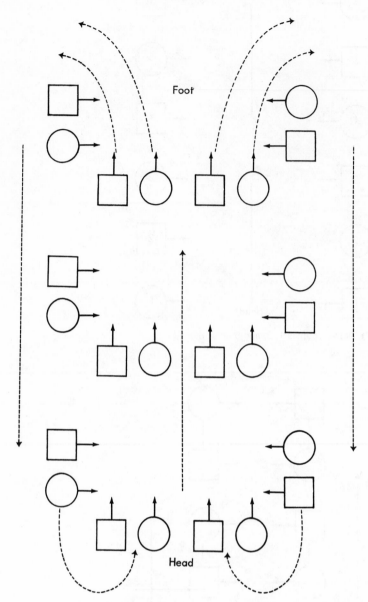

(16) Double contra: two couples in "grandstand" position progress down the set, side couples progress laterally.

dance swing it is necessary to lean away from partner.

Varsouvienne (Fig. 27): Couples stand side by side, left hands joined in front of man's body, with man's right arm behind partner's shoulders and holding partner's right hand above her right shoulder.

BASIC LOCOMOTOR FORMS

The 9 basic locomotor forms vary according to the manner in which the body weight is transferred to the supporting leg or legs. All dance steps are derived from a combination of these basic forms.

Walk, *run*, and *leap:* The body weight is transferred alternately from one foot to the other in even rhythm. In the walk the weight goes from one foot to both feet and on to the alternate single foot. In the run the weight is transferred from one foot to the other. In the leap both feet are momentarily off the floor in the process of weight transference.

Hop and *jump:* The weight is transferred to the same foot in the hop; in the jump the take-off is from one or both feet with the landing onto both feet.

Slide and *galop:* The weight is transferred in uneven rhythm with the leading foot starting the movement followed by a quick closing action of the other foot. The slide is smooth with slight or no elevation; the galop has greater elevation and force resulting in a leap-step or step-leap.

Skip and *step-hop:* In both of these the weight

Shoulder-waist (Fig. 24): Partners face, man places hands around girl's waist, and girl places hands on sides of man's shoulders. The arms bow out and both lean back slightly.

Side-car (Fig. 25): From a closed position, each dancer turns individually to his right until left hips are adjacent. This is also called "left parallel" position.

Swing (Fig. 26): From a closed position, each dancer turns individually to the left until right hips are adjacent. This is also called the "banjo" or "right-parallel" position. For the square

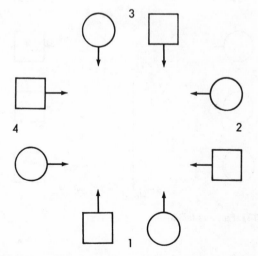

(17) Square of four couples: 1 and 3 head couples; 2 and 4 side couples.

(18) Closed position.

(19) Butterfly position.

(20) Facing.

(21) Open position.

(22) Promenade.

(23) Semi-closed position.

(24) Shoulder-waist position.

(25) Side-car or left-parallel position.

(26) Swing, banjo, or right-parallel position.

(27) Varsouvienne position.

Folk Dance   **387**

is transferred to the same foot, each being a combination of a step and a hop. The rhythm of the skip is uneven or long-short, while the rhythm of the step-hop is equal time value.

Combinations of these fundamental forms of locomotion offer an endless variety of step patterns. A few step patterns are used so universally in European and American dances that they are called traditional steps. The most common traditional steps are schottische, two-step, polka, waltz, and mazurka. Just as the music of each country or locality has its own unique characteristics, the steps are also executed somewhat differently by various ethnic groups.

TRADITIONAL DANCE STEPS

Schottische—4/4 *meter:* Take three smooth even running steps and a hop swinging the free foot forward; or step, close, step, hop. Each movement has the same time value. Schottische may be taken forward, sideways or in place. Two schottische steps are frequently balanced with four step-hops.

Two-step—2/4 *meter:* Step forward on L foot (ct. 1), close R to L taking weight (ct. &), step L again (ct. 2&). Repeat starting with R foot. The rhythm is quick, quick, slow. The two-step may be taken forward, backward, or turning.

Polka—2/4 *meter:* Similar to the two-step with the addition of a hop before the first step. Hop on R (ct. ah), step forward on L (ct. 1), close R to L taking weight (ct. &), step forward L (ct. 2&). The polka is a sprightly step in keeping with the gay music. It may be taken forward, backward, or turning.

Waltz—3/4 *meter:* Step L (ct. 1), step R (ct. 2), close L to R taking weight on L (ct. 3). The waltz is a smooth step with accent on the first beat. It may be danced in any direction or with a turn.

Mazurka—3/4 *meter:* Step L (ct. 1), bring R to L taking weight on R (ct. 2), hop R while bending L knee bringing L foot close to R instep (ct. 3). The accent is on the second beat.

OTHER BASIC STEPS

Balance—3/4 *or* 2/4 *meter:* Step on one foot (ct. 1), step with other foot beside it (ct. 2), then step in place (ct. 3). With 2/4 meter, the three steps are taken on cts. 1-&-2. In square and contra dancing, there are several ways to balance; a favorite one is to face partner and take two step-swings, starting right, either with or without right hands joined.

Box waltz: A box pattern is made by stepping forward on left foot (ct. 1), sideways with right foot (ct. 2), together with left (ct. 3); backward on right (ct. 1), sideways on left (ct. 2), together on right (ct. 3). Two measures are used to complete the pattern. The step may start either forward or backward, on either right or left foot.

Buzz: This step is frequently used in square and contra dancing for the partner swing. Step on the right foot on the accented beat and with the left foot make quick pushing movements to turn clockwise. The right foot stays in place with only the heel being lifted.

In Danish dancing the buzz step is used for travelling sideways in a circle formation as well as for the partner swing. Dancers, facing center of circle, cross one foot in front of the other and place the weight on the forward foot during the accented beat while bending the knees enough to give a slight up and down movement.

Canter—3/4 *meter:* The rhythm is long-short. Step (ct. 1), hold (ct. 2), and step bringing feet together (ct. 3). The same foot continues in the lead.

Chassé (*Shassay*): Partners move sideways once around each other with a gliding step. With each dancer facing the center of the square, the lady moves to her left in front of the man while the man moves to his right behind the lady.

Cross polka: The rhythm and step pattern are the same as in the polka but the free foot on the upbeat swings across in front of the foot taking the hop.

Cut step: A quick change of weight as the free foot displaces the supporting foot. The step may be taken forward, backward, or sideways.

Dip (*Corté*): Step forward or backward, bending the knee while other leg is extended in a straight line from the hip, with toe in contact with floor.

Gavotte: Three steps forward, then point the free foot to the floor. This step is similar to the minuet but more lively.

Grapevine: A sideward movement with the trailing foot crossing alternately in front and behind the leading foot, or behind and then in front. The step may start with a sideward step, the body moving in the same direction, or with a crossover step, the body moving in the direction of the crossing foot.

Heel and toe polka: The regular polka step is preceded by a light touching of the heel diagonally forward, then toe of the same foot backward near the supporting foot. The supporting foot may hop as the heel and toe touch.

Hopsa step: A small leap sideways (ct. 1), step on toe of other foot close in front (ct. &), step back onto the first foot (ct. 2). On the hopsa turn with the partner, the toe is placed behind rather than in front and it pushes for the turn.

Jig step: Alternate feet step and hop in place in even rhythm with the knees turned well outward and toes pointed. The free foot is swung in a small arc around the supporting ankle and then steps close behind the heel. To keep the body from moving backward, the hop is taken slightly forward.

Kolo step: The kolo step varies in different localities, but basically may be described as: moving sideways to the right, hop on left foot, leap on right, step on left foot behind right, step on right in place, and hop on right. Repeat moving to the left; the two hops together are very slight, the foot scarcely leaving the floor.

Pas de basque (pas de bas): The dancer describes an arc forward-sideways with the right foot, then leaps onto the right foot, steps on the ball of the left foot close in front of right, then steps backward on right foot. To repeat, leap onto the left foot. The step may be danced in place or progressing, starting with either foot.

Pivot: This step may be done individually or as a couple in closed position. To pivot individually, the dancer swings smoothly around on ball of foot, the free leg giving momentum for the turn. For the couple pivot the right foot is placed between partner's feet and one complete clockwise turn is taken with two steps (one measure) or three steps (waltz). It is easier if partners are fairly close to each other. Progress should be in the line of dance around the room on the pivot.

Varsouvienne—3/4 meter: This step consists of two phrases; a long phrase of four measures and a short one of two measures. The long phrase begins with a pick-up beat on the 3rd count. Sweep left foot diagonally across right instep with toe pointed downward (ct. 3), step left (ct. 1), step right bringing foot close to left heel (ct. 2); repeat sweep, step, together, with same foot leading. Sweep (ct. 3), step left (ct. 1), step right (ct. 2), step left (ct. 3), point right toe to floor (ct. 1, hold ct. 2). Then the long phrase is repeated starting with the other foot.

(28) Dance with group of three. (Courtesy of the Department of Physical Education for Women, Oberlin College.)

The short two-measure phrase begins with the sweep (ct. 3), then repeats the three steps and point of the last two measures of the long phrase. On each long and short phrase the man maneuvers the woman to the opposite side. When the left foot leads, the woman moves to the left of partner; when right foot leads she moves to the right.

Partners start with the same foot; the action may begin with either foot and may be danced moving forward, backward, or turning.

Yemenite step: Step on right to right bending knees (ct. 1), step left close to right straightening knees (ct. 2), step right across in front of left bending knees (ct. 3), hold, straightening knees (ct. 4).

BASIC FIGURES

All around your left hand lady, see saw your pretty little taw: The men dance a figure eight by passing to their left and behind their corner, around her, back to place passing in front of her, behind their partner and around her, and back to place, passing in front of partner. The ladies move slightly toward the center when the men pass behind them, and then the ladies return backward to place when the men pass in front of them.

Allemande left: Join left hands with the corner and turn once counterclockwise, ending in starting position.

Allemande thar: Men allemande left with corner, give right hand to partner, then with a left forearm-grasp with the next lady, men walk into center to form a backward right hand star. The star turns counterclockwise, the men moving backward, women forward. At caller's direction men break the star, progress counterclockwise, meeting next lady with the right hand and meeting the following lady with a left forearm-grasp. Men again form a backward right hand star, ladies moving forward. Allemande thar is an interrupted grand right and left. It may also be done with ladies in the center turning the backward star, each lady holding partner with left forearm-grasp.

Arming, arm right, arm left: Two dancers hook designated elbow, turning once around, and fall back to place.

Basket: Girls join hands in a circle and raise the joined hands over the head of the man on either side. Men join hands and raise the joined hands over the head of the girl on either side. The joined hands rest in the small of the adjacent dancer's back. Unless otherwise directed, the basket then moves to the left with the dancers using a buzz step.

Bend the line: Executed when dancers are in a line of four. Line breaks in the middle with centers backing up and ends moving forward to face the other half of the line.

Box the flea: Dancers who are facing join left hands. Lady turns right under man's raised arm and man turns left to be in lady's position. They have exchanged places and are facing each other.

Box the gnat: Dancers who are facing join right hands. Lady turns left under man's raised arm and man turns right to be in lady's position. They have exchanged places and are facing each other.

California twirl (whirl): With partner's inside hands joined, man walks clockwise around lady as lady turns left under man's raised arm. Partners are now side by side facing in opposite direction.

Circle left: The designated number of dancers join hands and, unless directed otherwise, make one complete circle moving to the left. If the circle left is to be repeated to the right it may be called "and back."

Cross trail: Couple crosses square, lady moving to her left in front of man while man moves to his right behind lady. Wait for next call.

Do paso: Turn partner with left forearm-grasp, corner with right, and partner with left in a courtesy turn.

Do-si-do (back to back): Two dancers face, move forward passing right shoulders, move to the right passing back to back, and fall back to places.

Down the center and back: The active or designated dancers in a contra set dance down the center, turning on the last two beats of the music to face up the set, and dance back up the center of the set to place.

Down the center and back and cast a place: With right hands joined, the couple dances down the center (4 steps), turns individually to the left with the lady turning under the joined hands (4 steps), dances back up the center (4 steps), separates with each casting off around the next person below. On the last four steps the couple below faces up and dances up into the active couple's place.

Down the center and up the outside: With inside hands joined, the couple leads down the center past two inactive dancers, separates and passes between the inactive dancers to the outside of the set, and dances up the outside of the set to place.

Down the outside and back: The active couples turn out, dance down the outside of the set, turn out again (8 steps), and dance back up the outside of the set to place (8 steps).

Down the outside and up the center: The active dancers turn out as in the foregoing figure and dance down the outside of the set by two inactive dancers, come into the center of the set, passing between the inactive dancers, and dance up the center to place.

Ends turn in: In a line of four, center two raise arms and ends duck under to face in opposite direction. Center two then execute California twirl to face in same direction as ends, with lady on the right.

Forward and back: Designated dancers dance four short steps forward and four steps back to place.

Forward and pass through: Designated dancers, usually couples or lines, dance eight steps forward, passing right shoulders with the opposite dancer.

Four ladies chain (ladies grand chain): Danced in the same manner as a ladies chain except that the four ladies form a right hand star to move to the opposite man, who turns them, and then dance another right hand star to return to partner, who also turns them to place. See Ladies chain.

Grand right and left: Partners face while in a single circle, men facing counterclockwise and women facing clockwise. Join right hands and pass right shoulders, join left hands with next dancer and pass left shoulders. Continue moving in the same direction, alternately passing right and left shoulders until partners meet or are back to place, or until the music allotted for the grand right and left is finished as called in the dance.

Grand square: A simultaneous movement where the heads are dancing one movement while the sides are dancing another. Heads dance into the center and turn to face partner (4 steps), back away to the side of the set and turn to face opposite (4 steps), back away to the corner of the set and turn to face partner (4 steps) and dance forward to place (4 steps), but do not turn. From this point the heads reverse the movement by backing away from partner to the corner of the square and turn to face the opposite (4 steps), dancing forward to meet opposite and turning to face partner (4 steps), dancing forward to center to meet partner and turning to face opposite (4 steps) and falling back to place (4 steps). The sides start by facing partner and dancing the last sixteen steps of the movement just described while the heads are dancing the first sixteen steps. While the heads are dancing the last sixteen steps, the sides dance the first sixteen steps. Whenever dancing beside another dancer, inside hands are joined.

Half promenade: This figure is danced by two couples facing. In promenade position, the couples dance forward, men passing left shoulder, and turn counterclockwise into the other couple's place, all in eight steps.

Half sashay: Man moves sideways to right behind lady as lady moves left in front of man to exchange places.

Honor: Men bow while ladies curtsy.

Ladies chain: This figure is danced by two couples who are facing. The women join right hands and turn until they can join left hands with the opposite man. With left hands joined with the opposite man, the women release right hands, and the men place their right arm around the ladies' waist. In this side-by-side position the two dancers wheel counterclockwise in place, leaving the men in their original places and

(29) Swing like thunder.

the women in the opposite woman's place; this wheeling movement is called the *courtesy turn*. This much of the figure is a half ladies chain. The right hand turn and wheel is then repeated, returning to own partner and original position. The entire figure requires sixteen beats to complete, four for the first right hand turn, four for the wheel, and eight for the repeat back to place. On the wheel, or courtesy turn, the women customarily place their right hands on their hips, palm out, and in the man's right hand, placing the left hand palm down on the man's left hand, which is held palm up.

Reel: A figure generally danced in a contra set where there is a progression from the head of the set to the foot. Head couple joins right elbow and turns once around (8 steps), passes partner and turns next person in opposite line with the left elbow (4 steps), returns to partner in the center of the set and turns again with the right elbow (4 steps), returns to the opposite line and turns the next person in line (4 steps), and so on, until the couple reaches the foot of the set.

Right and left through, or *right and left:* This figure is danced by two couples facing, who dance forward four steps passing right shoulder with the opposite dancer, then join inside hands and wheel counterclockwise in place to finish in the other couple's starting position. This much of the figure is called a Half Right and Left. The movement is then repeated to places. The figure requires sixteen beats to complete, four to pass through, four to wheel, and eight to repeat the movement back to place. In square dancing right hands are generally joined with opposites on the pass through and the turn. Hand positions on the turn are the same as in the Ladies chain.

Right hand star (right hand mill, right hands across), (left hand star): The four dancers (usually) join hands with the diagonally opposite dancer and move once around the circle clockwise if right hands are joined, and counterclockwise if left hands are joined. In either case the dancers face in the same direction they are moving. If two men join hands and two women join hands, the men's hands are above those of the women.

Right hand turn or *Left hand turn:* Two dancers join right or left hands as directed, turn once around clockwise or counterclockwise respectively, release hands, and fall back to places. As soon as hands are joined the direction of facing is the same as the direction of movement.

Roll: A turn to the right or left, progressing to the right or left respectively, generally made in four steps, or three steps and a touch or swing of the free foot.

Sashay: Partners move once around each other, the man moving sideways to the right behind the lady; the lady moves sideways to left in front of man. Dancers face center of circle throughout the Sashay.

Star promenade: Same as promenade except that the dancers on the inside form a star with the other hand around partner's waist. Either men or women may be in the center with either a right- or left-hand star. To reverse the star, the inside dancer backs out of the star while the outside dancer moves into the center to form another star. To spread the star out wide, couples slide away from partner to join inside hands.

Star thru: Executed when two couples are facing each other. Man takes opposite lady's left hand in his right, walks forward to exchange places with her making a quarter right face turn as lady makes a quarter left face turn under

man's raised arm. Couples have now changed partners and are facing former partners.

Swing: Couples assume designated position and turn in place until directed to dance another figure or until the music for the swing is finished.

Twirl: A roll made with leading hands joined.

Wheel: A turn by two dancers acting as a unit in which the dancer on the left backs around while the dancer on the right moves forward, with the pivot being at a point between the two dancers.

Classification of American Folk Dancing

Six types of folk dances have become American by adoption: squares, progressive circles, contras, round dances, mixers, and play party games, with a seventh type, international folk dancing, having wide participation in this country.

SQUARE DANCE

Square dance stems from two divergent sources: the quadrille, which originated in England and France, became popular in New England and some southern states; and the Kentucky Running Set, which derived from the chain dances of the British Isles and became established in the Appalachian Mountains. The quadrille, a square with four couples, is a quiet and dignified dance in moderate tempo. The dancers are reminded of the patterns by simple "prompt" or "cue" calls. The Kentucky Running Set is a vigorous four couple square in fast tempo with short calls that relate to the life of the people—for example: "The Wild Goose Chase," "Wind up the Ball Yarn," and "The Wagon Wheel." Western squares are akin to the Kentucky Running Sets in the vigorous style of the dance and the homespun nature of calls. The colorful patter of the Western caller has been a creative contribution to square dancing. This device, in addition to giving ornamentation, keeps the dancers together by clearly marking the number of beats allotted for a given movement. The sequence of patterns in Western squares is fast and is designed to have a minimum of waiting for the inactive couples.

In pioneer days singing calls were used occasionally in the eastern part of the United States. In such calls the dance directions, rhyming in couplets, fit the music like words of a song. Singing calls are now in common usage throughout the country, the music being popular hit tunes. The name of the dance may or may not have the same name as the music.

Square dance styles vary markedly in different sections of the country. When a person dances in a new area, it is wise to notice the differences and conform as nearly as possible. Some of the common variations are speed of the dance, dance step used, type of swing, position of hands in promenade and courtesy turn, use of twirls, hand or forearm grasp for allemande left, dip to partner in grand right and left. These variations may gradually disappear because increased travel, square dance workshops, national, district, and state conventions, and professional callers' associations tend to standardize square dance usage.

Listed here are suggested *American square dances*. The numbers in parentheses are references to the source books given at the end of this chapter. Dances in square formation from other countries are listed in the section on international dances.

Alabama Jubilee (1, 6)
Arkansas Traveler (6)
Birdie in the Cage (6)
Catch All Eight (6)
Chantez, Chantez (5)
Ends Turn In (6)
Figure 8 (5)
Forward Up Six, Left Hand Lady Under
   (6, 10, 12) (also called Camptown Races)
Four Gents Star (6)
Grand Square (9, 13)
Hot Time (6)
Hurry, Hurry, Hurry (5)
Inside Arch and Outside Under (6)
Jessie Polka Square (5, 6)
Manana (5, 6)
Marianne (5)
Polka on a Banjo (6)
Promenade the Outside Ring (6)
Shoot the Owl (6)
Sides Divide (6)
Somebody Goofed (5)
Split the Ring (6)
Texas Star (6, 13)

There's a Rainbow 'Round Your Shoulder
   (5)
Two Gents Swing with the Elbow Swing (5)

PROGRESSIVE CIRCLE DANCES

In progressive circle dances a couple faces another couple in a double circle around the hall. *Sicilian Circle* is a dance in which the facing couples dance various figures, then progress in the direction they are facing (being sure always to face in the original starting direction), to meet another couple (see Fig. 9, page 384). This formation is so universally used that it is called the "Sicilian Circle" formation. *Soldier's Joy* and *Portland Fancy* are examples of dances in this formation, the latter being a double version with two couples facing two couples, the woman always on the right of the man. The progressive circle is an excellent formation to use when learning dance basics such as ladies' chain, right and left through, right (or left) hand star, and so on.

Listed here are suggested *American progressive circle dances*. The numbers in parentheses are references to the source books given at the end of this chapter. Dances in progressive circle formation from other countries are listed in the section on international dances.

Circle Virginia Reel (1)
Fireman's Dance (4 face 4) (8, 9)
Portland Fancy (4 face 4) (1, 8, 9, 13)
Red River Valley (3 face 3) (1, 6, 12)
Sicilian Circle (1, 8, 13)
Soldier's Joy (8, 13)
Spanish Circle Waltz (1, 2, 8, 9)

CONTRAS OR LONGWAYS

Contra dance is a dance of opposition or line facing line (Figs. 12–16, pages 385–386). In such dances each figure is danced in the framework of the music. The dancer must hear the beat, feel the musical phrase, and execute the figure within the phrase.

Virginia Reel, the best known longways from pioneer days, illustrates how dances are slightly modified as they are transferred from one generation to the next. The same basic calls are used, but now each couple dances the figures with partner simultaneously instead of waiting while head and foot execute the patterns. The

(30) Many different formations are used in folk dances.

rest of the dance remains essentially the same as in the past.

In contrast to the Virginia Reel, which is a longways of any number of couples with a simple progression of the head couple going to the foot of the set, the duple minor contras are executed in two-couple units within the set. Certain contras are danced with the men in one line and women in the other (Figs. 12 and 13, page 385), whereas in others the actives cross over into the opposite line (Fig. 14). Triple minor contras, danced in units of three couples, are considered intermediate in difficulty and offer a delightful challenge after the duple pattern is well understood.

In every contra there is a progressive pattern for each couple to meet the next couple. The progressive figures are very ingenious; sometimes one is scarcely aware of having changed position in the line. The active couples (numbers 1, 3, 5) progress down the set while the inactives

(numbers 2, 4, 6) progress up the set. Upon reaching the foot, the active couple becomes "neutral" or waits for one repetition, and then is inactive to work up the set. Upon reaching the head, the inactive couple waits for one repetition, and then is active to dance down the set.

If the active couples crossed over at the beginning, it is necessary upon arrival at the foot to cross back; while the inactives, upon arrival at the head, must cross as they become active.

The basic step in contras is a walking step, with a buzz step for swinging with one's partner. It is best to limit the contra line to six to eight couples in order to give every couple opportunity to be active.

All contras can first be danced in Sicilian Circle formation, for this is an excellent device for quickly learning contra progression. Each couple then continues as active or inactive throughout the dance and is not confused by the need to learn the opposite pattern. Another suggestion is to stop the music after each progression to straighten out the active, inactive, and neutral couples.

Different figures, formations, and ways of progressing lend variety to contras. An example of progressing laterally (Fig. 15, page 385) is *Criss Cross Reel*; an example of the double contra with two couples in "grandstand" position is *The Tempest* (Fig. 16, page 386).

Listed here are suggested *American contra dances*; except for the *Virginia Reel*, all are duple minor. The numbers in parentheses are references to the source books given at the end of this chapter. Dances in contra formation from other countries are listed in the section on international dances.

> All the Way to Galway (6)
> Criss Cross Reel (6)
> Glover's Reel (8, 9)
> Haymakers' Jig (6, 9, 13)
> Hull's Victory (8, 9, 13)
> Lady of the Lake (8, 9)
> Lady Walpole's Reel (8, 13)
> Petronella (8, 9)
> Pop Goes the Weasel (8, 13)
> St. Lawrence Jig (6)
> The Tempest (8)
> Virginia Reel (8, 13)

ROUND OR COUPLE DANCES

Round dance is the term used in America for dances in which partners dance freely "round" the room in a counterclockwise direction; in other countries such dances are called "couple" dances.

In the "proper" European couple dances of the eighteenth century there was very little contact with partners—at most an occasional touching with one hand. When the German turning waltz in closed position appeared on the scene toward the end of the eighteenth century, the dancing masters and populace were shocked. Gradually, however, the populace became enraptured over this new free and joyous turning movement—to the great disgust of the dancing masters. Following in the wake of the waltz, other dance steps became popular. Germany is usually given credit for the schottische, Bohemia for the polka, Poland for the mazurka, whereas the source of the two-step is doubtful. These old-time dance steps

spread quickly through Europe and America, sparking renewed participation in round or couple dancing.

The interest in round dancing in America is shown by the number of clubs that specialize in this type of dance. The abundance of dances created to folk tunes, popular classics, or the latest swing music results in even the "dance of the month," being soon forgotten unless it is exceptional. These devised dances use such ballroom steps as grapevine, box step, dip, canter, two-steps, and waltz and pivot steps. Because both partners learn the sequence, the man does not need to be a skilled leader.

Easy rounds, called "square dancers' rounds," are frequently taught in dance clubs as breathers between tips. Intermediate rounds, spoken of as "round dancers' rounds," are taught in round dance clubs.

The schottische and polka are especially delightful free old-time dances. Couples enjoy the freedom of creating their own steps and sequence. The traditional dances are easy to do, give variety to a program of square dancing, and have stood the test of time.

Listed here are some of the older *American round dances*. The numbers in parentheses are references to the source books given at the end of this chapter. Couple dances from other countries are listed in the section on international dances.

> Black Hawk Waltz (4, 5, 6)
> Blue Pacific Waltz (4, 6, 13)
> California Schottische (5)
> Cotton Eyed Joe (2, 5, 6, 9)
> Glowworm (4, 6)
> Happy Polka (6)
> Heel and Toe Polka (13)
> Jessie Polka (6)
> Merry Widow Waltz (5, 6)
> Mexican Schottis (4)
> Mexican Waltz (6, 13)
> Old Time Schottische (6)
> Varsouvianna (6, 9, 13)

MIXERS AND ICEBREAKERS

Mixers are dances or activities in which partners are exchanged; icebreakers are nonpartner. Socially akin to the nonpartner dances are those involving three people, an especially useful grouping when the number of girls and boys is uneven. Even when there is no partner exchange, threes make for sociability.

Many round or couple dances may be adapted to change partners by the girl turning under the boy's arm, by partners separating with one going forward and the other backward, by facing partner followed by a quarter turn to meet a new partner, and so on. Many play parties are delightful mixers and icebreakers.

Listed here are suggested *American nonpartner dances, American couple-mixers,* and *American dances in groups of three.* Play parties will be found in the following section. Mixers and icebreakers from other countries, given in the section on international dances, include nonpartner circle and broken circle dances, couple-mixers, dances in groups of three, a dance in which a partner is secured by "stealing" at a certain point in the dance (*Gustav's Skoal*), and a dance based on a game element (*Little Man in a Fix*).

The numbers in parentheses are references to the source books given at the end of this chapter.

(31) Swing your partner.

Nonpartner
Bunny Hop (file or conga line) (5, 6)
Jessie Polka (line) (9)
Ten Pretty Girls (line) (5, 6, 9, 12)

Couple-Mixer
All American Promenade (5, 6)
Bingo (5)
Five Foot Two (6)
Mexican Waltz (10)
Oklahoma Mixer (2, 3, 9)
Patty Cake Polka (1, 5, 6)
Susan's Gavotte (3, 6, 9, 12)
   (also called Lili Marlene)
Teton Mountain Stomp (5, 6, 9)
White Silver Sands (6)

Groups of Three
Dashing White Sergeant (3 face 3) (8, 9)
Highland Reel (3 face 3) (8)
Red River Valley (3 face 3, ends change)
   (1, 6, 12)
Three Man Schottische (center progresses)
   (3, 9) (also called Oklahoma Mixer for
   Three)

PLAY PARTY GAMES

Play parties are derived from simple European folk dances with elements of a dance, game, or dramatic action. They were called "games" to meet the opposition of the Puritans to dancing. Because instrumental music was also frowned upon, singing and clapping became the accompaniment. These dance games were an important part of the recreation of our pioneer forefathers as they travelled westward. Play parties are a type of informal do-it-yourself recreation with the singing and clapping creating a friendly atmosphere. Because partners change often, even the shy become acquainted; and extra boys or girls may join in the action, adding to the game element.

Play parties are especially useful when the group is large and inexperienced, as well as when there is no other music available.

Listed here are suggested *play party games.* The numbers in parentheses are references to the source books given at the end of this chapter.

Alabama Gal (6, 10)
Bingo (10)
Come My Love (10)
Oh, Susannah (9, 10, 13)
Paw Paw Patch (13)
Shoo Fly (13)
Skating Away (10)
Skip to My Lou (13)

American Dance Styling

Each country has its own unique characteristics in dancing—the "style" of that country. Before one studies the specific styling of other countries, it is important to apply the basic principles of movement from the point of view of American dancing. Some specific suggestions for good appearance and efficiency are

1. Show enjoyment of the dance by smiling at your partner and other dancers.
2. Alignment of the body is of paramount importance. Stretch up tall, lift your head and chest. Work for a straight alignment from ankle to ear, pull in the abdomen and hips as though moving through a narrow passageway. Do not let the weight sag onto each foot but keep the body under control with an attitude of lightness. Put the toe to the floor first; keep the knees and ankles flexible.
3. Gravity can assist one and make dancing effortless if, when moving, one leans *slightly* from the *ankles* in the direction of desired movement; the legs and feet then move to support the body to prevent it from falling.
4. Relax! There are no serious mistakes on the dance floor except social ones. Keep shoulders poised but not tense. Tension increases the difficulty of leading or following your partner.
5. Feet should be kept close to the floor, but without scuffing. There should be a slight spring in the ankles, giving a rhythmical lift and fall on each step.
6. Keep your feet under the body at all times. Do not "over-stride" by taking steps that are so long that the body is not over the legs. When about to change direction, take a smaller step. When the tempo of a dance is fast, take small steps.
7. If the floor pattern and phrasing in a dance suggest moving through space, try to match the length of steps with the phrasing so as to complete the floor pattern in the time allotted. Taking short steps all the time is as undesirable as always taking long ones.
8. Keep as small a base as possible. When taking a two-step or sliding sideways, bring the feet *close together* for a split second before separating them.
9. Smooth natural movements, rather than ballet movements, of the arms and legs are used. The elbows should not be sharply bent; in some areas women let their arms hang naturally from the shoulder, in other regions the free hand holds the skirt to the side in certain movements. The arms may be put out to the side when it improves balance or assists one in turning, but the position should be without artificiality. High leg lifting or kicking is not done by women.
10. Always focus in the direction of movement. When sliding sideways, turn the head in the direction of the slide, keeping the rest of the body facing forward. When moving forward in a small arc, turn the head in the direction of the leading shoulder with hips in opposition. Natural opposition will aid balance.
11. Never look at your feet, unless you wish to emphasize the foot position (as when pointing the toe in the minuet).
12. When not moving, and locomotion is necessary in the succeeding figure, just before you are to move rise on your toes in place shifting the weight to one foot, so that you can step out on the first beat of the music with the free foot.
13. Avoid excess movement of the hips—either up and down or sideways—unless the dance calls for a "strut."
14. When joining hands with a partner or in a circle, man has palms up, woman palms down. When joining hands with people of the same sex, a simple way is to have the right hand palm up and left palm down. The person in back takes the hand of the forward person, thus avoiding the need to look backward for the joining.
15. When joining hands with a partner for a partner turn, or when circling in a group, mutual support is secured by bending the arms, elbows pointing downward, with body leaning slightly backward. If turning with a partner, each turns the other person; if in a group, each assists in the group circling.
16. When two people each have a hand joined overhead for the lady to turn under the joined hands, there must be a loose hold to permit the lady to pivot freely. The man cups two or three fingertips downward, around which the turning partner may pivot easily.
17. Arm movements as well as leg movements

must be smooth and rhythmical. When taking hands momentarily with different dancers such as in grand right and left, allemande left, star through, and so on, do not jerk the arm of the approaching person. Jerking is due to awkwardness and tension, and is more apt to happen when the calls are too fast for one's ability.

18. For the square dance swing, the movement should be smooth with no up-and-down action. It is possible to walk around, but the more highly skilled buzz step is preferred in most areas. For the buzz swing, the right foot is placed close to the partner's right foot so outside edges almost touch; the left foot gives a pushing action. For a smooth swing the right foot must not travel, but remains in place with only the heel being lifted as one pivots. If the woman wishes to change the speed of the swing, she can control it by pressure of her left hand on the man's shoulder. To accelerate the swing, the left hand is placed on the back of the man's shoulder, pressing toward one; to retard the swing, the left hand slips slightly in front of the man's shoulder pressing away from one.

International Folk Dancing

International folk dance is an ideal medium for the great adventure of learning about cultures different from our own. As we explore the dances, music, folk arts and festivals of the various ethnic groups, our understanding and appreciation of these cultures increase. Interest in the background of people from other lands has been stimulated through United Nations' organizations, councils on international affairs, student foreign exchange programs, and the increased use of jet travel.

Since folk dancing is related to the life of the people, it may be effectively integrated with many subjects, such as history, socioeconomic progress, language, art, music and musical instruments, handicrafts, and folk songs and lore. It is an enriching, horizon-widening experience.

The international folk dancer is challenged to portray the dances of each country in the spirit of the homeland. Each country has its own uniqueness. For authentic dancing, the native dances require as much study as the learning of a language. Variety in music, style of movement, and folk traditions give breadth as well as depth to study.

International folk dancing is increasing in popularity with many clubs now dancing only these dances. Some clubs even specialize in dances of a specific country or area, such as Israel or the Balkan countries.

A listing of suggested dances from various countries follows. This list includes sources for descriptions of the dances and includes available dance records. Also cited for each dance is the country of origin, the basic step and formation used, and the approximate difficulty of the dance classified according to beginner and intermediate levels of ability.

Classified Index of Suggested International Folk Dances

	Reference	Record	Nationality	Basic Step	Formation	Difficulty of Dance*
Alexandrovsky	4, 5, 6, 9, 13	Folk Dancer MH-1057	Russian	Waltz	Couple	I
Alunelul	3, 5, 11	MH-1120	Roumanian	Run, stamp	Circle, nonpartner	B
Apat-Apat	11	Folk Dancer MH-2031	Philippine	Walk	Couple-mixer	B
Ari-Ara	6	MH-1052	Israeli	3 step turn, skip	Couple-mixer	B
Black Nag	5, 11	HMV 9480; Folkkraft 1174	English	Walk, slide, set, and turn single	Set of 3 couples	I
Boston Two-Step	2, 9	Folk Dancer MH-3001	English	Pas de basque, 2 step	Couple-mixer	I
Čačak	11	Folk Dancer MH-3022	Serbian	Walk, step-hop, 2 step	Broken circle, Nonpartner	I
Cherkassiya (also as Tscherkessia)	6, 9	Kismet K-105	Israeli	Grapevine, scissors	Hora, nonpartner	B
Christ Church Bells	12	World of Fun M-109	English	Walk, slide	Contra	I

	Reference	Record	Nationality	Basic Step	Formation	Difficulty of Dance*
Corrido	4, 6, 13	Mexican Columbia 1613-C Star 8412	Mexican	Step-close, grapevine	Couple	I
Cshebogar	5, 9	Folkraft 1196	Hungarian	Slide, skip, hop-step turn	Circle	B
Cumberland Square Eight	2, 12, 13	World of Fun M-109	English	Slide, polka, buzz	Square	B
Danish Family Circle (also called Familie Sekstur)	3, 6, 11	Linden 703 Tanz EP 58402	Danish	Buzz, walk, swing	Couple-mixer	B
Danish Schottische	3, 11	RCA Victor 26-0017	Traditional	Schottische, step-hop	Couple-mixer	B
Dargason	11	HMV 8169 Methodist M 121	English	Setting, turn single	4 couples in file men facing women	I
Dashing White Sargent	9	RCA Victor LPM 1619	Scotland	Polka, pas de basque, reel step	3 face 3, progressive circle	I
Dodi Li	11	Arzi 770	Israeli	Walk, grapevine Yemenite step	Couple	I
Doudlebska Polka	3, 6, 9, 11, 13	Folk D. MH-3016	Czecho-slovakian	Polka	Couple-mixer	B
Dr . . . Gsatzlig	3, 6, 11	Folk D. MH-1114	Swiss	Schottische	Couple	B
Eide Ratas	2, 7, 9	Sonart M 303	Estonian	Leap-step-hop, waltz	Couple	B
Ersko Kolo	9	Folk D. MH-3020	Yugoslavian	Schottische	Broken circle, nonpartner	B
Espan	4	Kismet A-116	Russian	Waltz, step draw	Couple	I
Fado Blanquita	1, 2, 5, 11	RCA Victor LPM 1620	Portuguese	Buzz step, schottische	Single circle	B
Galopede	5, 9	Folkraft 1331	English	Polka	Longways 4-6 couples	B
Gathering Peascods	5	RCA Victor LPM 1621	English	Slide, walk	Single circle	B
Gay Gordons	5, 6, 13	Folkraft 1162	Scottish	Walk, two-step	Couple	B
Gerakina Syrto	6	Folkraft 1060	Greek	Walk, step hop	Broken circle, nonpartner	I
Geud Man of Ballingigh	3	World of Fun 120	English	Walk, set and turn single	Contra	B
Gustav's Skoal	5, 9, 12	Folkraft 1175	Swedish Game Dance	Walk	Square	B
Hambo	4, 6, 11, 13	Capitol T 10039	Swedish	Hambo step	Couple	I
Harmonica	6, 11	Folk D. MH-1091	Israeli	Grapevine, step-hop	Circle-nonpartner	I
Hasapikos	13	Folkraft F 1021 GB	Greek	Walk, hop, slide	Broken circle, nonpartner	I
Hole in the Wall		CDS 1 (directions with record)	English	Walk	Contra	I
Hora	5, 6, 9	RCA Victor LPM 1623	Israeli	Step, swing, run	Hora, nonpartner	B
Kalamatianos	11	Festival 3505	Greek	Walk, hop	Broken circle, nonpartner	I
Kalvelis	1, 5, 9	Folk D. MH-1016	Lithuanian	Polka	Couple-mixer	B
Kanafaska	5	Imperial 1089	Moravian	Slide, polka	Square	B
Karagouna	11	OL 24-13, Side 1 Band 5 "Picnic in Greece"	Greek	Walk, cross-over, brush	Broken circle, nonpartner	I
Karapyet	5, 9, 13	Folk D. MH-1058	Russian	Walk, two-step	Couple	I
Klumpakojis	6, 9	Columbia 16083F	Lithuanian	Walk, polka	Couple-mixer	B
Kohanotcha	2, 6, 7	Kismet A-106	Russian	Russian polka	Couple	B
Kontrasejre	11	Folk D. MH-1100 Columbia DD 624	Danish	Run, step-hop, buzz	Square	B
Korobushka	2, 5, 6, 12, 13	World of Fun M-108	Russian	Schottische	Couple-mixer	B
Kriči, Kriči, Tiček	11, 13	Folk D. MH-3021	Croatian	Walk, hop step-step	Couples in closed circle	I
Kuma Echa	5, 11	Folk D. MH-1150	Israeli	Schottische, grapevine	Circle, nonpartner	I
La Faira Da Strada	11	Folk D. MH-1112	Swiss	Step, close, step-bend	Couple	I
La Russe	5	World of Fun M-120	English	Swing, polka	Square	B
Little Man in a Fix	3, 5	Folk D. MH-1054	Danish	Run, waltz	2 couples, men's left elbows hooked together	I
Makedonka	5	Balkan 547	Macedonian	Walk	Broken circle, nonpartner	B
Man in the Hay	3, 5	Folk D. MH-1051	German	Slide, skip	Square	B

	Reference	Record	Nationality	Basic Step	Formation	Difficulty of Dance*
Masquerade (also called Swedish Masquerade)	3, 9, 11, 13	Folk D. MH-1019	Danish	Hopsa, waltz	Couple	I
Mayim	3, 4, 6, 13	Folkraft 1108	Israeli	Run, grapevine	Circle, nonpartner	B
Meitschi Putz di	2, 9, 13	Folk D. MH-1017	Swiss	Schottische, step-hop	Couple	B
Milanovo Kolo	5, 11	Stanchel 1011	Serbian	Schottische, walk	Circle, nonpartner	B
Miserlou	5, 6, 13	Columbia 10072	Greek-Amer.	Grapevine, walk	Broken circle, nonpartner	B
Napoleon	5	Folk D. MH-1054	Danish	Schottische, hopsa	Couple	B
Neda Grivne	3	Folk D. 1015	Serbian	Walk	Broken circle, nonpartner	B
Oslo Waltz	3, 5, 6, 11, 13	Folk D. MH-3016	English	Balance, waltz, step draw	Couple-mixer	I
Picking up Sticks	11	HMV B 9881	English	Run, siding, sheepskin hey	Set of 3 couples	I
Pljeskavac Kolo	6, 11	Folk D. MH-1009	Roumanian-Amer.	Walk, step-hop	Broken circle, nonpartner	B
Polka zu Dreien	9	Folk D. MH-1050	German	Polka	Groups of 3	B
Raksi Jaak	3, 5, 11	Folk D. MH-3007	Estonian	Polka	Line of 3, facing center	I
Road to the Isles	2, 6, 9, 12, 13	M-110	Scottish	Schottische	Couple	B
Rumunjsko-Kolo	5, 6, 11	Balkan 525	Roumanian	Step-hop, cut step	Broken circle, nonpartner	B
Seljancica Kolo	3, 4, 5, 6, 11, 13	Folk D. MH-1006	Yugoslavian	Walk, run	Broken circle, nonpartner	B
Sellinger's Round	5, 9	RCA Victor LPM 1621	English	Sliding, Setting, turn single, siding, arming	Circle	B
Shibolet Bassadeh	11	Folkraft 1109	Israeli	Slide	Broken circle, nonpartner	B
Siamse Beirte	6, 11, 13	Folkraft 1422	Irish	Schottische	Couple	I
Sicillian Tarantella	5, 7, 9	RCA Victor LPM 1621	Italian	Hop step, run, skip	2 couples	I
Sjampa Dans	3, 11	World of Fun M 121	Danish	Polka	Longways for 6 couples	B
Snurrbochen	6, 11	Aqua Viking V 200	Swedish	Polka	Couple	B
Sønderhoning	11	HMV AL 1358	Danish	Walk, Sønderho step	Couple	I
Sønderburg Double Quadrille	6, 11	Aqua Viking V 406	Danish	Walk, polka	4 face 4	I
Spinning Waltz	1, 2, 5, 9	World of Fun M 110	Finnish	Waltz, step-draw	Couple	B
Spinnradl	3, 5, 11	Zither Melodies 1897	Austrian	Waltz	Couple	I
Sudmalinas	3, 9	RCA Victor LPM 1621	Latvian	Polka, waltz	2 couple sets, mixer	I
Three Meet	6, 11	Folk D. MH-3025	English	Walk, buzz	Lines of 3 facing another 3	B
Totur	2, 6, 9, 13	Folk D. MH-1021	Danish	Walk, two step	Couple-mixer	B
Troika	1, 5, 6, 7, 9	Folk D. MH-1059	Russian	Run	Mixer in groups of 3	B
Ve' David	9	Folkraft 1432	Israeli	Walk	Couple-mixer	B
Vranjanka	11	MH 3020 B	Serbian	Walk	Broken circle, nonpartner	B
Waltz Country Dance	9	Folkraft 3363	English	Balance, waltz	Couple facing couple	I
Waves of Tory	1, 9	Folk D. Album FD-22	Irish	Walk	Contra	I
Zillertaler Laendler	4, 11, 13	Victor 25-4147	Austrian	Laendler waltz	Couple	I

* Difficulty of Dance: B = Beginner; I = Intermediate

Selected References

SOURCE BOOKS FOR FOLK DANCE

1. Eisenberg, Helen and Larry. . . . *And Promenade All*. Nashville, Tenn.: Fun Books, 1952. (Available through Tennessee Book Co., Nashville, Tenn.)
   Folk Dance Federation of Calif. *Folk Dances from Near and Far*, San Francisco, Calif., 1095 Market St. (This includes entries 2 to 4.)

2. International Series; Vol. A-1 (30 beginner dances), 1964;
3. International Series; Vol. A-2 (33 beginner dances), 1962;
4. International Series; Vol. B-1 (25 intermediate dances), 1960.
5. Hall, J. Tillman. *Dance! A Complete Guide to Social, Folk, and Square Dancing*. Belmont, Calif.: Wadsworth Publishing Co., 1963.

6. Harris, Jane A., Anne Pittman, and Marlys S. Waller. *Dance A While*. Minneapolis: Burgess Publishing Co., 1964.
7. Herman, Michael. *Folk Dances for All*. New York: Barnes & Noble, 1954.
8. Holden, Rickey, Frank Kaltman, and Olga Kulbitsky. *The Contra Dance Book*, American Square Dance Series No. 3. Newark, N.J.: American Squares, 1956. (Available through Frank Kaltman, 1159 Broad St., Newark, N.J.)
9. Kraus, Richard. *Folk Dancing*. New York: Macmillan; 1962.
10. Kraus, Richard. *Square Dances of Today*. New York: Ronald Press, 1950.
11. Lidster, Miriam, and Dorothy N. Tamburini. *Folk Dance Progressions*. Belmont, Calif.: Wadsworth Publishing Co., 1965.
12. Methodist World of Fun Series, 201 Eighth Ave. South, Nashville, Tenn.: Fun Books.
13. Wakefield, Eleanor Ely. *Folk Dancing in America*. N.Y.: J. Lowell Pratt and Co., 1966.

Folk Dance Record Outlets

Country Dance Society of America, 55 Christopher St., New York, N.Y.

Folk Dancer, 108 W. 16th St., New York, N.Y.

Folkraft Records, 1159 Broad St., Newark, N.J.

Methodist Publishing House, 201 Eighth Ave. South, Nashville, Tenn.

Sets in Order Records, 462 N. Robertson Blvd., Los Angeles, Calif.

Chapter 21

Modern Dance *Lucy McIver*

History. Goals. Costume. ELEMENTS OF MOVEMENT: *Force, Space, Time. Axial Movement. Fundamental Forms of Locomotion. Technique. Composition.*

From primitive man to his contemporary counterpart, the urge to communicate has been universal. This communicative need has resulted in varying degrees of artistic expression in speech, written language, drama, poetry, music, painting, sculpture, architecture, and dance. In dance, man uses his body as his instrument and movement as his medium for a creative nonverbal expression of his reaction to his environment.

All arts have elements in common—rhythm, color, design—and with each art form there is a specific medium for expressing content. In dance, movement is the medium. As the dancer studies his medium he learns to understand himself and his body: what movements are structurally possible; how physical forces such as gravity, acceleration, and momentum affect muscular force; and how inner feelings can be objectified in movement.

Few dancers reach the level of high art, but even a beginner may achieve great satisfaction

through creative expression in dance. Today's educators recognize in modern dance an effective means for developing individual expression, demanding as it does intellectual, physical, and emotional involvement.

History

The history of modern dance has special significance to Americans inasmuch as this country has contributed so richly to its development. At the turn of the twentieth century the formalism of established classical ballet was not attuned to the creative forces that were unfolding in this country. Isadora Duncan, an American whose work was largely done in Europe, was the first to break away. Her approach to dance was toward natural movement, simple Grecian-type costumes that followed body lines, and subject matter that reflected the inner self. Although flouting artistic discipline, she showed in her work a creative spark that kindled in others a dissatisfaction with the lack of freedom and the limited vocabulary of traditional ballet. For a time, the influence of Isadora Duncan caused dancers to reject all ballet movements and to search only for "natural" movements. After a while, however, dancers realized that the greatest possible variety of movement could be attained only by blending ballet and modern techniques.

Mrs. Lucy McIver, an assistant professor at the University of Idaho, is director of dance activities and advisor to the modern dance club. She received her B.A. at the University of Kansas and her M.A. at Ohio State University. She is a member of the Dance Notation Bureau and a Labanotator. Mrs. McIver has performed in works by Humphrey, Limon, Currier, Moore, and Payton, and has presented her own compositions at several universities.

This trend has in turn brought about a change in ballet, resulting in a more varied form of expression.

In the early 1900's Ruth St. Denis and Ted Shawn established in California the Denishawn School of the Dance. It has been called the "cradle of American modern dance." Doris Humphrey, Louis Horst, Charles Weidman and Martha Graham, acknowledged pioneers in modern dance, either attended or were on its faculty. The Denishawn School was especially interested in oriental themes and used a mystic approach to dance. This group was the first to tour the country successfully and to present American modern dance to the public. Ted Shawn also organized an all-male group of dancers, which received wide acclaim through such works as "The Labor Symphony." Through this group Shawn helped to restore the masculine role in theatrical dance.

Meanwhile, in Germany, Mary Wigman, a former pianist and actress, began to shape a new philosophy and technique entirely apart from the American movement, except for the influence of Isadora Duncan. Mary Wigman contributed a new understanding of the use of tension in dance and a broader concept of dynamic movement. Her dancers were strong and vital; beauty of movement was not an objective. She had studied with Rudolph von Laban, a pioneer in developing laws of human motion. (He later established a system of recording movement known as *Labanotation*.) Hanya Holm, Mary Wigman's most outstanding pupil, established her own school in New York and is now a Broadway choreographer.

In 1923, Martha Graham broke away from Denishawn, started her own school, and developed a philosophy of dance backed by a strongly defined system of techniques. She originated the "contraction and release" principle of movement: a strong impulse or contraction initiated in the center of the body flows outward to the extremities as the force is spent. She introduced a variety of ingenious movements to propel the body at low levels. Miss Graham insists that the dancer discipline the body instrument to the high level she holds for herself. She has travelled extensively, giving concerts alone as well as with her group, and continues her teaching in New York with an occasional public performance. Her mentor and accompanist for years was Louis Horst, musician, composer, and trusted advisor to many aspiring young dancers. Until his death in 1964, he edited *Dance Observer*, a perceptive magazine devoted to contemporary dance.

Meanwhile, Doris Humphrey and Charles Weidman started a school in New York, developing their own approach to modern dance. They, along with Martha Graham, rebelled against musical accompaniment. Dance had lost its identification and was simply impersonating the supporting music. In their choreography they experimented with the spoken word, incidental instrumental sounds, or complete silence as accompaniment.

Doris Humphrey, from her observation of the body in motion, used in her dances floating movements based on breath control and fleet footwork. She later worked breath rhythms into a theory of movement. One of her basic tenets was that gravity plays a major role in controlling movement and that all movement has degrees of relaxation and resistance to gravity. She used creatively those movements that are either falling with or resisting gravity. She experimented with dramatic and expressive sounds such as humming, shouting, buzzing. She was imaginative in her use of themes and stage effects. She was especially successful as choreographer for the Humphrey-Weidman group. After retiring as a performing artist, she continued to gain stature as artistic director for José Limón and his group.

Charles Weidman developed his own style, and much of his work has been satirical. With a "gift for observing and visualizing the vagaries of men and manners," he has found inspiration in abstracting normal gestures and giving them a touch of comedy.

The Humphrey-Weidman Company made an outstanding contribution to popular understanding of modern dance by the tours they took for many years throughout the country, giving

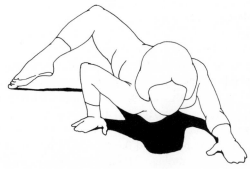

(1) The Weidman push-up.

concerts and conducting workshops in school auditoriums and gymnasia. Their willingness to go to the people has been one of the important growth factors in the interest of schools in modern dance; in general, dance in education has followed the trends of dance in the theatre.

While teaching at the University of Wisconsin, Margaret H'Doubler developed a course based on anatomy, kinesiology, physics, and psychology, which in 1926 became the first dance major in college physical education. Now many colleges offer this major. In 1933, Martha Hill, collaborating with Martha Graham, Doris Humphrey, Charles Weidman, Hanya Holm, Louis Horst, and John Martin, established at Bennington College a summer program in modern dance, which later moved to Connecticut College. These sessions, and other summer sessions now established throughout the country, for professional dancers, college teachers and students have done much to bridge the gap between lay and professional dancers and have greatly improved the level of teaching in the schools.

Inspired by the work of the pioneers of modern dance, a new group of dancers is developing. Today's dancers still search for valid expression, always seeking to relate dance to the changing environment. With the new governmental subsidies for the arts, including dance, there should be definite encouragement to talented young people to enter the profession. Choreography is employed in many theatre productions, and television programs of modern dance are increasingly popular. Many personalities are coming to the fore in this field, exploring and experimenting in untried areas.

Goals

The goals in modern dance vary with each individual, but for a beginning student the following are generally present: to gain experience in exploration of rhythmical movement and have opportunities for individual expression; to improve skills of balance, flexibility, strength, relaxation, and coordination in order to free the body and make it a more expressive instrument; to develop understanding and appreciation of music as it relates to dance.

Also, to understand the principles relative to selection of movement patterns and to their organization into an effective sequence, a fundamental creative process; to evaluate one's own solutions in relation to the efforts of others through problem-solving activities; and to experience opportunities both to lead and to follow by working in a group project.

Perhaps the most important outcome of participation in modern dance will be self-realization.

Costume

Most dancers wear leotards and tights. These must allow for freedom of movement. Tights should not cover the feet for one is less apt to slip when barefooted; shoes are generally not worn although ballet slippers or sandals may be used. Some dancers wear either short or long skirts.

A dancer with long hair should wear it held back from the face, because one cannot see and focus well with the movements of the dance if the hair is constantly in the eyes. Jewelry should not be worn as it detracts from the line of movement.

Elements of Movement

Movement is the medium of dance. To understand this medium it is necessary to analyze it into its component parts: force, space, and time or rhythm. Force or energy is expended by the use of muscular action controlling the body; space is utilized by spatial design; and time is consumed in the performance of a rhythmical pattern.

Dance involves a movement pattern that is executed through space with varying degrees of force and in a rhythmical sequence requiring time. Dance becomes creative through the way these elements are merged into a synthesis or form for communication.

FORCE

The way in which force is applied determines the quality of movement; it ranges from minimal to great stress, from tension to release. Variation lies in the application of the initial impetus as well as in the disbursement of the sequential force. When the amount of force increases along with speed and rhythm, the dynamic quality of a movement is heightened.

Force, as applied to movement, falls into the

(2) One learns to use force, space, and time in a leap.

following classifications: swinging, sustained, percussive, vibratory, suspended, and collapsing.

Swinging movement with its alternate tension and release has a great range of variation of tension. After such a movement is initiated, gravity assists; thus tension is released as momentum carries the movement to full range. At the peak of the swing muscles are strongly stretched; then the muscles relax and gravity pulls the weight down.

Sustained movements are smooth and evenly controlled. The muscular contraction necessary to perform the movement is only enough to initiate movement and oppose gravity. Then throughout the movement the tempo is slow as the energy needed remains constant and is concealed by the resistive forces.

Percussive movement is characterized by a sharp explosive use of force. It begins quickly and ends abruptly, using considerable energy both in starting and stopping.

Vibratory or small oscillating movements use energy in a repetitive percussive manner. Such movements have a high degree of tension.

Suspended movement results when the movement flow is momentarily arrested at the peak of resistance to gravity. This off-balance position gives emphasis as well as continuity because the suspended pause leads into the succeeding pattern.

Collapsing movement comes when the body or some part of it gives way to the pull of gravity; collapse or relaxation of the entire body results in a fall.

No dance uses only one type or quality of movement. A single classification may predominate, but it will be heightened by other qualities or uses of force. The contrast of one quality against another makes a dance composition more interesting.

SPACE

As the body moves in three-dimensional space, it creates a design giving form and shape to space. In studying the use of space, the following are to be considered.

Floor pattern: Variety is possible in floor pattern through use of straight, curved, or zigzag lines as well as a whole array of convolutions.

Direction: Movement may be forward, backward, or sideward, with various deflections of each, all offering possibilities of diversified spatial designs.

Focus: Planned eye focus is an important aspect of all movement, adding balance, significance, and emphasis.

Dimension: Size of movement varies from very small to large. A dynamic quality may be achieved by combining an increase in dimension, or size, of movement with increase in force and tempo.

Levels: Spatial possibilities are enriched by the use of all levels, from lying on the floor to the highest leap.

Body contour: Whether of an individual or a group, body lines are studied in relation to the front, or audience. Dancers may face or have their backs to the audience, be in profile, or in oblique facings; these, in combination with varying directions, afford innumerable possibilities for interest.

The dancer's arms and legs may be symmetrically balanced or, with the left side in a position different from the right, the body becomes asymmetrical. Symmetrical designs suggest stability whereas asymmetrical designs tend to create the impression of movement.

TIME OR RHYTHM

Time has to do with the rate of speed and the rhythmical structure with which a movement is performed. A span of time is necessary for development of the rhythmic patterns. Rhythm is the grouping of strong and light beats into units of time. Rhythmic factors include the following.

Tempo: The speed of a movement may vary from fast to slow.

Underlying beat: The pulsating beat provides

Modern Dance　　**405**

(3) The dancer experiments with an idea.

the measurement of time into regular intervals, with the accent at the beginning of each unit of time.

Accent: The grouping of strong and light beats determines the meter.

Phrasing: A musical sentence suggests a comparable unit of movement.

Duration: The period of time a rhythmic pattern takes.

Syncopation: The use of shifted accents gives variety and excitement to rhythm.

Classification of Movement

Movement falls into two classifications, axial and fundamental forms of locomotion.

AXIAL MOVEMENT

Axial movement is movement of the body, or any body segment, on a stationary base. This includes all movement at all levels when the base is constant. The movements that are possible due to the anatomical structure of the body are flexion and extension, rotation, abduction and adduction (moving a body part sideward away from and toward the central axis of the body), and circumduction (a circling of the torso or any part; a combination of the above move-

ments). These movements will vary in the way they are developed or distorted, and in the manner in which energy is released and expended.

FUNDAMENTAL FORMS OF LOCOMOTION

Locomotor movement involves changing the position of the body through space. Although there are various ways, such as rolling and crawling, for propelling the body without using the feet, the fundamental forms of locomotion are those methods which use the feet as the moving base. These forms vary in rhythm and the manner in which the body weight is shifted from one or both feet; and they are the bases of all movement in which the feet move the body through space.

Walk is a smooth even change of weight from one foot to the other, with one foot always in contact with the floor. In the normal walk the weight is transferred first to the heel and then to the ball of the foot; in the usual dance walk the ball contacts the floor first and then the weight is transferred to the heel. The walk may be done in any direction and to various meters.

Run is a fast even rhythm with alternate transference of weight. The ball of the foot touches the floor first, followed by the heel to absorb the jar. The movement of the legs directs the body upward as well as forward. Like the walk it may be done in any direction and to various meters.

Leap is a spring into the air from one foot to the other, with the body suspended in the air as both feet are off the floor. It is executed in even rhythm at a moderate tempo; either height or distance may be emphasized.

Hop is a pushing-off from one foot, lifting the body upward momentarily. The weight then returns to the same foot. It is done in even rhythm.

Jump is a spring into the air from one or both feet and landing simultaneously on both feet. It is executed in even rhythm in moderate tempo; either height or distance may be emphasized.

Gallop is a combination of a leap on one foot and a step on the other; the following foot comes to but not beyond the leading foot. This may be either leap-step or step-leap, and is executed in uneven rhythm usually in a forward direction.

Slide is similar to the gallop except the leading foot slides smoothly along the floor. The quick draw step of the other foot replaces the sliding foot by a cutting motion. It is uneven in rhythm and may be done in any direction.

Skip is a step and a hop on the same foot. The rhythm is uneven with the step taking the long time value, the hop the short. When repeated, the step and hop action alternates from one foot to the other; it may be done in any direction, and height or distance may be emphasized.

Step-hop is taken on the same foot, the feet alternating as the movement is repeated. The rhythm is even with the step and hop having the same time value. It may be taken in any direction or in place.

Combinations of these locomotor forms offer an endless variety of dance patterns by using them in different sequence, by varying the direction, tempo, size of movements, amount of force, and stylization.

Sample problems

Combine walk and run in any sequence changing direction on the run.

Combine walk, run, and leap in any combination covering as much space as possible, followed by using as little space as possible.

Perform 8, 4, and 2 running steps alternating with step-hops in equal amount of time.

Gallop and skip, alternating the leading foot each time on gallop.

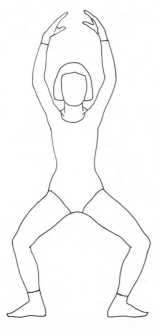

(4) Technique teaches control.

Walk, jump and hop in any sequence while clapping hands on each jump.

Slide and hop, and from the hop change into a new direction for each slide.

Stylize a walk by swinging the free leg straight forward before stepping.

Run while kicking the legs up behind and with the body leaning forward in a straight line from ankles.

Step-hop and bend the free knee and ankle to form sharp angles.

Traditional dance steps

The traditional dance steps are combinations of the fundamental forms of locomotion. After experimenting with various combinations of the fundamental forms, the more complex patterns of traditional dance steps, such as polka, schottische, two-step, and waltz, will offer further possibilities for exploration. Select a specific step and organize the movement pattern in relation to change of direction, focus, force, or stylization.

Modern Dance Technique

The purpose of exercises (techniques) in modern dance is to condition the body so that it can be free to accomplish all the movements one wishes to use in dance. It is helpful, with each dance session, to start with warm-up exercises using the large muscles of the torso. Then techniques for each part of the body are used, generally starting with exercises done while sitting and lying on the floor, then standing, then moving through space. Your group and your teacher will develop your own technique series to fit your needs and will want to work out variations to offer variety and challenge.

Composition

DEVELOPING MOVEMENT PHRASES

Each day of the modern dance class, simple problems will be presented which the student will attempt to solve either alone or in groups. She will be challenged to use her mind to direct her movements, and will discover many responses out of which she will select the best. The approach to individual creative response is to have, from the beginning, one or two specified factors while others are to be manipulated. For instance, under fundamental locomotor movements, the run and walk may be the two factors to be manipulated; and specified factors might be the floor pattern in a square with two measures of 4/4 meter to be taken on each side of the square with the focus constantly toward the center of the square. For more body involvement, clapping the underlying beat could also be specified. After working on this problem for a while, the class may be asked for suggestions for other ways to use the arms. After further experimentation, a movement phrase develops. Following are some examples of problems for development.

Problem: Use of levels with symmetrical and asymmetrical movement.

Specified: Floor pattern of a half circle, the ends connected by a zigzag line. The movement should start and end on the floor. One symmetrical movement is to be used that will be repeated at different levels; other movements will be asymmetrical.

Problem: Change of tempo and sustained movement.

Specified: Floor pattern is a figure eight with a large circle around it. A sustained movement done in place, then enlarged, moving through space as the tempo gradually increases; then the movement becomes smaller, followed by a sudden stop; after the stop, a change of direction with a different sustained movement.

Problem: Sustained movement with tension followed by release of tension in a series of sharp bursts.

Specified: Contrast of sustained with vibratory movement and a relaxed swing. Climax of either high tension or complete release in a fall.

Suggestions for compositional studies

There are many motivational approaches to dance. A dance may be based on an emotion, a poem, a painting, music, or an experience or idea which the dancer wishes to convey. Some suggestions are.

1. Select an emotion such as happiness or depression. Plan focus and direction of movement, the energy to be expressed, and a convincing climax.
2. Select a gesture, such as thumbing a ride. Stylize it and use the movement with varying dimension at different levels. Contrast expectation and disappointment by movement rather than pantomime.
3. Select a character to portray such as a debonair person, a dual personality torn between the conventional and risqué, a slap-happy pugilist. Analyze the gestures this character would use and plan in terms of space, time, and energy.
4. Imagine that you are moving an object that is very heavy or very light. Plan the amount of energy needed and think of pushing with parts of the body other than hands.
5. Listen for unusual sounds that have unique rhythm. Try to find sounds that are long, short, even, or uneven. Think of the kind of energies the sounds imply. Are any emotional states such as fear or restlessness suggested?

A SUGGESTED APPROACH TO COMPOSITION FOR DANCE

Modern dance composition requires creativity. The choreographer must first decide on an idea that she wishes to express; then she must use variety, innovation, and inventiveness to convey the idea. Nevertheless, even the novice in dance should begin to experiment with dance compositions of her own. Her experiences will bring satisfaction and a deeper insight into the potentials of dance.

Dance composition requires exploration into finding and selecting movements in relation to the dynamic principles of time, force, and space, and structuring the phrases to state and restate the central idea by such devices as contrast, diminution, augmentation, or rhythmic variation. The movements must be carefully planned to follow in a natural course of development with one movement growing out of another. As in any composition, there must be unity, not just a series of isolated movements that are strung together; repetition for emphasis; variety in movement quality; coherence with movements contributing to the central theme; and climax for a strong definitive ending.

In evaluating one's composition, one must remember the process is equally as important as the product.

There is no standard procedure or method for creating a dance, but the following problem is presented as one way to organize ideas and start to work on making a dance.

Organizing space

Figure 5 represents a floor pattern. Walk through the pattern by starting at *X*. Decide which direction to face on each part of the path and vary the walk to include sideward, backward, and diagonal as well as forward movements.

Add designs for body movement to the floor pattern. Include symmetrical and asymmetrical arrangements as well as high, middle, and low levels. Figure 6 indicates design stations for this planning. Designs should be simple to assume, and easy to move away from when going to the next part of the floor pattern. An example of design combinations follows

1. Asymmetrical, sitting or lying on the floor
2^1. Asymmetrical, standing, straight lines predominating
2^2. Same as 2^1, may change direction of facing
3. Asymmetrical, standing, with angles (different from 2)
4. Symmetrical, high level (on toes or in the air), with angles
5. Asymmetrical, low on floor, roll or crawl into circular path
5. Same as first 5
6. Symmetrical, standing, curved lines
7. Asymmetrical, kneeling, similar to 5
8. Asymmetrical, high level, straight lines.

Organizing time

Changes in the length of time it takes to get from one design to another and in the length of time the dancer stays in each design adds interest. Try the following changes in moving from one design to the next in Figure 6:

1 to 2. Move slowly
2 to 3. Moderate increase in speed
3 to 2. Move slowly
2 to 4 to 5. Continuous movement with increasing speed
5 to 5. Hold design 5, move slowly between
5 to 6 to 7. Increasing speed with continuous movement, hold 7 briefly
7 to 8. Very quickly move to 8 and hold.

Organizing energy

Energy change provides accents and contrast.

1 to 2. Use tension so that it appears difficult to move
2 to 3. Slight relaxation
3 to 2. Use tension so that the movement appears to be restricted
2 to 4 to 5. With the increase of speed progressively release tension in sharp bursts,

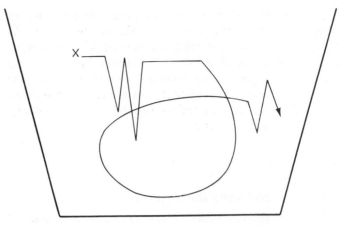

(5) Floor pattern for basic compositional study.

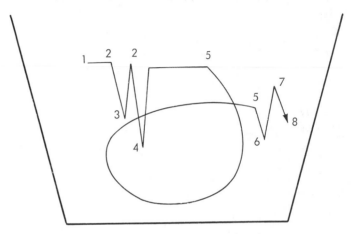

(6) Eight design stations for basic compositional study.

then completely relax and drop into design 5
5 to 5. Smooth and relaxed
5 to 6. Bursts of increasing tension, sharp movement comes to peak at 7
7 to 8. Continuous sharp movement into 8, hold with tension.

After the framework for a dance has been established, much practice is needed in order to achieve clarity in design and variation in intensity of energy.

The special problems of dance composition require exploration into finding and selecting movements in relation to the dynamic principles of time, force, and space, structuring the phrases to state and restate the central idea by such devices as contrast, diminution, augmentation, or rhythmic variation. Dance composition involves carefully planning the movements to follow in a natural course of development with one movement growing out of another. As in any art form, there must be unity—not just a series of isolated movements that are strung together; repetition for emphasis; variety for contrast; coherence with movements contributing to the central theme; and climax for a strong definitive ending.

Selected References

Hawkins, Alma. *Creating through Dance*. Englewood Cliffs, N.J.: Prentice-Hall, 1964.

H'Doubler, Margaret N. *Dance: A Creative Art Experience*. Madison, Wisc.: University of Wisconsin Press, 1962.

Horst, Louis. *Modern Form*. San Francisco: Impulse Publications, 1961.

Humphrey, Doris. *The Art of Making Dances*. New York: Rinehart and Co., 1959, and New York: Grove Press, Inc., 1959 (Paperback).

Lockhart, Aileene, and Esther E. Pease. *Modern Dance: Building and Teaching Lessons*. Dubuque, Iowa: William C. Brown, 1966.

Martin, John. *The Dance*. New York: Tudor Publishing Co., 1946.

Norris, Dorothy, E. Koch, and Reva P. Shiner. *Keynotes to Modern Dance*. Minneapolis: Burgess Publishing Co., 1965.

Pease, Esther E. *Modern Dance*. Dubuque, Iowa: William C. Brown, 1966.